The Elgar Companion to Post Keynesian Economics, Second Edition

Edited by

J.E. King

Professor of Economics, School of Economics, La Trobe University, Australia

Edward Elgar
Cheltenham, UK • Northampton, MA, USA

Published by
Edward Elgar Publishing Limited
The Lypiatts
15 Lansdown Road
Cheltenham
Glos GL50 2JA
UK

Edward Elgar Publishing, Inc.
William Pratt House
9 Dewey Court
Northampton
Massachusetts 01060
USA

A catalogue record for this book
is available from the British Library

Library of Congress Control Number: 2011934814

ISBN 978 1 84980 318 2 (cased)

Typeset by Servis Filmsetting Ltd, Stockport, Cheshire
Printed and bound by MPG Books Group, UK

Contents

Figures

Tables

Contributors

Altuzarra, Amaia: University of the Basque Country, Bilbao, Spain

Arestis, Philip: University of Cambridge, Cambridge, UK

Asada, Toichiro: Chuo University, Tokyo, Japan

Barba, Aldo: University of Naples, Naples, Italy

Baskoy, Tuna: Ryerson University, Toronto, Ontario, Canada

Bibow, Jörg: Skidmore College, Saratoga Springs, NY, USA

Blankenburg, Stephanie: School of Oriental and African Studies (SOAS), University of London, London, UK

Blecker, Robert A.: American University, Washington, DC, USA

Bloch, Harry: Curtin University, Perth, WA, Australia

Brown, Andrew: University of Leeds, Leeds, UK

Bunting, David: Eastern Washington University, Cheney, WA, USA

Carvalho, Fernando J. Cardim de: Universidade Federal de Rio de Janeiro, Brazil

Chick, Victoria: University College London, London, UK

Cornwall, Wendy: Mount Saint Vincent University, Halifax, Nova Scotia, Canada

Courvisanos, Jerry: University of Ballarat, Ballarat, Vic, Australia

Danby, Colin: University of Washington, Bothell, WA, USA

Dantas, Flavia: University of Missouri, Kansas City, MO, USA

Davidson, Paul: New School for Social Research, New York, USA

De Paula, Luiz Fernando: State University of Rio de Janeiro, Rio de Janeiro, Brazil

Dequech, David: Campinas State University, Campinas, Brazil

Dow, Sheila C.: University of Stirling, Stirling, Scotland, UK

Downward, Paul: Loughborough University, Loughborough, UK

Dullien, Sebastian: University of Applied Sciences, Berlin, Germany

Dunn, Stephen P.: NHS Midlands and East, Cambridge, UK

Dutt, Amitava Krishna: University of Notre Dame, Notre Dame, IN, USA

Fazzari, Steven: Washington University, St. Louis, MO, USA

Ferrari-Filho, Fernando: Federal University of Rio Grande do Sul, Brazil

Fine, Ben: School of Oriental and African Studies (SOAS), University of London, London, UK

Fontana, Giuseppe: University of Leeds, Leeds, UK

Forstater, Mathew: University of Missouri, Kansas City, MO, USA

Fujii, Gerardo: Universidad Nacional Autónoma de México, Mexico City, Mexico

Garnett, Rob: Texas Christian University, Fort Worth, TX, USA

Gerrard, Bill: University of Leeds, Leeds, UK

Glickman, Murray: Formerly University of East London, London, UK

Gu, Gyun Cheol: University of Missouri, Kansas City, MO, USA

Harcourt, G.C.: University of New South Wales, Sydney, NSW, Australia

Harvey, John T.: Texas Christian University, Fort Worth, TX, USA

Hayes, Mark: University of Cambridge, Cambridge, UK

Hein, Eckhard: Berlin School of Economics and Law, Berlin, Germany

Henry, John F.: University of Missouri, Kansas City, MO, USA

Hewitson, Gillian: University of Sydney, Sydney, NSW, Australia

Howard, M.C.: University of Waterloo, Waterloo, Ontario, Canada

Howells, Peter: University of Western England, Bristol, UK

Jefferson, Therese: Curtin University, Perth, WA, Australia

Jespersen, Jesper: Roskilde University, Roskilde, Denmark

Jo, Tae-Hee: State University of New York, Buffalo, NY, USA

Katzner, Donald W.: University of Massachussetts, Amherst, MA, USA

Keen, Steve: University of Western Sydney, Sydney, NSW, Australia

Kelton, Stephanie (*née* Bell): University of Missouri, Kansas City, MO, USA

King, J.E.: La Trobe University, Melbourne, Vic, Australia

Kriesler, Peter: University of New South Wales, Sydney, NSW, Australia

Lavoie, Marc: University of Ottawa, Ontario, Canada

Leclaire, Joëlle: State University of New York, Buffalo, NY, USA

Lee, Frederic S.: University of Missouri, Kansas City, MO, USA

Lodewijks, John: University of Western Sydney, Sydney, NSW, Australia

Marcuzzo, Maria Cristina: University of Rome 'La Sapienza', Rome, Italy

McCombie, John S.L.: University of Cambridge, Cambridge, UK

McKenna, Edward J.: Connecticut College, New London, CT, USA

Mearman, Andrew: University of the West of England, Bristol, UK

Melmiès, Jordan: University of Lille 1, Lille, France

Mitchell, William: University of Newcastle, Newcastle, NSW, Australia

Mongiovi, Gary: St. John's University, Jamaica, NY, USA

Mott, Tracy: University of Denver, Denver, CO, USA

Mouakil, Tarik: University of Cambridge, Cambridge, UK

Nersisyan, Yeva: University of Missouri, Kansas City, MO, USA

Nevile, J.W.: University of New South Wales, Sydney, NSW, Australia

Niechoj, Torsten: Hans Böckler Foundation, Düsseldorf, Germany

O'Donnell, Rod: University of Technology, Sydney, NSW, Australia

O'Hara, Phillip Anthony: Curtin University, Perth, WA, Australia

Pacella, Andrea: University of Sannio, Benevento, Italy

Palley, Thomas I.: New America Foundation, Washington, DC, USA

Palma, Gabriel: Cambridge University, Cambridge, UK

Panico, Carlo: University of Naples, Naples, Italy

Parsons, Stephen D.: De Montfort University, Leicester, UK

Perry, Neil: University of Western Sydney, Sydney, NSW, Australia

Pivetti, Massimo: University of Rome 'La Sapienza', Rome, Italy

Pollin, Robert: University of Massachussetts, Amherst, MA, USA

Pressman, Steven: Monmouth University, West Long Branch, NJ, USA

Priewe, Jan: University of Applied Sciences, Berlin, Germany

Razmi, Arslan: University of Massachussetts, Amherst, MA, USA

Realfonzo, Riccardo: University of Sannio, Benevento, Italy

Rider, Christine: St. John's University, Jamaica, NY, USA

Rochon, Louis-Philippe: Laurentian University, Sudbury, Ontario, Canada

Rodríguez-Fuentes, Carlos J.: University of La Laguna, Tenerife, Spain

Rossi, Sergio: University of Fribourg, Fribourg, Switzerland

Sardoni, Claudio: University of Rome 'La Sapienza', Rome, Italy

Sawyer, Malcolm: University of Leeds, Leeds, UK

Scott, Robert H., III: Monmouth University, West Long Branch, NJ, USA

Setterfield, Mark: Trinity College, Hartford, CT, USA

Shapiro, Nina: St. Peter's College, Jersey City, NJ, USA

Sherman, Howard J.: University of California, Los Angeles, CA, USA

Skott, Peter: University of Massachusetts, Amherst, MA, USA

Smithin, John: York University, Toronto, Ontario, Canada

Stockhammer, Engelbert: University of Kingston, Kingston-upon-Thames, UK

Studart, Rogério: World Bank, Washington, DC, USA

Tcherneva, Pavlina R.: Franklin and Marshall College, Lancaster, PA, USA

Thirlwall, A.P.: University of Kent, Canterbury, Kent, UK

Todorova, Zdravka: Wright State University, Dayton, OH, USA

Toporowski, Jan: School of Oriental and African Studies (SOAS), University of London, London, UK

Tortorella Esposito, Guido: University of Sannio, Benevento, Italy

Trigg, Andrew B.: The Open University, Milton Keynes, UK

Tymoigne, Éric: Lewis and Clark College, Portland, OR, USA

Ussher, Leanne: City University of New York, Flushing, NY, USA

Van Treeck, Till: Hans Böckler Foundation, Düsseldorf, Germany

Vercelli, Alessandro: University of Siena, Siena, Italy

Vernengo, Matías: University of Utah, Salt Lake City, UT, USA

Watts, Martin: University of Newcastle, Newcastle, NSW, Australia

Webster, Elizabeth: University of Melbourne, Melbourne, Vic, Australia

Winnett, Adrian: University of Bath, Bath, UK

Wolfson, Martin H.: University of Notre Dame, Notre Dame, IN, USA

Wray, L. Randall: University of Missouri, Kansas City, MO, USA

Zannoni, Diane C.: Trinity College, Hartford, CT, USA

Introduction

Much has changed in the decade since the first edition of this *Companion* was published. Most obviously, the illusory 'Great Moderation' has given way to the 'Great Recession' that was produced by the global financial crisis of 2007–8. (Like Karl Marx, I believe that 'there are no permanent crises' – only permanent contradictions.) These dramatic events have yet to engender any significant modifications to mainstream macroeconomic theory or any lasting change in macroeconomic policy in the rich, post-industrial economies of the Global North. Quite the reverse: the essentially pre-Keynesian theoretical apparatus of the New Neoclassical Synthesis, which had only recently emerged in 2003, has become much more deeply entrenched among academic economists and is today more dogmatically asserted and more vigorously defended against all fundamental criticism (see Sebastian Dullien's entry). Who would have thought, even 10 years ago, that a graduate text in macroeconomics could be published by an Ivy League press with no index reference to 'unemployment'? (The – deeply – offending text is Wickens 2008.) Politically, the only developed nations to swing noticeably to the left in the wake of the global financial crisis have been Denmark and Iceland. Elsewhere the pre-Keynesian shibboleths of sound finance and small government have made a remarkable comeback, sucking in centrists (the Liberal Democrats in England) and former social democrats (in Greece and Spain) as well as traditional conservatives.

Thus the Post Keynesian message is even more important today than it was at the beginning of the century – or, rather, Post Keynesian *messages*, since in my view Post Keynesianism always was, and remains, a broad church (King 2005; see Davidson 2005 for the opposing view). It will be evident from this volume that there are sharp differences of opinion between the contributors on some important issues and a subtle variety of philosophical perspectives and analytical approaches on many others. There is, however, agreement on the fundamentals, beginning with the principle of effective demand: in capitalist economies, output and employment are normally constrained by aggregate demand, not by individual supply behaviour. Since a decision not to have lunch today – as Keynes famously put it – does not entail a decision to have lunch tomorrow, investment drives saving and not the other way round. Moreover, there exists no automatic or even minimally reliable mechanism that will eliminate excess capacity and involuntary unemployment. Interest rates depend on monetary considerations rather than on the so-called 'real' forces of productivity and thrift; there is no 'natural rate of interest' to equilibrate investment and saving, so that an increase in the propensity to save will prove self-defeating, resulting in lower output and reduced employment but not in higher levels of saving.

Whatever they may disagree about, Post Keynesians concur in their rejection of the mainstream vision of a capitalist reality in which uncertainty is not inescapable, expectations are not tentative and often unreliable, money does not affect output as well as prices, and demand-deficient unemployment is not *the* central macroeconomic problem. They repudiate the mainstream notion of the long run as a sort of magic kingdom where the future is knowable (at least probabilistically), expectations are always fulfilled, money has no real significance and resources are fully employed. For Post Keynesians, then, 'New Keynesian' macroeconomics is not 'Keynesian' at all, in any genuine sense (see Wendy Cornwall's entry).

All of these issues are covered by entries (often by several entries) in this *Companion*. Many of them (69 in all) appeared in the first edition and have been more or less extensively revised and updated by their original authors; 43 are new, reflecting both the theoretical and policy challenges that I have referred to and the emergence of a new generation of Post Keynesian scholars, including (I am delighted to report) a significantly larger minority of women contributors. The central theoretical and policy issues that were dealt with in the first edition remain at the core of the book, but there have been some substantial changes. Much more attention is paid in this second edition to financial markets and their reform; a series of entries deals with Post Keynesian economics outside its traditional Anglo-American heartland; and previously neglected themes of gender and environmental policy are now included. A few of the contributors to the first edition were unable to update their entries, which have therefore been omitted. Remarkably, death has claimed only two of the original 83 contributors: John Cornwall, whose entry on 'Stagflation' has been revised by Mark Setterfield, and Egon Matzner, whose topic ('The Third Way') did not seem worth reviving. This edition is dedicated to them, and to the memory of the great Austrian heterodox economist Kurt Rothschild (1914–2010), who was an inspiration to so many of us.

I am extremely grateful to my hawk-eyed Japanese translator, Shozo Koyama, whose remarkably thorough scrutiny of the first English edition picked up an embarrassingly large number of errors; all, I hope, have now been corrected. I must also acknowledge the helpful comments of Peter Kriesler and Frank Stilwell on my entry on 'Australia'. Andrew Mearman wishes to thank Victoria Chick and Sheila Dow for comments on his entry; Phil O'Hara acknowledges the assistance of Harry Bloch, John

King, Peter Kriesler, Marc Lavoie and Douglas Vickers with his entry; and Gerardo Fujii thanks Armando Román-Zozaya for translating his entry from the original Spanish. The usual disclaimer applies to all of them.

References

Davidson, P. (2005), 'Responses to Lavoie, King, and Dow on what Post Keynesianism is and who is a Post Keynesian', *Journal of Post Keynesian Economics*, **27** (3), 393–408.

King, J.E. (2005), 'Unwarping the record: a reply to Paul Davidson', *Journal of Post Keynesian Economics*, **27** (3), 377–84.

Wickens, M. (2008), *Macroeconomic Theory: A Dynamic General Equilibrium Approach*, Princeton, NJ: Princeton University Press.

Agency

Agents are the sources of choices and decisions. Agency deals with the capacity that enables choices to be made. The provenance of this capacity, its nature, and the factors that enhance or limit it are the main questions of concern. For Post Keynesian economics, an additional question arises. An essential aspect of Post Keynesian economics is the adoption of the non-ergodicity postulate, which states that probability distributions are not stable over time. As a result, the future is unknown and unknowable. Thus, the Post Keynesian concept of agency is one that must be consistent with the postulate of non-ergodicity.

To speak of 'the Post Keynesian concept of agency' is perhaps too generous, for this is an area of work that is still in development. Indeed, some economists have advanced the claim that important aspects relating to the concept of agency are completely lacking in Post Keynesian economics (Hodgson 2004, p. 22). Nevertheless, a perusal of the work in this area clearly reveals a set of factors that will undoubtedly be at the core of any Post Keynesian concept of agency likely to develop in the near future.

Since agents make choices, they must possess a capacity that enables them to accomplish this. The idea of making a choice involves more than just a capricious action. To make a choice is to engage in an intentional act based upon reasons and beliefs. Thus, agents must be capable of having reasons and beliefs. Further, to act intentionally implies that one is attempting to bring about some result. An attempt to bring about a certain result is an attempt to structure the world in which the agent lives. To do so, an agent requires the ability to conceptualize the world both as it is, and as the agent would like it to be. Thus, agents must have the capacity to formulate a conception of the world and a conception of what a good life would entail.

Agents equipped with these endowments are able to make choices. What does the idea of 'making a choice' imply? While not an uncontroversial question, the basic idea is that an agent in a given situation could have selected an action different from that actually undertaken. This, however, does not imply that the agent makes unconstrained choices. A key feature of the Post Keynesian concept of agency is that agents make choices within the context of a social structure, where by social structure we refer to such things as rules, relationships and institutions. The introduction of the idea of the social structure raises a question: what is the relationship between an agent and the social structure? Two traditional answers have been given to this question. The first, the methodological individualist position, advances

1

the claim that structure is entirely the result of individual actions: structure is determined by individuals. The second, methodological collectivism (or holism), posits that individuals and their actions are entirely determined by the social structure. A hallmark of the Post Keynesian concept of agency is a rejection of both of these views. For Post Keynesians, individual agents are born into a social structure that deeply influences, indeed partly constitutes, the nature of the agent. However, it is equally true that the actions of agents help to reproduce and transform the social structure. Thus, agent and structure are mutually dependent upon, but not reducible to, each other. The fact that agent and structure are not reducible to each other means that each possesses powers and capabilities that are not solely derived from the other.

Agents, then, make choices in the context of a social structure. The fact that the social structure partly constitutes the individual agent means that the social structure does more than simply constrain the choices available to an agent. Rather, the social structure partly determines who an agent is. At a deep level, an agent is constituted by the meanings of the world he or she both holds and transforms. For Post Keynesians, meaning is not an objective fact about the world. Rather, meaning is both created and transformed as the result of social interaction within a social structure. Differing social structures enable differing types of social interaction that engender different meanings and understandings of the world, hence leading to different individuals. Likewise, different individuals with different understandings of the world will help to bring about different transformations of the social structure. Agents and structure are then engaged in a dynamic process of reproducing and transforming each other. We thus see the context for a frequently heard Post Keynesian expression, 'institutions and history (time) matter'. Moreover, the fact that the actions of agents will bring about a transformation of the social structure also provides an explanation for the existence of non-ergodicity. This follows once we are able to see that the future will be made by people on the basis of meanings that they will freely create, though in the context of the social structure.

This account of agency and institutions also makes available to Post Keynesians an understanding of economic rights that is precluded to those who cling to the notion that economics is a value-free domain. McKenna and Zannoni (2007), for example, have demonstrated that the right to a job follows naturally once it is understood that agents, in a non-ergodic world, will seek to create institutions that alleviate the possibility of unemployment. The fact that agents are responsible for the creation of institutions also has implications for the 'Luck Egalitarian' approach to moral responsibility and distributive justice, which posits that agents can only claim a right for that for which they are responsible (Cohen 1989).

The idea of a dynamic interaction between agent and structure helps illuminate another important aspect of Post Keynesian economics. While the world is non-ergodic, it nevertheless often remains fairly stable for significant periods of time. Post Keynesians partly account for this through the existence of conventions. In explaining how entrepreneurs make investment decisions in a world where the future cannot be known, Keynes expressed the view that agents tend to follow a convention by which they project into the future the present state of things, unless there is some specific reason for believing change likely. For Keynes, conventions are shared rules of behaviour that enable individuals to take actions in situations where the future results of actions are unknowable. From a Post Keynesian perspective, conventions exist because they are one of the elements agents use to give a coherent meaning to the world in which they live. Thus, conventions actually help create the world, hence the future. Moreover, conventions are formed on the basis of social interaction, which helps us to understand what Keynes meant when he wrote in regard to how expectations of the future are formed: 'We endeavour to fall back on the judgment of the rest of the world which is perhaps better informed' (Keynes 1973, p. 114).

It is one thing to state that individuals and social structure partly constitute each other without being reducible to the other. It is quite another to explain how this can be. It is clear that we wish to avoid complete reduction of the individual to the social structure, and vice versa. To conflate the individual with the social structure is to remove the possibility of free choice. To reduce the social structure to the individual is to deny the independent existence of physical, chemical and biological forces. Neither of these positions will do. However, to say that individuals and the social structure only partly constitute each other implies that each of these possesses some capabilities that are independent of the other. What explains these independent capabilities? Two different positions can be found in the literature.

The first is the Cartesian dualist position. According to this view, it is simply in the nature of things that there exist both material and intentional causes. The material causes deal with the physical, chemical and biological. Intentional causes are the basis of human agency. The existence of intentional causes, founded upon reasons, is what makes free choice possible. Intentional cause is a bedrock category in the sense that little more can be said concerning what causes intentional cause. As critics of this position would state, intentional cause is an uncaused cause.

There are a number of difficulties with this position. At the philosophical level, no generally accepted argument has been developed to explain how these two different types of causes can interact and cohere with each other. More importantly, from the Post Keynesian perspective, is the fact that the Cartesian view is at variance with the idea that individuals and the social structure partly constitute each other. According to the Cartesian position, materialist and intentional causes are independent, bedrock categories, with neither owing its existence to other factors. Under such a view, individual choices may be constrained by the materialist factors that explain the existence of the social structure, but individuals and the choices they make are not (even partly) constituted by the social structure, a view of the world that is more consonant with the neoclassical conception of economics. Finally, the idea of an uncaused cause strikes critics as being unscientific in that the idea rules out from the outset any possibility of further investigation.

The second position found in the literature is newer, and we shall refer to it as the 'evolutionary position' (Bunge 1980). According to this view, materialist and intentional causes are not independent of each other. Rather, intentional causes are 'emergent' properties of the material world. The idea here is that the human capability of intentional choice has evolved over time through the development of materialist (physical, chemical and biological) forces. The term 'emergent' is used in the following, somewhat special, sense. While human intentionality has evolved from materialist forces, it nevertheless possesses irreducible properties of its own. In other words, while intentionality evolves from materialist forces, it cannot be explained solely in terms of these forces.

While the evolutionary position avoids the strict dualism inherent in the Cartesian approach, it too suffers from a number of difficulties. There does not yet exist an adequate explanation as to how intentions actually evolve from materialist forces. More problematic, from the perspective of a social scientist, is the precise meaning of the term 'emergent'. Several questions arise here. First, what exactly does it mean to state that intention is only partly explainable in terms of materialist forces? Does this imply that some aspects of intention are not explicable in terms of anything else? If so, does this not raise the same types of objections that were raised against the Cartesian approach? If, on the other hand, intention can be fully explained by materialist forces, then a serious question is posed as to the existence of free choice. While those writing in the evolutionary camp are sensitive to this issue, it is also the case that the impression is often given that a complete explanation of intention in terms of other causes is what these writers truly seek. How this could be accomplished, while maintaining the possibility of free choice, is unclear. For example Hodgson, in criticizing the idea of an uncaused cause, writes approvingly of Darwin: 'A crucial point emerges here. It is part and parcel of Darwin's underlying philosophy that all intention has itself to be explained by a causal process . . . There can be no first and "uncaused cause"' (Hodgson 2004, p. 55). While Hodgson claims that free will and determinism are compatible, many see his claim as establishing that what is really compatible is the appearance of free choice and determinism, not the reality of free choice and determinism.

EDWARD J. MCKENNA
DIANE C. ZANNONI

See also:

Babylonian Mode of Thought; Choice Under Uncertainty; Critical Realism; Expectations; Institutionalism; Macroeconomic Methodology; Non-ergodicity; Time in Economic Theory; Uncertainty.

Bibliography

Bedau, M. and P. Humphreys (eds) (2008), *Emergence: Contemporary Readings in Philosophy and Science*, Cambridge, MA: MIT Press.
Bunge, M.A. (1980), *The Mind–Body Problem: A Psychobiological Approach*, Oxford: Pergamon.
Cohen, G.A. (1989), 'On the currency of egalitarian justice', *Ethics*, **99** (4), 906–44.
Hodgson, G.M. (2004), *Evolution of Institutional Economics*, London and New York: Routledge.
Keynes, J.M. (1973), *The Collected Writings of John Maynard Keynes. Volume XIV: The General Theory and After*, London and New York: Cambridge University Press for the Royal Economic Society.
Lawson, T. (1997), *Economics and Reality*, London and New York: Routledge.
McKenna, E.J. and D.C. Zannoni (1997–98), 'Post Keynesian economics and the philosophy of individualism', *Journal of Post Keynesian Economics*, **20** (2), 235–50.
McKenna, E.J. and D.C. Zannoni (2007), 'The right to a job: a Post Keynesian perspective', *Journal of Post Keynesian Economics*, **29** (4), 555–72.

Australia

Australia was once something of a Post Keynesian stronghold: 'the *General Theory* conquered Australia with a speed and thoroughness that would have impressed the Spanish Inquisition, so that by 1945 there was no more totally Keynesian economics profession in the world' (King 2002, p. 141; see also King 1997). One of the earliest and best reviews of Keynes's masterpiece was published in the *Economic Record*, written by the young Brian Reddaway on the boat out to Melbourne on a Bank of England scholarship. There were strong and long-established links with Cambridge, and a tradition of state intervention in the colonial and post-colonial economies that favoured a Keynesian approach to macroeconomic management. After 1945 the teaching of macroeconomics in Australia's (then) seven universities was overwhelmingly Keynesian in spirit, and Post Keynesian visitors such as Nicholas Kaldor and Joan Robinson (Millmow 2009) were welcomed with great appreciation. Down to the 1970s, at least, there was no bastion of pre-Keynesian thought in Australia, no 'Chicago of the South'. Broadly Post Keynesian ideas on the control of inflation and the operation of an effective and equitable wages policy were developed by Geoff Harcourt, John Nevile, Eric Russell and Wilfred Salter and influenced Commonwealth government policy for several decades (Harcourt 2001).

Harcourt himself was easily the most important of the early Australian Post Keynesians. A post-graduate student in Cambridge for three years, beginning in 1955, he returned to teach at the University of Adelaide, where he was co-author of a Keynesian textbook (Harcourt et al. 1967) and co-editor of *Australian Economic Papers* from 1967 until his return to Cambridge in 1983. Until it passed into mainstream hands in the late 1980s, *Australian Economic Papers* was an important outlet for both local and international Post Keynesian research at a time when more orthodox journals overseas were increasingly being closed to dissident voices. Harcourt himself remained a major influence on Post Keynesian thinking in Australia, frequently visiting his native country and supervising an impressive series of dissertations by Australian research students.

Peter Groenewegen's 1979 survey of 'radical economics' in Australia concluded that the prospects for Post Keynesianism were extremely bright (Groenewegen 1979, p. 205). In retrospect, this was much too optimistic, although Post Keynesian themes were prominent in the seven annual Political Economy conferences held at the University of Sydney between 1976 and 1982, and courses in Post Keynesian theory were being taught at the University of Sydney, the University of New South Wales and other institutions in the 1980s. In 1988 the University of New South Wales hosted a Post Keynesian conference, organized by Peter Kriesler, and an entire day was devoted to Post Keynesian papers at the 19th Conference of Economists at the same venue in 1990, with international speakers including Harcourt, Edward Nell and Jan Toporowski. As late as 1994, Paul Davidson was the international guest of honour at a two-day conference on 'Post Keynesian Economics: Theory and Policy Alternatives for Australia' at La Trobe University in Melbourne.

But the tide was already flowing very strongly in the other direction. First monetarism, then New Classical macroeconomics and finally the New Neoclassical Synthesis swept all before them in most university economics departments, and neoliberalism (under its peculiarly question-begging Australian title of 'economic rationalism') soon came to dominate public policy, most notably under the Hawke-Keating Labor government of 1983–96, which was deeply infiltrated by mainstream academic economists (Pusey 1991). The brightest young students were increasingly sent to the United States for postgraduate training instead of to Cambridge, which had in any case itself lost most of its Post Keynesian flavour. By the end of the 1980s it was apparent that the Australian economics profession was being Americanized (Groenewegen and McFarlane 1990). Some peculiarities of the (relatively highly regulated) Australian labour market continued to command attention, with the consequences of the rather sudden introduction of equal pay for women totally failing to reflect neoclassical expectations (Gregory and Duncan 1981). Significantly, the senior author of this important early paper in the *Journal of Post Keynesian Economics*, Bob Gregory, was on all other issues impeccably orthodox, and the Australian National University, where he spent the great majority of his career, was an early and continuing stronghold of economic rationalism.

By the beginning of the twenty-first century, 'Post Keynesianism remained powerfully entrenched at Sydney University and survived at most other institutions, albeit generally as an embattled minority' (King 2002, p. 145; see also Butler et al. 2009 on Sydney). At Sydney, Curtin University in Perth, and elsewhere in Australia, Post Keynesians cooperated happily with heterodox economists of other persuasions, and indeed often regarded themselves as being to some extent feminists, institutionalists, ecological economists and/or Marxists. A steady stream of Post Keynesian empirical and policy research was beginning to emerge from the Centre of Full Employment and Equity (CofFEE) at the University of Newcastle, New South Wales, established in 1997 under the direction of Bill Mitchell to promote the case for full employment and economic justice. Closely associated with similar research institutes at the University of Kansas City/Missouri and the University of Maastricht in the Netherlands, CofFEE promotes the case for the government to offer a 'job guarantee' to the unemployed, with the state acting as an employer of last resort in the same way that central banks function as lenders of last resort (Mitchell and Muysken 2007). Its annual conferences, held in early December when coastal south-eastern Australia is at its most beautiful, have attracted a steady stream of international visitors.

Since 2002 the CofFEE conference has dovetailed with the annual conference of the Society of Heterodox Economists (SHE), an informal umbrella organization established by Peter Kriesler on the model of the Association of Heterodox Economists in the UK. Like its British counterpart, SHE has no formal membership and no real existence outside the annual conference, which is now held (with financial support from the University of New South Wales) within sight of the beach at the Sydney suburb of Coogee; attendance is normally around 100. SHE is deliberately and proudly ecumenical, and Kriesler has gone to great lengths to ensure a regular feminist presence at the conferences and to encourage the participation of graduate students from economics and other social science departments. One weakness is that it is predominantly a Sydney affair, with rather limited involvement from Post Keynesians outside New South Wales; attempts to establish informal Post Keynesian associations in other states have never succeeded.

By 2011 there was a large and very ugly cloud on the horizon. Australia's propensity to adopt the least intelligent aspects of British politics, society and culture has been demonstrated yet again by the Antipodean version of the UK's Research Assessment Exercise (RAE); the acronym has been reshuffled to produce ERA ('Excellence in Research Australia'). At the time of writing (April 2011), ERA is still in its early stages, but Post Keynesian fears look like being very fully justified (Bloch 2010). Journals have been ranked in four categories (A*, A, B and C), with the divide between A and B being particularly critical. Articles in B-ranked journals count for little or nothing, and there is even a suggestion that academic managements will discourage staff from publishing in them for fear of 'pulling down the average'. No heterodox journals of any persuasion score A*, and of the handful that are ranked A, only two – the *Cambridge Journal of Economics* and the *Journal of Post Keynesian Economics* – publish Post Keynesian work on a regular basis. Books, and book chapters, which constitute a larger and more influential part of Post Keynesians' economists' published work than they do for the mainstream, seem to count for very little. Thus it came as no surprise that in the first round of evaluations, published in January 2011, institutions with a significant Post Keynesian presence came off badly. The medium- to long-run implications are obvious, and extremely unfavourable. As in the UK (Lee 2009, chapters 8–9), Post Keynesians in Australia will find it increasingly difficult to get appointed or promoted, and established Post Keynesians will be denied promotion, research funding and sabbaticals.

Geoff Harcourt's permanent return to Australia in 2010, just before his eightieth birthday, was very welcome, but it also served to underline the relative weakness of Post Keynesian influence among academic economists of the post-1945 baby boom, let alone generations X and Y. There are many productive individuals, including 16 contributors to the present volume, but most of them will not see 50 again (which is not true of many of the German and US contributors). Post Keynesian ideas remain influential in a few institutions, but most of these are not of the first rank (Curtin University, for example, and the University of Western Sydney), and there is little or no Post Keynesian presence in the more prestigious universities, at the annual mainstream Conference of Economists, or in the *Economic Record*. The rapid shift to the American system PhD from the old British system, which required little or no coursework, has confronted potential research students with daunting examination commitments in neoclassical theory and mainstream econometrics. Becoming a Post Keynesian is in any case not a good career move for a bright young economist in Australia, and the future for those who decide to make it is not at all bright.

Postscript: in mid–2011 the abandonment of the journal ranking system was announced. However, the damage had already been done, and it is likely that similar criteria will be applied informally in future research assessments, which will become even less transparent than the 2011 exercise.

J.E. KING

See also:

Cambridge Economic Tradition; Employer of Last Resort.

References

Bloch, H. (2010), 'Research evaluation down under: an outsider's view from the inside of the Australian approach', *American Journal of Economics and Sociology*, **69** (5), 1530–52.
Butler, G., E. Jones and F. Stilwell (2009), *Political Economy Now! The Struggle for Alternative Economics at the University of Sydney*, Sydney: Darlington Press.
Gregory, R.G. and R.C. Duncan (1981), 'Segmented labor market theories and the Australian experience of equal pay for women', *Journal of Post Keynesian Economics*, **3** (3), 403–28.
Groenewegen, P.D. (1979), 'Radical economics in Australia: a survey of the 1970s', in F.H. Gruen (ed.), *Surveys of Australian Economics*, Vol. 2, Sydney: Allen & Unwin, pp. 172–223.
Groenewegen, P.D. and B. McFarlane (1990), *A History of Australian Economic Thought*, London and New York: Routledge.
Harcourt, G.C. (2001), *50 Years a Keynesian and Other Essays*, Basingstoke: Palgrave.
Harcourt, G.C., P.H. Karmel and R.H. Wallace (1967), *Economic Activity*, Cambridge: Cambridge University Press.
King, J.E. (1997), 'Notes on the history of Post Keynesian economics in Australia', in P. Arestis, G. Palma and M.C. Sawyer (eds), *Capital Controversy, Post Keynesian Economics and the History of Economic Theory: Essays in Honour of Geoff Harcourt*, Vol. 1, London and New York: Routledge, pp. 298–309.
King, J.E. (2002), *A History of Post Keynesian Economics Since 1936*, Cheltenham, UK and Northampton, MA, USA: Edward Elgar.
Lee, F. (2009), *A History of Heterodox Economics: Challenging the Mainstream in the Twentieth Century*, London and New York: Routledge.
Millmow, A. (2009), 'The transition from Keynesian to monetarist economics in Australia: Joan Robinson's 1975 visit to Australia', *History of Economics Review*, **49**, 15–31.
Mitchell, W. and J. Muysken (2007), *Full Employment Abandoned: Shifting Sands and Policy Failures*, Cheltenham, UK and Northampton, MA, USA: Edward Elgar.
Pusey, M. (1991), *Economic Rationalism in Canberra: A Nation-Building State Changes Its Mind*, Cambridge: Cambridge University Press.

Austrian School of Economics

The publication of Carl Menger's *Principles of Economics* (*Grundsätze der Volkswirthschaftslehre*) marked the birth of the Austrian School of Economics. After the publication of the book, Menger became embroiled in the famous *Methodenstreit* with Gustav Schmoller, and it was left to others to develop his economic insights, most notably Eugen von Böhm-Bawerk and Friedrich von Wieser. The development of the Austrian School was further carried on by Ludwig von Mises and Friedrich von Hayek, and later by Murray Rothbard, Ludwig Lachmann and I.M. Kirzner. Other famous economists associated to various degrees with the school include Fritz Machlup, Oskar Morgenstern, Joseph Schumpeter and G.L.S. Shackle.

Although Mises continued Menger's investigations into methodological issues, he and Hayek are probably best known for their respective criticisms of centrally planned economies. While Mises focused on the problem of economic calculation in non-monetary economies, Hayek drew attention to the dispersed, partial, continually changing, and frequently contradictory information possessed by different economic agents in any advanced economy. Hayek argued that the nature of this information made it impossible for governments to direct economic activity with any semblance of economic efficiency. The problem was not merely a collection and computational problem, as information required interpreting and was continually altering. Hayek argued that this problem also raised questions for most attempts at governmental intervention in capitalist economies, thus continuing what has become something of an Austrian tradition of emphasizing the advantages of free markets.

Vaughn (1994) acknowledges two main strands in contemporary Austrian economics. The first strand, represented primarily by Kirzner, views Austrian economics as a necessary supplement to mainstream economics. On this account, Austrian economics is not directly concerned with equilibrium states, but with the processes through which equilibrium may be attained, with pride of place given to entrepreneurial discovery and creation. The second strand, represented by Lachmann (who greatly admired the work of Shackle), concentrates on uncertainty and divergent expectations, and is highly suspicious of any reference to the idea of equilibrium.

Despite these divergent strands, Vaughn claims that all contemporary Austrian economists subscribe to two views. First, social phenomena are to be explained in terms of the ideas and actions of individuals (methodological individualism). Second, human action takes place in time and under conditions of uncertainty. Thus Menger drew attention to the importance of 'time and error' in economics (Menger 1871 [1976], pp. 67ff.) and Mises emphasized 'the uncertainty of the future' (1966, p. 105) and argued that the ideas of human action and time are inseparable (pp. 99ff.). This leads to an emphasis on individuals possessing different knowledge and expectations, and also on the importance of institutions for the coordination of actions.

This second position clearly bears affinities with the emphasis on histori-cal time, uncertainty and expectation in Post Keynesian economics, as does Menger's argument that the demand for speculative balances formed a sig-nificant component of the demand for money (Streissler 1973) and Mises's dismissal of the 'spurious idea of the supposed neutrality of money' (Mises 1953, p. 398). However, despite some attempts, there has tended to be little cross-fertilization between the two schools. In part, this is no doubt expli-cable in terms of historical precedent. Thus Keynes thought that Hayek's review of his *Treatise on Money* was carried out with insufficient 'good will', responding by characterizing Hayek's book *Prices and Production* as 'an extraordinary example of how, starting with a mistake, a remorseless logician can end up in Bedlam' (Keynes 1973, p. 252). However, the differ-ences between the schools go deeper than lack of good will and the ques-tioning of sanity, and can be explored through focusing on the question of economic coordination.

In a discussion of Austrian economics, the Post Keynesian economist Paul Davidson draws attention to the tension between the two strands identified by Vaughn: 'Austrian subjectivists cannot have it both ways – they cannot argue for the importance of time, uncertainty, and money, and simultaneously presume that plan or pattern coordination must exist and is waiting to be discovered' (Davidson 1989, p. 468). Davidson here cor-rectly recognizes a problem in attempting to fuse the two strands into an 'Austrian view'. If entrepreneurs are formulating plans under conditions of uncertainty, with limited knowledge and divergent expectations, how can it be assumed that somehow these numerous different plans become coordi-nated? Given time and uncertainty, entrepreneurial action may move economies farther away from, not closer to, equilibrium conditions. In a recent attempt to resolve this dilemma, Kirzner argues that, although given uncertainty, entrepreneurs make mistakes, there are 'underlying objective realities [that] exercise their influence upon entrepreneurial production decisions' (Kirzner 1992, p. 34). Entrepreneurs may make mistakes, but it all comes out in the wash and thus entrepreneurs can still be viewed as suc-cessfully steering the economy towards equilibrium.

It is difficult to recognize this as a satisfactory solution, as it appears to remain impaled on the dilemma identified by Davidson. If market coordi-nation occurs through entrepreneurs being influenced by some 'underlying objective realities' then this coordination is reliant upon the *absence* of ignorance and uncertainty, as entrepreneurs presumably become aware of the nature of these 'realities'. Market coordination is explained through abstracting from the very feature that Vaughn identified as constitut-ing the Austrian approach – the emphasis on uncertainty. However, it is also not clear that the Post Keynesian approach is any more successful in combining explanations of economic coordination with an emphasis on uncertainty.

From a Post Keynesian perspective Davidson argues that, as reality is transmutable, where 'today's human action can create a new and different reality', then there is uncertainty where 'no relevant information exists today that can be used as a basis for scientifically predicting future events' (Davidson 1993, p. 430). Whereas Kirzner argued for the coordination effects of entrepreneurial action, Davidson argues that as entrepreneurs are acting under conditions of uncertainty, market coordination may not occur, and consequently there is a role for governments in creating the conditions whereby full employment might occur (Davidson 1989, p. 474). Hence 'through institutional and political changes, society can intelligently control and improve the performance of the economy compared with what would occur under laissez-faire' (Davidson 1993, p. 430).

However, if, given uncertainty, future events cannot be predicted, how can any government know what effects in the future any institutional and political changes made in the present will ultimately have? Again, economic coordination appears to be improved through abstracting from the very uncertainty that forms the initial focus. From an Austrian perspective, the problem here is not simply a mistaken reliance on the positive effects of governmental intervention in the economy. Rather, it seems to epitomize the 'rationalism' that Hayek criticized Keynes for: the belief that human affairs and problems could be fully known and resolved through the application of reason.

A further fundamental difference between the schools is that, while Post Keynesians would undoubtedly argue that the current economic crisis vindicates their view on unregulated free markets, from the Austrian perspective the crisis indicates problems arising from misguided policy interventions in the market. The crisis is thus identified as vindicating Austrian business-cycle theory (see Mises 1953). According to this theory, the Federal Reserve and the European Central Bank responded to the crisis following 11 September 2001 by lowering interest rates below the 'natural level'. In response, banks decide to expand credit and consumers borrow to make purchases, such as housing, which they would previously have been unable to afford. Similarly, business invests in the capital-goods industries. When interest rates eventually rise, consumers cannot repay debt and investments become unprofitable.

In his criticisms of centrally planned economies, Mises had drawn attention to the significance of institutions such as the institution of private property for economic efficiency. From the perspective of Jesús Huerta de Soto (2009a, 2009b) the question of property rights is also significant in the current crisis. First, in lending money that others have deposited, banks are exercising a privilege that contravenes property rights (Huerta de Soto 2009a, p. 144). Huerta de Soto argues that nobody should enjoy the privilege of lending something that has been deposited as a demand deposit, and hence the banking system should hold 100 per cent reserves.

Second, in the derivatives market, derivatives are not required by law to be recorded, tracked, or tied to assets (Huerta de Soto 2009b); hence ultimately no one knows who is financially accountable for them. Huerta de Soto thus argues that no economic activity based on trust should be allowed to operate outside property law. These two arguments both acknowledge that the efficiency of markets is dependent upon the assignment of property rights, where these rights are ultimately enforceable by the state. Consequently, the efficiency of the market is ultimately dependent upon governments being capable of determining and enforcing property rights.

Although the Austrian emphasis on time and uncertainty forms one defining difference from mainstream economic theory, there is another major difference between Austrian and mainstream theory. This difference is frequently only implicit, and also concerns action coordination. In his economic sociology, influenced by Austrian theory, Weber noted that '"rational economic action" requires instrumental rationality in this orientation, that is, deliberate planning' (Weber 1978, p. 63). As Lachmann later noted in his book on Weber, 'in social theory our main task is to explain observable social phenomena by reducing them to individual plans' (Lachmann 1971, p. 31).

In mainstream economic theory an instrumentally rational act is a utility-maximizing act, which can be explained solely in terms of individual desires (preferences) and beliefs. Assuming a causal account of action, then desires and beliefs alone give reasons for action, hence causing the relevant action. However, this is not how Weber understands an instrumentally rational act. For Weber, such an act can best be explained in terms of plans and future-directed intentions, and it is these, not preferences and beliefs, that cause action.

The significance of this is not merely that Weber offers an alternative account of instrumentally rational action, but that, unlike the mainstream account, Weber's model of action can explain intentional action coordination. Say a friend and I form future-directed intentions to meet in a week's time. When the time comes, will we meet? According to the mainstream account, we shall meet only if, at the time of action, meeting is the strictly preferred option of each. Consequently, if either has received a better offer in the meantime, he or she will not attend the meeting. Given normal rationality assumptions, each believes this of the other; hence it is unlikely either will meet as arranged. However, if intentions cause actions, and each believes this, each will meet as intended. Intentions thus act rather like promises, and in giving reasons for actions, facilitate intentional coordination. However, from a mainstream perspective, this is irrational.

STEPHEN D. PARSONS

See also:

Agency; Choice under Uncertainty; Equilibrium and Non-equilibrium; Expectations; Macroeconomic Methodology; Non-ergodicity; Time in Economic Theory; Uncertainty.

References

Davidson, P. (1989), 'The economics of ignorance or the ignorance of economics?', *Critical Review*, **3** (3–4), 467–87.
Davidson, P. (1993), 'Austrians and Post Keynesians on economic reality: a rejoinder to critics', *Critical Review*, **7** (2–3), 371–444.
Huerta de Soto, J. (2009a), *The Theory of Dynamic Efficiency*, London and New York: Routledge.
Huerta de Soto, J. (2009b), 'Toxic assets were hidden assets', *Wall Street Journal*, 25 March.
Keynes, J.M. (1973), *The Collected Writings of John Maynard Keynes. Volume XIII: The General Theory and After. Part I: Preparation*, London: Macmillan.
Kirzner, I.M. (1992), *The Meaning of Market Process: Essays in the Development of Modern Austrian Economics*, London and New York: Routledge.
Lachmann, L. (1971), *The Legacy of Max Weber: Three Essays*, London: Heinemann.
Menger, C. (1871), *Principles of Economics*, trans. J. Dingwall and B.F. Hoselitz, New York: New York University Press, 1976.
Mises, L. von (1953), *Theory of Money and Credit*, New Haven, CT: Yale University Press.
Mises, L. von (1966), *Human Action: A Treatise on Economics*, 3rd edn, Ithaca, NY: Contemporary Books.
Streissler, E.W. (1973), 'Menger's theory of money and uncertainty: a modern interpretation', in J.R. Hicks and W. Weber (eds), *Carl Menger and the Austrian School of Economics*, Oxford: Clarendon Press, pp. 164–89.
Vaughn, K.I. (1994), *Austrian Economics in America: The Migration of a Tradition*, Cambridge: Cambridge University Press.
Weber, M. (1978), *Economy and Society*, ed. G. Roth and C. Wittich, Berkeley, CA: University of California Press

Babylonian Mode of Thought

The expression 'Babylonian mode of thought' has been used in economics – and particularly in connection with Post Keynesian economics – in an attempt to identify a way of approaching economic analysis which is quite different from the mainstream. We start by tracing the use made of the term, and then discuss in more detail its meaning and significance.

But first we need to consider the term 'mode of thought'. It refers to the principles of knowledge construction and communication which underpin choice of methodology, and indeed daily life: 'As we think, we live' (Whitehead 1938, p. 87). A mode of thought is 'the way in which arguments (or theories) are constructed and presented, how we attempt to convince others of the validity or truth of our arguments' (Dow 1985, p. 11). It is important to dig down to this level, beyond the methodological level, since arguments about the relative merits of different methodologies (such as Post Keynesian and mainstream) can founder through lack of recognition that different modes of thought are also involved.

The term 'Babylonian' was used by Keynes (1933) in his biography of Isaac Newton, where he challenged the conventional understanding of Newton as the first of the age of reason. Instead '[h]e was the last of the magicians, the last of the Babylonians and Sumerians, the last great mind which looked out on the visible and intellectual world with the same eyes as those who began to build our intellectual inheritance rather less than 10,000 years ago' (1933 [1972], p. 364). Keynes contrasted the way in which Newton relied on intuition in order to arrive at explanations for natural phenomena, on the one hand, with the rational proofs he constructed after the fact, on the other.

The term 'Babylonian' then apparently fell into misuse until introduced to modern economics in Stohs's (1983) note on the subject of Keynes on uncertainty, which he argued could be developed further on Babylonian lines. He had picked up the Babylonian category from Wimsatt's (1981) discussion in terms of the social sciences in general, in juxtaposition to Cartesian/Euclidean thought. According to the Babylonian approach, 'there is no single logical chain from axioms to theorems; but there are several parallel, intertwined, and mutually reinforcing sets of chains, such that no particular axiom is logically basic' (Stohs 1983, p. 87).

Wimsatt in turn had developed the idea from Feynman's (1965) representation of what he called the Babylonian tradition in mathematics, which involved a range of starting-points for arguments, and thus a multiple derivability of physical laws. Feynman contrasted this with the Euclidean approach, which ties all arguments deductively to a set of axioms, and argued that the Babylonian approach was preferable for physics: 'The method of always starting from the axioms is not very efficient in obtaining theorems' (1965 [1992], p. 47). Indeed the context of this argument is a discussion of the limitations of mathematics for physics (ibid., pp. 56–70).

Following on from Stohs, Dow (1985) explored the nature and implications of Babylonian thought in order to understand the different underpinnings of mainstream economic methodology from those of the methodologies of other schools of thought. Post Keynesianism being one of those schools of thought, the idea of Babylonian thought came to be one of the ways by which Post Keynesianism has become identified in the various efforts to specify the philosophical and methodological underpinnings of Post Keynesian economics.

Feynman (1965) presented Babylonian mathematics as consisting of an array of chains of reasoning, not tied to any one set of axioms, but governed by the practicalities of the problem at hand. It is thus a realist approach to knowledge. Since no one set of axioms can be relied on as being true, long chains of reasoning simply serve to compound any inaccuracy. Rather than constructing a single general formal system, it is seen as preferable to segment reality for the purposes of constructing a range of partial analyses, which are incommensurate; if they were commensurate, the arguments could be formally combined. One chain of reasoning might focus on one segment of reality such that a particular variable is (provisionally) exogenous, which is endogenous to another chain of reasoning. One chain of reasoning might rely on statistical analysis, while another might rely on historical research, for example. Euclidean mathematics, by contrast, is a closed logical system built on one set of axioms using one, mathematical, method; it abstracts from practical problems in order to generate universal solutions within the domain of abstraction. The logical system is thus governed by internal rules rather than reference to reality. This deductivist style of reasoning is also associated with René Descartes, hence the term 'Cartesian/Euclidean'.

Cartesian/Euclidean thought is a closed system, such that all variables are pre-specified and categorized as endogenous or exogenous; what is not known is assumed to be random. The nature of the components and their interrelations is fixed. In order to satisfy these conditions for closure, Cartesian/Euclidean thought is characterized by dualism and atomism. Duals are the all-encompassing, mutually exclusive categories with fixed meaning typical of closed systems. Variables are endogenous or exogenous; values are known with certainty (or within a stochastic distribution whose moments are known with certainty) or are not known at all; relationships are either causal or random; economic agents are rational or irrational; and so on. Atomism involves building up a theoretical system on the basis of the smallest units, which are independent of one another and of the system of which they are a part – rational economic men.

Babylonian thought is an open system, where the identity of all the relevant variables and relationships between them is not known, and in any case the meaning of variables and their interrelations is subject to change. There is scope for creativity and discrete shifts, as well as for stability. Babylonian thought is neither dualistic nor atomistic. The categories used to account for social life in an evolving environment are not seen as readily falling into duals. Indeed, vagueness of categories is seen to have the benefit of adaptability within a changing environment where institutions, understanding and behaviour undergo change. In a system of thought with a variety of incommensurate strands of argument, variables may be exogenous to one strand but endogenous to another. Knowledge is in general held with uncertainty (by economic agents and by economists), so the analysis points to degrees of uncertainty. Further, some strands of argument may refer to individuals, and others to the group level, since causal forces may act in either direction. Indeed, individuals are not seen as independent, and their behaviour may change as the environment changes. Institutions and conventions provide the stability to allow decisions to be taken in an uncertain environment.

Babylonian thought therefore refers to a social structure which is understood to be organic, itself an open system. It is thus realist, and indeed holds much in common with the critical realist approach to economics (although not its philosophical foundations). While Lawson (1994) argues that critical realism does not in itself provide the basis for identifying schools of thought among those who adopt a critical realist approach, this need not be the case (see Dow 1999). The Babylonian approach suggests a basis for differentiation in the form of realist ontology adopted – whether the economist understands the economic process in terms of production or exchange, class or the rational individual, and so on. The case for the compatibility between Babylonian thought and critical realism was made by Arestis et al. (1999) in response to Walters and Young's (1997) critique; see also Dow (1999).

Similarly, Babylonian thought provides a rationale for pluralism. It justifies both methodological pluralism (methodologists analysing a range of methodologies) and pluralism of method (economists using a range of methods). If the real world is understood as organic, not governed by universal laws, then there is scope for a range of methodologies. Further Babylonian thought specifically supports the use of a range of different methods for different chains of reasoning. But, to be operational, both forms of pluralism are moderated by the way in which the open system of thought is specified. How the real world is understood will govern the particular choice of methodology, and in turn the range of methods to be used.

The original expression of the Babylonian mode of thought was misunderstood by some as the dual of Cartesian/Euclidean thought. Rather than generating a unified methodology, it was seen as encouraging methodological diversity in the extreme sense of eclecticism. Cartesian/Euclidean thought offers a closed axiomatic system, which yields certain conclusions given the axioms. When Babylonian thought was understood as an open system without axioms, with incommensurate methods and with uncertain conclusions, it was taken to imply the absence of methodological principles – an 'anything goes' approach. It was associated with pure pluralism in the sense of a range of methods with no appraisal criteria by which to assess them. This interpretation was restated forcibly by Davidson (2003–04), who insisted on the merits of expressing Post Keynesian ontology in terms of axioms. But while axioms imply deductive logic, Davidson like most Post Keynesians uses human logic, which is implicit in Babylonian thought (see Dow 2005).

The 'anything goes' interpretation is dualistic, according more with the Cartesian/Euclidean mode of thought. Rather, the Babylonian mode of thought requires some criteria by which to choose segmentations of the subject matter for analysis, the chains of reasoning to pursue, and the methods employed to pursue them. This means that pluralism in Babylonian thought is not 'pure pluralism', but rather structured (Dow 2004). The subject matter is regarded as too complex to be captured fully in any one analytical system, so a range of choices as to methodology is possible. Since Post Keynesians have a distinctive ontology, a distinctive methodology follows, which differs from the methodology of other schools of thought that also employ an open systems mode of thought. The corollary is that, while Post Keynesians can (and do) argue for their own methodology and theories, they recognize that others, with different ontologies, will choose different methodologies and theories. While thought progresses within Post Keynesianism, there is also evidence in the extent of Post Keynesian work which crosses boundaries with other schools of thought, that an open thought system fosters creative synthetic developments.

SHEILA C. DOW

See also:

Critical Realism; Econometrics; Macroeconomic Methodology; Non-ergodicity; Open Systems; Pluralism in Economics; Uncertainty.

References

Arestis, P., S.P. Dunn and M. Sawyer (1999), 'Post Keynesian economics and its critics', *Journal of Post Keynesian Economics*, **21** (4), 527–49.

Davidson, P. (2003–04), 'Setting the record straight on *A History of Post Keynesian Economics*', *Journal of Post Keynesian Economics*, **26** (2), 245–72.

Dow, S.C. (1985), *Macroeconomic Thought: A Methodological Approach*, Oxford: Blackwell; reprinted in a revised and extended version as *The Methodology of Macroeconomic Thought*, Cheltenham, UK and Brookfield, VT, USA: Edward Elgar, 1996.

Dow, S.C. (1999), 'Post Keynesianism and critical realism: what is the connection?', *Journal of Post Keynesian Economics*, **22** (1), 15–33.

Dow, S.C. (2004), 'Structured pluralism', *Journal of Economic Methodology*, **11** (3), 275–90.

Dow, S.C. (2005), 'Axioms and Babylonian thought', *Journal of Post Keynesian Economics*, **27** (3), 245–72.

Feynman, R.P. (1965), *The Character of Physical Law*, Cambridge, MA: MIT Press. Page references are to the Penguin edition, 1992.

Keynes, J.M. (1933), 'Newton the man', in J.M. Keynes, *Essays in Biography*; reprinted in J.M. Keynes, *Collected Writings volume X*, London: Macmillan for the Royal Economic Society, 1972, pp. 363–74.

Lawson, T. (1994), 'The nature of Post Keynesianism and its links to other traditions: a realist perspective', *Journal of Post Keynesian Economics*, **16** (4), 503–38.

Stohs, M. (1983), '"Uncertainty" in Keynes' *General Theory*: a rejoinder', *History of Political Economy*, **15** (1), 87–91.

Walters, B. and D.Young (1997), 'On the coherence of post Keynesian economics', *Scottish Journal of Political Economy*, **44** (3), 329–49.

Whitehead, A.N. (1938), *Modes of Thought*, Cambridge: Cambridge University Press.

Wimsatt, W.C. (1981), 'Robustness, reliability and overdetermination', in M.B. Brewer and B.E. Collins (eds), *Scientific Inquiry and the Social Sciences*, San Francisco, CA: Jossey Bass, pp. 124–63.

Balance-of-payments-constrained Economic Growth

The balance-of-payments-constrained growth model provides a Keynesian demand-oriented explanation of why growth rates differ. This approach stands in marked contrast to the neoclassical growth theory (whether of the Solow–Swan or the endogenous variety), with the latter's emphasis on the role of the supply side. The central tenet of the balance-of-payments-constrained growth model is that a country cannot run a balance-of-payments deficit for any length of time that has to be financed by short-term capital flows and which results in an increasing net foreign debt-to-GDP ratio. If a country attempts to do this, the operation of the international financial markets will lead to increasing downward pressure on the currency, with the danger of a collapse in the exchange rate and the risk of a resulting depreciation/inflation spiral. There is also the possibility that the country's international credit rating will be downgraded. Consequently, in the long run, the basic balance (current account plus long-term capital flows) has to be in equilibrium. An implication of this approach is that there is nothing that guarantees that this rate will be the one consistent with the full employment of resources or the growth of the productive potential.

The main elements of this approach are set out in Thirlwall's (1979) seminal paper. The growth of exports is determined by the growth of world income and the rate of change of relative prices. The growth of imports is specified as a function of the growth of domestic income, together with the rate of change of relative prices. Substituting these into the definitional equation for the balance of payments, expressed in growth rate form, gives the growth of domestic income as a function of the growth of world income, the rate of change of relative prices, and the growth of net international capital flows.

If the impact of the last two on economic growth is quantitatively negligible (as empirically is often the case), the growth rate of income consistent with balance-of-payments equilibrium (y_B) is given by $y_B = \varepsilon z/\pi = x/\pi$, where ε, π, z, and x are the world income elasticity of demand for exports, the domestic income elasticity of demand for imports, the growth of world income, and the growth of exports. These two expressions for y_B are alternative specifications of what has come to be known as Thirlwall's law. It can be seen that the key factor determining the growth of a country is the growth of the exogenous component of demand, that is to say, exports, which in turn is determined by the growth of world markets (strictly speaking the weighted income growth of the country's trading partners). Thus, the model is an extension of the export-led growth hypothesis, but where the balance-of-payments constraint is explicitly incorporated.

There are substantial differences between countries in their values of ε and π and hence in how fast these economies can grow without encountering balance-of-payments problems. The disparities in ε and π are interpreted as reflecting differences in non-price competitiveness (for example, differences in the quality of goods and services, the effectiveness of a country's distribution network, delivery dates, and so on). It also reflects the degree to which a country's exports are concentrated on those sectors for which world demand is growing fastest. Thus the supply side is important to the extent that these supply characteristics play a crucial role in explaining the growth of exports and, hence, income. This stands in marked contrast to the way in which the neoclassical approach emphasizes the supply side, where technical change and the growth of factor inputs are the causal factors in the growth process.

A necessary condition for the balance-of-payments constraint to be binding is that the rate of change of the exchange rate is ineffective in determining the growth of exports and imports. If this were not the case, then real exchange rate adjustments could ensure that the balance of payments was brought into equilibrium at any given rate of the growth of income, including the growth of productive potential. However, it should be emphasized that the balance-of-payments-constrained growth model does not imply that changes in relative prices have *no* effect on the current account. It may be that changes in these are sufficient to bring a current account deficit back into equilibrium when, for example, the economy is growing at, or near, its balance-of-payments equilibrium rate, but they are unlikely to be sufficient to raise the balance-of-payments equilibrium growth rate, *per se*. Given the multiplicative nature of the export and import demand functions, to achieve the latter would require a sustained rate of real depreciation.

There are a number of reasons why this is implausible. First, there may be real wage resistance, which makes it difficult for a continuous nominal depreciation to be translated into a corresponding sustained real depreciation. Second, firms may price to market so that imports and exports are unresponsive to any changes in the real exchange rate. Third, the values of the price elasticities of demand may be so low that the Marshall–Lerner condition is barely satisfied. If the absolute values of the price elasticities sum to one, then the rule $y_B = \varepsilon z/\pi$ holds, even if there is a substantial rate of change of relative prices. Manufactured goods and services that enter into international trade are for the most part highly differentiated and so their demand curves are relatively inelastic. Firms compete for sales predominantly by attempting to shift outwards the demand curve for their products through increasing their non-price competitiveness, rather than by moving down the demand curve through improving their price competitiveness. (See McCombie and Thirlwall 1994, chapter 4 for a discussion of the empirical evidence.) The effect of the growth of relative prices may be more important for the developing countries, especially for homogeneous commodity exports, but there may well be strong competition from other developing countries that limits the growth of such exports.

Thirlwall's law may be regarded as a dynamic version of Harrod's (1933) foreign trade multiplier. McCombie and Thirlwall (1994, chapter 6) demonstrated that, in a more complex Keynesian model than Harrod used, Thirlwall's law could be more generally regarded as the workings of the Hicks super-multiplier. An increase in export growth from, for example, a position of current account equilibrium, would increase the growth of income directly through the Harrod foreign trade multiplier. Moreover, at the same time, by generating an increasing current account surplus, it allows a further increase in the growth of other domestic components of demand to occur, thereby raising the growth rate even further, until the basic balance is re-established. The combined effect of these two mechanisms represents the operation of the Hicks super-multiplier in dynamic form.

There have been an increasing number of studies that have tested this approach to economic growth. The early literature is surveyed in McCombie and Thirlwall (1994), while the more recent studies are covered in McCombie and Thirlwall (2004) and Thirlwall (2011). The general methodology is to estimate the values ε and π for a particular country from export and import demand functions (which include relative price terms) using time-series data. In the original studies, ordinary least-squares was used, but recently more sophisticated econometric techniques have been adopted, for example those that test for stationarity and cointegration of the data and use a VAR framework. From the estimates of ε and π, a value for the balance-of-payments equilibrium growth rate can be obtained using the expression for Thirlwall's law, $y_B = \varepsilon z / \pi$. (Alternatively, $y_B = x / \pi$ is sometimes used.) The balance-of-payments equilibrium growth rate, when calculated over a period of a decade or longer, is often found to be very close to the actual growth rate and this has been confirmed by a variety of statistical tests. It is also commonly found that the estimates of the price elasticities in the export and import demand functions are either small or statistically insignificant, or both. This provides further evidence of the unimportance of price competition in international trade. Of course, not all countries will necessarily be simultaneously balance-of-payments constrained. At any one time, some countries (or trading blocs) may be policy constrained, where demand management policies have resulted in the actual growth of income being below the balance-of-payments equilibrium growth rate. Other countries may be growing so fast that they are resource constrained. The problem is that the balance-of-payments-constrained countries find that their growth rates are effectively limited by the growth of these policy- and resource-constrained countries. If, for example, a particular country curtails its growth for policy reasons, its major trading partners are going to find that their balance-of-payments equilibrium growth rates fall. Their actual rate of growth will then be curtailed, regardless of whether or not the conditions in their domestic market warrant this. McCombie (1993) presents a two-country theoretical model of this, while Nell (2003) tests a model using three regions that are closely linked by trade, namely South Africa, the rest of the South African Development Community (RSADC) and the OECD. He finds that South Africa is balance-of-payments constrained with respect to the OECD and the RSADC is balance-of-payments constrained with respect to South Africa.

The approach does not just apply to countries with national currencies, but the principle also holds at the regional level (McCombie and Thirlwall, 1994, chapter 8). This suggests that the formation of a monetary union, such as the European Economic and Monetary Union, will not remove the importance of export growth and the balance of payments in determining the overall growth rate of a country. This is especially true when there are few, if any, fiscal transfers between countries in the monetary union.

Araujo and Lima (2007) extend theoretically the balance-of-payments-constrained growth model by using Pasinetti's (1993) disaggregated structural economic dynamics. The latter, while emphasizing the importance of demand-led structural change, does not have a balance-of-payments constraint. The aggregate income elasticities of demand for exports and imports are the weighted elasticities of the respective individual sectors, where the weights should change over time. Using the latter, Araujo and Lima derive what they term the 'multi-sectoral Thirlwall's law'. They show that even though the individual sectoral income elasticities of demand for exports and imports are constant, the balance-of-payments-constrained growth rate can increase if a country over time specializes more in those sectors where the individual export income elasticities of demand are highest as well as in import-competing sectors where the income elasticity of demand is also greatest. As Thirlwall (2011, p. 24) puts it, 'this is what import substitution and export promotion policies are meant to achieve'.

Gouvea and Lima (2010) use this approach to analyse the growth rates of four Latin American and four Asian economies. They find that both the multi-sectoral and the original aggregate version of Thirlwall's law hold, with the exception of the latter for South Korea. Using the multi-sectoral approach, they show that the ratio of the aggregated sectoral export income elasticities of demand to the aggregated import income elasticities for the Asian countries increased over time, whereas this was not true of the Latin American countries (with the exception of Mexico). Thus, the acceleration of growth in the Asian economies was primarily due to their increasing specialization in those exports for which world demand was growing more rapidly. In conclusion, Davidson (1990–91, p. 303) has summarized this approach as a significant contribution to Post Keynesian economic theory in its demonstration that 'international payments imbalances can have severe real growth consequences, i.e., money is not neutral in an open economy'. Recent theoretical and applied developments in the subject have served to confirm this view.

JOHN S.L. MCCOMBIE

See also:

Exchange Rates; Export-led Growth; Growth Theory; International Economics; Multiplier.

References

Araujo, R.A. and G.T. Lima (2007), 'A structural economic dynamics approach to balance-of-payments-constrained growth', *Cambridge Journal of Economics*, **31** (5), 755–74.

Davidson, P. (1990–91), 'A Post Keynesian positive contribution to "theory"', *Journal of Post Keynesian Economics*, **13** (2), 298–303.

Gouvea, R.R. and G.T. Lima (2010), 'Structural change, balance of payments constraint and economic growth: evidence from the multisectoral Thirlwall's law', *Journal of Post Keynesian Economics*, **33** (1), 169–204.

Harrod, R.F. (1933), *International Economics*, Cambridge: Cambridge University Press.

McCombie, J.S.L. (1993), 'Economic growth, trade inter-linkages and the balance-of-payments constraint', *Journal of Post Keynesian Economics*, **15** (4), 471–505; reprinted in McCombie and Thirlwall, 2004.

McCombie J.S.L. and A.P. Thirlwall (1994), *Economic Growth and the Balance-of-Payments Constraint*, Basingstoke: Macmillan.

McCombie, J.S.L. and A.P. Thirlwall (2004), *Essays on Balance of Payments Constrained Growth: Theory and Evidence*, London and New York: Routledge.

Nell, K. (2003), 'A generalized version of the balance-of-payments growth model: an application to neighbouring regions, *International Review of Applied Economics*, **17** (3), 249–67; reprinted in McCombie and Thirlwall, 2004.

Pasinetti, L.L. (1993), *Structural Economic Dynamics*, Cambridge: Cambridge University Press.

Thirlwall, A.P. (1979), 'The balance of payments constraint as an explanation of international growth rate differences', *Banca Nazionale del Lavoro Quarterly Review*, **128** (791), 45–53; reprinted in McCombie and Thirlwall, 2004.

Thirlwall, A.P. (2011), 'Balance-of-payments constrained growth models: history and overview', paper presented at the conference 'Thirlwall's Law and the Balance of Payments Constrained Growth', Faculty of Economics, University of Coimbra, Portugal (June).

Banking

The behaviour of banks in the loan market is of major significance to Post Keynesian analyses of a monetary production economy. When the money supply is endogenous and the central bank sets the cost of wholesale funds (the base rate), and accommodates bankers' demands for liquidity at that rate, the direction of causation between loans and deposits embodied in the traditional exogenous money/money multiplier model is reversed. In Post Keynesian models, loans cause deposits and hence bring money into existence as an integral aspect of the operation of the 'real' economy. Thus banks are able to advance the financing for investment without the necessity for saving to have been accumulated beforehand. It follows that investment expenditures can be constrained by credit rationing but not by a shortage of saving. Banks and their ability and willingness to extend loans, then, are a key determinant of increases in the level of employment and output following an *ex ante* increase in the demand for investment goods. What has become starkly obvious as a result of the global financial crisis, which began in the US banking system, however, is that banks extend credit not only for the financing of investment but also for speculation in assets by their customers, and as speculators in their own right (see Jarsulic 2010).

To Post Keynesians, the banking system is in a constant state of innovating and evolving in response to the profit opportunities presented by 'the interaction of economic conditions with regulatory constraints' (Moore 1988, p. 31n; see also Minsky 1986, chapter 10; Chick 1992, chapter 12). Thus when banks were subject to reserve requirements, with which central banks endeavoured to control bank balance sheets and their capacity to lend by requiring banks to hold liquid asset reserves against their liabilities, new financing instruments and techniques associated with liability management emerged. Liability management refers to the ability of banks to vary interest rates to attract both wholesale and retail funds which can be used to finance lending activity. Negotiable certificates of deposit, security repurchase agreements, retail cash management accounts and the interbank market for short-term funds are examples of innovations which have increased the elasticity of the supply of financing relative to regulation intended to limit such responsiveness. In the more recent era of capital requirements, which are requirements to hold capital against categories of assets and off balance sheet risks, different techniques and instruments are used to minimize the banks' costs of regulation, primarily the securitization, or packaging and sale, of loans.

However, while these innovations have lowered the banks' costs of regulation and increased their ability to provide credit on demand, they have also increased the banking system's exposure to liquidity and credit risks. Individual banks may expand their balance sheets by matching potentially volatile sources of funds with new and relatively illiquid loans. The increasing liquidity of these loans through securitization, however, may reduce a bank's interest in the creditworthiness of individual loans and raise its attention to conditions within secondary markets for asset-backed securities. Whether or not US banks deliberately (fraudulently) made loans to homeowners which they knew could not be repaid, higher liquidity and credit risk have become a feature of the system (see Jarsulic 2010 on the role of subprime lending and securitization in the recent US housing boom and collapse). In the context of an asset-price inflation, banks are inherently speculating in lending on the basis of continued inflation. In the case of the recent US housing boom and subsequent financial crisis, as housing prices rose, lending standards fell, so that banks turned borrowers into Ponzi financing units: the banks increasingly disregarded future cash flows (indeed, mortgages were structured to minimize early repayments to raise eligibility), and relied on rising house prices to raise borrower equity and hence create the access to credit needed for mortgage repayments. Even more problematically, the Glass–Steagall Act 1933 was repealed by the Financial Services Modernization Act 1999, which meant that not only were banks creating new financial instruments to move loans off their balance sheets, but they could now speculate on their own account in those very instruments. It hardly need be noted that these securities were subprime mortgage-backed securities.

The Post Keynesian view of asset management should be distinguished from that implied by the orthodox account, where banks must either passively await new deposits made available by central bank purchases of government securities, or finance new loans with the proceeds of the termination of other assets, replacing a consumer loan with a small business loan, for example. In Post Keynesian economics, banks actively manage both sides of their balance sheets to minimize the cost of regulation and maximize profit.

Bankers' decision-making processes around these liquidity and credit risk issues are the subject of some debate among Post Keynesian monetary theorists. This debate can be framed as disagreement on the extent to which banks are quantity takers in their loan markets. In the case of the horizontalist position, as defined by Moore (1988), banks set the interest rate on loans as a profit-maximizing mark-up over the cost of funds. The mark-up equates the bank's marginal cost of borrowed funds and marginal revenue of lent funds. Bankers provide loans on demand at that rate: 'In their retail loan and deposit markets banks act as price setters and quantity takers' (ibid., p. 55). A shortage of funds is met by borrowing in the wholesale market, using the tools of liability management. As mentioned above, the cost of funds in the short-term wholesale market is determined by the central bank, which, as a market maker, will typically fully accommodate banks' demands. Should the stance of monetary policy tighten, the central bank's supply of funds will be restricted and the base rate will rise. In this scenario, the credit-money supply function is demand determined and perfectly elastic at the mark-up over the base rate, with the important implication that the liquidity preference theory of the interest rate is thereby invalidated (ibid., pp. 197–204).

Other Post Keynesians agree that the central bank implements monetary policy through its control of the base rate, but disagree that banks are quantity takers to the extent required by the pure horizontalist position. They argue that bankers respond to changes in their liquidity preference by systematically price- and quantity-rationing credit. Thus liquidity preference theory is essential to an explanation of how and why bankers vary the price and availability of credit for any given base rate (see, for example, Dow 1996). In part, this difference of opinion can be explained as somewhat semantic by pointing out that the horizontalist position is overstated in relation to the issue of the quantity rationing of credit. In fact, in the horizontalist account, banks impose credit limitations on *all* loan applicants and meet unreservedly only the *effective* demand for loans.

That is, before banks supply loans 'on demand', applicants have already been subjected to criteria which identify them as applicants to be either fully or partially restricted (see Moore 1988, pp. 55–6). Fully restricted applicants are those who fail to meet the minimum collateral and income and maximum risk requirements set by the bank. Partially restricted applicants are those who are approved for borrowing up to a specified limit. Thus 'the supply of credit by the banking system is perfectly elastic, *up to borrowers' allotted credit ceilings*' (ibid., p. 337, emphasis added; see also Lavoie 1996). It is therefore a matter of timing – when does credit rationing take place? – that determines whether one argues that banks are or are not unqualified quantity takers.

However, a perfectly elastic credit money supply function rules out price rationing at any particular base rate. This is justified by the need to clearly distinguish the Post Keynesian exogenous interest rate analysis from the loanable funds, endogenous interest rate, orthodoxy which predicts that an increase in investment necessarily raises the rate of interest (ibid., pp. 276–7). Lavoie (p. 279) argues that the base rate is indeed exogenous with respect to the income-generating process, and that it is a separate issue as to how bankers establish mark-ups over that rate. But he further insists that Post Keynesians must argue that there is no compulsion for banks to raise lending rates as economic activity expands. The opposing view is that, at a given base rate, banks will supply more credit to individual borrowers only if accompanied by an increasing loan rate, since borrowers' debt/equity ratios increase and hence lender's risk rises (Dow 1996, pp. 500–503; see also Minsky 1986, chapter 8). Yet it is certainly plausible that, in a period of optimism and inflated expectations with respect to future stock or flow returns from assets, bankers' perceptions of this increasing risk may be muted to the point of non-existence, at least within the relevant range. Indeed, this point is made by Dow (1996, p. 501, Fig. 1) and similarly by Minsky (1986, p. 193, Fig. 8.4). Moreover, the 'paradox of debt' may apply when considering not a single firm but industrial firms in aggregate. Specifically, leverage ratios of firms may fall as profits rise with rising investment during the upturn, frustrating firms' plans to finance their expansions with debt rather than equity, and eliminating the increase in lender's risk (Lavoie 1996, pp. 285–6). Furthermore, Lavoie (pp. 292–4) argues that liquidity preference goes by the name of 'animal spirits' in the horizontalist account, and so denies that there is a serious incompatibility between the views of horizontalists and others. Nevertheless, Dow (1996, pp. 502–4) does not agree that the supply of loans is necessarily perfectly elastic and suggests that, even if banks were to supply loans to creditworthy borrowers on demand for most of the business cycle, during a downturn the rising liquidity preference of the providers of wholesale funds, as well as the providers of the capital which banks must hold to meet risk-adjusted capital requirements, will cause bankers' liquidity preference, and hence their mark-ups, to rise.

The use of liquidity preference theory is all the more imperative when the business cycle is considered because it allows a cornerstone of Keynes's legacy – the existence of uncertainty – to play a central role in explaining the periodic crises which beset capitalist economies. These crises are characterized by significant increases in loan defaults and interest rate margins, and a collapse in the willingness of bankers to continue to extend credit, entailing a strong desire to move to more liquid balance sheets (a rise in banks' liquidity preference). The upturn which eventually follows the crash is characterized by the reverse of these events. Thus over the cycle, and independently of changes in the base rate, banks revise their views on creditworthiness and appropriate loan rates and, therefore, on quantity and price rationing (see Jarsulic 2010 on the lowering of lending standards in the lead-up to the recent global financial crisis). Orthodox models of credit rationing due to market failure in the form of asymmetric information between borrowers and lenders miss this key point: there simply is no full information case, so that default probabilities can only ever be subjectively determined. As Minsky (1986, pp. 239–40) stresses, the 'prudent banker' is faced not by objective probability distributions of returns but by uncertainty and hence the necessity of subjective evaluations of risks. These evaluations are not constrained by depositor monitoring, due to the absorption of risk by the monetary authorities (the classic moral hazard problem). Because the future is unknown and uncertain, rather than probabilistically known and risky, bankers and loan applicants may or may not suffer from asymmetric information but they will typically be making decisions under asymmetric expectations. That is, even if they have the same information (and even if they have the same risk preferences), they evaluate that information differently (Wolfson 1996, pp. 450–51).

A banker's evaluation of information about particular borrowers, their investment projects and their likelihood of repayment involves assessing a number of factors in relation to the bank's established standards or conventions. Factors such as the borrowing history of the applicant, the applicant's debt/equity ratio, the value of collateral, and expected future cash flows given the bank's view of the macroeconomic environment during the period of repayment, are all subjectively assessed. Whether or not these assessments lead to the provision of funds, and at what price, is a function both of conventions – what has happened in the recent past and the extent to which it is expected that the past will be repeated – and of the degree to which a banker is confident in the assessment. When the bank perceives an increase in the default risk of borrowers, due for example to a downturn in the economy, or when its own liquidity preference rises, it raises both the loan price and non-price requirements, so that some borrowers pay higher rates at the same time as other borrowers – those unable to meet the non-price requirements – are rationed (ibid., pp. 452–60). Thus the loan supply function is subject to shifts as bankers' perceptions move between pessimism and optimism, with their liquidity preference correspondingly rising and falling. Banks' extensions of credit are virtually unconstrained in the increasingly optimistic environment of the upturn, which leads them to finance increasingly fragile debt positions (see Minsky 1986, chapter 9). Central banks, as lenders of last resort, play an essential role in mitigating the crises which result from the inevitable reversals of expectations, liquidity preference and cash flows relative to cash commitments which end the growth of the debt pyramid. In short, banks are both destabilizing and indispensable to a monetary-production economy: banking 'is a disruptive force that tends to induce and amplify instability even as it is an essential factor if investment and economic growth are to be financed' (ibid., p. 229).

GILLIAN HEWITSON

See also:

Central Banks; Credit Rationing; Financial Instability Hypothesis; Liquidity Preference; Monetary Policy; Money; Rate of Interest; Uncertainty.

References

Chick, V. (1992), *On Money, Method and Keynes: Selected Essays*, edited by P. Arestis and S.C. Dow, New York: St. Martin's Press.
Dow, S.C. (1996), 'Horizontalism: a critique', *Cambridge Journal of Economics*, **20** (4), 497–508.
Jarsulic, M. (2010), *Anatomy of a Financial Crisis*, Basingstoke: Palgrave Macmillan.
Lavoie, M. (1996), 'Horizontalism, structuralism, liquidity preference and the principle of increasing risk', *Scottish Journal of Political Economy*, **43** (3), 275–300.
Minsky, H.P. (1986), *Stabilizing an Unstable Economy*, New Haven, CT: Yale University Press.
Moore, B.J. (1988), *Horizontalists and Verticalists: The Macroeconomics of Credit Money*, Cambridge: Cambridge University Press.
Wolfson, M. (1996), 'A Post Keynesian theory of credit rationing', *Journal of Post Keynesian Economics*, **18** (3), 443–70.

Bastard Keynesianism

More has been written about Keynes's *General Theory* than any other work in economics in the twentieth century. It has a reputation of being a difficult book to understand. Some of Keynes's greatest supporters were initially hostile in their reviews. The doyen of American economics, Paul Samuelson found the book so confusing it took him 12 to 18 months to begin to understand it, and then only when it was put in mathematical form. Popularizers had to simplify the book for mass consumption. In the process of simplification and interpretation, the *General Theory* was presented in a way that was comfortable to those brought up on the micro-economic supply and demand apparatus. Again there was a simple graphical presentation (either IS–LM or the Keynesian 'cross') and issues could be discussed in terms of shifts of curves, and slopes and elasticities, and marginal changes of variables. Its pedagogical attractiveness and simplicity soon ruled the textbooks (Schneider 2010).

However, while economics acquired a new macroeconomic model that was simple, easily grasped and teachable, it was also a model that omitted many important aspects of Keynes's ideas. Joan Robinson in 1962 called this vulgarization of Keynes 'Bastard Keynesianism' (Robinson 1971, p. 90). Sidney Weintraub (1977) called it 'Hicksian Keynesianism' or 'Classical Keynesianism'. 'Hydraulic Keynesianism' is another label used, as is 'Neo-Keynesian'. The term 'neoclassical synthesis' describes the process through which Keynes's *General Theory* was reconciled with pre-Keynesian thinking. The years from the mid-1950s through the 1960s were the golden age of the neoclassical synthesis, which in substance was the linking of the Keynesian income–expenditure system with neo-Walrasian general equilibrium analysis. During this period, the terms 'neo-Keynesian' and 'neoclassical' seemed interchangeable. Yet in this context Keynes's contribution was relegated to imposing several price rigidities which, however useful for policy purposes, were nevertheless theoretically trivial. It is this trivialization of Keynes that so offends his true disciples.

The process of simplification and systematization of Keynes began almost immediately. One can see this clearly in the titles of the articles and books published at the time. John Hicks's key article was titled 'Mr. Keynes and the Classics: A Suggested Interpretation'. James Meade's article was 'A Simplified Model of Mr. Keynes' System' and Alvin Hansen's book was *A Guide to Keynes*. Models comprising a small number of simultaneous equations, presented by Hicks, Hansen, Meade, Brian Reddaway, Roy Harrod, Franco Modigliani and Oscar Lange, came to symbolize the Keynesian revolution. The model was popularly known as the IS–LM model. It seemed to summarize whatever substantive message the interpreters took from Keynes's book in a system of simultaneous equations whose properties were similar to the standard partial-equilibrium supply–demand approach. Once the equations were translated into diagrammatic form (the Hicks–Hansen diagram) many of the apparent obscurities and ambiguities seemed to vanish. Furthermore, it provided a logical basis for activist policy proposals associated with the Keynesian revolution.

Paul Samuelson's response to the *General Theory* is instructive. While he acknowledged that it was a work of genius, it was also (he claimed) obscure, confusing, overly polemical and poorly organized. Keynes, he alleged, had no genuine interest in economic theory, although by intuition he seems to have stumbled on the right path. What was needed was to update and systemize the framework through a system of mathematical equations. Indeed, the IS–LM model was needed to comprehend what the *General Theory* was all about, something even Keynes may not have been sure of. While the IS–LM model was used for advanced students, a truncated version called the Keynesian cross was used for introductory students. Samuelson remarked that 'the intersection C(Y) + I with the 45 degree line gives us our simplest "Keynesian-cross", which logically is exactly like a "Marshallian-cross" of supply and demand' (cited in Weintraub 1977, p. 47).

The Keynesian cross and IS–LM became the two most popular ways through which students 'learned' Keynesian economics. Wide dissemination of the Keynesian cross was achieved through the various editions of Samuelson's introductory text. Relationships between aggregate variables constituted the foundations of the macroeconometric models generated. Aggregate flows of the economy were likely to grind out less than full-employment output levels through various rigidities and imperfections. Keynesians were not concerned with the structure of the economy, as all that was needed was to change a few dials to maintain adequate levels of aggregate demand. The most important dials were those associated with fiscal policy; hence early Keynesians were often called 'fiscalists'. Financial markets and monetary policy were neglected.

As IS–LM and the Keynesian cross became the dominant orthodoxy in macroeconomics, other issues vanished from the mainstream literature. But did these models convey the essential message that Keynes intended to convey in the *General Theory*?

The dissenters from the mainstream interpretation of Keynes all agree that IS–LM and the Keynesian-cross models miss the essence of Keynes, but provide contrasting views as to what that essential message is. Joan Robinson's critique is primarily methodological. She denies the legitimacy of using comparisons of equilibrium positions to analyse processes in actual time, and contrasts models in logical time and those in historical time. The 'Bastard Keynesians' assume microeconomic foundations so that markets behave as if they were Walrasian competitive ones, but agree that an economy can come to rest at an underemployment equilibrium, or move to full-employment equilibrium very slowly, due to deficient aggregate demand. Hence they support demand management policies. Robinson argues that one cannot fit Keynes into a neo-Walrasian framework because it can not handle historical time. Keynes did not think in terms of simultaneous determination: he was a cause and effect man;

investment determined saving, aggregate demand determined output and employment, and so on. Robinson contrasts the Marshallian micro model of Keynes with the Walrasian micro model of the Bastard Keynesians.

The *General Theory* stimulated the construction and testing of aggregative models. These models attempted to replicate the actual economy's behaviour through various systems of mathematical equations, the coefficients of which were derived from historical data. Lawrence Klein played a key role here in pioneering the path for a generation of quantitative research in Keynesian macroeconomics. The economics profession devoted substantial resources to the construction, estimation, testing and manipulation of these large-scale econometric models for forecasting and policy analysis. All the large-scale US models had properties similar to the IS–LM model. While these models were called 'Keynesian' the modellers seemed to have been unaware of Keynes's 1939 critique of Jan Tinbergen's econometric methods and he presumably would not have favoured this development.

Textbook Keynesianism has been subject to frequent attack, with perhaps Sidney Weintraub's (1977) critique being the clearest. Weintraub sees Keynesianism as only tenuously connected to Keynes. The Keynesian-cross income–expenditure analysis uses simple equations relating consumption to income, investment to the interest rate, and an equilibrium balance equation. When solved it leads to an equilibrium income that may or may not correspond to a full-employment level of income. However, in this model, with its inflationary and deflationary gaps, the economy could experience either inflation or unemployment but not both. It could not accommodate stagflation. A Phillips curve was then grafted on to the Keynesian-cross analysis and the Phillips curve became identified as an important part of Keynesianism via Robert Solow and Paul Samuelson. Yet one cannot find the Phillips curve in Keynes, and it would have been inconsistent with his approach to find a sustainable empirical relationship. Keynes would not have supported any stable, dependable, long-term relationship between inflation and unemployment. It was precisely these features of the model that were so successfully attacked by Milton Friedman and the monetarists (Forder 2010). Similarly it was the Keynesian macroeconometric models that were attacked by Robert Lucas and the New Classical macroeconomists. In both cases the attacks related to the Bastard Keynesians, *not Keynes*. Leijonhufvud (1968) highlights this distinction clearly.

Weintraub's alternative Keynesianism, using aggregate demand and aggregate supply analysis, would have avoided these confusions. Stagflation is inconsistent with IS–LM and the Keynesian cross, but not with aggregate demand and aggregate supply. Stagflation is not inconsistent with

Keynes's framework. Lorie Tarshis also provided an early text using this framework, but the aggregate supply curve was developed in an imperfectly competitive setting. This allowed an easier incorporation of the 'wage unit' into the analysis. Fiscalism is another concern for Weintraub. Sheila Dow notes that Keynes for most of his life was an endogenous money person and a monetary theorist (Harcourt 2001, p. 48). The neglect of monetary factors in the postwar period would not have been in the spirit of Keynes.

Paul Davidson (1972) and Hyman Minsky (1975) have both emphasized the important role Keynes placed on the financial sector. For Minsky, Keynesian economics as the economics of disequilibrium is the economics of *permanent* disequilibrium. He contends that the capital asset valuation process, in conditions of uncertainty, was central to Keynes's argument and that capitalism is inherently unstable due to its financial structure. Davidson, along with George Shackle and others, focuses on fundamental uncertainty. Decision making is undertaken in an uncertain environment, and we need to examine the psychologies of the main players – speculators, investors, consumers, wage-earners. Keynes almost never refers to isolated individuals; he speaks of the psychology of specific social groups. Davidson tries to integrate the monetary detail of Keynes's earlier *A Treatise on Money* with the effective demand features of the *General Theory*. The overriding importance of uncertainty in investment and money markets means that investment expectations are unquantifiable and unpredictable, and their volatility influences the economy's overall instability.

There are other critics of the Bastard Keynesians, such as Victoria Chick (1983), who focus on the misapplication of the policy prescriptions of the *General Theory*. Chick argues that fiscal stimulus was designed as shock treatment and not intended to sustain an economy over a long time period. She maintains that Keynes would not have approved of fine-tuning and would have supported the more selective use of fiscal policy, and not continuous budget deficits. The excessive preoccupation with the short run has ignored the long-run tendency to a lack of effective demand with involuntary unemployment. Less concern with fine-tuning and more attention to the long-run expansion of economic activity is required. Keynes's mention of the need for closer scrutiny of the level and composition of investment, or the 'socialization of investment', has also gone unheeded by the mainstream Keynesians.

To sum up the critique of the Bastard Keynesians, the so-called 'custodians' of the real message of the *General Theory* claim that Keynes's vision is too rich to be encapsulated in one graph or a few equations. Wage stickiness or liquidity traps are not essential components of Keynes's message. The 'economics of Keynes' cannot be analysed in timeless, perfect information, general equilibrium models. A world of fundamental uncertainty moving through historical time is essential to the message of Keynes. Interpreting Keynes through IS–LM is a distortion that forces the *General Theory* into the older neoclassical mould. Mainstream Keynesians such as Paul Samuelson and James Tobin reject these criticisms. Indeed, Robert Solow approves of the Bastard Keynesian label because to him it suggests 'hybrid vigour'!

The debate between the Bastard Keynesians and the true disciples has long been superseded by the attacks on Keynesians of any description by the monetarists and, more powerfully, by the New Classical macroeconomists. What one finds in the textbooks now is a far greater travesty of Keynes than anything the 'Bastards' did. For example, in Gregory Mankiw's *Principles of Macroeconomics* one finds a pre-Keynesian loanable funds model; all a budget deficit achieves is higher interest rates, crowding out and lower national saving. Mankiw (1998) presents the 'Treasury View' that Keynes so devastatingly attacked. In the unemployment chapter there is no mention of aggregate demand; the only causes of unemployment are minimum wage laws, unions, efficiency wages and job search. Unemployment appears to be always at the 'natural' rate, with deviations rare and transitory. A monetarist approach to inflation is provided. This text concentrates on the classical principles of macroeconomics and is a savage departure from the fundamental principles of any kind of Keynesian thought. The 'Treasury View', the quantity theory of money and Say's law are all found in modern guises. This is all presented as 'New Keynesianism'!

In this context, Geoffrey Harcourt (2001) made a plea for a united front with Keynesians of whatever type, including the Bastard Keynesians, to fight the monetarist/New Classical assault. His call for Keynesians of any persuasion to coalesce into a united front seems to have mollified the earlier Post Keynesian antagonism towards the Bastard Keynesians. This sentiment was to no avail as a new 'neoclassical synthesis' emerged that was accepted by New Keynesians and New Classical economists alike. Robert Lucas played a pivotal role in synthesizing neoclassical economics and 'efficient markets' finance theory into a dynamic stochastic general equilibrium macroeconomic framework utilizing rational expectations and representative agent models.

This cosy consensus was ruptured by the global financial crisis that hit in 2007–08. Such a crisis could not be captured by the models of the New Neoclassical Synthesis. This is powerfully documented by Taylor (2011) and popularly in Paul Krugman's 2009 *New York Times* piece, 'How did economics get it so wrong?'. Even a leading figure associated with the Chicago School, Richard Posner, acknowledged that 'Keynes is back' while Robert Skidelsky's (2009) book is titled *Keynes: The Return of the Master*. There is life yet in the debate over the 'bastardization' of Keynes.

JOHN LODEWIJKS

See also:

Econometrics; Effective Demand; Keynes's *General Theory*; Keynes's *Treatise on Money*; New Classical Economics; New Keynesian Economics; New Neoclassical Synthesis; Stagflation; Time in Economic Theory; Uncertainty; Walrasian Economics.

Bibliography

Chick, V. (1983), *Macroeconomics after Keynes: A Reconsideration of the General Theory*, Cambridge, MA: MIT Press.
Davidson, P. (1972), *Money and the Real World*, London: Macmillan.
De Vroey, M. and K.D. Hoover (eds) (2004), *The IS–LM Model: Its Rise, Fall, and Strange Persistence*, Durham, NC: Duke University Press.
Forder, J. (2010), 'Friedman's Nobel lecture and the Phillips curve myth', *Journal of the History of Economic Thought*, **32** (3), 329–48.
Harcourt, G.C. (2001), *50 Years a Keynesian and Other Essays*, Basingstoke: Palgrave.
Krugman, P. (2009), 'How did economists get it so wrong?', *New York Times*, 2 September.
Laidler, D. (1999), *Fabricating the Keynesian Revolution*, Cambridge: Cambridge University Press.
Leijonhufvud, A. (1968), *On Keynesian Economics and the Economics of Keynes: A Study in Monetary Theory*, London: Oxford University Press.
Mankiw, G. (1998), *Principles of Economics*, Sydney: Dryden.
Minsky, H.P. (1975), *John Maynard Keynes*, New York: Macmillan.
Robinson, J. (1971), *Economic Heresies*, New York: Basic Books.
Schneider, M. (2010), 'Keynesian income determination diagrams', in M. Blaug and P. Lloyd (eds), *Famous Figures and Diagrams in Economics*, Cheltenham, UK and Northampton, MA, USA: Edward Elgar, pp. 337–47.
Skidelsky, R. (2009), *Keynes: The Return of the Master*, New York: Public Affairs.
Taylor, L. (2011), *Maynard's Revenge: The Collapse of Free Market Macroeconomics*, Cambridge, MA: Harvard University Press.
Weintraub, S. (1977), 'Hicksian Keynesianism: dominance and decline', in Weintraub, *Modern Economic Thought*, Philadelphia, PA: University of Pennsylvania Press, pp. 45–66.

Behavioural Economics

'Behavioural economics' is an umbrella term, and the key question is which areas of economic research are included and how these differ from other approaches. John Tomer describes behavioural economics as including eight different approaches: (i) Herbert Simon and the Carnegie School; (ii) George Katona and the Michigan School; (iii) psychological economics; (iv) Harvey Leibenstein and X-efficiency theory; (v) George Akerlof and behavioural macroeconomics; (vi) Richard Nelson, Sidney Winter and evolutionary theory; (vii) behavioural finance; and (viii) Vernon Smith and experimental economics. The difficulty of succinctly defining behavioural economics arises partly because it has never been purposively framed as a single coherent research project. This is not necessarily seen as problematic, since 'post positivism means methodological pluralism' (Tomer 2007, p. 464). Tomer argues that the distinguishing feature of behavioural economists is that they 'practise and espouse scientific methods that are different, at least, from those typical of mainstream economists', and this arises from their 'different normative conceptions of economics as a science' (pp. 463–5). He concludes that behavioural economics does not 'have a clear, definite methodology and social philosophy'; if it is to be recognized as a school of thought, this might be at the level that 'behavioral economists by and large regard the key social evil or Great Problem to be the dominance of mainstream economics in the economic profession' (p. 478). Post Keynesian economics is also multifaceted, and it too might be regarded as treating mainstream economics as the 'great problem'. However, contributors to this area of economic thought have typically placed a high priority on a consistent methodology; plural *methods* might be accepted by Post Keynesians, but not plural *methodologies*.

Despite the varying and potentially incompatible methodologies contained under the label of behavioural economics, several Post Keynesian scholars have called for a closer engagement between Post Keynesian economics and behavioural economics. Indeed, Paul Davidson (2010–11) argues that John Maynard Keynes was in fact the first behavioural economist, since his emphasis on uncertainty, the role of conventions and the possibility of herd behaviour in a non-ergodic economic universe is entirely consistent with recent neurological research carried out by brain scientists into the way in which people actually make economic decisions. The potential for collaboration between Post Keynesians and neuroeconomists is an intriguing question, albeit one that has been, up to now, almost entirely unexplored.

In rather similar vein, Peter Earl has urged that economists grasp the opportunity of engaging with broader approaches to understanding consumer behaviour or 'run the risk that psychologists (or, perhaps consumer researchers from marketing) will do so instead and displace conventional economics for policy-making purposes' (Earl 2005, p. 911). Similarly, Marc Lavoie (2004) has noted potential synergies between findings from economic psychology and Post Keynesian consumer research, while Paul Downward, John Finch and John Ramsay have drawn attention to the patterns of behaviour identified in both behavioural and institutional economics, arguing that such patterns provide evidence of quasi-closure and that such patterns can legitimately form the basis of inductive inferences in economic analysis (Downward et al. 2002, p. 486). Sheila Dow has observed that economists' engagement with behavioural economics has been limited, but that a capacity exists to broaden this approach beyond the confines of constrained optimization utilized by some mainstream economists (Dow 2010; see also Fernández-Huerga 2008).

Despite these examples, the engagement of Post Keynesian economics with behavioural economics remains limited. One reason for this is the evident failure of the project foreshadowed by George Akerlof in his Nobel acceptance speech, which he entitled 'Behavioral macroeconomics and macroeconomic behavior' (Akerlof 2002). In fact behavioural macroeconomics seems to have made very little progress since 2002, and this impression is confirmed by the weaknesses of Akerlof and Robert Shiller's much-heralded book, *Animal Spirits* (2009), which is subtitled *How Human Psychology Drives the Economy, and Why It Matters for Global Capitalism*. The book begins with a long and glowing endorsement of Keynes, and there is even a bow to Hyman Minsky. Yet *Animal Spirits* is profoundly non-Keynesian in several important respects. First, it contains nothing on the determinants of business investment, and little or nothing on the savings–investment relationship, which in any serious macroeconomic analysis that claims to be 'Keynesian' must play the central role. Instead, Akerlof and Shiller come up with a caricature of a 'Keynesian' business cycle: 'left to their own devices, capitalist economies will pursue excess, as current times bear witness. There will be manias. The manias will be followed by panics. There will be joblessness. People will consume too much and save too little' (ibid., p. ix; original stress deleted).

Second, Akerlof and Shiller completely fail to understand the significance for Keynes of fundamental uncertainty, and in consequence also misunderstand his use of the phrase that they take for the title of their book. Keynes did not believe that animal spirits are synonymous with 'noneconomic motives and irrational behavior'; nor did he argue that animal spirits are 'the main cause of involuntary unemployment' (ibid., p. x). And he certainly would not have accepted Akerlof and Shiller's policy conclusion: 'Indeed if we thought that people were totally rational, and that they acted almost entirely out of economic motives, we too would believe that government should play little role in the regulation of financial markets, and perhaps even in determining the level of aggregate demand' (ibid., p. 173). There is no simple dichotomy in the *General Theory* between 'animal spirits' and 'rational behaviour'. In fact Keynes would probably have agreed with David Dequech in defining animal spirits as 'the optimistic disposition to face uncertainty' (Dequech 2003, p. 153).

Third, *Animal Spirits* reflects the overwhelming bias of twenty-first century behavioural economics towards the study of individual, rather than organizational, behaviour, with the individual viewed either as a consumer or (in the case of behavioural finance) as a player in the market for securities. *Real* investment, which is undertaken by *firms*, whose decisions depend upon organizational procedures and routines, is very largely neglected. Behavioural economists of a previous generation, such as Herbert Simon and his associates Richard Cyert and James G. March, had intended to construct a behavioural theory of the firm. This project appears to have been abandoned, reflecting the growing focus of mainstream economics on individual aspects of decision making, rather than social and organizational aspects. By contrast, the 'institutionalist–Post Keynesian' approach advocated by Eduardo Fernández-Huerga 'conceives of individuals as social beings who are immersed in a cultural environment' (Fernández-Huerga 2008, p. 710). In particular, cognitive processes are necessarily social, and conventions can only be learned through social interaction (ibid., pp. 714, 716, 718). The failure of mainstream economists to appreciate these simple but fundamental truths helps to explain the otherwise rather puzzling lack thus far of a serious behavioural macroeconomics.

This is one important example of a more general problem: the close association between some forms of behavioural economics and mainstream analysis. There is an extensive literature using the nomenclature of 'behavioural economics' that retains key assumptions of neoclassical economic theory, and this tendency has strengthened in the last two decades (Sent 2004). Peter Earl distinguishes between 'behavioural' and 'pseudo behavioural' economics, while Esther-Mirjam Sent (2004) discerns key differences between 'old behavioural' and 'new behavioural' economics. In both cases, the former is viewed as a challenge to mainstream economics and the latter is framed as a set of Lakatosian 'anomalies' waiting to be synthesized into mainstream analysis. Earl, an early advocate of the 'old' behavioural economics, has described his reaction to the 'new' variant in especially graphic terms: 'watching the rise of new behavioural economics is an experience akin to that suffered by a European art-house movie director whose film is re-made Hollywood-style and in the process is "dumbed down" and has its ending changed' (Earl 2010, p. 218).

However, 'old' behavioural economics does have significant strands that do not assume optimization, and most of the work discussed by Earl and Tomer relies on detailed empirical research and descriptions of observed behaviour. In broad terms, much of this literature is consistent with Dow and Victoria Chick's call for Post Keynesian engagement with plural research methods, and also with Tony Lawson's arguments for retroduction (Dow and Chick 2001; Lawson 2003). It may be significant in this context that Simon, one of the most important of the 'old' behavioural economists, fell foul of both his neoclassical Keynesian and proto-New Classical colleagues at Carnegie Tech in the 1960s (Franco Modigliani and John Muth, respectively), and in effect abandoned academic economics for the more welcoming disciplines of psychology, artificial intelligence and decision theory (Simon 1991, chapter 16). He might well have proved receptive to more heterodox economic ideas, had a fully developed Post Keynesian school been in existence at the time. At all events, the obstacles to closer engagement between Post Keynesians and advocates of the 'old' variant of behavioural economics do not seem insurmountable.

The existing Post Keynesian engagement with behavioural economics, such as it is, suggests that there are at least three types of contributions that can be further developed by careful and closer engagement between the two broad areas of thought. First, behavioural economics can be used to contribute to or evaluate the realism of the assumptions used in Post Keynesian analysis. Behavioural economics has contributed insights that call into question key mainstream economic assumptions relating to the behaviour of economic agents, particularly consumers and firms. At the same time, Post Keynesians have consistently rejected an instrumentalist approach to economic prediction in favour of understanding the causes underlying economic events. The use of behavioural insights to investigate and further develop the realism of Post Keynesian analysis remains one area for further engagement. One recent example of this approach is Sheila Dow's use of the literature in behavioural and emotional finance to shed light on problems originally raised in the work of Keynes and Hyman Minsky (Dow 2010).

Second, both Post Keynesians and behavioural economists emphasize the common use of heuristics, or short cuts, in decision making that are decisively influenced by our social context. These issues remain largely neglected in mainstream economics but have been extensively developed and discuss by John Harvey (1998, p. 49) who attempts to integrate the findings of behavioural economics into a comprehensive theory of decision making on which to base Post Keynesian analysis. Harvey takes specific findings from the psychology literature, including availability, representativeness, anchoring, framing and overconfidence, and integrates these into a five-stage model of decision making consisting of probability assignment, confidence assessment, decision-weight application, choice, and recollection and interpretation. Each of these stages is explained in some detail, with emphasis on the importance of social context on decision making. In addition, Harvey also discusses aspects of Post Keynesian theory that are not usually considered in the psychological literature. For example, he discusses how an awareness of non-ergodicity on the part of decision makers can operate to decrease the level of confidence of future predictions (ibid., p. 55). Harvey's arguments open a number of avenues for both micro- and macro-level investigations. His insights have contributed to his own analysis of foreign exchange rates and to Éric Tymoigne's analysis of financial instability (2007). Third, some Post Keynesians argue that analysis should include empirical research methods which extend our observations and inferences about the causes of economic events. Earl in particular argues that Post Keynesians should look to behavioural economics to include a broader range of research methods, including material 'from social science and marketing such as questionnaires, repertory grids/construct laddering techniques, protocol analysis and experimental research, in addition to traditional econometric tools' (Earl 2005, p. 916).

Thus there may be gains from closer engagement between Post Keynesians and the 'old' behavioural economics, which has in effect been repudiated by the mainstream. These go much further than drawing on behavioural economics for evidence that Post Keynesian theory has realistic assumptions. The multidisciplinary heritage of behavioural economics means that it reveals a wide range of methods of data collection and analysis. Post Keynesians could enhance their efforts to examine these (and other) methods, both to widen their research agenda and to extend existing theories to reflect more closely the dynamics of real-world twenty-first century economies (Fung 2010–11; Jefferson and King 2010–11). This might have the additional benefit of bringing Post Keynesians and institutional economists closer together, since many of these questions also occupy the attention of institutionalists.

THERESE JEFFERSON
J.E. KING

See also:

Agency; Choice under Uncertainty; Conventions; Institutionalism; Uncertainty.

References

Akerlof, G.A. (2002), 'Behavioral macroeconomics and macroeconomic behavior', *American Economic Review*, **92** (3), 411–33.
Akerlof, G.A. and R.J. Shiller (2009), *Animal Spirits: How Human Psychology Drives the Economy, and Why It Matters for Global Capitalism*, Princeton, NJ: Princeton University Press.
Davidson, P. (2010–11), 'Behavioral economists should make a turn and learn from Keynes and Post Keynesian economics', *Journal of Post Keynesian Economics*, **33** (2), 251–4.
Dequech, D. (2003), 'Conventional and unconventional behavior under uncertainty', *Journal of Post Keynesian Economics*, **26** (1), 145–68.
Dow, S.C. (2010), 'Psychology of financial markets: Keynes, Minsky and emotional finance', in D.B. Papadimitriou and L.R. Wray (eds), *The Elgar Companion to Hyman Minsky*, Cheltenham, UK and Northampton, MA, USA, pp. 246–62.
Dow, S.C. and V. Chick (2001), 'Formalism, logic and reality: a Keynesian analysis', *Cambridge Journal of Economics*, **25** (6), 705–21.
Downward, P., J. Finch and J. Ramsay (2002), 'Critical realism, empirical methods and inference: a critical discussion', *Cambridge Journal of Economics*, **26** (2), 481–500.
Earl, P.E. (2005), 'Economics and psychology in the twenty-first century', *Cambridge Journal of Economics*, **29** (6), 909–26.

Earl, P.E. (2010), 'Economics fit for the Queen: a pessimistic assessment of its prospects', *Prometheus*, **28** (3), 209–25.

Fernández-Huerga, E. (2008), 'The economic behavior of human beings: the institutional/ Post-Keynesian model', *Journal of Economic Issues*, **42** (3), 709–26.

Fung, M.V. (2010–11), 'Comments on "Can Post Keynesians make better use of behavioral economics?"', *Journal of Post Keynesian Economics*, **33** (2), 235–49.

Harvey, J.T. (1998), 'Heuristic judgement theory', *Journal of Economic Issues*, **32** (1), 47–64.

Jefferson, T. and J.E. King (2010–11), 'Can Post Keynesians make better use of behavioral economics?', *Journal of Post Keynesian Economics*, **33** (2), 211–34.

Lavoie, M. (2004), 'Post Keynesian consumer theory: potential synergies with consumer research and economic psychology', *Journal of Economic Psychology*, **25** (5), 639–49.

Lawson, T. (2003), *Reorienting Economics*, London and New York: Routledge.

Sent, E.-M. (2004), 'Behavioral economics: how psychology made its (limited) way back into economics', *History of Political Economy*, **36** (4), 735–60.

Simon, H.A. (1991), *Models of My Life*, New York: Basic Books.

Tomer, J.F. (2007), 'What is behavioral economics?', *Journal of Socio-Economics*, **36** (3), 463–79.

Tymoigne, É. (2007), 'Improving financial stability: uncertainty versus imperfection', *Journal of Economic Issues*, **41** (2), 503–50.

Brazil

In a paper prepared for the first meeting of the Brazilian Keynesian Association (AKB), Fernando Carvalho wrote:

> For many years it has been noted, with some surprise, that the thinking of Keynes and his followers exerts a strong influence on Brazilian economic thought. Even in the gloomy 1980s when, especially in North American academic circles, the so-called New Classical School emerged with a force as intense as it was ephemeral, the community of academic economists in Brazil continued to cultivate the legacy of great economists such as, but not only, Keynes, Kalecki and Schumpeter, to name just a few. (Carvalho 2008, p. 569)

The relationship between the application of heterodox anti-cyclical economic policies, and the Brazilian economy's performance is a matter of fact: in the period when Brazil's economy enjoyed vigorous growth (averaging around 7.0 per cent year between 1947 and 1980), there was active state intervention in the economy, and heterodox economic policies predominated. As a result, in that same period, Brazil's economy underwent important structural changes, although maintaining high levels of social inequality. Since the early 1980s, meanwhile, the Brazilian economy has been conspicuous for its stop-and-go performance and relatively slow growth (averaging 2.5 per cent per year between 1980 and 2008). That period is identified, on the one hand, with strongly accelerating inflation in the 1980s and failed heterodox stabilization plans and, on the other, in the 1990s, by the introduction of neoliberal stabilization policies – trade liberalization, market deregulation, privatization of state enterprises, and financial liberalization – a set of policy recommendations of what came to be known as the Washington Consensus. However, the vulnerability of the Brazilian economy (and other Latin American economies) to contagion by external crises, with adverse effects on production and employment, meant that by the late 1990s and the 2000s the policies advocated by the Washington Consensus were being called into question (Stiglitz 1999).

Brazil's economy after the Second World War can be considered broadly in two phases: the years 1950–1980, when the national-developmentalist model predominated and, following the interregnum of the 1980s, the neo-liberal model of the 1990s and 2000s, associated with the policies inspired by the Washington Consensus.

The national-developmentalist model, based on both tariff protection-ism to stimulate the import-substitution industrialization process and the state's playing an active role in planning, financing and directly producing in favour of industrialization as the basis for developing Brazil's heavy industry, was inspired strongly by the Economic Commission for Latin America and the Caribbean (ECLAC).

ECLAC was inspired by structuralism and it was greatly influenced by economists identified with Keynesian ideas, such as Raul Prebisch, Anibal Pinto and Celso Furtado. Prebisch introduced Keynes into Latin America, while Pinto and Furtado were great exponents of Keynes's ideas in Chile and Brazil, respectively. Furtado's classic book, *Formação Econômica do Brasil* (Furtado 1965), is a brilliant application of Keynes's macroeconomic approach to the process of change in Brazil from the primary-exporting model to the domestic market-oriented industrial model. Furtado showed that in the 1930s – even before Keynes's *General Theory* was published – the Brazilian government used a Keynesian anti-cyclical policy of major proportions to protect the coffee-exporting sector from losses, thus ena-bling Brazil's economy to weather the crisis of the 1930s.

After a period of strong growth between 1950 and 1970, the Brazilian economy, like others in Latin America, suffered the effects of the foreign debt crisis. That crisis eventually led the Brazilian state into serious fiscal crisis and caused inflation to accelerate extraordinarily. In the early 1980s, in response to the failure of monetarist policies to reduce inflation in Brazil, a structuralist-inspired theory of inertial inflation was formulated, explaining inflationary inertia in terms of the existence of formal and informal mechanisms of price and contract indexation, which rendered conventional stabilization policies ineffectual. Various policies were sug-gested in this regard, such as heterodox stabilization plans (basically, price freezes).

The failure of heterodox stabilization plans – as a result of difficulties stemming from the foreign debt problem in the environment of the 1980s –

led in a way to a 'failure' of heterodox and developmentalist policies in Brazil. Developmentalist policies came to be seen as outdated, and often pejoratively. In that regard, since the start of the 1990s, a process of trade and financial liberalization began in Brazil, accompanied by a strong reduction in the state's role in the economy. In 1994–95 the success of the 'Real Plan' in stabilizing the economy using orthodox and heterodox policy ingredients, such as de-indexation, an exchange anchor, monetary reform, financial deregulation and others, created fertile ground for neoliberal policies to become established in Brazil, with the consequent decline of Keynesian policies.

In 1999, after the collapse of the semi-fixed foreign exchange regime, Brazil adopted a tripartite economic policy strongly inspired by the 'New Consensus' in macroeconomics: a floating exchange rate, an inflation targeting regime and the pursuit of a primary fiscal surplus. Whether or not this new economic policy arrangement has been successful is a subject of controversy; in any case, from 2004 on, the commodity boom drove the Brazilian economy, making for economic growth without balance-of-payments constraints, a problem typical of developing countries that do not follow the export-led growth model.

The first Lula da Silva government (2003–06), partly as a reaction to the foreign exchange crisis of late 2002 and early 2003, was notable for its conventional orthodox economic policies. However, at the end of the first administration and in the second Lula da Silva government (2007–10), economic policy – and particularly fiscal policy – became relatively more flexible, with the launch of a programme of public spending on economic and social infrastructure: the 'Growth Acceleration Programme'. The floating exchange rate policy was maintained intact, however, although the Central Bank of Brazil went on to implement a foreign reserve accumulation policy, which was later to be important in fending off the financial crisis of 2008.

In 2008–09, Brazil was one of the economies that recovered most rapidly from the effects of the world financial crisis. This was achieved by means of both traditional Keynesian anti-cyclical instruments – monetary policy providing liquidity to the bank sector, and expansionist fiscal policy – along with unconventional policies, such as using federal public banks in anti-cyclical credit measures. For these purposes, the presence of developmentalist economists in the finance ministry and on the boards of federal public banks was fundamentally important for the formulation of anti-cyclic policies to address the crisis in Brazil.

One important area of concern to heterodox and Keynesian economists has been the discussion of the development model for Brazil and the role the state should play in that model. Their argument is that the national-developmentalist model has, to some extent, now played its part in Brazil's, economic development, but that in order to meet the present-day challenges facing a semi-mature economy like Brazil's, another development strategy should be designed as an alternative to the neoliberal strategy. Thus they stress the need to reconcile sustained economic growth with social equity and macroeconomic stability. To that end, the state has a fundamental role to play as the promoter of growth, by creating a suitable, stable institutional environment to encourage private investment and to reduce social inequalities, not just through growth, but also through both comprehensive and focused social policies. Also, the Keynesian–structuralist economists who advocate this new developmentalism underline the need to use a competitive exchange rate to overcome external constraints on growth and the risk of de-industrialization of Brazil's economy caused by currency appreciation (see Sicsú et al. 2007; Bresser-Pereira 2010).

Focusing on the spread of Keynesianism in the universities in Brazil, ECLAC was an important influence in the social sciences in the 1960s and 1970s. As part of that tradition, a postgraduate programme in economics was founded at Campinas State University (UNICAMP) in the 1970s. Its faculty included a number of economists who had served at the ECLAC. At the UNICAMP, the Marxist critique of ECLAC ideas of the 1970s led to support for Michał Kalecki and his version of the effective demand principle, which was appropriate to understanding the dynamism of the Brazilian economy driven by capitalist consumption. That is to say, they endeavoured to show that, contrary to Furtado's stagnationist view, growth was possible, even with a highly unequal income distirbution. In the 1980s and 1990s the UNICAMP was moving towards a broader heterodox outlook that was not purely Marxist, but included the ideas of Keynes and his followers. Luiz Beluzzo, Maria Tavares and Mario Possas all made particularly important contributions in this regard. At present, a number of professors at UNICAMP pursue their research from a (Post) Keynesian perspective.

Another school that was important in spreading heterodox and Keynesian thinking in Brazil was the Federal University of Rio de Janeiro (UFRJ), which was strongly linked, first in the 1980s, to UNICAMP and, later in the 1990s, to a Post Keynesian approach significantly influenced by North American authors such as Paul Davidson and Hyman Minsky. At the UFRJ a Money and Financial System Study Group was set up in 1997 under the coordination of Professor Fernando Cardim de Carvalho, with participation by professors from the UFRJ itself and from other universities, such as the Federal University of Rio Grande do Sul (UFRGS) and the State University of Rio de Janeiro (UERJ). An important milestone in the work of this group was the 1997 International Keynesian Conference at the UFRJ, with the participation of Philip Arestis, Gary Dymski, Steven Fazzari, Jan Kregel and Nina Shapiro.

In the course of the 1990s and 2000s, besides UFRJ, UFRGS and UERJ, other academic centres took on Keynesian researchers and many became important centres of heterodox thought, among them the Federal University of Minas Gerais (UFMG), the Federal University of Paraná (UFPR) and the Fluminense Federal University (UFF), along with other equally important centres at the State University of São Paulo (USP), the University of Brasília (UnB), the Getúlio Vargas Foundation (FGV-SP) and the Catholic University of São Paulo (PUC-SP). One important aspect of the spread of Keynesianism in Brazilian academic circles was that not only were researchers being trained with a Keynesian/heterodox outlook at important academic centres in several states in Brazil, but also from the mid-1990s onwards, a growing number of Keynesian economists were producing a large volume of academic papers in leading Brazilian and international heterodox journals.

In April 2008, the Brazilian Keynesian Association (AKB), a not-for-profit, 'civil society', was set up on the occasion of its first meeting, held at the UNICAMP. The founding of the AKB was made possible by the joint efforts of two groups that had been important in developing Keynesianism in Brazil: the Money and Financial System Study Group and the UNICAMP's Economics Institute. However, since its founding the Association has endeavoured to include on its board researchers from various leading universities in Brazil. One important aspect of its founding principles is that it was established at the outset that Keynesianism should be understood with sufficient breadth to encompass different theoretical colourings, and not only the Post Keynesian approach properly speaking. In that connection, the patrons of the AKB include Keynesian economists who are heterodox economists and mix Keynesian economics with other heterodox approaches. The AKB is a mainly academic forum for discussion of key issues of Keynesianism in Brazil and is also political, in the sense of contributing new ideas to Brazilian political discussions, especially concerning the directions set for Brazilian economy and society.

A longer version of this entry was published as De Paula and Ferrari-Filho (2010).

LUIZ FERNANDO DE PAULA
FERNANDO FERRARI-FILHO

See also:

Balance-of-payments-constrained Economic Growth; Development Economics; Development Finance; Export-led Growth; Latin American Structuralism; Pluralism in Economics.

References

Bresser-Pereira, L.C. (2010), *Globalization and Competition*, Cambridge: Cambridge University Press.

Carvalho, F.C. (2008), 'Keynes e o Brasil', *Economia e Sociedade*, **17**, 569–74 [in Portuguese].

De Paula, L. and F. Ferrari-Filho (2010), 'The spread of Keynesianism in Brazil: the origins and experience of the Brazilian Keynesian Association', *Intervention: European Journal of Economics and Economic Policies*, **7** (2), 248–55.

Furtado, C. (1965), *The Economic Growth of Brazil: A Survey from Colonial to Modern Times*, Berkeley, CA: University of California Press.

Sicsú, J., L.F. Paula and R. Michel (2007), 'Por que novo-desenvolvimentismo?', *Brazilian Journal of Political Economy*, **27** (4), 507–24 [in Portuguese].

Stiglitz, J. (1999), 'More instruments and broader goals: moving toward the Post-Washington consensus', *Brazilian Journal of Political Economy*, **19** (1), 94–120.

Bretton Woods

The Bretton Woods agreement was part of the reorganization process following the Second World War. The Bretton Woods system, named after the New Hampshire town where the conference was held in July 1944, was relatively short-lived. It extended from late 1946, when the declaration of par values by 32 countries went into effect, to August 1971, if one takes the closure of the gold window in the US as the end of the system, or late 1973, if one takes the breakdown of the Smithsonian agreement that held exchange rates fixed. This was a period of great prosperity. The Bretton Woods period exhibited the most rapid growth of output of any monetary regime (Bordo 1993). As a result, this period is usually referred to as the 'golden age' of capitalism.

The Bretton Woods agreement is mostly known for imposing fixed, but adjustable, exchange rates, on the basis of a gold–dollar system, and for the creation of two institutions with a mandate to provide finance for balance-of-payments adjustment (the International Monetary Fund, IMF) and for promoting development (the World Bank). Two main characteristics of the Bretton Woods system should be emphasized, namely the existence of a set of rules, which included fixed exchange rates, but also capital controls and domestic macroeconomic policy autonomy, on the one hand, and the hegemony of the US dollar, on the other.

The Bretton Woods system represented 'the first successful systematic attempt to produce a legal and institutional framework for the world economic system' (James 1996, p. 27). It must be noted that the system worked only because the US, the creditor country, was willing to pay the bill for reconstruction through the Marshall Plan. The Marshall Plan, in turn, was only possible in the environment of the Cold War. Post Keynesian authors have emphasized the importance of creditor countries in expanding demand on a global level (Davidson 1982).

The need for this legal framework was unanimously accepted as a way of avoiding the negative consequences of the interwar period financial speculation. Ragnar Nurkse forcefully presented the consensus view. According to Nurkse (1944, p. 16), 'the flow of short term funds, especially in the thirties, often became disequilibrating instead of equilibrating, or instead of simply coming to a stop'. This was partially true of the pre-1914 system, but the main difference was the absence of a hegemonic power capable of controlling capital flows through the variation of the interest rate (Kindleberger 1973). Further, according to Nurkse (1944, p. 22), 'in the thirties, there was a gradual but persistent change in economic opinion. The price-level came to be regarded more and more as a secondary criterion of economic stability. The state of employment and national income tended to become the primary criterion.' This change was to a great extent part of the effects of the Keynesian Revolution.

John Maynard Keynes was the chief British negotiator at the Bretton Woods conference. It is important to note, given the prominence of Keynes's views during the Bretton Woods conference, that he was not an advocate of either fixed or floating exchange rates. His main objective was always the management of the exchanges to achieve domestic policy goals. The development of the principle of effective demand led Keynes to support not only expansionary fiscal policies, but also low interest rate policies, whose ultimate impact would be to reduce the significance of the rentiers' income share, the so-called 'euthanasia of the rentier'.

To guarantee the euthanasia of the rentier, Keynes pointed out that the central bank should be able to set the rate of interest independently from any international pressures. Keynes especially insisted, as much as Harry Dexter White (Boughton 2002), his American counterpart in the Bretton Woods negotiations, who ultimately prevailed, upon the idea that movements of capital could not be left unrestricted. Keynes argued that 'we cannot hope to control rates of interest at home if movements of capital moneys out of the country are unrestricted' (Keynes 1980a, p. 276).

The fact that Keynes accepted, and even defended, the final agreement at Bretton Woods, which diverged in several points from his Bancor proposal, can be attributed to the maintenance of capital controls in the final document (Crotty 1983). The neoliberal thinking that came to dominate financial circles in the recent years had little standing at the Bretton Woods conference. Keynes (1980b, p. 17) was categorical in saying 'not merely as a feature of transition, but as a permanent arrangement, the plan accords to every member government the explicit right to control all capital movements. What used to be a heresy is now endorsed as orthodox.'

The control of capital flows means that the central bank does not need to use the bank discount rate to attract inflows of capital, or avoid capital flight. As a result the bank rate can be maintained as low as possible. A reduction of the bank rate leads to a transfer from the finance or rentier sector to the industrial capitalist and working classes, leading to an increase in consumption and investment spending. In addition, low rates of interest reduce the burden of debt servicing, so that active fiscal policies can be pursued by the state without leading to an explosive increase of the debt-to-GDP ratio. Thus, the prosperity of the golden age period is associated with the euthanasia of the rentier, which was an integral part of the Bretton Woods agreement.

Also the interwar period showed that greater capital mobility led to greater exchange rate instability (Nurkse 1944). The fact that increased capital mobility leads to higher volatility of exchange rates should not be read as a one-way relationship. Flexible rates allow the opportunity for speculators to profit from arbitrage; therefore profit-seeking speculation is an inevitable outcome of the abandonment of fixed rates. In that sense, a system of fixed but adjustable exchange rates is more conducive to a situation of reduced capital flows.

However, despite the intense preoccupation with capital controls, capital movements began to play an important role in the late 1960s. A pool of unregulated capital emerged as early as the late 1940s, when the Chinese communist government placed its dollar earnings with a Soviet bank in Paris. This was the origin of the so-called 'euromarket' (James 1996, p. 179). However, it was not until the late 1950s, with the return of the convertibility of the European currencies, and the removal of the current account restrictions, that the transition from a dollar shortage to a dollar surplus took place.

The growth of the euromarket is also directly connected to the expansion of US multinational firms, and the consequent expansion of the US banks abroad. The collapse of Bretton Woods is related to increasing speculative capital flows. According to Triffin (1960) this resulted from the fact that the US economy could not guarantee the convertibility of dollars into gold at the fixed parity. In this view, the collapse of the Bretton Woods system is directly connected to the increasing role of capital movements and the incapacity of the hegemonic country to control them.

Whereas this view is incorporated into the conventional view, the main cause of the demise of Bretton Woods is associated with the inflationary pressures brought about by the expansionary fiscal policies in the US, and the propagation of these inflationary pressures through the international system. The increasingly expansionary fiscal policies of the 1960s – resulting from both the Vietnam War and the Great Society experiment of the Kennedy–Johnson administrations – led to growing balance-of-payments deficits. The US deficits were initially considered instrumental for the working of an international monetary system that was desperately in need of dollars to obtain the essential imports of capital goods needed for reconstruction. However, by the late 1960s the accumulation of idle dollar balances started to put pressure on the money supply of the rest of the world, leading to inflation. That is, according to the neoclassical logic, inflation was caused by the US fiscal and monetary policies, and transmitted to the world as a result of the system of fixed parities.

The collapse of Bretton Woods is then related to the unwillingness of foreign countries to import US inflation. That eventually broke the credibility of the fixed exchange rate commitments, and the willingness of the several central banks to cooperate in order to maintain the fixed parities. In other words, the Bretton Woods system failed because the fixed parity commitment was not credible in the face of accelerating inflation.

An alternative explanation for the inflationary pressures of the 1960s is possible, though. This alternative explanation, compatible with the Post Keynesian view, would minimize the effects of the US expansionary fiscal policy in the demise of Bretton Woods. The golden age regime implied a commitment to full employment and the creation of a safety-net for unemployed workers. Additionally, the imposition of capital controls and the cheap money policies – which led to low real rates of interest – implied a favourable environment for workers. Parties with strong ties with the labour movement were in power in several Western countries, and this was tolerated, to a great extent, since it was considered a form of reducing the dangers of the Soviet menace. Furthermore, full employment tends to increase the bargaining power of the working class.

In this environment, workers' pressures for higher nominal wages would usually be expected. For a given real rate of interest, and a fixed nominal exchange rate, the only effect of rising wages would be higher prices. In sum, inflation was the result of wage pressures (cost–push) rather than the expansionary fiscal and monetary policies (demand–pull). In that sense, the abandonment of the fixed parities was not connected to the loss of credibility in the face of higher inflation, since the causes of inflation lay somewhere else.

Post Keynesians emphasize the role of financial liberalization in the collapse of the Bretton Woods regime. Paul Davidson (1982) argues that the US dollar represents the asset of ultimate redemption, and hence is used as the measure of international liquidity. As a result, the US benefits from a more liberal financial system, since the centrality of US financial market allows it to attract funds to finance persistent current account deficits. For that reason, beginning in the 1960s the US adopted a more self-centred financial policy, promoting financial openness in order to be able to face the growing current account deficits. It is the increasing financial openness

of the 1960s, built into the American support for the euromarket, that ultimately made the Bretton Woods system untenable (Helleiner 1994).

Arguably, the end of Bretton Woods and the advent of the so-called
'flexible dollar' standard (Serrano 2003) has intensified the hegemonic
position of the dollar, since with the closing of the gold window the dollar
became the first world fiat money. Some authors (for example, Dooley et
al. 2004) have argued that the emergence of relatively fixed and undervalued exchange rates in the Asian periphery, has allowed for a sort of revived
Bretton Woods. The absence of capital controls, the incredible accumulation of dollar reserves by the central banks of peripheral countries to
protect themselves from financial crisis and the global financial crisis of
2007–08 suggest that the Bretton Woods II system is *not* as stable as its
first incarnation.

The crisis has created what Ilene Grabel (2010) refers to as a 'moment of
productive incoherence', in which on the one side the US and the IMF try
to re-establish the pattern of pro-cyclical adjustments, and the old structures of governance, while capital controls become increasingly common
in the periphery. The impact of the crisis in Europe has also diminished
the chances that the dollar will be substituted as the key reserve currency
in the near future, while exacerbating the problems generated by global
imbalances, at the heart of the limitations of the dollar-centred system that
replaced Bretton Woods.

MATÍAS VERNENGO

See also:

Economic Policy; Exchange Rates; Inflation; International Economics; Stagflation.

References

Bordo, M.D. (1993), 'The Bretton Woods international monetary system: a historical over-
view', in Bordo and B. Eichengreen (eds), *A Retrospective on the Bretton Woods System*,
Chicago, IL: University of Chicago Press, pp. 3–108.
Boughton, J. (2002), 'Why White, not Keynes: inventing the post-war international monetary
system', in A. Arnon and W. Young (eds), *The Open Economy Macro-Model: Past, Present
and Future*, Norwell: Kluwer Publishing, pp. 73–96.
Crotty, J. (1983), 'On Keynes and capital flight,' *Journal of Economic Literature*, 21 (1), 59–65.
Davidson, P. (1982), *International Money and the Real World*, London: Macmillan.
Dooley, M.P., D. Folkerts-Landau and P. Garber (2004), 'The revised Bretton Woods system',
International Journal of Finance and Economics, 9 (4), 307–13.
Grabel, I. (2010), 'Not your grandfather's IMF: global crisis, "productive incoherence"
and developmental policy space', Working Paper No. 214, Political Economy Research
Institute, University of Massachusetts, Amherst, MA.
Helleiner, E. (1994), *States and the Re-emergence of Global Finance: From Bretton Woods to
the 1990s*, Ithaca, NY: Cornell University Press.
James, H. (1996), *Monetary Cooperation Since Bretton Woods*, New York: Oxford University
Press.
Keynes, J.M. (1980a), *The Collected Writings of John Maynard Keynes. Volume XXV:*

Activities 1940–1944, London: Macmillan and Cambridge University Press for the Royal Economic Society.

Keynes, J.M. (1980b), *The Collected Writings of John Maynard Keynes. Volume XXVI: Activities 1941–1946*, London: Macmillan and Cambridge University Press for the Royal Economic Society.

Kindleberger, C.P. (1973), *The World in Depression, 1929–39*, Berkeley, CA: University of California Press.

Nurkse, R. (1944), *International Currency Experience: Lessons from the Interwar Period*, Princeton, NJ: League of Nations and Princeton University Press.

Serrano, F. (2003), 'From static gold to floating dollar', *Contributions to Political Economy*, **22**, 87–102.

Triffin, R. (1960), *Gold and the Dollar Crisis: The Future of Convertibility*, New Haven, CT: Yale University Press.

Budget Deficits

Post Keynesians find that the federal budget should be in deficit up to the point at which additional federal government spending does not increase the number of jobs, or the amount of goods and services produced. When additional spending by the federal government no longer increases the number of jobs, or the number of goods and services produced, then federal deficit spending should be stopped. This means that the federal budget may always need to be in deficit to make up for investment fluctuations, population increases and technological changes (Keynes 1980, pp. 322–3). State and local government budgets should be balanced. The federal deficit is key in maintaining the overall standard of living in a capitalist economy where private investment naturally fluctuates due to uncertainty over future profits. When private investment falls short of what is required to maintain full employment, the federal government can use its ability to spend in order to increase total spending in the economy to the level that provides and maintains full employment of all resources, labour being the most important. Currently, widespread misunderstanding of government finances erroneously leads policy makers to chronically spend less than what is required to maintain a decent and equitable standard of living, even in the most developed nations. Lack of spending causes temporary and long-term job loss. This constitutes a waste of human energy that could be directed to improve our standard of living substantially (Minsky 1986 [2008], p. 326; Wray 1998, p. 184). We are therefore living well below our means.

The federal budget is divided into two parts, the capital and current accounts. The capital account includes government spending that takes place over time, such as investment in buildings and infrastructure. The current account includes spending that occurs on a day-to-day basis, such as spending on payroll and office supplies. Large investment projects occur over many years, and the annual cost of these projects is much lower than the overall cost. Because the tradition in many countries is to include the total cost of long-term projects on the books along with short-term spending costs, the federal budget appears to be in large deficit, when in fact, it is not. By way of analogy, a household does not consider the full value of its home in its monthly expenses. Does the household consider itself to be in a serious deficit position if the value of its home exceeds its ability to pay for it this month? Most homeowners consider their ability to pay the mortgage payment on their monthly expenses, rather than the full value of the home itself. For years, many policy makers have argued that the federal budget should be explicitly stated in terms of capital and current account spending. This would allow the federal budget to state the annual cost of investment projects alongside annual operating expenses. Current practice grossly overstates the size of the deficit. Post Keynesians agree (Keynes 1980, pp. 224–5, 277–8).

The financial sector balances provide a useful way of considering the position of the government balance, relative to the private sector and external balances. According to the financial balances approach, the sum of the government balance, the private sector balance and the external balance must equal zero by accounting identity (Godley and Lavoie 2007, pp. xxxvi–xxxvii). The government balance is given by government spending minus taxes. The private sector balance is private sector investment minus saving. The external balance is exports minus imports. An interesting conclusion that comes from looking at the economy from this financial perspective, is that when the external sector is balanced (exports = imports), then a deficit in the government balance would be perfectly mirrored by a surplus in the private sector balance. Conversely, when exports = imports, a private sector deficit would be perfectly mirrored by a government sector surplus. This means that if any sector is balanced, then one must have a deficit and the other must have a surplus. This holds under any condition. The more common case is that none of the sectors is balanced. A large deficit in the external sector can be offset by a small surplus in both the government balance and the private sector balance, or by a large surplus in the private sector balance, and a deficit in the government balance. There are a number of different combinations that can prevail. The most important element, though, of the financial balances approach is that it recognizes that what is happening in the government balance is related to the private sector balance and the external balance (see Leclaire 2008b, p. 141). The financial sector balances approach is based in part on Michał Kalecki's profits equation. Kalecki found that if an economy has an unbalanced budget and unbalanced trade, then private saving (which is synonymous with private profits) is equal to the sum of private investment, the budget deficit, and net exports (Kalecki 1933 [1971], p. 83). Thus, the budget deficit contributes to private saving (or profits) just as importantly as private investment and net exports. The government balance does not stand isolated in supporting national income. It is affected by (and affects) in a profound way what is happening in the private and in the external sector. When the government reduces the deficit, then the private sector pays the price (Leclaire 2008a, p. 53). This shows up as a reduction of surpluses in the private sector when government deficits fall. The policy implications are important. If the private sector is suffering from large deficits, then one way to improve the situation is to deliberately increase government deficits. Aiming spending directly at the domestic private sector will push the private sector towards surplus. Most of the time, the government fails to consider its relationship with the private sector from a financial perspective. Misunderstanding the relationship between the government's finances and the rest of the economy is only part of the reason why countries have failed to address some of our most serious social problems such as high and persistent levels of unemployment and poverty.

Another reason why federal deficit spending is not commonly advocated as a useful and powerful tool for solving social issues is because most policy makers and their advisers do not understand how government spending works. In supporting government deficit spending, Post Keynesians rely on an intimate understanding of what happens when the government spends. In keeping with the financial point of view, the federal government works with the central bank. The central bank will issue central bank liabilities (money) when a cheque is drawn on the federal government's account, and may choose to hold government bonds as corresponding assets. Both the bonds (assets) and the central bank notes (liabilities) are created *ex nihilo* (from thin air). Thus money is created and enters the economy through government spending of balances at the central bank. When taxes are paid, central bank liabilities return to the government's account at the central bank and reduce the central bank's liability in terms of outstanding central bank notes. This also means that the value of outstanding government bonds held by the central bank (if the central bank chooses to hold government bonds) must fall (Wray 1998, pp. 77–89; Bell 2000, pp. 614–15). A federal government deficit is the result of spending more over the course of a fiscal year than what is returned in the form of taxes. Thus, when government spending exceeds taxation, there is a deficit. Conversely, when taxes exceed government spending, there is a surplus.

Another often held but mistaken belief is that government bonds are held in large part by the public. The truth is that most government bonds never find their way into the economy proper. They are held internally by the central bank. A small proportion of government bonds outstanding are held by large financial institutions and countries. The latter have no impact on whether the government can pay for goods or services. They are essentially the byproduct of government spending and provide their bearers with an interest-bearing alternative to holding cash, just as purchasing a corporate bond would (Wray 1998, p. 87). Government bonds, depending on the government that issues them, are often considered to be the safest financial instrument next to cash.

The sum of federal deficits minus surpluses over time gives the value of the federal debt. The federal debt is equal to the value of outstanding government bonds (when bonds are issued as corresponding assets each time government spending takes place). For the central bank, the large financial institution or the country that holds the government bond, this 'debt' is considered an asset. The government bond is called a debt but it was not borrowed from anyone. It was created from nothing. Government debt is reduced when taxes exceed spending. Surpluses thus reduce the national debt by reducing government bonds outstanding. If the federal government ran persistent surpluses for long enough, all the central bank notes that existed in the economy would be returned to the central bank. This also means that all the bonds issued as corresponding assets would no longer exist.

This brings one to the question of why we pay federal taxes if the federal government can spend without cost. Taxes are used to drain excess money balances from the economy and prevent it from overheating (ibid., p. 115). It is possible that we might find ourselves in a situation where the government spends enough in the economy that additional spending creates no new jobs, or new goods and services. If additional deficit spending by the government does not create new jobs or goods and services, then prices of existing goods, services, and perhaps even wages, may increase. In this case, an increase in taxation can be used to draw out excessive money balances (Lerner 1943, pp. 39–40).

Up to this point, the topic of budget deficits has been handled from the federal point of view. However, there are important differences between federal and state and local finances. While the federal government creates money when it spends, state and local governments do not. Taxes and bond sales are used by state and local governments to finance their expenditures. For this reason, state and local government budgets should be balanced whenever possible. Federal spending can and should help offset deficits in state and local budgets when these deficits are due to economy-wide fluctuations.

It was shown that Post Keynesians support the use of budget deficit spending to offset fluctuations in investment spending due to uncertainty over future profits. Federal budget deficits may need to persist indefinitely to keep overall expenditures in the economy high enough to achieve and maintain full employment, of labour in particular. The way the federal budget is currently expressed grossly overstates budget deficits because the full costs of investment projects are counted as part of the annual budget, rather than spread over the lifetime of the project. Revising the way government investment projects are accounted for in the budget would provide a more accurate tally of the federal deficit. The financial sector balances approach shows that the federal budget deficit is mirrored by a private sector surplus, when we have balanced trade. Understanding how government spending works greatly increases our ability and desire to use deficit spending as a tool for solving our most pressing socio-economic problems. It was also clarified that while federal deficit spending is supported by Post Keynesians, state and local government budgets should be balanced because, in the last two cases, governments are limited by tax revenues and bond sales. In sum, federal budget deficits can and should be used to significantly improve the well-being of society.

JOËLLE LECLAIRE

See also:

Fiscal Policy; Kaleckian Economics; Money; Stock–Flow Consistent Modelling.

References

Bell, S. (2000), 'Do taxes finance government spending?', *Journal of Economic Issues*, **34** (3), 603–20.
Godley, W. and M. Lavoie (2007), *Monetary Economics: An Integrated Approach to Credit, Money, Income, Production and Wealth*, Basingstoke: Palgrave Macmillan.
Kalecki, M. (1933 [1971]), 'The determinants of profits', in Kalecki, *Selected Essays 1933– 1970*, Cambridge: Cambridge University Press, pp. 78–88.
Keynes, J.M. (1980), *The Collected Writings of John Maynard Keynes, Volume 27. Activities 1940–1946: Shaping the Post-War World: Employment and Commodities*, London: Macmillan.
Leclaire, J. (2008a), *The Great Deficit Debacle*, Saarbrucken: VDM Verlag.
Leclaire, J. (2008b), 'US deficit control and private sector wealth', *Journal of Post Keynesian Economics*, **31** (1), 139–49.
Lerner, A.P. (1943), 'Functional finance and the federal debt', *Social Research*, **10** (1), 38–51.
Minsky, H. (1986 [2008]), *Stabilizing an Unstable Economy*, New York: McGraw-Hill.
Wray, L.R. (1998), *Understanding Modern Money: The Key to Full Employment and Price Stability*, Cheltenham, UK and Northampton, MA, USA: Edward Elgar.

Business Cycles

The time path of aggregate output and its main components exhibits significant fluctuations around trend values, as do other important variables, including employment, productivity, prices, wages, interest rates and stock prices. These fluctuations are recurrent but not regular. The pattern of co-movements between the different variables, the amplitudes of the fluctuations and the length of the cycle vary over time. In fact, the delineation of cycle from trend raises many problems, and cycles of different length may coexist in the data; short-run fluctuations may take place with reference to a long-run cycle, rather than around a constant exponential trend. The term 'business cycles', however, usually refers to relatively short cycles, and the main focus in this entry will be on fluctuations in output and employment for a closed economy.

Business-cycle theories can be categorized in different ways. One common distinction concerns the 'exogeneity' or 'endogeneity' of the cycles. In some theories the fluctuations are caused by external shocks and the cycle, in this sense, is 'exogenous'. The shocks may be completely random and non-cyclical. They constitute the 'impulse', and the cyclical pattern is produced by 'propagation mechanisms' that spread out the effects of the impulse. A positive shock, for instance, may induce firms to increase their investment and, by raising the capital stock, this decision will affect future conditions.

Michał Kalecki (along with Ragnar Frisch and Eugene Slutsky) was a pioneer of the external shock approach. Most Post Keynesians, however, have followed a different line. According to this alternative approach, external shocks may indeed hit the economy and affect movements in economic activity, but fluctuations would occur even in the absence of shocks. The fluctuations in this sense are created endogenously.

It is sometimes claimed that a reliance on external shocks leaves the cycle unexplained and that endogenous theories are therefore intrinsically superior from a methodological perspective. The claim is not convincing. Unforeseen shocks do hit the economy; some of these shocks must be considered exogenous, and it is easy to set up plausible propagation mechanisms that convert random shocks into irregular cyclical fluctuations.

It should be noted also that the distinction between exogenous and endogenous cycles carries no implications for economic policy. Most neoclassical economists may take an external shock approach, but policy intervention is both feasible and desirable in some models of exogenous cycles, including some mainstream specifications. External shocks that require policy intervention, moreover, also appear in Post Keynesian analysis as in the case of the desirability of compensating for autonomous shifts in 'animal spirits'. Conversely, endogenous cycles can be generated in models in which markets are clear and outcomes are Pareto optimal, as well as in Post Keynesian models characterized by important market failures. Thus, the feasibility and desirability of policy intervention depend on the precise structure of the theory and its cyclical mechanisms.

In general, Post Keynesian theories stress the instability of markets and the need for both regulatory constraints and policy intervention. This emphasis on the inherent problems and limitations of free markets, rather than the exogenous/endogenous distinction, represents the substantive difference *vis-à-vis* most mainstream theories of the business cycle.

Endogenous business cycles can be generated in many ways, and at least four distinct sets of mechanisms have been used in the Post Keynesian literature. The mechanisms are not mutually exclusive, and some contributions combine several mechanisms.

The determination of investment is central to theories that focus on the *goods market*. As a main component of autonomous expenditure, high investment leads to high levels of aggregate demand and output. A high level of output, in turn, will be reflected in high rates of profitability and capital utilization, and this will tend to induce high levels of investment and output in the next period. If investment decisions are relatively insensitive to changes in utilization and profitability, the resulting time path for output will converge to a long-run equilibrium. A high sensitivity, on the other hand, makes this long-run equilibrium (locally asymptotically) unstable: following a slight displacement from the equilibrium position, the economy does not return to the equilibrium but moves further away.

Local instability of this kind can be turned into perpetual fluctuations, rather than cumulative and unbounded divergence, if there are appropriate 'nonlinearities' in the investment function and/or in other equations of the model. The existence of 'ceilings' and 'floors' represents a simple example of such 'nonlinearities' (gross investment cannot be negative, for instance, and output cannot exceed a full employment ceiling) but other, less crude nonlinearities may also keep the movements bounded and convert local instability into endogenous cyclical movements. Kaldor (1940) is a classic reference for nonlinear models in this multiplier-accelerator tradition, but variations on this theme also characterize early contributions by Roy Harrod, Michał Kalecki, Paul Samuelson, John Hicks, Joan Robinson and Richard Goodwin.

Investment needs to be financed, and *financial markets* are given a critical role in some aggregate-demand-based theories of the business cycle. The 'financial instability hypothesis' developed by Hyman Minsky represents a prominent example (for example, Minsky 1982). Suppose that, having recovered from past turbulence, the economy now appears to be approaching a smooth equilibrium path. Along this path expectations are largely being met and, using Minsky's terminology, there is 'financial tranquillity': borrowers are able to meet their financial commitments. This very state of tranquillity will induce changes in the risk assessments of both lenders and borrowers while, at the same time, financial regulators and policy makers may loosen the regulatory standards. Risk premiums fall; lenders start giving loans they would previously have rejected, and borrowers increasingly finance their projects in speculative and risky ways. These behavioural changes relax the financial constraints on the rate of investment and a boom ensues. Gradually, the 'fragility' of the financial system increases until a financial crisis causes a rapid rise in interest rates and a contraction of credit and investment. A return to cautious financial practices now follows and the process repeats itself, although the precise financial instruments and institutions may be new and different. Minsky's theories, not surprisingly, have received a lot of attention after the financial crisis of 2007, and a number of formalizations have been developed; a recent example is Ryoo (2010), whose model produces short cycles around a Minskyian long wave.

The role of *labour markets and income distribution* has been emphasized by a Marx-inspired literature, with Goodwin's (1967) model of a growth cycle as the most influential example. The model describes the dynamic interaction between the distribution of income and the accumulation of capital. When there is low unemployment – when the reserve army of labour is small, in Marx's terminology – workers are in a strong position and the real wage will be increasing. As real wages increase, however, profit rates suffer and the rate of accumulation declines. With a constant capital–output ratio, the growth rates of output and employment fall, too. Unemployment soon starts to increase, the balance of power starts shifting against workers, and, when the balance has shifted sufficiently, the share of wages stops increasing. Since the *level* of profitability is low, the rate of accumulation will also be low and the rate of unemployment keeps rising at this point. The capitalists now get the upper hand, the wage share starts falling, and profitability and accumulation gradually increase. This increase in accumulation gradually raises the rate of employment, workers once again gain wage increases, and the cycle is complete.

This model formalizes Marx's 'general law of accumulation' and, in Goodwin's original version, the model has no Keynesian features. It presumes that the capital stock is fully utilized at all times; output is determined by the supply side without reference to aggregate demand, and investment adjusts passively to the level of saving. Hybrid models have tried to overcome this weakness by including both Keynesian and Marxian features in the same model (for example, Skott 1989).

Political intervention may itself be a source of fluctuations. This is a position stressed by many free-market advocates, but the Post Keynesian argument for a *political business cycle* is different. The classic reference is a short paper by Kalecki (1943). In a technical sense, Kalecki argued, governments may have the ability to control aggregate demand at (near) full employment, but the maintenance of full employment generates cumulative changes in worker militancy. Increased militancy and inflationary pressures quickly bring together a powerful bloc of business leaders and rentiers and (supported by economists who 'declare that the situation is manifestly unsound') the government allows unemployment to rise. The result, Kalecki argues, is a political business cycle. Although applied by Kalecki to short cycles, the argument is arguably better suited to deal with longer-term fluctuations, and it has been used by a number of writers in relation to the rise in unemployment in the 1970s and 1980s.

Mathematical models have played an important role in the analysis of business cycles in both Post Keynesian and mainstream theory. Not all Post Keynesians are comfortable with the use of these formal techniques. Business cycles, however, involve complex, dynamic interactions and in a purely verbal analysis it is virtually impossible to keep track of these inter-actions and their implications. Without formalization it may be difficult to decide, for instance, whether a given argument implies that there will be persistent fluctuations, explosive divergence or convergence to a smooth path.

Most formal models of endogenous fluctuations are deterministic. This might seem a serious drawback. The empirical evidence shows irregular cycles and, from a theoretical perspective, it should be easy for both private agents and policy makers to forecast (and to take action to prevent) a cycle that was regular and deterministic.

This objection is not as powerful as it might seem. First, the endogenous view of cycles does not preclude external shocks, and the introduction of shocks (ranging from natural disasters to policy shocks and changes in animal spirits) may remove the regularity without affecting the underlying cyclical mechanism. Second, deterministic, nonlinear dynamic models can produce 'chaotic' outcomes that are hard to distinguish from those of a stochastic model. Prediction in these models is virtually impossible, since even the smallest change in initial conditions has dramatic effects on the subsequent movements (for example, Day 1994). Third, the incentives for individuals to try to uncover and take into account aggregate regularities may be small. Most decision makers face specific problems and uncertain-ties whose effects on the outcome of their decisions dominate the effects of movements in aggregate activity. With limited informational and cognitive resources, these boundedly rational decision makers may choose to ignore the possible influence of aggregate regularities altogether.

Finally, Post Keynesians, have always emphasized the historical contin-gency of economic models. Structural and institutional changes, such as the rise in the size of the public sector, the deregulation of the financial markets, or increased international trade and capital mobility influence the path of the economy and may necessitate a re-specification of the models.

The real-wage Phillips curve (a key element in the Goodwin model) may shift, for instance, as a result of changes in labour market legislation, and historical contingency also lies behind the Minsky argument for financial instability. It was changing institutional forms and new financial instruments that led many observers to perceive 'a far more flexible, efficient, and hence resilient financial system than the one that existed just a quarter-century ago' (Greenspan 2005). More generally, until the severe recession that followed the financial crisis in 2007, mainstream macroeconomists talked of a 'great moderation'. Fluctuations appeared to become milder, and the mainstream explanation focused on changes in monetary policy, deregulation and financial innovations.

Beliefs in the disappearance of business cycles may have been disproved by events since 2007, but the historical contingency and the complexity of business cycles have other implications. Small models, like the ones described above, highlight particular mechanisms. But no single mechanism and no single source of shocks fully explain the diverse patterns of fluctuations that have been observed, and the relative importance of the different mechanisms may vary across both time and place. Thus the different models should be seen as useful tools rather than as complete explanations of the business cycle.

PETER SKOTT

See also:

Equilbrium and Non-equilibrium; Financial Instability Hypothesis; Investment; Kaleckian Economics.

References

Day, R. (1994), *Complex Economic Dynamics*, Vol. 1, Cambridge, MA: MIT Press.
Goodwin, R.M. (1967), 'A growth cycle', in C.H. Feinstein (ed.), *Socialism, Capitalism and Economic Growth*, Cambridge: Cambridge University Press, pp. 54–8.
Greenspan, A. (2005), available at: http://www.federalreserve.gov/boarddocs/speeches/2005/20051012/default.htm.
Kaldor, N. (1940), 'A model of the trade cycle', *Economic Journal*, **50** (197), 78–92.
Kalecki, M. (1943), 'Political aspects of full employment', *Political Quarterly*, **14** (4), 322–31; reprinted in Kalecki, *Selected Essays on the Dynamics of the Capitalist Economy, 1933–1970*, Cambridge: Cambridge University Press, 1971, pp. 138–45.
Minsky, H. (1982), *Can 'It' Happen Again? Essays on Instability and Finance*, Armonk, NY: M.E. Sharpe.
Ryoo, S. (2010), 'Long waves and short cycles in a model of endogenous financial fragility', *Journal of Economic Behavior and Organization*, **74** (3), 163–86.
Skott, P. (1989), *Conflict and Effective Demand in Economic Growth*, Cambridge: Cambridge University Press.

Cambridge Economic Tradition

The starting-point must be Alfred Marshall (even though Keynes called T.R. Malthus 'the first of the Cambridge economists' and Keynes's successors were increasingly to draw on classical political economy and Marx for inspiration). Marshall, though, was responsible for the foundation of the Economic Tripos (in 1903) and also, in large measure and at least until very recently, for the approaches to economics in Cambridge even as we know them today. The Marshallian tradition has it that economists should explain how the world works and then, if it does not work well or fairly, do something about it (within well-defined limits). This should be done by theorizing, doing applied work and formulating plausible policies. The approach to applied economics emphasizes the importance of relevance in economics, incorporating the lessons of history, the institutional context and previous social and political conditions, gathered under the rubric of the 'rules of the game'. Theory and measurement are interdependent, feeding back and modifying and expanding one another. This tradition has characterized the contributions of the Faculty's Department of Applied Economics, a research institute which started in 1945 with Richard Stone (one of four Cambridge recipients of the Nobel Prize) as its first director. Alas, it no longer exists following an internal coup and takeover.

Marshall's major contribution was his huge *Principles of Economics*, first published in 1890. It went through eight editions in his lifetime, as Volume I for the first five as he initially intended to write two or three more volumes. What would have been the structure of Marshall's ideal *Principles*? In the first volume he wrote about the nitty gritty of economic life – what determines the prices and quantities of commodities produced, what determines the wages, salaries and employment of different sorts of labour, what determines the rates of profit in various industries, that is, a theory of relative prices and quantities. He introduced systematically into economics the use of supply and demand functions and curves in order to analyse the formation of prices and quantities in, principally, freely competitive markets.

His second great contribution was to recognize in a deep way that time is the most elusive, difficult yet relevant concept affecting economic life. To try to capture this insight Marshall used three analytical concepts: the market, the short and the long period. The first deals with existing stocks, the last two with flows. The short period is an analytical device which takes in a period long enough for employment and production but not for the number of firms, or the amount of machinery available and number of skilled labour to change; the long period is long enough for firms to enter or exit and for amounts of machinery available and supplies of labour to change (the methods of production known at the start of the long period, however, are not allowed to change). These are not one-to-one descriptions of real life, but analytical devices which exploit the concept of *ceteris paribus*. The economist decides what may or may not vary, in order to get a grip on intricate interconnecting processes and so develop theories of prices and quantities of commodities, and of the services of the factors of production. Money does not get a mention except as a ticket – something in which to measure things; it has little or no analytical role. Everything is done in real, relative terms. Although Marshall understood general equilibrium analysis and had a general equilibrium model in an appendix, he preferred to use partial equilibrium analysis, examining one firm or one industry only, in order to make the analysis manageable and obtain definite results (the limitations of which were explicitly stressed).

Money entered the scene properly when Marshall (in a never properly spelt-out second volume) developed the quantity theory of money in order to describe what determined the general price level. He argued that, at least in the long period, what was happening in the real sector and what was happening in the monetary sector of the economy – banks and the financial sector generally, the formation of the general price level – were independent of one another. Money was basically a veil. In the short period it was admitted that monetary matters could have real effects, though this was not worked out systematically because of the constraint of the dichotomy between the real and the monetary. The role of monetary institutions, including central banks, was to so control the monetary side of the economy that the underlying real factors operating in a competitive environment were not handicapped in their determination of the allocation of resources, with supplies and demands responding to each other and tending to bring about a sort of social optimum.

This was only a sort of social optimum. The Marshallian tradition did not contain an uncritical defence of *laissez-faire* – poverty, unemployment, unsatisfactory working conditions were all recognized, along with a limited role for government to tackle them. Nevertheless, *logically*, it was required to argue that, if there were competition, here were strong forces to ensure the production of goods and services that people wanted by business people who were able to employ their capital as they wanted and workers who could do the jobs they wished to. Only then was it possible to argue that in the long period it was the quantity of money which determined the general price level, as long-period levels of activity and employment could now be regarded as givens along with the long-period value of the velocity of circulation. As to the limitations of the outcome even in these circumstances it was A.C. Pigou, Marshall's successor, who developed the economics of welfare, analysing what happens, and what to do about it, if social costs and benefits were not matched by their private counterparts that the competitive system threw up. His influence is alive and well today under the guise of externalities. Pigou, drawing on his mentor, established another aspect of the Cambridge tradition, that our subject should be, first and foremost, fruit-bearing rather than only light-bearing. This view is to be found in the many editions of *The Economics of Welfare*. An interest in the causes of poverty and inequality, as well as in the distribution of income, reflects this strand. It is especially associated with the writings of James Meade, David Champernowne, Amartya Sen and Tony Atkinson (who explicitly acknowledges Meade's inspiration and example).

Keynes was Marshall's most distinguished pupil. He dominated Cambridge economics from the 1920s until his death in 1946, and beyond. His work in the late 1920s and in the 1930s significantly extended and radically changed the Marshallian tradition in which he was brought up. He was driven, as were/are all the outstanding Cambridge economists, by an intense seriousness: a desire to understand the world, especially why it malfunctioned, and how to make it a better place.

Trained as a mathematician, Keynes was also a fine philosopher as well as a great economist. He always regarded economics as a branch of moral philosophy. Three strands of his philosophical understanding are especially relevant for the Cambridge economic tradition: first, that in a discipline such as economics there is a spectrum of languages running from intuition and poetry through lawyer-akin arguments to formal logic and mathematics, all of which are relevant for particular issues, or aspects of issues, in the subject; second, that in the workings of complex economic systems, the whole may be more than the sum of the parts; and third, a lesson learnt from Marshall, what are the principles which guide sensible (sometimes not so sensible) people doing the best they can in situations of inescapable uncertainty and what are the systemic effects of their behaviour? The significance of these strands was made most explicit in the 1930s when Keynes was writing *The General Theory*. In the 1920s and especially the 1930s he started to rethink drastically how the world worked, initially with his close ally, Dennis Robertson, who is a bridge between Marshall and Keynes, but who, in the end, tragically split with Keynes (a personal tragedy for him and also a professional one for the development of economics).

As Keynes was rethinking Marshall's monetary theory, others at Cambridge were starting to rethink (and in the case of Piero Sraffa ultimately reject) Marshall's theory of the determination of prices and quantities at the level of the firm and industry. Sraffa published two fundamental papers in the mid-1920s, one in Italian and only recently available in an English translation, the other in the *Economic Journal* (Sraffa 1925, 1926). Both contained an attack on Marshall's method, that is, the extremely limited practical applications of partial equilibrium analysis (and, he thought then but for different reasons, general equilibrium analysis). But he also suggested that monopoly rather than free competition was the better model of how markets worked, that firms' prices and outputs were constrained by demand rather than by rising supply prices and costs. The appropriate model was therefore one of mini-monopolies surrounded by mini-monopolies so that they had to take account of their actions and other firms' reactions when setting prices. The 1926 paper helped precipitate the imperfect competition revolution developed by Gerald Shove, Richard Kahn and then Austin Robinson and especially, Joan Robinson. Her 1933 *Economics of Imperfect Competition*, though still Marshallian/Pigovian in construction, greatly altered the emphasis and details of the results in this tradition. Sraffa had refuted the tradition by 1930 and had started on the long trail which would lead through his edition (with the collaboration of M.H. Dobb) of Ricardo's works (published between 1951 and 1963) to *Production of Commodities* (1960), both a critique of the foundations of neoclassical theory and simultaneously a rehabilitation of the approach of classical theory, including Marx. Joan Robinson only joined him, more or less fully, in the postwar years, Kahn probably never fully and Shove and Austin Robinson not at all.

Keynes became more and more dissatisfied with Marshall's way of looking at the economy as a whole, especially the view that we could talk about prices and quantities independently of what was happening in the financial and monetary sectors generally. He also changed the emphasis from the long period, the central core of Marshall's economics, to the short period, including designing policies for other than that '*long run* [in which] we are all dead' (Keynes 1923 [1971], p. 65; original italics). *A Treatise on Money* (1930), two volumes, was meant to be Keynes's *magnum opus* but it was too constrained by the Marshallian tradition to be successful. So in the 1930s he started again, aided by the remarkable group of young economists in the 'circus', Kahn, James Meade, Austin and Joan Robinson, Sraffa, as well as by Roy Harrod in Oxford.

What did he do in his authentic *magnum opus*, *The General Theory*, published in 1936? The 1920s in the United Kingdom and then in the 1930s in much of the advanced industrialized world was characterized by mass unemployment. Economic theory, though, said that at least in the long term it could not occur if impediments to competition were removed. Keynes, working through his rational reconstruction of the traditional analysis, decided it was wrong, that there could be a failure of *overall* demand so that people and machines could be involuntarily idle for considerable periods of time and that there were not strong or indeed any forces at work in an unregulated economy that tended to redress these situations. Why? – principally because important expenditure decisions had to be made in situations of inescapable uncertainty about the future. This was especially true of investment decisions, the desire to accumulate, which drove capitalist systems along. Keynes showed that basically there were not persistent forces at work which, at least on average, could produce enough investment to absorb the resources released by what the community would voluntarily save at the full-employment level of income where all those willing to work under existing conditions would have jobs. In situations of unemployment there was no way in which those who were willing to work but who were involuntarily unemployed, could signal to employers that it would be profitable to employ them. And indeed, it would not be unless there were to be a simultaneous, *autonomous* rise in the total demand. It followed therefore that there was a coherent logical case for government intervention; Keynes had provided an explicit theory with which to rationalize the common-sense policies which were being put forward at the time.

A barrier to this being perceived before was the real–monetary dichotomy with money only a veil. But as it is also a store of value, people could hold it and other financial assets rather than spend. In Keynes's view this second reason for holding money plays an important part in determining the pattern of the rates of interest. The forces concerned may not be such as to give a pattern which induces a rate of accumulation of real things which offsets full employment saving. We now have an integrated theory of the real and monetary, of a monetary production economy.

All members of the 'circus' influenced Keynes but Kahn, his favourite pupil, was especially influential in the making of *The General Theory*: first, as a remorseless critic of the quantity theory as a causal explanation of the general price level; second, through his work on the short period in the late 1920s in which he made it a subject worthy of analysis in its own right (though still at the level of the firm and industry); and, third, with James Meade, through his 1931 article on the multiplier which provided an essential, crucial concept for Keynes's new system, showing how investment created saving and not the other way round, as in the traditional view (Kahn 1931).

The General Theory (and a few following articles) were Keynes's great theoretical contribution to economics in the last century and the Cambridge contribution has built on these foundations ever since: developing policies to run a war-time economy including keeping inflation in check, using Keynes's concept of the inflationary gap; designing the required international institutions for the postwar world at Bretton Woods, in order to remove the contractionary, deflationary biases built into the operation of much of the world economy (here Keynes leaves us, dead at the ridiculously early age of 62 in 1946); and, third, in the postwar period developing long-term theories of distribution and growth over time. With this last it was some of Keynes's colleagues in the circus – Kahn, Joan Robinson, Sraffa – together with Nicholas Kaldor (who came to Cambridge from the London School of Economics in the postwar years), Richard Goodwin and Luigi Pasinetti, who were the pioneers.

Within the postwar development of growth theory their work stands out as peculiarly Cambridge in that it draws on insights from the classical political economists, Marx and Keynes, initially in response to Harrod's original and seminal writings just before and after the Second World War (Harrod 1939, 1948). One basic question was whether capitalist economies could maintain full employment of labour and capital over time when both the employment- and capacity-creating effects of accumulation were taken into account, together with the classical concern with technical progress, embodied through accumulation itself. In the Cambridge approach (which includes Michał Kalecki's contributions, principally through Joan Robinson) investment led and saving responded, both through changes in output and distribution, taking note of differences in saving propensities at the margin as between wages and profits (and their recipients). (Kaldor flirted with being 'Jean Baptiste Kaldor' for over a decade (Samuelson 1964, p. 345) by assuming that growing economies were fully employed and letting changes in distribution do all the work.) The ultimate goal, probably only reached by Kalecki and Goodwin, was to model descriptively the movement of industrial societies over time.

Joan Robinson and Kahn prefaced this objective with 'golden age' analysis, walking before they ran, getting definitions and concepts clear and precise before tackling the much harder task of disequilibrium dynamic analysis. Ever impatient, Kaldor's writings in the 1950s and 1960s were meant to be descriptive analysis, theories to explain his famous 'stylized facts' of economic growth, increasingly in the 1970s and 1980s by cumulative causation processes. Neoclassical growth theorists, though similarly stimulated (irritated?) by Harrod's writings, tackled his conundrums – the instability of the warranted rate of growth (g_w), the unlikely correspondence of g_w with the natural rate (g_n) – by explicitly concentrating on the supply side and the long-term effects of substitution possibilities in production. Initially aggregate production function as well as multi-sector n-commodity models were used. This led to the Cambridge critique of capital and marginal productivity theory generally, associated especially with Kaldor's, Joan Robinson's and Sraffa's writings on value, distribution and capital theory. Also, through Sraffa's contributions and Joan Robinson's writings on Marx and her absorption of Kalecki's approach, the central classical/Marxist organizing concept of the surplus – its creation, extraction, distribution and use – was integrated into the Cambridge approach and tradition. Pasinetti's (1981) 'theoretical essay on the dynamics of the wealth of nations' is the most systematic and comprehensive development of the classical and Keynesian elements outlined above, thus making him the senior living heir of this strand of the Cambridge tradition; see Pasinetti (2007) for a comprehensive account of his take on the Cambridge tradition, his own approach and the best way forward.

Finally, the tradition is marked by an interest in the history of our subject and the relevance of our predecessors' writings for current issues. Marshall set the example; Keynes's biographical essays reflect it (he was not always the most accurate or reliable historian of theory); and Joan Robinson's writings (see Harcourt and Kerr 2009) are characterized by references to the insights of past economists, often in order to back up her current interests and interpreted accordingly! The two greats, though, are Kalecki's only two English gentlemen, one an Italian and the other a communist, Piero Sraffa and Maurice Dobb. Sraffa's edition of Ricardo's works and correspondence (with the collaboration of Dobb) and his attempt to rehabilitate the classical approach in *Production of Commodities* (1960) are extraordinary examples of scholarship and theory combined. Dobb was the foremost Marxist economist of his era and his writings and influence still diffuse through modern work, even when those affected are not aware of it. Dobb, together with Phyllis Deane and Robin Matthews and their colleagues, also left a distinctive stamp on our understanding of economic history.

I have tried to make clear what I understand to be the Cambridge tradition. I have to say that many of the present decision makers in the Faculty have done their best to suppress this tradition and to replace it with approaches which reflect what they see as the best practice of leading American departments.

G.C. HARCOURT

See also:

Capital Theory; Joan Robinson's Economics; Kaleckian Economics; Keynes's *General Theory*; Keynes's *Treatise on Money*; Keynes's *Treatise on Probability*; Sraffian Economics.

References

Harcourt, G.C. and P. Kerr (2009), *Joan Robinson*, Basingstoke: Palgrave Macmillan.
Harrod, R.F. (1939), 'An essay in dynamic theory', *Economic Journal*, **49** (193), 14–33.
Harrod, R.F. (1948), *Towards a Dynamic Economics*, London: Macmillan.

Kahn, R.F. (1931), 'The relation of home investment to unemployment', *Economic Journal*, **41** (162), 173–98.

Keynes, J.M. (1923), *A Tract on Monetary Reform*, London: Macmillan, two vols; reprinted as Volume VI of Keynes's *Collected Writings*, London: Macmillan for the Royal Economic Society, 1971.

Keynes, J.M. (1930), *A Treatise on Money*, London: Macmillan; reprinted as Volume IV of Keynes's *Collected Writings*, London: Macmillan for the Royal Economic Society, 1971.

Keynes, J.M. (1936), *The General Theory of Employment, Interest and Money*, London: Macmillan.

Pasinetti, L.L. (1981), *Structural Change and Economic Growth. A Theoretical Essay on the Dynamics of the Wealth of Nations*, Cambridge: Cambridge University Press.

Pasinetti, L.L. (2007), *Keynes and the Cambridge Keynesians: A 'Revolution in Economics' to be Accomplished*, Cambridge: Cambridge University Press.

Samuelson, P.A. (1964), 'A brief survey of post-Keynesian developments', in R. Lekachman (ed.), *Keynes's General Theory: Reports of Three Decades*, New York: St. Martin's Press, pp. 331–47.

Sraffa, P. (1925), 'On the relations between cost and quantity produced', in L.L. Pasinetti (ed.), *Italian Economic Papers*, Vol. 3, Oxford: Oxford University Press, 1999, pp. 323–63.

Sraffa, P. (1926), 'The laws of returns under competitive conditions', *Economic Journal*, **36** (144), 535–50.

Sraffa, P. (1960), *Production of Commodities by Means of Commodities. Prelude to a Critique of Economic Theory*, Cambridge: Cambridge University Press.

Capital Theory

'Capital theory' has been used as a shorthand term for the debate known as the Cambridge capital controversies. The reference to Cambridge follows from the dispute having mainly been conducted between prominent figures, or figureheads, attached or aligned to Cambridge, Massachusetts, especially MIT, and Cambridge, England. The two Cambridges stood, respectively, as representatives for mainstream neoclassical economics and its critics from radical political economy. A key initiating text was penned by Joan Robinson (1953–54), who was most closely identified with the early phase marking aggressive popularizing of the critique. Piero Sraffa's (1960) classic contribution, long delayed in publication, has served as a basis both for a critique of neoclassical economics – as was its intention – and as an alternative to Marxist value theory. The impact of the capital critique was at its height in the early 1970s, rising and falling with radical political economy. Today, as discussed below, despite the Cambridge critique having won the debate and wrung intellectual concessions from the mainstream, the latter proceeds in practice as if the controversy never occurred, replicating theoretical and empirical errors that were previously exposed and accepted as such.

The Cambridge critique raises a number of interconnected issues. Here, these will be reduced to, and represented by, three broad aspects. First, in mainstream economics, it has been standard to represent an 'economy' as if it were reducible to an aggregate production function, $F(K, L)$ say, where K is capital and L is labour, with $f()$ exhibiting the standard assumption of decreasing but positive marginal products and overall constant returns to scale. We place 'economy' in inverted commas because it could stand for a country, a sector, a single firm or any producing entity such as a household, with a corresponding production function. In each case, even if imputed for the household, it follows from a knowledge of $f()$ and the capital and labour in use, K and L, respectively, that the rate of profit, r, and the rate of wages, w, can be determined by taking marginal products (with assumptions of full employment and perfect markets for inputs). In particular, $r = f'(k)$ where f is the per capita version of F; $f(K/L) = F(K, L)/L$. It follows that the rate of profit falls with an increase in capital per worker as a result of the presumed diminishing marginal product of capital.

One way of interpreting the Cambridge controversy is in terms of whether this stylized *one-sector* model (there is only one good, with the capital input identical to the output) is capable of being representative of a more complicated economy with more than one good. In other words, it is a discussion about *models* – specifically, are models with more than one good reducible to an 'as if' one-good model? The unambiguous answer is no, unless special assumptions are made about the more complicated economy that essentially make it equivalent to a one-good economy (all outputs are produced with the same input proportions). The presence of more than one good more or less completely undermines the results derived from the one-sector model. First, distribution is not 'determined' by technology alone – what techniques are available and which are in use (by analogy with the one sector, knowledge of F and the technique in use, that is, which particular K/L). I have placed 'determined' in inverted commas because there is only a one-to-one *association* between technology and distribution if there is no double switching or reswitching, briefly elaborated in the next paragraph. If you tell me which technology is in use, I can tell you distribution and, it should be added, vice versa. But this says nothing about causation from one to the other or by other factors altogether.

Double switching or reswitching is difficult to explain briefly, so an attempt will be made to do so through use of present value curves that are assumed to be familiar to the reader. Figure 1 shows a number of present value curves, T1, T2 and T3, each representing a technique for producing output. Note, when the rate of profit/interest (the two are treated interchangeably), $r = 0$, the corresponding intercept on the present value axis is net output (gross output over and above inputs without discounting).

It might be presumed, incorrectly, that higher net output (for T1 over T2 and for T2 over T3) means higher capital intensity. But, even if this

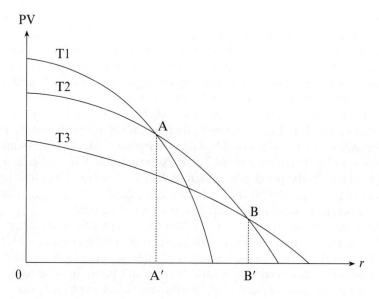

Figure 1   No reswitching

sort of one-dimensional statement is to make sense (there are different capital outlays at different points in time), it all depends upon the profile over time of streams of costs and benefits. Even so, at low rates of interest, OA′, technique 1 would be chosen; along A′B′, technique 2; and beyond B′, technique 3. So a *switch* is made from technique 1 to 2 at A, and from technique 2 to 3 at B. At any rate of interest, there is a corresponding technique and vice versa. We could also add more and more techniques, filling out an envelope, along which there could be continuous switching from one technique to another as the rate of interest changes.

This is fine as far as it goes as long, as previously mentioned, as there is no reswitching. The latter is illustrated in Figure 2. At C, technique 3 switches to technique 4 and, at D, technique 4 switches back to technique 3. There is no necessary one-to-one correspondence between technique in use and rate of interest. By knowing all techniques available and the actual one in use, we are not able to 'determine' the rate of interest/profit as suggested by reference to the marginal product of capital for the 'as if' one-sector model (with inputs and outputs assessed at different points in time making the present value curves equivalent to having more than one good).

In addition, we cannot write down a sensible production function for the economy as a whole since, even if we can do so for individual sectors in terms of physical quantities of inputs and outputs, aggregating over sectors will require an evaluation of the weight of each sector. This cannot

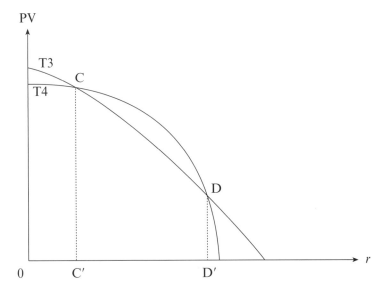

Figure 2   Reswitching

be done in a way that preserves the results of the one-sector model – in particular, that there is an inverse relationship between the measure of capital and the rate of profit. With reswitching, as in Figure 2, it is possible for the same technology to be in use at two different rates of profit. For the results of the 'as if' one-good model to carry over to the more complicated model, the same physical quantities of capital would have to be measured as lower (higher) for the higher (lower) rate of profit. In short, we cannot aggregate capital sensibly to give rise to an 'as if' aggregate production function.

The aspect of the capital controversy just covered is purely technical in content – the one-good model is not representative of a model with more than one good. A second aspect concerns the empirical implications. For, within mainstream neoclassical economics, it has been standard to estimate the economy as if it were represented by a one-sector production function, a practice often also to be found in use to suit in radical political economy. This is most notable in the residual method used to measure the contribution of technical progress to economic growth, as opposed to the contribution made by growth of inputs. In such work, even on the assumption of full employment and perfect competition in all markets, capital is usually aggregated by weighting it at current prices. As the previously reported technical results suggest, this is entirely arbitrary. Indeed, because the economy is being treated as if it only had one good, any change in prices, for whatever reason and in favour of a capital good relative to a consumption good say, will be measured as if the quantity of capital had increased. Accordingly, even though technology will not have changed, it will appear as though output had remained the same despite use of more capital. Technical progress will appear, falsely, to have been negative.

Again this is difficult to explain briefly. But refer to Figure 1 again. As we go round the outside of the curves, the envelope traced by the available techniques including others not shown, there is no technological advance, just switching from one technique to another. But, associated with these, for the 'as if' one-good world, there will be changes in measured output over and above (or below) those attached to technique. This is due to changes in relative prices (which cannot be distinguished from changes in quantities of input and output in the 'as if' one-good world). In short, changes in quantities and prices are treated as if they were purely changes in quantities. It is simply empirical nonsense, as if the changes in the area of a rectangle could be measured by reference to one side (as if it were a circle with that radius, for example, or a square).

In short, the standard methods for measuring total factor productivity are invalidated by the Cambridge critique. Further, this can be shown to have nothing to do with reswitching – the conflation of price and quantity effects pertains even if no technique were preferred at two different rates of profit. Despite this, empirical work on the basis of an aggregate production function has proceeded without regard to this totally destructive critique, with only an occasional acknowledgement of the critique, often then with an irrelevant and unexamined appeal to whether reswitching exists in practice.

The third aspect of the capital controversy concerns its wider signifi- cance for economic method and the choice between schools of thought. For some, it seemed as if the whole of neoclassical mainstream economics were invalidated by the critique. This is simply false, as the mainstream does not depend upon a one-sector model of the economy. Indeed, the latter is a very special case for, in the absence of more than one good, the model is effectively without demand (lest it be for choice of consumption over time) and utility theory, a central component of the orthodoxy. The results of the Cambridge critique can be accepted and incorporated within a model of general equilibrium, in which there can be no presumption of simple inverse relations between quantities of capital and rates of profit. For, suppose there is an increase in physical quantities of all capital goods, the rate of profit could rise if demand conditions are such that there is an even greater increase in demand for capital-intensive goods or more capital- intensive techniques to produce them. What this does mean, though, is that all the intuitions attached to the one-sector model do not hold.

The debate was entirely conducted in terms of choice between linear technologies. Essentially, the last aspect reveals that the debate is about how to close such a model of supply. The mainstream can retreat into general equilibrium and a utility-based demand theory. This, however, leaves it floundering for a notion of capital other than as a physical quantity of inputs, initial endowments, that provides for a stream of utility. The alternative offered by many from within the critique, as well as the critique itself, has been inspired by Sraffa. He showed that there is a trade-off between the rate of profit and the level of wages, as previously posited by David Ricardo. Hence, the terms 'Sraffian' and 'neo-Ricardianism' are often used interchangeably to suggest that technology (and technique in use) alone do not determine distribution, only what is available to redistribute. However, there is a difference between these two closures in method. Sraffa (and Sraffians) model in terms of *physical* conditions of production, input–output matrices and the wage–profit trade-off they sustain (although Sraffa's own preference for closure was via a profit rate related to a distinct rate of interest determined by monetary factors). Neo-Ricardians retain an attachment to the labour theory of value. In either case, with a linear technology, it is possible to close the system by appeal to a trade-off between the rate of profit and the level of real wages, motivated by the idea that capital and labour confront each other over distribution. In addition, the Sraffian approach has been used as a critique of Marxist value theory, arguing that prices diverge from labour values, even if modified by their transformation into prices of production.

As observed, capital theory attained its greatest prominence in the 1970s when radical political economy was considerably stronger than it is today. Despite the veracity of its empirical and theoretical results, and their acceptance by the mainstream (who conceded that empirical measurement of performance ought to include both supply and demand and not just supply), the mainstream now proceeds as if the Cambridge critique never existed and shamelessly deploys aggregate production functions as if they are without problems. This is particularly notable in the 'new' or endogenous growth theory, where aggregate production functions are used for theoretical and empirical work. It is a particularly appropriate symbol of the analytical weaknesses of mainstream economics, and its ignorance even of its own most recent history as a discipline, since the new growth theory generally proceeds on the assumption that the economy as a whole can be understood as if it were made up of a single sector (apart, occasionally, from a separate sector to generate productivity increase in the 'as if' one-good economy). This is also indicative of the extent to which the mainstream's supposed mathematical rigour is always sacrificed in deference to its prior commitment to longstanding techniques, methods and goals (Fine and Milonakis 2009).

BEN FINE

See also:

Cambridge Economic Tradition; Growth and Income Distribution; Income Distribution; Joan Robinson's Economics; Marginalism; Production; Sraffian Economics.

Bibliography

Arestis, P., G. Palma and M.C. Sawyer (eds) (1997), *Capital Controversy, Post-Keynesian Economics and the History of Economics: Essays in Honour of Geoff Harcourt*, Volume I, London and New York: Routledge.

Bliss, C. (1975), *Capital Theory and the Distribution of Income*, Amsterdam: North-Holland.

Cohen, A. and G.C. Harcourt (2003), 'Whatever happened to the Cambridge capital theory controversies?', *Journal of Economic Perspectives*, **17** (1), 199–214.

Fine, B. (1980), *Economic Theory and Ideology*, Chapters 5 and 6, London: Edward Arnold.

Fine, B. (2000), 'Endogenous growth theory: a critical assessment', *Cambridge Journal of Economics*, **24** (2), 245–65, a shortened and amended version of identically titled SOAS Working Paper, No. 80, February 1998.

Fine, B. (2006), 'New growth theory: more problem than solution', in Jomo and Fine (eds), pp. 68–86.

Fine, B. and D. Milonakis (2009), *From Economics Imperialism to Freakonomics: The Shifting Boundaries Between Economics and Other Social Sciences*, London and New York: Routledge.

Han, Z. and B. Schefold (2006), 'An empirical investigation of paradoxes: reswitching and reverse capital deepening in capital theory', *Cambridge Journal of Economics*, **30** (5), 737–65.

Harcourt, G.C. (1972), *Some Cambridge Controversies in the Theory of Capital*, Cambridge: Cambridge University Press.

Harcourt, G.C. (1976), 'The Cambridge controversies: old ways and new horizons – or dead end?', *Oxford Economic Papers*, **28** (1), 25–65.

Hodgson, G. (1997), 'The fate of the Cambridge capital controversy', in Arestis et al. (eds), pp. 95–110.

Jomo, K. and B. Fine (eds) (2006), *The New Development Economics: After the Washington Consensus*, Delhi: Tulika and London: Zed Books.

Robinson, J. (1953–54), 'The production function and the theory of capital', *Review of Economic Studies*, **21** (1), 81–106.

Sraffa, P. (1960), *Production of Commodities by Means of Commodities: Prelude to a Critique of Economic Theory*, Cambridge: Cambridge University Press.

Symposium (2005), on 'Aggregate production functions', *Eastern Economic Journal*, **31** (3), 421–92.

Central Banks

Central banks are institutions in charge of multiple functions. Existing central banks are, in some cases, a spontaneous product of historical evolution, like the Bank of England, or the result of social engineering, as in the case of central banks created during the twentieth century, like the Federal Reserve in the US. In both cases, central banks were created, or ended up with the power, to manage the stock of national currencies. Orthodox economists tend to see the main (or the sole) responsibility of a central bank as the control of the available *quantity* of money in order to preserve its purchasing power. Keynesian economists, on the other hand, stress the fact that by controlling the ultimate source of liquidity in a modern economy, a central bank is responsible for the smooth operation of the financial system. For Keynesians, thus, a central bank is first and foremost to operate as the *lender of last resort* for the financial system, particularly for the banking system, which creates means of payment in the form of demand deposits.

Post Keynesian economists, in particular, approach a modern market economy as one organized around the existence of forward money contracts (see Davidson 1978). These contracts are essential to allow entrepreneurs to face the uncertainties that plague a market economy. Contracts, however, create obligations to be discharged in the future by the delivery of money from the debtor to the creditor. This simple fact is the foundation of liquidity preference: facing the uncertainty of being able to pay debts when they come due, the possession of money serves to lull a debtor's disquietudes, to borrow Keynes's expression. Money in these economies exists either as currency or as its perfect substitute, demand deposits created or accepted by banks, which are private liabilities that have the characteristic of being redeemable on demand, at par. The acceptance of these substitutes, however, depends on confidence that they will *actually be redeemable* on demand, at par. The only institution that can give this guarantee is the central bank, when it makes known its willingness to trade bank deposits for currency on those terms. This makes the central bank the lender of last resort to the banking system.

This view, proposed by Walter Bagehot in his famous *Lombard Street*, was accepted by Keynes and is the foundation of the Post Keynesian approach to central banking. In fact, the key role of a lender of last resort was, if anything, strongly underlined by the current global financial crisis. Major central banks, like the Federal Reserve in the United States and the European Central Bank, even extended their support from the banking sector to securities markets, becoming buyers of last resort as well for almost everything, from subprime mortgage securities to sovereign bonds. That central banks perform this role confirms Keynes's and Post Keynesian views that they should not be confined to pursuing inflation targets, as became fashionable in recent years. There are some important differences among Post Keynesians, however, in the way the performance of this function is seen to constrain central banks' behaviour.

Keynes himself believed that central banks, besides performing their defensive function of lender of last resort, could also actively manage the supply of money. In his *Treatise on Money* (1930 [1971]), Keynes stated that '[t]he first necessity of a central bank, charged with responsibility for the management of the monetary system as a whole, is to make sure that it has an unchallengeable control over the total volume of bank money created by its member banks' (p. 201). In that book, Keynes criticized the 'monetary heretics' who maintained that 'in some way the banks can furnish all the real resources which manufacture and trade can reasonably require without cost to anyone' (p. 194). A bank performed a dual function, being 'a provider of money for its depositors, and also as a provider of resources for [its] borrowing customers' (p. 191). This meant that the creation of money by banks had to take into consideration its effects on the value of money. Central banks should use the interest rate as an instrument to control bank reserves, since 'the aggregate volume of the deposits of the member banks of a modern banking system depends on the reserve ratio which the members aim at keeping, and the amount of reserves (in the shape of cash and deposits at the central bank)' (p. 43). Keynes recognized that the central bank could be *forced* to supply reserves to banks, since there were situations in which it had to purchase assets 'in virtue of an obligation, of law or custom, to purchase such an asset if it is tendered on specified conditions' (p. 202). However, the central bank could compensate for these operations and regain initiative through the investments it could make: '[t]he amount of the central bank's investments, since these are purchased and sold on its own initiative, is entirely within its own control. Action directed towards varying the amount of these is now usually called "open-market policy"' (p. 202).

In sum, for Keynes, a central bank should act as a lender of last resort to the banking system, but this would not necessarily prevent it from also managing the volume of means of payment available in the economy. The central bank uses an interest rate as an instrument to control the volume of reserves of the banking system, but sets its aims both in terms of interest rates and in terms of the volume of reserves.

Keynes's approach was emphatically rejected by Nicholas Kaldor. Kaldor argued that Keynes never completely abandoned the quantity theory of money, which led him to attribute a definiteness to the concept of money that it lacked in modern economies and to give it an importance that it did not have. According to Kaldor, money was not a precise concept, since the public can use many instruments to make payments. Liquidity was a better concept, but liquidity is an attribute shared by many types of vehicles in different degrees. To single out 'money', in Kaldor's view, as means of payment would falsify the nature and operation of the payment systems since it would imply confining the attribute of liquidity entirely to an arbitrarily chosen asset (Kaldor 1982). As a result, for Kaldor it was a mistake to assume that a central bank could control the supply of money. It should be concerned exclusively with interest rates, because these affect the actual liquidity premium of the several assets, since they affected supply and demand for each of them. Thus a central bank should set the interest rates over which it had direct control, and freely supply the volume of reserves that were demanded by banks at those rates. As a result, the money supply curve should be represented by a horizontal line, in the space money/interest rate, originating at the level of the interest rate set by the central bank.

Kaldor argued that to perform the role of a lender of last resort did not allow the central bank any room for pursuing an active reserve policy. Any attempt to regulate the volume of reserves could threaten the solvency of banks and, thus, put in jeopardy the supporting role of the central bank. Kaldor's later followers, such as Basil Moore, extended Kaldor's argument, which was centred around the use of the discount window to open-market policies, suggesting, in opposition to Keynes, that central banks were constrained to supply a given amount of reserves also through open-market operations. Also, somewhat differently from Kaldor, modern-day *horizontalists* tended to focus on the non-controllability of money supply, rather than on the concept of money itself, as being the main feature to characterize an approach as Post Keynesian. As a result, it becomes harder to differentiate orthodox approaches that nevertheless accept the assumption of endogenous money from certain strands of Post Keynesian monetary theory (see, for example, Lavoie and Seccareccia 2004).

The horizontalist approach created by Kaldor represents, however, a more extreme view that is not shared by all Post Keynesians. In fact, authors such as Paul Davidson, Hyman Minsky, Jan Kregel and Victoria Chick advance approaches more faithful to Keynes's own views, emphasizing, in different degrees, the capacity a central bank has of taking initiatives in terms of reserve policies, while recognizing that one of its essential functions remains that of a lender of last resort. Davidson, for instance, actually defines two strategies available for a central bank at any time in terms of creation of reserves: (i) the *income generating method*, by which the central bank accommodates the demand for reserves made by banks in order to satisfy market demands for credit; and (ii) the *portfolio change method*, by which the central bank takes the initiative to use interest rates to induce a desired change in the amount of reserves at the disposal of banks (Davidson 1978). In the first case, the central bank acts in a more passive way, validating the demands coming from the credit market. In the second, though, the central bank tries to implement its own strategies in terms of reserves, through open-market operations, as Keynes suggested. Moreover, a more refined analysis of the relationship between money and finance, based on the concept of liquidity preference as proposed by Minsky (1986), also leads to a richer analysis of the role of central banks in support of financial stability. Lessons derived from Minsky's analyses have been particularly important to understand the financial crisis initiated in the United States in 2007 and its repercussions throughout the world. In particular, the role of central banks as financial regulators and supervisors, which has always been stressed as a crucial function by Post Keynesians, has been increasingly acknowledged by other strands of monetary theory.

FERNANDO J. CARDIM DE CARVALHO

See also:

Banking; Financial Instability Hypothesis; Kaldorian Economics; Keynes's *Treatise on Money*; Liquidity Preference; Monetary Policy; Money; Rate of Interest.

References

Davidson, P. (1978), *Money and the Real World*, 2nd edn, London: Macmillan.
Kaldor, N. (1982), *The Scourge of Monetarism*, Oxford: Oxford University Press.
Keynes, J.M. (1930), *A Treatise on Money. The Applied Theory of Money*; reprinted in *The Collected Writings of John Maynard Keynes*, Volume VI, London: Macmillan, 1971.
Lavoie, M. and M. Seccareccia (eds) (2004), *Central Banking in the Modern World*, Cheltenham, UK and Northampton, MA, USA: Edward Elgar.
Minsky, H.P. (1986), *Stabilizing an Unstable Economy*, New Haven, CT: Yale University Press.

Chartalism

Chartalism is an approach to monetary economics that portrays money as 'a creature of the state' (Lerner 1943) rather than as a market outcome, which is by opposition the approach pervading more orthodox economics (see, for instance, Menger 1892). The chartalist school can be traced back to the work of Knapp (1924) as well as Schumpeter (1954). Indeed the former aimed at explaining money's validity in respect of law and institutions, while the latter put aside money's historical origins to focus on its logical origin conceptually (Rossi 2007, chapter 1).

The chartalist theory of money originated as a critique of metallism, which (in neoclassical economics) is the view that purports money to be 'a creature of the market', that is to say, a result of agents' search for a 'lubricant' in order to reduce 'frictions' in exchange (Niehans 1978). In light of the historical evidence that some forms of 'money' existed independently of market processes, for instance in cases of socially obligatory donation or redistribution in the local community for individual or group production, chartalists argue that the essence of money as a unit of account and means of payment stems from a sovereign act establishing – by law or social convention – what object(s) people may dispose of in order to settle any of their debt obligations (see Keynes 1930 [1971], p. 4).

This argument is further refined by introducing the state explicitly into monetary analysis, that is to say, the power to levy taxes linked to the definition of the means of payment accepted by the fiscal authority in that respect. Wray (2003, p. 89) dubs this view as 'the sovereignty approach' to money, 'because it links the state's ability to issue a currency denominated in the unit of account it has chosen . . . to a fundamental power that is directly associated with sovereign nations'.

As a matter of fact and conceptual logic, money does not need to be reified into a precious metal in order for it to be a final means of payment, to wit, an instrument that any kind of agent (both in the private and in the public sector) may use to pay for their debt obligations finally. All that is required in this respect, indeed, is that a 'third party', such as a bank or a clearing house, keeps a double-entry book by means of which all economic transactions are recorded and settled through a purely book-entry device (see Rossi 2007, chapter 2).

Now, the essential question is to understand the nature of this numerical means of payment, as it is plain that no economic agent will ever agree to dispose of a good or service in order to obtain a mere number in exchange for them. Metallists argue in this connection that bank money – which they recognize as fully immaterial – has a purchasing power only because it is the 'general equivalent' of the set of goods and services on sale on the mar-ketplace. The general equilibrium framework supports this alleged prop-erty of modern money, only in so far as the latter is included in the set of commodities available within the economic system. As national account-ants well know, however, money is a 'non-commodity': nobody would ever include it in the set of goods and services used to measure produced output and income within a given economic space (usually a country). To be true, money is the (numerical) means to express in economic terms the value of total production within the given space (and time). It is therefore the 'social form' of value, particularly because it allows one to participate in income distribution, or to enter into 'the great social store of all goods [that are exchanged against it]' (Schumpeter 1954, p. 289). This raises thereby the issue of understanding the workings of our monetary economies of pro-duction and exchange in the light of banks issuing money when recording agents' debts and credits in their accounting books.

The chartalist argument in this regard amounts to a theoretical 'middle ground' between so-called 'exogenous' and 'endogenous' money. As Wray (1998, p. 80) puts it,

> [w]hen the government creates fiat money to purchase goods and services . . . this shows up on the books of the public as a credit of fiat money and a debit of goods and services sold to the government . . . This is 'net money creation' because it is not offset by a private sector liability. This 'net money' (also called 'outside money') is available to pay taxes.

The state's IOUs are thus created exogenously with respect to the so-called 'needs of trade' in the private sector, and deposited into the banking system by their recipients. This creates bank reserves, which might then give rise to an expansion of banks' assets and liabilities endogenously. This amounts to saying that state money is exogenous and that bank money is an endogenous multiple of it, similarly to orthodox money multiplier stories (see ibid., p. 111).

Abstracting from this collision with traditional macroeconomics, chartalism turns economic policy objectives upside down with respect to the mainstream view: contrary to orthodox analysis, chartalists argue that fiscal policy determines the so-called 'money stock' (which is the total sum of deposits in the banking system, composed of a central bank and the set of banks participating in the relevant payment and settlement system), while monetary policy determines interest rates through open-market operations whose major objective is the sale (purchase) of government bonds in order for the central bank to drain (inject) reserves from (into) the banking system and thereby attain the targeted rate of interest. In this perspective, the general government sector does not need to collect taxes or sell sovereign bonds to earn the purchasing power that it needs to finance public spending in factor or goods markets: it can buy whatever is on sale just by issuing the relevant number of money units through the central bank (see ibid., 1998, p. ix). The amount of 'money supply' would thus depend on fiscal policy eventually, that is, on the power to fix and collect taxes, as the state determines by taxation the number of money units that it deems appropriate to satisfy agents' demand for money as a liquid stock of purchasing power (hoarding). This is tantamount to saying that government deficits are the norm in monetary economies of production, for private sector agents need 'always and everywhere' a store of wealth 'to lull them from their inquietude' in regard to the (uncertain) future (see Keynes 1936 [1973], chapter 17).

As Wray (2003, p. 97) observes, however, '[t]his does not mean that deficit spending is always desirable, nor does it mean that government should ignore impacts of deficits or exogenously set low interest rates on domestic inflation or on exchange rates'. According to this view, in fact, there are some limits (mainly institutional or linked to confidence) to any government's ability to create money without inducing inflation at the same time. 'If the tax system breaks down, the government's fiat money can become worthless – which is manifested as "hyperinflation"' (Wray 1998, p. 85). Also, the extent to which government debt-financed spending refers to production activities rather than public consumption has an impact on the purchasing power of money as well as on the causes of inflation. Indeed, (state) money created to finance public sector consumption gives rise to some inflationary pressures on retail prices, whereas money created to finance the production of public goods or services has no such effect, since in this case the money–output relation is not affected by the latter creation.

As interesting as chartalism may be, it does not yet provide a sound alternative to orthodox monetary economics on a number of fundamental points, such as the way money is created and the objective (by contrast to the subjective) value of (book-entry) money. To be sure, in both the metallist and chartalist traditions, the money-creation process is an act involving an agent selling any goods or services (including labour services) and some other agent buying them, in an exchange whereby the latter creates the very means of payment that s/he uses to settle her/his debt obligations. This is so, particularly with regard to the general government sector, because there is a confusion between the payer (the treasury) and the book-keeper (a central bank), which Wray (2003, p. 92) considers indeed as 'husband and wife within the household'. In fact, as Hicks (1967, p. 11) recognized, '[e]very transaction involves three parties, buyer, seller, and banker'. Conflating the payer and the record-keeper of the result of the relevant transaction implies that the payment recorded in the books is just promised, rather than finalized, a final payment meaning that 'a seller of a good, or service, or another asset, receives something of equal value from the purchaser, which leaves the seller with no further claim on the buyer' (Goodhart, 1975 [1989], p. 26). If so, then chartalism is grounded in a 'seigniorage approach' that clashes with the chartalists' intention to provide an alternative to more orthodox monetary thinking (see Wray 2003).

The conceptual proximity of chartalism to metallism, and to neoclassical economics more generally speaking, stems also from the common view that considers the purchasing power of money as depending on agents' decisions to use money as a means of settling their debts. Orthodox economists claim indeed that money is a valueless 'token' that agents accept to use, as it avoids the burden of searching for the famous 'double coincidence of wants' that characterizes barter trade. Analogously, the chartalist view is that money is a form of debt (by the state or a bank) that agents accept only in so far as there is a monetary law or a social convention that attributes a purchasing power to money, even though the latter is essentially an acknowledgement of debt – and 'nobody can pay through a mere promise of payment', as a popular adage recalls cogently (see Rossi 2007, p. 19).

All in all, chartalism offers a tentative explanation of money's origin and purchasing power that really does not provide an alternative to more orthodox monetary thinking, because it is trapped in many conventional views that ramify into every corner of a large majority of the economists' minds – to paraphrase a famous statement by Keynes (1936 [1973], p. viii). A more promising avenue would consist in exploring the emission of money as a triangular flow occurring in every payment between the payer, the payee, and the banking system as a whole, linking it to production directly (for payments on the factor market) or indirectly (for any payments on the product or financial markets) (see Rossi 2007 for analytical elaboration).

SERGIO ROSSI

See also:

Banking; Liquidity Preference; Monetary Policy; Money.

References

Goodhart, C.A.E. (1975 [1989]), *Money, Information and Uncertainty*, 2nd edn, London and Basingstoke: Macmillan.
Hicks, J. (1967), *Critical Essays in Monetary Theory*, Oxford: Clarendon Press.
Keynes, J.M. (1930 [1971]), *A Treatise on Money* (Volume I: *The Pure Theory of Money*), in *The Collected Writings of John Maynard Keynes*, Volume V, London and Basingstoke: Macmillan.
Keynes, J.M. (1936 [1973]), *The General Theory of Employment, Interest and Money*, in *The Collected Writings of John Maynard Keynes*, Volume VII, London and Basingstoke: Macmillan.
Knapp, G.F. (1924), *The State Theory of Money*, London: Macmillan (first German edition 1905).
Lerner, A.P. (1943), 'Functional finance and the federal debt', *Social Research*, **10** (1), 38–51.
Menger, K. (1892), 'On the origin of money', *Economic Journal*, **2** (6), 239–55.
Niehans, J. (1978), *The Theory of Money*, Baltimore, MD and London: Johns Hopkins University Press.
Rossi, S. (2007), *Money and Payments in Theory and Practice*, London and New York: Routledge.
Schumpeter, J.A. (1954), *History of Economic Analysis*, London and New York: Routledge, 1994.
Wray, L.R. (1998), *Understanding Modern Money: The Key to Full Employment and Price Stability*, Cheltenham, UK and Northampton, MA, USA: Edward Elgar.
Wray, L.R. (2003), 'Seigniorage or sovereignty?', in L.P. Rochon and S. Rossi (eds), *Modern Theories of Money: The Nature and Role of Money in Capitalist Economies*, Cheltenham, UK and Northampton, MA, USA: Edward Elgar, pp. 84–102.

Choice under Uncertainty

Mainstream choice theory is based on a complete map of preferences and fully known income. This is extended into the future by invoking state-contingent preferences. Under these conditions there is only one possible 'choice'. There is perfect knowledge or its stochastic equivalent, and therefore no uncertainty. The exercise of this 'choice' is seen as evidence of rationality. The identification of rationality with perfect knowledge goes back to the Greeks (Vercelli 1991), but the requirement of perfect knowledge flies in the face of rationality in the sense used in everyday life. Perfect knowledge of the present and past is beyond the capacity of any human brain, and the fact that certain knowledge of the future is impossible is acknowledged by all who are rational in the ordinary sense. Although perfect-knowledge rationality is used as the benchmark in mainstream evaluations of theory, to believe that we possess it is irrational in the extreme. Indeed, if you were in a situation of certainty, how would you know? (Dow 1995).

The tendency in mainstream economics is to regard any lapse from perfect knowledge as total ignorance and from full-information rationality as irrationality. Uncertainty would leave the decision maker in paralysis or motivated by pure emotion. Our starting-point, by contrast, is the acceptance that we live and make decisions in what Shackle (1972, pp. 68–9) called the 'epistemic interval' between these two extremes: in this interval we have some knowledge of the past and present and some limited ability to imagine and evaluate probable outcomes in an intrinsically uncertain future. In this interval, uncertainty does not paralyse us and our cognitive faculties are still useful to us.

Keynes's attempt to model rigorously the process by which one might prepare decisions under uncertainty (or partial knowledge) was perhaps the first to claim the attention of heterodox economists. He framed his enquiry (Keynes 1921) in terms of evidential propositions, h, and the conclusions, a, which may follow from them with a probability α. Symbolically, $a/h = \alpha$. If $\alpha = 1$, the connection is certain; if $\alpha = 0$, there is no connection. In between, there is some probability that a follows from h which allows decision makers to make inferences, albeit uncertain ones – to have a 'degree of rational belief' in the results of their actions. Clearly, most of the time this probability cannot be assigned a numerical value; but the probabilities of different conclusions following from their evidential propositions can be ranked under certain circumstances (Keynes 1921 [1973], pp. 40–43).

There is scope for varying degrees of confidence in these inferences depending on the weight of argument supporting the belief, that is, the amount of relevant evidence relative to the amount of relevant ignorance. But the understanding both of the evidence itself and of its relevance is a matter of judgement. Further, being based also on conventional judgement and on psychological factors, judgement is prone to discrete shifts. Keynes referred to a range of conventions to deal with uncertainty, such as assuming that the past is a better guide to the future than we know to be the case. But other powerful conventions are distinctly social, such as following the market view.

When Shackle turned to the question of decision under uncertainty, he stressed the role of imagination and also of emotion: 'Choice', he said, 'is a business of the whole psyche' (1972, p. 85). First, he chose the opposite benchmark: not the degree of certainty but the extent of doubt, embodied in his concept of 'potential surprise' in contemplating both positive and negative outcomes. His reason was that 'degrees of belief' offered little scope for gradation, whereas surprise allowed for a rich range. He was interested in how one might go about evaluating a single project; therefore Keynes's scheme of comparisons of probability across relations was no use to him. It is also notable that surprise, even imagined surprise, is something that the entrepreneur would *feel*. There are a range of outcomes in the area around a neutral outcome which would occasion no surprise. He then finds a way to derive two points which command the maximum attention. He calls these 'focus gain' and 'focus loss': the outcomes combining desirability (positively) and surprise (negatively) which represent the maximum reasonable hope of gain and fear of loss. Having standardized these, they are compared to 'gambler indifference curves', and the combination which gives the highest anticipated yield will determine the project selected.

This is quite a rigmarole (explained fully in Shackle 1961), and it is plainly not how any entrepreneur actually thinks – certainly not consciously. Its purpose is to try to make explicit the intuitive processes based on partial knowledge and previous experience in making decisions in an uncertain world. The concept of focus points usefully addresses the need for economy in the use of mental resources when faced with the complexity of such decisions. Shackle's construction dispenses with probability of any kind.

We come to the application of decision under uncertainty in the context of wider theory. This was such an innovation at the time that Hicks (1936) regarded Keynes's *General Theory* (1936) as having introduced a new method, the method of expectations. Yet Keynes's theory of expectations was disregarded in the 1970s when rational expectations theorists introduced their own new method of expectations addressed to the experience at the time of rising inflation. This method focused on agents basing their quantified probabilistic forecasts on the same (closed) models as those generated by economists; there was no scope for surprise. This framework is unable to address decision making under the uncertainty which necessarily follows from the economic system being open, as Keynes himself had argued (Loasby 2003).

Of the four contexts in which Keynes referred to expectations (investment, output, user cost and liquidity preference), the role of uncertainty is best understood in the case of investment. Keynes sets out a calculation, relying on expected profits over the life of an investment project, to be compared to the rate of interest to assess the project's viability. But he cautions that these expectations are very uncertain, the more so the longer-lived the equipment, and that it would be unlikely for any investment to be undertaken were not entrepreneurs full of 'animal spirits', the spontaneous urge to action which can override the doubts attached to these calculations. The introduction of temperament does not invalidate the calculations: they are complementary (Dow and Dow 1985).

Having raised the term 'animal spirits', it is worth noting two things about the recent book of that title (Akerlof and Shiller 2009). The first and most important is that they lump together all sorts of responses not covered by traditional full-information maximizing under that title (whereas Keynes's use of it was quite precise). The second is that these are all accounted as irrational responses or non-economic preferences. Although the recognition of factors beyond utility maximization is welcome, there is no idea that they might serve a complementary role in a theory of behaviour which is rational in the ordinary sense of the term. This would entail describing these factors as lying in another dimension from full-knowledge rationality, not as its negation (although there is a hint of this in their use, when discussing confidence, of the expression 'beyond rationality' rather than 'irrationality'). Nuti (2009) goes further: he argues that the factors Akerlof and Shiller place under the umbrella of 'animal spirits' are analysed in economics already under other names.

While Keynes also discussed expectations in relation to output deci-sions and user cost (Chick 1983, 1992), the expectations formed by the speculators in financial markets, who form part of the analysis of liquidity preference, are of a different order. While there is a social element even to individual entrepreneurs' expectations formation, social convention is much more powerful in financial markets. Agents are betting on capital gains and losses on securities or equities. This translates into forming expectations not about some fundamental rate of return but about likely movements in market sentiment, as these affect changes in equity prices or the rate of interest (the inverse of bond prices). When the market as a whole is in substantial agreement, asset prices can be quite unstable, for stability comes from having traders on both sides of the market: 'Best of all that we should know the future. But if not. . .it is important that opinions should differ' (Keynes 1936 [1973], p. 172).

Since, as explained above, expectations in Keynes are substantially con-ventional and subject to discrete shifts, there is no such thing as a 'true' valuation of assets. Indeed, in a very important, short piece, Townshend (1937) pointed out that all prices are influenced by expectations and specu-lation. This implication of Keynes's theory of choice under uncertainty is critical for analysis of financial markets. Behavioural finance is currently being developed to explain swings in asset prices away from their 'true' values in terms of various forms of modification to mainstream choice theory to take account of what they deem 'irrational' factors. This work is to be distinguished from the original behavioural economics spearheaded by Simon (1955), whose notion of bounded rationality followed not just from cognitive limitations but also from the open nature of social reality. It is important to note that an absence of true valuations does not leave asset prices completely up in the air, since reason and evidence are generally employed as far as possible in exercising judgement; this is bounded rationality. Nevertheless the ebb and flow of conventional judgement in a creative environment means that market valuations normally fluctuate (see Frydman and Goldberg 2011). In all of this the emotional element in exercising judgement is inescapable. Psychological theory has been used to explain how this can go too far: reason and evidence can be suppressed, allowing full rein to emotion and leading to wilder swings in asset valuation (see Tuckett and Taffler 2008).

Theories of decision making under uncertainty present a variety of approaches by which one might come to a reasonable estimate of the consequences of projected actions. But they have in common a connection with the wider society and its conventions, and with the individual's hopes and fears, as integral elements in the decision process.

VICTORIA CHICK
SHEILA C. DOW

See also:

Agency; Behavioural Economics; Conventions; Efficient Markets Hypothesis; Expectations; Fundamentalist Keynesians; Investment; New Classical Economics; Open Systems; Uncertainty.

References

Akerlof, G.A. and R.J. Shiller (2009), *Animal Spirits: How Human Psychology Drives the Economy, and Why it Matters for Global Capitalism*, Princeton NJ: Princeton University Press.
Chick, V. (1983), *Macroeconomics After Keynes: A Reconsideration of the General Theory*, Cambridge, MA: MIT Press.
Chick, V. (1992), 'The small firm under uncertainty: a puzzle of *The General Theory*', in B. Gerrard and J. Hillard (eds), *The Philosophy and Economics of J.M. Keynes*, Aldershot, UK and Brookfield, VT, USA: Edward Elgar, pp. 149–64.
Dow, S.C. (1995), 'Uncertainty about uncertainty', in Dow and J. Hillard (eds), *Keynes, Knowledge and Uncertainty*, Aldershot, UK and Brookfield, VT, USA: Edward Elgar, pp. 117–36.
Dow, A.C. and S.C. Dow (1985), 'Animal spirits and rationality', in T. Lawson and H. Pesaran (eds), *Keynes's Economics: Methodological Issues*, London: Croom Helm, pp. 46–65.
Frydman, R. and M. Goldberg (2011), *Beyond Mechanical Markets: Asset Price Swings, Risk, and the Role of the State*, Princeton NJ: Princeton University Press.
Hicks, J.R. (1936), 'Mr Keynes' theory of employment', *Economic Journal*, **46** (182), 238–82.

Keynes, J.M. (1921), *A Treatise on Probability*; reprinted in Keynes, *Collected Writings*, Volume VIII, London: Macmillan for the Royal Economic Society, 1973.

Keynes, J.M. (1936), *The General Theory of Employment, Interest and Money*; reprinted in Keynes, *Collected Writings*, Volume VII, London: Macmillan for the Royal Economic Society, 1973.

Loasby, B.J. (2003), 'Closed models and open systems', *Journal of Economic Methodology*, **10** (3), 285–306.

Nuti, D.M. (2009), 'Akerlof and Shiller, *Animal Spirits*: a misnomer for their sound economics', Department of Economics, University of Rome 'La Sapienza', *Short Notes* No. 1.

Shackle, G.L.S. (1961), *Decision, Order and Time*, Cambridge: Cambridge University Press.

Shackle, G.L.S. (1972), *Imagination and the Nature of Choice*, Edinburgh: Edinburgh University Press.

Simon, H. (1955), 'A behavioral model of rational choice', *Quarterly Journal of Economics*, **69** (1), 99–118.

Townshend, H. (1937), 'Liquidity premium and the theory of value', *Economic Journal*, **47** (185), 157–69.

Tuckett, D. and R. Taffler (2008), 'Phantastic objects and the financial market's sense of reality: a psychoanalytic contribution to the understanding of stock market instability', *International Journal of Psychoanalysis*, **89** (2), 389–412.

Vercelli, A. (1991), *Methodological Foundations of Macroeconomics: Keynes and Lucas*, Cambridge: Cambridge University Press.

Circuit Theory

The debate on Keynes has mainly focused on the principle of aggregate demand and on the analysis of macroeconomic equilibrium with involuntary unemployment. This is in homage to the traditional interpretation, which holds that Keynes's innovative force exploded with the *General Theory* (1936), the work in which he broke with neoclassical theory and with most of his own earlier work. However, it is also possible to maintain that the *General Theory* should be read as a continuation of the analysis put forward by Keynes in *A Treatise on Money* (1930) and in other works before and after the *General Theory*. According to this interpretation, Keynes's analysis should be considered part of the theory of the monetary circuit (what Keynes called the 'monetary theory of production'), which should also include contributions from the first half of the twentieth century by, among others, Knut Wicksell, Dennis Robertson and Joseph Schumpeter (Realfonzo 1998).

In the second half of the century, starting in particular from the teachings of Keynes and Schumpeter, the theory of the monetary circuit was put forward again and developed mainly by Italian- and French-speaking scholars, such as Augusto Graziani, Marc Lavoie, Alain Parguez and Bernard Schmitt. It has subsequently been supported by Riccardo Bellofiore, Biagio Bossone, Alvaro Cencini, Francis Cripps, Giuseppe Fontana, Guglielmo Forges Davanzati, Claude Gnos, Wynne Godley, François Poulon, Riccardo Realfonzo, Louis-Philippe

Rochon, Sergio Rossi, Elie Sadigh, Mario Seccareccia and others. The theory of the monetary circuit has aroused growing interest, generating productive debates (for instance, see Deleplace and Nell 1996; Rochon and Rossi 2003; Fontana and Realfonzo 2005) and further historical and analytical studies. While significant differences persist on specific points, most of the theoreticians of the monetary circuit follow substantially the same approach, remaining within the sphere of Post Keynesian theory.

As far as the basic analytical approach is concerned, the theoreticians of the monetary circuit reject the methodological individualism typical of neoclassical doctrine and adopt a socio-historical method: the study of individual behaviour is subordinate to the macro approach.

The simplest model of the monetary circuit, with a closed economy and no state sector, can be described in the following way. Let us consider three macro agents: banks, firms and workers. Banks have the task of financing the production process through the creation of money, and of selecting business plans; firms, through access to credit, buy factors of production and direct the production process, making decisions on the quantity and quality of output; workers supply labour services. The working of the economy is described as a sequential process, characterized by successive phases whose links form a circuit of money. A clear understanding of the circuit theory can be obtained from Figure 3:

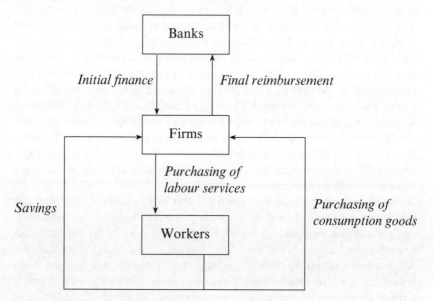

Figure 3   The monetary circuit

The phases in the circuit are:

1. banks grant (totally or in part) the financing requested by firms, creating money (opening of the circuit);
2. once financing has been obtained, firms buy inputs; considering firms in the aggregate, their expenditure coincides with the total wage bill; at this point money passes from firms to workers;
3. once labour services have been purchased, firms carry out production; in the simplest case, firms produce homogeneous goods;
4. at the end of the production process, firms put the goods on the market. It can be envisaged that firms set the sale price following a *mark-up* principle. Supposing workers have a propensity to consume equal to one, firms recover the entire wage bill and maintain ownership of a proportion (corresponding to the mark-up) of the goods produced. If the propensity to consume is less than one, once the workers have purchased consumer goods they must make a further choice about how to use their savings, either hoarding (increase in liquid reserves) or investing (purchase of shares). If all the money savings are invested in shares on the financial market, firms manage to recover the whole wage bill;
5. once goods and shares have been sold, firms repay the banks (closure of the circuit).

Starting from this synthetic description, the remarks below concern the nature and role of monetary variables, the volume of production and employment, the distribution of income and macroeconomic equilibrium (Graziani 1989, 2003; Lavoie 1992; Parguez 1996; Realfonzo 1998, 2006).

According to the theory of the monetary circuit, money is a pure symbol – merely a book-keeping entry (or a certificate) – with no intrinsic value, created by the bank in response to a promise of repayment. The bank is defined as the agent that transforms non-monetary activity into activities that are money. This approach therefore holds that it is the decision to grant credit that generates deposits ('loans make deposits'). The money supply is endogenous, in that it is essentially determined by the demand. On a theoretical level, the banking system could create money endlessly. In its turn, the demand for money can be broken down into two distinct parts: the demand for money to finance production (which Keynes called the 'finance motive') and the demand for liquid reserves (dependent on the well-known transactions, precautionary and speculative motives). According to the theory of the monetary circuit, what mainly distinguishes entrepreneurs is their access to bank credit. In fact, money – as Schumpeter said – is the lever through which power over real resources is exercised. From what has been said, it follows that monetary circuit theory rejects traditional principles of the exogenous nature of the money supply and the neutrality of money, as well as the quantity theory of money.

The volume of production is autonomously fixed by firms, based on the expected level of aggregate demand. Naturally, production decisions taken by firms may or may not be supported by banks. If there is credit rationing by banks, firms are unable to translate their production plans into real production processes. To make the matter more complicated, it can be shown that the production decisions taken by firms are also influenced by the possibility of equity rationing. One conclusion drawn by theoreticians of the circuit is that the financial structure of firms is not neutral with respect to production decisions. The employment level depends on firms' production decisions and therefore on aggregate demand. The labour market is thus described, according to Keynes's teaching, as the place where any shortage in aggregate demand is dumped (generating involuntary unemployment). Macroeconomic equilibrium is compatible with the presence of involuntary unemployment.

According to the theory of the monetary circuit, as in Keynes's original work, in the labour market bargaining concerns only money wages. In fact, the price level (and therefore the real wage) is known only at a later phase, when workers spend their money wage in the goods market. This obviously does not mean that, at the time when they bargain for their money wage, workers have no expectations about the price level, but their expectations are not necessarily confirmed by the market. Consequently, there may be a difference between the *ex ante* real wage (expected by workers) and the *ex post* real wage (the actual real wage). If workers' expectations about the price level are confirmed, the expected real wage coincides with the actual real wage. In a model with two types of goods (consumer goods and investment goods) this happens when voluntary saving equals investment. When investment exceeds voluntary savings there is a positive gap between the expected real wage and the actual real wage, which gives rise to forced saving.

As far as the firm's profit is concerned, monetary circuit theory accepts the thesis that firms as a whole 'earn as much as they spend'. In fact, given the mark-up (which in turn may be made to depend on the industrial concentration ratio), the higher the level of production (and therefore the expenditure on inputs), the higher the firm's real profit. In a model with two types of goods – consumer goods (wage goods) and investment goods – decisions about the composition of production determine the distribution of income. The higher the demand for and production of investment goods, the higher the profits for firms. Thus scholars of the monetary circuit reject the marginal theory of distribution in favour of a Kaleckian–Post Keynesian approach.

In the theory of the monetary circuit there is a strict distinction between the money market and the financial market, and between the two interest rates that are set there. In the money market, banks and firms negotiate and the interest rate constitutes the price firms have to pay to obtain initial finance. The money interest rate is basically a 'levy' on the gross profit of entrepreneurs. It should be underlined that, in the simple model here described, firms can at most repay the initial finance to banks but not the interest as well. If there is hoarding, firms will not even be able to repay the initial loan in money. It is possible to envisage that in this case firms may decide either to settle their debt with the banks in goods, or to remain indebted to them. It is worth emphasizing, however, that this inability on the firm's part to repay the debt in money terms is not an inevitable feature of monetary circuit models. Indeed, as soon as one moves on to more complex models – with a state sector and/or an open economy, or to models in which firms start production at different times (not simultaneously) – this feature disappears and in theory it is possible that, at the closure of the circuit, firms are able to repay their entire debt (interest included).

In the financial market, workers and firms negotiate and the interest rate constitutes the price firms have to pay to raise the money not spent on the goods market. It is, in fact, through the goods market and the financial market working in conjunction that firms try to obtain the final finance, in other words to recover the liquidity initially spent on purchasing inputs. From what we have seen, it can be deduced that for circuit theorists there is a sort of logical hierarchy between the money market and the financial market. In fact, the financial market could not operate at all unless the money market had already been operating. This means that while the individual firm can freely choose whether to get financing through the money market or through the financial market, for firms as a whole no such choice is possible. This is so unless there is a public spending deficit and/ or a surplus in the balance of payments such that enough money will flow, through workers' decisions to buy securities, into the financial market.

Within the contemporary theoretical debate about fiscal and monetary policies, monetary circuit supporters criticize the prescriptions of the so-called 'New Consensus model' (Forges Davanzati et al. 2009). According to the circuit theory, output is demand driven both in the short and in the long run, and there is no endogenous mechanism that guarantees full employment. For this reason, fiscal policy is effectual for increasing the level of economic activity and employment. In particular, an expansive fiscal policy increases – thanks to the wide multiplier of state expenditure – aggregate demand, firms' expectations, private investments and employment. However, the size of the effects of fiscal policies on production and prices depends also on the way public expenditure is financed (through taxation, government bonds or the creation of money). At the same time, state interventions promoting high levels of the Employment Protection Legislation Index determine an increase in real wages, and hence in labour productivity and output. The New Consensus arguments are also criticized on the side of monetary policies. According to the monetary circuit approach, monetary policy cannot guarantee price stability. In fact, restrictive monetary policies could not reduce demand and inflation if agents have positive expectations; at the same time, those policies could be very counter-productive since they could generate a negative effect on output in the long run. On the contrary, inflation can be controlled by public policies aimed at a reduction of degree of concentration of firms, monopoly power and the mark-up.

RICCARDO REALFONZO

See also:

Banking; Fiscal Policy; Italy; Keynes's *Treatise on Money*; Monetary Policy; Money; New Neoclassical Synthesis.

References

Deleplace, G. and E.J. Nell (eds) (1996), *Money in Motion*, Basingstoke: Macmillan.
Fontana, G. and R. Realfonzo (eds) (2005), *The Monetary Theory of Production: Tradition and Perspectives*, Basingstoke: Palgrave Macmillan.
Forges Davanzati, G., A. Pacella and R. Realfonzo (2009), 'Fiscal policy in the monetary theory of production: an alternative to the "new consensus" approach', *Journal of Post Keynesian Economics*, **31** (4), 605–21.
Graziani, A. (1989), 'The theory of the monetary circuit', *Thames Papers in Political Economy*, Spring.
Graziani, A. (2003), *The Monetary Theory of Production*, Cambridge: Cambridge University Press.
Lavoie, M. (1992), *Foundations of Post-Keynesian Economic Analysis*, Aldershot, UK and Brookfield, VT, USA: Edward Elgar.
Parguez, A. (1996), 'Financial markets, unemployment and inflation within a circuitist framework', *Économies et Sociétés*, **30** (2–3), 163–92.
Realfonzo, R. (1998), *Money and Banking: Theory and Debate (1900–1940)*, Cheltenham, UK and Northampton, MA, USA: Edward Elgar.
Realfonzo, R. (2006), 'The Italian circuitist approach', in P. Arestis and M. Sawyer (eds), *A Handbook of Alternative Monetary Economics*, Cheltenham, UK and Northampton, MA, USA: Edward Elgar, pp. 105–21.
Rochon, L.-P. and S. Rossi (eds) (2003), *Modern Theories of Money: The Nature and Role of Money in Capitalist Economies*, Cheltenham, UK and Northampton, MA, USA: Edward Elgar.

Competition

The importance of competition is a central tenet of economics. Its benefits figure prominently in the standard texts of the discipline, where competition perfects the performance of markets. Their outcomes are 'Pareto optimal' under competitive conditions; resources are fully and efficiently employed, and allocated to their most valuable uses. Markets provide the products consumers desire most at the lowest possible cost, output is at its full-employment level, and there is no change in resource usage, or government intervention, that would improve the welfare of everyone, or benefit some without harming others.

But while the competition highlighted in economics has ideal outcomes, competitive markets can fail also. Demand for products need not be high enough for full employment, for, as Keynes and the Post Keynesians emphasize, the competition of markets does not make them 'self-adjusting'. It does not keep the demand for products in line with the supply, or the supply in line with the labour available for their production. Labour can be unemployed, and products in excess supply, under competitive conditions also, and while the competition of firms can hold down their prices, it cannot keep up their production. Indeed, it may in fact 'ruin' them (Eichner 1969).

Price competition squeezes the profits of firms, and this is the case even if the wages of their workers fall with their prices (as is traditionally assumed), for labour costs are not the only costs of production. Firms have the expenses of their plant and equipment, and the service charges on their debt, as well as the 'sunk costs' of their product development. These fixed costs are as prevalent as the 'variable' costs highlighted in the microeconomic texts, and when those costs are high – as they are in modern industry – and the investments of firms irreversible, price competition can wipe out profits and finances. It can drive prices down below costs, 'expropriating' the capital invested in production (ibid.). That fixed capital cannot be taken out of industries when prices fall, and as long as prices stay above the average variable costs of production, firms will be better off selling products at a loss than not selling them at all.

While ruinous price competition is identified in economics with oligopoly, it is more in keeping with the conditions of perfect competition than those of oligopoly. It is when the products of firms are homogeneous that they must match the price cuts of competitors regardless of the costs, and it is when their numbers are large, and market shares similar, that they cannot effectively 'fix' their prices. There is no dominant firm to enforce their price-fixing agreements, and it makes little sense for the firms to honour them when prices can be undercut and sales lost. And while perfectly competitive firms are small, and their productive capacity limited, they can have fixed costs also. Indeed, their products could not be homogeneous if they were not produced by machinery, and their fixed costs will lock them into a ruinous price war whenever their sales revenue falls short of the amount needed for the recoupment of costs.

The perfect competition idealized in economics is far from ideal – it bankrupts firms and volatilizes prices. The worst-performing markets of the economy are the ones that come closest to the perfectly competitive markets of the economic texts (Kaldor 1985), and it is because firms cannot operate under the price competition of those commodity markets that they consolidate their industries and differentiate their products (Eichner 1969).

The pricing power of firms is essential to their survival, and their investment depends on it also. They could not generate the revenue that investment requires if they could not hold up their prices, for profits would not be high enough for the funding of investment (Eichner 1976). Firms would not be able to finance investment with the profit from their products, or secure (and repay) the loans needed for the external financing of investment projects. And since the profit from their products would be precarious as well as small, their long-run expectations could not be positive (Shapiro 2005). They could not expect to make a profit on a product long enough to recoup the costs of a plant and equipment or product development investment. Those long-lived investments are not profitable when prices are variable and sales insecure, and in the absence of the 'frictions' and 'restrictions' of markets, there would be little investment in their products (Richardson 1990).

The entry barriers of industries increase and stabilize the investment in products, and while they also lessen competition, they do not end it. Oligopolists compete also – they have the same profit drive as other capitalist enterprises. They want to expand their markets and market shares, and their product competition can be as beneficial as the price competition of less protected enterprises. Indeed, it can be more beneficial, for product competition increases the investment in products (Shapiro 2005).

The product changes that update and differentiate products require equipment changes and, in some cases, installation of new production lines, and the advertisement that publicizes the differences in products is an investment in them also. It increases the investment of firms, as does the product innovation undertaken for the purposes of competitive advantage. Firms differentiate their products through product improvement as well as advertisement, and it is through this innovation only that they can retain their markets. These are protected not by the prices charged for products, but by their improvement and extension of their uses.

Oligopolists, as Eichner (1976) notes, compete through their investments, and their competition improves production as well as increasing investment. Productivity improvements are 'embodied' in the new capital goods they develop and market, and technology advanced through their patent 'races'. Research and development is an integral part of their operations, and while their product competition necessitates this innovation, their profits provide the requisite finance (Galbraith 1967). The productivity growth of modern industry would not be possible in the absence of this 'monopoly' profit, and, as Galbraith emphasizes, it is precisely because its firms are large, and markets controlled, that its productivity growth is historically unprecedented.

This is not to say that the oligopolization of industry is without cost. The profit margins of firms can be too high as well as too low, exceeding the level needed for the funding of their investment. Their investment is not determined by their savings – it depends on their expectations also – and if their profit margins rise without a corresponding rise in their investment, the demand for their products will fall, reducing production and increasing unemployment (Steindl 1976).

But the pricing power of the oligopolist is not 'absolute' (Kalecki 1971). It is limited by the competition of its industry, the substitutes for its products, and the risk of drawing new firms into its market. The substitution and entry effects of its price increases limit the mark-up on its product (Eichner 1976), and the firm will not increase prices in line with costs unless the prices of competitors rise also. There is no automatic transmission of costs into prices.

The fact that the price competition of oligopolists is tempered by the conditions of their industries does not mean that there is no competitive pressure on prices. And while oligopolists eschew price wars, they do not eschew price reductions. Prices are reduced when competition requires it, to meet the prices of new competitors or drive them out of markets. Competition does not have to be 'perfect' for it to bring down prices, and prices can be reduced for reasons other than the protection of markets or increases in competitiveness.

Price reductions can expand markets as well as increase market share, as reductions in prices make products more affordable. They increase both the number of those that can afford the product, and the amount of the product they can afford, while increases in sales bring down costs, realizing the scale economies of product development, advertisement and production. And when productivity improvements reduce labour costs, the profit from these innovations can be used in the interests of market growth and development. Instead of increasing the mark-up on the product, the firm can reduce the price, pricing the product with its long-term rather than short-term profitability in mind (Steindl 1976).

Prices can also fall under oligopoly, and real wages rise with increases in productivity. And while competition is beneficial, and nations would be poorer without it, there can be too much competition in industry as well as too little. Perfect competition is not optimal.

Nina Shapiro

See also:

Equilibrium and Non-equilibrium; Galbraith's Economics; Innovation; Investment; Market Governance; Price Rigidity; Prices and Pricing; Welfare Economics.

References

Eichner, A.S. (1969), *The Emergence of Oligopoly*, Baltimore, MD: Johns Hopkins University Press.
Eichner, A.S. (1976), *The Megacorp and Oligopoly*, Armonk, NY: M.E. Sharpe.
Galbraith, J.K. (1967), *The New Industrial State*, Boston, MA: Houghton Mifflin.
Kaldor, N. (1985), *Economics Without Equilibrium*, Armonk, NY: M.E. Sharpe.
Kalecki, M. (1971), *Selected Essays on the Dynamics of the Capitalist Economy*, Cambridge: Cambridge University Press.
Richardson, G.B. (1990), *Information and Investment*, Oxford: Oxford University Press.
Shapiro, N. (2005), 'Competition and aggregate demand', *Journal of Post Keynesian Economics*, **27** (3), 541–9.
Steindl, J. (1976), *Maturity and Stagnation in American Capitalism*, New York: Monthly Review Press.

Consumer Debt

Consumer debt has existed for thousands of years. In the most recent thirty years, however, the consumer credit market has expanded. Many people are accumulating increasing amounts of revolving consumer debt – using expected future income for current spending (cars, education and medical expenses). More importantly, deregulation of the financial industry has created underwriting standards for consumer loans that favour lenders and hurt borrowers by allowing lenders to charge exorbitantly high interest rates and fees. This, mixed with recent changes to personal bankruptcy laws, makes it easier for people to accumulate consumer debt and harder to discharge once they have it. This is an issue John Maynard Keynes did not discuss in great detail because consumer debt of the types that are prevalent today was less common while he was alive. Also, Michał Kalecki's models of aggregate profits assumed negligible working-class debt, so that Wages = Workers' Consumption. Today, however, working-class debt is no longer negligible. While the growth in consumer debt–spending does not change Keynes's or Kalecki's conclusions, Post Keynesians are addressing both the causes and consequences of high consumer debt levels on individuals and the macroeconomy in order to modernize the work of Keynes, Kalecki and others (Kalecki 1971; Palley 1994, 2002).

Consumer debt is more of a problem in the United States than in other countries – though credit card debt, inflation and other consumer debt-related issues are affecting a growing number of people worldwide. Post Keynesians attribute the rise in consumer debt in the United States over the past thirty years to several factors, the primary cause being the rise of inequality of income and wealth (Galbraith 1998). Growing inequality has forced many people to accumulate consumer debt in order to maintain their standard of living. At the same time, rising inflation in the cost of housing, higher education and medical services has stretched many budgets. While the rich over the past thirty years have seen their taxes decrease and incomes rise significantly, the large majority of incomes have decreased or been stagnant (in real terms). For example, during this thirty-year period the minimum wage rate decreased in real terms and many middle-class manufacturing jobs were outsourced to countries with less expensive labour. This has eroded the union workforce and kept wages flat for most people. Unlike in previous decades, people with low incomes can now build up high levels of consumer debt because banks (and other institutions) have realized that it is profitable to lend to riskier borrowers at high interest rates, which has happened in concert with deregulation of the banking industry.

Keynes argued in the *General Theory* (1936) that stable wages help stabilize prices, and that income distribution has a direct effect on aggregate demand and employment. Easy access to consumer credit, however, means that people can spend more than they make in income (raising their marginal propensity to consume above 1 for debtor households). During the thirty-year period of stagnant (or decreasing) wages many people have substituted their lost income with consumer debt. Also, many people have a tendency to want to live above their current means, and consumer debt lets them buy automobiles, vacations and houses they cannot currently afford. People will take on too much debt (a) when they are optimistic about the future, and (b) when they have no other option but to borrow money and need to pay bills when faced with income shortages (for example, divorce, illness, or job loss). Whatever the reason, consumer debt will raise aggregate demand in the short run. But the lasting effects of the consumer debt burden (shifting income from high to low marginal propensity to consume households) will result in a dampened aggregate demand caused by the payments to service outstanding debt, which will not subside until the debt is repaid – often taking many years (Palley 1994).

Hyman Minsky (1986) argued that debt spending is observable in the macroeconomy and is a significant driver of business cycles (Palley 1994). While Minsky did not write much on consumer debt at the individual level, his financial instability hypothesis offers a good explanation of the macroeconomic effects of consumer debt-financed spending. At the start of a cycle people take a 'hedge' position where their incomes are able to repay interest and principal. Then as their optimism grows (or they have an unexpected reduction in income) they move to a 'speculative' position where their income can repay only interest but not principal – thus creating revolving debt. Lastly, as optimism heightens (or their financial situation worsens) they move to a Ponzi position where their income is unable to repay interest or principal, so the only options are to increase debt (if possible), sell assets (personal possessions), or file for bankruptcy (which is expensive, time-consuming, and not guaranteed to work). Minsky's hypothesis, with regard to consumer debt, is a structural problem where banks are incentivized to lend as much money to as many people as possible. Little concern is paid to whether people can afford to pay back their debt. Over time this lending model becomes too fragile and the debt pyramid collapses. Rather than regulate financial institutions to make sure they are allocating credit properly, however, the Federal Reserve (and other regulatory agencies) have remained stoic in the face of growing consumer debt burdens (much as they ignored the housing bubble that burst in 2008). Post Keynesians argue for more proactive regulations that stabilize the credit market by protecting borrowers and holding creditors accountable when they engage in risky lending practices.

Deregulation of the financial system, starting in the 1980s, eventually led to a predatory lending environment. From payday loans to high-interest credit cards, banks (and other lending institutions) were allowed to charge desperate borrowers usurious interest rates and high fees. Worse yet, these institutions found that many people accepted their terms because they needed money and had no other option. This has turned out to be a profitable model. This is a long way from Keynes's proposal for the euthanasia of the rentier in chapter 24 of the *General Theory*. Post Keynesians understand that the bailout of the financial system starting in 2008 saved creditors not debtors, which is the reverse of what Keynes recommended. Instead of euthanizing the rentier, creditors were rewarded for reckless risk taking, which has hurt debtors and helped pull the economy deeper into recession.

Credit card debt is another form of consumer debt that barely existed during Keynes's time. Credit cards have become popular in the past thirty years. In the early 1980s banks' credit card operations were essentially deregulated, and were allowed to move their operations to states with less stringent usury laws. This means that credit card companies can charge any interest rate they want. Credit card companies then started promoting cards and encouraging their use. In 2009 there were around 1.6 billion credit cards (roughly nine cards for every cardholder) in circulation in the United States, and were used to spend roughly $2.5 trillion. In that same year, revolving consumer debt totalled almost $900 billion (with an average interest rate of over 15 per cent). Credit card companies profit by both brokering debt and securitizing it (into asset-backed securities: ABSs) and selling it to institutional investors (Brown 2007). This is one more example of what Post Keynesians call the 'financialization' of the economy. The rise in consumer debt has created opportunities for investors to gamble on people's credit risk, which has helped increase the rate of financialization.

The United States (like other countries) has replaced many of its manufacturing jobs with service sector jobs. Employment skills demanded by companies, therefore, have changed. No longer is a high school diploma adequate to get a middle-class income. Instead, people need college degrees to compete for good jobs. As the need for more and better higher education increases, the number of students attending college is increasing. At the same time, however, state and federal support for higher education is decreasing. Few students who graduated from college a generation ago had any education debt. In 2008 over 67 per cent of graduates had an average debt of $23,200, which was an increase of more than 70 per cent from 10 years previously (National Center for Education Statistics 2009). In the 1980s free market (neoliberal) proponents started arguing that students were not paying enough for their education. This led to significant increases in the number of student loans and a reduction in government grants for higher education (see Bousquet 2008). Similar trends are observable in other countries (for example, England).

This change in policy is contrary to Post Keynesian economics and Keynes's (1936) concept of *social investment*. From the 1940s to the 1980s higher education was considered a public good, funded in a way Keynes would have approved. The creation of a government-supported student loan market (via Sallie Mae) has added unnecessary costs to getting a college degree. The added expense nearly doubles the cost of a college degree, which gets passed on to students (but is profit in the loan market). By moving away from loans and back to a grants-based system for higher education the government would spend only a marginal amount more – yet there would be direct economic benefits to students and colleges (and probably the macroeconomy as well, since students will have more money to spend during their early years out of college). Again, college loans are securitized and sold to investors, but the government can guarantee payment in case of default. This further promotes the financialization of the economy.

The last significant category of consumer debt is medical care. The price of medical care has risen as fast as higher education. Post Keynesians acknowledge that the health-care industry is too heavily controlled by health insurance companies. Private insurers are for-profit businesses that maximize profits when they can increase premiums and decrease payouts for care. As a result, it is in their interest to approve the least amount of care claims and limit the amount of money they have to pay out when costs get excessive. This has led to significant health-care debt. Even a minor health problem with no insurance (or a major health problem with insurance) can easily result in thousands of dollars of debt. Medical debt is often listed as the main reason why someone files for personal bankruptcy in the United States. Since a majority of people in the United States are covered under some form of government medical care coverage (Medicare, Medicaid, or veterans' care) it is generally agreed that some form of universal health care is not only possible but much more efficient than the current system. Social safety-nets such as Social Security and health care are important. Funding these programmes may require more aggressive fiscal policy; but if the purpose is to improve social safety-nets then Post Keynesians agree that this is an important objective for government.

Consumer spending affects economic growth more now than ever. As consumer debt levels rise, however, the ability to raise aggregate demand (especially during recessions) lessens because a portion of many people's income is going toward maintaining outstanding consumer debt. This also means that multipliers are lower than they appear. As a result, economic downturns will be deeper and more persistent than in the past. People are less likely to increase spending if they are uncertain about the economy, and carrying consumer debt heightens their uncertainty. Greater social investment in higher education and health care will reduce imminent consumer debt burdens. In addition, the United States (and other countries) must create and maintain greater income equality. Many people take on consumer debt to replace lost income. Greater income equality will reduce many people's dependency on consumer debt to maintain their basic living standards.

ROBERT H. SCOTT, III

See also:

Consumption; Economic Policy; Financial Instability Hypothesis; Financial Reform; Financialization.

References

Bousquet, M. (2008), *How the University Works: Higher Education and the Low-Wage Nation*, New York: New York University Press.
Brown, C. (2007), 'Financial engineering, consumer credit, and the stability of effective demand', *Journal of Post Keynesian Economics*, **29** (3), 427–53.
Galbraith, J. (1998), *Created Unequal*, Chicago, IL: University of Chicago Press.
Kalecki, M. (1971), *Selected Essays on the Dynamics of the Capitalist Economy 1933–1970*, Cambridge: Cambridge University Press.
Keynes, J.M. (1936), *The General Theory of Employment, Interest and Money*, London: Macmillan.
Minsky, H. (1986), *Stabilizing an Unstable Economy*, New Haven, CT: Yale University Press.
National Center for Education Statistics (2009), *Digest of Education Statistics 2008*, available at: http://nces.ed.gov/pubs2009/2009020.pdf.

Palley, T.I (1994), 'Debt, aggregate demand, and the business cycle: an analysis in the spirit of Kaldor and Minsky', *Journal of Post Keynesian Economics*, **16** (3), 371–90.
Palley, T.I. (2002), 'Economic contradictions coming home to roost? Does the US economy face a long-term aggregate demand generation problem?', *Journal of Post Keynesian Economics*, **25** (1), 9–32.

Consumer Theory

Few efforts have been made by Post Keynesians to explain how consumers make choices. Does that mean that Post Keynesians accept the neoclassical axioms of consumer choice? The answer is no. Although there have been few contributions on consumer behaviour by Post Keynesian authors, there is a certain degree of coherence among them. The few pieces that exist – by well-known Post Keynesians such as Joan Robinson, Luigi Pasinetti, Edward Nell and Alfred Eichner – fit, like a puzzle, with the rest of Post Keynesian theory. These pieces, however, must also be tied to the work of various social economists, marketing specialists, dissident orthodox authors and institutionalist authors such as Thorstein Veblen and John Kenneth Galbraith. It has also been realized that consumer choice in Post Keynesian theory and ecological economics carries a great deal of overlap, since both are inspired by the works of Nicholas Georgescu-Roegen.

The common ground of Post Keynesian consumer theory can be presented under the form of seven principles (Lavoie 2004, 2009).

1. the principle of procedural rationality;
2. the principle of satiable needs;
3. the principle of separability of needs;
4. the principle of subordination of needs;
5. the principle of the growth of needs;
6. the principle of non-independence; and
7. the principle of heredity.

The principle of *procedural rationality* asserts that agents lack perfect knowledge and the ability to process a large amount of information. Agents devise means to avoid complex calculations and considerations, and procedures enabling decisions to be taken despite incomplete information. These means and procedures include rules of thumb, the acceptance of social conventions, and reliance on the hopefully better informed opinion of others. Seen from the perspective of neoclassical substantive rationality, procedural rationality may seem to be 'ad hocery', but procedural responses are the only sensible answer to an environment characterized by bounded knowledge and computational capabilities, time constraints and fundamental uncertainty. It could also be called the principle of *reasonable rationality* (see the entries on 'Non-ergodicity' and 'Uncertainty').

In the case of consumer behaviour, it has long been established by marketing specialists that consumer choice usually involves simple procedures (Earl 1986, p. 58). Very often there is no decision process to speak of: purchases are made on recommendations, in conformity to social norms, with the consideration of few alternatives, and on the basis of few criteria. Some of the procedures that we follow are conscious – we may then speak of rules or conventions – while others are unconscious – we may refer to them as habits or routines, as in the case of a large part of our repetitive spending on non-durable consumption goods.

The second principle – *satiable needs* – can be likened to the neoclassical principle of diminishing marginal utility, but it takes a particular meaning in the Post Keynesian theory of the consumer. Here satiation arises with positive prices and finite income. There are threshold levels of consumption beyond which a good, or its characteristics, brings no satisfaction to its consumer. Beyond the threshold, no more of the good will be purchased, regardless of its price.

One has to carefully distinguish wants from needs, as do Lutz and Lux (1979). There is a hierarchy of needs, where some are more basic than others, which implies that they must be fulfilled in order of priority. All needs are not equal. Some needs are bound to be satiated much earlier than others. Needs are subjected to a hierarchy classification and are the motor of consumer behaviour. By contrast, wants evolve from needs. They can be substituted for each other and constitute 'the various preferences within a common category or level of need' (ibid., p. 21). This leads to the next two principles of a Post Keynesian consumer theory.

The principle of the *separability of needs* asserts that categories of needs or of expenditures can be distinguished from each other. In the case discussed by Kevin Lancaster (1991), with goods described by a matrix of consumption technology with various characteristics, a separate need will be associated with a submatrix of goods and characteristics arising out of a decomposable matrix. The principle of the separability of needs is illustrated by the widely used econometric models of consumer demand, which assume that broad categories of expenditures enter separately into the overall utility function. In the utility-tree approach, the principle of separability is pushed one step further, since these broad categories of expenditures are further subdivided into several branches.

The separability of needs allows the consumer to divide the decision-making process into a series of smaller multistage decisions. Consumers first make an allocation of their budget among needs, and then spend that allocation among the various wants or subgroups of each need, independently of what happens for the other needs. Changes in the relative prices of goods within a given category of wants will have no effect on the budget allocation between various needs, while a fall in the overall price of a group of goods corresponding to a given need will have repercussions on the budget allocation of all needs. The principle of the separability of needs imposes substantial restrictions on the neoclassical principle of price substitution, since separability severely limits the degree of substitutability between goods in different groups. Indeed, a substantial amount of empirical evidence shows that general categories of consumption expenditures have quite negligible own-price elasticities and cross-elasticities.

Further restraints may be added if one goes beyond the principle of separability of needs, by introducing a fourth principle, the principle of the *subordination of needs*. With this principle, utility cannot be represented by a unique catch-all utility measure; it can only be represented by a vector. The principle of the subordination of needs is often associated with the notion of a *pyramid* of needs – a *hierarchy* of needs – as described by the humanistic school of psychology (Lutz and Lux 1979). The integration of the principles of separability and subordination leads to Nicholoas Georgescu-Roegen's principle of *irreducibility*.

In the case of utility-tree analysis, the first-stage budgeting problem is resolved by assuming that money is allocated first to necessities and then to discretionary needs. There is no substitution between the budget categories apportioned to necessary needs and discretionary ones. All the principles previously invoked culminate in this hierarchy: needs are separable and the most basic needs are first taken care of in their order of priority, until they are satiated at some threshold level. This is reminiscent of the classical distinction between necessaries and luxury goods and the Sraffian distinction between basic and non-basic commodities (see the entry on 'Sraffian economics').

There have been some formal representations of the above principles. Hierarchical behaviour is known under the name of 'lexicographic preference ordering', owing to its similarity with searching for a word in a dictionary. Strict lexicographic ordering, however, is unlikely, and more sophisticated orderings of a lexicographic nature have been suggested, with consumers setting targets and thresholds (Earl 1986). These non-compensatory ordering schemes are not only reasonable but also compatible with procedural rationality, since a complete utility map is not required. Decisions about the most basic needs can be taken quite independently of the informational requirements of the higher needs. Consumers need know nothing whatsoever about the prices of the goods that are part of the higher needs, and they need not rank alternatives which they cannot attain or which are beyond their satiation levels (Drakopoulos 1994).

Neoclassical authors deny that needs are subject to the principle of subordination. This, it must be presumed, is mainly due to the devastating consequences of the irreducibility of needs for neoclassical theory and its substitution principle. Irreducible needs imply that they are incommensurable and therefore that 'everything does not have a price'. A trade-off is not always possible. The axiom of continuity, or of indifference, does not hold any more. Nor does the axiom of Archimedes (meaning that if we add enough of a good in a bundle, that bundle will be chosen), so popular with choice theorists (Earl 1986, p. 249), or the axiom of gross substitution (Eichner 1987, p. 632), so often invoked among general equilibrium theorists.

Having assumed that indeed there exists a hierarchy of needs, how do consumers move up the steps of the pyramid? The basic answer is that individuals move upwards in the hierarchy due to income effects. Beyond the principle of satiation, lies the principle of the *growth of needs* – our fifth principle.

When a need has been fulfilled, or more precisely when a threshold level for that need has been attained, individuals start attending to the needs which are situated on a higher plane. There are always new needs to be fulfilled. If they do not yet exist, consumers will create them through innovation. To be satisfied, needs often require additional income. The fulfilment of new needs, and therefore the purchase of new goods or new services, is thus related to income effects. This is the microeconomic counterpart of the Post Keynesian focus on effective demand, that is, on macroeconomic income effects instead of substitution effects. The latter play only a minor role in a static analysis of consumer behaviour, when similar goods or goods fulfilling the same wants are being considered. Indeed, changes in relative prices have an impact on the budget allocation between needs only in so far as they have an impact on real income. What is being asserted is that income effects, status, customs and habits are crucially important in explaining the evolution of expenditure on goods. Indeed, this has become even more evident with the generalization of consumer credit and the rise in household debt (Brown 2008) (see the entry on 'Consumer debt').

The expansion of consumerism has brought to the fore the role of the learning process in consumption theory, and in particular the principle of *non-independence*, put forth by John Kenneth Galbraith. Decisions and preferences are not made independently of those of other agents. Consumers watch and copy other consumers, in particular those of higher ranks in the consumers' hierarchy. The composition of demand depends on socio-economic classes. A household's pattern of consumption will reflect the lifestyle of the other households that constitute its social reference group. Marketing officers, through publicity, will attempt to make sure that households follow the appropriate lifestyle.

Preferences are not exogenous. They are influenced by past experience. Habit formation can be seen as a particular case of path dependency and even of hysteresis, which are key features of Post Keynesian macro-economics. Past decisions will have an effect on future choices. This is the seventh principle, the principle of *heredity*, put forth by Georgescu-Roegen (1954), a consequence of which has been found in several behavioural studies showing that agents attribute more value to the loss of something than to the gain of this same thing.

The upshot of this Post Keynesian analysis of consumer choice may now be noted. Macroeconomic models based on the analysis of income classes and on income effects are a legitimate outgrowth of a Post Keynesian theory of the consumer where price substitution effects are not important or severely constrained to goods which respond to similar characteristics, and where increases or changes in demand are mostly determined by increases in real incomes or the introduction of new positional goods. To ignore substitution effects, based on relative prices, appears to be much less disastrous than to ignore income effects and threshold levels.

Marc Lavoie

See also:

Agency; Behavioural Economics; Choice under Uncertainty; Consumer Debt; Consumption; Environmental Economics; Institutionalism; Non-ergodicity; Sraffian Economics; Uncertainty.

References

Brown, C. (2008), *Inequality, Consumer Credit and the Saving Puzzle*, Cheltenham, UK and Northampton, MA, USA: Edward Elgar.
Drakopoulos, S.A. (1994), 'Hierarchical choice in economics', *Journal of Economic Surveys*, **8** (2), 133–53.
Earl, P.E. (1986), *Lifestyle Economics: Consumer Behaviour in a Turbulent World*, Brighton, UK: Wheatsheaf.
Eichner, A.S. (1987), *The Macrodynamics of Advanced Market Economies*, Armonk, NY: M.E. Sharpe.
Georgescu-Roegen, N. (1954), 'Choice, expectations and measurability', *Quarterly Journal of Economics*, **48** (4), 503–34.
Lancaster, K. (1991), 'Hierarchies in goods-characteristics analysis' in Lancaster, *Modern Consumer Theory*, Aldershot, UK and Brookfield, VT, USA: Edward Elgar, pp. 69–80.
Lavoie, M. (2004), 'Post Keynesian consumer theory: choice', *Journal of Psychological Economics*, **25** (5), 639–49.
Lavoie, M. (2009), 'Post Keynesian consumer choice theory and ecological economics', in R.P.F. Holt, S. Pressman and C.L. Spash (eds), *Post Keynesian and Ecological Economics*, Cheltenham, UK and Northampton, MA, USA: Edward Elgar, pp. 141–7.
Lutz, M.A. and K. Lux (1979), *The Challenge of Humanistic Economics*, Menlo Park, CA: Benjamin/Cummings.

Consumption

Accounting for 70 per cent or more of total spending on final goods and services, consumption is by far the most important component of aggregate demand. The modern theory of aggregate consumption dates from John Maynard Keynes, who proposed that a 'propensity to consume' governs the functional relationship between a given level of income and expenditures on consumption out of that level of income. Keynes thought the propensity to consume was a 'fairly stable function so that, as a rule, the amount of aggregate consumption mainly depends on the amount of aggregate income'. The propensity to consume itself is largely determined by a 'fundamental psychological law' that consumer units ('men' originally) tend to reduce their rate of consumption (C) as their income (Y) increases; that is, $dC/dY < 1$ with $C = C(Y)$.

Keynes's proposed relationship was quickly subjected to empirical testing, using whatever data were available and whatever specification seemed reasonable. Some anomalies were soon uncovered. First, estimates of marginal propensities using cross-sectional household data ranging from 0.4 to 0.8 could not be reconciled with those derived from time-series aggregate data clustering around 0.9. Second, when transformed into an average consumption model, the linear Keynesian model predicted a long-run declining spending rate not found in the actual data. Third, cross-sectional functions showed shifting or ratcheting spending from one dataset or year to another, behaviour not predicted by cross-sectional specifications or found with time-series data. Although the actual historical development of these anomalies is more complex, they soon became 'a fashionable feature of many macroeconomic textbooks and survey articles' (Thomas 1989, p. 131), generating an enormous literature and motivating many resolutions.

Nearly all these resolutions focused on the 'consumption function paradox', or differences between estimates of cross-sectional and times-series spending behaviour. The best known of these, the life-cycle theory of Franco Modigliani and Richard Brumberg and the permanent income hypothesis of Milton Friedman (reviewed in Deaton 1992; see also Carroll 2001 and Muellbauer and Lattimore 1995), were essentially similar explanations developed from the neoclassical theory of household behaviour. Like individual consumers, the aggregate or representative consumer unit seeks to maximize the utility from lifetime consumption, an effort constrained by the present value of lifetime income plus any original endowments minus any bequests. Since consumption decisions are motivated by lifetime considerations, the relevant income for these decisions is expected lifetime or 'permanent' income rather than current or 'transitory' income. While these distinctions are nebulous – permanent to one is transitory to another, in the context of aggregate spending – average income was identified as permanent income and any other income as transitory. Thus, in the neoclassical view, in its simplest form, when interest and time discount rates are assumed to be zero, average consumption is a function of average income. Since average data are time-series data, the appropriate marginal propensities are the time-series ones, and since the Keynesian consumption function utilizes current or cross-sectional data, it can be dismissed as reflective of transitory, not permanent, spending behaviour.

While simply a semantic exercise, the neoclassical reformulation of the Keynesian consumption function seemed compelling. It was reasonable, for obviously consumption is determined by more than current income. It was grounded in the microfoundations underlying the education of all economists. Its theoretical, mathematical and econometric complexities, such as determining appropriate or tractable utility functions and measuring permanent income, offered research possibilities for the ambitious. By having consumption determined by long-run considerations, it found favour with anti-Keynesians. But, most importantly, proponents of the Keynesian view offered no effective counter-arguments to the permanent/transitory distinction. As a consequence, macroeconomics shifted away from the implications of current spending behaviour and the Keynesian consumption function was relegated to honorific status, largely serving to motivate extensions of the neoclassical consumption model.

In fact, it is the case for the Keynesian view that is compelling. First, the alleged consumption function paradox simply reflects confusion about the geometric implications of cross-sectional and time-series data. The usual diagrammatic representation of the paradox is shown in Panel A of Figure 4, with the slope of the cross-sectional (CS) function less than that of the time-series (TS) one. The functions cross at Y^*, average income for either. In the neoclassical view, income different from Y^* is transitory. Hence, in the absence of transitory income, all incomes equal average income and fall on the TS function, and the CS function disappears.

None the less, CS functions still exist for every time period; two are shown in Panel B. Even if the transitory notion is correct, the slopes (marginal propensities) of the CS and TS functions must differ, because the slope of the TS line connecting points on the CS lines cannot equal the slope of either CS line.

Second, the alleged predictive failure of the Keynesian formulation reflects the failure to distinguish carefully between cross-sectional and time-series data. CS functions exist for every time period:

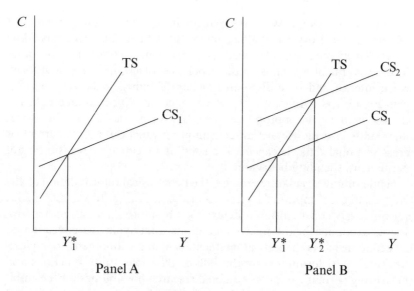

Figure 4   *The consumption function*

$$c_{ti} = a_t + b_t y_{ti}, \text{ where } i = 1, \ldots, m \text{ consumer units.}$$

When transformed into an average function, the average propensity to consume converges on b_t as CS income increases. Similarly, a TS function exists covering all years:

$$C_t = \alpha + \beta Y_t, \text{ where } t = 1, \ldots, n \text{ years.}$$

When transformed into an average function, the average propensity converges on β as TS income increases. The objection that the Keynesian model produced incorrect predictions about the average propensity is simply the consequence of introducing time-series values into the cross-sectional function. When appropriate income data are used, the CS function predicts a declining average propensity as income increases in any time period while, following the conventional assumption of $\alpha = 0$, the TS function predicts a constant propensity over time. Both these predictions are consistent with the historical record.

Finally, the effects of the definitional relationship between cross-sectional and time-series data have not been realized (Bunting 2001). Like corporations, time-series data are soulless, having no existence beyond the individual consumption and income observations from which they are constructed. But these individual data are the cross-sectional data. Thus, since $C_t = \Sigma c_{ti}$ and $Y_t = \Sigma y_{ti}$, average consumption and income used for TS estimation are also CS averages. This implies that, with average data, the CS function can be stated as:

$$C_t = a_t + b_t Y_t,$$

and the TS marginal propensity is:

$$dC_t/dY_t = da_t/dY + db_t Y_t/dY.$$

From the TS function, the TS marginal propensity is also:

$$dC_t/dY_t = \beta.$$

Assuming constant CS marginal propensities,

$$\beta = da_t/dY_t + b.$$

In words, the CS and TS marginal propensities differ only because of shifts in the cross-sectional functions.

Time-series coefficients are determined by two factors: an induced component, reflecting cross-sectional consumption behaviour, and an autonomous component, reflecting shifts in that behaviour. The induced component simply indicates that time-series behaviour requires behaviour in every time period, while the autonomous component is necessary for time-series data to exist. With direct estimation, it is not possible to determine whether changes in time-series behaviour are the result of actual behavioural changes or the result of autonomous, unknown influences. Since the time-series coefficient is exactly defined by these two components, time-series behaviour is meaningless – after eliminating autonomous and induced effects, the time-series coefficients are zero.

For their part, Post Keynesians have not shown much interest in expanding or extending Keynes's basic ideas. Since the consumption function is derived from individual data, it actually shows how the distribution of income affects consumption: for example, the rate of spending declines as income rises. This also can be shown by calculating consumption and income shares, $w_i = c_i/\Sigma_i c_i$ and $v_i = y_i/\Sigma_i y_i$. Because every consumer unit must have its own consumption function, the CS marginal propensity is an income-weighted average of the individual propensities, $b_t = \Sigma b_i v_i$, implying that changes in the distribution of income produced by alterations in the business cycle or by public policy will change the overall marginal propensity. Autonomous influences are also important, yet these simply indicate that unknown factors influence spending. Determining these factors has obvious merit. Quite possibly they could be demographic and sociological factors, suggesting that the consumption function has a much larger social dimension than is commonly recognized.

The Keynesian view that current income largely determines current consumption is commonly attacked as myopic and unrealistic. Consumer units spend and earn over their lifetimes; most are not fooled by unanticipated changes in current income caused by fortuitous or adverse events. Instead they plan consumption, schedule purchases, set retirement goals, save for rainy days, and the like. It is this focus on individual behaviour that forms the basis of the neoclassical critique of Keynes's theory. As an explicit theory of individual spending behaviour, this perspective is relevant for those able to save, who constitute half or less of all consumer units. For this group, spending could very well be based on lifetime considerations. However, for the other half or more, those unable to save, annual consumption is simply a question of annual survival and lifetimes are determined year by year.

Unfortunately for the neoclassical critique and for those concerned about myopic spending, regardless of form, Keynes developed a theory of aggregate, not individual, consumption. In macroeconomics (as opposed to microeconomics) individual consumption decisions are revealed in the aggregate data. The motivation for these decisions, or how they fit into some individual lifetime spending plan, is of no consequence. Instead, the aggregate data reveal the annual relationship between consumption and income. While incompletely understood, suffering misrepresentation by its critics and neglect by its adherents, this relationship none the less governs the operation of any aggregate economic system.

DAVID BUNTING

See also:

Effective Demand; Multiplier; Saving; Time-series Econometrics.

References

Bunting, D. (2001), 'Keynes' law and its critics', *Journal of Post Keynesian Economics*, **24** (1), 149–63.
Carroll, C.D. (2001), 'A theory of the consumption function, with and without liquidity constraints', *Journal of Economic Perspectives*, **15** (1), 23–46.
Deaton, A. (1992), *Understanding Consumption*, New York: Oxford University Press.
Muellbauer, J. and R. Lattimore (1995), 'The consumption function: a theoretical and empirical overview', in M.H. Pesaran and M.R. Wickens (eds), *Handbook of Applied Econometrics: Macroeconomics*, London: Blackwell, pp. 221–311.
Thomas, J. (1989), 'The early history of the consumption function', in N. de Marchi and C. Gilbert (eds), *History and Methodology of Econometrics*, Oxford: Clarendon Press, pp. 131–49.

Conventions

Emphasizing strong forms of uncertainty poses at least two interrelated challenges to social scientists interested in economic issues. First, is it possible to theorize without falling into an extreme subjectivism and explaining everything *ex post* by variations in what John Maynard Keynes called 'animal spirits' and the like? Second, how to explain the considerable degree of coordination among separate agents and of stability that one observes in real economies? An important part of the answers involves institutions and, among them, conventions.

Under conditions of fundamental uncertainty, with the possibility of non-predetermined structural changes, how do economic agents form expectations about the future and behave? In the *General Theory*, while discussing investment, Keynes argued that they follow a convention, which consists in projecting the current situation into future, unless they have specific reasons for expecting a change. A similar idea appeared in his 1937 *Quarterly Journal of Economics* article, where Keynes also referred to an attempt to conform to the majority or average opinion. Following Keynes's lead, early Post Keynesians such as Paul Davidson and Hyman Minsky also mentioned conventions, but the notion started gaining focused attention from the 1980s on. Regardless of the ambiguities in Keynes's insightful treatment and of the controversies surrounding it (Dequech 2011), one can develop the idea both conceptually and theoretically, and then use it in the study of various relevant issues.

What is a convention? It can be broadly conceptualized as a socially shared pattern of behaviour and/or of thought with two characteristics: (a) when followed consciously, a convention is followed at least in part because other people are following it (or are expected to follow it), and not, or not only, because there is external pressure to comply; and (b) it is to some degree arbitrary, in the sense that an alternative is conceivable that is not clearly inferior to the pattern actually adopted. These properties can be called, respectively, conformity with (expected) conformity and arbitrariness. They are often implied by many concepts of convention in the economic literature – including the one that was itself only implicit in Keynes's writings. A convention as defined above may be not only a behavioural rule, that is, a way of behaving, as in more restrictive concepts that are frequent in economics, but also a way of thinking, as in Keynes's work. In turn, as a shared mental model, a convention may be a way of forming rather precise expectations, like Keynes's projective convention, or a vaguer or broader model, which can be used for selecting, organizing and interpreting information, as well as for supplementing it. In addition, under this broad concept, a convention need not be unanimously adopted.

Nor is there an implication that everybody should conform to the existing convention when all the others are expected to conform, or that one is subject to punishment if one does not conform. This concept leaves enough room for deviation.

Using the idea of conventions allows one to theorize about economic situations marked by fundamental uncertainty without falling into an extreme subjectivism. By influencing individuals and being used by them, conventions, together with other institutions, facilitate coordination and help provide some stability to the social world.

Partly in reaction against claims that economic theorizing is incompatible with strong forms of uncertainty, Post Keynesians and other economists have argued for the rationality of conventional behaviour. Some have even identified following conventions as *the* form of rationality under such uncertainty. People's knowledge about conventions and the fact that they are shared by many agents do indeed provide rationales for conventional behaviour. On the other hand, conventions do not completely eliminate fundamental uncertainty, and one should not assume that all agents follow all the relevant conventions all the time. Otherwise, there would be no innovations in goods markets and, in the case of Keynes's projective convention, no divergence of opinions and therefore no transactions in speculative financial markets. Some agents do deviate from existing conventions. Moreover, they are not necessarily less rational than those conforming with the conventions. The possibility of deviant behaviour, particularly in the form of the introduction of technological or institutional innovations, is a very important source of fundamental uncertainty. For the sake of both realism and coherence with the notion of fundamental uncertainty, this possibility should not be neglected in the theory of economic behaviour.

All this can be better understood in light of the following scheme of determination of expectations and confidence, which is in part inspired by Keynes, but introduces different elements and relations and uses some of Keynes's terms in a sense that may be different from, or more explicit than, what he meant (see Dequech 1999 for a detailed presentation, with a diagram on p. 418 that synthesizes and clarifies these points). The state of expectation refers to the use of expectations in practice, and therefore directly depends not only on expectations themselves, but also on the confidence with which expectations are held. Expectations are forecasts or images of the future. They depend on knowledge, spontaneous optimism and creativity. Let us briefly consider each of them. Since fundamental uncertainty does not imply complete ignorance about the future, individuals may have some knowledge about the future (even making imprecise and not fully reliable judgements of probability). This knowledge is, however, very incomplete and is explicitly or implicitly supplemented by something else. It is useful to distinguish between two supplementary factors: spontaneous optimism and creativity. Spontaneous optimism is the factor through which animal spirits are reflected in expectations. It is spontaneous in the sense of not being based on knowledge. It varies in quality and intensity along a spectrum, ranging from intense pessimism (very negative) to intense optimism (very positive). In contrast, creativity, when applied to expectations, is the ability to imagine a future that is structurally different from the present, in some relevant aspect (for example, technology or institutions). It also varies along a spectrum, from absent (no structural changes imagined), through weak, to very strong. The best economic example of creativity is imagining an innovation, which means at least a microeconomic change in market structure. The following example helps illustrate the difference between spontaneous optimism and creativity: when creativity in expectations is absent, one imagines a future economy with an otherwise unchanged structure in comparison with the present, but the expectations about the level of demand in this economy will be greater the more spontaneously optimistic one is.

To recapitulate, expectations depend on knowledge, spontaneous optimism, and creativity. In its turn, confidence (the other immediate determinant of the state of expectation) is the willingness or unwillingness to act on expectations despite uncertainty. It depends on uncertainty perception and uncertainty aversion (especially regarding fundamental uncertainty). Uncertainty aversion – which can be related to courage or fear – is essentially a matter of animal spirits; the perception of uncertainty is influenced by knowledge, namely the knowledge of uncertainty itself and of the factors that affect the degree of uncertainty (for example, institutions). Animal spirits therefore influence both expectations (through spontaneous optimism) and confidence (through uncertainty aversion). So does knowledge, including knowledge of conventions and formal institutions. Expectations and confidence can thus vary with changes in knowledge, even if animal spirits – or creativity – do not change. In addition, animal spirits and creativity are not purely subjective.

The selection, organization and interpretation of information, so that it may be transformed into some form of knowledge, as well as the combination of knowledge with spontaneous optimism and creativity, is made through (and manifested in) a mental model. Mental models may be socially shared and, more specifically (when they have the properties of conformity with conformity and arbitrariness), conventional, or not.

People do have some knowledge, which may be shared, including knowledge of existing conventions. However, differences in knowledge (reflecting differences in information or in its handling and interpretation through mental models), as well as differences in animal spirits (affecting both expectations and confidence) or creativity, among other factors, may lead some agents to deviate from some of these conventions. Important examples are the innovative agent, the investor who is more optimistic or confident than the average in a product market, and the speculator who flouts the projective convention in a financial market (Dequech 2003). Their actions help explain how conventions may be destroyed and replaced. These agents do not, however, break with all conventions at once, which would be extremely difficult. They keep following many conventions, while at the same time deviating from one or a few others.

When agents supposedly do follow a convention, this should not be assumed to be, or formalized as if it were, unconditional. Under strong forms of uncertainty, one has to explicitly consider the confidence held by agents in their expectations or in their expectational patterns, as well as the possibility of changes in this confidence. Otherwise the adequate treatment of liquidity and money is jeopardized. As Keynes suggested, the liquidity premium of money (and other liquid assets) is a barometer of our lack of confidence in our calculations and conventions about the future. This can be generalized to unconventional expectations: their adoption as guides to action also depends on confidence and, when these expectations lead to a departure from liquidity, the liquidity premium of any liquid asset is also inversely related to confidence in them.

Where should we apply the concept of convention? There is no doubt that Keynes used it when discussing the stock exchange. He also explicitly referred to the interest rate as a conventional phenomenon. His interpreters disagree, however, on whether Keynes also considered (or should have considered) the existence of conventions outside the context of financial markets. Once again, regardless of how one interprets Keynes's original writings, the idea of convention can be used and developed in the study of a broad set of issues. Several Post Keynesians have at least briefly referred to conventions when dealing with (physical) investment, production, pricing, consumption, wage bargaining, money and bank lending. Specifically concerning macroeconomic theory, some authors have identified conventions and other institutions as the foundation for such a theory (for example, Crotty 1994). Detailed work on conventions in different markets and contexts has been developed within the economics of conventions, an institutionalist approach originated in France. Even in financial markets they have gone beyond Keynes, with André Orléan's notion of financial convention as a qualitative and normative model of evaluation in the stock exchange. Other approaches in economics have also begun to study conventions. As informal institutions, conventions have in part benefited from the surge of interest in institutions among economists in recent decades. Much more is yet to be done, with due attention to the specificity of each market or context.

Indeed, the concept and the theory of conventions provide potentially useful links between different approaches that emphasize institutions, in economics as well as in other disciplines. One can mention Post Keynesianism, the economics of conventions, the original institutional economics, some branches of the new institutional economics, neo-Schumpeterian economics, and the regulation school. In other disciplines, there is, for example, the new institutionalism in organization studies, as well as part of economic sociology and of the interdisciplinary field of political economy. Moreover, even work that does not explicitly refer to conventions or informal institutions can be connected to them, when it considers imitation, herd behaviour, strategic complementarities or increasing returns to adoption.

DAVID DEQUECH

See also:

Agency; Behavioural Economics; Choice under Uncertainty; Expectations; Institutionalism; Keynes's *Treatise on Probability*; Liquidity Preference; Non-ergodicity; Uncertainty.

Bibliography

Crotty, J. (1994), 'Are Keynesian uncertainty and macrotheory compatible? Conventional decision making, institutional structures, and conditional stability in Keynesian macro-models', in G. Dymski and R. Pollin (eds), *New Perspectives in Monetary Macroeconomics*, Ann Arbor, MI: University of Michigan Press, pp. 105–42.

Davis, J.B. (1994), *Keynes's Philosophical Development*, Cambridge: Cambridge University Press.

Dequech, D. (1999), 'Expectations and confidence under uncertainty', *Journal of Post Keynesian Economics*, **21** (3), 415–30.

Dequech, D. (2003), 'Conventional and unconventional behavior under uncertainty', *Journal of Post Keynesian Economics*, **26** (1), 145–68.

Dequech, D. (2011), 'Financial conventions in Keynes's theory: the stock exchange', *Journal of Post Keynesian Economics*, **33** (3), 473–94.

Dow, S. (1996), *The Methodology of Macroeconomic Thought*, Cheltenham, UK and Brookfield, VT, USA: Edward Elgar.

Lawson, T. (1985), 'Uncertainty and economic analysis', *Economic Journal*, **95** (380), 909–27.

Runde, J. and S. Mizuhara (eds) (2003), *The Philosophy of Keynes's Economics: Probability, Uncertainty and Convention*, London and New York: Routledge.

Credit Rationing

The theory of credit rationing developed by Joseph Stiglitz and Andrew Weiss (1981) has received much attention in the economic literature. However, this New Keynesian approach assumes asymmetric information, in which there is a precise probability distribution of returns from potential investment projects known by the borrower but not by the lender. In contrast, the Post Keynesian approach to credit rationing is based on the assumption of Keynesian uncertainty, a non-ergodic future about which both borrower and lender simply 'do not know'. In addition to uncertainty, the Post Keynesian approach builds upon the following concepts:

Borrower's risk and lender's risk   In the *General Theory*, Keynes (1936, p. 144) defined borrower's risk as due to doubts about 'actually earning the prospective yield for which he hopes'. Lender's risk was related to either voluntary default by the borrower (moral hazard) or involuntary default 'due to the disappointment of expectation'.

Financial fragility   As Hyman Minsky (1986, p. 213) has argued, 'the successful functioning of an economy within an initially robust financial structure will lead to a structure that becomes more fragile as time elapses'. This increase in financial fragility is likely to occur during the expansion phase of the business cycle or over the course of a series of relatively mild business cycles.

Endogenous development of expectations   The endogenous development of financial fragility, particularly if accelerated by rising interest rates and falling profit rates (two typical developments near the end of the business-cycle peak), leads to a corresponding change in bankers' willingness to lend. This endogenous development of expectations (Crotty 1994) is likely to lead to a reduction in bank lending.

Sheila Dow builds upon these concepts to argue for a Post Keynesian theory of credit rationing. She argues that this theory contradicts the horizontalist interpretation of endogenous money: 'a theoretical case is made for amending the horizontalist position to allow for systemic credit rationing, referring particularly to the business-cycle' (1996, p. 498). It would appear that the idea of endogenous money, if interpreted to mean a horizontal supply curve such that bankers accommodate all demands for loans, would indeed be in conflict with a concept of credit rationing in which bankers do not accommodate demands for loans.

Dow argues that, over the course of the business cycle, financial institutions become increasingly less willing to lend. Building upon Minsky's (1975) discussion of borrower's and lender's risk, she asserts that 'the demand for borrowed funds and the supply of borrowed funds are less interest elastic the greater is the perceived borrowers' risk and lenders' risk, respectively' (Dow 1996, p. 500). A more sharply rising supply curve meets a more sharply falling demand curve, with the result being a reduction in the amount of credit extended.

These developments in the economic and financial systems result in a reduced availability of credit, which Dow identifies with credit rationing. She recognizes that there may be an issue in equating these two terms: 'It is a matter of semantics whether or not the resulting availability of credit is termed "rationing"' (ibid., p. 499). None the less, she uses this analysis to make her main point, which is that this reduction in credit availability is incompatible with a 'horizontalist' view of endogenous money that assumes accommodating credit behaviour on the part of the banking system.

Martin Wolfson (1996), however, attempts to develop a framework to analyse credit rationing that incorporates a horizontal endogenous money supply curve. Marc Lavoie (2010) points out that the compatibility of these two concepts was established by Alfred Eichner in a perceptive article with Philip Arestis (Arestis and Eichner 1988).

Wolfson defines credit rationing as 'any situation in which the bank refuses to lend to a particular borrower, despite the borrower's willingness to pay a higher interest rate' (1996, p. 463). In his analysis, he uses the following additional Post Keynesian concepts:

The fringe of unsatisfied borrowers In the *Treatise on Money*, Keynes (1930, Volume I, p. 212) referred to 'an unsatisfied fringe of borrowers' that is refused credit. In this way, Keynes argued, the banks can increase or decrease the volume of their loans (and thus investment) 'without there being necessarily any change in the level of bank-rate [or] in the demand-schedule of borrowers'. Keynes's concept clearly implies a banking system that does not accommodate all demands for credit. Moreover, his reference to changing the volume of loans in the context of both an unchanged interest rate and an unchanged demand schedule would seem to imply a movement *off* the borrowers' demand curve, rather than along it.

Asymmetric expectations Wolfson introduces this term to make the point that the source of credit rationing is the existence of an uncertain future, one in which borrowers and lenders come to different conclusions about future events. It is not necessary to rely on either asymmetric information or even the assumption that lenders are less risk averse than borrowers. Just different, or asymmetric, expectations will lead to a situation in which borrowers will have some projects that they regard as risky, whereas lenders don't, while borrowers will have other projects that they regard as safe, whereas lenders don't. The first group of projects will never be seen by lenders, while the second group will be rationed (refused credit).

Wolfson draws upon surveys conducted by the Federal Reserve (the Survey on Bank Lending Practices and the Survey on the Terms of Bank

Lending) to understand how banks actually ration credit. He concludes (1996, pp. 459–60):

1.   Banks classify borrowers according to perceived risk, and use these risk classifications to set both price and non-price terms of lending. (Price terms refer to explicit charges, such as the cost of credit lines or the spread of loan rates over a base rate; non-price terms involve other aspects of the loan agreement, such as requirements for collateral, loan covenants, or the size of credit lines.)
2.   Higher price terms imply a higher spread over the reference rate, except for borrowers with loan commitments (in the short run).
3.   Higher non-price terms raise requirements on existing loans, but also provide the basis for denying credit to those borrowers judged to be insufficiently creditworthy.
4.   Banks give preference to borrowers with whom they are familiar.

These observations lead to an important conclusion: since banks increase both price and non-price terms in response to perceptions of higher risk and since higher non-price terms are the basis for denying a loan, spreads over reference rates and credit rationing move together. This is interesting because for those borrowers who are rationed, the bank has denied them credit rather than increasing the interest rate charged.

Wolfson builds upon these observations to develop a framework for understanding credit rationing. In doing so, he introduces two additional concepts:

Notional demand curve   The notional demand curve expresses the desire for loans by borrowers. It is the traditional demand curve used in most situations to analyse the interaction between supply and demand for a commodity. However, the demand for bank loans is different from the demand for most other commodities. To obtain a bank loan, it is necessary to achieve the consent of the lender. In a situation of credit rationing, it is precisely this consent that is not given. Thus the borrower's demand curve is simply a notional (theoretical, not effective) demand curve for the bank.

Creditworthy demand curve   What the bank uses is the creditworthy demand curve. This represents the bank's judgement about the proportion of borrowers desiring loans who are creditworthy. (In the 1996 article, Wolfson used the term 'effective demand curve', rather than 'creditworthy demand curve'. However, as pointed out by Peter Skott and Marc Lavoie, use of the term 'effective demand' is unwise, since it already has a specific meaning within Keynesian economics. 'Creditworthy demand' is a better term (Wolfson 1997; see also Rochon 1999, p. 283).)

Wolfson emphasizes that the judgements made by the bank are those made in the context of uncertainty. Thus they are subject to two concepts discussed by Keynes (1936): a *state of confidence* about any particular forecast of the future, and lending *conventions* that bankers seize upon in the absence of any firm knowledge of the future. Both of these are subject to change. They can change gradually and endogenously over the course of the business cycle, but they can also change dramatically and suddenly during more turbulent times.

Wolfson's ideas can be illustrated with the use of Figure 5. Here L indicates bank loans, r the interest rate charged by the bank, $D^N D^N$ the notional demand curve, $D^C D^C$ the creditworthy demand curve, C the bank's cost of funds, S_A the average spread over the cost of funds charged the borrower (so that $S_A + C$ represents the interest rate paid by the borrower), and ABD the horizontal 'endogenous money' supply curve. The bank accommodates all creditworthy demands for credit, and rations the rest. Thus BD represents the amount of credit rationing, or the 'fringe of unsatisfied borrowers' who would be willing to pay a higher interest rate, but who are refused credit.

If the bank increases its average spread to S_B, then the amount of credit rationing would increase to FG. However, Wolfson indicates that the main

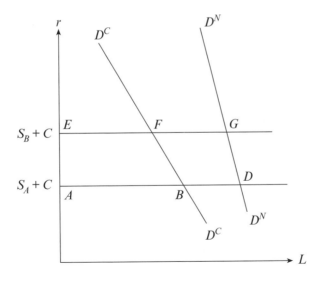

Figure 5   Credit rationing

'action' in the model would have less to do with relatively small changes in interest rates at a given point in time, and more to do with factors that affect banks' expectations of the future. He gives three examples: the 'boom and bust' lending in the 1970s and 1980s, the typical change from optimism to pessimism (discussed by Minsky and Dow) that occurs as the business-cycle expansion nears its peak, and the quick collapse of lending that accompanies financial crises.

Indeed, the most dramatic change in expectations and collapse in lending in recent times occurred in connection with the financial crisis following the failure of investment bank Lehman Brothers in September 2008. In its Senior Loan Officer Opinion Survey on Bank Lending Practices, covering the fourth quarter of 2008, the Federal Reserve Board found that 83.6 per cent of bank respondents had tightened lending standards for its commercial and industrial (C&I) loans to large and medium businesses (see Figure 6). The Federal Reserve also inquired about other types of loans, with

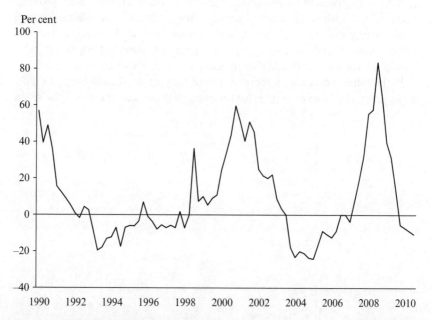

Note: Net percentage of domestic respondents tightening standards for C&I loans to large and medium businesses.

Source: Federal Reserve Board Senior Loan Officer Opinion Survey on Bank Lending Practices, 8 November 2010, available at: http://www.federalreserve.gov/boarddocs/ snloansurvey/201011/fullreport.pdf.

Figure 6   Fluctuations in credit rationing

similar results: the fourth quarter of 2008 saw the most dramatic tightening of lending standards for C&I loans to small businesses (74.5 per cent), commercial real estate loans (87.0 per cent), and subprime residential loans (100.0 per cent).

It is important to note that Figure 6 shows simply the change in lending standards for a particular quarter; it does not represent the overall degree of credit rationing in the banking system. As long as more banks are tightening standards than loosening them (the net percentage of banks tightening standards is positive), it will be more difficult for borrowers to obtain credit. Accordingly, it was not until the beginning of 2010 that credit standards began to ease in the banking system following the financial crisis of 2008.

Martin H. Wolfson

See also:

Banking; Effective Demand; Efficient Markets Hypothesis; Multiplier; Saving.

References

Arestis, P. and A.S. Eichner (1988), 'The post-Keynesian and institutionalist theory of money and credit', *Journal of Economic Issues*, **22** (4), 1003–22.
Crotty, J. (1994), 'Are Keynesian uncertainty and macrotheory compatible? Conventional decision making, institutional structures, and conditional stability in Keynesian macro-models', in G. Dymski and R. Pollin (eds), *New Perspectives in Monetary Macroeconomics*, Ann Arbor, MI: University of Michigan Press, pp. 105–39.
Dow, S. (1996), 'Horizontalism: a critique', *Cambridge Journal of Economics*, **20** (4), 497–508.
Keynes, J.M. (1930), *A Treatise on Money*, New York: Harcourt, Brace & Company.
Keynes, J.M. (1936), *The General Theory of Employment, Interest and Money*, New York: Harcourt, Brace & World.
Lavoie, M. (2010), 'Eichner's monetary economics: ahead of its time', in Lavoie, L.P. Rochon and M. Seccareccia (eds), *Money and Macrodynamics: Alfred Eichner and Post-Keynesian Economics*, Armonk, NY: M.E. Sharpe, pp. 155–71.
Minsky, H.P. (1975), *John Maynard Keynes*, New York: Columbia University Press.
Minsky, H.P. (1986), *Stabilizing an Unstable Economy*, New Haven, CT: Yale University Press.
Rochon, L.P. (1999), *Credit, Money, and Production: An Alternative Post Keynesian Approach*, Cheltenham, UK and Northampton, MA, USA: Edward Elgar.
Stiglitz, J. and A.Weiss (1981), 'Credit rationing in markets with imperfect information', *American Economic Review*, **71** (3), 393–410.
Wolfson, M.H. (1996), 'A Post Keynesian theory of credit rationing', *Journal of Post Keynesian Economics*, **18** (3), 443–70.
Wolfson, M.H. (1997), Letter to Marc Lavoie, 12 March.

Critical Realism

Though known to economists through the work of Tony Lawson and others since the late 1980s, critical realism has a long history and cannot adequately be characterized by the work of any single author or by application within any one discipline. With that caveat, key features are presented below: (i) the basic tenets of critical realism, systematized by Roy Bhaskar, which remain definitive of critical realism; (ii) a very brief indication of the development of critical realism since its inception; and (iii) the impact of critical realism in (especially Post Keynesian) economics.

Bhaskar (1975) articulates a philosophy of natural science that he terms 'transcendental realism'. This philosophy proposes that objects of science – cells, molecules, atoms, sub-atomic entities and so on – have an intrinsic structure ('real essence') and associated modes of activity ('mechanisms'). Bhaskar criticizes the received view, enshrined in the 'covering-law' model of scientific explanation, that scientific laws refer to event regularities. He argues, instead, that laws refer to the aforementioned mechanisms and that only under conditions of experimental control does a mechanism necessarily produce an event regularity. Outside of experimental conditions a mechanism acts as an enduring tendency, interacting with other tendencies, to produce the flux of events. In other words reality is an 'open system', whereas the controlled environment of experiment creates a 'closed system'. Furthermore, if laws *did* refer to event regularities, then their application to reality would require that (atomistic) event regularities are ubiquitous *outside* of experiment; that is, it would imply that reality is a closed system such that experiment is unnecessary. Bhaskar opposes such reductionism, which he sees as a legacy of 'positivism'. He proposes, instead, that reality is 'stratified'. Higher strata, such as the molecular level (or, higher still, the cellular level) are causally *irreducible* to the lower strata from which they 'emerge'.

Bhaskar (1979) also offers a philosophy of social science, termed 'critical naturalism'. He argues that social structures and agents are each emergent strata, irreducible to the natural realm, or to each other. On Bhaskar's view social structures, defined as ensembles of social relations, are reproduced (or transformed), often unintentionally, by agents. For example, by getting married a couple unintentionally help to reproduce the institution of marriage; by going to work the worker unintentionally helps to reproduce the social relation of wage labour/capital; by paying rent the tenant unintentionally helps to reproduce the social relation of landlord/tenant. Thus social structures *constrain and enable* the very practices through which they are reproduced. A problem for social science is that experiment is largely impossible. The 'compensator' for this inability to undertake experiment is the social scientists' preconception, gained through their ongoing social activities, of social structures (however distorted it may be). To take one example, agents must, in order to participate in the economy, have concepts of 'money' and 'capital'. The social scientist (who is also an agent within society) uses such preconceptions as premises for hypothesizing the 'deep' social structures that give rise to, or condition, agents' pre-conceptions. This explanatory move, from preconception to 'deep' social structure, is termed 'retroduction'. Through the 1980s Bhaskar's ideas gained considerable currency. They were developed and debated by radical philosophers, sociologists and other social scientists, and became known as 'critical realism' (a combination of '*critical* naturalism' and 'transcendental *realism*').

Since the late 1980s, Tony Lawson, followed by a group of economists originally based at Cambridge University, has given voice to critical realism in economics. The most comprehensive statement of their common position (beyond the consolidation of the basic tenets noted above) is found in Lawson (1997, 2003). Lawson has added significantly to the critical realist method. Whereas Bhaskar argued simply that 'preconceptions' provide the key to social scientific retroduction, Lawson argues that the social world gives rise to 'partial' or 'demi-' event regularities. It is such 'demi-regs', rather than simple 'preconceptions', that, in general, enable retroduction, according to Lawson. These 'demi-regs' do not presuppose an atomistic reality, as in positivism. Instead, they serve to direct social scientists' attention to where underlying social structures and mechanisms may be located. Lawson gives as an example the 'demi-regularity' of the historically poor comparative productivity performance of the UK. This 'demi-reg' initiates an investigation into the underlying social structures that may account for it; Lawson's previous work argued that one such social structure is the system of industrial relations.

Lawson has used critical realism to criticize mainstream economics. He argues that the essence of mainstream economics is the extensive deployment of a method to which statements of the *form* 'whenever x then y' (where x and y refer to events or states of affairs) are central. To explain something is to deduce it from axioms, assumptions and conditions that require statements of the aforementioned form (this is a variant of the 'covering law' model of explanation). Lawson criticizes this 'deductivist' method, and hence mainstream economics, according to Bhaskar's general critique of positivism: the method fails to acknowledge that social science is concerned primarily with 'deep' social structures and agents rather than with event regularities. In attempting to 'close the system', the content of mainstream economics is pushed towards a conceptual world of ubiquitous event conjunctions among atomistic individuals. Yet the real social world is an open system of social structures and agents, not a closed system of atoms. Until deductivism is jettisoned, in favour of methods adequate to open social reality, mainstream economics (both econometrics and economic theory) will remain broken-backed.

Lawson (1994; Symposium 1999) has contributed to ongoing debate regarding the coherence of Post Keynesian economics. He argues that most, perhaps all, key Post Keynesian 'nominal manifestations', such as opposition to the mainstream, emphasis on making method explicit, focus on uncertainty and history, upholding of genuine human choice, allowance of competing substantive perspectives, and association with certain classical economists, can be rendered 'intelligible' by critical realism. Accordingly, he suggests that Post Keynesian economics is made coherent if grasped as upholding an ontology that is redolent of critical realism. Two significant corollaries are: (i) it would appear to be difficult to distinguish Post Keynesian economics from much (old) institutional, Austrian, Marxian and other radical economics, which are likewise redolent of critical realism, in their acknowledgement of open systems; and (ii) the neo-Ricardian commitment to the deductivist method would appear to exclude it from Post Keynesianism.

According to Lawson (2003, 2006) the critical realist social ontology of internally related social structures, mechanisms, agents, processes and systems is common across the social world and so does not admit of a separate economic sphere (or political sphere or sociological sphere, and so on). Economics and the other disciplines should therefore be seen as a division of labour within a single social science. Synthesizing the respective accounts of John Stuart Mill, Alfred Marshall and Lionel Robbins (accounts usually thought to be mutually exclusive), Lawson conceives of economics as characteristically concerned with social structures and processes that bear upon the material conditions of well-being. Specific traditions within heterodox economics are then differentiated, according to Lawson, by their different respective choices of substantive foci, not by the unit of analysis – so, for example, Post Keynesian economics might be seen to choose to focus on uncertainty whereas evolutionary economics might be considered to choose to focus on processes of change.

Largely as a result of the Cambridge group's efforts (including the weekly Cambridge Realist Workshop, ongoing since 1990, whose list of speakers reads as a 'Who's Who' of the economic methodology discipline), there has been a remarkable rise to prominence of critical realism within: (i) non-mainstream economics, especially within Post Keynesianism; and (ii) the discipline of economic methodology. Taking, first, Post Keynesians, there has been a general, though cautious, acceptance of critical realism by leading Post Keynesians. Arestis explicitly characterizes Post Keynesianism as critical realist; Dow has suggested that her 'Babylonian' method is largely compatible with critical realism. The more critical reactions from within Post Keynesianism, notably Davidson (Symposium 1999), have tended to focus on issues of strategy and style (critical realism certainly does contain awkward neologisms). Walters and Young (Symposium 1999) argue for a rejection of the marriage of critical realism and Post Keynesian economics but do so from *outside* of Post Keynesianism. Jefferson and King (2011), in an important article claiming compatibility of Michał Kalecki and critical realism, go so far as to suggest that it would have been a 'cause for concern' had Kalecki – as a major figure in Post Keynesianism – proved incompatible with critical realism.

Of course, by no means every detail of the Cambridge group's arguments is endorsed, and a major area of controversy concerns econometrics and mathematics, where non-Cambridge-based critical realists have claimed, *contra* the perceived position of the Cambridge group, that critical realism is compatible with econometrics and mathematical modelling. Related debate has concerned the conceptualization of open and closed systems and of event regularities. Lawson (2003) now stresses that 'quite' strict event regularities *do* occur in the social realm but that they are not the *causal* regularities that are required by econometrics and mathematical modelling – instead they are merely concomitant associations, typically at a high level of generality, for example, 'whenever shops in the UK attach prices to their products today, they do so tomorrow'. Critical realism has very little to say about the notion of 'systems' beyond their being either closed (displaying event regularities) or open (no event regularities) – a deficiency according to some authors (for example, Mearman 2006).

A number of other criticisms have been levelled against critical realism in economics (see Symposium 1999; Lewis 2004; Fullbrook 2009). Lawson's replies to criticisms (and those by other members of the Cambridge group) have been robust but there is clearly a range of areas that it remains for critical realists to develop. From the above-mentioned collections, and elsewhere, the following criticisms can be noted. Critical realism: (i) does not add much to economic methodology since economics does not posit unobservable entities, beyond those that are trivial; (ii) undertakes a misplaced critique because mainstream modelling does not deal in 'events' at all and hence cannot be deductivist; (iii) misleadingly assimilates very different levels of analysis under the single rubric of 'retroduction'; (iv) employs an unhelpful notion of 'transcendental deduction' in philosophy; (v) employs an opaque notion of social structure; (vi) puts forward a tautological and banal conception of social structure and agency; (vii) illicitly and unwisely cleaves economic theory from philosophy and methodology; (viii) falsely states that event regularities of interest to science seldom occur outside of experiment; and (ix) provides little methodological *help* to the social scientist.

From a critical realist perspective, many of these criticisms appear to miss the main point of critical realism in social science: social science should be concerned with ensembles of social relations and with their reproduction or transformation by agents. Some critics do not offer anything like this persuasive description of economic reality, and their criticisms appear myopic as a result. They appear to maintain the philosophical bias against ontology (the theory of being) that critical realism exposes. Indeed, it is not the philosophical justification, but rather the appeal to intuition, that has most likely attracted economists and others to critical realism. While philosophical arguments are important, it is only once they are allied to fruitful methodological and substantive arguments that they are likely to make a real impact. In this vein, Brown et al. (2002) and Brown (2007) reproduce some of the aforementioned criticisms, and make other criticisms, as part of a positive agenda that embraces the intuitive appeal of critical realism.

Critical realism has made much ground within economics. It seems that it will continue to do so in the future, not only through the efforts of the Cambridge group, but also through the many new converts to critical realism who are now engaged in actively promoting and developing it.

ANDREW BROWN

See also:

Babylonian Mode of Thought; Econometrics; Keynes's *Treatise on Probability*; Macroeconomic Methodology; Open Systems; Sraffian Economics; Time-series Econometrics.

References

Bhaskar, R. (1975), *A Realist Theory of Science*, Leeds: Leeds Books.
Bhaskar, R. (1979), *The Possibility of Naturalism: A Philosophical Critique of the Contemporary Human Sciences*, Brighton: Harvester.
Brown, A. (2007), 'Reorienting critical realism: a system-wide perspective on the capitalist economy', *Journal of Economic Methodology*, **14** (4), 499–519.
Brown, A., G. Slater and D.A. Spencer (2002), 'Driven to abstraction? Critical realism and the search for the "inner connection" of social phenomena', *Cambridge Journal of Economics*, **26** (6), 773–88.
Fullbrook, E. (ed.) (2009), *Ontology and Economics: Tony Lawson and his Critics*, Abingdon and New York: Routledge.
Jefferson, T. and J.E. King (2011), 'Michał Kalecki and critical realism', *Cambridge Journal of Economics*, **35** (5), 957–72.
Lawson, T. (1994), 'The nature of Post Keynesianism and its links to other traditions: a realist perspective', *Journal of Post Keynesian Economics*, **16** (4), 503–38.
Lawson, T. (1997), *Economics and Reality*, London and New York: Routledge.
Lawson, T. (2003), *Reorienting Economics*, London and New York: Routledge.
Lawson, T. (2006), 'The nature of heterodox economics', *Cambridge Journal of Economics*, **30** (4), 483–505.
Lewis, P. (ed.) (2004), *Transforming Economics: Perspectives on the Critical Realist Project*, Abingdon and New York: Routledge.
Mearman, A. (2006), 'Critical realism in economics and open-systems ontology: a critique', *Review of Social Economy*, **64** (1), 47–70.
Symposium (1999), 'Symposium on critical realism', *Journal of Post Keynesian Economics*, **22** (1), 3–129.

Development Finance

Development finance refers to the use and allocation of domestic and external resources necessary for economic growth and social progress. It is often associated with the issue of investment finance in developing economies, where capital needs are high and financial structures are often underdeveloped. In our view, a Post Keynesian development finance theory should be based on Keynes's (1936) monetary production economy and Minsky's (1982) financial fragility hypothesis.

The starting-point of Keynes's analysis is his rejection of Say's law through his theory of effective demand, particularly his identification of investment as the *causa causans* in the determination of output, employment and aggregate income. This logically implies that aggregate saving is a residue in the income creation process, and thus cannot be a constraint on investment (Studart 1995). Indeed, for Keynes investment could be restricted by lack of finance, or the willingness of the banking sector to actively create deposits and credit – an assumption deeply rooted in his description of the evolution of the banking system in his *Treatise on Money*. If banks hold a key position in the transition from a lower to a higher scale of activity (Keynes 1937, p. 668), what is the role of savers, non-bank intermediaries and securities markets in such an approach? This is where the issue of *funding* comes into the story.

Investment funding has to do with maturity transformation of investors' bank debts into long-term liabilities and/or equity, and is an important part of a threefold process: investment finance allows for long-term undertaking to materialize and initiate the income-multiplier process; this in turn generates an aggregate saving that equals investment; and finally, additional saving is intermediated by non-bank financial intermediaries and markets to become a long-term source of funding. Of course, this circuit is associated with a specific institutional framework: a financial structure which possesses developed primary and secondary markets for long-term securities – where primary securities markets promote the matching of supply and demand for long-term saving; while an active secondary market gives the liquidity to otherwise illiquid assets. In an uncertain environment (in a Knightian sense), this provision of liquidity is fundamental to make long-term bonds and securities attractive to savers – who, as Davidson (1986) has rightly put it, are searching for safe 'liquidity time-machines', and rarely wish to be locked in to holding an asset for a long period of time.

From a Post Keynesian perspective, it may be said that the lack or underdevelopment of funding mechanisms can have two undesirable consequences. First, if funding is not available, banks may refrain from expanding their lending and/or may ration credit – as they will almost certainly prefer short-term loans (to finance consumption, working capital and/or speculation) rather than longer-term, and hence, riskier investment projects. Second, in this case, both firms and banks tend to assume speculative positions – as investment growth can be sustained if some investing firms borrow short, hoping to repay by borrowing until their investment matures and begins to produce additional cash inflows (using Minsky's terminology, more and more investors and financiers will adopt speculative, and even Ponzi scheme-type strategies). Third in this case, growth would necessarily lead to higher financial fragility of banks and investors – and rising risks of a Minskian type of instability occurring.

Because the weight of speculative finance tends to increase with the rise of investment, in times of growth, credit-based systems – which prevail in developing economies – are extremely vulnerable to shifts in interest rates. If the financing of long-lived assets is supplied mainly through short-term renewable loans, a change in the rate of interest will represent a significant rise in the firms' financial expenditures; and if firms try to adjust by cutting other expenditures simultaneously, this may set in motion a vicious circle of financial reactions which could reduce effective demand even further.

The Post Keynesian approach allows for an interesting conclusion regarding the *functionality* (as defined in Studart 1995) of different financial structures. It implies that whether the financial system is a good platform to support growth and development does not depend on a specific structure, but on the existence of appropriate mechanisms to finance and fund investments. Thus, for instance, successfully developed economies such as the United States and United Kingdom possess capital-market-based financial structures, where the mechanisms to finance and the mechanisms to fund were, until recently, segregated; whereas in most other developed economies (including Germany and France) and some successful emerging market economies (such as South Korea, India, Brazil and China), the supply of finance with different maturities is provided by universal banks – and therefore finance and funding are provided within the banking sectors. When it comes to the ownership of financial intermediaries, the differences are also wide, and there is no indication whatsoever that ownership matters when it comes to the aggregate supply of finance and funding, and/or the capacity to avoid financial instability (Stallings and Studart 2005). The issue of how the financial sector is owned by itself quite irrelevant in a Post Keynesian approach. What matters is not so much whether the economy possesses a credit-based system or a capital-market-based system, or whether the ownership of the domestic institutions is private or public, but the existence of appropriate mechanisms to finance and fund investment and to avoid financial instability.

The policy implications of a Post Keynesian approach are quite different from those found in most mainstream development finance literature. Just to remind the reader, since the 1970s and until recently, this literature has been dominated by the Shaw–McKinnon approach. The underlying assumptions of such an approach are twofold. First, market-based financial arrangements are assumed to be the most efficient way to allocate resources intertemporally – an assumption that was enhanced by the so-called 'efficient markets hypothesis'. Second, financial repression (through interest rate ceilings, directed credit and so on) is seen as the main cause for lower domestic saving and financial underdevelopment, and possibly unnecessary dependency on external saving. Financial deregulation or liberalization would in turn unleash financial market forces, and lead to higher domestic saving, investment and growth – and a lower need for external saving (for a survey, see Agénor and Montiel 1996). This mainstream approach has been contradicted by the fact that many successful emerging economies managed to increase their levels of investment finance and growth, despite their often significantly regulated financial sector – sometimes dominated by public financial institutions and relatively small securities markets. In addition, financial liberalization in most developing countries did not lead to financial deepening – that in many cases resulted in financial instability and crisis (Stallings and Studart 2005). Such contradictory evidence prompted criticism and searches for alternative approaches, even before the current world economic crisis (2008–09), frequently seen as a consequence of financial deregulation in developed economies throughout the 1980s and 1990s.

In the 1990s, New Keynesian models of asymmetric information had already challenged the view that financial markets are efficient allocators of capital, and made way for interventionist views that are foreign to the liberal wave that has dominated development finance literature since the 1970s. However, these models are still based on the view that the role of financial markets is to allocate saving – seen as a constraint on growth and development. They also had little to say about why financial liberalization has often been followed by financial instability in developing and developed economies or about policies to foster financial deepening. Here is where a Post Keynesian approach seems to have significant advantages.

Indeed, the implicit assumption prevailing in mainstream thinking, that financial liberalization *per se* promotes financial development and deepening, or that capital account liberalization allows for wider and better access to external saving, is not warranted in the Post Keynesian approach. On the contrary, financial deregulation tends to create further uncertainties and volatility of interest rates, which in credit-based systems are recipes for, respectively, further credit rationing and financial instability.

Financial development is thus much more an issue of appropriate policies and regulation – a position that is far from the *laissez-faire* mainstream view. In the long run, market-enhancing policies are required if private mechanisms to finance and fund investment are to evolve – and there are significant experiences in both developed and developing economies of successful market-enhancing economies. While such mechanisms are not developed, private credit (and equity) rationing is likely to be a pervasive problem of developing economies. This gives support for directed credit policies, especially to developing sectors that, due to their long maturity horizon (for example, long-term fixed capital accumulation) and/or risk characteristics (for example, technology-related investments and small and medium-sized enterprises), are likely to have little access to private financing. And, given that most developing countries have a bank-based financial structure, appropriate regulation and low and stable interest rates are an important requirement to avoid the inherent financial fragility, associated with the resulting maturity mismatches, evolving into undesirable processes of financial instability and crises. Financial deepening should come with the process of growth, but the development of mechanisms to fund investment will most likely depend on policies – from distributive policies that stimulate household savings to intelligent regulation and policies to promote the evolution of securities markets.

Finally capital flows are not seen in a Post Keynesian approach as directly associated with the use of external saving. These flows can have important roles in mitigating balance-of-payments constraints in the process of development, allowing the importation of capital goods and the transfer of technology and knowledge often needed in the process of development; but their usefulness will ultimately depend on their being conduits of domestic investment finance and funding – for instance, on the maturity of the capital flows or their long-term impact on domestic financial intermediation. Capital account deregulation should not be assumed to be able to boost access to external financial markets *per se*, not to mention to increase access to sustainable, long-term sources of finance and funding. In contrast, given that capital account opening adds currency mismatches to the problem of maturity mismatches, caution should be used to avoid volatile foreign capital flows affecting domestic financial stability. Indeed, intelligent regulation of capital flows should be a better means to attract capital from abroad that can actually contribute to investment and development.

ROGÉRIO STUDART

See also:

Credit Rationing; Efficient Markets Hypothesis; Financial Instability Hypothesis; Financial Markets; Financial Reform; Keynes's *Treatise on Money*; Monetary Policy; New Keynesian Economics.

References

Agénor, P.R. and P.J. Montiel (1996), *Development Macroeconomics*, Princeton, NJ: Princeton University Press.
Davidson, P. (1986), 'Finance, funding, saving and investment', *Journal of Post Keynesian Economics*, **9** (1), 101–10.
Keynes, J.M. (1936), *The General Theory of Employment, Interest and Money*, London: Macmillan.
Keynes, J.M. (1937), 'The "ex-ante" theory of the rate of interest', *Economic Journal*, **47** (188), 663–9.
Minsky, H.P. (1982), 'The financial-instability hypothesis: capitalist processes and the behavior of the economy', in C.P. Kindleberger and J.P. Laffargue (eds), *Financial Crises*, Cambridge: Cambridge University Press, pp. 13–39.
Stallings, B. and R. Studart (2005), *Finance for Development: Latin America in Comparative Perspective*, Washington, DC: Bookings Institution Press.
Studart, R. (1995), *Investment Finance in Economic Development*, London and New York: Routledge.

Econometrics

Perhaps because of an emphasis upon drawing theoretical rather than methodological differences with neoclassical and New Keynesian economists, from its inception, Post Keynesian economics exhibits widespread use of econometric methods. In the seminal era of the 1980s, Alfred Eichner with various research partners presented results associated with estimating various 'blocks' of structural equations for a short-period Post Keynesian model of the US economy. Likewise, Philip Arestis undertook a comparable exercise for the UK. More recently, perusal of the *Journal of Post Keynesian Economics* would suggest that Post Keynesian economists are still prepared to use a variety of econometric methods, though concerns with methodological issues, financial instability and the macroeconomy prevail. It is also true that unlike mainstream economics, Post Keynesian scholars are more likely to use other forms of data analysis, such as descriptive statistics, as a central feature of their analysis. The reasons for this are not just accidental. While Post Keynesian economics does not draw upon Keynes's ideas only, in the case of econometrics his somewhat ambiguous sentiments are strongly echoed in the literature. Keynes's essentially philosophical argument, that 'the main *prima facie* objection to the application of the method of multiple correlation to complex economic problems lies in the apparent lack of any adequate degree of uniformity in the environment' (Keynes 1939, p. 567) is pertinent. Yet Keynes (1973b, p. 300) also stresses the need for 'messy acquaintance with the facts'. From this perspective it is not surprising that in the Post Keynesian literature, tension exists between an explicit discussion of the philosophical pronouncements and the practice of economics.

Post Keynesian economics broadly presents itself as accepting an 'open-system' philosophical approach from three main perspectives, that are not always perceived to be consistent (Davidson 1999, 2003–04; Dow 1999, 2003; Lawson 1999). These are critical realism, associated with Tony Lawson, a 'Babylonian' or structured-pluralist perspective associated with Sheila Dow, and an 'encompassing' approach associated with Paul Davidson. Critical realism in economics is primarily associated with the work of Lawson (1997, 2003), who argues that neoclassical economics has its roots in the philosophical system of positivism – and in particular embraces an ontology – where reality comprises the constant conjunction of atomistic events in a closed system. Here, broadly speaking, the intrinsic condition of closure (ICC) – that each cause produces the same effect – and the extrinsic condition of closure (ECC) – that each effect has the same cause – allow an epistemology based on deduction. Thus theoretical explanation can comprise statements of the form 'whenever event "X" then event "Y"', allowing also for stochastic errors. Consequently the mathematical modelling of individual agency is emphasized in neoclassical economics, coupled with econometric testing. Lawson (1997, 2003) describes this approach as 'empirical realism'.

In contrast, an open-system approach presents an organic ontological perspective, which implies that human agency is embedded in a social context. Behaviour is thus irreducible to individual action *per se* but, on the contrary, is both conditional on, and results in, multiple modes of the determination of events. Furthermore, critical realists argue that reality is stratified into three domains. These are the level of actual events, the empirical level of experience and sense impression, and the level of the real, where causal relations are located. Accordingly, critical realism maintains that at best there will be a plurality of partial regularities and processes underlying events, and not predictable or universal event regularities. Econometric inferences are thus inherently problematic.

Davidson's (1996, 1999) methodological approach broadly shares these sentiments. He argues that, in general, the neoclassical research programme invokes the axiom of 'ergodicity'. This implies that the world is predetermined and immutable. In the case of probabilistic inferences, therefore, as the past is a good guide to the future, objective or subjective probabilities will ultimately converge on the true values of the parameters of the probability distribution. For Davidson, the ergodicity axiom is the reason why neoclassical economists emphasize probabilities and statistical/econometric inference in their analysis. In contrast, Davidson argues that Post Keynesians embrace a non-ergodic and transmutable reality view of the world in which probabilities, and thus econometric inference, are not reliable guides to the future. Finally, while echoing the critical realist perspective in stressing the organic nature of society, Dow's (1990, 2005) 'Babylonian' or structured pluralist approach argues that evidence is validly provided by a variety of sources, such as questionnaire and historical sources. This approach also allows for qualified econometric testing, however, because theories cannot be judged according to the principles of a *particular* theoretical structure and because theoretical and empirical diversity is a logical consequence of open-system thought.

For the purpose of further discussion, though adopting the particular language of critical realism, it is maintained here that Post Keynesian philosophical deliberation leads to the rejection of 'empirical realism'. However, the practice of Post Keynesian economics admits of the need for empirical analysis. Herein lies the central tension of this discussion, however. It is clear that both the estimation of regression coefficients and an emphasis upon drawing statistical inferences require the invocation of the closure conditions noted earlier. The ICC is equivalent to assuming the underlying homogeneity of nature and the atomistic combination of objects. This is required to ensure that the coefficients, or functional form, of a regression are constant over time (or space). The ECC implies that all of the causal factors have been included in an econometric study, or that the effect of external factors on internal factors is constant (see also Downward and Mearman 2002; Downward 2007). This last point is equivalent to assuming that countervailing factors are constant. As noted above, the fact that Post Keynesians, like mainstream economists, employ econometric methods, as well as descriptive data, suggests a possibility of logical inconsistency between the methodological aspirations and the practices of Post Keynesians.

In fact, though not clearly articulated in the literature, the employment of econometrics could also reflect the need for Post Keynesians to adopt an appropriate 'rhetoric' in order to engage in critical discussion with neoclassical economists. It has often been argued that Post Keynesian economics only has coherence in terms of an opposition to neoclassical economics. In a related way econometrics might also act as a vehicle for them to demonstrate comparable technical virtuosity with neoclassical economists.

Yet these are rather unsatisfactory and defensive arguments. Post Keynesians have also sought to present a positive case for employing econometric methods that confronts the issues raised by Post Keynesian philosophical concerns. Summarizing a number of arguments, Downward and Mearman (2002) explore the variety of econometric methods, arguing that not only does a burgeoning set of techniques exist for the researcher to calculate statistics, but that they also form part of various inferential frameworks.

Thus, for example, the 'average economic regression' or textbook approach presents a maintained hypothesis that is assumed to capture a correct specification. Following estimation, the random error terms are analysed and transformations of the model then follow to eliminate any problems. In contrast, the David Hendry/LSE approach stems from developments in time-series econometrics. Central to Hendry's research programme is a continual interaction between theory and data; thus knowledge appears to arrive from a complex interaction of deduction and induction. This is demonstrated, for example, in the focus upon error-correction models in the cointegration analysis of time series. Theory describes the long-run relationship, while the data reveal the short-run dynamics of adjustment.

Moreover, in the latter case, it can be argued that the 'average economic regression' approach has its roots in Haavelmo's (1944) influential essay. For Haavelmo the essence of econometrics was to build, identify, estimate and assess various models conforming to the optimizing behaviour given by neoclassical precepts. Importantly, he writes, 'the question is not whether probabilities exist or not, but whether – if we proceed as if they existed – we are able to make statements about real phenomena that are correct for "practical purposes"' (Haavelmo 1944, p. 43). On such a basis, econometrics can be described as a form of instrumentalist reasoning. In contrast, at times Hendry argues that the literal process that generates data – the data-generating process – can be measured by probabilities as a 'statistical generating mechanism'. However, he also stresses that the 'proof of the pudding lies in the eating' as far as econometric models are concerned.

Other econometric methods draw upon Bayesian inferential logic or 'atheoretical' vector-autoregression analysis. In the former case Ed Leamer's (2010) *modus operandi* is to formulate a general family of models, decide what inferences are of importance, which need not be structural relations, express these in terms of parameters, and form prior distributions summarizing any information not in the dataset. The sensitivity of inferences to a particular choice of distributions should be analysed to explore their 'fragility'. In the latter case the concept of exogenous variables is rejected and analysis proceeds in terms of simultaneous relationships between jointly endogenous variables. Finally, there now exists a large-scale microeconometrics literature comprising a broad set of cross-sectional and panel-data methods. For example, LOGIT and PROBIT estimators are employed in cases in which the dependent variable is presumed to reflect simple dichotomous categories, or rank orders. Poisson and Negative Binomial models are now estimated for models which maintain that dependent variables reflect discrete rather than continuous values (that is, comprise integers or counts), along with 'zero-inflated' counterparts to allow for the potential double meaning to zero values in a survey, stemming from either a genuine choice, or one that was constrained by opportunity at the time of the survey.

Other and related developments include allowing for truncated or censored distributions in the dependent variable of non-count data. The seminal example of this is the TOBIT model. Under these circumstances, the assumption is usually that the dependent variable is drawn from a normal distribution but that there is a qualitative break in the measurement of the variable. The TOBIT model has been extended into a double-hurdle model and 'Heckman' sample-selection models. In these cases, separate processes are said to underpin the choice to engage in an activity and the intensity of that activity. They differ in as much that the double-hurdle model effectively treats 'zero' choices as genuine, but unlike the TOBIT case has different potential determinants. In contrast, the Heckman models assume that this is not the case and analyse only the strictly non-zero values in the intensity equation. As this represents a constraint, selection bias needs to be addressed in making inferences from the non-zero subsample.

Interestingly, these latter approaches particularly indicate that econometricians have thought quite deeply about ontological issues. Estimators have been refined in connection with presuppositions about the purported character and context of phenomena such as choices. Further, there has been much debate about the need for econometrics to emphasize research design more, and to try to focus on 'causality' through the use of instrumental variables for the analysis of real and natural experiments, and 'difference-in-difference' approaches on repeated observations, such as panel data to control for omitted variable bias (Angrist and Pischke 2009; Heckman 2010; Leamer 2010). Despite these differences and innovations, however, Downward and Mearman's (2002) position is that the underlying inferential logic of econometric techniques, as typically and currently applied, appeals essentially to measurable probabilities either through the research design and statistical inference, or the latter in more traditional approaches. It follows that embracing the philosophical discourse in Post Keynesian economics means that inferences cannot simply proceed by such an approach.

However, Downward and Mearman also argue that the assumptions involved in estimating coefficients are shared with all (even descriptive) empirical analyses. If this is so, then logically any empirical analysis advocated by Post Keynesians can embrace econometric *estimation*. As far as inferences are concerned, Keynes emphasized the importance of rational belief rather than knowledge as a basis of argument (Keynes 1973a, p. 10). To avoid the problem of induction, Keynes argued that one should examine a particular phenomenon in different contexts, thus engaging in a process of 'negative analogy'. If a phenomenon appears to be a common element between various contexts, then ultimately this can add weight to a particular account of that phenomenon.

From an operational perspective this suggests that various empirical insights should be 'triangulated', that is, compared to insights produced elsewhere. This idea has resonance with, or can be combined with, the tenets of critical realism. Critical realism strongly argues that analysis should pay explicit attention to ontology and, in particular, explanation should focus, by a process of 'retroduction', on elaborating the underlying causal mechanisms of events. Crucially, these are not likely to be synchronized with empirical statements about the events. Consequently, Downward and Mearman (2002, 2007) argue that while descriptive and historical analysis might be employed to explore suggested causal mechanisms, it follows that the effects of their action can be assessed, and hence the purported causal mechanism supported, with reference to more quantitative analysis conducted by econometric techniques. Thus econometric methods can potentially perform a very helpful task in codifying events at the empirical level, suggesting issues for further causal investigation and helping to assess the legitimacy of existing causal claims.

It should be clear from this that Post Keynesians do not accept that explanation and prediction are synonymous, as implied by much neoclassical presentation of econometrics. In Post Keynesian thinking, any quantitative prediction becomes merely a scenario whose legitimacy will rest upon the robustness of the claimed causal mechanism that is tentatively identified and/or supported by econometric estimation. Predictions from an econometric model will always be open to revision.

In closing, it should be emphasized that philosophy and applied economics need to coexist and to develop from mutual discourse, in terms of both articulating the problems of adequately capturing real elements of economic processes and working towards concrete analysis and policy prescription. Some compromise with a purely philosophical inclination seems inevitable in applying econometric, and indeed other empirical, methods.

PAUL DOWNWARD

See also:

Agency; Babylonian Mode of Thought; Critical Realism; *Journal of Post Keynesian Economics*; Keynes's *Treatise on Probability*; Macroeconomic Methodology; Non-ergodicity; Open Systems; Time-series Econometrics.

References

Angrist, J.D. and J.S Pischke (2009), *Mostly Harmless Econometrics, An Empiricist's Companion*, Princeton, NJ and Oxford: Princeton University Press.

Davidson, P. (1996), 'Reality and economic theory', *Journal of Post Keynesian Economics*, **18** (4), 479–508.

Davidson, P. (1999), 'Taxonomy, communication and rhetorical strategy', *Journal of Post Keynesian Economics*, **22** (1), 125–30.

Davidson, P. (2003–4), 'Setting the record straight on "A History of Post Keynesian Economics"', *Journal of Post Keynesian Economics*, **26** (2), 245–72.

Dow, S.C. (1990),'Post Keynesianism as political economy: a methodological discussion', *Review of Political Economy*, **2** (3), 345–58.

Dow, S.C. (1999), 'Post Keynesianism and critical realism: what is the connection?', *Journal of Post Keynesian Economics*, **22** (1), 15–34.

Dow, S.C. (2003), 'The Babylonian mode of thought', in J.E. King (ed.), *The Elgar Companion to Post Keynesian Economics*, Cheltenham, UK and Northampton, MA, USA: Edward Elgar, pp. 11–15.

Dow, S.C. (2005), 'Axioms and Babylonian thought: a reply', *Journal of Post Keynesian Economics*, **27** (3) 385–91.

Downward, P.M. (2007), 'Method, quantitative', in M. Harwig (ed.), *Dictionary of Critical Realism*, Abingdon and New York: Routledge, pp. 311–12.

Downward, P.M. and A. Mearman (2002), 'Critical realism and econometrics: constructive dialogue with Post Keynesian economics', *Metroeconomica*, **53** (4), 391–415.

Downward, P.M. and A. Mearman (2007), 'Retroduction as mixed-methods triangulation in economic research: reorienting economics into social science', *Cambridge Journal of Economics*, **31** (1), 77–99.

Haavelmo, T. (1944), 'The probability approach in econometrics', *Econometrica*, **12** (Supplement), 1–115.

Heckman, J.J. (2010), 'Building bridges between structural and program evaluation approaches to evaluating policy', *Journal of Economic Literature*, **48** (2), 356–98.

Keynes, J.M. (1939), 'Professor Tinbergen's method', *Economic Journal*, **44** (195), 555–68.

Keynes, J.M. (1973a), *The Collected Writings of John Maynard Keynes. Volume VIII: A Treatise on Probability*, London: Macmillan for the Royal Economic Society.

Keynes, J.M. (1973b), *The Collected Writings of John Maynard Keynes. Volume XIV: The General Theory and After. Part II: Defence and Development*, London: Macmillan for the Royal Economic Society.

Lawson, T. (1997), *Economics and Reality*, London and New York: Routledge.

Lawson, T. (1999), 'Connections and distinctions: Post Keynesianism and critical realism', *Journal of Post Keynesian Economics*, **22** (1), 3–14.

Lawson, T. (2003), *Reorienting Economics*, London and New York: Routledge.

Leamer, E.E. (2010), 'Tantalus on the road to asymptopia', *Journal of Economics Perspectives*, **24** (2), 31–46.

Economic Development

Post Keynesian economics is not primarily known for its contribution to development economics. There is little of direct relevance to the problems of 'catching-up' development in J.M. Keynes's *General Theory*, although this problematic was, of course, part of his concern with international economic and financial reform after the Second World War. This emphasis on the economics of advanced capitalism and on international economic relations has remained characteristic of Post Keynesian economics since. It would, however, be wrong to conclude that Post Keynesian economists have not made important contributions to the theoretical and practical concerns of late economic development. Quite the contrary, leading first-generation Post Keynesians such as Nicholas Kaldor (1967), Joan Robinson (Harcourt and Kerr 2009, chapter 9) and Michał Kalecki throughout his working life actively participated in ongoing debates on economic development, not least as advisers to developing country governments. Later Post Keynesian analysis has mainly focused on trade and finance issues of late development, but has tended to neglect Kalecki's explicit focus on the internal socio-economic and political transition dynamics of developing economies. This increasingly important debate has therefore been dominated by economic traditions from outside Post Keynesianism.

Post Keynesian approaches to economic development have been informed by general features of Post Keynesian economics in three main respects. First, investment is causally prior to savings in that it does not depend on accumulated savings. Investors and savers also act independently of one another, and there is therefore no presumption that (capitalist) savings are automatically re-invested. This differentiates Post Keynesian development economics both from classical (Ricardian)-inspired dualist development theories, such as those advanced by Arthur Lewis, as well as from neoclassical capital market theory. Second, Post Keynesians reject the Miller–Modigliani 'irrelevance theorems' that suggest a total dichotomy between finance and the real economy and hold that firm performance is entirely determined by real variables. For the case of developing economies, the non-validity of these theorems is not simply a matter of friction in existing capital markets, for example through a high liquidity preference of banks and the vulnerability of developing country financial systems to changes in credit conditions. More basically, the transformation of financial flows (often from abroad) into a concrete stock of capital, that can sustain long-term capital accumulation, faces systematic learning, administrative and institutional–political constraints. Debt, once contracted, cannot be dealt with through deflation and 'decumulation', as in neoclassical and Austrian business-cycle theory – that is by 'getting prices right' internally – since the underlying problem is not one of a temporarily inefficient allocation of existing resources, or even of the endogenous instabilities of self-sustaining capitalist accumulation paths, but one of structural socio-economic obstacles to industrialization. Third, a corollary of the above is that Post Keynesians reject the neoclassical argument in favour of free international trade as the main route to a successful insertion of developing economies into the world economy. Since prices are not a reliable measure of true economic scarcity and economic agents do not act solely as choice-theoretic automatons but also as members of social groups, comparative advantage is not a reliable driver of international integration.

This opposition of basic elements of Post Keynesian perspectives on economic development to neoclassical theory has its counterpart in the important role early Post Keynesian contributions have played for structuralist analysis (Palma 1978; Blankenburg et al. 2008; Rodríguez 2009). This Post Keynesian-cum-structuralist approach to economic development builds on three main propositions: Post Keynesians as well as structuralists argue that economic growth is both sector and activity specific, where the concept of sector refers to manufacturing or agriculture and that of activity to, say, R&D activities or education (Palma 2005). In this view, informed by the Kaldor–Verdoorn law, overall productivity growth is a function of output growth in the manufacturing sector due to this sector's propensity to high static and dynamic increasing returns to scale. Activities matter in the sense that their overall impact on growth depends on the nature of the sector in which they operate. By contrast, conventional neoclassical growth analysis with constant returns to scale, but also more recent 'endogenous' AK growth models with constant returns to hybrid (human-cum-physical) capital, are both sector and activity indifferent. Later neoclassical developments are activity specific in that constant returns to (hybrid) capital are attributed to research-intensive activities in horizontal and vertical innovation efforts, but they remain sector indifferent in that these activities are not associated with the material properties of any particular sector. Kaldorian-style cumulative growth dynamics through embodied technological change are explicitly rejected (Aghion and Howitt 1998).

Second, the world economic system is regarded as divided into a centre and a periphery intrinsically related to each other through dynamic interaction largely driven by their different productive and sectoral structures. Many of the periphery's problems in catching up with advanced capitalism, such as poor infrastructure, structural unemployment and inflation and rising foreign indebtedness are the result of an economic structure that has at least partially been determined by its interaction with the centre. While the centre's productive structure has become homogeneous and diversified, the periphery's structure of production remains heterogeneous and specialized. Heterogeneous because economic activities with significant productivity differences continue to exist alongside each other, such as a high productivity commodity-export sector and subsistence agriculture with a highly inelastic supply (Kaldor 1957). Specialized because the export sector, typically concentrated on unprocessed primary products, represents a high proportion of GDP but has very limited linkages.

Finally, given this structural heterogeneity, macroeconomic imbalances and growth divergence are bound to accelerate in the absence of policy intervention. Structural unemployment will persist in developing economies so long as the modern sector has to carry the heavy burden of absorbing not only the growth of active population but also labour displaced from traditional sectors. Given its excessive specialization, the periphery will also have to rely on a substantial proportion of its demand for manufactured products being serviced via imports. With high income elasticities for these imports and low income elasticities for imports of primary products from the periphery, there is a material limit to the rate of growth of real income in the periphery relative to that of the centre. Although this challenge can be met temporarily by an international financial system that tolerates sustained trade deficits arising from domestic industrialization, a long-term solution can only be achieved by a policy space within developing nations that allows for a switch from import substitution to export diversification towards more income-elastic products. Latin America tried the former line to its detriment in the 1970s, and East Asia has succeeded along the latter line largely because of a unique constellation of internal political and external economic factors.

Kaldor (1967) largely built on these considerations to provide an ideal-type argument for sector-specific export-led growth in catching-up economies. What was required was a switch from import substitution in the initial stages of light industrialization for which domestic markets would suffice, to export-led growth once the manufacturing sector had grown sufficiently to become reliant on export demand. Kaldor (1959) did not hesitate to propose unpopular measures to support high rates of domestic investment – for example, a tax reform for Chile that would penalize dividends and idle land, while incentivizing profits retained for real investment – but he did not embark on a systematic analysis of the obstacles to the implementation of such reforms in developing economies. Kalecki shared the view that the core problem of catching-up development was the organization of manufacturing and infrastructure investment, and that the key leakage of development finance arose from the disparity between product- and sector-specific income elasticities of import between the centre and the periphery (Kalecki 1951, 1963). Kalecki's account of structural (rather than demand-led) inflation in developing countries became central to structuralist analysis and was also taken up by Kaldor (1967). This was based on the distinction between basic and luxury goods, and argued that unless the supply of (initially largely agriculturally produced) necessities could keep pace with the growth of an industrial workforce and industrial investment, the resulting inflationary pressures would reduce historically low real wages and see workers carry the main burden of industrialization. More explicitly than Kaldor, Kalecki analysed the political determinants of late development. He saw land reform as a core requirement of late industrialization since, without it, increased agricultural incomes due to a higher demand for necessities would be absorbed by landed rentiers. Since, in his view, domestic private investment was unlikely to be attracted to high-risk investment on the scale required for late industrialization, and foreign investment by large multinationals was expensive, for example due to transfer pricing (Kalecki 1954), Kalecki advocated state-led planned industrialization. This, he thought, was most likely to be carried through by 'intermediate regimes' (Kalecki 1964), dominated by the lower middle classes with little stake in land ownership and at least the potential to resist big business and foreign investor demands. In retrospect, it is clear that Kalecki, who had mainly Nasser's Egypt in the 1950s and 1960s in mind, both overestimated the political autonomy of 'intermediate regimes' and underestimated the role of potentially repressive military leadership.

Subsequent Post Keynesian contributions to the debates on economic development have largely focused on four aspects: Kaldor's export-led growth model and the implications of a foreign exchange constraint on economic development (for example, McCombie and Thirlwall 1994), the analysis of development finance (Chick and Arestis 1995; Eshag 2000), the specific nature of (Minskian) financial fragilities in developing countries (Burlamaqui and Kregel 2005; Taylor 2010), and international economic reform to facilitate a productive insertion of developing economies into the world economy (Davidson 2009). Most of these contributions have retained the focus of early Post Keynesian analysis on middle-income developing economies. Apart from an application of Post Keynesian thought on late economic development to low-income developing economies, probably the largest lacuna to date is a lack of further systematic analysis of the internal transition dynamics of these economies. Confronted with the widespread failure of IMF structural adjustment programmes to promote economic development during the 1980s and early 1990s, neoclassical theory has shifted its argument from 'getting prices right' to 'getting institutions right'. Its 'good governance agenda' identifies as the main obstacle to economic development the (unexplained) corruption of developing country institutions and their consequent inability to implement market-friendly reforms. Clearly, from a Post Keynesian perspective that takes history seriously, the answer to underdevelopment cannot be the formal prescription of market-friendly liberal institutions across the board. An integration of the sector-specific dynamic growth perspective of Post Keynesian thought – including apart from Kaldor's and Kalecki's founding contributions also the work of close relatives to Post Keynesianism, such as Albert Hirschman – with a similarly dynamic and context-specific analysis of institutional change under catching-up conditions would therefore certainly constitute a relevant future contribution of Post Keynesianism to heterodox development economics.

STEPHANIE BLANKENBURG
GABRIEL PALMA

See also:

Balance-of-payments-constrained Economic Growth; Brazil; Development Finance; Export-led Growth; Growth Theory; Innovation; Kaldorian Economics; Kaleckian Economics; Latin American Structuralism.

References

Aghion, P. and P. Howitt (1998), *Endogenous Growth Theory*, Cambridge, MA: MIT Press.
Blankenburg, S., J.G. Palma and F. Tregenna (2008), 'Structuralism', in S. Durlauf and L. Blume (eds), *The New Palgrave Dictionary of Economics*, Vol. 8, Basingstoke: Palgrave Macmillan, pp. 69–74.
Burlamaqui, L. and J. Kregel (2005), 'Innovation, competition and financial vulnerability in economic development', *Brazilian Journal of Political Economy*, **25** (2), 5–22.

Chick, V. and P. Arestis (eds) (1995), *Finance, Development and Structural Change: Post-Keynesian Perspectives*, Aldershot, UK and Brookfield, VT, USA: Edward Elgar.

Davidson, P. (2009), *The Keynes Solution: The Path to Global Prosperity*, Basingstoke: Palgrave Macmillan.

Eshag, E. (2000), *Fiscal and Monetary Policies and Problems in Developing Countries*, Cambridge: Cambridge University Press.

Harcourt, G.C. and P. Kerr (2009), *Joan Robinson*, Basingstoke: Palgrave Macmillan.

Kaldor, N. (1957), 'La inflación chilena y la estructura de la producción' ['Chilean inflation and the structure of production'], *Panorama Económico*, **180**, November.

Kaldor, N. (1959), 'Economic problems of Chile', in Kaldor, *Essays on Economic Policy*, Vol. II, London: Duckworth, 1964, pp. 233–87.

Kaldor, N. (1967), *Strategic Factors in Economic Development*, Ithaca, NY: New York State School of Industrial and Labor Relations.

Kalecki, M. (1951), 'Report on the main current economic problems of Israel'; reprinted in J. Osiatynski (ed.), *Collected Works of Michał Kalecki. Volume V: Developing Economies*, Oxford: Oxford University Press, 1993, pp. 95–121.

Kalecki, M. (1954), 'The problem of financing development'; reprinted in J. Osiatynski (ed.), *Collected Works of Michał Kalecki. Volume V: Developing Economies*, Oxford: Oxford University Press, 1993, pp. 23–44.

Kalecki, M. (1963), 'Problems of financing economic development in a mixed economy'; reprinted in J. Osiatynski (ed.); *Collected Works of Michał Kalecki. Volume V: Developing Economies*, Oxford: Oxford University Press, 1993, pp. 45–60.

Kalecki, M. (1964), 'Observations on social and economic aspects of "intermediate regimes"'; reprinted in J. Osiatynski (ed.), *Collected Works of Michał Kalecki. Volume V: Developing Economies*, Oxford: Oxford University Press, 1993, pp. 6–12.

McCombie, J.S.L. and A.P. Thirlwall (1994), *Economic Growth and the Balance of Payments Constraint*, London: St. Martin's Press.

Palma, J.G. (1978), 'Dependency: a formal theory of underdevelopment, or a methodology for the analysis of concrete situations of underdevelopment?', *World Development*, **6** (7/8), 881–924.

Palma, J.G. (2005), 'Four sources of de-industrialisation and a new concept of the Dutch Disease', in J.A. Ocampo (ed.), *Beyond Reforms: Structural Dynamics and Macroeconomic Vulnerability*, Stanford, CA: Stanford University Press, pp. 71–116.

Rodríguez, O. (2009), *El Estructuralismo Latinoamericano* [*Latin American Structuralism*], Mexico City: Siglo XXI.

Taylor, L. (2010), *Maynard's Revenge: Keynesianism and the Collapse of Free Market Macroeconomics*, Cambridge, MA: Harvard University Press.

Economic Policy

The general approaches to economic policy arise out of analyses of the economy and the issues and problems identified by the analyses. The features of Post Keynesian macroeconomic policy are derived from the basic insight of Michał Kalecki and John Maynard Keynes for the workings of industrialized market economies, namely that a *laissez-faire* market economy will not usually generate full employment. The essential cause of that failure to create full employment is not some rigidities or 'imperfections' of monopolistic competition, trade unions and so on, which could potentially be removed through government policy. It is rather that a *laissez-faire* market economy would exhibit elements of instability with booms and busts, and periods of crisis. Further, a market economy would not usually generate a level of aggregate demand consistent with full employment. Arestis and Sawyer (2010b, 2011) present the features of a Post Keynesian analysis from which they draw a range of policy conclusions. The achievement of full employment is a major policy objective for Post Keynesian economists through the inherent desirability of full employment and because their analysis identifies it as a general feature of a market economy. Post Keynesian policies in this direction then require policies and institutional arrangements supportive of high levels of demand.

The Post Keynesian approach to fiscal policy is informed by the relationship:

$$(\text{Savings} - \text{Investment}) = (\text{Exports} + \text{Net Income} - \text{Imports}) + (\text{Government Expenditure} - \text{Taxation}),$$

where (Exports + Net Income − Imports) is the current account surplus, and equal to the deficit on capital account. If savings and investment intentions were equal and consistent with full employment, and if the exchange rate (or other variable) ensured a current account balance, then the budget deficit could be zero and full employment realized. But the Post Keynesian approach is that there are no market forces ensuring that savings and investment are in balance at full employment, and indeed in general the perception that there is a tendency for savings to exceed investment. In the case where savings would exceed investment at full-employment income, then some combination of trade surplus and government budget deficit would be required to balance the excess of savings over investment to maintain full employment, and indeed to permit the savings intentions to be realized. Running a budget deficit in these circumstances helps to sustain full employment, but it can also be seen that the excess of savings over investment funds the budget deficit. Hence there is no 'crowding out', or upward pressure on interest rates.

Lerner put the case for what he termed functional finance, which 'rejects completely the traditional doctrines of "sound finance" and the principle of trying to balance the budget over a solar year or any other arbitrary period' (1943[1966], p. 355), and adjustment of total spending to eliminate both unemployment and inflation. 'No matter how much interest has to be paid on the debt, taxation must not be applied unless it is necessary to keep spending down to prevent inflation. The interest can be paid by borrowing still more' (ibid., p. 356). Lerner summarized the answers to arguments against deficit spending by saying that the national debt does not have to keep on increasing, and that even if it does the interest does not have to be paid from current taxes. Further, interest payments on bonds are an internal transfer.

The use of fiscal policy and budget deficit provides a major way through which high levels of economic activity can be secured (Arestis and Sawyer 2010a). But there may be other ways. Although monetary policy has in recent years been focused on inflation targeting, it is intended to do so through the impact of interest rates on the level of economic activity. Post Keynesians have taken different positions on the effectiveness of interest rates on the level of demand, with some seeing interest rates as having little effect (Sawyer 2006) through to those who have seen them as potentially having greater impact though with the limit of zero nominal interest rates. Post Keynesians have generally advocated low interest rates for reasons of impact on demand and the distributional implications of interest rates. Smithin (2007), for example, defends a monetary policy which is 'an attempt to stabilize the real policy rate at some "low" level, [as] the best option for monetary policy. It is also the most consistent with the traditional Keynesian advocacy of cheap money' (p. 101; see also Symposium 2007).

A fruitful way of considering other alternatives is to consider Kalecki's discussion of 'three ways to full employment' (Kalecki, 1944). His three ways were budget deficits, stimulation of investment and redistribution of income, where each of those would serve to stimulate the level of demand. Kalecki argued that there were limits to the promotion of investment. This can be summarized by a consideration of $I/Y = (\Delta K/K).(K/Y)$ where I is net investment, equal to the change in the capital stock ΔK, and K/Y is the capital–output ratio. The share of investment in GDP is then given by the multiple of the underlying growth rate (which sets the growth of the capital stock $\Delta K/K$) and the capital–output ratio. A higher share of investment would involve creation of spare capacity and a likely decline in the rate of profit, which would limit the possibilities (and there are severe environmental limitations of faster growth). The redistribution of income from profits to wages, from high to low-income earners, would tend to raise the propensity to consume and lower the propensity to save. Additions can be made to Kalecki's list – for example, policies designed to lower the propensity to save would help raise the level of demand.

Some Post Keynesian authors (for example, Wray 1998) have advocated the policy of 'employer of last resort' (ELR) whereby the government stands ready to employ anyone at a predetermined money wage (which may be set to ensure that the wage is sufficient to remove the worker from poverty). It is argued that such a policy would not be inflationary (since the wage paid by the government as ELR remains unchanged) and secures full employment (in that anyone who wishes to work is able to do so, albeit at the ELR wage).

There would be a concern to ensure that the international financial system was conducive to high levels of aggregate demand. In the context of the Bretton Woods fixed exchange rate system, this concern was translated into policy arrangements which sought to ensure that countries which were running trade deficits were not forced into deflationary policies to correct the trade deficit. Keynes (1980, p. 176) sought to design an international payments system which transferred 'the onus of adjustment from the debtor to the creditor position' and aimed 'at the substitution of an expansionist, in place of contractionist, pressure on world trade'. Davidson, building on the work of Keynes, proposed a 'new international payments system' (1992, p. 157) designed 'to resolve payments imbalances while simultaneously promoting full-employment economic growth and a long-run stable international standard of value' (ibid., p. 153). These proposals included the unit of account and reserve asset for international liquidity being the International Money Clearing Unit (IMCU), with each nation's central bank committed to guarantee one-way convertibility from IMCU deposits at the clearing union to its domestic money. Davidson advocated 'an overdraft system to make available short-term unused creditor balances at the Clearing House to finance the productive international transactions of others who need short-term credit', and 'a trigger mechanism to encourage any creditor national to spend . . . "excessive" credit balances accumulated by running current account surpluses' (p. 160). Finally, 'if a country is at *full employment* and still has a tendency toward persistent international deficits on its current account, then this is *prima facie* evidence that it does not possess the productive capacity to maintain its current standard of living' (p. 163; original emphasis).

The era of floating exchange rates has led to a different set of concerns, namely the effects of the large flows across the currency exchanges and the volatility of exchange rates. The volatility of exchange rates (and indeed of prices in financial markets more generally) comes as no surprise to Post Keynesians. In a world of uncertainty, where the equilibrium price in a market is unknowable (and indeed may not exist in any meaningful sense), traders will not (and cannot) hold 'rational expectations' of future prices. They will be influenced by the views of others, and by a variety of information, including recent trends in price. One policy proposal which addresses these concerns is the 'Tobin tax'.

Inflation, or the fear of inflation, may be seen as limiting the achievement of full employment, though Post Keynesian analysis would cast doubt on the existence of any immutable 'natural rate of unemployment'. In so far as there is an 'inflation barrier' such that lower unemployment would tend to have inflationary consequences, this barrier is structuralist in nature arising from shortage of capacity, and would change over time and can be influenced by appropriate economic policies (Arestis and Sawyer 2005). Post Keynesian views on the endogenous nature of money and its creation through the credit process would deny any causal role for money in the inflationary process. Deflation (whether brought about through fiscal or monetary policies) is seen as a blunt and inefficient instrument for the control of inflation. Some would envisage that any inflationary problems could be addressed through incomes policy of the social contract form or through tax-based incomes policy, while others would point to the importance of institutional arrangements and the creation of sufficient productive capacity.

The attainment of high levels of productivity requires an appropriate work intensity and commitment on the part of the labour force as well as the provision of sufficient capital equipment, training, skills and management. In many market economies, unemployment (and more particularly the threat of it) serves as a significant mechanism for imposing a high level of work intensity (Kalecki 1943). Unemployment is seen as performing a systemic function (of aiding the disciplining of workers). This is not to argue that unemployment is *necessary* to ensure work effort; indeed, unemployment heightens fear and brings demoralization, which serve to undermine it, and different market economies have drawn on mechanisms other than unemployment.

The factors which influence investment and thereby the size of the capital stock (such as profitability and capacity utilization) are generally rather different from the factors which determine the size of the workforce (mainly demographic). From that crude observation, we could say that there is no particular reason to think that the capital stock will be adequate for the provision of full employment. There are rather limited opportunities, especially in the short run, for substitution between labour and capital. We would expect that after a period of prolonged slow growth (such as the past two decades) investment may have fallen short of what would be required to sustain full employment.

The pace of growth is generally seen as driven by the growth of demand, with supply (of labour, capital equipment and so on) adjusting to the growth of demand. The effective supply of labour can vary through changes in labour force participation rates, training and skill acquisition and movement of workers from areas of disguised unemployment and low productivity. The amount of capital equipment is determined through the cumulative effect of investment.

The foreign trade position can constrain the rate of growth, in that a growing deficit will emerge if there is a tendency for the growth of imports to exceed the growth of exports. When the (domestic) income elasticity of demand for imports is greater than the (world) income elasticity of demand for the country's exports, then the maintenance of a non-exploding trade deficit requires that the domestic growth rate is sufficiently below the world growth rate so that actual imports and exports grow in line with one another (McCombie and Thirlwall 1997). One policy implication which can be drawn is that continuing growth of output requires growth of exports, and supply-side policies (such as industrial policy) can be required to ensure the production of goods and services for which there is a strong export demand.

Post Keynesian analysis views the market economy as prone to cycles and to instabilities, and nowhere more so than in the financial sector. Post Keynesian analysis has generally been sceptical of the benefits of financial liberalization, and Post Keynesians have argued for effective regulation of the banking industry and the financial sector.

The general Post Keynesian approach would be based on the view that the creation of high levels of aggregate demand is necessary for the achievement of full employment. The creation of high levels of aggregate demand can proceed directly through higher government expenditure and/or lower taxation, indirectly through the stimulation of investment and the redistribution of income towards higher spending groups, and through the encouragement of institutional arrangements which are conducive to high levels of demand. But a high level of aggregate demand is a necessary, though not sufficient, condition. Policies to ensure adequate capacity, the creation of a low-inflation environment, an equitable distribution of productive activity and a sustainable balance of trade position are also required.

MALCOLM SAWYER

See also:

Balance-of-payments-constrained Economic Growth; Bretton Woods; Budget Deficits; Employer of Last Resort; Exchange Rates; Financial Reform; Financialization; Fiscal Policy; Full Employment; Inflation; Monetary Policy; Rate of Interest; Tobin Tax; Unemployment.

References

Arestis, P. and M. Sawyer (2005), 'Aggregate demand, conflict and capacity in the inflationary process', *Cambridge Journal of Economics*, **29** (6), 959–74.
Arestis, P. and M. Sawyer (2010a), 'The return of fiscal policy', *Journal of Post Keynesian Economics*, **32** (3), 327–46.
Arestis, P. and M. Sawyer (2010b), '21st century Keynesian economic policy', in Arestis and Sawyer (eds), *21st Century Keynesian Economics*, Basingstoke: Palgrave Macmillan, pp. 81–119.
Arestis, P. and M. Sawyer (2011), 'A new paradigm for macroeconomic policy', *International Journal of Public Policy*, **7** (1–3), 22–39.
Davidson, P. (1992), 'Reforming the world's money', *Journal of Post Keynesian Economics*, **15** (2), 153–79.
Kalecki, M. (1943), 'Political aspects of full employment', *Political Quarterly*, **14** (4), 322–31.

Kalecki, M. (1944), 'Three ways to full employment', in Oxford University Institute of Statistics, *The Economics of Full Employment*, Oxford: Blackwell, pp. 39–58.

Keynes, J.M. (1980), *The Collected Writings of John Maynard Keynes, Volume XXVII. Activities 1940–1946. Shaping the Post-War World: Employment and Commodities*, London: Macmillan for the Royal Economic Society.

Lerner, A. (1943), 'Functional finance and the federal debt', *Social Research*, **10** (1), 38–51; reprinted in M.G. Mueller (ed.), *Readings in Macroeconomics*, New York: Holt, Rinehart & Winston, 1996 pp. 353–60 (citations refer to the reprint).

McCombie, J.S.L. and A.P. Thirlwall (1997), 'The dynamic Harrod foreign trade multiplier and the demand-oriented approach to economic growth: an evaluation', *International Review of Applied Economics*, **11** (1), 5–26.

Sawyer, M. (2006), 'A Kaleckian analysis of monetary policy', *Intervention: European Journal of Economics and Economic Policies*, **3** (2), 331–50.

Smithin, J. (2007), 'A real interest rate rule for monetary policy?', *Journal of Post Keynesian Economics*, **30** (1), 101–18.

Symposium (2007), 'The state of Post Keynesian interest rate policy', *Journal of Post Keynesian Economics*, **30** (1), 3–141.

Wray, L.R. (1998), *Understanding Modern Money: The Key to Full Employment and Price Stability*, Cheltenham, UK and Northampton, MA, USA: Edward Elgar.

Effective Demand

Effective demand is a concept of central importance in Post Keynesian economics. The principle of effective demand states that the level of economic activity – that is, aggregate nominal income and employment – is determined by the level of effective demand, which is, in turn, determined by the conjunction of aggregate supply and demand conditions. Demand conditions are held to play a leading role in this relationship.

The determination of effective demand, and hence the levels of nominal income and employment, results from the interaction of aggregate supply and demand functions that describe relationships between levels of employment and levels of business proceeds. Business proceeds constitute receipts from the sale of final goods and services net of an allowance for the use of capital equipment and thus represent, in the aggregate, the total income of the community. The aggregate supply function describes a relationship between expected proceeds and the levels of employment that firms are willing to offer on the basis of these expectations. The aggregate supply function, then, suggests that firms base their employment offers on the value of goods and services that they think they can sell. Not surprisingly, as expected proceeds rise, so, too, do employment offers (see schedule *Z*, Figure 7). The aggregate supply function so described can be formulated on the basis of either Marshallian or Kaleckian microfoundations. In the first case, firms equate short-run price expectations with the marginal costs of production in order to determine the profit-maximizing level of output, on which employment offers are then based. In the second case, firms set

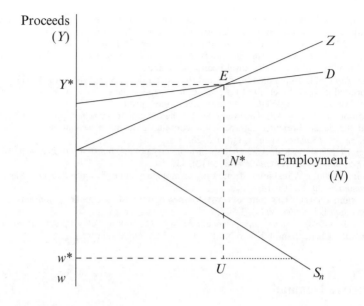

Key
D = aggregate demand function
Z = aggregate supply function
E = point of effective demand
Y = business proceeds (aggregate nominal income)
N = employment
w = real wage
U = involuntary unemployment
S_n = labour supply

Figure 7   The principle of effective demand and labour market outcomes

prices as a mark-up over average costs, with both expected proceeds and consequent employment offers then determined by the volume of output that firms expect to sell at these prices (Asimakopulos 1991, pp. 53–7).

The aggregate demand function, meanwhile, describes a relationship between received proceeds and the levels of employment that generate these receipts. It therefore relates aggregate expenditures in the economy to the level of employment, which is a determinant of household income. According to the aggregate demand function, higher levels of employment are associated with higher household income, and hence higher aggregate expenditures and business proceeds (see schedule *D*, Figure 7). As this description suggests, some of the components of aggregate demand are endogenous – that is, influenced by the levels of income and employment that they, in turn, help to determine. However, other components of aggregate demand are autonomous – that is, determined independently of the levels of income and employment.

Two important properties of the aggregate demand function mean that it will not, in general, be identical to the aggregate supply function. The first concerns the behaviour of endogenous components of aggregate demand. Although the principle of effective demand associates an increase in employment with both an increase in output and an increase in expenditures, the additional expenditures associated with any increase in employment are understood to constitute only a fraction of the value of the additional output (and hence income) that this increase in employment generates. This is due to Keynes's 'fundamental psychological law', according to which the marginal propensity to consume out of additional income is less than one (Keynes 1936, p. 96). Hence the slope of the aggregate demand function differs from (specifically, is smaller than) that of the aggregate supply function, as illustrated in Figure 7.

The second important property of the aggregate demand function concerns the behaviour of autonomous components of aggregate demand. According to the principle of effective demand, autonomous expenditures are genuinely independent of endogenous expenditures, so that there is no automatic tendency for variations in the latter to be offset by changes in the former. This can be understood most simply in the context of a closed economy with no active government sector, in which case it reduces to the proposition that saving does not create investment. This is so for two reasons. First, in a money-using economy, saving does not in and of itself constitute a current demand for goods, as it does in a barter economy. In other words, saving is not identical to investment. (Indeed, saving does not even constitute a demand for consumption goods in some specific future period. In an environment of uncertainty, a decision to avoid commitment to goods and services in the present – that is, to save – represents an indefinite postponement of expenditure.)

Second, saving – considered now as distinct from investment – has no direct impact on the rate of interest, to which investment is, in principle, sensitive. Hence an increase in saving cannot automatically create offsetting investment expenditures through variations in the interest rate (as, for example, in the classical loanable funds theory). An important feature of the principle of effective demand, then, is its treatment of the interest rate as a monetary variable, the determination of which is relatively autonomous from the income-determination process. This autonomy is achieved in Keynes (1936) by the liquidity preference theory of the interest rate, and in contemporary Post Keynesian theory by central bank determination of short-term interest rates in an endogenous money environment. Note that the interest rate need not be *absolutely* autonomous from the income-generation process. It is quite possible for changes in income to have some impact on the interest rate via changes in liquidity preference or via a central bank reaction function. Neither alters the operation of the principle of effective demand, however. What ultimately emerges from this analysis is a system in which the level of income (and by extension, employment) rather than the interest rate is the key adjustment variable responsible for equating investment and saving, according to a strict causal schema in which changes in investment spending cause (via their impact on the level of income) changes in saving (Amadeo 1989, pp. 1–2).

The level of effective demand is determined by the point of effective demand, at which the aggregate supply and demand functions intersect (point E in Figure 7). The proceeds resulting from this effective demand and the associated volume of employment constitute the economy's equilibrium levels of income and employment. Because the former is a nominal magnitude, both the price level and the level of real output can be recovered from the point of effective demand, so that the principle of effective demand is a theory of *both* price *and* quantity determination (see Hartwig 2006). The point of effective demand is an equilibrium in the sense that, at this point, the expected proceeds necessary to encourage firms to offer a particular level of employment (as determined by the aggregate supply function) are exactly equal to received proceeds at this level of employment (as determined by the aggregate demand function). However, the importance attached to historical time and uncertainty in Post Keynesian economics necessitate that care is taken when interpreting the precise nature of this equilibrium relative to equilibrium constructs found in other approaches to economics (Kregel 1976; Chick 2002).

Several salient features of the principle of effective demand as described above are worthy of note. First, because the aggregate supply function will, in general, coincide with the aggregate demand function at only one level of income and employment, the principle of effective demand refutes Say's law, according to which supply always creates its own demand. Say's law is, in fact, revealed to be a special case, in which the aggregate demand and supply functions are identical. In this special case, the resulting indeterminacy in the levels of income and employment is resolved by the equation of labour supply and demand – so that variations in the real wage, by establishing a market-clearing level of employment, determine aggregate income (see Figure 8). In general, however, the aggregate supply and demand functions will coincide at only one level of employment, at which point the level of income and the value of the real wage are also determined. (The real wage may, in fact, be constant along the aggregate supply function if the latter is based on Kaleckian microfoundations, but will systematically decline as the level of employment rises if the aggregate supply function is based on Marshallian microfoundations.) Whether or not the level of employment and real wage so established correspond to a point on the economy's labour supply schedule is an open question. In general it will not, and the resulting deficient demand for labour will give rise to involuntary unemployment (see Figure 7). In the general case, then, variations in effective demand cause changes in income, employment and the real wage (to the extent that this is non-constant), and there is no automatic tendency for the labour market to clear.

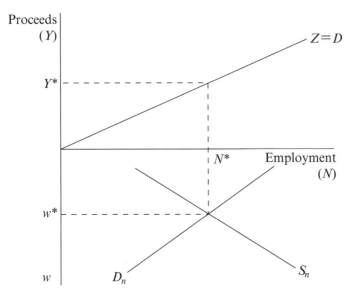

Key
D = aggregate demand function
Z = aggregate supply function
Y = business proceeds (aggregate nominal income)
N = employment
w = real wage
S_n = labour supply
D_n = labour demand

Figure 8   The special case of Say's law

Implicit in the contrast above is the observation that, according to the principle of effective demand, the volumes of employment and production depend on firms' anticipations of the value of output that they can sell, rather than the equation of the marginal physical product and marginal disutility of labour. This draws attention to a number of other salient features of the principle of effective demand: the importance that it attaches to the goods market rather than the labour market as the proximate determinant of the scale of economic activity; the central role it ascribes to firms in actively setting employment and output, rather than passively responding to labour market outcomes; and the epistemological significance of explaining economic activity in terms of *expected* future sales revenues rather than the *known* productive capacities of factors of production.

Several important controversies surround the principle of effective demand. In the first place, and partly as a result of Keynes's original exposition, the terms 'aggregate demand' and 'effective demand' are frequently confused, and there is a longstanding debate as to whether the aggregate demand function describes the proceeds *actually* received by firms at different levels of employment, or the proceeds they *expect* to receive at these various levels of employment (see, for example, Hartwig 2007). As regards the first of these issues, it should be clear from the foregoing discussion that aggregate demand is a *schedule* (which describes the relationship between levels of employment and received proceeds), whereas effective demand is a *point* (specifically, the point where the aggregate demand and supply functions coincide) (see also Chick 1983, pp. 64–5). As regards the second issue, the aggregate demand function can be thought of as describing either actual or expected magnitudes. Indeed, it is useful to think of two different aggregate demand functions, one describing actual and the other expected proceeds (Amadeo 1989; Allain 2009) – although particular microfoundations are required in order to generate an expected aggregate demand function that is upward sloping (Asimakopulos 1991, pp. 43–4). Where the expected aggregate demand function intersects the aggregate supply function determines the level of employment within any production period; where the actual aggregate demand function intersects the aggregate supply function determines the equilibrium position described earlier, at which expected sales proceeds equal proceeds actually received. This equilibrium will actually be achieved when the expected and actual aggregate demand functions and the aggregate supply function all coincide at a single level of employment (see Figure 9).

A further controversy concerns Pasinetti's (1997, 2001) claim that standard expositions of the principle of effective demand succeed only in identifying a *point* of effective demand, rather than anything meriting description as a *principle*. Pasinetti (1997, pp. 98–100) identifies the *principle* of effective demand with the proposition that changes in demand result in changes in output (at least until full capacity is reached), and argues that this principle operates at a deeper or more fundamental level than is suggested by the behavioural relations commonly used to describe a point of effective demand (ibid., p. 100; 2001, pp. 386–9; see also Boitani and Delli Gatti 2001). That the principle of effective demand is associated with the

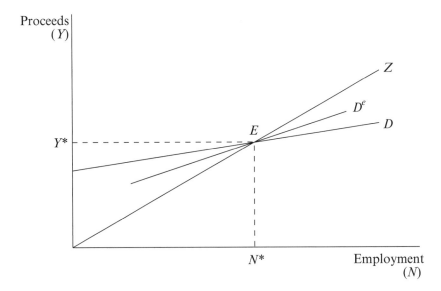

Key
D = aggregate demand function
Z = aggregate supply function
E = point of effective demand
Y = business proceeds (aggregate nominal income)
N = employment
D^e = expected aggregate demand function

Figure 9   The interaction of expected and actual aggregate demand, and aggregate supply

proposition that macroeconomic activity is demand determined is not controversial. But Pasinetti's suggestion that this principle can be articulated at a 'more fundamental' level of analysis than that associated with specific behavioural relations and a particular institutional context is contentious. It raises the issue of methodological divisions within Post Keynesian economics, between those who favour a long-period method of analysis in which certain 'core' relationships obtain independently of short-term events (in the determination of which institutions *do* play a part), and those who argue that there are no long-period positions defined and reached independently of the sequence of (behaviourally and institutionally specific) short-run outcomes leading up to them. It is not surprising, then, to find critics of Pasinetti's position re-asserting the fundamentally behavioural and institutionally specific nature of the principle of effective demand. Davidson (2001, p. 393), for example, defines the *principle* of effective demand as the proposition that the behavioural determinants of the aggregate demand and supply functions differ in the institutionally specific context of a money-using economy.

A final controversy concerns use of the D–Z framework in Figure 7 to express the principle of effective demand. Colander (2001) and Lavoie (2003) call for its abandonment, in favour of expositions in the more conventional price–output space. Much of their concern is with principles of pedagogy, and how best to communicate Post Keynesian thinking to students of economics. To this end, Fontana and Setterfield (2009) show how the Post Keynesian principles of demand formation and (on the supply side) pricing and production that inform the D–Z framework can be represented in price–quantity space in a simple macroeconomics teaching model. But the D–Z framework is the preferred apparatus for representing Post Keynesianism in Galbraith and Darity's (1994) macroeconomics textbook. And interest in the framework remains strong in Post Keynesian research, as evidenced by the number of recent contributions investigating its properties (see, for example, Hartwig 2006, 2007; Hayes 2007; Allain 2009).

MARK SETTERFIELD

See also:

Employment; Expectations; Investment; Keynes's *General Theory*; Liquidity Preference; Rate of Interest; Saving; Say's Law; Sraffian Economics; Unemployment.

References

Allain, O. (2009), 'Effective demand and short-term adjustments in the *General Theory*', *Review of Political Economy*, **21** (1), 1–22.
Amadeo, E. (1989), *Keynes's Principle of Effective Demand*, Aldershot, UK and Brookfield, VT, USA: Edward Elgar.
Asimakopulos, A. (1991), *Keynes's General Theory and Accumulation*, Cambridge: Cambridge University Press.
Boitani, A. and D. Delli Gatti (2001), 'Effective demand and coordination failures', *Journal of Post Keynesian Economics*, **23** (3), 411–40.
Chick, V. (1983), *Macroeconomics After Keynes*, Cambridge, MA: MIT Press.
Chick, V. (2002), 'An equilibrium of action: a new approach to the long period in Keynes', University College London, mimeo.
Colander, D. (2001), 'Effective supply and effective demand', *Journal of Post Keynesian Economics*, **23** (3), 375–81.
Davidson, P. (2001), 'The principle of effective demand: another view', *Journal of Post Keynesian Economics*, **23** (3), 391–409.
Fontana, G. and M. Setterfield (2009), 'A simple (and teachable) macroeconomic model with endogenous money', in Fontana and Setterfield (eds), *Macroeconomic Theory and Macroeconomic Pedagogy*, London: Palgrave Macmillan, pp. 144–68.
Galbraith, J. and W. Darity (1994), *Macroeconomics*, Boston, MA: Houghton Mifflin.
Hartwig, J. (2006), 'Explaining the aggregate price level with Keynes's principle of effective demand', *Review of Social Economy*, **64** (4), 469–92.
Hartwig, J. (2007), 'Keynes vs. the Post Keynesians on the principle of effective demand', *European Journal of the History of Economic Thought*, **14** (4), 725–39.
Hayes, M.G. (2007), 'The point of effective demand', *Review of Political Economy*, **19** (1), 55–80.

Keynes, J.M. (1936), *The General Theory of Employment, Interest and Money*, London: Macmillan.

Kregel, J. (1976), 'Economic methodology in the face of uncertainty: the modelling methods of Keynes and the Post Keynesians', *Economic Journal*, **86** (342), 209–25.

Lavoie, M. (2003), 'Real wages and unemployment with effective and notional demand for labor', *Review of Radical Political Economics*, **35** (2), 166–82.

Pasinetti, L. (1997), 'The principle of effective demand', in G.C. Harcourt and P.A. Riach (eds), *A 'Second Edition' of The General Theory Volume 1*, London and New York: Routledge, pp. 93–104.

Pasinetti, L. (2001), 'The principle of effective demand and its relevance in the long run', *Journal of Post Keynesian Economics*, **23** (3), 383–90.

Efficient Markets Hypothesis

Although something of a chameleon (Findlay and Williams 2008), the efficient markets hypothesis (EMH) reduces to a claim that 'you can't beat the market'. In its weak form, it holds that past financial data are no guide to the future. In its stronger forms, it maintains that financial asset prices represent 'fundamental value', except to the extent that they are deflected by temporary departures from rationality. Despite the various financial crises during the period of financial liberalization, together with much academic criticism based on empirical evidence as well as the actual practices of professional investors, the hypothesis remains tenacious. This persistence reflects its intimate relationship with the core concept of rational expectations that underpins mainstream macroeconomics and financial economics.

The Post Keynesian perspective is that there is no such thing as fundamental value, except with hindsight. However efficient may be the transmission to investors of all available information about the real economy, the future events which will determine the *ex post* value of long-term assets are inherently unknowable. Expectations about the long-term future are intractably uncertain in the sense which John Maynard Keynes and Frank Knight distinguished uncertainty from statistical random variation. This difference in perspective leads to differences in the interpretation of the empirical evidence and in policy recommendations.

The weak form of EMH emerged as a theoretical response to the empirical evidence that stock market prices follow a 'random walk' so that they cannot be predicted from patterns in past data, for example by charting – it holds that such information is already reflected in the price. Further evidence was sought through 'event studies', which analyse the price movement before and after a price-sensitive announcement, such as an unexpected increase or drop in earnings. These studies largely confirm that new information is rapidly incorporated in the price, although they also provide evidence of specific patterns of psychological response which have become the stuff of behavioural finance (see below).

The stronger forms of EMH take this evidence to mean that, outwith periods of collective madness, prices reflect fundamental value, that is, the present value of the future cash flows on which the security is a claim. In other words, prices reflect rational expectations based ultimately on the general equilibrium parameters of endowment, technology and preferences. Thus prices will display random variation as news comes in of random shocks to the parameters, which are by definition unpredictable. The semi-strong variant of EMH allows that insiders may have advance knowledge of such news and can (illegally) profit thereby.

However this evidence is equally, if not more, consistent with the Post Keynesian view that securities prices are a matter of convention. In the absence of a reliable basis for forming long-term expectations, what matters are the expectations and intentions of other investors (Glickman 1994). A conventional valuation is the price that balances the bullish and the bearish tendencies in the market (and indeed in the minds of particular investors) and represents the average opinion or conventional wisdom as to the correct price, given the current information (Keynes 1936, chapters 12 and 13; Hayes 2006). This price should therefore continue to prevail until there is change in the information – or, of course, in average opinion. The convention typically extends not just to the price itself but to the 'model' such as a conventional price/earnings ratio. A change in the news may thus affect the price without a change in convention, and as Keynes points out, 'we should not conclude that everything depends on waves of irrational psychology. On the contrary, the state of long-term expectation is often steady' (Keynes 1936, p. 162). Conventional valuations may normally be fairly robust and bear some steady relationship to the changing information that becomes available, although always open to discontinuous shifts.

In principle, fundamental value can be identified in retrospect by observing the market interest rates and the money yield of an asset over its economic life. However the attempt to estimate that value in advance faces the insuperable obstacle of the irreversible, historical nature of time. As Keynes puts it:

> The outstanding fact is the extreme precariousness of the basis of knowledge on which our estimates of prospective yield have to be made. Our knowledge of the factors which will govern the yield of an investment some years hence is usually very slight and often negligible. If we speak frankly, we have to admit that our basis of knowledge for estimating the yield ten years hence of a railway, a copper mine, a textile factory, the goodwill of a patent medicine, an Atlantic liner, a building in the City of London amounts to little and sometimes to nothing; or even five years hence. (Ibid. p. 149)

The problem is the durable character of physical capital assets: if the expectations upon which an investment was based prove mistaken, it is not possible either to reverse the investment today or to go back in time, adjust the original investment decision, and then check the revised results in the present. It is only in a stationary or steady state (allowing for stochastic risk, an 'ergodic' system) that adjustments made today might (given stable dynamics) be expected to have the same effect in the future as the same adjustments, made in the past, would have had today. So the convergent feedback mechanism necessary for supply and demand to generate a set of long-term equilibrium 'normal' prices, as a fundamental basis for the prospective yield of a capital asset, is absent in a world subject to unforeseeable change.

Perhaps the decisive empirical test which discriminates between the efficient markets and Post Keynesian hypotheses is the variance bounds test (Shiller 1981). The logic of this test is that if prices are a good *ex ante* estimator of fundamental value, the volatility of prices should not exceed the volatility of *ex post* fundamental value. Using US data for 1871–1980, Shiller found that price volatility was at least five times the volatility in fundamental value, rather than less, as the stronger EMH predicts. Much ink has been spilt in an effort to overturn Shiller's claim, motivated presumably by the correct instinct that investors do not normally behave irrationally. Yet if price volatility reflects variation in conventions as well as in the news about technology, preferences and endowment, Shiller's result is fully to be expected, since conventions may change frequently without a descent into irrationality. Furthermore, equity prices will follow a random walk, if news is random and *a fortiori* if changes in conventions are also random.

Behavioural finance theory offers a critique of the EMH on a different tack from the Post Keynesian position, as well as a positive model of investor psychology that provides an explanation of apparently irrational behaviour. A weakness of behavioural finance is its continued adherence to the concept of *ex ante* fundamental value, if only as a reference point. The implication is that any departure from fundamental value is in some sense irrational, in contrast with the Post Keynesian argument that conventional valuation may be the only rational response to an unknowable future.

The behavioural finance critique of the EMH centres on the limits to arbitrage by the 'smart money' (that is, investors with rational expectations) in offsetting irrational trading by 'noise traders' (that is, investors who trade on the basis of 'non-news' or 'pricing models' with no rational foundation). Risk-averse arbitrageurs will not be able to hold the market to its fundamental value, partly because they are unable to hedge the market as a whole over time; and also because the noise traders may push the market further away from fundamental value before it reverts, while credit costs and limits tend to prevent arbitrageurs from taking longer-term positions. Worse still for the purposes of the EMH, the 'smart money' may egg on, rather than bet against, the 'feedback traders' (that is, a species of noise trader who buys when prices rise, and sells when they fall), supporting rather than preventing the expansion of a bubble.

The positive contribution of behavioural finance theory lies in providing a basis in investor psychology for the behaviour of noise traders. Drawing upon work in experimental psychology, the observed behaviours of trend following and of under and over-reaction to news, can be explained in terms of 'conservatism' and 'representativeness' (Shleifer 2000, pp. 112–30). Conservatism means that investors are slow to revise their expectations, effectively discounting the relevance of individual news items until they are corroborated. This tendency manifests itself in event studies which show that excess returns are recorded for a considerable period (60 days) after the announcement (under-reaction). Conversely, representativeness means that investors form perceptions of particular shares as 'winners' or 'losers' based on a run of good or bad returns, rather than ascribing the observed sequence to chance, and thus rating the shares higher or lower than the EMH would warrant, manifested in lower or higher future returns (over-reaction). Taken together these two tendencies provide a behavioural foundation for positive feedback, with a run of good returns encouraging bullish expectations, which are then slow to react to disappointment. There may well be scope for research incorporating the insights of behavioural finance into the formation of conventions.

The EMH has provided part of the theoretical foundation for the ideology of financial liberalization and globalization. Deregulation of financial markets and the abolition of capital controls are justified ultimately by the idea that competitive financial markets allocate capital efficiently and spread risk. Deeper still, the understanding of probability that underlies the EMH, reducing the uncertain future to calculable risk, encouraged the shift to securitization and the proliferation of increasingly opaque derivatives that faced their nemesis in 2008.

The Post Keynesian perspective on the financial sector is very different. First, there is recognition of the well-established empirical evidence that the vast majority of physical capital formation or accumulation is financed from the internal cash flow of large corporations supplemented to some extent by bank credit lines. The social purpose of the stock market is not to finance new physical investment but to permit transfers of existing assets, including corporate control. Second, there is recognition of a tendency to financial fragility, driven partly by the speculative opportunities provided by the equity market, but also by those of the housing market in certain countries such as the UK and the US, and of currency and commodity markets at other times and places. Third, there is full recognition that exchange rates do not reflect fundamentals and furthermore that equilibrium in the balance of payments need not be consistent with full employment.

From this perspective flow detailed policies, which in present circumstances look radical but in certain respects are a reversion to older wisdom. These include high transaction taxes on capital transfers, the reform of corporate governance, alternative financial institutions designed in fact to channel long-term savings into physical investment, nationalization or close regulation of institutions offering retail financial products (such as deposits and pensions) that carry an explicit or implicit state guarantee, and a reassertion of the right of states to regulate capital flows and exchange rates together with the need for reform of the international financial institutions.

Post Keynesians would, in the words of Winston Churchill, see finance less proud and industry more content. The comfortable hypothesis that asset prices are, on average, reliable indicators of fundamental value has proved exceedingly dangerous.

MARK HAYES

See also:

Banking; Behavioural Economics; Choice under Uncertainty; Conventions; Financial Instability Hypothesis; Financial Reform; Financialization; Investment; Non-ergodicity; Uncertainty.

References

Findlay, M.C. and E.E. Williams (2008), 'Financial economics at 50: an oxymoronic tautology', *Journal of Post Keynesian Economics*, **31** (2), 213–26.
Glickman, M. (1994), 'The concept of information, intractable uncertainty, and the current state of the "efficient markets" theory: a Post Keynesian view', *Journal of Post Keynesian Economics*, **16** (3), 325–49.
Hayes, M.G. (2006), 'Value and probability', *Journal of Post Keynesian Economics*, **28** (3), 527–38.
Keynes, J.M. (1936), *The General Theory of Employment, Interest and Money*, London: Macmillan.
Shiller, R.J. (1981), 'Do stock prices move too much to be justified by subsequent movements in dividends?', *American Economic Review*, **71** (3), 421–36.
Shleifer, A. (2000), *Inefficient Markets: An Introduction to Behavioral Finance*, Basingstoke: Palgrave.

Employer of Last Resort

The employer of last resort (ELR) is a proposal for a government-funded programme in which the government employs all of the jobless who are ready, willing and able to work in a public sector project at a base wage.

The proposal stems from the Post Keynesian understanding that unemployment is a monetary phenomenon and that profit-driven capitalist economies consistently fail to produce and maintain anything close to true full employment. Keynes himself had argued that governments must do everything that is humanly possible to produce 'a reduction of the unemployed to the sort of levels we are experiencing in wartime . . . that is to say, an unemployed level of less than 1 per cent unemployed' (Keynes 1980, p. 303). This tight definition of full employment is at the heart of the ELR proposal. Although calls for the government to become the employer of last resort were popular as early as the 1930s, contemporary scholarship has formalized the proposal as follows.

First, ELR offers an infinitely elastic demand for labour. ELR is not a depression solution. There are people looking for work even in expansions, and this permanent and voluntary programme hires the unemployed irrespective of the phase of the business cycle. Since government is the only institution that can divorce the profitability of hiring from the decision to hire, the programme would eliminate unemployment by taking workers 'as they are' regardless of their work experience, race, age or gender.

Second, ELR hires off the bottom. Unemployment is eliminated by direct job creation, not by 'pump priming' or by raising aggregate demand. It is a bottom-up policy that offers an employment safety-net to those individuals who tend to be last hired and first fired from private sector work – normally the least skilled and least educated. By contrast, pro-growth pro-investment aggregate demand policies always increase demand for the highly skilled, highly educated and highly paid workers first. Once the economy begins to recover, demand starts to trickle down to other workers, but never far enough to reach all of those who wish to work. Instead of targeting some level of investment or output growth (which may or may not produce true full employment), the ELR programme goes to the heart of the problem and closes the demand gap for *labour* by guaranteeing a job at a base wage.

Third, ELR operates as a buffer stock. The key countercyclical stabilization feature is its buffer stock mechanism, where labour in the ELR programme is the buffer stock that fluctuates with the cycle. In recessions, workers who are laid off from the private sector find jobs in the ELR programme, expanding government spending countercyclically. Once the economy recovers, they are hired away from the public sector into better-paying private sector jobs, reducing public expenditure.

Fourth, ELR stabilizes wages and prices. As with any buffer stock programme, ELR stabilizes the price of the buffer stock – in this case, wages at the bottom. An ELR worker will be hired by a private employer at a margin above the ELR wage and, thus, the ELR wage becomes the effective minimum wage. Although it should not compete with wages in the private sector, some argue that it should be set at the living-wage level that establishes a minimum wage-benefit standard for the economy. To the extent that wages are a cost in every producible and reproducible commodity in the economy and the ELR programme stabilizes them at the bottom, the programme would also help stabilize prices. Other price stabilization features include the countercyclical mechanism which alleviates both inflationary and deflationary pressures in the economy as a whole, as well as the programme's supply-side effects. In contrast to income-support programmes, ELR directly increases both the demand for workers and the supply of goods and services. That supply can be directed to satisfy the very needs of the previously unemployed and poor, thereby absorbing part of the ELR wage.

Fifth, ELR spending is always at the appropriate level. With pro-growth pro-investment pump-priming policies, economists never know exactly how much stimulus is needed to produce genuine full employment. Producing effective demand consistent with full employment is particularly difficult with such policies because the determinants of effective demand (investment, saving and portfolio allocation) are highly subjective and not under the direct control of policy makers. With ELR, however, government spending will be no more and no less than what is necessary to hire all who wish to work.

Sixth, ELR operates with loose labour markets. The programme must be flexible enough to absorb new entrants into the ELR pool but also to let them go when they find private sector employment, without major disruptions to the public sector projects. A careful programme design will produce a database of such tasks that can easily be shelved when there is little demand for ELR work. But it will also permit some level of experimentation if there is an unexpected influx of workers into the ELR pool. Keynes's own view was that macroeconomic stability and full employment would be achieved by hiring the jobless directly into a long-term programme for the socialization of investment, where a considerable amount of investment would be under public or semi-public auspices (Keynes 1936 [1964], p. 378). This means that at any given time, the pool of public sector workers would be quite large. But should unemployment unexpectedly develop, the state would play the role of 'entrepreneur in chief' to provide enough employment opportunities. In the absence of a sizeable socialization of investment, however, the ELR programme would serve essentially the same function of delivering macroeconomic stabilization and full employment through direct hiring into socially useful projects. Thus some have compared the ELR programme to a universal public service employment scheme (for example, Forstater 2004).

Seventh, ELR has key preventive features over the long run. It is one thing to maintain full employment over the long run through private and public employment schemes (including traditional public sector work and ELR employment) and an entirely different task to eliminate unemployment once it has developed in the absence of such programmes. In the latter case, the policy response is always too small and always too late and, without a plan for direct employment, unemployment always accelerates far too quickly. Furthermore, much greater policy intervention is needed to produce job growth through pump-priming policies, which never garner sufficient support to generate anything close to true full employment.

Eighth, ELR maintains and enhances human capital. Unlike cash transfers, this employment safety-net does not waste human potential by keeping the unemployed and poor in idleness and misery. Instead, it mobilizes their manpower for the public good. Even the poorest and least-educated individual has something to contribute to his/her community. ELR aims to find such individuals decent work that provides both on-the-job training and other educational opportunities that prepare them for post-ELR work.

Ninth, ELR workers perform socially useful work. ELR supplies public goods and services that the private sector generally fails to provide. There is no shortage of needs that require attention in any community, no matter if it is poor or relatively wealthy. The job of policy makers is to carefully assess those needs and the available resources to adequately address them, as well as to improve upon current projects and implement others that may be deemed more beneficial.

Tenth, ELR is an institutional vehicle to achieve other socio-economic goals. ELR can be used as a strategic tool for addressing pressing socio-economic problems, beyond that of unemployment. Research on direct job creation has identified some potentially transformational effects on poor women and destitute communities of such programmes. Some advocate that ELR take the form of a Green New Deal or a Green Jobs Corps that launches a massive environmental renewal effort and public investment in green technology (Forstater 2004).

Eleventh, ELR is financially sustainable over the long run in sovereign currency nations. ELR proposals are normally linked to the Post Keynesian modern money and functional finance literature, which argues that countries with freely floating non-convertible currencies face no solvency problems or technical constraints in funding these programmes in perpetuity. More than that, ELR itself can serve as a benchmark for the value of such fiat currencies. Currency values are determined in a highly complex manner, but they essentially reflect what one can buy with the currency. Advocates argue that the ELR hourly wage pins down a basic conversion rate between labour and the currency. In other words, a $10/hour ELR wage, for example, anchors the currency in labour power and sets the value of the dollar to be equal to six minutes of work. If the wage were doubled, then as a benchmark (recall that ELR stabilizes all wages at the bottom), one dollar will exchange for three minutes of work or will erode in value by half. So when the emitter of the currency (the government) sets the exchange rate between the currency and the labour in the countercyclical buffer stock pool, it helps stabilize the value of its currency. Freely floating non-convertible currencies today have no equivalent anchors. Finally, ELR advocates argue that in the absence of a solvency problem, the effects of government policy must be evaluated according to the principles of functional finance, namely by the programme's real effects on the economy and not by its financial costs.

One common objection to ELR deals with the administration and management of such programmes. One can look no further than nationwide wartime armament policies or the management of the military in peacetime, to see that governments have the ability, but perhaps are unwilling, to embark on similarly ambitious efforts for the purposes of civilian production and public service. But the more serious criticisms of ELR question its ability to deliver macroeconomic stabilization through full employment and price stability in practice. Several studies have looked at a recent direct job creation programme in Argentina (*Plan Jefes*) that was explicitly modelled after ELR proposals in the US and Australia and find that, although the programme was not universal (it was open to heads of households only) and had a number of other shortcomings (for example, a small educational component), it exhibited virtually all of the above-mentioned features of the ELR proposal (Tcherneva and Wray 2005a,b).

History has witnessed few long-term policies for full employment (most notably in postwar Sweden). Most direct job creation programmes, such as Argentina's and the US New Deal in the 1930s, are normally implemented as emergency measures and, therefore, are short-lived. In Argentina, for example, despite its enormous success, the programme was phased out after three years under heavy political pressure. Thus perhaps the most persuasive criticism of ELR is a political one, stemming from the Kaleckian argument that full-employment policies in general tend to be strongly opposed by the captains of industry. Nevertheless, in 2005 an ELR-type policy was codified into law in India (the National Rural Employment Guarantee Act), suggesting that the social, environmental and economic benefits of the programme, at least in one country, are deemed more important than whatever drawbacks businesses may see in it, to warrant its mass support and implementation.

PAVLINA R. TCHERNEVA

See also:

Economic Policy; Employment; Environmental Policy; Fiscal Policy; Full Employment; Money; Unemployment.

Bibliography

Forstater, M. (1998), 'Flexible full employment: structural implications of discretionary public sector employment', *Journal of Economic Issues*, **32** (2), 557–64.

Forstater, M. (2004), 'Green jobs: addressing the critical issues surrounding the environment, workplace and employment', *International Journal of Environment, Workplace and Employment*, **1** (1), 53–61.

Keynes, J.M. (1936), *The General Theory of Employment, Interest and Money*, New York: Harcourt Brace & World, 1964.

Keynes, J.M. (1980), *Activities 1940–46. Shaping the Post-War World: Employment and Commodities. Collected Works, Volume XXVII*, London: Macmillan for the Royal Economic Society.

Minsky, H.P. (1986), *Stabilizing an Unstable Economy*, San Francisco, CA: Chandler Publishing.

Mitchell, W.F. (1998), 'The buffer stock employment model and the NAIRU', *Journal of Economic Issues*, **32** (2), 547–56.

Sawyer, M. (2003), 'Employer of last resort: could it deliver full employment and price stability?', *Journal of Economic Issues*, **37** (4), 881–908.

Tcherneva, P.R. (2011), 'Permanent on-the-spot job creation – the missing Keynes Plan for full employment and economic transformation', *Review of Social Economics*, forthcoming.

Tcherneva, P.R. and L.R. Wray (2005a), 'Is Argentina's *Plan Jefes* an Employer of Last Resort Program?', Working Paper No. 43, Center for Full Employment and Price Stability, University of Missouri–Kansas City, Kansas City, MO.

Tcherneva, P.R. and L.R. Wray (2005b), 'Gender and the job guarantee: the impact of Argentina's *Jefes* Program on female heads of poor households', Working Paper No. 50, Center for Full Employment and Price Stability, University of Missouri–Kansas City, Kansas City, MO.

Wray, L.R. (1998), *Understanding Modern Money: The Key to Full Employment and Price Stability*, Cheltenham, UK and Northampton, MA, USA: Edward Elgar.

Employment

Involuntary unemployment is a pervasive, and undesirable, property of capitalist economies. Employment is determined by the level of effective demand. The key determinants of demand are thus also the determinants of employment. While there is some feedback from the labour market to the goods market, this feedback is weak and often perverse. In private market economies employment has no built-in tendency to return to full employment. Therefore government activity is called for. In the following we present the Post Keynesian analysis of the macroeconomics of (un) employment and clarify the rejection of (traditional) neoclassical arguments as well as its relation to the (more recent) 'New Keynesian' NAIRU (non-accelerating inflation rate of unemployment) theory.

The assertion that employment depends on the level of effective demand is one of the cornerstones of Keynesian economics (Keynes 1936, 1937). This is in contrast to the neoclassical emphasis on real wages as the key determinant of employment. According to Keynes, firms will hire the number of workers that will allow them to produce expected sales, which in turn depend on demand. The single most important variable determining effective demand is investment expenditures, which depend on business sentiment ('animal spirits') or expectations not reducible to optimizing behaviour.

The standard (neoclassical) prescription for unemployment is cutting wages. In Chapter 19 of the *General Theory*, Keynes goes to great lengths to argue that a reduction in wages will not necessarily reduce unemployment. First, he notes that in labour markets typically it is not the real wage that is agreed on, but the nominal wage. There is no straightforward market mechanism to cut real wages. A wage cut, in practice, will be a nominal wage cut. Second, if there is a reduction in nominal wages, the key question is how this will affect aggregate demand. Only if a wage cut stimulates demand can it be expected to also stimulate employment. In fact there will be complicated effects depending on how open the economy is, how expectations about future wage developments react, and to what extent the nominal wage cut will also translate into price cuts. While the nominal wage cut may stimulate demand via net exports or (if the money supply is exogenous) by lowering interest rates, there are also reasons to expect it to actually lower aggregate demand. First, in so far as the wage reduction translates into a redistribution of income from wage incomes to profit incomes, it will reduce consumption demand because wage incomes will typically be associated with a higher propensity to consume than profit incomes. Second, to the extent that wage cuts also lead to deflationary pressures, they will increase the real value of debt and may thereby decrease demand. Third, if firms expect wages to decline further, they will postpone hiring.

In Keynes's vision of the labour market, nominal wages are set in wage bargaining and effective demand determines the level of employment. Competitive forces will then determine prices such that the real wage equals the marginal product of labour. A nominal wage cut will have complicated effects on aggregate demand. The real wage is not the equilibrating variable in the labour market, but rather an outcome that critically depends on the level of aggregate demand (Lavoie 2003).

Keynes thus rejects one important tenet of neoclassical (Walrasian) economics: that the real wage equilibrates the labour market. However, he maintains two other standard features: the assumption of a production function and the assumption of perfect competition in the goods market. Arguably, both assumptions are made in order to maintain comparability with the mainstream rather than for realism. However, many Post Keynesian economists have abandoned these assumptions. Regarding the production function, in the short run, actual changes in the capital–output ratio are best interpreted as changes in the utilization of capacity rather than as a substitution with full utilization of available resources (as is implicitly assumed when a production function is utilized). Regarding the long run, Post Keynesians have highlighted inconsistencies of the neoclassical theory of distribution and production in the course of the Cambridge capital controversies, and therefore some Post Keynesians reject the theoretical usefulness of the concept of an aggregate production function. Moreover, it can be shown that estimated (aggregate) labour demand functions deliver spurious results (with respect to the underlying coefficients of the production function) because of accounting identities (Felipe and McCombie 2009).

While Keynes himself assumed perfect competition in the goods market, many Post Keynesians nowadays prefer the more realistic assumption of firms with market power that was pioneered by Michał Kalecki. In Kalecki, prices (for non-primary goods) are set as a mark-up on (normal) unit costs after wage bargaining. Real wages are thus independent of nominal wages. These models have been developed further into so-called 'conflict inflation models' (Rowthorn 1977; Arestis and Sawyer 2005), where the outcome of wage bargaining depends on the level of unemployment and other factors determining the bargaining position of labour unions, and prices are set by firms which may not be able to pass on nominal wage increases in full. Inflation, or indeed wage–price spirals, are the outcome of unresolved distributional conflicts (rather than a result of increases in the money supply). These models are similar to NAIRU models.

The NAIRU model has become an important reference model in today's macroeconomic discussion of unemployment. It is a rather general imperfect competition model of the labour and the goods market that contains some Keynesian features. Nominal wages are the outcome of a bargaining process and will react negatively to unemployment. Prices are set by firms with some degree of market power. From this a short-run trade-off between inflation and unemployment, that is, a short-run Phillips curve, can be derived and, by implication, the NAIRU at which inflation is stable. NAIRU models are non-Walrasian in that there is no tendency to full employment, but many NAIRU models feature a supply-side-determined equilibrium rate of unemployment, the NAIRU. Stockhammer (2008) argues that, with different assumptions regarding the properties of the aggregate demand function and regarding the endogeneity of the NAIRU, the model can be given a Neoclassical-New Keynesian Synthesis (NNKS) or a Post Keynesian interpretation.

There are two important differences between NNKS and Post Keynesian NAIRU models. First, regarding the demand function, NNKS models typically assume a well-behaved aggregate demand function, where increases in inflation lead to a decrease in aggregate demand (often because of the interest rule adopted by the central bank), whereas Post Keynesians highlight the real debt effect and limitations in the effectiveness of monetary policy once inflation gets close to zero. Inflation (below hyperinflation) can have expansionary effects because it lowers the real debt burden, and the ability of central banks to affect the real interest rate may be limited once inflation gets close to zero. As a consequence, while the NAIRU is an attractor for actual unemployment in NNKS models, the NAIRU equilibrium will be unstable in Post Keynesian models (in particular at low inflation rates).

Second, in the Post Keynesian view the NAIRU will be endogenous in the medium term because income claims are based on social norms subject to various hysteresis mechanisms (Skott 2005), because investment expenditures have supply-side effects and because mark-ups may be interest elastic. While there is a well-defined short-run NAIRU (and a short-run inflation unemployment trade-off) in Post Keynesian models, in the medium term the NAIRU is endogeneous and will move along with wherever effective demand pushes actual unemployment to. In contrast, in (most, but not all) NNKS models, the NAIRU itself is determined only by labour market institutions and is thus effectively an exogenous supply-side phenomenon. In this view the economy is anchored in a supply-side equilibrium characterized by involuntary unemployment in the medium run. Empirically, Post Keynesians have argued that capital accumulation and interest rates are more powerful in explaining changes in medium-term unemployment than labour market institutions (for example, Stockhammer and Klär 2011).

The differences in policy implications of the Post Keynesian and NNKS theories are stark. An NNKS version of the NAIRU has been adopted by economic policy institutions such as the European Commission, the IMF and the OECD in their pursuit of policies of labour market deregulation. This is a distinctly anti-Keynesian reincarnation of the old neoclassical claim that only wage cuts can cure unemployment. Post Keynesian theory, on the other hand, concludes that, without government intervention, there is no long-run equilibrium rate of unemployment in which the economy is anchored. As a consequence, government intervention is required to achieve full employment. This should be done by means of demand management, with fiscal policy usually featuring prominently to stabilize short-run fluctuations and industrial policy and financial regulation to encourage investment growth.

ENGELBERT STOCKHAMMER

See also:

Capital Theory; Economic Policy; Effective Demand; Employer of Last Resort; Full Employment; Income Distribution; Inflation; New Keynesian Economics; New Neoclassical Synthesis; Production; Unemployment; Wage Deflation; Walrasian Economics.

References

Arestis, P. and M. Sawyer (2005), 'Aggregate demand, conflict and capacity in the inflationary process', *Cambridge Journal of Economics*, **29** (6), 959–74.
Felipe, J. and J. McCombie (2009), 'Are estimates of labour demand functions mere statistical artefacts?', *International Review of Applied Economics*, **23** (2), 147–68.
Keynes, J.M. (1936), *The General Theory of Employment, Interest and Money, The Collected Writings of John Maynard Keynes, Volume VII*, Cambridge: Macmillan, 1973.
Keynes, J.M. (1937), 'The general theory of employment', *Quarterly Journal of Economics*, **41** (2), 209–23.
Lavoie, M. (2003), 'Real wages and unemployment with effective and notional demand for labour', *Review of Radical Political Economics*, **35** (2), 166–82.
Rowthorn, R. (1977), 'Conflict, inflation and money', *Cambridge Journal of Economics*, **1** (3), 215–39.
Skott, P. (2005), 'Fairness as a source of hysteresis in employment and relative wages', *Journal of Economic Behavior and Organization*, **57** (3), 305–31.
Stockhammer, E. (2008), 'Is the NAIRU a Monetarist, New Keynesian, Post Keynesian or Marxist theory?', *Metroeconomica*, **59** (4), 479–510.
Stockhammer, E. and E. Klär (2011), 'Capital accumulation and unemployment in the medium run', *Cambridge Journal of Economics*, **35** (2), 437–57.

Environmental Economics

Over the past quarter-century or so environmental economics from being a fringe activity has become one of the most active areas of economic research. (In this entry the term 'environmental economics' is used broadly, to include the closely related area of natural resource economics.) It has become a major, even dominating, influence within significant areas of policy debate, encompassing momentous global issues such as climate change and biodiversity loss. Mainstream environmental economics is currently dominated by the neoclassical paradigm in the ways in which it formulates and analyses the two key areas with which it is concerned: the valuation of environmental assets and the design of policy instruments to manage those assets. These are brought together in the study of sustainable development: how is it to be defined and achieved – if, indeed, it is desirable? Thus environmental economics is conventionally seen as essentially a branch of applied welfare economics. In some respects, environmental economics represents a rather extreme interpretation of the neoclassical paradigm, with its belief in the possibility of extending, with reasonable reliability, individual valuations to all sorts of non-marketed 'commodities', with its definition of environmental problems as essentially flowing from market 'failures', and with its advocacy of the efficacy and desirability of incentive-based policy instruments to correct for these failures (as discussed in the entry on Environmental Policy).

Partly due to its somewhat extravagant faith in the neoclassical paradigm and partly, also, because of the necessary interface between environmental economics and the natural sciences, mainstream environmental economics has not been without its critics. Some of this criticism is simply misplaced and easily rebutted by any well-trained neoclassical environmental economist. A leading example is that standard environmental economics cannot properly account for the full life cycle of products. (This example also happens to be pertinent to Post Keynesians: life-cycle assessments utilize what are, in effect, diagonal input–output matrices, familiar to students of Piero Sraffa and Luigi Pasinetti, with little recognition of their limitations and a great deal of agonizing over the definition of process boundaries as a result.) But some is fundamental. This is especially true of those criticisms that challenge the foundations of neoclassical approaches to the environment, and that thence seek alternative accounts of sustainability based on physical or natural processes intrinsic to the environment, such as energy usage (Georgescu-Roegen 1971) or biological resilience (Common and Perrings 1992). Some of these accounts aspire to create an entirely new form of economics based, for example, on a redefinition of the concept of scarcity or value.

Leaving this aside, for the moment, what was conspicuously lacking in the debate until quite recently was a serious attempt to draw ideas from heterodox schools of thought *within* economics, broadly defined, in order to criticize and reformulate environmental economics. This has now changed (2011) with some major contributions (notably those in Holt et al. 2009; many of those represented in that volume have also published elsewhere). The only significant exceptions were as follows. First, some moves were made to extend neo-Ricardian models of production and growth to incorporate some process-related natural resource and environmental components (Kurz and Salvadori 1995, chapter 12). Second, richer psychologically-based or socially-embedded accounts of human behaviour were drawn on to criticize the appropriateness of attempts to extend neoclassical valuation processes over non-market domains (Sagoff 1988; Kahneman and Knetsch 1992). However, beyond these, it seems obvious that Post Keynesian economics can provide insights which have the potential to provide a powerful critique of neoclassical environmental economics and pointers to a reformulation of the subject. It is the area of socio-behavioural research that has been the subject of particular recent attention – as, for example, in the recent work of Marc Lavoie (see his contribution to Holt et al. 2009). But the production-process, capital and growth aspects have regrettably received much less attention than the socio-behavioural issues: this is a serious deficiency.

The present entry attempts to outline a few of the existing insights and also to suggest ways forward. Thus it uses the term 'Post Keynesian economics' in a comprehensive sense, so as to include and develop both the steps just mentioned, along with others. All this is tentative and very much represents work-in-progress.

But first, a little more on recent thinking. There has been rapidly growing interest post-2008 on the possible synergies between Post Keynesian and (heterodox) environmental economics, especially ecological economics. But perhaps more caution is needed in the discussion of both theory and policy than is sometimes apparent. Some versions of 'environmentalism' are conceptually questionable and, not unrelated, socially regressive, especially in their neo-Malthusianism; they are not easy bedfellows with Post Keynesianism. But the underlying agenda makes some sense: financialization and, even more broadly, the monetization of all human activities, has obviously contributed to both economic and environmental problems. However, there is a need for serious analysis to take us beyond these vapid generalities: here Post Keynesians could contribute. (There have been attempts to argue that Keynes's broader social and moral vision embodied what we now regard as sustainability and that this informed his economics: this seems tenuous.) The more immediate policy agenda post-2008 has focused on the linkage of Keynesian fiscal stimulus and environmental investment: the so-called 'Green New Deal'. This again looks like an obvious synergy between Post Keynesianism and environmentalism (Lawn 2009). But caution is once more needed: Post Keynesians should be attuned to the path dependency of longer-run outcomes from immediate investment decisions in areas such as new energy technologies.

This is the broad-brush background. This entry now focuses on more analytical issues. In the neoclassical view, environmental problems are just one species of externality and are to be costed at the price which an efficient market would impute to them: they would not exist if markets were complete and in equilibrium. This seems to many to fail, in some sense, to grasp the real existence of environmental problems independent of their specification in an economic model. It might be a reason for adopting one of the alternative accounts, mentioned above, of what might be called environmentally embedded sustainability in order to define the nature of environmental problems, with all the foundational issues thus entailed. The present entry proceeds more pragmatically, and attempts in part to formulate a debate between neoclassical and possible Post Keynesian perspectives on the environment.

Does the Post Keynesian approach encompass the concept of externalities? Presumably not. To use two (or three) arguments, which may or not be consistent with each other: what sense would the neoclassical notion of allocative efficiency make in, first, a (non-trivial) monetary economy where markets were necessarily incomplete or in continuous disequilibrium, or, second, in an economy where prices were (re)production prices, Sraffian or Kaleckian, and not indices of scarcity? To this it might be objected that neoclassical general equilibrium is an ideal-type construct which specifies the necessary conditions for allocative efficiency, and this normative status is untouched by Post Keynesian arguments. This raises deep questions about the nature of economic models, which are not pursued further here.

A Post Keynesian argument which appears more secure against this sort of objection might run as follows. The Post Keynesian perspective on the nature of prices would apply to the attempt to use supposedly allocatively efficient prices to value environmental assets and damage to them. In many, perhaps most, of the cases which are of most interest to environmental economists, there are no observable or even imputable prices of any sort to use in such valuations. One widely used procedure in such cases is to use the so-called 'contingent valuation method', eliciting prices by questioning people about their willingness to pay for environmental benefits or to accept losses. As noted above, this has provoked a variety of criticisms, partly because of what appear to be irreducible anomalies, but a Post Keynesian one might run along these lines. The answers given in contingent valuation surveys could represent an attempt by respondents to formulate a response based on the prices that people know in their everyday economic lives. So what if these prices are not, for one or other of the reasons given above, to be interpreted as meaningful indicators of underlying preferences and relative scarcities? We might ask: where does a person's notion of an appropriate price come from if not from social practice?

It is indisputable that many environmental problems, however defined, involve lengthy time horizons and extreme uncertainty, and that these are closely related. This is fertile territory for Post Keynesians. In mainstream environmental economics, time is routinely dealt with by discounting. This is a source of much criticism from environmentalists, for familiar practical and ethical reasons (Broome 1992). For Post Keynesians, similar arguments might be made as in the case of prices in general. In what sense can an efficient interest rate be defined, bearing in mind, say, the capital controversies or the concept of the interest rate as an essentially monetary phenomenon? Here, an attempted neoclassical rebuttal would not be so convincing: the notion of an interest rate which somehow encapsulates intertemporal efficiency would be regarded by many Post Keynesians as simply meaningless. Needless to say, this is contentious.

In dealing with risk, standard environmental economics generally assumes a world of calculable probabilities. Post Keynesians would, of course, reject this in favour of radical uncertainty, which undoubtedly characterizes many environmental problems. Not only does this undermine the specifics of much environmental modelling, forecasting and management, but it also links with the foregoing questions to do with the nature of interest rates and prices so as to lend additional support to a more comprehensive critique of neoclassical environmental economics.

More positively, there is a need for a proper integration of natural resources and environmental assets into a well-formulated model of a monetary economy. Here Post Keynesians have a real chance to develop an innovative approach, perhaps building on an own-rates analysis.

The standard neoclassical model of efficient resource extraction relies on asset valuations based on arbitrage across asset returns. Financial instruments are introduced as simple comparator assets. A Post Keynesian would regard this as a quite inappropriate way to capture the essential characteristics of a monetary economy.

Sustainability is a highly debatable concept (and is discussed more fully in the entry on Sustainable Development). Its status within neoclassical environmental economics is not entirely clear: it is essentially a side-condition, rather than intrinsic to the logic of the model. At all events, the core of the concept is that some measure of welfare is bounded from below over time. This is often expressed in terms of maintaining an appropriate aggregate capital stock. Welfare is ultimately dependent on the return to this stock. The capital stock is very broadly defined, to include natural resource and environmental assets, alongside physical, human and even social capital. It should be noted that this framework is very widely used, even by those who are dismissive of neoclassical environmental economics. Indeed, one of the more common *mistaken* criticisms of environmental economics is that it does not use a comprehensive enough definition of capital. (This needs to be distinguished from the criticism that the market-based values used in aggregation are inappropriate.) A Post Keynesian would argue, instead, that such aggregation procedures are inherently flawed. There is a need, however, to explicitly extend the so-called 'Cambridge critique' to encompass natural resources and environmental capital. In addition, the problems, already discussed, with assigning allocatively efficient prices to the components of such capital stocks, and uncertainties in future stocks, would be further ingredients in a comprehensive critique.

Many of the mainstream accounts of sustainability-as-maintaining-aggregate-capital strengthen the criterion by requiring some individual components of the aggregate to be maintained as well, on the grounds that the weaker criterion overestimates the possibilities of substitution within the economy, though others are more sanguine. A Post Keynesian would presumably have no problem with models of production that assume limited substitutability. But introducing it as an assumption does raise questions about the coherence of the neoclassical model of sustainability, which do not seem to be very clearly appreciated.

In understanding the possibilities for long-run sustainability, an area which needs further exploration is the integration of natural resource and environmental assets into growth models, especially those with endogenous innovation (Aghion and Howitt 1998, chapter 5). Some of the newer work on endogenous innovation and growth has strong similarities, in some respects, with Kaldorian models, but otherwise relies on questionable neoclassical modelling of representative agents. One particular aspect that has barely been investigated, which again has a strong Kaldorian flavour, is the relationship between environmental performance and the sectoral and spatial structure of the economy. What are the relative natural resource and pollution intensities of production and consumption processes in the primary sector, in manufacturing and in services, and at various population densities? The last is a particularly interesting issue for Post Keynesians. There is an anti-urban bias in much environmentalism, often justified by utilizing 'environmental foot-printing'; but this widely deployed analysis ignores the economies of scale – static and, especially, dynamic – from agglomeration familiar to students of Kaldor and Myrdal.

ADRIAN WINNETT

See also:

Capital Theory; Economic Policy; Environmental Policy; Kaldorian Economics; Production; Rate of Interest; Sustainable Development; Time in Economic Theory; Uncertainty.

References

Aghion, P. and P. Howitt (1998), *Endogenous Growth Theory*, Cambridge, MA: MIT Press.
Broome, J. (1992), *Counting the Cost of Global Warming*, Cambridge: White Horse Press.
Common, M.S. and S.C. Perrings (1992), 'Towards an ecological economics of sustainability', *Ecological Economics*, **6** (1), 7–31.
Georgescu-Roegen, N. (1971), *The Entropy Law and the Economic Process*, Cambridge, MA: Harvard University Press.
Holt, R.P.F., S. Pressman and C.I. Spash (eds) (2009), *Post Keynesianism and Ecological Economics: Confronting Environmental Issues*, Cheltenham, UK and Northampton MA, USA: Edward Elgar.
Kahneman, D. and J.L. Knetsch (1992), 'Valuing public goods: the purchase of moral satisfaction', *Journal of Environmental Economics and Management*, **22** (1), 57–70.
Kurz, H.D. and N. Salvadori (1995), *Theory of Production: A Long-period Analysis*, Cambridge: Cambridge University Press.
Lawn, P. (ed.) (2009), *Environment and Employment. A Reconciliation*, Abingdon and New York: Routledge.
Sagoff, M. (1988), *The Economy of the Earth*, Cambridge: Cambridge University Press.

Environmental Policy

The Post Keynesian approach to environmental economics calls into question the orthodox environmental economics concept of an efficient pollution level and its prioritizing of price-based mechanisms over direct controls. An environmental tax may have a role to play in Post Keynesian environmental policy, but its effectiveness requires a suite of complementary policies to overcome the Post Keynesian realities of limited substitution effects, fundamental uncertainty and the problem of financing new investment.

As a branch of neoclassical welfare economics, orthodox environmental economics views pollution as a resource allocation problem. Firms and consumers do not consider the social costs of their actions (external costs) because environmental services are not priced. The obvious solution is to create a price using a Pigovian tax system or tradable emission permit scheme, which will internalize the externality and restore the optimal resource allocation.

Whether it is a tax or permit scheme, the orthodoxy prefers the price mechanism to direct controls (the command and control approach) because it achieves the optimal pollution level at minimum cost. Orthodox economists identify the optimal level of pollution using the concepts of marginal social damage (MSD) from pollution and marginal abatement cost (MAC). The optimal level of pollution is the level at which MSD equals MAC. The minimum-cost method of achieving the optimal pollution level requires that the MAC is equal across all firms. From this perspective, the command and control approach – where firms face direct controls on their actions and fines for non-compliance – is more costly than a tax or permit scheme because policy makers cannot know the MAC curves for individual firms and must set uniform standards for all firms. In this case, some high-cost firms will abate more than the optimal level and some low-cost firms will abate less. Cost minimization will only be achieved with a common price on pollution. The single issue facing policy makers, then, is to choose the tax level or quantity of permits that equates MSD and MAC.

Post Keynesian economists are critical of the concept of an efficient pollution level because the MSD curve is not well defined. The MSD curve relates the quantity of emissions to the monetary damage of those emissions. To find the monetary damage, orthodox economists must determine the willingness to pay to avoid the health and environmental damages of pollution, using contingent valuation studies or other methods of environmental valuation. But these methods implicitly assume the efficiency of all prices in the economy because the willingness to pay values are imputed from the value of other goods (see the entry on Environmental Economics).

If the prices used to impute the health and environmental damages are not efficient, the MSD curve does not reflect the true social cost of pollution. Post Keynesians contend that prices are set by business enterprises and therefore are not the 'efficient' prices achieved by a Walrasian auctioneer. By extension, the MSD curve has no relevance to the resource allocation problem the orthodoxy is trying to solve, and the optimal emission level is not really optimal. To a Post Keynesian economist, the appropriate level of environmental improvement must be decided by scientists and the community. Keynes (1930 [1952], p. 373) himself implied this in his vision of the future: to reach our economic bliss we must, in part, 'entrust to science the direction of those matters which are properly the concern of science'.

The MAC curve – which relates emission abatement to the cost of that abatement – is also problematic and cannot be used to confirm the cost-minimization properties of taxes and permits in preference to direct controls. First, underlying the MAC curve is the assumption that producers have perfect knowledge about abatement methods and choose the least-cost method to abate each additional emission level. If information is not perfect, the firms' MAC curves will be above the least-cost MAC curves and, to a Post Keynesian economist, this is to be expected. Second, abatement can occur by installing new technology which abates non-marginal quantities at a constant cost, whereas the theory assumes increasing costs for marginal changes in abatement. This results in a disjointed, rather than a smooth, MAC curve. With these two considerations, two firms with identical (theoretical) MAC curves will, in reality, abate to two different levels in response to a common emission price. Their theoretical and actual MAC values will be different and thus a common emission price is not cost-minimizing.

Post Keynesian environmental economists are also critical of the singular reliance on the price mechanism to achieve environmental improvement. Except in times of environmental crisis, the theoretical policy recommendation of the orthodoxy is either a permit or a tax system, not both, and certainly not accompanied by other direct controls. But this conclusion depends on a faith in the price mechanism which rests on the core assumptions of perfect competition and information, zero transaction costs and unlimited substitution possibilities. For example, considering a new tax on emissions, producers respond by either reducing output or substituting a new technology. Producers have perfect knowledge about substitution opportunities and it becomes profitable to install environmentally friendly technology. Again with perfect knowledge, consumers assist in the process by substituting from the more expensive dirty consumption items to green alternatives.

Post Keynesian economists criticize these core assumptions and the conclusions which the orthodoxy draws from them. In particular, the irrelevance of substitution possibilities for consumers and producers renders the price-based policies much less effective than the orthodoxy claims. The Post Keynesian consumer has limited substitution possibilities within narrow bands of consumption items, current choices are dependent on past decisions, and publicity, fashion, brand loyalty and other cultural factors determine consumer desires (Lavoie 2009, p. 145). Changing relative prices will not immediately, effectively or definitively cause changes in consumption decisions.

Given this Post Keynesian reversal of causality between preferences and society, the effectiveness of taxes or permits must come from producers substituting among their factor inputs. However, in the short run, Post Keynesian economists assume fixed production coefficients. In a Kaleckian model of the economy, an environmental tax or other price on carbon constitutes a prime cost similar to a wage tax. Producers will simply mark up this extra cost, which results in a stable share of profits in value added (Perry 2010). This means that producers have little need, along with no ability, to change their production mix in the short run.

In the long run, producers can change production coefficients through investment. The composition of industries can also change due to the growth and contraction of firms. A Kaleckian model of tax incidence can be used to show that an environmental tax will lead to changes in the composition of industry (ibid.). Green firms will become larger and more dominant and dirty firms will either fade away or adjust by switching to environmentally friendly technology. The end result is a greener economy. This occurs even with consumers maintaining their existing spending patterns and with fixed production coefficients in the short run. However, important Post Keynesian principles impede the growth of green firms, and these principles include fundamental uncertainty and the role of the banking sector in financing new investment.

It is because of these and other principles that Post Keynesian economics recommends a suite of policies to deal with environmental problems. An environmental tax system may have a role to play, but other policies are needed to complement it. In particular, the impediments to the growth in green firms must be removed. Fundamental uncertainty regarding the future state of technology and future environmental policy could be alleviated using a sustainable development version of Michał Kalecki's 'perspective planning', a state structural adjustment programme which would provide certainty for firm-level investment strategies (Courvisanos 2005, p. 192). The second impediment to the growth of green firms is the banking sector. Not surprisingly, orthodox environmental economics has little to say about the role of the banking sector in environmental degradation and the financing of green investments. However, the financing of investment and non-neutrality of money are fundamental issues in Post Keynesian economics. The banking sector favours existing, large and dirty firms and technologies over new, small and green firms and technologies. The removal of this impediment through the use of government loan guarantees for green technology and firms is an important Post Keynesian policy to complement environmental taxes.

Other complementary policies naturally arise from a Post Keynesian approach to environmental policy. First, consumers can be encouraged to change consumption habits. For example, Earl and Wakeley (2009, pp. 169–72) use the analogy of addictive behaviour. Rather than using the price mechanism, information policies, labelling and obstructive policies have been used to reduce cigarette smoking, and obstructive policies such as parking or road access restrictions can be used to reduce automobile use and emissions. Similar policies to reduce energy consumption and consumerism form part of the Post Keynesian approach to environmental policy. The establishment of free green information centres and a green workforce can also help consumers change their habits, and could be incorporated within the Post Keynesian employer-of-last-resort initiative.

Second, and particularly in times of recession, deficit spending can be used to complement environmental taxes. For example, Holt (2009, p. 154) explains that Keynesian public spending could be directed towards the public provision of the environment to help stabilize the economy and promote sustainable development. While Keynes famously suggested that people be employed to dig holes during times of recession, this could have environmental benefits if people are employed, for example, to dig contour banks to reduce soil erosion.

Third, direct controls become valid in Post Keynesian economics. For example, Bird (1982, p. 588) suggests that direct controls have the advantage of lower information requirements with more assured effects. Earl and Wakeley (2009, p. 172) discuss the role of product standards, such as automobile fuel-efficiency standards, which, unlike the price mechanism, achieve environmental outcomes even when consumers are habit driven and have limited information. Product standards also provide clear guidelines about the products required in the future, which reduces uncertainty and aids green investment (ibid., p. 173). Finally, direct controls are preferred on the basis of equity, an important consideration in Post Keynesian economics, because all consumers, and not simply the poor, must change their behaviour (ibid., p. 174).

The Post Keynesian approach to environmental policy requires a suite of policies to achieve a scientifically determined appropriate pollution level. Above all else, these policies must deal with corporate power. Corporations will rally against any of the above policies because they limit corporate power. However, this highlights the fact that Post Keynesian environmental economics is part of the broader programme of Post Keynesian economics, rather than simply a branch of it. As Post Keynesians act to reduce the power of corporations, and as they act to promote the public interest, growth and employment, and an equitable income distribution, they can also improve the environment with policy measures that work because they fundamentally recognize economic realities such as uncertainty, fixed production coefficients, and habit-driven consumers.

NEIL PERRY

See also:

Consumer Theory; Economic Policy; Employer of Last Resort; Environmental Economics; Fiscal Policy; Kaleckian Economics; Prices and Pricing; Sustainable Development; Welfare Economics.

References

Bird, P.J.W.N. (1982), 'Neoclassical and Post Keynesian environmental economics', *Journal of Post Keynesian Economics*, **4** (4), 586–93.
Courvisanos, J. (2005), 'A Post-Keynesian innovation policy for sustainable development', *International Journal of Environment, Workplace and Employment*, **1** (2), 187–202.
Earl, P.E. and T. Wakeley (2009), 'Price-based versus standards-based approaches to reducing car addiction and other environmentally destructive activities', in R.P.F. Holt, S. Pressman and C.L. Spash (eds), *Post Keynesian and Ecological Economics: Confronting Environmental Issues*, Cheltenham, UK and Northampton, MA, USA: Edward Elgar, pp. 158–77.
Holt, R. (2009), 'The relevance of post-Keynesian economics to sustainable development', in P. Lawn (ed.), *Environment and Employment: A Reconciliation*, Abingdon and New York: Routledge, pp. 146–60.
Keynes, J.M. (1930), 'Economic possibilities for our grandchildren'; reprinted in Keynes, *Essays in Persuasion*, London: Hart-Davis, 1952, pp. 358–73.
Lavoie, M. (2009), 'Post Keynesian consumer choice theory and ecological economics', in R.P.F. Holt, S. Pressman and C.L. Spash (eds), *Post Keynesian and Ecological Economics: Confronting Environmental Issues*, Cheltenham, UK and Northampton, MA: Edward Elgar, pp. 141–57.
Perry, N. (2010), 'A Post Keynesian Theory of Environmental Taxes', *Proceedings of the Ninth Australian Society of Heterodox Economics Conference*, University of New South Wales, Sydney, Australia, December 6–7.

Equilibrium and Non-equilibrium

Three facts relating to economic analysis in general are relevant in understanding equilibrium and non-equilibrium. First, the primary purpose of economic analysis is to explain real economic phenomena (prediction, of course, may be a byproduct). Second, one common method by which economic explanation proceeds is through the construction of economic models. And third, model building necessitates abstracting from reality and concentrating on the 'smallest' number of forces that adequately represent what is actually happening. In this context, consider the notion of equilibrium first.

Equilibrium is a feature of a model. A collection of variables is in equilibrium if they are 'at rest'. That is, all forces or laws in operation that might influence the values those variables take on balance each other out and there is no tendency for the variable values to change. The idea of equilibrium was imported from the physical sciences where it was (and is) applied with respect to the properties of physical, non-sentient objects. In the economic context, the focus of equilibrium has been, and continues to be, on human action derived from mental decision processes. Thus equilibrium obtains when no decision maker, to the extent that his/her action has been appropriately captured in the model, has even the slightest motivation to change any plan or action.

Traditionally, the notion of equilibrium has been one of the most, if not the most important organizing feature of economic analysis. In many instances, either equilibrium in a model is thought to prevail, or it is taken to be the end towards which everything is moving. Explanation based on the former often interprets observations of the real economic world as equilibria. Thus, for example, each price–quantity data point arising in an isolated market may be construed as located at the intersection of the demand and supply curves assumed to be in play at the moment it was observed, and may therefore be explained as the outcome of the interaction of the forces of demand and supply. Explanation founded on the latter frequently interprets observations as lying on a time path that converges to equilibrium, as is the case when, say, cobweb models with stable equilibria are taken as the representation of reality. And from either perspective the end result (here, the equilibrium), is independent of the movement towards it (should that movement be relevant).

Since the presence of equilibrium requires no change in the variable values at equilibrium, and since change, or a lack thereof, can only be discerned over time, the idea of time is fundamental to that of equilibrium. Moreover, the nature of the concept of time employed has to be such as to make it possible to recognize circumstances in which change in the relevant variable values is absent. The notion of time usually invoked for this purpose is called 'logical time'. Logical time merely provides a way of ordering events without reference to the actual passing of time. Although, in this manner of representing reality, past events come before present events and present events come before future events, the different possibilities and significances for the spacing of those events, along with the fact that past, present and future events all have different qualities in relation to human abilities to know and experience them, are ignored. All events (past, present and future) are assumed to be completely knowable, at least probabilistically. This means that plans can be assumed to be carried out on the basis of correct knowledge and expectations that will, on average, turn out to be correct. As a consequence, it is possible to envisage behavioural and expectational variable values that reflect realized plans and hence do not require alteration as the system represented by the model moves across past, present and future states. Logical time, then, along with the requirement of full knowledge that goes with it, is essential to the traditional concept of equilibrium as described above. In this form, equilibrium has been invoked by economists independently of time (though time, as just described, is implicit), as existing through time, as temporary or changing as time passes, in terms of unchanging growth rates and full-employment growth paths, and in reference to the short and long runs and to both microeconomic and macroeconomic phenomena.

But in spite of its usefulness in, and widespread appearance over almost two centuries of economic discourse, the concept of equilibrium has little place in Post Keynesian economics. This is because Post Keynesian economics, in part, views the workings of the real economic system as a 'process of continuous and organic change' (Galbraith 1978, p. 8) that is so fundamental, pervasive and dynamic that that system cannot be corralled by any notion of equilibrium. The vehicle for the expression of this change, in addition to a more sensitive regard for the institutional structures in relation to which the actual economy operates, is the vision of historical, as opposed to logical, time that informs virtually all Post Keynesian analytical constructions.

By the phrase 'historical time' is meant time that is actually experienced by human beings, in which each moment in history is unique, in which knowledge of past events is necessarily fragmentary and variable depending on each person's perception of them, and in which the occurrence of future events and their properties is not only unknown even probabilistically, but is also unknowable. As time passes, individuals change not only with respect to the knowledge in their possession or in their epistemic status, but they also experience unforeseeable modifications in their economic endowments and in their perceptions of external institutional structures, environments, and the possibilities of action taken by others. Because planned behaviour continually changes with these variations, it is not possible for behavioural variables to remain constant through time. Hence the concept of equilibrium, at least in its conventional connotation, is both irrelevant and meaningless.

The organizing feature that replaces the notion of equilibrium in Post Keynesian Economics may be referred to as 'non-equilibrium'. An analysis is organized in reference to non-equilibrium if the notion of time upon which it rests is historical. Because of the changing nature of the subjects

of inquiry, because of the fluidity of economic endowments and expectations that market processes generate, and because of the continually
evolving character of institutional structures, such an analysis constructed
for any moment or period is different from that constructed for any other.
Moreover, non-equilibrium analyses permit the end result of a process (not
an equilibrium) to be influenced by the means of achieving it (for example,
Shaikh 2011). They also allow for the presence of non-probabilistic uncertainty and are capable of including in their explanatory reach phenomena
that are subject to that uncertainty (for example, Jefferson and King 2010–
11, pp. 218–19). Thus, for example, in the context of decision making that
accounts for (non-probabilistic) ignorance of the future, a richer complex
of forces can be incorporated into the analysis and description of economic phenomena. And the recognition of money as a historical time and
non-probabilistic uncertainty phenomenon, in which actual time passes
between the receipt and disposal of funds, permits us to address the reality
that the set of forces obtaining at the time of the funds' receipt might be
different from those at the time of their disposal. The latter, in turn, may
give rise to changes in liquidity preference and in the level and stability
of expenditure streams, and macroeconomic problems in which labour
markets do not clear may result. Like traditional economics, explanation
from the Post Keynesian perspective may also proceed by constructing
models. But, as this discussion suggests, these models are rather different
in character from those of traditional economics. (For a more complete
discussion, see Katzner 1998.)

At first, in the construction of an explanation of a phenomenon for, say,
the period between moments t^0 and t^1, where $t^0 < t^1$, Post Keynesian or
'non-equilibrium analysis' may be conceived of as proceeding analogously
to that which would arise under the equilibrium alternative: a model may
be built up, its solutions or time paths studied, and one time path identified
with observed reality between t^0 and t^1. Then, by pursuing the latter time
path beyond t^1, one possible description of what could happen next may
be provided. It is important to understand, however, that although non-
equilibrium-analytic models constructed in this way might seem similar
to their equilibrium-analytic counterparts, the difference between them
remains significant and far-reaching. For unlike the models of 'equilibrium
analysis', a non-equilibrium-analytic model itself, that is, the variables,
parameters and relations from which it is formed, would be thought of
as time dependent. Once t^0 or t^1 changes, one could not, for the reasons
described above, expect the same model to be appropriate. Hence the
'fixed' parameters do not remain fixed, and the structural relations themselves dissolve: if t^1 were to increase, then the history of reality is modified
by the passage of time and explanations of occurrences after t^0 undergo

such profound change (due to the unforeseen and unpredictable novelty at t^1 that enters the fabric of real life after t^1) that the analytical structures of those explanations are unlikely to hold up in its wake. Shackle (1974, p. 42) has referred to this process in general as 'kaleidics'. Clearly the methodology of non-equilibrium analysis does not allow formal prediction as permitted by the methodology of equilibrium analysis.

Still, stretches of time may unfold during which real-world newness does not appear to impinge substantively on the particular phenomena under investigation. The lack of impact could be reflected in at least two ways. First, it may be that the equations of a model seem to be roughly stable over time in the sense that for a while, as t^1 expands, a single time path (stationary or otherwise) generated by the model continues to approximate observations of reality reasonably well. Here traditional equilibrium analysis, though coming from a different methodological perspective while using the same variables, parameters and relations, provides a formal picture of the real world identical to that furnished by Post Keynesian or non-equilibrium analysis. Furthermore, it is only in unusual cases like these that the possibilities, exposed by the model, of what could happen in the future actually transpire.

Second, and perhaps even less likely, stability over time could also arise with respect to the solution values of the variables even as the equations of the model modify. Thus it may happen that all observed values between t^0 and t^1 are 'essentially' similar. Hence reality between t^0 and t^1 could be viewed as in a pseudo-stationary state: novelty occurs, but either not to a sufficient extent or not in the ways that significantly affect the values of the variables in the analysis. Bausor (1982–83, pp. 173–7) calls this 'historical equilibrium'. In such a case, what is seen can be explained either in terms of a traditional equilibrium analysis with a single model containing a unique stationary state and with all of the assumptions that that entails or, in the language of non-equilibrium analysis, with a 'model' whose equations might modulate but whose solutions remain essentially the same over time.

During periods of transformation, the two approaches clearly supply quite distinct explanations of real-world phenomena. On the one hand, traditional equilibrium analysis can only explain unforeseen change by asserting, after the fact, that 'outside' forces caused alteration in functions or parameter values. But the idea of a continually modulating equilibrium responding to, say, repeated parametric variation is not a very satisfying way of conceptualizing the effects of novelty. Non-equilibrium analysis, on the other hand, cannot provide much of an understanding of unforeseen change either. Yet the acknowledgement of such change is part of the internal structure of its methodological tissue. Non-equilibrium analysis expects change and leaves room for it. Its emphasis is on process and the present state, and on what might happen subsequently. By comparison, equilibrium analysis, with its focus on the end result towards which time paths, if not already there, converge, makes room for change only after it has been observed.

DONALD W. KATZNER

See also:

Agency; Behavioural Economics; Choice under Uncertainty; Conventions; Efficient Markets Hypothesis; Macroeconomic Methodology; Non-ergodicity; Time in Economic Theory; Uncertainty; Walrasian Economics.

References

Bausor, R. (1982–83), 'Time and the structure of economic analysis', *Journal of Post Keynesian Economics*, **5** (2), 163–79.
Galbraith, J.K. (1978), 'On Post Keynesian economics', *Journal of Post Keynesian Economics*, **1** (1), 8–11.
Jefferson, T. and J.E. King (2010–11), 'Can Post Keynesians make better use of behavioral economics?', *Journal of Post Keynesian Economics*, **33** (2), 211–34.
Katzner, D.W. (1998), *Time, Ignorance, and Uncertainty in Economic Models*, Ann Arbor, MI: University of Michigan Press.
Shackle, G.L.S. (1974), *Keynesian Kaleidics*, Edinburgh: Edinburgh University Press.
Shaikh, A. (2011), 'Reflexivity, path-dependence and disequilibrium', *Journal of Post Keynesian Economics*, **33** (1), 1–16.

Exchange Rates

The central feature of the Post Keynesian approach to exchange rates is the belief that capital flows play an active, autonomous role in the economy. This view is key in terms of both their explanation of currency price determination and policy prescription; it is also what most distinguishes Post Keynesian scholarship from orthodox. This entry begins with a review of the latter.

Mainstream theories of exchange rates, though there are several, ultimately agree that the underlying forces driving foreign currency prices are the 'Fundamentals'. Unfortunately, little effort is expended in explaining these determinants (see Harvey 2001). Definitions range from simple lists of potential candidates to circular references to them as 'those variables suggested by economic theory'. In reviewing this literature it becomes apparent that the unifying theme among the seemingly disparate approaches is that the fundamentals represent that set of variables guaranteeing the efficient operation of the foreign currency market. Orthodoxy is therefore assuming the optimality of the outcomes created by real-life foreign exchange operations; to them the task at hand is to identify these undiscovered variables.

A second feature of the mainstream approach is its acceptance of Say's law and consequent relegation of monetary factors to irrelevance. No orthodox exchange rate model treats portfolio capital flows as anything but transitory factors, serving merely to finance trade flows. If short-term investment moves a currency price, this is merely a reflection of the fundamental factors in the economies in question. Thus, though capital is undeniably the largest factor in the balance of payments today, it can be safely ignored. It is no more responsible for *determining* prices than the mechanism that affixes stickers to cans of soup at the grocery store (or, to offer a more modern analogy, resets the register's interpretation of the Universal Price Code symbol).

As a result of these dispositions, orthodox exchange rate theory focuses almost exclusively on trade flows as the determinant of currency prices. Note that if currency prices are indeed driven by trade flows, trade imbalances must represent an excess demand for the money of the surplus nation. A corollary to the orthodox approach is therefore that balanced trade can be expected to prevail over the long run.

Empirical tests of mainstream exchange rate models have fared very poorly, even by the admission of supporters. Trade does not tend towards balance, capital flows appear to have enormous influence on currency markets, and exchange rates have been far too volatile for their only determinants to have been fundamental in origin. This has led to considerable questioning within the orthodox school, the basic result of which has been the conclusion that short-term currency movements may be irrational and therefore 'non-economic'; economists' time, they conclude, is best spent focusing on long-term movements. Note the striking similarity of this position to that of the classicals criticized by Keynes in *The General Theory*.

The Post Keynesian view is driven by their rejection of Say's law (which results from Keynesian uncertainty) and the consequent belief that finance plays a substantive role in determining output and employment. Within this context, Post Keynesians argue that currency prices are a function of international investors' portfolio decisions. Monies of nations whose assets are in greatest demand will tend to appreciate; those in least demand will depreciate. While the value of international assets may be related to trade flows in some indirect manner (which would tend to return us to the orthodox position), it is primarily financial considerations that underlie agents' decision making. Greatest among these is the potential for capital gain from selling an asset in the future. Expectations therefore play a central role in the Post Keynesian explanation. However, unlike the 'rational expectations' employed by the orthodox school, which simply passively observe and predict outcomes (the latter being generated by the fundamentals), those posited in the Post Keynesian view *create* the objective variable. If market participants expect (in aggregate level) that Japanese assets will become more valuable, investors will enter the market to purchase those assets and thus cause their (and the yen's) appreciation. The trick to earning profits becomes guessing the behaviour of the rest of the market.

How do agents form their expectations? That, of course, is the key question. It is also a very difficult one. In their search for a realistic formulation of agents' expectation-formation processes Post Keynesians have turned in part to other disciplines. The work of the psychologists Daniel Kahneman and Amos Tversky has provided an excellent starting-point. In their view, people make decisions on the basis of simple heuristics, the most important of which are availability, representativeness and anchoring. Among the many implications of these rules of thumb are that agents overemphasize the importance of events that are more recent or dramatic (leading to overreaction in financial markets), they tend to place undue confidence in making decisions based on scant information (which combined with the Post Keynesian characterization of decision making in an environment of uncertainty tends to create volatility), and that they will tend to accept the current rate as the standard against which to consider future movements (as in Keynes's 'convention'). Furthermore, there is a great deal of support from the psychological literature for the existence of bandwagon effects in financial markets. This is key because it helps to explain what appear to be self-sustaining trends and the existence and popularity of technical analysis. Recent work done by the psychologist Thomas Oberlechner has added to the Post Keynesian arsenal, suggesting, among other things, that feedback loops between financial reporters and currency dealers give rumour an air of credibility: dealers hear rumours, dealers tell reporters, reporters publish the rumours, dealers read the published rumours as facts and repeat them to reporters, and so on. He also argues that dealers care far less about the veracity of stories than in getting the information first, consistent with Keynes's view that speculation dominates over enterprise in financial markets. Extensive surveys conducted by Oberlechner and his colleagues (Oberlechner and Hocking 2004; Oberlechner et al. 2004) show that the metaphors employed by foreign exchange dealers lead to a view of the market as interactive and organic, like the ocean or a living being – emotional, subject to waves of irrationality, and dwarfing the impact of any single agent. Again, the psychological research fits Keynes much more closely than the mainstream.

In summary, the Post Keynesian view of exchange rates is based on the empirical fact that currency prices are driven by short-term capital flows. Those flows are in turn a function of agents' expectations, which are best modelled using a combination of standard Post Keynesian tools (Keynes's convention, uncertainty and so on) and some borrowed from psychology. The picture that emerges is not one of a market characterized by stability, efficiency and optimality (all benevolently guided by the invisible hand of the fundamentals), but of an institution where agents' imperfectly considered actions create currency prices. Those actions may be marked by stability for long periods of time (though with whipsaw patterns created by the interactions of the cash-in and bandwagon effects) as agents rely on convention to anchor to stable levels or rates of change; but because they are subject to availability and bandwagon effects they are apt to rapid revision in the face of salient events (even when those events may seem inconsequential to cooler heads).

Currency markets affect world welfare in a number of ways. First, international commerce (especially trade) is discouraged by the volatility of exchange rates. Though one could correctly argue that this instability has hardly brought import and export activity to a halt, it has at the very least caused a shift of world resources away from productive activities and into pecuniary ones. Ironically, the change in focus entailed by that shift has no doubt exacerbated the problem by increasing the size and importance of international capital.

Second, if one of the goals of an international monetary system is a tendency to balanced trade, then our current arrangements do not and cannot deliver. Simply put, one price cannot except by coincidence clear two markets. Were there no capital flows in the world then (assuming minimal government intervention) trade imbalances would represent market disequilibria. Current-account deficits and surpluses would soon be eliminated. Alternatively, were capital flows very small as compared to trade flows, then agents in the former would have a vested interest in tracking the latter; they would operate to anticipate current-account activities and to offer liquidity on a timely basis. However, given that the overwhelming majority of international commercial activity takes the form of portfolio investment, there is no reason to believe that events in the world's current account are of more than minor interest to the agents acting in the capital account. Even when a nation is heavily indebted and one might expect a massive depreciation/devaluation to take place to correct an accompanying trade deficit, investors have come to rightly anticipate that the more normal course of action will be emergency loans and grants that allow a continuation of the status quo. There is no automatic stabilizer operating in the post-Bretton Woods world.

As a consequence of their understanding of the foreign exchange market the most common recommendation of Post Keynesian economists with respect to the organization of the international economy is that we control the flow of capital. This notion is hardly new. Keynes argued at the

Bretton Woods conference that nations must reserve the right to control all capital movements. His recommendation was not entirely ignored, but the efforts made were half-hearted and, in the end, easily circumvented by investors. Of course, addressing this shortcoming has now been complicated by the fact that the *laissez-faire* attitude prevails among policy makers and academics.

But reforming the international monetary system will require more than simply slowing the rate of international portfolio investment flows. In recognition of this fact, Paul Davidson has recommended a comprehensive plan that addresses both currency and broader macro issues. At its core is a recognition that Say's law does not operate in the real world and that we must therefore undertake policy to generate full employment. The system would feature a fixed exchange rate (as a means of making international transactions prices more predictable) and provisions to control capital flows (so that those fixed rates could be defended). Furthermore, it would place the burden of resolving trade imbalances on the *surplus* country. This is logical, according to Davidson, because in a less-than-full employment world where Say's law does not hold, surplus nations are antisocial drains on world employment. This proposed system will thereby avoid the inherent deflationary biases of those based on orthodox understandings of the currency market.

JOHN T. HARVEY

See also:

Bretton Woods; Conventions; Economic Policy; Efficient Markets Hypothesis; Expectations; International Economics; International Financial Reform; Say's Law; Tobin Tax.

Bibliography

Davidson, P. (1999), 'Global employment and open economy macroeconomics', in J. Deprez and J.T. Harvey (eds), *Foundations of International Economics: Post Keynesian Perspectives*, London and New York: Routledge, pp. 9–34.
Davidson, P. (2009), *The Keynes Solution: The Path to Global Economic Prosperity*, New York: Palgrave Macmillan.
Harvey, J.T. (2001), 'Exchange rate theory and "the fundamentals"', *Journal of Post Keynesian Economics*, **23** (1), 3–15.
Harvey, J.T. (2009), *Currencies, Capital Flows, and Crises: A Post Keynesian Analysis of Exchange Rate Determination*, London and New York: Routledge.
Oberlechner, T. and S. Hocking (2004), 'Information sources, news, and rumors in financial markets: insights into the foreign exchange market', *Journal of Economic Psychology*, **25** (3), 407–24.
Oberlechner, T., T. Slunecko and N. Kronberger (2004), 'Surfing the money tides: understanding the foreign exchange market through metaphors', *British Journal of Social Psychology*, **43** (1), 133–56.
Schulmeister, S. (1987), 'An essay on exchange rate dynamics', Discussion Paper 87-8, Wissenschaftszentrum Berlin für Sozialforschung [Research Unit Labour Market and Employment], Berlin.

Expectations

One of the intrinsic properties of our world is that the future is uncertain. This uncertainty affects the way decisions are made because economic actors (entrepreneurs, bankers, employees, governments) have to define their priorities by relying on their expectations about the future so as to anticipate it (that is, to act in advance of what they think will happen). In *The General Theory*, Keynes explains how and why expectations influence the current and future states of capitalist economic systems and how expectations are formed.

The first problem when dealing with expectations is to understand how and why they matter. Because we live in a monetary production economy, the most influential expectations are those of entrepreneurs and of the financial sector. Keynes distinguishes between short-term expectations, long-term expectations and confidence in these expectations. The first consist of expectations of costs and sale proceeds induced by a certain level of production, for a given level of capital equipment (new capital assets are not available for production yet). The aim is to find progressively the point of effective demand, that is to say, the point at which production is expected to generate the highest monetary profits. This point represents the current equilibrium position (by which Post Keynesians mean state of rest and not market clearing) induced by a given state of long-term expectations. The short term refers to the 'shortest interval after which the firm is free to reverse its decision as to how much employment to offer' (Keynes 1936 [1973], p. 47). These short-term expectations are gradually revised in the light of current economic results so that 'if we suppose a state of expectation to continue for a sufficient length of time for the effect on employment to have worked itself out . . . completely . . . the steady level of employment thus attained may be called the long-period employment corresponding to that state of expectation' (p. 48). To simplify the analysis, one can consider that entrepreneurs 'do not, as a rule, make wildly wrong forecasts of the equilibrium position' (p. 182), and Keynes considers that 'the theory of effective demand is substantially the same if we assume that short-term expectations are always fulfilled' (Keynes 1937b [1973], p. 181). With this simplification, the level of production is always at the point of effective demand.

What really matters for the economic system are the past and current states of long-term expectations (Kregel 1976). These concern the future net cash flows provided by old and new capital assets. The past states of long-term expectations are reflected in the current amount and composition of the capital equipment. In the simple Keynesian economic model, the current state of long-term expectations (named E in a draft of *The*

General Theory) determines the expected level of expenditures for investment (*I*) and consumption (*C*). Indeed, *E* is a key variable for the marginal
propensity to consume (and so *C*), but also, and mainly, for the marginal
efficiency of capital assets, their user cost and the interest rate (and so *I*).
Therefore, the aggregate demand curve (*D*) and aggregate supply curve
(*Z*) are drawn for a given *E*. Minsky (1975) complemented this analysis by
showing how the state of long-term expectations affects the level of investment. Thus, for two different states of long-term expectation with short-
term expectations realized, see Figures 10 and 11.

P_{Id} is the demand price of capital assets, that is, the price entrepreneurs
are ready to pay for acquiring capital equipment. This price depends on
the price of existing capital equipment as quoted in financial markets and
in mergers and acquisitions (P_K), and on the entrepreneur's (or borrower's)
risk. The latter is the entrepreneur's sentiment about the viability of his/
her project (or, at the macroeconomic level, entrepreneurs' opinion about
the current and future states of the economy). Thus, P_{Id} is determined by
entrepreneurs' expectations about the future net cash flows $E(\Pi_{IF})$ generated by a certain level of investment. P_{Is} is the supply price of capital assets.
This price depends on the unit price (P_I) charged by producers of capital
assets, which in turn depends partly on the user cost of capital assets, that
is, the amount of expected profits forgone by producers from using their
available capital equipment now rather than later. In addition, when the

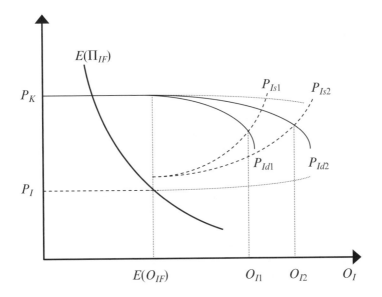

Figure 10   Determination of the level of investment

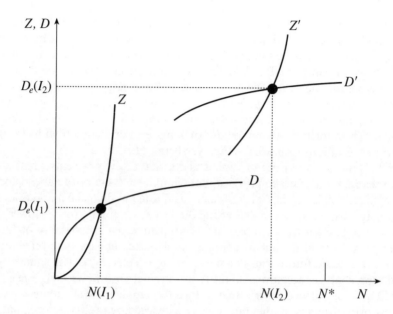

Figure 11   Determination of the level of employment

quantity of investment is not expected to be completely internally funded ($O_I > E(O_{IF})$), the supply price also depends on the expected cost of external funds, which adds a mark-up over the producer price. The cost of external funds is influenced by the lender's risk, which is the lender's opinion about the creditworthiness of entrepreneurs and so the expected net cash flows provided by capital assets.

As long as economic conditions are favourable ($P_{Id} > P_{Is}$), the equalization of the two prices generates a positive level of investment ($I = P_I O_I$). The more optimistic entrepreneurs and lending institutions are, the higher the desired use of leverage and the higher the level of investment are, leading to a higher level of effective demand (and so of production and employment).

It is sufficient for the state of long-term expectations of one community (entrepreneurs, financial analysts or banks) to be degraded to decrease the level of investment. This depressive effect may grow because entrepreneurs and lending institutions are influenced by each other while determining their long-term expectations. Thus, more pessimistic (optimistic) expectations from one community can lead to more pessimistic (optimistic) in the other: P_{Id} and P_{Is} are related (Keynes 1936 [1973], p. 145).

Actually, the reality is worse than that because the two prices do not depend only on the lending institutions' expectations and entrepreneurs' expectations. Indeed, the expectations of speculators are also very important. Kaldor (1939 [1960]) shows in great detail how speculation may generate economic instability. Speculators make portfolio arbitrages to earn short-term capital gains, so they are not interested in future rents provided by a capital asset during its entire life. For speculators, buying financial assets is a game that consists in trying to anticipate what the main opinion of the financial community will be in the short run. This is the famous beauty contest situation described by Keynes in chapter 12 of *The General Theory*. Each judge of the contest is not asked to try to find the most beautiful woman (that is, the most economically viable capital asset), but rather the woman that other judges consider the most beautiful (that is, an asset that others will buy in the near future). The problem is that this kind of behaviour has a tendency to become generalized in financial markets; it is possible to make quick capital gains and, by not adopting this behaviour, one may make capital losses. Thus speculators can lead both lending institutions and entrepreneurs to adopt speculative behaviour (forecasting the psychology of the participants of the financial market) instead of enterprising behaviour (that is, acting in expectation of future income streams provided by the productive use of capital assets). Therefore, the state of long-term expectations, which is already very fragile because it depends on forecasts of economic variables in the long run about which we know very little (wages, interest rates, tastes of consumers, the degree of competition and other variables), is still more precarious because it depends on fads and fashions in the financial markets. This, however, does not mean that the state of long-term expectations is completely unstable. It means only that this state can change very abruptly for insignificant or purely cyclical reasons. These changes are largely independent of the realization or not of short-term expectations, because 'it is of the nature of long-term expectations that they cannot be checked at short intervals in the light of realized results' (Keynes 1936 [1973], p. 51). As explained below, this is important for policy purpose.

However, for Keynes and Post Keynesians the real problem is elsewhere (Kregel 1976). What matters for employment is neither the fulfilment or not of expectations, nor the instability of long-term expectations. It is, instead, the level of the latter that is important because high unemployment ($N^* - N_i$) results from an insufficient level of effective demand (D_e). Stated alternatively, because economic actors are not optimistic enough, their spending is too low to implement a level of production that is consistent with full employment. This shows that the conditions of equilibrium are determined endogenously by economic actors' actions, which are based on their expectations. There is no predefined, or 'natural', state that the economy can reach; this state is created and modified by economic actors' anticipations (Kregel 1986 [1998]). At the macroeconomic level, economic actors are responsible for their own economic situation. Thus, pessimism may be so high that economic actors cannot solve their problems by themselves, or economic actors can be too optimistic and indulge in dangerous behaviour leading to doubtful investment and financial fragility. Indeed, during 'a boom the popular estimation of the magnitude of both . . . borrower's risk and lender's risk, is apt to become unusually and imprudently low' (Keynes 1936 [1973], p. 145). The government should thus do everything to limit and to regulate the economic impact of pessimism and optimism. Indeed, this economic actor has the financial and technical ability to anticipate the macroeconomic consequences of the current anticipations of private agents. Entrepreneurs are only concerned with expectations of profits of their own activities; and it is not their job to take into account the macroeconomic consequences of their own decisions.

For some Post Keynesians, the fact that unemployment mainly exists because the state of long-term expectations of employers in the private sector is usually stubbornly too low to give them an incentive to employ everybody willing to work, has some important policy implications. For example, this casts doubt that fine-tuning policies can achieve full employment because long-term expectations are largely independent of the current state of the economy; and expected demand, rather than current demand, drives employment. The only thing that fine-tuning can achieve more or less successfully is to smooth the business cycle. As a consequence, some Post Keynesians are for a direct involvement of the government in generating full employment through an employer of last resort programme. This programme would decouple the achievement of full employment from the state of long-term expectations prevailing among entrepreneurs and financial institutions (Wray 1998).

The preceding has shown how expectations influence the current state of the economy (determination of the level of production, the level of spending, the amount of external finance and the current level of capital equipment) and why they are important (unemployment or unsustainable economic patterns). It is now necessary to look at how the state of expectations is formed to understand how it evolves. Here 'the *confidence* with which we make this forecast' (Keynes 1936 [1973], p. 148; original italics) becomes important.

Once again it is necessary to make a distinction between short- and long-term expectations. Concerning the former, Keynes agrees that they can quite easily be formed by using probability calculus. To find the effective scale of production, an entrepreneur will make 'several hypothetical expectations held with varying degrees of probability and definiteness' (ibid.,

p. 24 n. 3). The constant overlapping between short-term expectations and current results (ibid., p. 50) makes this probabilistic calculation quite easy because it is based on a routine process.

If probabilities can be used more or less easily for short-term expectations, long-term expectations cannot be based mainly on this kind of method of decision. The mathematical expectation is, at best, an element among others in the process of decision. Indeed, to apply probability calculus with confidence and to base his or her actions only on this method of decision, an economic actor has to assume that the economic system is ergodic. This means that the properties of the system in which decisions are made are not modified by these decisions (Davidson 1991). However, investment spending is a crucial decision (Shackle 1955) because it leads to irreversible qualitative changes in the economic system. Thus future possibilities and properties of the economic system evolve as new technologies and methods of production are introduced. There is another important reason why long-term expectations cannot rely essentially on probabilities: these expectations depend on factors that we know little about, so that the state of confidence plays a dominant role in the formation and change of the state of long-term expectations. This implies that, contrary to probability calculus, probability and confidence do not necessarily move in the same way and have to be clearly separated. It is not because more information is available that confidence is increased.

Thus 'the *state of confidence*, as they term it, is a matter to which practical men always pay the closest and most anxious attention' (Keynes 1936 [1973], p. 148; original italics). To evaluate this state of confidence, economic actors refer to the prevailing convention concerning the present and future states of the economy. This means that, to take crucial decisions, they rely heavily on the past and current economic situations, and that they judge the current opinion of the majority as the best (Keynes 1937a, [1973]). However, entrepreneurs can also go against the convention in place and let their instinct dominate their decisions. Long-term expectations then depend on different elements that are related but have little to do with probability (Dequesh, 1999): animal spirits, creativity and uncertainty perception are three of them. It follows from this that conventions are fragile and subject to sudden changes. However, they are usually stable enough for entrepreneurs whose optimism and animal spirits push them to invest. Moreover, this uncertainty about the future is less an obstacle than a stimulus to investment. Uncertainty leaves the system open to the imagination of entrepreneurs regarding profit opportunities. If investment depended on 'nothing but a mathematical expectation, enterprise [would] fade and die' (Keynes 1936 [1973], p. 162).

ÉRIC TYMOIGNE

See also:

Conventions; Employer of Last Resort; Investment; Keynes's *Treatise on Probability*; Non-ergodicity; Uncertainty.

References

Davidson, P. (1991), 'Is probability theory relevant for uncertainty?', *Journal of Economic Perspectives*, **5** (1), 129–43.

Dequesh, D. (1999), 'Expectations and confidence under uncertainty', *Journal of Post Keynesian Economics*, **21** (3), 415–29.

Kaldor, N. (1939), 'Speculation and economic stability', *Review of Economic Studies*, **7** (1), 1–27; reprinted and revised in Kaldor, *Essays on Economic Stability and Growth*, London: Duckworth, 1960, pp. 17–58.

Keynes, J.M. (1936), *The General Theory of Employment, Interest and Money*; reprinted in *The Collected Writings of John Maynard Keynes*, Vol. 7, London: Macmillan for the Royal Economic Society, 1973.

Keynes, J.M. (1937a), 'The general theory of employment', *Quarterly Journal of Economics*, **51** (2), 209–23; reprinted in *The Collected Writings of John Maynard Keynes*, Vol. 14, London: Macmillan for the Royal Economic Society, 1973, pp. 109–23.

Keynes, J.M. (1937b), 'Ex post and ex ante', 1937 lecture notes; reprinted in *The Collected Writings of John Maynard Keynes*, Vol. 14, London: Macmillan for the Royal Economic Society, 1973, pp. 179–83.

Kregel, J.A. (1976), 'Economic methodology in the face of uncertainty: the modeling methods of Keynes and the Post-Keynesians', *Economic Journal*, **85** (342), 209–25.

Kregel, J.A. (1986), 'Conceptions of equilibrium: the logic of choice and the logic of production', in I. Kirzner (ed.), *Subjectivism, Intelligibility, and Economic Understanding*, New York: New York University Press, pp. 157–70; reprinted in P. Boettke and D. Prychitko (eds), *Market Process Theories, Volume 2: Heterodox Approaches*, Cheltenham, UK and Northampton, MA, USA: Edward Elgar, 1998, pp. 89–102.

Minsky, H.P. (1975), *John Maynard Keynes*, London: Macmillan.

Shackle, G.L.S. (1955), *Uncertainty in Economics*, Cambridge: Cambridge University Press.

Wray, L.R. (1998), *Understanding Modern Money*, Cheltenham, UK and Northampton, MA, USA: Edward Elgar.

Export-led Growth

The standard Post Keynesian framework is demand driven. It is not surprising then that, as a source of international demand for domestic products, *net* exports play a major role in output and growth determination. Indeed, exports could be seen as *special* in the sense that these boost demand while simultaneously having a positive impact on the trade balance. Recent development literature outside of Post Keynesian circles, in part motivated by the East Asian example, has energetically debated the special nature of tradables in general, and exports in particular. The emphasis on the demand constraint, as opposed to an endowment constraint, however, is largely what distinguishes the Post Keynesian school from this body of literature.

In the traditional Keynesian multiplier approach with fixed output prices and an infinite price elasticity of supply on the part of (domestic and foreign) producers, an autonomous export expansion works through the multiplier process to create expanded output that is only partially crowded out by imports. Since the respective national producers set prices in their domestic currency (that is, producer currency pricing) and adjust supply in response to demand, a nominal devaluation translates into a real devaluation. Assuming that the Marshall–Lerner condition is satisfied, net exports rise, setting in motion the expansionary process.

The model of export-led growth that has arguably attracted the most attention among Post Keynesians is the one developed by Thirlwall (1979). In a departure from most preceding Post Keynesian work, the balance-of-payments-constrained growth (BPCG) model, building on Nicholas Kaldor's work, emphasizes the external constraint; indeed it emphasizes it almost to the exclusion of other constraints. The basic idea is simple, and its roots can be traced back both to mercantilist literature and to the more recent work on foreign exchange gap models. In Thirlwall's words:

> If a country gets into balance of payments difficulties as it expands demand, before the short term capacity growth rate is reached, then demand must be curtailed; supply is never fully utilised; investment is discouraged; technological progress is slowed down, and a country's goods compared to foreign goods become less desirable so worsening the balance of payments still further, and so on. A vicious circle is started. By contrast, if a country is able to expand demand up to the level of existing productive capacity, without balance of payments difficulties arising, the pressure of demand upon capacity may well raise the capacity growth rate. (Thirlwall 1979, p. 46)

Thus the external balance constraint acts to limit supply-side growth. More specifically, and ignoring relative price changes, the BPCG growth rate is defined as the rate of growth of domestic exports divided by a country's income elasticity of demand for imports. Thirlwall interprets this as the dynamic version of the Harrod foreign trade multiplier. The key then to long-run growth is to make one's exports more attractive to the rest of the world relative to imports, in the non-price dimension. Put differently, a country grows rapidly by exporting products that have a high income elasticity of international demand and importing goods that have a low income elasticity of demand. Thirlwall and others have argued that the pattern of specialization involved captures supply-side effects through the respective income elasticities, which should be understood, perhaps, as slowly evolving state variables rather than parameters. The policy implications are clear. A country specializing in sophisticated manufactures and importing agricultural products, would, for example, grow at a healthy pace, assuming that the income elasticity of demand for the former is much higher. The parallels to the Prebisch–Singer hypothesis are obvious.

One could argue that, since trade is assumed to be balanced, the BPCG model is not really an export-led growth model. Rather, the growth of exports creates room for the economy to grow without running into balance-of-payments problems. In this sense, zero export growth accompanied by zero import growth will have the same effect as a high growth rate of exports accompanied by an equally high growth rate of imports. Put differently, an economy that does not require imports for growth will not require exports for growth either.

A recurring critique of the BPCG model involves the absence of relative price effects in a demand-side model that focuses on long-run growth; such an assumption for a price-taking *small* country would perhaps be less controversial, but that would not sit well with the demand-side emphasis of the model. Prices need not be fixed, however, in the Post Keynesian framework. In the cumulative causation models associated with the Kaldorian tradition, an initial shock involving greater export demand for domestic products translates into output growth (see Setterfield and Cornwall 2002 for a concise formulation). The latter, in turn, leads to productivity growth in the presence of Verdoorn effects. Productivity growth, assuming that it is not completely offset by rising wage costs, then results in increased competitiveness and exports, thus completing the first loop of a virtuous cycle. Conversely, a negative shock to exports could set into motion a vicious cycle. Notice again that the economy does not suffer from supply-side constraints as it expands. The supply of labour, capital and other factors adjusts endogenously in response to the environment. Notice also, that the demand stimulus need not arise from exports. Indeed, in the absence of a trade balance constraint, an internal stimulus, such as an increase in consumption, will achieve similar results. One could argue, however, that the presence of economies of scale makes access to international markets important, especially for economically small economies. Further, one would be inclined to give exports a special role in this schema in light of Thirlwall's summary of Kaldor's growth laws, according to which 'the growth of manufacturing output is . . . fundamentally determined by demand from agriculture in the early stage of development and exports in the later stages' (Thirlwall 1983, p. 346). In this sense, the Kaldor–Verdoorn cumulative causation framework can be interpreted as supporting the case for export-led growth.

Razmi (2011) explicitly introduces exportables, importables and non-tradables, deriving the BPCG hypothesis as a special case of a more general framework. The possibility of domestic production of importables and consumption of exportables makes the effect of an exogenous increase in world demand for a country's exports less certain, both in qualitative and quantitative terms. Moreover, the *internal* structure of the economy may constrain the externally constrained growth rate, and thus the prospects for export-led growth, below that predicted by the traditional BPCG hypothesis. Finally, since the BPCG framework is based on the 'imperfect substitutes' model, pursuit of tradable production implies pursuit of exportable production. As discussed below, in many small open economies sectoral allocation between tradables and non-tradables is an important consideration, pointing to a greater role for the real exchange rate, that is, the price of tradables relative to non-tradables.

The pursuit of export-led growth raises interesting distributional issues in a Post Keynesian framework. For example, in an environment of mark-up pricing with wage stickiness, a currency devaluation aimed at boosting exports will, at a given level of employment, shift income towards profits. Blecker (1999) uses a Kaleckian framework, which incorporates differences in saving behaviour between workers and capitalists to highlight some interesting implications. For example, trade surpluses have the same positive effect on profits as government deficits. This, in Kalecki's view could help explain the puzzle of 'economic imperialism'. In so far as net exports involve boosting domestic profits at the expense of the rest of the world, this message resonates in the more recent trade literature on *strategic* profit shifting. The impact of increased export competitiveness via lower real wages on growth will depend on the economic structure. An economy that is 'stagnationist' in its (hypothetical) autarkic state will be less likely to experience export-led growth since the negative effect on aggregate demand of a shift towards capitalists (that is, the savers) will dominate the positive effect of increased exports. For the same reason, however, the positive effect on the trade surplus is likely to be greater in such an economy. Based on similar logic, Blecker (2002) shows that an economy open to trade is more likely to be 'exhilarationist' than a closed one.

That growth in Post Keynesian models that is driven by aggregate demand creates a logical problem in the form of a 'fallacy of composition' at the global level. In a world with limited global demand, individual countries can grow through net exports only if they 'steal' demand from others by pursuing a beggar-thy-neighbour policy. Export-led growth from the demand side is thus a policy that the whole world cannot simultaneously pursue since there is no neighbour left to beggar. Put differently, an economically large country, or a group of small countries exporting similar products, cannot pursue export-led growth without experiencing significant negative terms-of-trade effects. Is the expansion of tradable production, therefore, a zero-sum game? This question raises interesting supply-side issues traditionally underexplored by Post Keynesians, to which we now turn.

As mentioned earlier, the real exchange rate can be defined as the relative price of tradables. Manufactures tend to constitute a large part of the tradable sector while services are largely non-tradable. Combining these two observations with the hypothesis that there is something special about the manufacturing sector, whether it be the presence of learning externalities, economies of scale, or greater scope for accumulation and technological progress, implies that real exchange rate undervaluation (an increase in the relative price of tradables) may have additional important benefits apart from export promotion. For example, Rodrik (2008) provides a supply-side-oriented explanation for why undervalued real exchange rates could spur growth. The explanation centres on two problems that are widespread in many developing countries: (i) institutional weaknesses and (ii) market failures. The paper argues that these features characterize the tradable sector to a greater extent, leading to suboptimal resource allocation. By boosting profitability in the tradable sector, an undervalued exchange rate acts as a second-best policy. The study finds robust econometric support for the hypothesis that undervalued exchange rates promote growth but mainly in developing countries. Razmi et al. (2009) model a small open dual economy with open (Keynesian) and hidden unemployment. Tradable sector output requires imported capital goods. Growth-promoting policies, therefore, have implications for the external balance. By ensuring that an expanding tradable sector does not cause external balance problems, the real exchange rate can serve as one of those instruments. Since the country is a price taker in international markets and trade is balanced, a fallacy of composition does not arise. The paper finds empirical support for the hypothesis that real undervaluations are a useful instrument for the pursuit of accumulation and growth, although again the evidence is more robust for developing countries.

Once one introduces supply-side considerations, interesting questions arise concerning the nature of export-led growth at more disaggregated levels of analysis. Recent non-Post Keynesian literature has, following Melitz (2003), analysed the relationship between firm heterogeneity and trade. Empirical work has established at least three relevant stylized facts: (i) plants are heterogeneous in the productivity dimension, (ii) exporters sell most of their output domestically, and (iii) exporting firms tend, on average, to be larger and more productive. The last finding suggests either that more productive firms self-select into export markets (due to extra costs imposed by the process of exporting), and/or that firms that export grow more productive due to economies of scale, learning, technological spillovers, competitive pressures and other factors. Causality, in other words, could flow in either direction. While empirical evidence for self-selection tends to be quite robust, that for learning-by-exporting appears to be significant only for developing countries. This is not surprising, since these countries tend to be farther from the technological frontier and, therefore, tend to have greater scope for learning. Pedro and Yang (2009) provide a survey of related literature.

At least two broad lessons can be derived from Post Keynesian and more mainstream work on export-led growth. First, the balance-of-payments constraint does seem to bind in many cases. Second, there does seem to be something special about the tradable sector, especially in the case of developing countries. What makes the tradable sector a driver of growth? Is it indeed the tradable sector in general that has interesting characteristics or are these specific to exports? In cases where exports raise economy-wide productivity, is it through Verdoorn effects or the reallocation of resources through the exit of less-productive firms? Does the process of export-led growth work through specialization or diversification? Why do undervaluation and export growth tend to have more significant effects in developing countries? What are the costs of export-led growth in terms of income redistribution, forgone consumption, resource misallocation and global crowding out, and do these costs render export-led growth unsustainable over the long run? These and related questions raise exciting possibilities for future work in the Post Keynesian tradition.

ARSLAN RAZMI

See also:

Balance-of-payments-constrained Economic Growth; Exchange Rates; International Economics; Kaldorian Economics.

References

Blecker, R. (1999), 'Kaleckian macro models for open economies', in D. Johan and J.T. Harvey (eds), *Foundations of International Economics: Post Keynesian Perspectives*, London and New York: Routledge, pp. 116–49.

Blecker, R.A. (2002), 'Distribution, demand and growth in neo-Kaleckian macro models', in M. Setterfield (ed.), *The Economics of Demand-Led Growth: Challenging the Supply-Side Vision of the Long-Run*, Cheltenham, UK and Northampton, MA, USA: Edward Elgar, pp. 129–52.

Melitz, M. (2003), 'The impact of trade on intra-industry reallocations and aggregate industry productivity', *Econometrica*, **71** (6), 1695–725.

Pedro, M. and Y. Yang (2009), 'The impact of exporting on firm productivity: a meta-analysis of the learning-by-exporting hypothesis', *Review of World Economics*, **145**, 431–45.

Razmi, A. (2011), 'Exploring the robustness of the balance of payments-constrained growth idea in a multiple good framework', *Cambridge Journal of Economics*, **35** (3), 545–67.

Razmi, A., M. Rapetti and P. Skott (2009), 'The real exchange rate as an instrument of development policy', Working Paper 2009–07, University of Massachusetts, Amherst, MA, June.

Rodrik, D. (2008), 'The real exchange rate and economic growth', *Brookings Papers on Economic Activity*, **2**, 365–412.

Setterfield, M. and J. Cornwall (2002), 'A neo-Kaldorian perspective on the rise and decline of the golden age', in Setterfield (ed.), *The Economics of Demand-Led Growth: Challenging the Supply-Side Vision of the Long Run*, Cheltenham, UK and Northampton, MA, USA: Edward Elgar, pp. 67–86.

Thirlwall, A.P. (1979), 'The balance of payments constraint as an explanation of international growth rate differences', *Banca Nazionale del Lavoro Quarterly Review*, **32** (128), 45–53.

Thirlwall, A.P. (1983), 'A plain man's guide to Kaldor's growth laws', *Journal of Post Keynesian Economics*, **5** (3), 345–58.

Financial Instability Hypothesis

Hyman Minsky had a long and distinguished career that spanned almost four decades, during which he developed a number of key insights into the workings of modern financial economies. Minsky's work is complex and rich, and attempts to model the real world in which financial institutions play a key role. It has had a definite influence, not only on Post Keynesians, but also on institutionalists and Marxists. Moreover, while there have always been scattered references to Minsky in the mainstream literature, the recent financial crisis has certainly multiplied these references, as many economists, in particular those in the New Keynesian tradition, try to understand what exactly has transpired.

For Minsky, orthodox theory is best described as a 'village market' where bartering one good for another is the principal economic activity. A capitalist economy, in contradistinction, is much closer to a 'Wall Street' system where agents, businessmen and bankers deal with investment financing and capital assets. It is within this setting that Minsky's financial instability hypothesis is developed. It deals with a capitalist economy of production, in Keynes's sense, where finance and financial institutions play a key and decisive role.

Among Minsky's many important contributions, the financial instability hypothesis remains his most important. It explains the inherent cyclical nature of modern financial economies, and how economic booms can sow the seeds for an eventual downturn, that is, how stability breeds instability. Capitalist economies cannot be studied without referring to their monetary and financial nature.

Minsky's work on financial instability incorporates aspects of John Maynard Keynes, Michał Kalecki and Irving Fisher. First, Minsky's work is set within an environment of Keynesian uncertainty. Businesses and banks operate in an uncertain environment in Keynes's sense, and hence their expectations and decisions are made in a world devoid of reliable knowledge. Second, Kalecki's principle of increasing risk is another central component of Minsky's work, according to which firms and the macroeconomy become more fragile as their level of debt increases. As it expands, the economy becomes increasingly fragile. In this sense, financial cycles are endogenous. Finally, as the economy collapses, deflation may ensue, implying that debt incurred during the expansionary phase of the cycle may not be reimbursed. This may then lead to debt-induced bankruptcies and a deepening recession. However, expansionary fiscal policy and a central bank acting as a lender of last resort may help in limiting the scope of the recession.

For Minsky, the early stages of an economic cycle are best described as periods of caution, as agents remember the last phases of the previous cycle. Coming out of a recession, firms tend to undertake safe investment projects where the expected revenues exceed the necessary debt repayments. Agents' liability structures are very liquid and the debt/equity ratio of firms is relatively low, or at least within respectable or acceptable levels. Firms expect good returns and expectations are generally fulfilled. In this stage, the economy is in a tranquil phase of 'hedge finance'. Firms tend to finance their investment initially through retained earnings, or at least internal financing is much greater than external financing.

As the boom continues, however, firms decide to undertake additional investment. Minsky (1982, pp. 120–24) refers to this phase as 'economic euphoria'. The optimism is fuelled by growth, and is shared by banks (ibid., p. 121). This is a key element. As firms invest more than their retained earnings allow, they will seek access to bank credit. Provided that banks are as optimistic as firms, they will finance new investment. Simultaneously, asset prices start rising as speculators enter the market. These 'Ponzi financiers' tend to borrow heavily to purchase assets in the hope of selling them at higher prices.

As both firms and speculators become more indebted and less liquid, interest rates start to rise, as rates are positively correlated with debt/ equity ratios. It is the illiquidity of both banks and firms that fuels the rise in interest rates. This rise of interest rates places the economy at risk, as firms may not be able to meet their debt commitments. Refinancing existing debt is made at a higher rate of interest, implying that cash outflows are greater than cash inflows. Debt burdens are increasing. Higher interest rates and less liquid balance sheets also imply growing fragility of the banking system. This is when the economy moves into a situation of 'Ponzi finance'. Financial euphoria slowly leads to financial panic, and a crisis may be at hand. At this point, asset prices and gross profits collapse; investment falls or even stops. The economic boom is now replaced by an economic downturn.

The degree to which the economy spirals downward will depend largely on the role of prices, but also on fiscal and monetary policy. If price inflation is high, firms' revenues may be sufficient to permit them to honour part of their debt commitments. If price inflation is low, however, accumulated debt will be too much of a burden, and the economy will continue to spiral downward.

Minsky's work on financial instability carries important policy implications in the Keynesian tradition. Since it discusses the inherent tendency for economies to go from booms to busts, it addresses the specific roles of fiscal and monetary policies in constraining the dynamic nature of capitalist economies. In fact, since Minsky's work relies on developed modern institutions, it can be used to explain why large-scale depressions have not occurred since the 1930s. Since the public sector was small, fiscal policy could not have prevented the Great Depression. It is in this sense that Minsky's work is insitutionally sensitive.

Today, however, the story is much different and governments are active and important players in the real world. Fiscal policy can have an important role in preventing further economic malaise, as fiscal deficits can translate into larger gross profits, enabling firms to honour their cash commitments on outstanding debt. Moreover, fiscal deficits may also limit the extent to which debt deflation occurs. According to Minsky (1982, p. xx): 'A cumulative debt deflation process that depends on a fall of profits for its realization is quickly halted when government is so big that the deficit explodes when income falls'. Furthermore, the central bank can have an important role in preventing runs on banks. It does so by expanding the monetary base to allow sufficient liquidity. It can also relax certain regulatory rules, such as reserve requirements. In doing so, a liquidity crisis can be avoided. Both policies can help in preventing continued deterioration of money profits, which are important for debt validation and asset prices. Minsky's reliance on modern institutions explains in fact why 'It' has not happened again.

In Minsky's world, capitalism is not a system that tends naturally to stability. It is fraught with chaotic episodes and tendencies to periodic booms and slumps. This is characteristic of financial and monetary economies in an uncertain world. This does not mean that a depression cannot happen again. Governments and central banks may choose not to act. Moreover, sound fiscal and monetary policies do not eliminate the financial phases of economic cycles, as these are endogenous to the cycle. Policy cannot inhibit the existence of Ponzi speculators.

Minsky's financial instability hypothesis has raised some concern among Post Keynesians. Key to this criticism is the fact that Minsky's analysis of financial fragility is essentially based on the microeconomic behaviour of the bank and the firm and is devoid of macroeconomic significance. This has led Lavoie and Seccareccia (2001) to question the 'missing macroeconomic link'.

Minsky's analysis of the notion that economic expansion leads to higher debt/equity ratios that translate automatically into higher interest rates may be applicable to the individual firm or bank. As their debt/equity ratios increase, banks may perceive them as riskier and may charge a higher rate of interest to cover the higher risk. Minsky's analysis, however, may not necessarily hold for the macroeconomy. In other words, as the economy expands, it may not necessarily become more fragile or riskier, and there is no reason why rates of interest need to increase, especially in an environment of endogenous money with exogenous rates of interest. These are set by the central bank.

Minsky, in fact, provides only one example of his financial fragility hypothesis in a macroeconomic setting. It can be found in an early article in the *American Economic Review* (1957). The only problem is that the argument is set within the loanable funds approach (Lavoie 1996; Rochon 1999; Lavoie and Seccareccia 2001), which would explain why interest rates automatically increase during expansions.

Furthermore, Minsky's early analysis is silent on Kalecki's profit equations (although they figure in his later writings, see Minsky 1977). Had Minsky taken note of these equations, he would have perhaps realized that debt/equity ratios might not rise during expansions, which would then imply that the economy does not necessarily become increasingly fragile. As Lavoie and Seccareccia (2001, p. 84) argue, 'There is a missing link. Minsky does not provide any rationale to justify his rising leverage ratio thesis at the macroeconomic level'.

On a last note, what can be said about the financial crisis, which started in 2007/08? Was this a Minsky moment? Has 'It' happened again? To many observers, both in the mainstream and within the Post Keynesian tradition, this was indeed a classic Minsky moment. For others, the answer is not so clear-cut. First, this crisis deals in a very real way with financial fraud on a large scale committed by the banking sector. Minsky never envisaged fraud as a mitigating factor in his instability hypothesis. Second, and perhaps more to the point, Minsky's hypothesis deals with the inability of firms to service their debt and their increasing fragility. Yet, during this last crisis, households in the end were left holding the debt bag, not firms. So for these two reasons, it is doubtful whether the crisis which started in 2007/08 was a Minsky moment.

LOUIS-PHILIPPE ROCHON

See also:

Banking; Business Cycles; Central Banks; Financial Markets; Financial Reform; Fiscal Policy; Global Financial Crisis; Kaleckian Economics; Liquidity Preference; Monetary Policy; Money Manager Capitalism; Rate of Interest; Uncertainty.

Bibliography
Bellofiore, R. and P. Ferri (eds) (2001a), *Financial Keynesianism and Market Instability: The Economic Legacy of Hyman Minsky, Volume I*, Cheltenham, UK and Northampton, MA, USA: Edward Elgar.
Bellofiore, R. and P. Ferri (eds) (2001b), *Financial Fragility and Investment in the Capitalist*

Economy: The Economic Legacy of Hyman Minsky, Volume II, Cheltenham, UK and Northampton, MA, USA: Edward Elgar.

Lavoie, M. (1996), 'Horizontalism, structuralism, liquidity preference and the principle of increasing risk', *Scottish Journal of Political Economy*, **43** (3), 275–300.

Lavoie, M. and M. Seccareccia (2001), 'Minsky's financial fragility hypothesis: a missing macroeconomic link?', in Bellofiore and Ferri (eds) (2001b), pp. 76–96.

Minsky, H. (1957), 'Monetary systems and accelerator models', *American Economic Review*, **47** (6), 859–83.

Minksy, H. (1977), 'The financial instability hypothesis: an interpretation of Keynes and an alternative to "standard" theory"', *Nebraska Journal of Economics and Business*, **16** (1), 5–16.

Minsky, H. (1982), *Can 'It' Happen Again: Essays on Instability and Finance*, Armonk, NY: M.E. Sharpe.

Minsky, H. (1986), *Stabilizing an Unstable Economy*, New Haven, CT: Yale University Press.

Nasika, E. (2000), *Finance, Investment and Economic Fluctuation: An Analysis in the Tradition of Hyman P. Minsky*, Cheltenham, UK and Northampton, MA, USA: Edward Elgar.

Rochon, L.-P. (1999), *Credit, Money and Production: An Alternative Post-Keynesian Approach*, Cheltenham, UK and Northampton, MA, USA: Edward Elgar.

Financial Markets

In mainstream economics, financial markets provide the conduit through which savers channel their savings towards investment, permitting the economy to allocate resources to their best uses through time. Guiding the so-envisaged intertemporal allocation of resources, the prices of financial instruments determined in financial markets are held to properly reflect 'fundamentals'. As saving finances investment, on this view, unlocking the economy's supply-side potential requires fully mobilizing the economy's saving pool. As competitive markets are efficient, on this view, maximum productivity of the economy is best served by a quest for market 'completeness' – the ideal of Arrow–Debreu contingent contracts spanning the whole space of states of nature, supposedly allowing an optimal spreading of risks. This vision of well-behaved financial markets anchored by fundamentals complements a notion of money as an arbitrary *numéraire* and mere convenience, facilitating exchange though otherwise 'neutral', that is, not determining anything 'real'.

The empirical finance literature is awash with puzzles challenging the 'efficient market hypothesis' and related beliefs. Most important of all is the experience of recurrent financial crises severely disrupting real-world economies, sharply contradicting any notion of financial markets as naturally tending towards stability and equilibrium. Yet there is remarkably little concern that mainstream economics may provide an altogether flawed depiction of the role of finance in real-world economies. Financial markets are indeed at the heart of the flaw in neoclassical economics diagnosed by Keynes in the *General Theory* (Bibow 2009).

Post Keynesian economics offers a refreshing alternative that is inspired by Keynes's path-breaking insights into the role of liquidity and finance in 'monetary production economies'. The starting-point is that 'human decisions affecting the future . . . cannot depend on strict mathematical expectation, since the basis for making such calculations does not exist' (Keynes 1936, pp. 162–3). Especially regarding investment decisions that require a look into the faraway future, Keynes emphasizes that about many relevant factors there is 'no scientific basis on which to form any calculable probability whatever. We simply do not know' (Keynes 1937 [1973], p. 114; see also Runde 1998).

'Fundamental (or Keynesian) uncertainty' is a critical factor considering financial markets (Kahn 1972; Chick 1983; Kregel 1998). The spreading of risks becomes a complicated matter when bankruptcy is a real possibility, but an event of unquantifiable probability. Specialized financiers may be willing to attach a price to 'risks' of intrinsically uncertain magnitude, but individual non-standardized risks are generally non-marketable. On the other hand, given the interconnectedness among economic units woven by financial markets through debt contracts that span over time, bankruptcies may easily spread, with contagion leading to systemic harm far beyond what seemed reasonable and objective estimates of individual default risks.

It is in the presence of fundamental uncertainty that liquidity attains a special attractiveness by offering some degree of safety and flexibility to the individual who fears price volatility of alternative assets and prefers keeping options open for the time being. Liquid assets may, therefore, trade at a premium over alternative assets. This is despite the fact that staying liquid is not an option for society as a whole, since society as a whole is permanently committed to any real investment once it is made. The *General Theory* focuses on the issue of satisfying 'liquidity preference' through financial markets and how this affects the economy in attaining full employment. The point is that waste of resources through underutilization results from any widespread urge to abstain from real investment commitments. How society chooses to deal with fundamental uncertainty is thus a crucial public policy matter. Financial markets may contribute to the spreading of risks, but coping with important uninsurable risks is an altogether different kind of challenge. Keynes emphasizes that public policy is crucial:

> Unemployment develops, that is to say, because people want the moon; – men cannot be employed when the object of desire (i.e. money) is something which cannot be produced and the demand for which cannot be readily choked off. There is no remedy but to persuade the public that green cheese is practically the same thing and to have a green cheese factory (i.e. a central bank) under public control. (Keynes 1936, p. 235)

As this quotation pinpoints, on a scale of liquidity, money represents 'liquidity par excellence', offering a fully known nominal value to its holder at any time. At the same time, it is the command over money and finance that equips entrepreneurs and entrepreneurial investors with the power to issue orders for production and investment. The contracts involved in recruiting labour services and obtaining the finance to pay for them are commitments to make future payments in terms of money, featuring money as a unit of account. The financial system intermediates between those who have a choice in holding their wealth in the form of money or other financial instruments and those who wish to acquire money in order to initiate production and/or the acquisition and management of assets. The financial system creates and channels the liquidity that is the precondition for economic activity and growth. In the fictitious exchange economy of mainstream economics any commodity may serve as *numéraire* and finance cannot play any substantial role when expected future income is included in the budget constraint upon which intertemporal optimization is set to operate. By contrast, in monetary production economies, both the money of account function and the property of money as liquidity *par excellence* are central to the functioning of the financial system and economy at large (Pasinetti 2007). In this twofold way, then, 'the importance of money essentially flows from its being a link between the present and the future' (Keynes 1936, p. 293). Other financial assets meet liquidity needs to some degree.

Regarding financial intermediation, there is an obvious attraction in being in a position to acquire higher-yielding assets by issuing lower-yielding liabilities, including monetary financial instruments that are substitutes for money issued by the sovereign. Specialized financial institutions may be engaged in various kinds of intermediation services aiming at profit maximization. In general, if unrestrained, the forces of competition and innovation may flourish, perhaps excessively so, in the creation, issuance and trading of financial instruments designed to transfer monetary units and associated risks. Financial stability presupposes sustainable business models of financial intermediation and arbitrage activities. The lure of short-term profit in an industry that literally deals in bridging an uncertain future has produced a history of finance that is scattered with fraud, instability and crises. Regulation of financial instruments and supervision of financial intermediaries are thus essential public policy functions.

The private sector has largely captured the profitable business of issuing liquidity *par excellence*, supported by public safety-nets. Bank deposits dominate notes and coins in the portfolios of the general public, with peace of mind provided by government-guaranteed deposit insurance.

And banks themselves economize their liquidity and normally hold deposits at the central bank only at whatever minimum may be required of them, assured that systemic liquidity is underwritten by the central bank as 'lender of last resort'. As a 'dealer in money and debts' (ibid., p. 205), the central bank has the power to swiftly adapt the size and composition of its balance sheet. Extending the scope of debt management techniques as applied to the public debt, typically providing an important collateral asset and the benchmark against which private risks are priced, monetary policy represents the most powerful public tool for applying immediate influence over financial conditions (Goodhart 1995).

Under normal conditions monetary policy consists of setting the short-term rate of interest, the price rather than the quantity of base money, and an important price for the financial system indeed, strongly influencing the profitability of financial intermediation in particular (Dow 1997). While the 'short-term rate of interest is easily controlled by the monetary authority' (Keynes 1936, p. 203), the challenge of monetary policy lies in guiding financial conditions more generally, and in a way that is conducive to achieving the goals of public policy. As an example, Keynes uses open-market operations to illustrate the role of expectations and market conventions in determining longer-term interest rates. In practice, the interaction between the central bank and financial market players is a longstanding, two-way, and rather complex one – making monetary policy an art as well as a science. With monetary policy tactics employing both words and deeds, Keynes stresses the pivotal role of banks, which, in his view, 'in general . . . hold the key position in the transition from a lower to a higher level of activity' (Keynes 1937, p. 222). Banks (perhaps also operating as 'shadow banks' if the authorities allow) can create the liquidity that the real economy requires to function and grow.

To pinpoint the flaw that Keynes identified in the 'classical' system, and to illuminate how Post Keynesian and mainstream perspectives differ, note here that the determination of 'the' rate of interest (rather: financial conditions), has nothing to do with equilibrium in some imaginary 'capital market' balancing saving and investment flows. Instead, the rate of interest is determined by portfolio equilibrium in asset markets at any given short-term policy rate: at current prices all existing marketable financial instruments are willingly held, with a given pool of liquidity – as provided by the banking system – supporting interest rates and asset prices at their current levels. While the outcome at any given time reflects the interaction between the monetary authorities and financial market players, there is no direct and immediate way in which 'fundamentals' may find their supposedly uniquely correct expression in asset prices. Under Keynesian uncertainty the idea of uniquely correct asset prices determined by fundamentals is philosophically fallacious. Tomorrow's realities supposedly reflected in uniquely correct asset prices today are yet to be determined. The point is that financial markets – however guided – are a real factor in shaping tomorrow's realities; not by channelling saving flows arising from given incomes though, but by creating and channelling liquidity, thereby determining national income and employment.

In short, money and finance condition the real economy, not the other way round. It is the financial system that grants, or declines, the command over the money units needed to meet money contracts. The price at which it does so is the money rate of interest – accordingly described by Keynes as 'ruling the roost' (Keynes 1936, p. 223) in setting the pace of capital accumulation and economic activity. While regular cash flows from the circular flow of production and spending may seem to keep the channels filled, this overlooks the fact that dated debts need to be rolled over, giving lenders the option to deny finance at their discretion. Reference to the prominence of retained earnings over external sources in financing corporate investment misses the point that fresh external finance is vital in sponsoring growth in spending, growth upon which the well-functioning of capitalism appears to depend. If growth is driven by corporate investment, the corporate sector can be expected to be in continuous need of fresh external finance: the situation that Keynes took for granted. Alternatively, apart from public 'deficit spending', more temporary growth stimuli can also arise from positive trade balances and household sector credit-financed spending, with financial markets catering for correspondingly different needs in each case.

Under Keynesian uncertainty, public policy is vital in anchoring financial markets. When let off the hook, endogenous processes of credit creation and asset market play may easily feed bubbles and lead to financial fragility, intrinsically entwined with powerful real economy feedback loops (Minsky 1975 [2008]). Liquid financial markets serve both individual and social purposes, but the 'fetish of liquidity' may also generate overtrading and underinvestment. Keynes knew from intimate experience that 'markets can remain irrational for longer than you or I can remain solvent' (attributed) and that professionals may find it safer to anticipate 'what average opinion expects the average opinion to be', rather than try to 'defeat the dark forces of time and ignorance' (Keynes 1936, pp. 155–6). Warning that 'when the capital development of a country becomes a by-product of the activities of a casino, the job is likely to be ill-done' (ibid., p. 159), he also suggested that the dynamism of monetary production economies depends on entrepreneurial animal spirits meeting some corresponding support from 'spontaneous optimism' in financial markets.

JÖRG BIBOW

See also:

Banking; Efficient Markets Hypothesis; Financial Instability Hypothesis; Financial Reform; Financialization; Investment; Keynes's *General Theory*; Liquidity Preference; Monetary Policy; Money; Rate of Interest; Uncertainty.

References

Bibow, J. (2009), *Keynes on Monetary Policy, Finance and Uncertainty*, London and New York: Routledge.
Chick, V. (1983), *Macroeconomics after Keynes*, Cambridge, MA: MIT Press.
Dow, S.C. (1997), 'Endogenous money', in G.C. Harcourt and P. Riach (eds), *A 'Second Edition' of The General Theory*, London and New York: Routledge, pp. 61–78.
Goodhart, C.A.E. (1995), *The Central Bank and the Financial System*, Cambridge, MA: MIT Press.
Kahn, R.F. (1972), *Selected Essays on Employment and Growth*, Cambridge: Cambridge University Press.
Keynes, J.M. (1936), *The General Theory of Employment, Interest and Money*, London: Macmillan.
Keynes, J.M. (1937), 'The general theory of employment', *Quarterly Journal of Economics*, **51** (2), 209–23; reprinted in *The Collected Writings of John Maynard Keynes*, Vol. 14, London: Macmillan for the Royal Economic Society, 1973 pp. 109–23.
Kregel, J. (1998), 'Aspects of a Post Keynesian theory of finance', *Journal of Post Keynesian Economics*, **21** (1), 111–33.
Minsky, H.P. (1975 [2008]), *John Maynard Keynes*, New York: McGraw-Hill.
Pasinetti, L.L. (2007), *Keynes and the Cambridge Keynesians: A 'Revolution in Economics' to be Accomplished*, Cambridge: Cambridge University Press.
Runde, J.H. (1998), 'Uncertainty, Keynesian/Knightian', in J. Davis, D.W. Hands and U. Mäki (eds), *Handbook of Economic Methodology*, Cheltenham, UK and Northampton, MA, USA: Edward Elgar, pp. 513–16.

Financial Reform

Walter Bagehot states that 'the briefest and truest way of describing Lombard Street is to say that it is the greatest combination of economical power and economical delicacy the world has ever seen' (Bagehot 1873 [1978], p. 49). The greatness of the delicacy is easy to understand. From a *laissez-faire* position, any proposal to make the management of such economical power an exception to the general rule that competition should be free from any government intervention is hard to swallow. Yet few would maintain that the financial market is a market like any other. Differences of opinion about financial reform mainly depend on the different reasons on which this position is based.

According to a recent influential report on financial regulation, when one asks about the goals of regulators,

[t]raditional economic theory suggests that there are three main purposes. 1. to constrain the use of monopoly power and the prevention of serious distortions to competition and the maintenance of market integrity; 2. to protect the

essential needs of ordinary people in cases where information is hard or costly to obtain, and mistakes could devastate welfare; and 3. where there are sufficient externalities that the social, and overall, costs of market failure exceed both the private costs of failure and the extra costs of regulation. (Brunnermeier et al. 2009, pp. 1–2)

Points 1 and 2 constitute the rationale for regulation in every economic sector. And, until the recent financial crisis, the prevailing view was that the financial sector ought to be regulated in roughly the same way as private utilities, the only exception being that for the financial sector point 2 was considered much more important than point 1. After the eruption of the crisis, the previously neglected issue of externalities (systemic contagion) has become dominant, and the idea that the set of rules which guarantee sound management of a single institution also ensures that the stability of the system as a whole has been dismissed. Therefore, in the recently reformulated traditional conception of financial market regulation, these markets are seen as atypical because for them points 2 and 3 are stronger than in other markets. If the costs of a less than perfect information and contagious failures are larger than the costs of regulation, the government can step in.

From what might be called a Keynesian perspective, once it is recognized that financial markets are affected by problems of asymmetric information and systemic contagion, the most important issue concerns a clear understanding of the peculiarities which these markets display, regardless of so-called 'micro' and 'macro' failures. Financial institutions do not match the demand and the supply of a fixed loanable fund available to finance investment, for the theory that there is a fixed loanable fund available to finance investment which exactly corresponds to the volume of saving at full employment (or at some non-inflationary level of unemployment) is denied. The function of financial intermediaries should be singled out, instead, considering that: (a) the financial system is not forced by savings to limit the volume of credit, being able to freely adjust its supply to the needs of industry and trade; (b) it is possible, by monetary means, to ensure *additional* expenditure which need not cause any diversion from other expenditures. Money is endogenous and is able to affect the level of economic activity. In short, the interest rate should be viewed as a purely monetary phenomenon.

Moving from the notion of the rate of interest as a purely monetary phenomenon, financial institutions have to be conceived as the link through which central bank monetary impulses are transmitted to the economy. These impulses, in turn, might affect current output, and therefore also the amount of new savings. At any given interest rate, the supply of loans has to be such as to meet the community's fluctuating demand for borrowing.

However, this does not imply that financial institutions are passively engaged in the riskless business of satisfying any demand for credit money, marking up the price set by the central bank. There are, in fact, 'certain limitations on the ability of the monetary authority to establish any given complex of rates of interest for debt of different terms and risk' (Keynes 1936, p. 207). If in principle nothing prevents central banks from dealing in debts of every maturity and risk, as a matter of fact this is a practice central banks could endorse only in exceptional circumstances. Otherwise, a private system of credit management would be totally relieved of any lender's risk, freeing financial institutions from any profitability and liquidity constraints, thus removing any impulses towards the selection of trustworthy borrowers. On the one hand, if financial intermediaries were forced to act as middlemen in the proper sense, there would be a poor match between lenders and borrowers who are interested in different maturities, risks and scales of funds (or, which is the same thing, the premium required by lenders to depart from liquidity would be unreasonably variable). On the other hand, if financial institutions were unconditionally assisted by the government, there would be no incentive to prevent the borrowers' tendency towards overindebtedness, due 'either to moral hazard, that is, voluntary default or other means of escape, possibly lawful, from the fulfilment of the obligation, or to the possible insufficiency of the margin of security, i.e. involuntary default due to disappointment of expectations' (ibid., p. 144). The crucial issue in the debate on financial reform is how to find a satisfactory balance between these two contrasting requirements. Government depositors' insurance, minimum reserves, regulations over capitalization and accounting, access to the facilities of the lender of last resort, all this regulatory framework can be seen as a way of preventing the consequences of irresponsible borrowing without leaving the determination of the interest rate to market forces. While trying to contain maturity and risk transformation, these measures make it, at the same time, possible.

Starting with the deregulatory 'Big Bang' of the beginning of the 1980s, the tendency towards unrestricted levels of credit money supply has prevailed. Because of a substantial increase in the instability of the financial system, central banks became systematically involved in dealing in debts of every maturity and risk. At the same time, due to the widespread use of financial instruments such as options, swaps and asset-backed securities, financial institutions made liquid what were once illiquid positions. The market was considered able to manage risk which had been traditionally contained within banks. The risk would be assumed by the less risk averse, while the needed liquidity would have been assured by the market and not by financial intermediaries assisted by the government. When the financial crisis erupted in 2007–08, it became clear that the market had been completely unable to evaluate the riskiness of a large class of assets intensively used as collateral in a process of credit money creation. Market liquidity evaporated, up to the point of generating a classic banking panic on short-term deposits (the repo market). The market was dominated by financial intermediaries engaged in a sort of asset-based credit multiplication, a multiplication completely unbounded, sensitive to marked-to-market evaluation and thus strongly pro-cyclical, and able to infiltrate and destabilize all the segments of the market. In the end, the financial industry was saved by the intervention of the lender of last resort, on which every system of credit intermediation must rest.

Back to the role of the government as the pillar of the creation of liquidity, something that the market can assure only to individuals, since 'there is no such thing as liquidity of investment for the community as a whole' (ibid., p. 155). And in fact the central bank was forced to act indefinitely as the market maker of last resort for a variety of assets no longer required by the market (the only attempt of the lender of last resort to discriminate between illiquidity and insolvency, a distinction completely meaningless in an interconnected and overleveraged market-oriented financial infrastructure, gave rise to the collapse of Lehman Bros. in September 2008, precipitating the crisis to an unprecedented scale). The new system contained the cost of loan capital partly by hiding the risk in a maze of intra-sector transfers, partly by parking it in the balance sheet of government-supported agencies, and partly by discharging it onto naive investors. Many are inclined to say that this is the result of greed and of inappropriate regulation in a market which is very far from the ideal state of perfect competition. An adequate regulatory framework could have helped the market to move towards that ideal state of affairs. But what if, thanks to an appropriate regulatory framework, lenders had been fully aware of the risks of securitized loans? If financial markets had functioned perfectly, the price of loan capital would have been unaffordable.

After the crisis, proposals to contain credit money supply spread, in response to the increased burden that government efforts to stop financial disorders were placing on the shoulders of taxpayers. Whence the proposal of separating commercial from investment banking in order to prevent retailers from engaging in proprietary trading (the Volcker rule). Second, the proposal of separating deposit-taking from credit-granting firms. Banking regulation is conceived here as restricted to the task of running a stable payment system (Tobin 1985; Kay 2009). Then there is the idea of limited-purpose banking (LPB), the most extreme form of narrow banking, according to which the debt-based financial intermediation system must be shut down, and replaced by an equity-based financial system (Kotlikoff 2010). Here, the reaction to financial disorder has reached the point of envisaging not only the possibility of disconnecting the dual function of bankers, but also of denying that banks can make maturity and risk transformation. Financial intermediation should take place through mutual funds only, without engaging in the management of maturity and risk mismatch. It is worthwhile to compare the proposals for segregating deposit-taking institutions and LPB. For the former, the pillar of financial reform is to draw a line between fully state-insured institutions – which should provide a safe store of value for risk-averse investors and a proper working of the payments system – and an uninsured and lightly regulated area of financial businesses, in which *caveat emptor* should apply. For the latter, no firewalls should be built around traditional banking activities, since not only deposit-taking institutions but also credit-granting firms should not be leveraged.

From both points of view, in order to avoid financial disorders, the damaging externalities due to the 'too big to fail' problem must be internalized, putting the burden of financial crises on the shoulders of those who benefited by lending in a risky – and thus more rewarding – financial environment. Yet, while according to the segregated funds proposal a market-oriented leveraged system of risk management could freely develop in the non-segregated environment, according to the more radical LPB proposal maturity and risk transformation is useless and should not be allowed. It is in the radicals' field that the influence of the traditional conception of the role of financial intermediaries is more strongly felt. Envisaging the avoidance of maturity and risk transformation as the scope of financial reform, it has lost sight of the fact that such transformation is what reduces the cost of capital. The LPB appears viable because it denies that the cost of capital has to be managed with a view to the real economy. Looking at the issue from the standpoint of the loanable fund theory and of money neutrality, such management is harmful. Leverage can only generate a discrepancy between the money rate of interest and the natural rate of interest, with the sole negative effect of inflating output and asset prices. From a Keynesian perspective, however, LPB would simply mean that the long-term interest rate would not be governed by the monetary authority, but by fluctuating factors which are outside its direct control.

The idea of segregating and strongly regulating only deposit-taking institutions apparently mediates between the conflicting purposes of allowing the needed supply of credit money and assuring the stability of the most essential functions of the credit system. But it does so at the price of reducing the functions of regulated financial institutions to the running of the payments system, delegating entirely to the market the task of providing credit in the due amount: 'The activities of managing maturity mismatch, and spreading and pooling risks, which once needed to be conducted within financial institutions, now can, and should, be conducted through markets' (Kay 2009, pp. 46–7). In essence, supporters of narrow banking have faith in the virtues of a market-based financial system. The Basel agreement is seen, from their perspective, as a failed exercise in functional segregation. Following a long-lasting trend away from liquidity ratios towards capital requirement ratios, the Basel agreements focus on the externally imposed requirement that banks have common equity equal to some percentage of their risk-weighted assets. However, due to the possibility of organizing transactions outside the regulatory border, non-bank financial intermediaries were stimulated by the Basel rules to leverage freely in a financial market regulated by the *caveat emptor* principle.

During the financial turmoil, the risk-adjusted capital measure has proved quite unable not only to prevent the influence of financial disorders on the real economy, but also to protect traditional banks – which have by now become financial conglomerates heavily engaged in the use of new financial instruments – from the financial chaos. According to narrow-banking supporters, a forcefully implemented ring-fencing regime would have protected deposit-taking institutions. Nevertheless, that unregulated institutions will be able to assure the needed credit supply in a stable financial environment, even without access to the retail deposit base and the related explicit government assistance, remains a completely unsettled issue. A central bank strongly committed to abstain from supporting the market would make much less easy the terms on which the financial system was ready to lend; the price of loan capital could cease to be a sort of administered price. Moreover, recurrent failures of institutions which are forced to operate in a highly unregulated competitive market could create intolerable disorders, even if the payment system remains sheltered.

It is interesting to note here that, even in the aftermath of the recent financial crisis, putting a check on leverage and insulating the unregulated segment of the market are not considered compelling priorities. This is not so much because the incoming Basel III rules will only go into effect over the next decade, or because Basel III remains centred on the idea that it is equity capital and not liquid assets that provides a cushion against the drying up of liquidity in times of crisis. The point is that the perimeter of the new agreement remains restricted to the already regulated banking activities, and these activities remain strongly interconnected with the market-based intermediation process. Faced with a choice between regulation and insulation, the Basel agreements reject both. The proposal to forbid useless financial transactions regardless of the intermediaries involved in them, in fact, has never received due attention. This is not surprising, given that considering the credit supply which is employed for purely financial purposes as distinct from that employed for the purposes of new current output is entirely unacceptable when speculation is not seen as destabilizing, but instead as the very activity that allows the market to discover the right prices and provide the needed liquidity.

It is in this light that the issue should be discussed of whether it is impossible to regulate bankers because regulation pushes financial transactions outside the regulatory perimeter. Of course, that all financial intermediaries cannot be regulated if governments do not have the political strength to do it (because of the enormous power of some intermediaries or because a single government can control only a national regulatory perimeter) is a big issue. It remains true, however, that financial reform, quite apart from its political feasibility, has to be considered practicable according to the economic functions that financial intermediaries are called upon to perform. Banks must transmit, as neutrally as they can, central bank monetary impulses to the economy. In doing so, they must bear some risk, otherwise there would be no need to look for solvent borrowers. This management of risk cannot be delegated to the market, and it becomes more difficult when conditions in the real economy are such as to require increasing doses of credit money, overstretching the role of the financial sector. After all, the causes of financial disorders have to be traced back to the real economy. A private sector in debt overhang, higher income inequalities, a very poor incentive to invest, coupled with shrinking public expenditure, could make the coexistence of a privately managed financial system and a financial environment not plagued by recurrent disorders a 'delicacy' very hard to handle.

ALDO BARBA

See also:

Banking; Central Banks; Economic Policy; Financial Markets; Liquidity Preference; Monetary Policy; Money; Rate of Interest.

References

Bagehot, W. (1873), *Lombard Street: A Description of the Money Market*, in *The Collected Works of Walter Bagehot. Volume 9*, N. St John-Stevas (ed.), London: The Economist, 1978.
Brunnermeier, M., A. Crockett, C. Goodhart, A.D. Persaud and H. Shin (2009), 'The Fundamental Principles of Financial Regulation', Geneva: International Centre for Monetary and Banking Studies (ICMB) and London: Centre for Economic Policy Research (CEPR), *The Geneva Reports on the World Economy*, no. 11.
Kay, J. (2009), 'Narrow Banking: the Reform of Banking Regulation', London: Centre for the Study of Financial Innovation (CSFI).
Keynes, J.M. (1936), *The General Theory of Employment, Interest and Money*, London: Macmillan.
Kotlikoff, L.J. (2010), *Jimmy Stewart is Dead: Ending the World's Ongoing Financial Plague with Limited Purpose Banking*, New York: Wiley.
Tobin, J. (1985), 'Financial innovation and deregulation in perspective', in Tobin, *Policies for Prosperity: Essays in a Keynesian Mode*, P.M. Jackson (ed.), Brighton: Wheatsheaf Books, 1987, pp. 255–64.

Financialization

Even before the global financial crisis starting in 2007–08, it was widely recognized that the growing weight of finance in the US and world economies had become a determining characteristic of the era we live in (see, for example, Epstein 2005). In recent years, the interdisciplinary literature on 'financialization' has become one of the most rapidly developing areas in the social sciences, including (Post Keynesian) macroeconomics (see Hein and van Treeck 2010 for a survey). In particular, the concept of financialization is grounded in the stages-of-development approach that is inherent in many Post Keynesian and regulationist analyses of capitalism. In this view, the 'finance-led' or 'finance-dominated' growth regime can be understood as the successor model to the 'Golden Age of Capitalism' or the 'Fordist growth model' of the postwar decades. As such, the Post Keynesian concept of financialization is a structuralist alternative to the largely ahistorical, neoliberal notions of 'financial deregulation' or 'financial liberalization' that had dominated economic literature during the decades before the global financial crisis starting in 2007–08.

In principle, one can distinguish between a supply-side and a demand-side economic analysis of financialization. Historically, the call for financial deregulation, gaining support in the 1970s, was mainly justified based on supply-side arguments. Broadly speaking, it was argued that deregulated financial markets, rather than traditional banks, were best suited to spur product innovation and technical progress by improving corporate governance and providing diverse forms of finance to young and dynamic firms. Essentially, this view can be seen as an outflow of the 'financial repression/liberalization' hypothesis formulated primarily in the context of developing countries. It can also be traced back to the New Institutional Economics literature, which highlighted the importance of deregulated and innovative financial markets for disciplining management (see, for example, Jensen and Meckling 1976). Today, however, many of the early proponents of financial liberalization seem to be somewhat disillusioned in light of the questionable effects of deregulated financial markets on business practices such as 'short-term performance obsession' (Rappaport 2005) and corporate scandals and 'value destruction' (see, for example, Jensen 2005).

While the supply-side dimension of financialization has potentially important implications for economic growth and, more generally, human development, Post Keynesian authors have focused primarily on demand-side and distributional implications of financialization. In what follows, we shall first describe sequentially how far financialization can be expected to affect the business and personal sectors. Then, we shall place these partial effects of financialization in the context of the Post Keynesian model of growth and distribution, and discuss different macroeconomic growth regimes potentially associated with financialization.

In the context of a closed private economy, we can define financialization as, broadly speaking, a combination of: a primary orientation by firms towards shareholder value; increasing income and wealth inequalities between shareholders and higher management on the one hand, and ordinary employees on the other; and easier access to credit for private households, including low-income groups.

As far as firms' investment and financing decisions are concerned, financialization can be hypothesized as having two main effects, from a Keynesian perspective (but also in line with the new institutional economics). First, firms' preference for expansion is weakened as a result of remuneration schemes based on short-term profitability and financial market results. Second, shareholders impose higher profit payouts (higher dividends and share buybacks) and resist new issues of equities (which tend to lower stock prices and reduce earning per share). Both these effects increase the firm's dependence on debt.

Historically, the political objective of shareholder value orientation was to prevent 'empire building' and 'overinvestment' by unconstrained management, which became a major concern of shareholders whose interests had been largely ignored by the managerial 'technostructure' throughout the Fordist postwar period: 'Among the manifestations of this lack of control over management were the pursuit of market share and growth at the expense of profitability' (OECD 1998, p. 17). It was argued that by imposing a higher distribution rate of profits and higher leverage on firms, the 'free cash flow' at the disposal of managements, and hence their capacity to 'shirk' and (over)invest, should be reduced. Moreover, the permanent threat of hostile takeovers and stock market-oriented remuneration schemes should penalize bad and reward good management practices.

A further potential effect of shareholder value orientation in corporate governance, particularly in so far as it is typically accompanied by labour market deregulation, is that the bargaining position of (blue-collar) workers deteriorates, as the Fordist 'manager–worker alliance' is replaced by a 'shareholder–manager alliance'. This leads to a redistribution of income in favour of profits and management remuneration at the expense of ordinary wages. In essence, in a financialized economy shareholders dominate (or co-opt) managers in the investment and financing decision, while shareholders and managers dominate workers in the conflict over income distribution (see, for example, Dallery and van Treeck 2011).

Moving to the private household sector, the following changes in the pattern of personal consumption may be expected as a result of financialization. First, consumption will be affected positively as firms distribute more profits to shareholders but negatively by lower ordinary wages and higher income inequality within the household sector. Second, the increase in wealth, relative to income, may lead to a decrease in the personal saving rate. Third, the deregulation of the credit market will lead to an increase in the overall propensity to consume out of income and wealth, in so far as social norms also develop towards a 'debt culture'.

At the macroeconomic level, the effects of financialization on aggregate demand and growth are ambiguous. Clearly, at the microeconomic level, shareholder value orientation was perceived by its proponents as a way to boost profitability at the firm level. However, at the macroeconomic level, a lower desire of firms to invest and the redistribution of income at the expense of lower-income groups will have adverse effects on aggregate production, and hence on profits, *ceteris paribus*. To see this, recall the following simple accounting identities:

$$\text{Production} = \text{Investment} + \text{Consumption}, \qquad (1)$$

$$\text{Income} = \text{Profits} + \text{Wages}, \qquad (2)$$

and hence

$$\text{Profits} = \text{Investment} + \text{Consumption} - \text{Wages}, \qquad (3)$$

or

$$\text{Profits} = \text{Investment} + \text{Consumption out of capital income} \\ - \text{Savings out of wages.} \qquad (4)$$

Equation (4) is Kalecki's well-known profit equation and the accounting basis of the 'Cambridge equation', which is the centrepiece of all Post Keynesian models of growth and distribution. The Cambridge equation says that the growth–profit trade-off may exist at the firm level but does not simply carry over to the macroeconomic level: when many firms attempt to increase their profitability by reducing investment (accumulation), in the absence of compensating forces they will collectively experience an actual decline in profits (the profit rate), due to the adverse aggregate demand effect. Similarly, when shareholder value orientation puts pressure on wages, then profits may actually decline, if the associated negative effects on consumption and aggregate demand are not compensated for by some other means. This phenomenon is well known in the Post Keynesian literature as the paradox of costs.

However, with financialization, there are a number of new channels allowing firms to increase profitability at the macroeconomic level despite a decline in the rate of capital accumulation (which has been an important stylized fact in many developed economies over the past two or three decades) and despite the surge in income inequality (another important stylized fact of the era of financialization in many countries) that should normally depress consumption and aggregate demand. These channels include increased consumption out of distributed profits by shareholders as a result of higher dividends and share buybacks, as well as the debt financing of consumption by workers and wealth-owners facilitated by financial deregulation and a rising wealth-to-income ratio. However, these effects then raise a number of interesting stock–flow issues, in the sense that the interaction between investment and consumption flows on the one hand, and the stocks of wealth and debt on the other, become crucial elements in explaining overall macroeconomic developments, with questions of sustainability arising.

In terms of economic modelling, these effects can best be analysed with the help of so-called stock–flow consistent (SFC) models (Godley and Lavoie 2007). Intuitively, an economy can be 'debt led', when the positive aggregate demand effects of higher consumption out of distributed profits and personal credit dominate the contractionary effects of a higher debt burden on the part of both businesses and private households. But it can also become 'debt burdened', when the positive flow effects of rising credit are overwhelmed by the negative stock effects of rising debt (through higher debt-servicing costs, lower creditworthiness and liquidity constraints, and increased overall financial fragility).

Retrospectively, many commentators have recognized the relevance of the Post Keynesian financialization hypothesis for explaining the deeper origins of the US and global financial crises starting in 2007–08. In fact, it can be argued that the US economy was essentially debt led during much of the past decades. Especially since the second half of the 1980s, both private households and corporations have increased their debt ratios considerably. For the business sector, this was partly the result of the hostile takeover movement of the 1980s and of important equity repurchases. While firms had previously borrowed to close the financing gap between internal means of finance and real investment expenditure, they now increasingly used credit to make financial investments. This contributed to the rise in personal financial wealth and capital income, which in turn boosted private consumption. Interestingly, the highest-income groups in the US seem to have reduced their saving rate considerably during the new economy boom of the 1990s, indicating the importance of the so-called 'wealth effect' on consumption in the US. At the same time, lower-income households had increasingly easy access to credit, which allowed them, up to a point, to expand consumption expenditures despite the stagnation of their real incomes. This led to a remarkably robust expansion of aggregate demand (and hence profits) despite the very volatile and often rather sluggish private real investment activity and despite rising inequality. When the new economy stock market bubble burst in 2001, the housing market boom almost immediately 'took over' and allowed for a further decline in the personal saving rate. An important implication of the credit-driven demand expansion in the US was very large and increasing current account deficits, with the US operating as the 'spender of last resort' for the world economy. Yet, at some point the economy turned 'debt burdened', and, when house prices eventually stopped increasing, a severe economic downturn and global financial crisis became inevitable.

Today, the non-functionality of the finance-led growth regime is clearly visible. From a Keynesian stages-of-development perspective, a new type of 'managed capitalism' should now be developed, in which financial market speculation would be contained through effective political regulations and primary concern would be given to the promotion of a stable real sector expansion facilitated by a more active public sector and a more equitable distribution of income.

TILL VAN TREECK

See also:

Consumer Debt; Economic Policy; Financial Markets; Financial Reform; Galbraith's Economics; Growth and Income Distribution; Growth Theory; Income Distribution; Market Governance; Stock–Flow Consistent Modelling; Wage- and Profit-led Regimes.

References

Dallery, T. and T. van Treeck (2011), 'Conflicting claims and equilibrium adjustment processes in a stock–flow consistent macro model', *Review of Political Economy*, **23** (2), 189–211.
Epstein, G. (ed.) (2005), *Financialization and the World Economy*, Cheltenham, UK and Northampton, MA, USA: Edward Elgar.
Godley, W. and M. Lavoie (2007), *Monetary Economics. An Integrated Approach to Credit, Money, Income, Production and Wealth*, Basingstoke: Palgrave Macmillan.
Hein, E. and T. van Treeck (2010), 'Financialisation in Post-Keynesian models of distribution and growth – a systematic review', in M. Setterfield (ed.), *Handbook of Alternative Theories of Economic Growth*, Cheltenham, UK and Northampton, MA, USA: Edward Elgar, pp. 277–92.
Jensen, M. (2005), 'Agency costs of overvalued equity', *Financial Management*, **34** (1), 5–19.
Jensen, M.C. and W.H. Meckling (1976), 'Theory of the firm: managerial behavior, agency costs and ownership structure', *Journal of Financial Economics*, **3** (4), 305–60.
OECD (1998), 'Shareholder value and the market in corporate control in OECD countries', *Financial Market Trends*, **69**, 15–38.
Rappaport, A. (2005), 'The economics of short-term performance obsession', *Financial Analysts Journal*, **61** (3), 65–79.

Fiscal Policy

Fiscal policy is concerned with the economy-wide effects of government expenditure and revenue raising. Post Keynesians believe that there is no endogenous mechanism in a capitalist economy which will ensure that economic activity tends to full employment, even in the long run. Hence, fiscal policy is important as a major way in which the government can raise aggregate demand to the full-employment level. In a justly celebrated article, Lerner (1943) argued that fiscal policy should not be based on 'sound finance' in which expenditure was balanced by revenue over a year or some other arbitrary period. Instead, fiscal policy should be based on 'functional finance'. Government expenditure and revenue should be determined so that total expenditure in an economy is at the rate which will produce full employment without inflation. This is to be done without any concern about whether the resulting budget is in surplus or deficit.

With the neoclassical resurgence in the 1970s and succeeding decades, 'sound finance' was again adopted by many economists and policy makers as the over riding guide to good fiscal policy. While Post Keynesian economists generally have a more complex theory of inflation than that implied by Lerner in 1943, they share his rejection of 'sound finance'. In the last three decades of the twentieth century, one major strand in Post Keynesian writing on fiscal policy was designed to counter neoclassical arguments against budget deficits. Nevile (2000) contains a survey of these neoclassical arguments and the counters to them.

Among the neoclassical arguments, crowding-out theory and the twin deficits hypothesis are of particular importance as each have had a substantial impact on actual policy making. Crowding-out theory maintains that an increase in the deficit will cause a fall in private investment expenditure of (almost) the same size as the rise in the deficit. If the government borrows to finance the deficit this, it is argued, will force up interest rates, reducing private investment. Moreover, even if the various multiplier effects are such that economic activity increases, more money will be demanded by the public to carry out this increased economic activity. They will try to borrow this extra money, forcing up interest rates further until the increase in gross domestic product is reversed. An assumption underlying this crowding-out thesis is that the monetary authorities are successful in maintaining a constant stock of money. However, even before financial deregulation the monetary authorities in developed economies did not maintain a constant volume of money. Since financial deregulation, the volume of money is endogenous.

The second influential argument, the twin deficits hypothesis, maintains that if a budget deficit is created or increased, the balance-of-payments current account deficit will increase by a very similar amount so that all the expansionary impact will go overseas through increased imports. The social accounting identities ensure that this will happen if other things do not change, but this proves nothing unless one has a theory to support the implied *ceteris paribus* assumption. Supporters of the twin deficits hypothesis usually have no theoretical foundations for their arguments and those that have been put forward hold only in very long-run equilibrium situations, making them largely irrelevant to anti-cyclical policy making. Moreover, empirical evidence does not support the twin deficits hypothesis. For example, from 1990 to 1993 in G7 countries on average budget deficits more than doubled and the current account deficits fell to zero. This was not an isolated incident. A similar story applies to the years from 1980 to 1983.

There is an obvious contradiction between these two theories. If any increase in government expenditure results in an equal increase in imports, it cannot crowd out private domestic expenditure. Of course, like expenditure in the private sector, government expenditure does have a marginal propensity to import, but Post Keynesian economists believe that in most countries neither the government nor the private propensities are big enough to prevent countercyclical discretionary fiscal policy being effective.

The severe slump in economic activity, which started in the United States in 2008 and rapidly spread to many other countries, produced widespread and rapid conversions to the merits of fiscal policy. Most of those advocating or implementing fiscal policy were not Post Keynesians and there was a variety of programmes to counter the slump. Post Keynesians emphasized the need for quick implementation of cash transfers to households, particularly to low-income households. Apart from equity considerations, these households have a high propensity to spend and their expenditure has a lower import content than is usual for the expenditure of the rich. Then over time the fiscal stimulus should change to spending on both physical and human capital. This will not only increase aggregate demand but will also help on the supply side and, if projects are carefully selected, will help overcome bottlenecks. More generally, since lengthy spells of unemployment are destructive of work skills, fiscal stimulus expenditure, whatever it is spent on, will increase potential output just by reducing unemployment. Projects that are specifically designed to increase physical and human capital will increase potential output even more. The consequent increase in GDP will raise taxable capacity so that the expenditure is effectively self-financing (Nevile and Kriesler 2011).

Even before the events of 2008, Post Keynesian writing on fiscal policy was not just defensive. Lerner's arguments of 1943 were developed and qualified in important ways that relate to inflation, external balance and the public debt. Much has been done on indicators of the stance of fiscal policy and the contribution, if any, fiscal policy can make to the solution of structural problems has been analysed.

For a while after the Second World War it did seem possible that there was a narrow zone of economic activity compatible with both full employment and a very low rate of inflation. However, as more and more workers were younger, with no memories of the Depression of the 1930s, the situation predicted by Michał Kalecki emerged. Full employment reduced substantially employers' power to discipline workers, leading to declining efficiency and inflationary wage demands. Most Post Keynesian economists argued that, if fiscal policy was to be successful in maintaining the economy at, or close to, full employment, it had to be supplemented with an incomes policy. (See, for example, Cornwall 1983, chapters 11 and 12.) As well as specific incentives or penalties in tax-based incomes policies (see ibid., pp. 272–5) fiscal policy can support incomes policies at the macro level, for example, through a general trade-off between wage rises and tax cuts and/or increased expenditure on the 'social wage'. Experience with incomes policies suggests that even successful ones are only effective for a limited period of time, which can usually be measured in years rather than decades. Ongoing innovation in designing incomes policies is important if fiscal policy, together with other policies, is to maintain full employment without inflation.

In a number of countries rising public debt is perceived to be a major problem as a consequence of budget deficits incurred to provide a fiscal stimulus. There are two aspects to this: general problems that could occur in any country, and problems for countries in the euro area caused by the nature of that currency union. In general, if a country's public debt is held by its own citizens, the liability (to taxpayers) is balanced by the assets of those who hold the debt. Nevertheless, the consequences for income distribution may be important. In theory these could be overcome through tax and other fiscal measures for redistribution. In practice, if the interest bill is large, this may not be feasible for political and even administrative reasons. A large public debt relative to GDP reduces the freedom of action with respect to fiscal policy and may impose other burdens. A quasi 'sound finance' argument, that the budget should be balanced not over a year but over the business cycle, is too strict as it ignores the effects of inflation and economic growth. If nominal GDP is growing there can be a positive budget deficit on average over the business cycle without any upward trend in the ratio of public debt to GDP. Most Post Keynesians argue that a deficit on average is usually necessary for the health of an economy (see, for example, Bougrine 2000, various chapters).

Continuing large budget deficits, especially if accompanied by large current account deficits, may lead financial markets to fear an increase in the rate of inflation in a country and to withdraw financial investment, leading to a decline in the value of the country's currency on the foreign exchange market. The resulting inflationary pressure can put stress on any incomes policy and could lead to a depreciation/inflation vicious circle. Whether or not the concerns about budget deficits are well founded, the actions of financial markets cannot be shrugged off. If more than one equilibrium position is possible this may result in an economy reaching an equilibrium position with a high rate of unemployment. This is particularly the case where equilibrium is path determined. While most Post Keynesians focus on the disequilibrium path in the short to medium run, rather than on some longer-term equilibrium position, the conclusion is the same: namely that fiscal policy may have to be modified to meet the fears of financial markets, for example by ensuring that the budget is balanced or in surplus when the level of economic activity is high. The importance of international financial markets was underlined by events in the widespread severe slumps starting with that in the United States in 2008.

As far as the problems facing countries in the eurozone such as Greece, Portugal and Spain are concerned, Post Keynesian economists start by pointing out two facts. The first is that the Maastricht Treaty sets out clearly that price stability rather than full employment is the overriding priority in macro policy within the eurozone. Price stability is defined as an inflation rate between zero and 2 per cent. The European Central Bank is expected to achieve this in the medium term (see, for example, Jespersen 2002). The second is that the limit on the size of budget deficits, namely a ratio of 3 per cent between the budget deficit and GDP, was not based on any theory or empirical research but is completely arbitrary and unnecessarily low. Hence fiscal policy is shackled, unable to achieve anything worthwhile in the face of significant rises in unemployment. Given these two facts, and since countries such as Greece are in a currency union that prevents them from devaluing, any fiscal stimulus to reduce unemployment must be paid for by the taxpayers in the large more-competitive countries, the most important of which is Germany. Given the obsession about the risk of inflation in Germany, any significant amount of expenditure to help, say Greece, reduce its level of unemployment would have to be matched by increased taxation. German taxpayers are not receptive to tax increases for this purpose.

Since Post Keynesian economists believe that fiscal policy is a major tool in the very important task of managing aggregate demand, they are particularly interested in measuring the effects of fiscal policy. The discussion has centred on the construction of a single-number indicator of the stance of fiscal policy. Most would agree that single-number indicators are very inadequate, given the varying multipliers that are attached to different categories of government expenditure and taxation. However, it seems impossible to move media discussion and political arguments past a single-number indicator, with the nominal budget deficit the most often used despite its manifest flaws (see Eisner 1986). Attention has therefore focused on alternative measures of the budget deficit. It is well known that, while fiscal policy affects the level of economic activity, the level of economic activity affects the outcome of fiscal policy, with tax revenues falling during recessions and government expenditure on transfer payments automatically increasing. An alternative measure of the stance of fiscal policy is the structural deficit, or the size the deficit would be at a benchmark level of high employment, but with the current expenditure and taxation laws. Most commentators agree that the sale of public assets should be excluded when calculating the structural deficit. Post Keynesians argue that the decline in the value of the government debt (including currency) due to inflation should be subtracted from the deficit. Eisner adds an additional point, arguing that not only must one correct for inflation, but it is also necessary to look at the market value of the public debt, not its face value. The former fluctuates with changes in the interest rate. Most ignore this point, which strictly speaking relates to monetary policy, not fiscal policy. Any calculation of structural deficits involves making a judgement about what level of economic activity should be taken as a benchmark. While this may not affect year-to-year changes in the structural deficit, it will certainly determine the size of this deficit and often will determine whether fiscal policy is judged expansionary or contractionary. The selection of the benchmark is affected by the relative weight one gives to the dangers of inflation and unemployment. Hence, no calculation of the structural deficit is completely objective.

J.W. NEVILE

See also:

Budget Deficits; Economic Policy; Full Employment; International Economics; Investment; Monetary Policy.

References

Bougrine, H. (ed.) (2000), *The Economics of Public Spending: Debts, Deficits and Economic Performance*, Cheltenham, UK and Northampton, MA, USA: Edward Elgar.
Cornwall, J. (1983), *The Conditions for Economic Recovery: A Post-Keynesian Analysis*, Oxford: Martin Robertson.
Eisner, R. (1986), *How Real is the Federal Deficit?*, New York: Free Press, Macmillan.
Jespersen, J. (2002), 'Why do macroeconomists differ on the consequences of the Euro?', in P. Arestis, M. Desai and S. Dow (eds), *Money, Macroeconomics and Keynes: Essays in Honour of Victoria Chick, Volume 1*, London and New York: Routledge, pp. 193–204.

Lerner, A.P. (1943), 'Functional finance and the federal debt', *Social Research*, **10** (1), 38–51.
Nevile, J.W. (2000), 'Can Keynesian policies stimulate growth in output and employment?', in S. Bell (ed.), *The Unemployment Crisis in Australia: Which Way Out?*, Cambridge: Cambridge University Press, pp. 149–74.
Nevile, J. and P. Kriesler (2011), 'Why Keynesian policy was more successful in the fifties and sixties than in the last twenty years', *Economic and Labour Relations Review*, **22** (1), 1–16.

Full Employment

> Blessed are the extravagant, for theirs shall be full employment.
> (Lekachman 1966, p. 94).

The term 'full employment' can be traced back to William Petty's 1662 work, *A Treatise on Taxes and Contributions*, in which he argued that non-productive labour could be supported as a consequence of the capacity of producers of consumption goods to generate a surplus over and above their own subsistence. The classical economists did not consider full employment specifically, but Jean-Baptiste Say (1803) denied that a production economy could ever suffer a general glut which would otherwise have led to unemployment. Say's law that 'supply creates its own demand' became the epithet of classical and neoclassical theory, and its underlying reasoning still dominates orthodox macroeconomics today. There was not a denial that unemployment could occur but it was considered to be a manifestation of a temporary disruption, rather than being a generalized tendency of a capitalist production system. A lack of consumption would become by definition an act of investment. Moreover, it was argued that there was a strict separation between output and price theory – the so-called 'classical dichotomy'. So the existence of money posed no special problems. While J.C.L. Simonde de Sismondi and Robert Malthus demurred and argued that generalized gluts could occur even if the savings–investment identity held, their analyses were flawed. It was Karl Marx, in his critique of Malthus, who provided a modern Post Keynesian rationale for generalized gluts. Marx understood that money could be held as a store of value and that this behaviour interrupted the sequence of sale and purchase. He also laid the foundations of multiplier theory by arguing, in *Theories of Surplus Value*, that, once this unity of sale and purchase was disturbed, the chain of contractual relationships between suppliers became threatened and overproduction, and then bankruptcies and unemployment, became widespread.

So, by 1900, there were two broad views about the possibility of full employment: (a) Marxian views of crisis and the reserve army of unemployed, which saw capitalism as being incompatible with a fully employed working class; and (b) the dominant (marginalist) view that unfettered market operations would ensure that all those who wanted to work at the equilibrium real wage could find it because Say's law held. Full employment became equivalent to the equilibrium intersection between the demand for and supply of labour, which in turn reflected the productive state of the economy driven by technology and the unconstrained preferences of the population. By definition, any workers who were idle were voluntarily enjoying leisure and could not reasonably be considered unemployed. Mass unemployment was considered to be a transitory disturbance.

The advent of the Great Depression made it hard to justify the view that the persistently high unemployment was due to changing preferences of workers (increased quits in search of leisure), excessive real wages (in the face of money wage cuts), and/or a temporary interruption to market efficiency. For the first time, notwithstanding Marx's inspiring insights, Western economists articulated a macroeconomics that could define a coherent concept of full employment and also explain mass unemployment in terms of the inherent tendencies of monetary capitalism. The clue lay in recognizing the unique role that money could play in resolving the tensions that uncertainty created in the decision-making calculus of decentralized agents, but also in realizing that the fallacy of composition was endemic in the prevailing (micro) explanations of unemployment.

Whether the 1930s marked the birth of Post Keynesian notions of full employment is debatable. Post Keynesian theory has fractured origins, with some practitioners seeing the labour market in Marxian, then Kaleckian terms and others tracing their ancestry to Keynes and his *General Theory*. Certainly, the attack against the marginalist faith in self-equilibration mounted by Keynes (1936) and his monetary analysis was path-breaking. It also more clearly outlined what we now mean by the term 'full employment'.

Keynes linked full employment to national income levels, such that full employment occurred at the level of output when all who want to work at the going money-wage rates can find a job. Full employment was the absence of involuntary unemployment. This was defined by the following thought experiment: if a rise in nominal demand with constant money wages increased the price level (of wage goods) but also resulted in both the demand for and supply of labour increasing beyond the existing volume of employment, then those who gained the new jobs were involuntarily unemployed. Involuntary unemployment was to be expected in a monetary economy subject to uncertainty, because the act of holding money as a source of liquidity provided the type of interruption to the output-spending balance that Marx had clearly envisaged.

Consequently, the maintenance of full employment required government policies to maintain levels of aggregate demand sufficient to achieve output levels consistent with all available labour being employed. Significantly, a departure from full employment was construed as a systemic failure, rather than an outcome related to the ascriptive characteristics of the unemployed and/or the prevailing wage levels. Consistent with this notion was the coexistence of unfilled vacancies and unemployed workers as part of the normal daily resolution of hiring and quits. Accordingly, full employment arose when all unemployment was frictional. Beveridge (1944) defined full employment as an excess of vacancies at living wages over unemployed persons. The emphasis was on jobs.

Macroeconomic policy in the postwar period was designed to promote full employment. Beveridge (ibid., pp. 123–35) argued that 'The ultimate responsibility for seeing that outlay as a whole, taking public and private outlay together, is sufficient to set up a demand for all the labour seeking employment, must be taken by the State'. In the following years, a number of Western governments, including those in Britain, Australia and Canada, made a commitment to at least 'high and stable' employment, if not full employment. The US government was more circumspect, with its 1946 Employment Act aiming only to ensure that employment opportunities were maintained. From 1945 to the mid-1970s, most governments used countercyclical budget deficits and appropriately designed monetary policy to maintain levels of demand sufficient to maintain full employment. Unemployment rates in Western economies were at historical lows throughout this period.

In the 1950s, however, the emphasis on jobs was replaced by a concern for inflation. Although only a subtle change, the redefinition of full employment in the early 1950s in terms of an irreducible minimum unemployment rate (see Mitchell 2001) gave way soon after to the Phillips curve revolution. The Keynesian orthodoxy considered real output (income) and employment as being demand determined in the short run, with price inflation explained by a negatively sloped Phillips curve (in both the short run and the long run). Policy makers believed that they could manipulate demand and exploit this trade-off to achieve socially optimal levels of unemployment and inflation. The concept of full employment had been redefined to be the rate of unemployment that was politically acceptable, given the accompanying inflation rate.

Milton Friedman's 1968 American Economic Association address and the supporting work from Phelps (1967) provided the basis for the expectations-augmented Phillips curve, which spearheaded the resurgence of pre-Keynesian macroeconomic thinking in the form of monetarism. Underpinning the natural rate hypothesis (NRH) was a unique cyclically invariant natural rate of unemployment (NRU), which was consistent with stable inflation. There was no long-run, stable trade-off between inflation and unemployment. The concept was broadened in the 1970s to incorporate a number of structural labour market impediments, and the term 'Non-Accelerating-Inflation-Rate of Unemployment' (NAIRU) become popular.

The acceptance of these new ideas was aided by the empirical instability of the Phillips curve in most OECD economies in the 1970s following the OPEC oil price rises. Unemployment was again considered voluntary and the outcome of optimizing choices by individuals between work (bad) and leisure (good). Full employment would prevail (with unemployment at the NAIRU), given the operation of market forces, unless there were errors in interpreting price signals. There was no discretionary role for aggregate demand management. Full employment as conceived by Beveridge had been abandoned. Only microeconomic reform would reduce the NAIRU. Accordingly, the policy debate became increasingly concentrated on deregulation, privatization, and reductions in the provisions of the welfare state while monetarist 'fight-inflation-first' strategies ensured that unemployment persisted at high levels. NAIRU proponents responded by claiming that steady-state unemployment rate must have risen due to worsening structural impediments, but strongly pro-cyclical quits undermined these claims.

The modern Post Keynesian approach to the NAIRU is represented by the hysteresis and persistence literature. Hysteresis or path dependence was traced to cyclical fluctuations that occurred in the labour market. Steady-state unemployment rates rose after a long downturn, but aggregate demand expansions could reduce it again, so that full employment could be restored at relatively low unemployment rates without ever-accelerating inflation. Empirical work has cast doubt on the robustness of the cyclically invariant NAIRU story and provided strong support for a hysteretic–asymmetric interpretation of the inflation–unemployment relationship which is driven by private sector caution but could be countered by stimulatory fiscal policy (Mitchell and Muysken 2008).

During the late 1990s and into the twenty-first century many developed economies experienced slowly declining official rates of unemployment, but high rates of labour underutilization persisted, given higher rates of underemployment and discouraged unemployment (ibid.). The mainstream profession coined the phrase 'The Great Moderation' and declared the business cycle to be dead, with policy makers urged to further deregulate and allow markets to self-regulate and flourish.

That misplaced optimism did not last long. In 2008, eurozone countries and others, notably the UK and the USA, suffered significant increases in their unemployment rates in the aftermath of the global financial crisis. Central banks reduced interest rates to close to zero early in the crisis, which limited their scope for further easing, and countries, in particular the UK, Japan and the USA undertook quantitative easing. Most nations undertook fiscal stimulus measures which attenuated the rise in unemployment. The International Monetary Fund (IMF) and the Organisation for Economic Co-operation and Development (OECD), which had previously championed the rejection of fiscal policy as a countercyclical stabilizing tool, were forced to acknowledge the positive role played by the stimulus measures although their arguments were never clearly articulated (Watts 2010). Importantly, their responses represented a concession with respect to their long-held supply-side explanations for unemployment.

However, what had started as a private debt crisis was soon reconstructed by the IMF, the OECD and mainstream economists as a sovereign debt crisis, even though the rising deficits and debt to GDP ratios were, in part, reflecting the operation of automatic stabilizers as private spending collapsed. The pressure on governments from the conservative media to rein in fiscal policy became intense, despite entrenched mass unemployment, and austerity programmes were implemented. The public debate became centred on the erroneous but widely accepted analogy between prudent households needing to finance their expenditures and national governments, which were obliged to engage in budgetary restraint to satisfy their intertemporal budget constraints. This argument ignored the fact that governments in most advanced nations issue fiat currency as monopolists and face no revenue constraint. Supply-side measures to reduce structural constraints continued to be advocated. The concept of a 'fiscal contraction expansion' became popular and was based on the claim that the private sector was 'Ricardian' in outlook. Accordingly, it would not increase spending until budget deficits were cut because of the fear of higher future tax liabilities. The evidence does not support these claims. The governments that adopted fiscal austerity the earliest have seen their economies deteriorate most (Mitchell 2011).

With their voluntary fiscal constraints, albeit temporarily relaxed, and the need to formally finance deficits denominated in a transnational currency, eurozone countries, particularly Greece, Ireland and Spain, were under extreme pressure and, at the time of writing (April 2011), Greece and Ireland had both received international loans and Portugal was about to negotiate one. Given the restricted policy options for these countries in the pursuit of lower unemployment, increased international competitiveness via wage cuts was advocated for these countries (for example, Leddin 2010, with respect to Ireland), which was reminiscent of misguided UK policy after the First World War to attempt restore sterling to the Gold Standard at the pre-war exchange rate.

Thus the global financial crisis has led to the extraordinary situation of leading economic organizations and economists advocating pro-cyclical fiscal policy when in the past they had used the possibility of such as a major part of their criticism of the use of fiscal policy. Fiscal austerity has further reinforced the fact that policy makers now use unemployment as a policy tool rather than a policy target. Accounting imperatives drive the clamour for fiscal consolidation, with no consideration of public purpose, specifically full employment (Mitchell 2010).

Despite the global financial crisis, which in principle provided the greatest challenge to the prevailing macroeconomic policy consensus for over 30 years, there has been little debate among Post Keynesians about policies to achieve and maintain full employment. Some appear to be opposed to full employment *per se*, claiming that it will be inflationary and/or environmentally damaging and/or cause a balance-of-trade deficit leading to an unsustainable foreign debt to GDP ratio.

Economies which avoided the plunge into high unemployment in the 1970s all maintained a sector that provided an employer of last resort capacity to redress the flux and uncertainty of private sector spending. In most countries through the 1950s and 1960s, the public sector played this role, which ceased when the monetarists began attacking the public sector on (orthodox) efficiency grounds (Mitchell and Muysken 2008). Accordingly, some Post Keynesians propose a job guarantee (Mitchell 2001) or an employer of last resort (Wray 1998), where the public sector maintains a constant fixed-wage job offer to anyone who cannot find employment elsewhere. An employment guarantee is precisely calibrated to the level of unemployment, thereby avoiding the lead and lag problems associated with the design of *ad hoc* stimulus measures which can cause demand–pull inflation or ongoing unemployment. Wray and Mitchell argue that deflationary fiscal and monetary policy which drives employees out of the private sector into the lower-paid guaranteed jobs provides an adequate counter-inflation policy if required. Other Post Keynesians (including Sawyer 2003, 2005; but see also Forstater 2005 and Mitchell and Wray 2005) eschew this approach for a range of reasons, including the likelihood of professional workers being invisibly underemployed, low-productivity guaranteed employment and reduced private sector employment under stable inflation.

Employment guarantees present a serious challenge to orthodox thinking that persistent budget deficits are unsustainable (IMF 2010; OECD 2010), due to the impact on long-term interest rates and the imperatives of the intertemporal budget constraint. Wray and Mitchell argue that the issue of government securities is designed to sustain the target interest rate, set by monetary policy, rather than being required *ex ante* to finance expenditure (see also Terzi 2010). Some Post Keynesians remain unconvinced, including Arestis and Sawyer (2006) and Aspromourgos (2010), who appear to view the non-government sector as being required to provide finance for bond purchases. Any disinclination on their part, it is suggested, will lead to higher long-term rates. Yet, if the central bank equates the support rate to the target rate, debt issue is unnecessary.

Over the past 30 years the NAIRU concept has obfuscated the debate over the capacity of capitalist economies to achieve and maintain full employment, as traditionally understood. While concessions have been made in respect of the cyclical sensitivity of the NAIRU following the global financial crisis, the alleged demands of fiscal sustainability are now the ostensible reason for full employment being off the policy agenda. At the same time the Post Keynesian literature remains divided, which has undermined any sustained challenge to orthodoxy.

WILLIAM MITCHELL
MARTIN WATTS

See also:

Budget Deficits; Economic Policy; Effective Demand; Employer of Last Resort; Employment; Fiscal Policy; Global Financial Crisis; New Classical Economics; Say's Law; Unemployment.

References

Arestis, P. and M. Sawyer (2006), 'Fiscal policy matters', *Public Finance*, **54** (3), 1–15.
Aspromourgos, T. (2010), 'The great financial crisis, the (brief?) revival of Keynesianism, and the question of public debt', *Australian Review of Public Affairs*, **3**, September.
Beveridge, W. (1944), *Full Employment in a Free Society*, London: Allen & Unwin.
Forstater, M. (2005), 'Reply to Malcolm Sawyer', *Journal of Economic Issues*, **39** (1), 245–55.
IMF (2010), *World Economic Outlook: Rebalancing Growth*, Washington, DC: International Monetary Fund.
Keynes, J.M. (1936), *The General Theory of Employment, Interest and Money*, London: Macmillan.
Leddin, A. (2010), 'More public sector deflation will help recovery', *Irish Times*, 12 November, available at: http://www.irishtimes.com/newspaper/finance/2010/1112/1224283150597.html.
Lekachman, R. (1966), *The Age of Keynes*, Harmondsworth: Penguin.
Mitchell, W.F. (2001), 'The job guarantee and inflation control', in E. Carlson and W.F. Mitchell (eds), *Achieving Full Employment*, Supplement to the *Economic and Labour Relations Review*, **12** (1), 10–26.
Mitchell, W.F. (2010), 'People are now dying as the deficit terrorists ramp up their attacks', *Billy Blog*, 6 May, available at: http://bilbo.economicoutlook.net/blog/?p=9632.
Mitchell, W.F. (2011), 'Beyond austerity', *The Nation*, 4 August, available at: http://www.thenation.com/article/159288/beyond-austerity.
Mitchell, W.F. and J. Muysken (2008), *Full Employment Abandoned: Shifting Sands and Policy Failures*, Cheltenham, UK and Northampton, MA, USA: Edward Elgar.
Mitchell, W.F. and L.R. Wray (2005), 'In defense of employer of last resort: a response to Malcolm Sawyer', *Journal of Economic Issues*, **39** (1), 235–44.
OECD (2010), *Restoring Fiscal Sustainability: Lessons for the Public Sector*, Paris: OECD Publications.
Phelps, E.S. (1967), 'Phillips curves, expectations of inflation and optimal unemployment over time', *Economica*, **34** (135), 254–81.

Sawyer, M. (2003), 'Employer of last resort: could it deliver full employment and price stability?', *Journal of Economic Issues*, **37** (4), 881–908.
Sawyer, M. (2005), 'Employer of last resort: a response to my critics', *Journal of Economic Issues*, **39** (1), 256–64.
Say, J.-B. (1803), *A Treatise on Political Economy*, Library of Economics and Liberty, available at: http://www.econlib.org/library/Say/sayT0.html (accessed 30 June 2002).
Terzi, A. (2010), 'The "Keynesian moment" in policymaking, the perils ahead, and a flow-of-funds interpretation of fiscal policy', Working Paper No. 614, Levy Economics Institute of Bard College, Annandale-on-Hudson, NY, August.
Watts, M.J. (2010), 'The role of the OECD in the design of macroeconomic and labour market policy: reflections of a heterodox economist', Centre of Full Employment and Equity, University of Newcastle, Newcastle, NSW, mimeo.
Wray, L.R. (1998), *Understanding Modern Money: The Key To Full Employment*, Cheltenham, UK and Northampton, MA, USA: Edward Elgar.

Fundamentalist Keynesians

The term 'fundamentalist Keynesians' originates with Coddington to describe 'those who have seen Keynes's work as a frontal assault on the whole reductionist programme' (1976, p. 1259). The fundamentalist Keynesians are those radical/Post Keynesians who see Keynes's *General Theory* as a rejection not only of the theories and policy prescriptions of neoclassical economics but also of its analytical (reductionist) methods. In particular, the fundamentalist Keynesians interpret Keynes as emphasizing the importance of uncertainty in economic behaviour and, as a consequence, rejecting the usefulness of both the optimization calculus and equilibrium analysis.

Coddington associated the fundamentalist strand of Keynesianism primarily with George Shackle and Joan Robinson. Both Shackle and Robinson believed the essence of Keynes's revolutionary contribution to be his analysis of the effects of uncertainty on investment in Chapter 12 of the *General Theory*, a theme that Keynes highlighted in his subsequent (1937) *Quarterly Journal of Economics* article. Both also argued that Keynes's analysis implies the need for a fundamental change in the analytical methods employed by economists. Robinson summarized the methodological argument very succinctly: 'As soon as the uncertainty of the expectations that guide economic behaviour is admitted, equilibrium drops out of the argument and history takes its place' (1979, p. 126). Shackle considered Keynes to have invented a scheme of thought for dealing with the effects of uncertainty on economic behaviour. Shackle called this scheme of thought 'the *kaleidic* analysis of a development through time in which one situation or event grows out of another' (1967, p. 151; emphasis in original). More recently, Davidson (1991) has restated the methodological argument as the rejection of the ergodic axiom that allows uncertainty to be modelled as a well-defined probability distribution. From Davidson's perspective, Keynes's concept of uncertainty represents a non-ergodic process in which economic behaviour consists of crucial decisions and unique events such that individuals cannot specify a complete set of possible future outcomes and associated probabilities.

Coddington dismissed the fundamentalist Keynesians as purely nihilistic as regards the development and practical application of economic theory. He argued that the fundamentalists give too much emphasis to those parts of Keynes's thought that are merely a ground-clearing exercise. For Coddington, fundamentalist Keynesians are on the slippery slope towards subjectivism, driving a wedge between behaviour and circumstance that negates analysis and renders economic theorizing impossible.

There is some validity in the criticism of early fundamentalist Keynesians as rather nihilistic, emphasizing mainly the negative aspect of Keynes's work. But Coddington himself was guilty of an excessive emphasis on the negative aspect of Keynesian fundamentalism. He ignored, for example, Shackle's attempts to construct an alternative theory of decision making under uncertainty using the concept of potential surprise. Coddington also wrongly implied that Keynes's concern with uncertainty was a transitional phase. Keynes had a longstanding interest in probability theory dating back to his undergraduate days. He published *A Treatise on Probability* in 1921 and explicitly referred back to this work in his discussion of uncertainty in chapter 12 of the *General Theory*.

The recognition of the centrality of probability and uncertainty throughout Keynes's thought led to the emergence of a 'new' Keynesian fundamentalism that sought to ground Keynes's later economic analysis in his early philosophical thought, especially *A Treatise on Probability*. This new Keynesian fundamentalism originated with Lawson (1985) and the subsequent books by Carabelli (1988), Fitzgibbons (1988) and O'Donnell (1989). A central theme of the new fundamentalists is the relationship between Keynes's analysis of uncertainty in the *General Theory* and the logical theory of probability that Keynes developed in *A Treatise on Probability*. Although the emphasis of the new fundamentalists is on the task of interpretation, there is a clear implication that Keynes's logical theory of probability may provide the basis for the development of an alternative economic theory of behaviour under uncertainty.

Keynes's logical theory of probability was an attempt to generalize beyond the frequency theory of probability. Keynes defined probability as the rational degree of belief in a proposition given the available evidence. A probability is a rational degree of belief in the sense of being objectively derived by logic rather than a matter of individual subjective evaluation. Keynes's concept of probability is epistemic in the sense of pertaining to the nature of knowledge. In contrast, frequency theory treats probability as an aleatory concept relating to the nature of the world. For Keynes, relative frequencies are a special type of quantitative data from which a numerical degree of belief in a proposition can be derived. Indeed, Keynes argued that numerical probabilities are a special case that had been over-emphasized because of their amenability to mathematical manipulation. Keynes considered probabilities to be typically non-numerical and, in some cases, non-comparable.

As well as the notion of probability as a rational degree of belief, Keynes also introduced the concept of the weight of an argument. The weight of an argument is a measure of the amount of evidence on which a proposition is based. For the most part, Keynes considered the weight of an argument to be the amount of relevant evidence. The weight of an argument is independent of its probability. As additional relevant evidence is acquired, the weight of an argument increases but the rational degree of belief in the proposition may increase, decrease or remain unchanged. However, Keynes is not entirely consistent in his definition of the weight of an argument. He also referred to the weight of argument as the degree of completeness of evidence, as well as the balance of absolute amounts of relevant knowledge and relevant ignorance. These two alternative definitions of the weight of argument imply the possibility that additional relevant evidence may reduce weight if the assessment of relative ignorance is revised upwards. Despite the conceptual difficulties in formalizing the definition of the weight of an argument, Keynes stressed that weight as well as probability is relevant to practical decision making.

Keynes's emphasis on the importance of the weight of an argument is a key element in his critique of the doctrine of mathematical expectation as a theory of human behaviour under uncertainty. The doctrine of mathematical expectation implies that alternative courses of action are evaluated by weighting the value of the outcome with its probability. Keynes considered this approach to be too limited as a theory of human behaviour under uncertainty. He argued that any such theory must incorporate not only the value of the outcome and its probability as determinants of human behaviour, but also the weight of the available evidence and the risk attached (that is, the possible losses associated with any course of action). Keynes considered the possibility of amending the doctrine of mathematical expectation by weighting the value of the outcome with what he termed the 'conventional coefficient' instead of the probability. The conventional coefficient depends not only on the probability of the outcome but also on weight and risk. The conventional coefficient would tend towards the probability as weight tends towards unity and risk tends towards zero. However, Keynes concluded that the conventional coefficient is too restrictive in its formalization of the effects of probability, weight and risk on uncertain choices between alternative courses of action.

In attempting to interpret Keynes's later economic writings as grounded in his earlier philosophical thought, a crucial issue is the extent to which his philosophical position remained unchanged in any fundamental way between *A Treatise on Probability* and the *General Theory*. The 'continuity-or-change?' debate has focused on four principal pieces of textual evidence: a biographical essay on F.Y. Edgeworth published in 1926; a letter to F.M. Urban, the German translator of the *Treatise*, also written in 1926; a review of Frank Ramsey's *Foundation of Mathematics* in 1931; and Keynes's autobiographical essay, 'My early beliefs' which was read to the Bloomsbury Group in 1938. These texts are ambiguous and subject to radically different interpretations. There remains considerable controversy regarding whether Keynes retained both the logical theory of probability and the belief that the inductive method is only applicable to atomistic (as opposed to organicist) systems. Disputes over interpretation such as these cannot be resolved in any definitive way by textual evidence, since ultimately they represent differences over the appropriate frame of reference. The only closure possible to the question 'what did Keynes really mean?' is to recognize the possibility of multiple answers and to move on to another question. From the perspective of constructing an alternative non-neoclassical theory of economic behaviour under uncertainty, the relevant question is whether or not Keynes's analysis in the *General Theory* can be developed by reference back to *A Treatise on Probability*. In this case the emphasis shifts to the possibility of theoretical continuity rather than its actuality in Keynes's own intellectual development.

Keynes's analysis of economic behaviour under uncertainty is fundamental to the logic of the *General Theory*. Keynes rejected the two foundations of neoclassical theory, namely, the aggregate labour market and Say's law that supply creates its own demand, the latter justified theoretically by the loanable funds theory of the rate of interest as the equilibrating mechanism ensuring that planned savings and investment are equated. Keynes proposed the principle of effective demand in which the level of income (and, in turn, output and employment) would adjust via the multiplier process to bring savings automatically into line with the volume of investment. Hence, ultimately, the level of employment depends on the determinants of the volume of investment, *ceteris paribus*. Keynes argued that the investment decision depends on prospective monetary yields (that is, the marginal efficiency of capital) exceeding the rate of interest. But prospective yields on investment depend on the state of long-term expectations. There is, therefore, an essential link between uncertainty and involuntary unemployment. If business is highly uncertain about future investment

prospects, the volume of investment will fall, leading to downward multiplier effects on income, output and employment. It is this essential link that
is emphasized by the fundamentalist Keynesians.

Keynes drew a crucial distinction in the *General Theory* between short-
term and long-term expectations. Short-term expectations relate to day-
to-day production decisions. These expectations are subject to continual
revision in the light of market outcomes. Mistaken short-term expectations
can cause temporary departures from the full-employment equilibrium, as
had been recognized by neoclassical economists prior to Keynes. In particular, underestimation of current market demand is one of the causes of
frictional unemployment. Mistaken short-term expectations do not cause
involuntary unemployment.

In contrast, long-term expectations relate to the estimation of the prospective monetary yields from investment projects. Keynes conceived of
the state of long-term expectations as consisting of two components: the
most probable forecast and the state of confidence. The latter refers to
the degree of uncertainty attached to the most probable forecast. It is at
this point that Keynes explicitly referred back to *A Treatise on Probability*
and the concept of the weight of an argument to clarify the meaning of
uncertainty. It is also consistent with his earlier criticism of the doctrine
of mathematical expectation as too limited. The investment decision
depends not only on the probability of alternative outcomes but also on
the degree of confidence attached to these probability estimates, based on
an assessment of the amount of relevant evidence. This insight provides
the basis for the construction of an alternative theory of economic behaviour under uncertainty. Keynes argued further that business recognizes the
precariousness of its estimates of prospective yields and, as a consequence,
investment decisions are not based purely on mathematical calculations.
He recognized that there are crucial non-rational elements in investment
behaviour, namely, an innate urge to action over inaction (that is, animal
spirits) as well as falling back on the conventional belief that the existing
state of affairs will continue unless there are specific reasons to expect
particular changes.

Keynes's analysis of economic behaviour under uncertainty in the
General Theory required a change in the method of equilibrium analysis.
Keynes retained the notion of equilibrium in the general sense of a position of rest but rejected the specific neoclassical definition of equilibrium
as a market-clearing allocative outcome. Keynes set out a three-stage
'shifting equilibrium' analysis (see Gerrard 1997). The first stage is to
determine the point of long-period equilibrium given a particular state of
long-term expectations. The second stage is the logical-time analysis of the
process of transition from one long-period equilibrium to another conse-

quent on a shift in the state of long-term expectations. The final stage is the dynamic analysis of historical time consisting of a complex of overlapping transitional processes arising from a multitude of changes in long-term expectations.

So far, we have followed Coddington in adopting a 'narrow' definition of fundamentalist Keynesianism as an emphasis on the role of uncertainty in the *General Theory* and the radical implications for neoclassical methods of analysis. This narrow view of the domain of fundamentalist Keynesianism has tended to go hand-in-hand with a 'broad-church' view of Post Keynesianism as encompassing a number of radical alternatives to mainstream neoclassical economics including most prominently neo-Ricardian and Kaleckian strands of thought as well as fundamentalist Keynesianism. The broad-church view of Post Keynesianism is exemplified by Hamouda and Harcourt (1988) and King's history of Post Keynesianism (2002). However, Davidson (2003) rejects the broad-church view of Post Keynesianism and makes the case for a 'wider' definition of fundamentalist Keynesianism that goes beyond a concern for uncertainty and methods of analysis, and provides the definitive demarcation criterion that differentiates Post Keynesianism from other schools of thought. For Davidson, fundamentalist/Post Keynesians are defined as following Keynes in rejecting the three classical axioms of money neutrality, ergodicity and gross substitution and constructing an alternative economic theory based on the four fundamental building blocks of Marshallian microfoundations, a monetary theory of interest, a marginal product of labour that does not represent a demand for labour, and a non-probabilistic, non-ergodic concept of uncertainty. Davidson argues that since neo-Ricardians and Kaleckians retain one or more of the three classical axioms rejected by Keynes and, as a consequence, reject one or more of the four fundamental building blocks, they should not be considered as part of the Post Keynesian school of thought. Whether or not one accepts Davidson's restricted view of the domain of Post Keynesian economics, his arguments emphasize the centrality of fundamentalist Keynesianism to any radical alternative to mainstream neoclassical economics.

The financial crisis of 2008 and subsequent global economic downturn with the obvious parallels to the 1930s has triggered a revival of interest in Keynes's insights by some mainstream economists concerned by the inadequacy of orthodox explanations of recent economic history. Two preeminent mainstream economists, George Akerlof and Robert Shiller, have emerged as persuasive advocates of the theoretical and practical significance of the fundamentalist aspects of Keynes's contribution. In their book, *Animal Spirits* (2009), Akerlof and Shiller argue that the fundamental contribution of Keynes is the recognition that people often act on the basis of non-economic motivations and respond in non-rational ways. Akerlof and Shiller use the term 'animal spirits' as a catch-all term for non-rational/non-economic influences on behaviour including confidence, fairness, corruption, money illusion and story-telling. They show how these behaviour patterns can explain why the macroeconomy does not always act as a self-adjusting invisible-hand system tending towards full employment. Akerlof and Shiller believe that Keynes's fundamentalist message was progressively emasculated by IS–LM Keynesianism, New Classical economics and New Keynesianism and is only now being rediscovered by mainstream economists through recent developments in behavioural economics. It is to be hoped that this emerging congruence between behavioural economics and fundamentalist Keynesianism can provide a basis for the constructive development of a more realistic and grounded economic theory inspired by Keynes's fundamental insights into the human nature of the economic process, a process of cognition and intuition, of self-interest and collective action undertaken in a monetary context in the face of inescapable non-ergodic uncertainty and subject to waves of optimism and pessimism.

BILL GERRARD

See also:

Behavioural Economics; Choice under Uncertainty; Conventions; Equilibrium and Non-equilibrium; Expectations; Keynes's *General Theory*; Keynes's *Treatise on Probability*; New Classical Economics; New Keynesian Economics; Non-ergodicity; Say's Law; Time in Economic Theory; Uncertainty.

References

Akerlof, G.A. and R.J. Shiller (2009), *Animal Spirits: How Human Psychology Drives the Economy, and Why It Matters for Global Capitalism*, Princeton, NJ: Princeton University Press.
Carabelli, A. (1988), *On Keynes's Method*, London: Macmillan.
Coddington, A. (1976), 'Keynesian economics: the search for first principles', *Journal of Economic Literature*, **14** (1), 1258–73.
Davidson, P. (1991), 'Is probability theory relevant for uncertainty? A Post Keynesian perspective', *Journal of Economic Perspectives*, **5** (1), 129–44.
Davidson, P. (2003), 'Setting the record straight on *A History of Post Keynesian Economics*', *Journal of Post Keynesian Economics*, **26** (2), 245–72.
Fitzgibbons, A. (1988), *Keynes's Vision: A New Political Economy*, Oxford: Clarendon Press.
Gerrard, B. (1997), 'Method and methodology in Keynes's General Theory', in G.C. Harcourt and P.A. Riach (eds), *A 'Second Edition' of The General Theory. Volume 2*, London and New York: Routledge, pp. 166–202.
Hamouda, O.F. and G.C. Harcourt (1988), 'Post Keynesianism: from criticism to coherence', *Bulletin of Economic Research*, **40** (1), 21–50.
Keynes, J.M. (1937), 'The general theory of employment', *Quarterly Journal of Economics*, **51** (2), 209–23; reprinted in *The Collected Writings of John Maynard Keynes*, Vol. 14, London: Macmillan for the Royal Economic Society, 1973, pp. 109–23.
King, J.E. (2002), *A History of Post Keynesian Economics Since 1936*, Cheltenham, UK and Northampton, MA, USA: Edward Elgar.
Lawson, T. (1985), 'Uncertainty and economic analysis', *Economic Journal*, **95** (380), 909–27.

O'Donnell, R.M. (1989), *Keynes: Philosophy, Economics and Politics*, London: Macmillan.
Robinson, J. (1979), 'History versus equilibrium', in Robinson, *Contributions to Modern Economics*, Oxford: Basil Blackwell, pp. 126–36. (First published in *Thames Papers in Political Economy*, London, 1974.)
Shackle, G.L.S. (1967), *The Years of High Theory: Invention and Tradition in Economic Thought 1926–1939*, Cambridge: Cambridge University Press.

Galbraith's Economics

John Kenneth Galbraith (1908–2006) was a distinguished Harvard economist, an accomplished diplomat, a political activist, a confidant and adviser to presidents, a memoirist and novelist, and one of the best-selling economic writers of his time. Galbraith was one of the leading progressive intellectuals of the post-Second World War period who, though part of the establishment, was happy to point out its self-serving interests and convenient myths. But he was more than just a gadfly. He was an original economic theorist whose contributions are now so widely assimilated that their original and lasting force is easily overlooked.

Galbraith was born on 15 October 1908 in Iona Station, a small town on the northern shore of Lake Erie, and he grew up in Southern Ontario, part of Scotch Canada. Galbraith was born into a family of farmers – his parents owned two modest farms totalling 150 acres. In the fall of 1926, Galbraith enrolled at Ontario Agricultural College to study agricultural economics. During his last year there, Galbraith successfully applied for a research assistant position at Berkeley that was sponsored by the Giannini Foundation of Agricultural Economics.

In the spring of 1933, Galbraith accepted an offer from Harvard, where – apart from an unhappy sojourn in Princeton and a stint as an editor of *Fortune* magazine – he spent the rest of his academic life, albeit with much time off to pursue his political and his writing interests. At Harvard Galbraith moved beyond agricultural economics, engaging with the New Dealers and the new economics of imperfect competition. In 1937 Galbraith ventured to Cambridge, England, where he spent time with the Cambridge Circus, but not Keynes (who was convalescing from a heart attack).

Returning to Harvard in 1938, Galbraith was asked to head a commission to review the public works programmes of the New Deal. In 1941, as the US was becoming more deeply involved in the Second World War, Galbraith was asked for his help in facilitating economic stabilization and resource mobilization by controlling prices in the war economy – becoming the 'Price Czar'. After being removed from office Galbraith joined the editorial staff of *Fortune* magazine, honing his ability to write.

During the fall of 1948, Galbraith returned to Harvard and academic life. His teaching responsibilities included agricultural economics and industrial organization, but his focus was more on writing and politics. Galbraith worked on the Stevenson (1952, 1956) and Kennedy (1960) campaigns and was subsequently chosen by John F. Kennedy to be his Ambassador to India. He also took an early stand against the Vietnam War. In the 1950s and 1960s Galbraith also started to write for a popular audience, churning out *American Capitalism* (1952a), *The Great Crash, 1929* (1955), *The Affluent Society* (1958 [1967]) and *The New Industrial State* (1967 [1972]).

In the 1970s and 1980s Galbraith began to wind down his political activities, concentrating more on educating the general public with *Economics and the Public Purpose* (1973) and his television series 'The Age of Uncertainty'. Galbraith continued to be active professionally during this period. He provided both the 'moral and financial support' to help start the *Journal of Post Keynesian Economics* (King 2002, p. 135), which began publishing in 1978 under the joint editorship of Paul Davidson and Sidney Weintraub. Immediately the journal became one of the major publishing outlets for Post Keynesian economists, with Galbraith serving as the Chairman of the Honorary Board of Editors from its inception until his death. In the 1990s and right up until his death, Galbraith also continued to write and comment on social trends and economic affairs.

For Galbraith the aim of economics was to be in touch with the great problems of our time. Galbraith (1958 [1967], 1967 [1972], 1973) argued, however, that the conventional wisdom fails to shed light on many contemporary concerns such as the overproduction of private goods and the underproduction of public goods; the increasingly superfluous nature of much technical innovation directed at socially less irrelevant commodities; the failure of economic growth to ameliorate enduring social problems; the uneven distribution of government expenditure, reflected in excessive spending on the military and other forms of social infrastructure (for example, roads), to the relative neglect of others (health care and education); the increasingly skewed income distribution between different sectors and personnel; the enduring distinction between the high- and low-wage industries; the unresponsiveness of the modern corporation and international institutions to public pressure and opinion; the problems of economy-wide coordination; and the continuing fear of inflation as opposed to deflation. Galbraith (1958 [1967], 1967 [1972], 1973) sought, however, to explain these concerns, presenting an analysis of the substantial economic power that large firms possess and outlining a programme of civilized responses.

Galbraith's principal theoretical contribution is foreshadowed in *American Capitalism* (1952a), and unfolds more clearly into view in his trilogy: *The Affluent Society* (1958 [1967]), *The New Industrial State* (1967 [1972]) and *Economics and the Public Purpose* (1973). At its core Galbraith's thesis is that the economic ideas that once interpreted the world of poverty have made little adjustment to the world of affluence, which has been ushered in by the modern corporation. Throughout these works Galbraith focused on the concentration of economic power and the challenge to consumer sovereignty, the dynamics of the large corporation, the control, role and influence of the 'technostructure' and the resultant social and environmental imbalance.

Galbraith's analysis centred on the impact of highly concentrated economic power and its nexus to technology. As technology advances, increasingly large amounts of time, money and specialized personnel are increasingly required. Threats to such investments must be protected. The market and the forces of competition generate too much uncertainty for the large firm. To thrive, firms must seek to control the market rather than being subservient to it. The large firm thus emerges as a planning response to the uncertain nature of markets. The firm 'must replace the market with planning' (Galbraith 1967 [1972], p. 41). This, according to Galbraith, is a primary reason for the observed growth of the large firm and its nexus to the political apparatus.

The uncertainties of the market are mitigated in a variety of ways (ibid. pp. 43–5; see also Dunn 2011 for a detailed discussion). Mergers and takeovers – vertical, horizontal or conglomerate integration – minimize competition and augment size, which provides greater control over the firm's destiny. Similarly, through spending money on advertising the firm attempts to manipulate the consumer and manage the demand for its products. Likewise, in entering into long-term contracts denominated in money, the large firm can insulate itself from market fluctuations. Alternatively it can lobby for state spending 'to give certainty to this planning and to protect the technostructure' (Galbraith 1967 [1972], p. 229).

Small firms populate the other half of the economy: what Galbraith referred to as 'the market system'. Like the large firms that populate 'the planning system' they wish to escape the uncertainty of the market. However, their power is held in check by free competition. Both the market and the planning systems are interdependent structures that form part of Galbraith's (1977) bimodal view of mature economies.

On this view the planning system dominates the market system. The result is unequal economic development. The oligopolistic planning system, in contrast to neoclassical predictions, produces too many goods, and the market system produces an inadequate supply of goods. The bimodal view serves to identify the virtuous and vicious cycles of cumulative causation that reinforce the divergences of incomes and lifestyles of those who populate the planning and market systems. Moreover, given its lack of economic power the market system is at a disadvantage relative to the planning system, with the consequence that lower and less secure income characterizes its inhabitants (Galbraith 1973, pp. 65–6). Firms in the market system confronted by the large monopsonies must sell their goods at lower prices to the planning system, but are confronted by monopoly providers and are thus forced to buy goods from the planning system at higher prices. What is more, those who work in the planning system are richly rewarded, while those who work in the market system are somewhat exploited. Income is determined by power and not by marginal productivity.

According to Galbraith it should be no surprise that the large corporation focuses more on producing goods and services for those affluent consumers and members of the technostructure who can both afford to purchase its wares and have moved beyond relative subsistence such that they are more susceptible to manipulation. The consequence is that they will naturally produce fewer goods for low-income households. What is more, the whole climate of consumerism, perpetuated through the relentless advertising propaganda, combines to further elevate private production over the provision of merit and public goods, leading to private affluence amid impoverished and underprovided basic and essential public services (see Dunn 2011). Finally, greater power by the technostructure and large firms combines to inhibit fiscal redistribution. Being clearer in expression, more resourceful and better organized, the large firm can articulate its needs in a way that other members of society cannot, with the natural consequence that the state embodies an in-built propensity to reduce its support for the poor, while at the same time lowering the taxes it collects from the very wealthy.

Galbraith's analysis allows policy makers to ascertain and respond to the planning system's dominance over society. The evolution of the modern corporation is not wholly malign; it encourages technological development and, by so doing, contributes to (uneven) improvements in our standard of living. Breaking up such large corporations, as liberals typically demand, is not merely futile but would also undermine prosperity. Only big business could make the large-scale investment in new processes, expensive equipment and basic research required by a different kind of economy. Better to limit the power of large firms through the state than destroy the basis of (uneven) advance and development: 'This consists in disciplining its purposes – in making it serve, not define the public interest' (Galbraith 1973, p. 240).

The response of the good society is to ensure a strong welfare state that provides benefits such as job protection and basic income guarantees, as well as an acknowledged and legitimate role for unions. It must ensure that the provision of public goods and services keeps pace with the production of private goods (Galbraith 1958 [1967]). The good society must divert public resources away from supporting the middle classes – the technostructure – to help the poor (Galbraith 1967 [1972]). And the symbiotic nexus between the state and the technostructure must be broken.

Of course, all these activities have to be paid for. Funds must be channelled away from the promotion and acquisition of increasingly irrelevant and superfluous commodities to the provision of public goods that address unmet public needs. Accordingly Galbraith advocated higher sales taxes in order to finance the important sorts of government spending (for example, public transport, health, education, police protection). Galbraith also advocated greater income taxes, holding that the tax system must be made progressive enough so that the rich protest loudly and vehemently. For Galbraith that was the only way to know that the taxes imposed on the rich are high enough!

In contrast to neoclassical theory, Galbraith argued that the opportunity cost of such redistribution should not be that great. For an affluent economy, Galbraith maintained, the lost private goods are not nearly as important as the public goods and poverty reduction that come from government fiscal efforts. But ignoring the distributional problem comes with large costs. Years of favouring private production and neglecting the provision of public goods have created a situation of private affluence and public squalor (Galbraith 1958 [1967]).

Galbraith (1958 [1967], 1967 [1972], 1973, 1977) also considered the macroeconomic consequences of these institutional changes. For example, he noted the differential impact of tight monetary policy on the distribution of income across the planning and market systems. High interest rates benefit the technostructure and the rich, who can lend money and earn high interest rates at the same time that high rates tend to protect its real wealth from inflation. On the other hand, poor and middle-class households are generally borrowers and debtors, and so high interest rates hurt them. Tight monetary policy also favours the strongest parts of the economy (large corporations with plenty of cash and easy access to financial markets) and disfavours the weakest and less developed parts of the economy (smaller firms lacking cash reserves and access to credit at the lowest possible interest rates.

A related consequence of the 'bimodal image' of the modern economic system is its inflationary bias. Galbraith (1952b, 1973, 1977) rejected the monetarist account of inflation, instead expounding a 'cost–push' view of inflation and adopting an endogenous money approach. Galbraith argued that it is no surprise that the emergence and dominance of the modern corporation occurs at the same time that inflation emerges as a major macroeconomic policy issue. The development of power blocs makes the economic system more inflationary, and the greater the market power, the greater the forces in the economy tending to push up prices. For this reason Galbraith argued for the development of appropriate institutions, such as wage and price controls, so as to minimize inflation and facilitate employment expansion. The alternative, uncivilized strategy is to create a pool of unemployed resources to discipline wage and price claims and maintain price stability (see also Kalecki 1943).

Galbraith, like Keynes before him, also identified the instability of modern capitalism in terms of the drive to accumulate excessive wealth and the fragile nature of the financial system. Galbraith argued that an unfettered, competitive capitalist system, operating on pure free-market principles, was inherently cyclical and unstable, requiring robust regulation and active government. In *The Great Crash, 1929* Galbraith (1955) set out his bubble thesis in which a perceived fundamental change in the economy arouses euphoria and heightened expectations of return, leading to excess, fraud and collapse. The expansion in business activity feeds entrepreneurial and speculative behaviour in the financial sectors. It drives monetary innovation and the new forms of financing structures that are contrived to allow firms to participate in the boom.

Heightened expectations stimulate a credit boom, with the banking system keen to cash in on the new situation. As Galbraith (1955) and Keynes (1936) before him warned, such speculation inevitably leads to euphoria or overtrading in which rising asset prices encourage speculative excess. As debt accumulates, soon it can only be serviced by the issue of new liabilities. As long as the financial markets are booming, it is possible to sustain low levels of cash inflow by issuing new stocks and securities to finance current liabilities.

When the financial markets slow their expansion, organizations that have covered their future liabilities through issuing more debt are forced to sell assets to meet their liabilities. These 'distress' sales cause asset prices to fall, at which point the financial markets, and businesses with exposure to those markets, collapse. The next phase, in which investors try to get their money back out of the markets, naturally gives way to one of 'panic'. This is the essence of the great financial crashes. At this stage, prices freefall and asset markets break down. This is precisely what happened in the great crash of 2008. Given these lasting contributions, it should be no surprise that many economists are avidly reading Galbraith once more.

STEPHEN P. DUNN

See also:

Competition; Economic Policy; Income Distribution; Inflation; Market Governance; Monetary Policy; Prices and Pricing; Welfare Economics.

References

Dunn, S.P. (2011), *The Economics of John Kenneth Galbraith: Introduction, Persuasion and Rehabilitation*, Cambridge: Cambridge University Press.
Galbraith, J.K. (1952a), *American Capitalism: The Concept of Countervailing Power*, London: Hamish Hamilton.
Galbraith, J.K. (1952b), *A Theory of Price Control*, Cambridge, MA: Harvard University Press.
Galbraith, J.K. (1955), *The Great Crash, 1929*, Boston, MA: Houghton Mifflin.
Galbraith, J.K. (1958 [1967]), *The Affluent Society*, 2nd edn, Harmondsworth: Penguin.
Galbraith, J.K. (1967 [1972]), *The New Industrial State*, 2nd edn, Harmondsworth: Penguin, 1972.
Galbraith, J.K. (1973), *Economics and the Public Purpose*, Harmondsworth: Penguin.
Galbraith, J.K. (1977), 'The bimodal image of the modern economy: remarks upon receipt of the Veblen–Commons award', *Journal of Economic Issues*, **11** (2), 189–200.
Kalecki, M. (1943), 'Political aspects of full employment', *Political Quarterly*, **14** (4), 322–31.
Keynes, J.M. (1936), *The General Theory of Employment, Interest and Money*, London: Macmillan.
King, J.E. (2002), *A History of Post Keynesian Economics since 1936*, Cheltenham, UK and Northampton, MA, USA: Edward Elgar.

Gender

While feminist economics has developed a large and varied literature, its intersection with Post Keynesianism is too nascent to delineate 'the' Post Keynesian approach to gender. I begin with the most developed literature in that intersection, gendered structural macroeconomics. I then develop a distinction between 'mapping' and 'making' approaches to gender. *Mapping* approaches treat gender as a social map of a biological distinction between sexes, stable enough in its properties that it can be regarded as a structural fact. Most work in gendered macroeconomics falls into this category. *Making* approaches, by contrast, treat gender as something *produced* socially, in various institutional contexts. In this category fall more recent Post Keynesian writings which address gender as a question of subject formation.

The gendered macroeconomics literature treats gender as 'structure' in a manner analogous to Kaleckian models of class: men and women may be distinguished in their wages and access to employment, consumption and savings behaviour, share in household distribution, access to finance, and ownership of property. The Kaleckian heritage may also be seen in a preference for non-equilibrium models with substantial excess capacity (Seguino and Grown 2006). In addition, a number of economists have sought to incorporate 'labor as a produced input' (Çağatay et al. 2000, p. 1148) in order to capture caring labour and a variety of non-monetized domestic tasks generally grouped under the heading 'household'. One drops the assumption of an 'infinitely elastic' supply of household services, as Diane Elson (1993, p. 238) put it, and asks how workers are fed and clothed and looked after in the short term, and how they are reproduced in the long term via the raising of children. A 'household sector' of this kind may be added via a two-sector model, or in other ways linked to a gender-disaggregated macro model, for example via the higher proportion of women's earnings that is typically devoted to spending on children (Çağatay et al. 2000). For-market production may be gender disaggregated if men and women, as entrepreneurs, face differential access to output and factor models (Floro and Dymski 2000). Some categories of for-market production may overlap unpaid domestic labour (Benería and Roldán 1987; Floro 1995).

Much of this work stems from investigation of the impact of structural adjustment policies in the 1980s. As Benería and Roldán's (1987) canonical study of working-class Mexicans showed, productive activity shifted quickly back and forth across the line between market and non-market, and households changed shape as people moved in together. Many women ended up doing substantially more work cooking, cleaning and caring, and traipsing to distant markets for bargains, while coping with declining household infrastructure and diminished public services.

Gendered macroeconomics tends to treat gender as exogenous, as pregiven 'structure' through which processes of macro adjustment work. It has to assume that gendered behaviours and constraints are common across national populations and constant across significant spans of time. The gendered macroeconomics literature generally, sometimes explicitly, theorizes the concept via the sex|gender distinction: 'sex' stands for biology and 'gender' handles whatever part of being a man or woman cannot be explained biologically, or in common jargon, that which is 'socially constructed'. Gender is thus a *mapping* of sex. To elaborate: in mapping theories of gender, a biological male|female divide (that is, 'sex') is presented as obvious, inherently dichotomous and complementary. *Gender* is then treated as a set of social distinctions and cultural meanings attached to, conceptualizing and culturalizing, this natural division. Depending on how tightly you think biology constrains social-cultural mappings, you can then generate either 'nature' or 'nurture' views: tight constraint gets you biological determinism, loose constraint produces social constructivism. Mapping theories of gender typically assume that 'family' rests on the natural substrate of a heterosexual breeding pair plus its progeny, a biological nature that humans share with, say, seagulls. Thus assumptions about biology do a lot of work in mapping theories, even those hostile to biological determinism. Those assumptions generate a nuclear, heteronormative family, a unit already *presumed* to be bounded, stable and heterosexual, and allow the generalization of those properties across human history and societies.

(Note that the typical microfoundational move in the gendered macro literature is to husband–wife bargaining models.)

Critiques of the mapping approach have converged from cultural anthropology, 'Queer Theory', and a range of feminist scholarship (see Danby 2007 for more extended argument and references). Rigorously biological accounts of human sexual differentiation turn out to be elusive. Kinship lacks a universal template; depictions of family as always built on a standard heterosexual couple (or even a primal mother–child bond) are ersatz ideological projections. Moreover, the constitutive link between gender and *heteronormativity* becomes clearer once you question the obviousness of heterosexuality. (Critique of heteronormativity is not a matter of being nicer to gay people, commendable though that is. It asks the more fundamental question of why sexuality gets partitioned into straight and gay, and how these categories emerged as distinct identities.) A heteronormative theory of gender (men and women are complementary family-makers) underlies a heteronormative theory of 'the' family, and vice versa: the tautological circle makes each appear obvious by virtue of the other.

The alternative to mapping I shall shorthand as *making*. Here is the argument: when you step in front of a classroom, participate in a meeting, or join a family dinner, you *perform* a gender. A 'biological male' who performs convincingly as a woman *is* a woman: she deploys the requisite scripts, rules of bodily comportment and social behaviour to be treated as a woman. What makes a performance successful or unsuccessful is its recognition by others. Gender performance is social, happens (repeatedly) in particular institutional contexts, and may vary depending on context (Charusheela 2010).

Performative or 'making' approaches are especially good at explaining why the display of gender is often anxious or showy, why we may be disciplined for inadequate gender performance. They are well-adapted to studying the impacts of regulation and control *on* gender. In this approach, 'gender' figures as an *outcome* rather than an input or cause. It thus becomes less stable. The practical and political consequences are large: in both the nature and nurture variants of mapping, gender is something that happened to you. In the nature variant it was built into your body, in the socially constructivist or nurture variant, it was trained into you as a child. As an adult, there is not much you can do about it. What is stable for the individual is stable for the society: any significant shift in gender norms and behaviour would require decades of changes in training and socialization. In a making approach, we look for the institutions that create and shore up gender, and consider the possibility that different institutions may be at cross-purposes. A person's 'gender' may be a disparate set of performances enabled, required, or thwarted in different settings.

This question opens a link to Post Keynesians via their interest in institutional instability. Workers, rentiers and entrepreneurs play distinct roles in a Post Keynesian world, but those roles are neither products of nature, nor generated by a social order of guaranteed stability. John Maynard Keynes denounced the complacent assumption that these roles are natural or stable; Michał Kalecki discussed the political conditions for particular configurations of class society. In the words of Charusheela (2010, p. 1153):

> Just as Keynes highlighted the extent to which plans for the future rest on others' actions, so too did feminists highlight the extent to which our performative acts rest on others' recognition. Just as post-Keynesians emphasised the role of rumour, expectations and the 'news' in constituting the grounds on which plans are made, feminists examine the role of discourse in setting the parameters of gender expectations. Both traditions are interested in desire and anxiety, and the ways in which plans cohere or fail to, neither tradition assumes that there is any automatic or natural equilibrium that produces coherence. ... if we argue that the world is marked by enough contingency and open-endedness that there is no necessary stability, the project becomes one of asking if and when we do see stability, how does it come about? What, in a given historical setting, at a specific place and time, are the repeated actions, the constantly, persistently repeated efforts, that make something stable in an unstable world?

Post Keynesians have taken an interest in the ways in which states structure national economies; as Charusheela shows, one of those roles may be via the regulation and disciplining of the very category 'household'. Governments have determined who may cohabit and under what conditions, what kinds of familial relations are required for access to government services or immigration, and under what conditions children may be confiscated from the people raising them. Thus not only gender but 'the household' itself may be co-created consequences of state action. Some of these points can be linked back to Benería and Roldán (1987): the production of householdness and the production of gender were joint projects; households themselves are contingent, unstable and contested projects that can fail. Household boundaries are porous.

Related points can be made about the gendering of entrepreneurs and firms. Van Staveren has drawn attention to the gendered nature of the standard neoclassical subject, and the point can be extended to Post Keynesian entrepreneurs. In what ways are firms, markets and finance not only gender structured, but also gender producing?

Lest the divide appear too stark, I conclude by listing points that would be accepted across economists working in the 'mapping' and 'making' approaches to gender. First, gender matters at the individual level: whether other people understand us to be men or women affects, all over the world, our access to employment, our pay, and how we are treated in the workplace.

It conditions our abilities to borrow, to acquire and to hold property, and to form commercial ties that facilitate buying and selling. It structures the relationships in which we perform care work and receive care. Second, there is sufficient regularity in the way gender matters to permit at least cautious aggregation; certainly there is no reason to think of the 'macro' as ungendered. The differences between the mapping and making approaches track the distinction between the Kaleckian and uncertainty-emphasizing tendencies within Post Keynesianism at large: how much structure to assume, how much to throw in doubt? But there is no reason not to see these approaches as complementary. (Todorova 2009, for example, links structure and subject-formation via institutionalist concepts.)

The constraints of a handbook entry preclude a full bibliography. On the gendered macroeconomics literature, readers are exhorted to consult Çağatay et al. (2000), another introduction by the same authors to a 1995 symposium in *World Development* (Vol. 23, No. 11), the articles in both symposia, and Grown and Seguino (2011). See van Staveren (2010) for a wide-ranging discussion of links between Post Keynesian and feminist economics.

COLIN DANBY

See also

Agency; Households; Institutionalism.

References

Benería, L. and M. Roldán (1987), *The Crossroads of Class and Gender: Industrial Homework, Subcontracting, and Household Dynamics in Mexico City*, Chicago, IL: University of Chicago Press.
Çağatay, N., D. Elson and C. Grown (2000), 'Introduction', *World Development*, **28** (7), 1145–56.
Charusheela, S. (2010), 'Gender and the stability of consumption: a feminist contribution to post-Keynesian economics', *Cambridge Journal of Economics*, **34** (6), 1145–56.
Danby, C. (2007), 'Political economy and the closet: heteronormativity in feminist economics', *Feminist Economics*, **13** (2), 27–53.
Elson, D. (1993), 'Gender-aware analysis and development economics', *Journal of International Development*, **5** (2), 237–47.
Floro, M.S. (1995), 'Economic restructuring, gender and the allocation of time', *World Development*, **23** (11), 1913–29.
Floro, M.S. and G. Dymski (2000), 'Financial crisis, gender and power: an analytical framework', *World Development*, **28** (7), 1269–83.
Grown, C. and S. Seguino (2011), *Gender and Economics*, Basingstoke: Palgrave Macmillan.
Seguino, S. and C. Grown (2006), 'Feminist–Kaleckian macroeconomic policy for developing countries', Working Paper No. 446, Levy Economics Institute of Bard College, Annandale-on-Hudson, NY, available at: http://www.levyinstitute.org/pubs/wp_446.pdf.
Todorova, Z. (2009), *Money and Households in a Capitalist Economy*, Cheltenham, UK and Northampton, MA, USA: Edward Elgar.
Van Staveren, I. (2010), 'Post-Keynesianism meets feminist economics', *Cambridge Journal of Economics*, **34** (6), 1123–44.

Germany and Austria

Although Keynesian ideas inspired both politics and academia in Germany and Austria after the Second World War, *Post* Keynesian thinking influenced political and theoretical development only to a limited degree.

After the Second World War, whereas in East Germany a centrally administered economy inspired by Marxist ideas was established, the dominant school of thought in West Germany was *ordoliberalism*, with its economic policy concept of a social market economy. This concept combined the notion of free markets, kept functional by competition policy, with the aim of a high level of social security. After a period of ongoing and rising prosperity, West Germany had to face an economic downturn after an overheating period in 1966 which, from the point of view of today and of the development in other countries at that time, was normal but was perceived as a crisis. This brought into power a Grand Coalition of Christian Democrats and Social Democrats, which introduced and institutionalized tripartite economic governance with Keynesian elements to stabilize the economy (Schanetzky 2007). Pushed by the social democrat Karl Schiller – then minister of economics and later also finance minister – the government implemented the Law for Promoting Stability and Growth in the Economy in 1967. It included the so-called 'Magical Square' of four goals to be achieved: price stability, high employment, balanced foreign trade and payments, and adequate and continuous growth, where 'magical' refers to the potential conflicts between the targets. Moreover, the government tried to control inflation by the corporatist 'Concerted Action', bringing together government, trade unions, employers and the German central bank in regular meetings. This attempt, however, failed – its symbol of failure being wildcat strikes in September 1969. In the 1970s, West Germany had to deal with a period of stagflation, which deeply undermined trust in Keynesian reasoning.

After this episode of Keynesianism, in the next decades liberal ideas – in the form of monetarism and supply-side economics – dominated again. Although the accession of East to West Germany in 1990 led to a massive monetary redistribution from West to East in combination with high deficit spending, this followed neither a coherent nor a Keynesian economic policy concept. Since the late 1990s, under Social Democrat-led governments, social pacts and since 2003 labour market reforms – the so-called 'Hartz reforms' – were implemented, promoting wage restraint and contributing to low wage increases, even real wage decreases in some years. Moreover, fiscal policies were restrictive.

In Austria, the economy prospered, similarly to Germany after the Second World War. From the early 1970s to the mid-1990s, economic policy in Austria followed – normally not explicitly in official statements of the government but de facto – a Keynesian approach, *Austro-Keynesianism* (Chaloupek and Marterbauer 2008). It was mainly characterized by countercyclical fiscal policy, wage increases oriented to productivity growth plus inflation, and the Austrian currency, the schilling, was closely tied to the German Deutschmark, the regional anchor currency of that time. As a result, for two decades unemployment performance was considerably better than the average of what is now the euro area. Moreover, real wages increased significantly. Both international competitiveness and strong domestic demand were achieved. This outcome was crucially dependent on a special Austrian socio-political setting based on corporatism and two co-ruling major parties, the Social Democrats and the Christian Democrats. Through the close links between the government on the one side, and trade unions and employers' organizations and their involvement in economic policy on the other, a consensus could emerge to keep wage developments distribution-neutral and unit labour costs constant. Also, public employment and investment were kept high and public subsidies for credits reduced the burden of interest rates for companies.

The continuing advancement of the European single market and especially the formation of the euro area in 1999 changed the economic framework for both countries substantially. Monetary policy is the sole responsibility of the European Central Bank at the European level, and aims primarily at price stability based on an inflation target of below but near 2 per cent. Fiscal policies are loosely coordinated by the Stability and Growth Pact for the member states of the European Union, institutionalizing two deficit criteria – public debt has to be below 60 per cent of GDP and the annual budget deficit below 3 per cent – which are enforced by a so-called 'excessive deficit procedure'. This economic policy concept and its institutionalization is clearly more inspired by the New Consensus view and supply-side economics than by Post Keynesian ideas (Arestis 2009). Although it did not alter this view completely, the financial crisis starting in 2007 led to a gain in influence of Keynesian ideas and policy proposals; fiscal stabilization programmes were established, the trend to financial market deregulation was stopped, and the central bank began to use unorthodox methods such as quantitative easing and purchase of government bonds.

Contributions to the development of Keynesian and explicitly Post Keynesian thinking were made by several German and Austrian authors. Moreover, in one case a distinct (sub-)school of Post Keynesian economics has been developed.

In criticizing the approach that certain aims such as full employment could be reached by a fine-tuned application of instruments without relevant side-effects on prices and quantities, Hajo Riese (2001) has developed a monetary theory of production without the mechanical tone of the hydraulic standard Keynesianism of the 1960s. Riese himself publishes almost exclusively in German, which has restricted his international influence. For him, economic policy has to acknowledge that it can act only as a market participant signalling prices, but cannot intervene in markets to change quantities. Similar to other Post Keynesian approaches, he and his Berlin group emphasize the monetary aspects of Keynes's theory: money is not a veil but matters; inflation is a phenomenon mainly based on wage–price spirals; and money is endogenous. The *differentia specifica* of this Berlin school might be seen in its interpretation of Keynes's liquidity premium as determining the credit supply. Lending money means parting with liquidity, which requires compensation in terms of the rate of interest. The latter sets the standard for the rate of profit. Therefore, the credit market dominates the goods and the labour market.

In their economic policy writings, the Berlin school has criticized what they call the German neo-mercantilist strategy of stability-oriented devaluation. In their view, this is a beggar-thy-neighbour strategy aiming at export surpluses, which is characterized by a focus on price stability and on restrictive fiscal and monetary policies. Moreover, they have produced a broad literature on transformation problems of Third World countries and of East Germany, concentrating on monetary and exchange rate issues.

Gunnar Heinsohn and Otto Steiger from Bremen have proposed a connected but not identical approach, taking property and the relationship between creditors and borrowers as the crucial starting-point for economic reasoning, discarding the exchange paradigm of neoclassical economics (Heinsohn and Steiger1996 [2009]). In their view, the existence of property creates money, interest and profit; markets, competition, business cycles, technical progress and so forth are seen as derivative phenomena.

Two Austrian intellectuals have had a distinct influence on the development of Post Keynesian Economics. Josef Steindl extended the work of Michał Kalecki in the fields of distribution, growth and business cycles. After emigration during fascism he returned to Austria and the Austrian Institute of Economic Research (WIFO). His influence, however, was not restricted to the Austrian scene but was also eminent in the English-speaking area (Harcourt 1994). In his works, Steindl tried to explain the stagnationary tendencies of the US interwar period, applying and modifying this reasoning to the declining growth rates in the 1970s after the exceptional period of the 'golden age'. In doing this, he emphasized political factors leading to a farewell to full employment and the implementation of macroeconomic policies focused on price stability and balanced budgets.

Three years before Steindl, Kurt Rothschild returned to Austria after emigrating and became the focal point of the Austrian Post Keynesian development. Despite several important contributions in English, for example on oligopoly and the Kaldorian growth model, interest in his person and works was more limited to Austria, as in the case of Steindl. As King (1994) points out, this might be caused by his broader range of interests – covering methodology, price theory and the labour market as well as bargaining and power – and his interest in economic policy.

Since the 1970s, researchers from both countries – notably Heinz D. Kurz, Peter Kalmbach, Harald Hagemann and Bertram Schefold – developed a synthesis of Piero Sraffa and Keynes and contributed substantially to the capital controversy and the neo-Ricardian approach in general. Moreover, they are well known for their contributions to the history of economic thought.

Post Keynesians in Germany and Austria now focus on European economic policies and issues of financialization, that is, an increasing financial market orientation within capitalism. The Bhaduri–Marglin model and stock-flow consistent models are preferred tools of younger Post Keynesians such as Engelbert Stockhammer and Eckhard Hein.

Despite their theoretical productivity, younger members of the Post Keynesian camp are not easy to find at universities and large public research institutes in Germany. However, at the two Berlin universities of applied sciences, Post Keynesian teaching and research is quite prominent. Outside the universities, the trade union-related Macroeconomic Policy Institute (IMK) at the Hans Böckler Foundation in Düsseldorf is a Keynesian institute that also utilizes the Post Keynesian approach. In Austria, at the universities and at the Austrian Institute of Economic Research WIFO, the largest and tripartitely financed research institute of Austria, there are some researchers with a Post Keynesian background.

Several societies and networks support (Post) Keynesian thinking. In Germany, the Memorandum group, a collaboration of economists and trade unionists with Marxian and/or Keynesian backgrounds, has issued counter-opinions to the reports of the state-commissioned German Council of Economic Experts in 1975 and from 1977 annually (see http://www.memo.uni-bremen.de). Jörg Huffschmid, one of the members of this group, also initiated the pan-European Euromemorandum group, founded in 1995. Founded in the 1970s, the Arbeitskreis Politische Ökonomie ('Working Group on Political Economy'; see http://www.iim.uni-flensburg.de/vwl/front_content.php?idcat=1696) gathers researchers from different schools, including monetary Keynesians and neo-Ricardians, at conferences and within a series of yearbooks. Since 1997, the originally German-based but now internationalized Research Network Macroeconomics and Macroeconomic Policies (FMM) has existed as a platform for analysis, research and discussion of macroeconomic issues with a clear focus on Post Keynesian positions. It has organized annual conferences in Berlin, issues a book series and has started to provide an introduction to Post Keynesian economics through summer schools for young researchers and students (see http://www. network-macroeconomics.org). Loosely connected to the research network, the peer-reviewed English-language journal *Intervention. European Journal of Economics and Economic Policies*, existing since 2004, serves as a forum for studies in macroeconomic theory, economic institutions and economic policies, to a large extent from a Post Keynesian perspective (see http://www. journal-intervention.org). The main focus of the German Keynes Society is to popularize information on Keynes and Keynesian thinking for the German-speaking region (available at http://www.keynes-gesellschaft.de/); the society also organizes conferences and issues a book series.

In Austria, BEIGEWUM, a private advisory council for social, economic and ecological alternatives, integrates members of several economic disciplines but has a focus on public budgets, distribution and European integration, and often uses Post Keynesian arguments (see http://www. beigewum.at). It issues a journal, *Kurswechsel*, and further publications on an irregular basis.

TORSTEN NIECHOJ

See also:

Economic Policy; Financialization; Inflation; New Classical Economics; Stagflation; Wage Deflation.

References

Arestis, P. (2009), 'New Consensus macroeconomics and Keynesian critique', in E. Hein, T. Niechoj and E. Stockhammer (eds), *Macroeconomic Policies on Shaky Foundations. Whither Mainstream Economics?*, Marburg: Metropolis Publishers, pp. 165–85.
Chaloupek, G. and M. Marterbauer (2008), 'Was bleibt vom Austro-Keynesianismus? Dauerhafte Wirkungen der postkeynesianischen Wirtschaftspolitik in Österreich 1970–1995' ['What is left of Austro-Keynesianism? Lasting effects of Post Keynesian economic policy in Austria'], in H. Hagemann, G. Horn and H.-J. Krupp (eds), *Aus gesamtwirtschaftlicher Sicht. Festschrift für Jürgen Kromphardt [From a Macroeconomic Point of View: Festschrift for Jürgen Kromphardt]*, Marburg: Metropolis, pp. 45–67.
Harcourt, G.C. (1994), 'Josef Steindl, April 14, 1912–March 7, 1993: a tribute', *Journal of Post Keynesian Economics*, **16** (4), 627–42.
Heinsohn, G. and O. Steiger (1996 [2009]), *Eigentum, Zins und Geld. Ungelöste Rätsel der Wirtschaftswissenschaft [Property, Interest and Money: Some Unsolved Puzzles in Economics]*, Marburg: Metropolis.
King, J.E. (1994), 'Kurt Rothschild and the alternative Austrian economics', *Cambridge Journal of Economics*, **18** (5), 431–45.
Riese, H. (2001), *Grundlegungen eines monetären Keynesianismus. Ausgewählte Schriften 1964–1999 [Foundations of a Monetary Keynesianism: Selected Papers 1964–1999]*, two vols, Marburg: Metropolis.
Schanetzky, T. (2007), *Die große Ernüchterung. Wirtschaftspolitik, Expertise und Gesellschaft in der Bundesrepublik 1966 bis 1982 [The Great Disillusionment: Economic Policy, Expertise and Society in the Federal Republic, 1966–1982]*, Berlin: Akademie Verlag.

Global Financial Crisis

The global financial crisis (GFC) started in the US in August 2007 when short-term inter-bank lending in the money markets first dried up. It escalated following the failure of the US investment bank Lehman Brothers in September 2008, temporarily threatening the global financial system with full-scale collapse. This was prevented by rapid and massive state intervention in the US and major Western European economies to effect large-scale capital injections into their banking systems alongside state guarantees for inter-bank lending and partial bank nationalizations. While this emergency response succeeded in averting a chain reaction of bank failures, it was insufficient to kick-start bank lending and to prevent the worst recession in advanced economies since the Second World War.

The most salient feature of the GFC is its sheer size. Following Alan Greenspan, if one adds to the losses of the financial and listed corporate sector 'the thousands of billions of dollars of losses of equity in homes and losses of non-listed corporate and unincorporated businesses, that could easily bring the aggregate equity loss to well over US$40 trillion, a staggering two-thirds of last year's global gross domestic product' (Greenspan 2009). Conservative estimates for outstanding credit defaults swaps (CDS) in 2009 put these at $60 trillion, with the risk embodied after discounting mutually off-setting contracts still as high as $14 trillion (Tett 2009, p. 264). In 2009, world output in advanced economies fell by 3.4 per cent and the volume of world trade in goods and services by 10.7 per cent (IMF *World Economic Outlook*, January 2011). The International Labour Organization (*Global Employment Trends* January 2011) reported a global rate of unemployment of 6.2 per cent for 2010, or an increase of 27.6 million officially registered job-seekers compared to 2007. Despite a halting recovery of some macroeconomic indicators in 2010, unemployment in advanced economies continued to rise to 8.8 per cent in 2010 from 8.4 per cent in 2009.

While developing countries were not at the centre of the GFC, they have been adversely affected by the reduction of their exports to the US and the European Union area following the onset of debt deflation in these economies. Volatile commodity markets and growing speculation in staple food markets since 2008 have further increased the economic vulnerability of developing countries and thus also the risk of substantial political instability. This increased vulnerability occurs in the context of an international financial system that, for three decades prior to the GFC, has systematically concentrated net foreign currency debt in poor economies.

Mainstream economics has been widely criticized for failing to predict the GFC; it has since struggled to explain the systemic nature of the crisis (Crotty 2009; Skott 2010). Austrian and neoclassical economists have blamed the state, in particular Greenspan's easy money policy in response to the IT bubble of the early 2000s and the failure of successive US governments to rein in the US current account deficit. In addition to policy-induced global excess liquidity, 'irrational exuberance' (including fraudulent behaviour) has been a favourite explanation of the GFC by those subscribing to the 'efficient market hypothesis'. Paradoxically, from a perspective in which, over the long period, deviations from perfect foresight in rational agents are random, financial markets passively discount a predictable future, prices reflect all available information at any point in time, and the composition of corporate finance will not affect the value of a company, the only explanation of a financial crisis, apart from policy mismanagement or other exogenous shocks, is a sudden outbreak of 'folly' and the proverbial 'bad apple'. Consequently, mainstream (and Austrian) economists favour a policy approach to the aftermath of the GFC that will restore free markets to their presumed efficient state. This ranges from support for austerity programmes to address the (nationalized) debt overhang from the GFC to structural reforms aimed at reducing the future economic role of the state, for instance, by opening up public sectors to private competition.

By contrast, Post Keynesian explanations of the GFC have focused on the endogenous inability of liberalized financial markets to assess systemic risk. Central to Post Keynesian analyses of the GFC is Hyman Minsky's work on the instability of finance capitalism (Minsky 1986, 1993). In this view, the GFC is the predictable (and predicted) outcome of the rise of money manager capitalism since the 1980s. The core characteristic of money manager capitalism is a financial structure dominated by intermediaries that hold highly leveraged positions to maximize capital gains (rather than underlying income flows). This kind of financial structure not only commits large parts of cash flows to debt validation, but also encourages corporate control mechanisms that prioritize the full pricing of corporate liabilities in the financial markets over trade and production profits. The overall tendency is for risk to be heavily underpriced and, ultimately, transferred from financial investors to society at large. For Post Keynesians, money manager capitalism *per se* is not a recent phenomenon, having also been instrumental in the build-up to the Great Crash of 1929. There are, however, a number of specific features of contemporary money manager capitalism that explain the devastating nature of the GFC, with some Post Keynesians arguing that the GFC may signal the end of money manager capitalism (Wray 2009).

First, the high-technology nature and sheer extent of modern securitization (the bundling of debt into bonds that are sold in capital markets) was essential to the accelerated pace of financial globalization since the 1980s. As Minsky (1987, pp. 2–3) pointed out, 'there is a symbiotic relation between the globalization of the world's financial structure and the securitization of financial instruments'. Securitization creates 'border-free' dollar-denominated assets attractive for global investors in search of capital gains, and the globalization of financial institutions enhances 'the ability of creditors to capture assets that underlie the securities' (ibid.). Second, new techniques of risk management – apart from securitization *per se*, in particular the increased use of derivatives and portfolio diversification based on financial engineering – facilitated the creation of an opaque banking structure. The so-called 'originate and distribute' model of banking basically eliminated (reliable) capital backing as well as secondary liquidity cushions from the banking structure (Kregel 2008). Under this model, bank profits derived mainly from loan origination fees (rather than interest rate spreads) and banks' liquidity management relied heavily on leverage and securitization. Banks not only had every incentive to relax due diligence in assessing the creditworthiness of borrowers, but also the opportunity to take high-risk debt off their balance sheets into subsidiary financial institutions (or special investment vehicles) to reduce required capital backing for outstanding loans. In addition, conventional secondary reserves, such as access to money market funding and extensive holdings of government obligations, were replaced by complex bond insurance schemes or credit default swaps (CDS) for mostly highly illiquid mortgage-backed packaged securities. Finally, private credit rating agencies, increasingly beholden to fee income from banks interested in obtaining credit enhancements through insurance via high ratings on their senior liabilities, failed to provide due diligence on the products and structures they insured.

When real estate prices in the US eventually began to fall, insurers lacked capitalization to an even greater extent than banks. With the insolvency of securitized structures soon becoming evident, a rush for margin liquidity ensued that revealed the insolvency of the entire financial system, bringing it to the brink of collapse. In the end, '[t]he chain that linked a synthetic CDO of ABS [a credit default obligation of asset backed securities], say, with a "real" person was so convoluted it was almost impossible for anybody to fit that into a single cognitive map – be they anthropologist, economist or credit whizz' (Tett 2009, p. 299).

While Post Keynesians have stressed the role of financial deregulation in the rise of money manager capitalism, it is important to emphasize that from a Post Keynesian perspective excessive deregulation cannot be explained, as in New Keynesian economics, in terms of potentially avoidable coordination and information failures between banks, businesses and regulatory bodies. Instead, Minsky's famous verdict that 'stability is destabilizing' suggests that capital market liberalization was the inevitable outcome of thirty years of relative economic prosperity and stability prior to the 1980s, reflecting *shared* optimistic expectations of the dominant political classes and economic decision makers that explain their refusal to make use of available policy tools to regain control of credit-fuelled financial speculation.

Alongside Marxists and Schumpeterians, Post Keynesians have also highlighted the importance of structural factors to explain the severity of the GFC and the Great Recession. While Marxists emphasize politico-institutional determinants of the evolution of finance capital (Crotty 2009), and Schumpeterians have placed the GFC in the context of long-term technical change and financial innovation (Perez 2009), Post Keynesians have focused on the radical shifts in income distribution that have occurred in most advanced capitalist economies since the 1980s (Palley 2009; Palma 2009). 'Wage-less productivity growth' against the background of the dismantling of welfare-statist social security and employment protection, together with the regressive effects of housing inflation on income distribution (Toporowoski 2010), meant that economic growth in many advanced economies prior to the GFC was primarily driven by credit-fuelled consumer expenditure and/or export demand. Once debt deflation set in, these economies therefore lacked any 'real cushion' of 'reserve' effective demand.

Post Keynesians have been highly critical of current policy responses to the GFC. They argue that conventional reflationary measures are insufficient to address the extent of excess debt and the structural flaws of the 'originate and distribute' banking model. In their view, the failure to restore bank lending for productive purposes through the recapitalization of banks and monetary policies aimed at restoring asset and goods prices, is unsurprising since it ignores the need for structural reforms of a financial system in which banks had long ceased to be conventional lenders as well as the desire of firms and households to pay off debt (Kregel 2009; Toporowski 2010). Post Keynesians have been similarly critical of the Obama administration's investment schemes as only very indirectly targeted at household incomes, and are sharply opposed to the austerity programmes adopted in most European economies in response to rising government debt. Apart from their excessive social cost, the latter are likely eventually to raise the GDP-to-debt ratio due to their negative impact on GDP growth, falling tax revenue and rising social security expenditures. Instead, Post Keynesians advocate policies that tackle the underlying structural problems revealed by the GFC: this includes structural reforms of the international monetary and financial system to restore risk management in the interest of long-term growth and rectify core global macro-economic imbalances, as well as long-term income policies to rebalance income distribution in advanced capitalist economies in favour of lower-income classes.

STEPHANIE BLANKENBURG

See also:

Banking; Budget Deficits; Consumer Debt; Economic Policy; Efficient Markets Hypothesis; Financial Instability Hypothesis; Financial Markets; Financial Reform; Fiscal Policy; Income Distribution; International Financial Reform; Money Manager Capitalism.

References

Crotty, J. (2009), 'Structural causes of the global financial crisis: a critical assessment of the "new financial architecture"', *Cambridge Journal of Economics*, **33** (4), 563–80.
Greenspan, A. (2009), 'We need a better cushion against risk', *Financial Times*, 26 March.
Kregel, J. (2008), 'Minsky's cushion of safety. Systemic risk and the crisis in the U.S. sub-prime mortgage market', Highlights 93 A, Levy Economics Institute of Bard College, Annandale-on-Hudson, NY.
Kregel, J. (2009), 'Why don't the bailouts work? Design of a new financial system versus a return to normalcy', *Cambridge Journal of Economics*, **33** (4), 653–63.
Minsky, H. (1986), *Stablizing an Unstable Economy*, New York: McGraw-Hill.
Minsky, H. (1987), 'Securitization', Policy Note 2008/2, Levy Economics Institute of Bard College, Annandale-on-Hudson, NY.
Minsky, H. (1993), 'Finance and stability: the limits of capitalism', Working Paper No. 93, Levy Economics Institute of Bard College, Annandale-on-Hudson, NY.
Palley, T. (2009), 'After the Bust. The outlook for macroeconomics and macroeconomic policy', Public Policy Brief No. 97, Levy Economics Institute of Bard College, Annandale-on-Hudson, NY.
Palma, J.G. (2009), 'The revenge of the market on the rentiers. Why neoliberal reports of the end of history turned out to be premature', *Cambridge Journal of Economics*, **33** (4), 829–69.
Perez, C. (2009), 'The double bubble at the turn of the century: technological roots and structural implications', *Cambridge Journal of Economics*, **33** (4), 779–805.
Skott, P. (2010), 'The great detour', *Homo Oeconomicus*, **27** (3), 338–43.
Tett, G. (2009), *Fool's Gold: How Unrestrained Greed Corrupted a Dream, Shattered Global Markets and Unleashed a Catastrophe*, London: Little Brown.
Toporowski, J. (2010), *Why the World Economy Needs a Financial Crash and other Critical Essays on Finance and Financial Economics*, London: Anthem Press.
Wray, R. (2009), 'The rise and fall of money manager capitalism: a Minskian approach', *Cambridge Journal of Economics*, **33** (4), 807–28.

Growth and Income Distribution

The determinants of growth were a major concern of the classical econo-mists, who related growth to income distribution, which affects the saving and investment decisions of the different classes. Adam Smith and Karl Marx also underlined the role of technical progress, presenting a broad analysis of this subject, which can be considered an antecedent of the modern cumulative causation and evolutionary approaches.

The rise of the neoclassical school in the second half of the nineteenth century brought about a change of perspective in economic theory. Allocation of resources became the major concern and the problem of distribution was seen as one aspect of the general pricing and allocation process. Neoclassical economists argued that competitive forces, operating through variations in relative prices and factor substitution, generate a tendency to full employment and to the exploitation of the growth potential of the economy. These market mechanisms were examined in what Keynes called the 'real department of economics'. The 'monetary department' dealt instead with the price level and with business fluctuations, arguing that the working of the credit system cause or amplify them.

The severity of the Great Depression changed the course of these events. As Roy Harrod pointed out (see Young 1989, pp. 30–38), previous recessions had not cast doubt on the belief that the economy is able to return to full employment. The Great Depression, instead, endangered political stability and raised the problem of a new political approach and of a new economic theory able to clarify whether market forces can lead the economy towards full employment or government intervention is required to restore it.

Moving along these lines, in 1932 Keynes introduced the concept of a 'monetary theory of production' to attack the neoclassical separation between the real and the monetary departments of economics and the idea of a tendency to full employment. Harrod, on the other hand, began in 1933 to develop economic dynamics. His work was stimulated by the will to extend Keynes's ideas to the dynamic context. The seminal 'An essay in dynamic theory' thus conceived modern growth theory as a Keynesian theory: it developed the views that the economic system does not tend necessarily to full employment and that the rate of growth may be affected by the autonomous components of aggregate demand, coming from the government, the private and the foreign sectors.

In opposition to Harrod's views, in 1956 Solow presented a dynamic version of neoclassical theory. He argued that variations in relative prices and factor substitution led the economy to a full employment steady growth path. The debate on capital theory, enhanced by the publication in 1960 of Piero Sraffa's *Production of Commodities by Means of Commodities*, scrutinized Solow's conclusions. Some outstanding neoclassical economists acknowledged the validity of the criticisms raised against their theory. In the summing up of the Symposium in the *Quarterly Journal of Economics* (1966) Samuelson recognized that in the long-period analysis of an economy where more than one commodity is produced, the occurrence of 'reverse capital deepening' is the general case. This conclusion undercut the neoclassical 'parables' that extended to a multi-commodity economy the conclusions from the analysis of a one-commodity world and challenged the view that price variations and factor substitution lead the economy to full employment.

During the same years Kaldor (1955–56) and Pasinetti (1962) developed the Post Keynesian theory of growth and distribution by assuming that market forces operate along lines different from those envisaged by neoclassical authors and similar to those described by the classical economists. Like the latter, Kaldor and Pasinetti assumed that the propensities to save of different income earners (or classes, or sectors of the economy) are not equal, and argued that variations in income distribution bring about changes in total saving and aggregate demand, leading the economy to steady growth. The Post Keynesian theory of growth and distribution introduced the 'Cambridge equation' and the 'Pasinetti theorem', which state that in steady growth the rate of profit is equal to the ratio between the rate of growth and the capitalists' propensity to save, and does not depend on technology or on the workers' propensity to save. In 1966 Samuelson and Modigliani challenged this conclusion and proposed the 'anti-Pasinetti' or 'dual' theorem. They argued that in steady growth, if the capital owned by the capitalist class is zero, the capital–output ratio is equal to the ratio between the workers' propensity to save and the rate of growth, while the rate of profit depends on the technological relation connecting this variable to the capital–output ratio. Whether the 'Pasinetti' or the 'dual' theorem applies depends on this technological relationship too.

By focusing on the role of income distribution in the growth process, and underlining the links with the classical economists and the differences with neoclassical authors, the theory proposed by Kaldor and Pasinetti failed to emphasize that there is no automatic tendency to full employment. However, developments in the Kaldor–Pasinetti theory, which have examined the role of the demand coming from the government sector, atone for this failure.

Kaldor's 1958 Memorandum to the Radcliffe Commission shows many similarities with the views on the role of government policy proposed by Harrod and other Keynesian authors. Kaldor considered government policies to be necessary to pursue stability and growth. For him, monetary policy is the appropriate tool against economic fluctuations, while fiscal policy is relevant to the long-range objective of sustained growth. He proposed to use the Cambridge equation to determine the tax rate compatible with both the full-employment rate of growth and the rate of interest fixed by the monetary authority. In doing so he showed awareness of the complexity of the growth process, when he made some anticipations of the view, which he developed some years later, that a fiscal policy that tends to increase the share of consumption in aggregate demand may cause problems for the international competitiveness of the economy and for the maintenance of sustained growth in the future.

Kaldor did not present his conclusions on the role of government policy in a formalized way. The first formal presentation of the Post Keynesian theory of growth and distribution, which explicitly introduces the government sector, was provided by Steedman in 1972. He assumed a balanced budget to show that the Cambridge equation – in a revised form that takes into account the existence of taxation – holds in a larger number of cases than the dual theorem of Samuelson and Modigliani. By the late 1980s, Fleck and Domenghino (1987) and Pasinetti (1989) started a debate on the validity of the Cambridge equation when the budget is *not* balanced. The debate examined a large number of cases, showing when the Cambridge equation holds. It confirmed the conclusions previously reached by Steedman (see Panico 1997), showing how the views presented by Kaldor to the Radcliffe Commission can be formally developed and clarifying some features of his proposals. Moreover, the debate shows the existence of some other common elements between the classical and the Post Keynesian traditions, allowing the reconciliation of two approaches to distribution, which had previously been considered alternative. These are the approach proposed by Kaldor and Pasinetti in their theory of growth and distribution and that implied by Sraffa's hint in *Production of Commodities* to take the rate of profit, rather than the wage rate, as the independent variable (determined, in turn, by money interest rates) in the classical theory of prices and distribution.

Another line of development in the Keynesian literature focuses on the demand coming from the private sector in the form of autonomous investment and presents several investment-driven growth theories based on different specifications of the investment function.

The neo-Keynesian theory, proposed by Joan Robinson and Kaldor, assumes a direct functional relationship between investment and the rate of profit. This theory, which determines growth and distribution simultaneously, extends to long-period analysis the 'paradox of thrift', according to which an increase in the propensity to save causes a reduction in the rate of profit and in the rate of growth. Moreover, it underlines the existence of an inverse relationship between the real wage rate and the rate of growth.

The Kaleckian theory, inspired by Michał Kalecki and Josef Steindl, assumes that (i) productive capacity is not utilized at its 'normal' level, (ii) the profit margin is an exogenous variable depending on the degree of monopoly enjoyed by oligopolistic firms, (iii) prices are determined through a mark-up procedure, and (iv) investment is positively related to the rate of profit, which is a proxy for the state of expected profitability and the availability of internal finance, and the degree of capacity utilization, which reflects the state of aggregate demand. This theory confirms the neo-Keynesian conclusion on the paradox of thrift and argues, in opposition to the neo-Keynesian theory, for the existence of a positive relationship between the real wage rate and the rate of growth in the presence of underutilization of capacity. This result, known as the 'paradox of costs', is due to the fact that the rise in the real wage rate brings about an increase in demand and capacity utilization, which has a positive effect on the rate of profit and on investment.

The Kaleckian theory has been subsequently amended by work inspired by Bhaduri and Marglin (1990), which takes into account the different effects on investment of the rate of profit, the profit margin and capacity utilization. By introducing an investment function positively related to the profit margin and to capacity utilization, these works identify a wage-led and a profit-led growth regime. In both cases, a rise in the real wage rate reduces the profit margin and increases capacity utilization. However, in the wage-led regime the overall effect of an increase in the real wage rate on growth is positive, as in the Kaleckian paradox of costs, because the positive effect on growth generated by the increase in capacity utilization is assumed to be greater than the negative effect on growth generated by the decrease in the profit margin. In the profit-led regime the opposite result holds, because the positive effect on growth generated by the increase in capacity utilization is assumed to be lower than the negative effect generated by the decrease in the profit margin.

Following these lines, Boyer (2000) introduced a finance-led growth regime, opening the way to a set of Kaleckian theories trying to interpret the recent phenomena of 'financialization' of the economy and increased inequality in income distribution. These theories focus on the changes in the relations among workers, managers and shareholders that occurred after the monetarist counter-attack to the labour movement of 1979–82. Boyer describes the new institutional forms brought about by these changes and formalizes a model in which the choice of the managers to increase dividend payouts, as demanded by shareholders, plays a central role in this analysis. It increases capital gains and the earnings of financial rentiers, generating a negative influence on investment, but a positive one on the ability to borrow of the household sector. Owing to this positive effect, consumption can increase and counteract the negative influence on investment enhancing effective demand, growth and profits.

Other works have further elaborated this line of research, sometimes combining the Kaleckian assumptions with those of a Steindlian (Dutt 2006) and a stock–flow consistent framework (Lavoie and Godley 2001–2; Taylor 2004). They have added to the 'finance-led' regime, a 'profits without investment' regime and a 'contractive' regime (see Hein 2009).

A neo-Ricardian theory of growth, which starts from a classical theory of prices and distribution can also be found in the literature. This theory, in opposition to the neo-Keynesian and Kaleckian ones, assumes that the investment function depends on the discrepancies between actual and normal capacity utilization and underlines the need to develop the analysis of growth through the comparison of long-period positions. Moreover, it makes the rate of profit depend on the money rate of interest, as suggested by Sraffa in *Production of Commodities*.

The last line of development of Keynesian literature focuses on the influence on growth of demand coming from the foreign sector, a problem already considered by Harrod in the 1930s. This literature plays down the role of distributive variables and is intertwined with the analysis of growth as a 'cumulative process'.

In a series of essays written between 1966 and 1972, Kaldor used the notion of 'cumulative causation' to describe the actual performance of economies. He attributed to the demand coming from the foreign sector the primary role in setting in motion the growth process. The domestic sources of demand mainly influence, instead, the competitiveness of the economy and the intensity with which an external stimulus is transmitted to the rate of growth. According to Kaldor, the composition of output and demand has an important influence on the rate of change of productivity, owing to the presence of variable returns in the different sectors of the economy and to the fact that increasing returns occur mainly in the capital-goods sector. For Kaldor, high ratios of investment to aggregate demand and of the capital-goods sector in the productive structure enhance productivity changes, which, in turn, improve the international performance of the economy, setting up and intensifying cumulative processes. He distinguished between the concepts of 'consumption-led' and 'export-led' growth. The latter, he argued, is more desirable than the former, which tends to have negative long-run effects on productivity and international competitiveness, since it increases the weight of non-increasing returns sectors in the productive structure of the economy. This distinction was at the basis of Kaldor's claim, noted above, that the maintenance of sustained growth in the future may be endangered by the use of fiscal policy, which, according to him, tends to increase the share of consumption in aggregate demand.

In 1975, Dixon and Thirlwall presented an 'export-led growth model', which formalized some aspects of Kaldor's views. Thirlwall (1979) and Thirlwall and Hussain (1982), on the other hand, worked out a dynamic analysis showing how growth may be constrained by the equilibrium of the balance of payments, disregarding the operation of cumulative processes. In spite of this simplification, the empirical applications of the new analysis, which are able to account for differences in the rates of growth among countries and the cumulative divergence in their GDP levels, have produced more satisfactory results than those of the 1975 export-led model. Recently Moreno Brid (1998–99) and McCombie and Thirlwall (1999) have extended Thirlwall's new analysis to take into account the impact of the persistent accumulation of external debt on the economy's long-term rate of expansion. These extensions have opened new areas of research into the financial restrictions imposed by international credit institutions on the long-term economic growth of countries with persistent trade balance deficits.

CARLO PANICO

See also:

Cambridge Economic Tradition; Capital Theory; Export-led Growth; Financialization; Growth Theory; Income Distribution; Kaldorian Economics; Kaleckian Economics; Sraffian Economics; Wage- and Profit-led Regimes.

References

Bhaduri, A. and S. Marglin (1990), 'Unemployment and the real wage: the economic basis for contesting political ideologies', *Cambridge Journal of Economics*, **14** (4), 375–93.
Boyer, R. (2000), 'Is a finance-led growth regime a viable alternative to Fordism? A preliminary analysis', *Economy and Society*, **29** (1), 111–45.
Dixon, R. and A.P. Thirlwall (1975), 'A model of regional growth-rate differences on Kaldorian lines', *Oxford Economic Papers*, **27** (2), 201–14.
Dutt, A.K. (2006), 'Maturity, stagnation and consumer debt: a Steindlian approach', *Metroeconomica*, **57** (3), 339–64.
Fleck, F.H. and C.M. Domenghino (1987), 'Cambridge (UK) versus Cambridge (Mass.): a Keynesian solution to the "Pasinetti Paradox"', *Journal of Post Keynesian Economics*, **10** (1), 22–36.
Hein, E. (2009), 'A (Post-)Keynesian Perspective on "Financialisation"', *IMK Studies*, 1/2009, Macroeconomic Policy Institute (IMK), Hans Boeckler Foundation, Düsseldorf.
Kaldor, N. (1955–56), 'Alternative theories of distribution', *Review of Economic Studies*, **23** (2), 83–100.
Lavoie, M. and W. Godley (2001–02), 'Kaleckian models of growth in a coherent stock–flow monetary framework: a Kaldorian view', *Journal of Post Keynesian Economics*, **24** (2), 277–311.
McCombie, J. and A.P. Thirlwall (1999), 'Growth in an international context: a Post Keynesian view', in J. Deprez and J.T. Harvey (eds), *Foundations of International Economics: Post Keynesian Perspectives*, London and New York: Routledge, pp. 35–90.
Moreno Brid, J.C. (1998–99), 'On capital flows and the balance-of-payments constrained growth model', *Journal of Post Keynesian Economics*, **21** (2), 283–98.
Panico, C. (1997), 'Government deficits in the Post Keynesian theories of growth and distribution', *Contributions to Political Economy*, **16**, 61–86.
Pasinetti, L.L. (1962), 'Rate of profit and income distribution in relation to the rate of economic growth', *Review of Economic Studies*, **29** (4), 103–20.
Pasinetti, L.L. (1989), 'Government deficit spending is not incompatible with the Cambridge theorem of the rate of profit: a reply to Fleck and Domenghino', *Journal of Post Keynesian Economics*, **11** (4), 640–47.
Samuelson, P.A. and F. Modigliani (1966), 'The Pasinetti paradox in neoclassical and more general models', *Review of Economic Studies*, **33** (4), 269–302.

Solow, R. (1956), 'A contribution to the theory of economic growth', *Quarterly Journal of Economics*, **70** (1), 65–94.

Steedman, I. (1972), 'The state and the outcome of the Pasinetti process', *Economic Journal*, **82** (328), 1387–95.

Taylor, L. (2004), *Reconstructing Macroeconomics: Structuralist Proposals and Critiques of the Mainstream*, Cambridge, MA: Harvard University Press.

Thirlwall, A.P. (1979), 'The balance of payments constraint as an explanation of international growth rate differences', *Banca Nazionale del Lavoro Quarterly Review*, **128**, pp. 45–53; reprinted in J.S.L. McCombie and A.P. Thirlwall, *Economic Growth and the Balance of Payments Constraint*, Basingstoke: Macmillan, 1994, pp. 232–61.

Thirlwall, A.P. and M.N. Hussain (1982), 'The balance of payments constraint, capital flows and growth rate differences between developing countries', *Oxford Economic Papers*, **34** (3), 498–509.

Young W. (1989), *Harrod and His Trade Cycle Group*, London: Macmillan.

Growth Theory

Sustained but irregular and unevenly distributed growth in output has been a defining aspect of capitalism. An equally defining aspect of Post Keynesian economic analysis has been its desire to realistically confront this complex phenomenon. The undeniable difficulty of this task in part explains why the Post Keynesian literature on growth is as irregular and uneven as its subject matter.

Post Keynesian growth models range from those that focus solely on the phenomenon of growth and eschew the analysis of cycles, to others in which cycles and growth are inseparable. However, most if not all Post Keynesian growth models are distinguishable from neoclassical models by considering at least two of the factors of growth, cyclicality and distribution (where the last factor concerns social classes, or different sectors of industry, or both). There is therefore a strong overlap between Post Keynesian treatments of growth, cycles, distribution and industrial structure. All are intrinsically entwined in Post Keynesian analysis and the real world.

Harrod set the tone for subsequent work by Post Keynesians when, in criticizing the neoclassical proclivity to treat growth and cycles as independent phenomena, he stated that 'the trend of growth may itself generate forces making for oscillation' (Harrod 1939, pp. 14–15). His single-sector model of unstable growth was driven by a savings function that depended upon the level of output, and an investment function that depended upon the rate of change of output. From this he derived a formula that equated the savings to output ratio to the product of the rate of growth and the ratio of investment to change in output (the latter is known as the incremental capital to output ratio, or ICOR). This equality applied both to the actual recorded rate of growth and ICOR, and the desired rate of growth and desired ICOR that together fulfilled capitalist expectations. If the actual rate of growth exceeded the desired rate, then the actual level of investment would be below the desired level – which then led to an increase in investment that accelerated the rate of growth even further; the reverse mechanism applied if recorded growth was below the desired rate.

Joan Robinson, Nicholas Kaldor, Luigi Pasinetti, Richard Goodwin and Edward Nell set off different analytic streams subsequent to Harrod's seminal contribution. Each stream involved some compromise forced by the difficulty of modelling the dynamic process of growth, though none compromised realism as completely as was commonplace in neoclassical theory. Today a substantial new band of nonlinear modellers are slowly blending these historic roots with modern nonlinear mathematical methods and computational analysis.

Robinson overcame the pre-computer inability to model growth processes out of equilibrium with the mental device of comparative 'golden age' economies. The structure of an economy was clearly specified in terms of classes (workers, capitalists, rentiers), sources of income (wages, profits, rent/interest), expenditures (consumption, investment, placement), industry sectors (consumption, investment) and fundamental rates of change (population growth, technical progress). The proportions between these variables that would be needed to ensure the highly unlikely outcome of stable growth were then worked out, and two economies were assumed to be in this golden age (sometimes with differing key values, such as the level of real wages). A change in behaviour could then be postulated in one economy (for example, an increase in birth rates leading to a rise in unemployment, or an increase in technical progress in investment goods) that would move it off its golden path, and the change in systemic behaviour was evaluated with respect to the economy that continued in its golden state. Kregel (1975) gives a very accessible overview of Robinson's method, and provides a useful survey of the rival approaches of Kaldor and Pasinetti.

Kaldor extended Harrod's model by incorporating the topic of income distribution between workers and capitalists, where capitalists had a higher propensity to save than workers. Using the extreme assumption that workers do not save and capitalists do not consume, he linked the rate of profit to the rate of growth. Kaldor eschewed the concept of an aggregate measure of capital, and argued that since technical progress was embodied in new machines, capital in use would have a profile from the most profitable new machinery to the near-obsolete that would earn a zero rate of profit.

However, while Robinson's approach emphasized the extreme improbability of any economy ever being on a 'golden path', and Harrod's model had an unstable equilibrium, Kaldor made the opposing assumptions that long-run growth had to involve the full employment of labour, and that the long-run equilibrium was stable. His reason for these assumptions – that growth concerns long-period analysis and only a full-employment equilibrium could prevail in the long term – would not be accepted today, since it is well known that models of complex systems do not have to converge to an equilibrium but can remain indefinitely in a 'far-from-equilibrium' state. This assumption also drove a wedge between Kaldor's short-run Keynesianism and his long-run analysis. Pasinetti corrected Kaldor's model to allow for workers owning a proportion of profits, but concluded that the rate of growth was nevertheless determined by the accumulation decisions of capitalists alone.

Kaldor also contributed a 'weather vane' to economic analysis by arguing that there were a number of 'stylized facts' that any theory of growth had to explain if it were to be regarded as prima facie tenable. These included the primacy of the rate of growth of the manufacturing sector in determining overall growth via the technological progress and increasing returns to scale that emanate from this growth, the decline in agricultural employment over time, and the relative constancy of income shares over time. Subsequent Post Keynesians have added effective demand growth as a key constraint on overall growth, a secular decline in manufacturing and rise of service employment in advanced economies, and the need for models of growth in which the monetary and financial system plays a crucial role.

Goodwin's growth cycle (Goodwin 1967), published in the centenary year of Marx's *Capital*, gave a mathematical rendition of Marx's Chapter 25 verbal model of a growth cycle driven by a struggle over the distribution of income between workers and capitalists in which the rate of unemployment acted as a check upon workers' wage demands. Technically the model was a descendant of the 'predator–prey' model first developed in biology by A.J. Lotka and V. Volterra, while economically it included the complete panoply of growth, cycles and income distribution. Though criticized in some quarters for structural instability and a lack of empirical verification, it has been used as a basis for many more general models and is still a fruitful basis for further research. Blatt (1983) provides a clearer explanation of this model than can be found in Goodwin's original writings.

Kaldor aside, most Post Keynesian work on growth has presumed that the main constraint on the rate of economic growth comes not from supply-side issues as in neoclassical theory, but from effective demand constraints and the non-neutrality of money. Post Keynesians have also been interested in explaining why growth occurs, as well as finding means to model it. Kornai (1990) argues that firms in capitalist economies are constrained not by resources and productivity, as in the neoclassical model, but by limits to effective demand. This demand constraint means that firms operate with significant excess capacity, since without this they can neither respond to changes in the structure of demand, nor take advantage of problems that might beset competitors. As a result, production costs do not vary with output, and firms compete by product innovation rather than via price: price competition is the exception rather than the norm.

Product innovation in turn requires research, development and investment, which both generates growth and gives rise to waves of Schumpeterian 'creative destruction' that give growth in capitalist economies its cyclical nature. This analysis thus grounds technical progress and growth in productive capacity in the competitive interactions of firms vying for profit and market share.

Nell (1998) emphasizes the transformational nature of growth in a capitalist economy – growth involves not merely quantitative increase, but also qualitative change in the composition of output, the nature of economic institutions, and the state of economic expectations. Like Kornai, Nell stresses the role of real, historical markets in promoting increased productivity, social change, and growth. He also attempts to integrate Sraffa's appreciation of the multisectoral nature of output into a dynamic model of the economy.

Failures in growth also attract Post Keynesian attention, with the most notable failure being the Great Depression. The most cogent explanation here has come from Hyman Minsky's blending of Irving Fisher's 'debt deflation' hypothesis with Keynes's analysis of the formation of expectations under uncertainty. Minsky (1982) developed the hypothesis that a period of stable economic growth will lead to capitalists and bankers revising their risk aversions, leading to an increased willingness to take on debt to finance expansions that will inevitably result in a period of financial stress and a collapse in the growth rate. This hypothesis that 'stability is destabilizing' neatly returns us to the Harrodian foundations of Post Keynesian growth theory, by providing a link between the rate of growth and the development of capitalist expectations – and hence their rate of investment.

Nonlinearity and 'chaos theory' (or, more properly, complexity theory) are playing an increasing role in modern Post Keynesian work on growth. Nonlinear relations arise naturally in economics out of interactions between variables (for example, by the multiplication of the wage rate times the level of employment to determine the wage bill) and obvious nonlinear social relations (such as the relationship between the rate of growth of the economy and profits and the willingness of capitalists to invest). When put into mathematical models of growth – using difference or differential rather than simultaneous equations – these nonlinearities in turn generate the stylized fact that distinguishes the Post Keynesian approach to growth theory from the neoclassical: unstable, cyclical growth. It is thus possible to have models of the long run in which the system continues to fluctuate, and in which the system never converges to an equilibrium. Chiarella and Flaschel (2000) is a very sophisticated example of this approach, using building blocks that would be acknowledged by traditional Keynesians as well as Post Keynesians.

These models can be partially characterized by the mathematical properties of their equations, but modern computer technology has also added the possibility of numerically simulating the behaviour of complex, high-dimensional models with far-from-equilibrium dynamics. This technology obviates the need to make simplifying assumptions, such as constancy of income shares, which were previously used to make dynamic reasoning tractable.

A comprehensive Post Keynesian theory of growth would clearly involve the following elements: a treatment of the causes of innovation in a market economy, where competition is primarily in product differentiation rather than price; multiple industry sectors rather than the abstraction of homogeneous output, so that the disproportional growth of the real economy is mirrored by the model, and the impossibility of producing an aggregate measure of capital is explicitly acknowledged; a relationship between the rate of technical progress and the income distributional and effective demand constraints inherent in a capitalist economy; a key role for non-neutral monetary factors, with the possibility that debt accumulation dynamics may on occasions retard and even reverse the process of growth; and a resulting model that generates both endogenous cycles and endogenous growth, with a significant possibility of economic breakdown under the weight of financial factors. While the many strands of Post Keynesian thought to date have provided most of the necessary strands, it remains true that blending an overall tapestry remains a research project for future Post Keynesians.

Recent progress towards this aim has taken two broad directions: the development of multi-agent complex systems models from which macroeconomic growth and cycles result as emergent phenomena – behaviour at the aggregate level that cannot be predicted from the behaviour of individual agents within the model; and structural macroeconomic models designed to achieve the consistency in the treatment of stock and flow dynamics. The modelling of the interaction of heterogeneous agents in a computer simulation that generates a simulation of permanent macroeconomic disequilibrium is an essential feature of the approach (Dosi et al. 2008). The consequent need for skills in computer programming has meant that much of the work in this area is being done by 'econophysicists' (see, for example, Di Guilmi et al. 2008), since today's economists lack training in this area.

The latter approach was inspired by Godley's insistence that meaningful macroeconomic growth models had to properly specify relevant stocks and account for flows between them (Godley and Lavoie 2007), and his development of the stock–flow consistent (SFC) approach to dynamic modelling to enable this (see Taylor 2008 for a survey). This approach, which employs difference equations, now has a large following among younger Post Keynesian researchers. A related explicitly monetary approach by Keen (2011) uses differential equations and is based on Goodwin's growth cycle, combined with Minsky's financial instability hypothesis (Minsky 1982) and the theory of the monetary circuit (Graziani 2003).

The fact that neoclassical models completely failed to anticipate the 'Great Recession', while the only economic modellers to predict it (see Bezemer 2009) were Godley (Godley and Izurieta 2002) and Keen (2007), has given added prominence to Post Keynesian economics. The time is ripe for further development of this still underdeveloped but fertile field.

STEVE KEEN

See also:

Business Cycles; Financial Instability Hypothesis; Growth and Income Distribution; Innovation; Kaldorian Economics; Stock–Flow Consistent Modelling.

References

Bezemer, D.J. (2009), '"No one saw this coming": understanding financial crisis through accounting model', Faculty of Economics, University of Groningen, Groningen.
Blatt, J. (1983), *Dynamic Economic Systems: A Post Keynesian Approach*, Armonk, NY: M.E. Sharpe.
Chiarella, C. and P. Flaschel (2000), *The Dynamics of Keynesian Monetary Growth*, Cambridge: Cambridge University Press.
Di Guilmi, C., M. Gallegati and S. Landini (2008), 'Economic dynamics with financial fragility and mean-field interaction: a model', *Physica A: Statistical Mechanics and its Applications*, **387** (15), 3852–61.
Dosi, G., G. Fagiolo and A. Roventini (2008), 'The microfoundations of business cycles: an evolutionary, multi-agent model', *Journal of Evolutionary Economics*, **18** (3–4), 413–32.
Godley, W. and A. Izurieta (2002), 'The case for a severe recession', *Challenge*, **45** (2), 27–51.
Godley, W. and M. Lavoie (2007), *Monetary Economics: An Integrated Approach to Credit, Money, Income, Production and Wealth*, Basingstoke: Palgrave Macmillan.
Goodwin, R. (1967), 'A growth cycle', in C.H. Feinstein (ed.), *Socialism, Capitalism and Economic Growth*, Cambridge: Cambridge University Press, pp. 54–8.
Graziani, A. (2003), *The Monetary Theory of Production*, Cambridge: Cambridge University Press.
Harrod, R.F. (1939), 'An essay in dynamic theory', *Economic Journal*, **49** (193), 14–33.
Keen, S. (2007), 'Deeper in debt: Australia's addiction to borrowed money', Occasional Papers, Centre for Policy Development, Sydney, SSN 1835-0135, available at: http://cpd.org.au/wp-content/uploads/2007/09/KeenCPD_DeeperInDebt_FullDoc_1.pdf.   http://cpd.org.au/2007/09/deeper-in-debt/.
Keen, S. (2011), 'A monetary Minsky model of the Great Moderation and the Great Recession',

Journal of Economic Behavior and Organization, DOI: 10.1016/j.jebo.2011.01.010, available at: http://www.sciencedirect.com/science/article/B6V8F-5230PMJ-3/2/92723a633380 b2d8e131c0fa0fd6df07.

Kornai, J. (1990), *Vision and Reality, Market and State: Contradictions and Dilemmas Revisited*, London and New York: Routledge.

Kregel, J.A. (1975), *The Reconstruction of Political Economy: An Introduction to Post-Keynesian Economics*, London: Macmillan.

Minsky, H.P. (1982), *Can 'It' Happen Again? Essays on Instability and Finance*, Armonk, NY: M.E. Sharpe.

Nell, E.J. (1998), *The General Theory of Transformational Growth*, Cambridge: Cambridge University Press.

Taylor, L. (2008), 'A foxy hedgehog: Wynne Godley and macroeconomic modelling: review article', *Cambridge Journal of Economics*, **32** (4), 639–63.

Households

In Post Keynesian economics households are conceptually different institutions from business enterprises (Fuller 1996; Hanmer and Akram-Lodhi 1998; Lee 2009; Todorova 2009, pp. 52–3). Conceptualization of households within the Post Keynesian paradigm has benefited from intersections with other heterodox approaches – specifically feminist economics (Hanmer and Akram-Lodhi 1998; van Staveren 2010); feminist and institutional economics (Todorova 2007, 2009); and post-structuralist feminist thought (Charusheela 2010). Some problems of importing ready-made household theories such as the household production function approach and household bargaining models into Post Keynesian theory have also been discussed (Todorova 2009, pp. 41–9). However, many of the Post Keynesian discussions of households have predominantly involved sector balance sheet analyses (Godley and Wray 1999; Papadimitriou et al. 2006; Parenteau 2006; Brown 2008; Wray 2008). These particular works have arrived at one of the most adequate insights about the role of households in the most recent economic turmoil – the unsustainability of growth driven by household debt. They do not, however, provide discussion of households as institutions. An exception is Brown (2008), who also offers an institutional analysis of evolving habits in household consumption, saving and borrowing. Also, Todorova (2009) provides sector, gender and institutional discussion of households, utilizing a particular combination of institutional, feminist, Post Keynesian and chartalist analysis.

One explanation of the relatively sparse work on households in the Post Keynesian tradition is perhaps the lack of sufficient attention paid to the social embeddedness of capitalist production, and particularly to gender. While acknowledging the broader social and historical context of economic activity, social relations underlying the market process are still to be explored in the Post Keynesian tradition. Consequently, there is a place for relevant collaborations with other heterodox approaches and disciplines that could enhance Post Keynesian analysis.

Another reason why Post Keynesians for the most part have not shown interest in that area is perhaps related to the finding that saving is of a residual nature, which renders households passive with respect to determining the level of investment, and thus seemingly unimportant. At the macroeconomic level, households' saving cannot increase before banks make loans. With no government deficits, households' demand deposits can be created only if business enterprises request loans and banks extend loans. Thus, both business enterprises' willingness to take positions in productive assets and banks' liquidity preference determine households' demand deposits. This is the same as saying that saving is a residual of investment, and that households have a passive role in that process. Such an important point, however, need not preclude explorations of the household as a social institution of importance for analysis of the monetary production economy.

In particular, Post Keynesian theory of demand for consumer goods necessitates the conceptualization of decision making by the social institution of the household rather than by an asocial individual, as in the case of neoclassical thought. This presupposes a theory of the household and specifically of household relations. For example, particular notions of masculinity and femininity within the household will inform consumption decisions. These notions are historically and culturally specific, and are influenced by the activities of the business enterprise and the state. We can say that the household is the basis of spending decisions, but these take the form of consumption activities (Fuller 1996) that are part of gender and the monetary production process (Todorova 2009) and are constituted in and through mechanisms of disciplining heteronormativity (Charusheela 2010).

The household has been conceptualized as an effect of disciplinary and regulatory mechanisms practised by the public at large and the state. 'Consumption spending is performative, since we engage in acts of consumption as part of our efforts to meet an "ideal" imagination of what it means to be a good provisioner, a good mother or father, a properly raised child or adult who shows appropriate race, class or ethnic markers' (ibid., pp. 1153–4). '"The household" is thus the effect of the series of underlying processes that normalise and constitute gender' (p. 1150). One historical example given by Charusheela (p. 1150) that illustrates this point is the state's project for agricultural development in the USA, constituting homemakers in rural areas who espoused urban middle-class values. A similar example involving colonial taxation is discussed by Forstater (2002) and Todorova (2009). Both cases illustrate how households are historically specific and regulated by the 'public' sphere, particularly the state, and how their evolution involves transition from self-subsistence to monetary production, as well as an alteration of the gender division of labour and the formation of new gendered roles and domains of activity.

In Charusheela's formulation, gender performances are stabilized into gender identities and into households as an effect. 'The historical evolution of the biopolitical mechanisms of discipline and sanction that underlie the contemporary heteronorm in advanced industrial societies, such as the USA, generate consumption stability as an effect of the stabilisation of gender performance' (Charusheela 2010, p. 1153). Thus, she argues that post-structuralist feminist theory can explain the stability of the consumption function: 'The heteronormative grid does not simply provide multiple types of consumption through which to signal multiple types of identities. By stabilising household forms, it stabilises both the unit of decision-making and the patterns of spending in predictable directions' (p. 1154). State regulation and social discourse within and beyond households are mechanisms of disciplining heteronormativity in contemporary industrial societies. Furthermore, business enterprises advertise based on the heteronormative desire to maintain a proper identity. Thus, 'the "private" realm of household that provides us with the consumption function is constituted in and through the "public" realm of state regulation and public social discourse in all spaces, within and beyond the "home"' (ibid ., p. 1155). Consequently, households' decisions are based on specific constructions emerging out of events that take place in historical time, and the consumption function given by households, and the macroeconomy is theorized as 'gendered'.

A similar discussion is offered by Todorova (2009), who grounds her analysis in Thorstein Veblen's theory of ceremonial and instrumental valuation to argue that household relations are manifestations of gender and monetary production processes. Veblen's notion of 'canons of decency' is used to discuss gender canons of decency, which are shown to be historically specific and contingent to particular business enterprise and state practices. There is a synergy between the functioning of a monetary production economy and the fear of deviation from these 'canons'.

The needs of households are driven by habits (Brown 2008), and are qualitatively distinct, separable, and thus specified in terms of a consumption basket of heterogeneous goods. The basket contains routine and discretionary goods, and it changes with income and the desirable socioeconomic status of the household. Conspicuous consumption is a routine consumption too, because it is part of the process of achieving a social status and acceptability. Because of lexicographically ordered needs based on separability and hierarchy, consumer goods differ significantly. This necessitates the conceptualization of heterogeneous households and goods (Lee 2009; Todorova 2009). Household heterogeneity has been discussed by Todorova (2009) in terms of three types of households based on their liquidity positions and heterogeneous unpaid household work, business enterprises, consumer goods and regions. This type of analysis brings forward households as more than sites of consumer demand.

Unpaid activities including domestic work and care activities taking place within households are part of the production process. Labour power is itself a produced input (Picchio 1992; King 2002). Households must obtain money through participation in the market process. Money can be used as a store of value, which restricts production; there is no market mechanism that ensures that households will obtain a livelihood. Unlike in neoclassical analysis, prices and the wage structure are administered by business enterprises – households have a limited role in their formulation. Furthermore, business enterprises launch product lines in order to achieve various business goals, which may or may not correspond to the households' need to secure a livelihood. A decrease in the demand for capital assets will cause a decrease in the demand for paid labour power, and will lead to an increase in the demand for unpaid household work, which would be used as a buffer to partially offset the worsened households' financial positions.

However, in a monetary production economy unpaid household work cannot entirely replace money wages. Households are not self-sufficient in capitalist economies – they need money to buy goods and services, and to pay their tax obligations. They rely on the output, income and employment provided by business enterprises and the state. In addition, the labour power that provides the unpaid household work itself needs to be produced and maintained. In the absence of adequate state policy, 'private' household crises translate into a macroeconomic problem not only through depressed effective demand but also through the mechanism of labour force 'reproduction'. Thus, households are not part of a separate 'private' sphere (Charushela and Danby 2006; Todorova 2009).

Some additional areas of investigation with respect to households are the consideration of global production, including paid domestic service and immigration; the ecological impact of household activities; and the nexus between household, state and business practices/objectives, neighbourhood formation, and inequalities, among others. It should be expected that while engaging in articulation of the socio-cultural embeddedness of the monetary production process, Post Keynesians would follow multiple paths, which should be welcomed as long as these enhance our understanding of capitalism.

ZDRAVKA TODOROVA

See also:

Agency; Consumer Debt; Consumer Theory; Gender; Institutionalism.

References

Brown, C. (2008), *Inequality, Consumer Credit and the Saving Puzzle*, Cheltenham, UK and Northampton, MA, USA: Edward Elgar
Charusheela, S. (2010), 'Gender and the stability of consumption: a feminist contribution to post-Keynesian economics', *Cambridge Journal of Economics*, **34** (6), 1145–56.

Charusheela, S. and C. Danby (2006), 'A through-time framework for producer households, *Review of Political Economy*, **18** (1), 29–48.

Forstater, M. (2002), 'Bones for sale: "development", environment and food security in East Africa', *Review of Political Economy*, **14** (1), 47–67.

Fuller, C. (1996), 'Elements of Post Keynesian alternatives to "household production"', *Journal of Post Keynesian Economics*, **18** (4), 595–607.

Godley, W. and L.R. Wray (1999), 'Can Goldilocks survive?', Policy Note 1999/4, Levy Economics Institute of Bard College, Annandale-on-Hudson, NY.

Hanmer, L. and A.H. Akram-Lodhi (1998), 'In the house of the spirits: toward a Post Keynesian theory of the household?', *Journal of Post Keynesian Economics*, **20** (3), 415–33.

King, J. E. (2002), 'Some elements of a Post Keynesian labour economics', in S. Dow and J. Hillard (eds), *Keynes, Uncertainty, and the Global Economy*, Cheltenham, UK and Northampton, MA, USA: Edward Elgar, pp. 68–87.

Lee, F. (2009), 'Alfred Eichner's missing "complete model": a heterodox micro–macro model of a monetary production economy', in M. Lavoie, L.-P. Rochon and M. Seccareccia (eds), *Money and Macrodynamics: Alfred Eichner and Post-Keynesian Economics*, Armonk, NY: M.E. Sharpe, pp. 22–42.

Papadimitriou, D., E. Chilcote and G. Zezza (2006), 'Are housing prices, household debt, and growth sustainable?', Strategic Analysis, Levy Economics Institute of Bard College, Annandale-on-Hudson, NY, January.

Parenteau, R. (2006), 'U.S. household deficit spending: rendezvous and reality', Public Policy Brief No. 88, Levy Economics Institute of Bard College, Annandale-on-Hudson, NY.

Picchio, A. (1992), *Social Reproduction: The Political Economy of the Labour Market*, Cambridge: Cambridge University Press.

Todorova, Z. (2007), 'Deficits and institutional theorizing about households and the state', *Journal of Economic Issues*, **51** (2), 319–26.

Todorova, Z. (2009), *Money and Households in a Capitalist Economy: A Gendered Post Keynesian–Institutional Analysis*, Cheltenham, UK and Northampton, MA, USA: Edward Elgar.

Van Staveren, I. (2010), 'Post-Keynesianism meets feminist economics', *Cambridge Journal of Economics*, **34** (6), 1123–44.

Wray, L.R. (2008), 'Demand constraints and big government', *Journal of Economic Issues*, **42** (1), 153–75.

Income Distribution

The dominant theory of income distribution in modern economics is the neoclassical marginal productivity approach, also known as the 'supply and demand' approach. Marginal productivity theory conceives capital as a productive factor, and it argues for the existence of an inverse monotonic relation between the profit rate and the quantity of capital employed in the production process. This relation constitutes the demand for capital schedule. The supply of capital is determined by households' portfolio demands for capital, and the equilibrium rate of profit and quantity of capital are then determined by the intersection of the supply and demand curves for capital.

The process of wage determination is entirely analogous to that determining the profit rate. Labour is also viewed as a productive factor, and there exists an inverse monotonic relation between the wage rate and the quantity of labour employed. This relation constitutes the demand for labour schedule. The supply of labour is determined by households' utility-maximizing choice over leisure and market income, and the equilibrium wage rate and employment level are determined by the intersection of the supply and demand curves for labour.

Perfect competition is the hallmark of the marginal productivity theory of income distribution. Departures from perfect competition can be introduced to explain such phenomena as discrimination in labour markets. This introduces 'economic' and 'monopoly' rents, with some factors being paid more than they would in a competitive market. This is also the neoclassical approach to trade unions. However, these modifications retain the basic marginalist approach to income distribution, interpreted as the outcome of an exchange process based on choices at the margin in a world in which production is described by a continuous concave function that is homogeneous of degree one.

The concept of a production function is crucial to neoclassical theory, providing the basis for marginal products from which are derived the demand for labour and capital schedules. The logical foundations of this concept formed the initial focus of a debate that became known as the Cambridge capital controversies. The controversy was kicked off by Joan Robinson's (1954) article challenging the existence of an aggregate production function on the grounds that it is impossible to aggregate heterogeneous capital.

Another criticism of neoclassical marginal productivity theory that is post-modernist in character, emphasizes the social construction of marginal products (Palley 1996a, pp. 64–7). Within existing accounts of marginal productivity theory, factors are paid their marginal products, which are objectively measurable. That assumes that objective measurement is possible. Yet measurement is intrinsically social, being an act of interpretation based upon socially negotiated rules. These rules attribute value and are derived from understandings that are themselves socially derived. As knowledge, beliefs and social arrangements change, so too will measurements. Who does the measuring affects the measurement outcome. Such considerations introduce a radical subjectivism into neoclassical production theory that parallels ordinal utility theory, which introduced radical subjectivism into neoclassical consumer theory in the 1930s. As a result, even if well-defined production functions exist, income distribution can never be the result of a purely technical process and is always inevitably tainted by social forces.

A key feature of the neoclassical supply and demand approach is that it is a joint theory of employment and factor price determination. Supply and demand schedules determine both prices and quantities, and the downward-sloping labour demand schedule imposes a binding trade-off whereby real wages can only increase if employment falls. The neo-Ricardian framework, developed by Piero Sraffa, aims to sunder the link between wages and employment. The Sraffian system has a number of appealing properties. The determination of the normal wage reflects social and historical forces, opening the way for the introduction of bargaining power concerns. It also breaks with the labour demand curve notion that the level of real wages constrains the level of employment. Instead, in the Sraffian system the real wage constrains the profit rate, and the binding trade-off is between the profit rate and wages. Since the model does not use aggregate capital, but instead only requires a competitively maintained common rate of profit on the value of inputs, it is not subject to Robinson's (1954) capital critique.

The traditional Marxian approach to income distribution is constructed through the lens of the labour theory of value, and the focus is on the extraction of surplus value. In this framework, concern lies with the rate of surplus value, which measures the degree of exploitation of labour. Over the last 35 years there has developed a distinctive American neoclassical school of Marxism, leading figures of which are Samuel Bowles, Herbert Gintis and John Roemer. These economists accept the existence of a well-defined neoclassical production function, but they break with the neoclassical assumption that technology is exogenous. Instead, they argue that it is endogenously selected. The significance of this argument is choice of technology now involves human agency and social context.

The importance of control for distributional outcomes signals the importance of 'power'. This brings into play the issue of perfect competition, which is another assumption embedded in neoclassical marginal productivity theory. Perfect competition ensures that both capital and labour have no power. It is not that the two are equally powerful, but rather that neither has any power. Removing the perfect competition assumptions of costless mobility and perfect free information restores power to centre stage.

The above neoclassical Marxian concerns link with the macroeconomics of Michał Kalecki (1942). A central component of Kalecki's macroeconomics is the mark-up, and its determination constitutes a key element of the Kaleckian research programme. In the standard Kaleckian model output is produced through a linear production function involving labour, and prices are a mark-up over average cost. The mark-up determines the wage and profit shares, bringing to the fore the question of what determines the mark-up. A modern neoclassical industrial organization perspective would focus on the degree of monopoly in product markets. Neoclassical Marxism focuses on control and bargaining power issues.

Keynesian economics emphasizes the significance of aggregate demand, which figures centrally in the Post Keynesian approach to income distribution developed by Kaldor (1956). Kaleckian macroeconomics takes the mark-up and income distribution as given, and income distribution then affects equilibrium income via its effect on aggregate demand. Kaldor reversed this logic and has income distribution adjusted so that aggregate demand equals normal income. This makes saving and investment behaviour critical to the determination of income distribution. Investment must equal saving, and income distribution must therefore be appropriate to support the right level of saving. If investment spending goes up, a higher profit share is needed to generate additional saving. If the propensity to save goes up, a lower profit share is needed to reduce total saving.

Pasinetti (1962) expanded Kaldor's (1956) model to include a capitalist–worker class structure, using the assumptions that (i) workers have a lower propensity to save than capitalists, (ii) capitalists' only source of income is profit income, (iii) workers receive both wage and profit income – wage income for supplying labour and profit income on their saving – and (iv) the rate of interest is equal to the rate of profit. The assumption that workers have a lower propensity to save ensures that their saving out of wage and profit income does not drive capitalists' ownership share of the capital stock to zero. Given these conditions, Pasinetti shows that steady-state income distribution is unaffected by workers' saving behaviour. The economic logic is simple. In a steady state, the capitalists' share of the capital stock is constant, and they must save sufficient to maintain this ownership share. Consequently, the profit share must be such that it can support a share of saving appropriate to maintaining the capitalists' ownership share. Viewed in this light, the Post Keynesian theory of income distribution might better be thought of as a theory of wealth ownership.

Pasinetti's theorem regarding the irrelevance of worker saving behaviour has been remarkably robust with regard to the introduction of other sources of saving. It holds when government saving is introduced via the government budget constraint and also in the presence of life-cycle saving behaviour. However, there are a number of limitations to the Post Keynesian approach to income distribution. First, it is an exclusively real theory of the interest rate, which is determined by the profit rate, and this is at odds with Keynesian theory, which emphasizes liquidity preference. Introducing monetary factors into the analysis invalidates Pasinetti's theorem regarding the irrelevance of the workers' propensity to save for steady-state distributional outcomes. To the extent that money balances are disproportionately held by workers, they must save more to maintain their share of the money stock, which influences steady-state income distribution. Palley (1996b) introduces financial intermediation and inside debt, and demonstrates that Pasinetti's theorem holds if lending is done via a loanable funds market, but is invalidated if done through a banking system with endogenous credit money.

The Kaldor–Pasinetti approach to distribution focuses on the dynamics of capital accumulation within classes. Yet, despite introducing class, it makes no mention of class conflict in the form of labour market struggle. Nor is there any mention of product demand conditions, in the form of the rate of capacity utilization.

These limitations are partially addressed in the neo-Kaleckian growth model (Lavoie 1995) that makes income distribution a function of capacity utilization, which is determined by saving and investment conditions. That sets up a loop whereby distribution affects capacity utilization, and capacity utilization affects distribution. A critique is that long-run capacity utilization is not free to vary and instead converges to a normal rate.

The neo-Marxian approach can also be synthesized with Keynesian demand considerations and provides an alternative to the neo-Kaleckian appraoch. Palley (1998) presents a short-run neo-Marxian model in which labour market bargaining conditions determine the distribution of income, and aggregate demand conditions determine the state of labour market conditions. Because aggregate demand is affected by income distribution, owing to Kaleckian differences in the propensity to consume out of wage and profit income, there is a feedback loop between aggregate demand (the goods market) and income distribution (the labour market). The canonical long-run version of the neo-Marxian–Keynesian model is by Goodwin

(1967), who constructs a model in which labour market conditions drive profit rates, profit rates drive the rate of accumulation, and the rate of accumulation feeds back to affect labour market conditions. When placed in a multiplier–accelerator framework, this generates cyclical growth, with a full-employment profit rate squeeze sending the economy into a phase of slower growth with rising unemployment that lasts until the profit rate has recovered.

The theory of distribution is more than just a matter of social and ethical interest. It also profoundly affects the way in which we view the economy. The neoclassical marginal product of labour is interpreted as the labour demand curve, and this enforces an inexorable trade-off between wages and employment. This trade-off drives opposition to minimum wages and unions, and it also drives macroeconomic policy recommendations that aim to lower unemployment by weakening employee protection and making wages downwardly more flexible. Yet all of these policy stances are predicated on a theory whose microeconomic foundations are deeply controversial. Moreover the validity of these policies is also questioned by macroeconomic monetary analyses that show why lower real and nominal wages may not increase employment.

The theory of distribution lies at the core of theories of output and employment determination. Seen in this light, it provides a window on the range of theories explaining the operation of modern capitalist economies. The fact that marginal productivity theory is the only theory taught in most university classrooms is telling about the closed and ideological state of contemporary economics.

THOMAS I. PALLEY

See also:

Capital Theory; Growth and Income Distribution; Kaldorian Economics; Marginalism; Sraffian Economics.

References

Goodwin, R.M. (1967), 'A growth cycle', in C.H. Feinstein (ed.), *Socialism, Capitalism, and Economic Growth*, Cambridge: Cambridge University Press, pp. 54–8.

Kaldor, N. (1956), 'Alternative theories of distribution', *Review of Economic Studies*, **23** (2), 83–100.

Kalecki, M. (1942), 'A theory of profits', *Economic Journal*, **52** (206–7), 258–67.

Lavoie, M. (1995), 'The Kaleckian model of growth and distribution and its neo-Ricardian and Marxist critiques', *Cambridge Journal of Economics*, **19** (6), 789–818.

Palley, T.I. (1996a), 'Out of the closet: the political economy of neo-classical distribution theory', *Review of Radical Political Economics*, **28** (3), 57–67.

Palley, T.I. (1996b), 'Inside debt, aggregate demand, and the Cambridge theory of distribution', *Cambridge Journal of Economics*, **20** (4), 465–74.

Palley, T.I. (1998), 'Macroeconomics with conflict and income distribution', *Review of Political Economy*, **10** (3), 329–42.

Pasinetti, L. (1962), 'Rate of profit and income distribution in relation to the rate of economic growth', *Review of Economic Studies*, **29** (4), 267–79.
Robinson, J. (1954), 'The production function and the theory of capital', *Review of Economic Studies*, **21** (2), 81–106.

Inflation

The Post Keynesian theory of inflation is eclectic in a way that the neo-classical or orthodox theory is not. It allows for multiple causes of, and explanations for, inflationary phenomena, as opposed to the virtually mono-causal nature of orthodox theory. The main reason for this is a more realistic view of the credit creation process, namely the theory of endogenous money (Wray 2001; Smithin 2012). This implies that any factor that tends to raise money costs has the potential to cause an increase in the general level of prices, as entrepreneurs incurring the costs will have access to newly created financial resources to pay for the increases. In orthodox theory, at least when the money supply is assumed fixed, it is only possible to discuss changes in relative prices.

Originally, the backbone of the orthodox theory of inflation was the equation of exchange from the quantity theory of money, $MV = PY$. In principle this is an identity, but if it is assumed that the money supply, M, is exogenous (controlled by the central bank), the velocity of circulation, V, is more or less a constant, and that money is neutral and super-neutral (so that monetary changes will not affect the level or growth rate of real GDP, Y), it also produces a simple theory of the aggregate price level, P. Letting lower-case letters represent proportional rates of change, we would have:

$$p = m - y \qquad (1)$$

According to this the inflation rate, p (the proportional rate of change of the price level, P) will be mainly determined by the rate of growth of the money supply, m, less the rate of growth of real GDP, y. This is a 'mono-causal' theory in the sense that (almost all) of the variations in inflation that occur in practice are attributed to variations in the rate of monetary growth.

There are some obvious problems with the theory, however. For example, how to define the money supply precisely in an era of rapid financial innovation? Also, how can the money supply sensibly be regarded as 'exogenous', as soon as any type of banking system, with the capacity for credit creation, is in place? One such problem is that in practice the monetary policy instrument is usually a short-term interest rate of some kind (such as the Federal Funds Rate in the USA), rather than any quantitative measure of the monetary base or money supply. Contemporary central bankers therefore seem to have had a practical theory of inflation owing more to the nineteenth-century Swedish economist Knut Wicksell, than to quantity theorists such as Irving Fisher or Milton Friedman. For example, a theory such as:

$$p = \alpha(r^N - r)y \qquad \alpha > 0 \qquad (2)$$

where the term r stands for the policy-determined interest rate set by the central bank expressed in real terms (that is, adjusted for inflation), r^N is Wicksell's 'natural rate', and α is a positive coefficient. The natural rate of interest is supposedly determined in the market for 'real capital' independently of any monetary influences. If the policy-determined rate is set 'too low' this provides an incentive for continued borrowing from the banks as long as the discrepancy exists, and hence for an endogenous increase in the money supply and ultimately inflation. If the policy rate is set 'too high', there will be a deflation. 'Wisdom' in monetary policy now entails searching for the correct setting of the policy rate to precisely match the natural rate adjusted for economic growth. In these circumstances, there would (supposedly) be no inflation, and the unemployment rate and the real GDP growth rate would also be at their 'natural' levels. The extensive discussion of 'interest rate rules' in the 1990s and early twenty-first century can plausibly be interpreted in precisely these terms. If this is not exactly a mono-causal theory of inflation, there are still only a limited number of possible inflation sources. Inflation/deflation is caused by a gap between the natural and policy determined interest rates, which can be created either by deliberate monetary policy, or by a change in the natural rate not matched by the monetary authority.

Contrary to the above, according to Joan Robinson (1979, p. xix), 'one of the important insights of the Keynesian revolution was . . . that the general level of prices in an industrial economy is determined by the general level of *costs*, and . . . the main influence upon costs is to be found in the relation between money-wage rates and output per unit of employment' (emphasis added). This can be illustrated by the formula $P = KW/A$, a rival to the orthodox equation of exchange, associated with the work of the Post Keynesian economist Sidney Weintraub (Davidson 1994). Here W is the average nominal wage rate, A is average labour productivity, and K is the mark-up factor. The term K is equal to $1 + k$, where lower-case k is the profit share. According to this, prices will rise if money wages rise, or if the mark-up rises, or if productivity falls. If further, it can also be assumed that the profit share stays more or less constant, this gives the theory of inflation suggested by Robinson, that inflation is caused mainly by a rate of increase of money wages faster than productivity growth. This can be written:

$$p = \dot{W}/W - \dot{A}/A \tag{3}$$

where $\dot{W}/W$ is the rate of wage inflation and $\dot{A}/A$ is the rate of productivity growth. The remedy for inflation, then, would not be changes in rate of money supply growth or interest rates, as suggested by monetarists or neo-Wicksellians, but specifically an *incomes policy* of some kind: in other words, regulations or agreements restricting the growth of nominal incomes (Davidson 2009). Such polices, of course, will have their own problems of implementation, including the need to gain public support for the restrictions. In particular, a concern of labour whenever incomes policies are suggested is that 'wage and price controls' should not turn out to be wage controls only. Although the quote from Robinson identifies the 'main influence' on costs as being that of changes in money wages, it should also be mentioned that the general Post Keynesian approach clearly leaves open the possibility that other cost increases would have similar effects. Therefore, this is not a mono-causal theory. This must, in fact, be the case as soon as it is admitted that the money supply is endogenous, although this point seems not to have been grasped by neo-Wicksellian writers in the modern era.

One loose end in the argument for the generic wage-/cost–push model concerns the motivation for the ongoing *nominal* wage push. Just to assume an exogenously given rate of increase in nominal wages may not be very convincing, as surely workers are interested primarily in real wages? If so, the motivation for asking for an increase in nominal wages must be the hope that this will be a *lasting* increase relative to prices, and will not be completely offset by an increase in inflation as soon as it has occurred. This sort of insight therefore leads on to another version of the cost–push argument which has been called 'conflict inflation' (Rowthorn 1977; Lavoie 2007; Smithin 2012). In this argument, inflation is caused by (or, rather, is a spillover from) conflict over real income shares. To illustrate, let us suppose that wage bargainers do have a target real wage in mind, and that they will always ask for a nominal wage increase sufficient to compensate for price-level increase in the previous period. Therefore:

$$(W/P)_0 = W/P_{-1}. \tag{4}$$

If they want to improve their relative position, therefore, they will try to increase the value of the target real wage, $(W/P)_0$, itself. The nominal wage rate will then be given by:

$$W = (W/P) \, P_{-1}. \tag{5}$$

Then, using (5) in the expression $P = KW/A$, and taking logs:

$$p = k + w_0 - a, \tag{6}$$

where a is the logarithm of average labour productivity ($a = lnA$), w_0 is the logarithm of the target real wage [$w_0 = ln(W/P)_0$], and k is the profit share [$k = lnK = ln(1+k)$]. Therefore the inflation rate, p, increases if either the mark-up or the target real wage increases, and falls if productivity increases. The money supply continues to adjust endogenously.

This model of inflation can be graphed in inflation/output space as a *horizontal* straight line. Meanwhile, the level of output in a Keynesian model is always determined by the principle of effective demand and this will show up as a *vertical* line in the same graph. This is illustrated in Figure 12. The main point to notice about the conflict inflation analysis in the figure is that if firms want to increase the mark-up k *now* – or if workers want to increase the real wage rate w_0 *now* – and then maintain that same situation in the future, this will lead to a *permanent* increase in inflation (as shown in the figure by an upward shift of the horizontal line). The inflation will continue even if they do not aim for continuous increases in their real share, and only seek to maintain the new higher relative level. Essentially the *same* conflict over real incomes will be

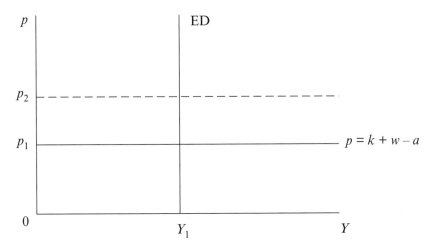

Figure 12   Aggregate demand and supply in p, Y space for a 'Post Keynesian' conflict inflation model

repeated every period. Therefore any increase in the profit share, or the real wage, causes an increase in the inflation rate now, and continuing in the future. An increase in average labour productivity, conversely, will allow inflation to fall, given the existing profit share and real wage rate. In that case there is 'more for all' and less reason for there to be conflict.

One way of making a brief 'shorthand' summary of the differences between the orthodox and Post Keynesian approaches to inflation would be to invoke the old distinction between demand–pull and cost–push inflation. This used to be a staple in the textbooks, but is now frequently neglected. Looking at it from this point of view, the orthodox theory would have inflation determined by demand, and output determined on the supply side. The simplest version of the Post Keynesian theory, however, reverses this, and has inflation determined on the supply side via cost push, and output and employment determined via effective demand. There would clearly be some truth in this characterization, and it is also true that the 'Phillips curve' explanation of inflation, postulating a trade-off between inflation and unemployment/growth that might be exploited by policy, has always had an ambiguous status among Post Keynesians (Davidson 1994).

However, it would be going too far to say that the Post Keynesian school neglects the concept of demand–pull inflation. The key underlying assumption of endogenous money allows for an eclectic view in this respect. Suppose, for example, that there is some positive slope to the inflation/output relationship as in Figure 13. This, by the way, need have nothing to do with the logic of the Phillips curve argument. It does not imply a causal relationship between inflation and output (Smithin 2012) – it is the other way round – the implication is simply that costs tend to increase with the level of output for the obvious sorts of reasons. In this case, the cost–push or conflict explanation would still go through if the inflation/output relationship were again to shift upwards. In addition, however, an increase in effective demand will increase output and employment, but at the same time now causes some increase in the inflation rate. This could be called a demand–pull inflation.

Inflation is a complex social process, and it seems unlikely on the face of it that there is any one explanation of the phenomenon that is valid for all times and places. Empirically, all possible combinations of growth and inflation have been observed in reality. That is, high growth with high inflation (an inflationary boom), low growth with low inflation (a depression), low growth with high inflation (stagflation), and, more benignly, non-inflationary growth. The Post Keynesian approach may therefore ultimately have an advantage over more orthodox explanations of infla-

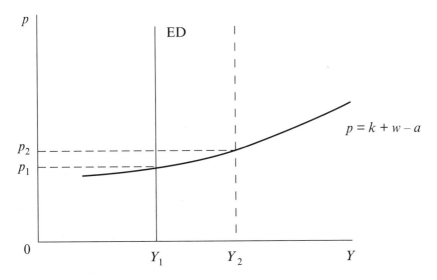

Figure 13   The potential for demand–pull inflation

tion because of its open-ended and eclectic nature. The key features are money supply endogeneity and the rejection of all natural rate concepts (of the interest rate, the GDP growth rate, or the unemployment rate). This therefore allows for coherent explanations for most of the empirical possibilities.

JOHN SMITHIN

See also:

Full Employment; Money; Rate of Interest; Stagflation.

References

Davidson P. (1994), *Post Keynesian Macroeconomic Theory: A Foundation for Successful Macroeconomic Policies for the Twenty-First Century*, Aldershot, UK and Brookfield, VT, USA: Edward Elgar.

Davidson, P. (2009), *The Keynes Solution: The Path to Global Economic Prosperity*, London: Palgrave Macmillan.

Lavoie, M. (2007), *Introduction to Post Keynesian Economics*, London: Palgrave Macmillan.

Robinson, J. (1979), 'Introduction', in Alfred S. Eichner (ed.), *A Guide to Post Keynesian Economics*, White Plains, NY: M.E. Sharpe, pp. xi–xixi.

Rowthorn, R. (1977), 'Conflict, inflation and money', *Cambridge Journal of Economics*, **1** (2), 213–39.

Smithin, J. (2012), *Essays in the Fundamental Theory of Monetary Economics and Macroeconomics*, Singapore: World Scientific Publishing, forthcoming.

Wray, L.R. (2001), 'Money and inflation', in R.P.F. Holt and S. Pressman (eds), *A New Guide to Post Keynesian Economics*, London and New York: Routledge, pp. 79–91.

Innovation

As the research field of economics deepened over more than two centuries since the Industrial Revolution, the linkage between innovation, growth and economic development – which early classical writers emphasized – has become more tenuous. Only economists examining the economy as a vast interconnected 'open systems' canvas continued to maintain this link, notably Karl Marx, Rosa Luxemburg, Michał Kalecki and Joseph Schumpeter. In the 1990s this situation altered dramatically, with an enormous expansion of research into innovation from many perspectives. Post Keynesian economics, after some early efforts in this area, has tended to neglect this issue as its emphasis on short-term economic outcomes places innovation into the autonomous forces of long-term growth (Bellais 2004).

Innovation can be defined as the application of knowledge by the enterprise in a new form to increase the set of techniques (or processes) and products commercially available in the economy. This knowledge application can be technologically or organizationally (human resource) based within the enterprise, operating in a cooperative mode (Shapiro 1991). The forms innovation can take are (i) continuous incremental (or *Kaizen*); (ii) radical discontinuous based on research and development (R&D); (iii) technological systems change based on a cluster of innovations; and (iv) techno-economic paradigm shift due to major structural change (for example, the steam engine, information technology). Forms of innovation can dovetail into higher order innovation, thus becoming increasingly more important to society.

Contemporary innovation research has taken two approaches. One is broad-based evolutionary change in the long-term structure of capitalism, focusing on the impact of innovation on the economy. The other is narrow-based entrepreneurship studies at the firm and industry levels, focusing on the individual entrepreneur or firm in managing innovation. Although both approaches acknowledge that innovation is deeply rooted in the uncertainty of the future world that brings change, their theoretical models acquit the issue through appeals to historical patterns or market adeptness, respectively. Post Keynesian analysis, identifying the sole source of uncertainty as the unexpected variations in aggregate demand arising from business cycles, provides the basis for analysing innovation as the precondition to investment decision making. Innovation in the form of knowledge and creativity is embodied as technology through investment in new capital stock. Thus effective demand variation and accompanying cyclical volatility, signalled through profits as the reaction coefficient to the investment function, sets up successful innovation. This entry focuses on analysis of innovation that is based on this Post Keynesian perspective and incorporates research from both broad and narrow approaches.

Attempts in economics generally to incorporate investment into the theoretical analysis of innovation have been limited. Two major exceptions to this are Salter (1960) from the neoclassical perspective, and Freeman and Perez (1988) from the evolutionary perspective. Both innovation studies set up economic 'snapshots', which provide case study patterns to show the plausibility of the theoretical relations they derive with respect to investment. Due to their primacy of investment, Post Keynesian writers have used these two works to begin fleshing out their innovation framework.

Salter examines technical change arising from process innovation only and its implications for means of production increments at the margin in different industry sectors. In an exceptionally insightful manner, Salter recognizes the gap between available process innovation and its application via investment. He uses market signals to indicate possible postponements in the use of introduction of more innovative means of production and consequent delays in scrapping old means of production; thus the capital stock becomes 'fossilised' (Salter 1960, p. 154). This exposes technical change to different rates of productivity growth between industries. The leading Post Keynesian, Geoffrey Harcourt, used this Salter approach to technical change in a number of significant articles in the decade 1965–75, culminating in Harcourt and Kenyon (1976) with an analysis of the impact on pricing behaviour of investment decisions incorporating technical change.

Freeman and Perez (1988) take a dynamic structural adjustment view of the economy with respect to innovation as a whole, and note the mismatch of current investment to new available technology. Rather than market signals, this study examines the variations in the climate of confidence related to the type of innovation and the life cycle of the industries which account for this mismatch, leading to intensified investment instability. Courvisanos (1996) has extended this work by incorporating the life cycle of innovation, from embryonic R&D to sustainable incremental change, into the investment instability of business cycles.

The classic proposition of an investment model with innovation comes from Joseph Schumpeter, who recognized that the investment function responds to waves of optimism and pessimism that create clusters of innovation, and thus 'bunching' of investment. Courvisanos (ibid.) shows how this leads to susceptibility to unstable investment cycles and the development of a trigger mechanism to initiate fundamentally new innovation systems with trend 'long-wave' implications. In his final attempt at modelling investment, Kalecki (1968) identifies this cycle-trend pattern that innovation has on the investment function as due to higher profitability of more advanced means of production based on new innovation systems. Thus the intensity of innovation, in terms of the extent to which high profits from investment can be generated, affects the amplitude of investment cycles and shifts the trend path – or trajectory – of investment growth. Virtuous circle effects occur as innovation intensity rises, increasing the amplitude of the upper turning-point of the investment cycle and shifting the trend path upwards. Vicious circle effects increase the amplitude of the lower turning-point and shift the trend downwards. The pace of innovation is a shift parameter in the Kaleckian investment function. Courvisanos and Verspagen (2004) provide empirical evidence of this cycle-trend pattern.

Gomulka et al. (1990, p. 535) attempt to provide ergodic closure to the Kalecki trend and cycle theory. This study argues that Kalecki's central role of innovations in preventing the trend rate of unemployment from increasing is unsupportable, as 'the balanced growth rate which Kalecki took to be stable is, in fact, unstable, rendering it unsuitable to serve as the trend growth rate'. Lavoie (1992, pp. 297–327) examines Kalecki's innovation and investment analysis at the theoretical level and rejects the ergodic closure assumption which ties this theory back to the neoclassical mainstream. Kalecki clearly assumes that the rate of capacity utilization may diverge from its full-capacity rate even in the long run, with the 'reserve army of the unemployed' as the typical feature of capitalism for a considerable part of the cycle. This asserts instability, as the dynamic non-ergodic business cycle has innovation-creating conditions that move the trend growth away from any analytical 'stability' and into the world of uncertainty.

The cause of clustering of innovation and subsequent bunching of investment ('clust-bun') is in debate. The prerequisite for clustering is deep depressions or breakthroughs in technology; both reflect reactions by private and public sectors to deep problems in the downswing of the previous business cycle. Then the bunching requires effective demand stimulus through widespread diffusion of the cluster effect, which can only be done through the availability of a surplus for investment (private profits and public deficit spending). Impediments to this 'clust-bun' effect reside in the institutional frameworks of nations, particularly the ones that have still-dominant mature industries with older technologies (Freeman and Perez 1988, pp. 58–65). Increased uncertainty arising from large investment in the new technology systems also adds a further impediment through increased macroeconomic volatility, slowing down the diffusion process.

The causality sequencing of innovation and investment is reversed by work done by Nicholas Kaldor and Joseph Schmookler, with the rate of investment determining the rate of innovation. Kalecki also recognizes this sequence, despite having identified the innovation-driven process. Kalecki places this investment-driven process clearly into an appropriate context by viewing this innovation process as 'part and parcel of "ordinary" investment' (Kalecki 1954, p. 158), or endogenous innovation.

Instead of unidirectional causality, the discussion above clearly leads to a circular flow where one innovation process feeds into the other. Kaldor's principle of cumulative causation is the 'self-reinforcing dynamic' in the circular process of investment demand leading to innovation that then stimulates further investment. The distinction between endogenous and exogenous innovation specifies how innovation enters this cumulative causation process. In this context, R&D expenditure is central to the endogenous innovation process, where large firms with strong profit results have the ability to activate large R&D spending, with patents reflecting the clustering of innovations, while exogenous innovation relates to techno-economic paradigm shift.

In Kalecki's view of innovation, endogenous innovation is of secondary importance from the scientific standpoint, coming as it does from: (i) slight adaptations of previous capital equipment (process innovation); (ii) cosmetic improvement in old products (product innovation); and (iii) extension of previous raw material sources. Such continuous incremental innovation is called endogenous because it is the cycle itself that induces the innovation and, with it, higher levels of investment orders. With endogenous innovation occurring in a Kaleckian macroeconomy, the analysis can focus on how such innovation affects the firm/industry level, leading to an increased degree of oligopoly and higher market concentration (Shapiro 1991), which has also been supported by evolutionary economics studies.

The firm's R&D expenditure is a form of intangible investment to be incorporated in the long-term business investment plan. This enables the firm to hold a stock of innovations that are ready to be applied when susceptibility to investment risk is relatively low. In this way endogenous innovation can be generated and directed by a process of investment. Assume that a firm decides to increase investment at relatively low susceptibility, that is, with low vulnerability to unstable investment cycles due to restricted past investment commitments in quantity (of 'dollars') and in quality (of innovation intensity). Then, under competitive pressures and higher costs of postponement, the R&D investment in the past makes these innovations abundantly ready to implement. R&D investment effectively increases the strategic productive capacity of the firm. In an industry where innovation is a regular competitive strategy, R&D expenditure would be large and would vary under the same susceptibility pressures as capital expenditure. In an industry where innovation is only occasionally implemented, R&D expenditure would be small and constant over the investment cycle. Geroski (1994) provides evidence from the UK in the 1970s that radical innovation out of such R&D reduces market concentration.

The endogenous creation of innovations out of low susceptibility makes some means of production obsolete and thus not part of excess capacity calculation. Also, oligopolistic firms (and industries) lobby for the assistance of governments in reducing private costs of production (through subsidies, tax concessions or protection) when these firms attempt to expand their market by innovations in order to utilize new, and decommission old, idle productive capacity. Such innovation and underwriting of the related risks reduces the rate of increase in susceptibility and encourages an investment recovery.

R&D amounts in aggregate to a large body of investigation going on continuously (at different rates of intensity). This large R&D spending and related individual entrepreneurial activity are bound to lead to some major new 'discovery' or 'invention' which is related to the total aggregate R&D and innovation support funding, rather than any one particular R&D project. This discovery is linked to possible small developments in various laboratories and informal networks between individuals, firms and industries, eventually coming to fruition in some way divorced from any specific competitive behaviour. New technological paradigms come out of such aggregate developments and are the basis of structural change to a new long wave of boom and prosperity (Freeman and Perez, 1988, pp. 47–58). Changes in technological systems and paradigms arise only after all the minor improvements (endogenous innovation) are squeezed out of the old systems and paradigms by 'monopoly capital' protecting existing means of production and delaying the new paradigm from taking over. There is also a 'log jam' in endogenous innovations based on the new paradigm, which compounds the latter's slow initial adoption. This occurs when established powerful capitalists, with much old means of production, cannot justify the entire shake-up of industries, since not enough interrelated clusters have been formed.

Technological paradigm shift leads to exogenous innovation input, affecting the investment cycle. The introduction of a new paradigm produces a large exogenous boost to industry investment at low susceptibility points. This investment boom relates to paradigm changes in large, important industry sectors that adopt new technology systems (for example, petrochemical innovations), or in the whole economy (for example, steam engine innovations). Either way, the investment boom is strong and resilient over a series of future cycles in susceptibility.

As the institutional framework slowly adapts to the new technological system, entrepreneurs' reactions against uncertainty of profits come from competitive pressures and growing inefficiencies of old means of production. This induces adaptation (by industries) and imitation (within industries) to technological trajectories that are totally new, establishing, at very low susceptibility, the new investment upturn. It is creating a new investment boom and at the same time re-establishing the conditions for a new phase of steady development. A paradigm shift occurs when the new adapted technological systems pervade the whole economy. Many from the evolutionary school of economics identify such a shift with the beginning of a new long wave in the economy's development

This analysis links together the two types of innovations described by Baran and Sweezy (1966), namely 'normal' (or endogenous) and 'epoch-making' (or exogenous). A period of secular decline in economic development can now be associated with the limitations of scale production in oligopolistic competition, as the old technology systems are running out of possible new adaptations. Diffusion of the old systems through endogenous innovation slows down, and imitators become considerably fewer. The large powerful corporations, with support from the state, attempt to protect existing capital values and ignore the new technological systems being developed on the fringe of the corporate world. This tends to exacerbate the mismatch between new technologies and the powerful private and public institutions based around monopoly capital, which Courvisanos (2009) named 'political aspects of innovation' after Kalecki (1943). Steindl, using a Kaleckian model back in 1952, recognized this secular decline as the incentive to reduce surplus capacity and invest in established monopoly capital sectors. In his 1976 introduction to the second edition of his 1952 book, Steindl stated that he was 'ready to admit a possibility which I denied in my book: that it might be the result of exhaustion of a long technological wave' (1952 [1976], p. xv). In this way, the conclusions of the Kaleckian and evolutionary traditions can be integrated.

JERRY COURVISANOS

See also:

Business Cycles; Growth Theory; Institutionalism; Investment; Kaldorian Economics; Kaleckian Economics; Technology and Innovation.

References

Baran, P. and P.M. Sweezy (1966), *Monopoly Capital*, New York: Monthly Review Press.
Bellais, R. (2004), 'Post Keynesian theory, technology policy, and long-term growth', *Journal of Post Keynesian Economics*, **26** (3), 419–40.
Courvisanos, J. (1996), *Investment Cycles in Capitalist Economies: A Kaleckian Behavioural Contribution*, Cheltenham, UK and Brookfield, VT, USA: Edward Elgar.
Courvisanos, J. (2009), 'Political aspects of innovation', *Research Policy*, **38** (7), 1117–24.
Courvisanos, J. and B. Verspagen (2004), 'Innovation and investment in capitalist economies 1870–2000: Kaleckian dynamics and evolutionary life cycles', in L.R. Wray and M. Forstater (eds), *Contemporary Post Keynesian Analysis*, Cheltenham UK and Northampton, MA, USA: Edward Elgar, pp. 205–26.
Freeman, C. and C. Perez (1988), 'Structural crises of adjustment, business cycles and investment behaviour', in G. Dosi, C. Freeman, R. Nelson, G. Silverberg and L. Soete (eds), *Technical Change and Economic Theory*, London: Pinter, pp. 38–66.

Geroski, P. (1994), *Market Structure, Corporate Performance and Innovative Activity*, Oxford: Oxford University Press.
Gomulka, S., A. Ostaszewski and R.O. Davies (1990), 'The innovation rate and Kalecki's theory of trend, unemployment and the business cycle', *Economica*, **57** (228), 525–40.
Harcourt, G.C. and P. Kenyon (1976), 'Pricing and the investment decision', *Kyklos*, **29** (3), 449–77.
Kalecki, M. (1943), 'Political aspects of full employment', *Political Quarterly*, **14** (4), 322–31.
Kalecki, M. (1954), *Theory of Economic Dynamics*, London: George Allen & Unwin.
Kalecki, M. (1968), 'Trend and business cycle reconsidered', *Economic Journal*, **78** (310), 263–76.
Lavoie, M. (1992), *Foundations of Post-Keynesian Economic Analysis*, Aldershot, UK and Brookfield, VT, USA: Edward Elgar.
Salter, W.E.G. (1960), *Productivity and Technical Change*, Cambridge: Cambridge University Press.
Shapiro, N. (1991), 'Firms, markets and innovation', *Journal of Post Keynesian Economics*, **14** (1), 49–60.
Steindl, J. (1952 [1976]), *Maturity and Stagnation in American Capitalism*, 2nd edn, New York: Monthly Review Press.

Institutionalism

Institutionalism is an approach to economics that sees economic life as taking place within a social context. In contrast to neoclassical economists, institutionalists see human behaviour as determined more by social factors than by deliberative individual thought.

Behaviour depends on the habits, the routines, and the customs of economic actors. These actors are households, workers, and business firms, as well as the government and its policies and regulations. Their habits, routines and customs are the rules they use to make decisions. They are matters of law or tradition; and they get passed along by example, by society's expectations, and by the power of the state. People tend to follow these rules because they see everyone else doing so. People also follow these rules because they provide a simple way to deal with the uncertainty and the complexity of everyday life (Hodgson 1988).

When most people follow institutional rules, behaviour becomes more certain and individuals are less likely to feel foolish by acting differently or by being wrong when they make important choices. Institutional rules thus provide for stability in a world of uncertainty.

Post Keynesians believe that methodological individualism prevents economists from seeing the impact of social phenomena on individual choice and also keeps them from providing useful guidance to society. By adopting an institutionalist or social perspective on individual choice, Post Keynesians can analyse how the perceptions of economic agents are moulded by institutions and habits. It also lets them address important economic and social issues that are assumed away by neoclassical theory.

Institutions appear at several key places in Post Keynesian economic analysis. First, institutional factors help explain the consumption behaviour of households. Second, institutions help us understand the investment decisions of business firms. Third, institutional considerations lead to the creation of money in capitalist economies and are responsible for the unique role of money. Finally, they help us understand the stability of capitalism, and how and why economic policy can improve economic outcomes. We consider these items in turn.

Institutionalists see consumer preferences and consumer spending stemming from learned social behaviour rather than from any innate utility functions. Consumer spending is determined by what is necessary to maintain a lifestyle similar to one's friends and neighbours, and possibly a lifestyle that is a bit more lavish than that of one's friends and neighbours. This argument goes back to the work of Veblen (1899 [1908]), regarded as one of the founding fathers of institutionalist thought.

These behavioural dispositions help explain why consumption is stable and also why fiscal policy is able to expand or contract the economy. Consumption is stable because it depends on spending habits. For most middle-class households, this means spending most, if not all, of one's regular paycheck. As a result, the propensity to consume additional income will be stable over time and also have a relatively high value.

A stable and high propensity to spend means that consumers will usually spend a large fraction of any extra money that they receive. This has important policy implications. Tax cuts, even temporary tax cuts enacted during a recession, will increase individual spending nearly dollar for dollar; likewise government spending will increase income (and therefore spending) by some fraction of any additional state expenditures. For this reason, fiscal policy can be counted on to affect the overall macroeconomy in a fairly predictable manner.

On the neoclassical approach, business investment is a rational and maximizing decision. Firms compare the costs of investing (interest lost due to borrowing or employing retained earnings) with the benefits (future earnings discounted for the time value of money). If benefits exceed costs, the firm will undertake the new investment project; otherwise there will be no new investment.

For Keynes, business investment was *not* undertaken on this basis, because firms are unable to make the calculations required of them. Future earnings are inherently uncertain. Post Keynesian economists also stress the uncertainty of the investment decision; such decisions must be made on the basis of educated guesses, gut feelings, or 'animal spirits'. These decisions arise not out of individual contemplation, but rather from a collective process where everyone watches what everyone else is doing (Skidelsky 2009, pp. 91–5).

Firms will invest if and only if a lot of other firms are investing and greater investment seems to be a safe choice. In contrast, when 'animal spirits' are pessimistic, few firms will invest. Under these circumstances, any single firm that invests will experience sluggish sales and low or non-existent profits. Here, the investment decision will turn out to have been a mistake. For this reason, negative expectations by some firms quickly translate into negative expectations by most firms, and little investment takes place. With little investment there will be high unemployment, expectations will remain poor, and the economy will remain mired in recession.

Money, for Post Keynesians, is an institutional construct that helps reduce uncertainty. Holding money reduces uncertainty for the firm because workers must be paid with money and debts must be repaid with money; it reduces uncertainty for people because households know that they will be able to pay for necessities in the future with the hoarded money. In addition, money (unlike stocks and other assets) does not change in value much from day to day and from month to month. By holding money, households will not be subject to sharp declines in net worth in the future.

Because it is a refuge from uncertainty, people and business firms will want to hold or hoard money in difficult economic times rather than spend it. But this demand for money creates macroeconomic problems that lead to even greater uncertainty and greater demand for money.

According to Davidson (2007, chapter 7), money has two essential characteristics that lead to unemployment in a world with an unpredictable and unknowable future. Money helps create unemployment because it has zero elasticity of production and because there are no substitutes for money. The former characteristic refers to the fact that no one is hired to produce money when people want money rather than goods. The second property refers to the fact that there is no substitute for money to pay off debts; even if the return to holding money falls to zero, people still need money. When people fear for the future, they desire to hold money. But because no one is hired to produce money, workers get laid off, businesses cannot sell goods, and everyone is more fearful about the future.

In Post Keynesian analysis, the state serves as an important institution that can counteract other forces undermining spending and leading to unemployment. It does this by employing fiscal and monetary policies to help control unemployment. The state can also help by creating institutional structures that tend to stabilize the economy – property rights, a central bank that operates as a lender of last resort, and stable international economic relationships.

In addition, and in contrast to more traditional views of the state, Keynes argued that the state was itself an important economic institution. As Skidelsky (1989) and Pressman (2006) have argued, Keynes saw the state as a set of institutions that would provide for public goods and benefits, the prime benefits of which would be full employment and important public goods and services that business firms were unwilling or unable to provide. It fills in for other social institutions when these institutions fail.

There are several mechanisms by which the state can fulfil these institutional functions. First, the state helps convert uncertainty and discontinuity into calculable risk. It gives economic actors confidence that the future will be like the past. The state provides the laws and regulations that are necessary for capitalist production to take place. It also provides for stability and security in life. This includes monetary stability, exchange rate stability, welfare benefits, old-age pensions and deposit insurance. Deposit insurance, in conjunction with central banks operating as a lender of last resort, reduces the likelihood of bank runs and financial collapse. Universal expenditure programmes (such as family allowances) and a progressive tax system provide a foundation for middle-class living standards in developed nations (Pressman 2007). And government policies that promote full employment and that provide safety-nets during hard times give people confidence to spend, since they know that they are not likely to starve when unemployed. State welfare systems are institutions which recognize that the market, the family and social networks sometimes are not enough to generate individual security. People may not spend if fearful of the personal consequences of becoming unemployed. A viable social safety-net alleviates this concern (Larson 2002).

Second, the state also provides an anchor for decision making. Firms can have more confidence in their own investment decisions when they know that the government will help maintain aggregate investment and full employment. This greater confidence will, in turn, generate more private business investment.

For Keynes, it did not matter how the state spent its money; what mattered was that the money got spent. In a much-quoted passage, Keynes writes about the need for more houses, hospitals, schools and roads. But, he notes, many people are likely to object to such 'wasteful' government expenditures. Another approach was therefore necessary. If the Treasury were to fill old bottles with banknotes, bury them at suitable depths in disused coal mines which are then filled up to the surface with town rubbish, private enterprise would dig the notes up and there need be no more unemployment (Keynes 1936 [1964], p. 129).

Keynes (p. 378) preferred, however, 'a somewhat comprehensive socialization of investment'. What he was advancing here was government spending policies to stabilize the aggregate level of investment in the national economy. For Keynes, the state needed to run deficits and invest in education, infrastructure, health care and so on during times of high unemployment. And during boom times, the government would need to reduce its investment spending and run budget surpluses. By following these budgetary rules, the economy would be more stable, businesses and consumers would face less uncertainty, and both groups would spend more (Pressman 1987, 2006).

In brief, employed correctly, monetary policy and fiscal policy function as uncertainty-reducing institutions. They give business firms the confidence to invest, knowing the chances are good that production from any new plants will be sold at a profit. They also give consumers confidence in the future, and keep them from hoarding money in fear of bad economic times. Other institutional arrangements created by the state that tend to stabilize the economy will have similar beneficial effects.

STEVEN PRESSMAN

See also:

Agency; Consumer Debt; Consumer Theory; Conventions; Economic Policy; Galbraith's Economics; Gender; Households; Investment; Money; Uncertainty.

References

Davidson, P. (2007), *John Maynard Keynes*, Basingstoke: Palgrave Macmillan.
Hodgson, G. (1988), *Economics and Institutions: A Manifesto for a Modern Institutional Economics*, Philadelphia, PA: University of Pennsylvania Press.
Keynes, J.M. (1936 [1964]), *The General Theory of Employment, Interest and Money*, New York: Harcourt Brace.
Larson, S. (2002), *Uncertainty, Macroeconomic Stability and the Welfare State*, Aldershot: Ashgate.
Pressman, S. (1987), 'The policy relevance of *The General Theory*', *Journal of Economic Studies*, **14** (1), 13–23.
Pressman, S. (2006), 'A Post Keynesian theory of the state', in Pressman (ed.), *Alternative Theories of the State*, Basingstoke: Palgrave Macmillan, pp. 113–38.
Pressman, S. (2007), 'The decline of the middle class: an international perspective', *Journal of Economic Issues*, **41** (2), 181–200.
Skidelsky, R. (1989), 'Keynes and the state', in D. Helm (ed.), *The Economic Borders of the State*, Oxford: Oxford University Press, pp. 144–52.
Skidelsky, R. (2009), *Keynes: Return of the Master*, London: Penguin.
Veblen, T. (1899 [1908]), *Theory of the Leisure Class*, New York: Macmillan.

International Economics

The conventional approach to international economics divides the subject into two separate branches. The 'micro' part, called *international trade*, analyses the determinants of countries' exports and imports, and the effects of alternative trade policies on economic welfare (including income distribution), using purely 'real' or barter models. The 'macro' part, called *international finance*, analyses balance-of-payments adjustment and exchange rate determination using aggregative models that emphasize monetary and financial factors. The 'pure' trade theory assumes that automatic financial and macroeconomic adjustment mechanisms effectively ensure the conditions (balanced trade with full employment) under which trade follows comparative advantage and all nations gain from free trade.

Post Keynesians reject this bifurcated approach to international economics, and especially the implied neutrality of monetary and financial factors with regard to 'real' trade. Although Post Keynesian analyses may focus on either the trade or the financial side of the subject, the Post Keynesian approach emphasizes how international trade and financial relations impact on each other (Deprez and Harvey 1999). Especially, in line with the general view of a 'monetary production economy' in which the financing of economic activity has non-neutral or real effects, Post Keynesians deny the existence of automatic adjustment mechanisms that maintain balanced trade and full employment as assumed in the standard pure trade theory, especially mechanisms that would operate via price changes. This opens the door to theories that emphasize the causes and consequences of trade imbalances in relation to output, income and employment.

These theoretical distinctions are of vital importance because of their implications for trade and financial policies. The conventional argument for mutual benefits to all countries from free trade, based on the theory of comparative advantage, is rooted in the 'pure' trade models that assume balanced trade and full employment as well as capital immobility. If any of these assumptions are dropped, the theory of comparative advantage breaks down, and it can no longer be presumed that free trade policies are always in a nation's best interest (although positive Post Keynesian analyses of trade policies remain poorly developed to date). On the financial side, the absence of automatic monetary adjustment mechanisms implies the need for activist government policies and international cooperative arrangements (such as managed exchange rates and/or capital flow restrictions) in order to foster more balanced and mutually beneficial trade and to promote global full employment.

One core Post Keynesian idea that links international trade and finance is Joan Robinson's concept of international conflict over limited global markets, which she called 'the new mercantilism' (see Blecker 2005b). In a world with inadequate aggregate demand and involuntary unemployment, countries often seek to run trade surpluses in order to boost their own output and employment. Since not all countries can run surpluses at the same time, the countries that succeed in obtaining them effectively compel other countries to run deficits, which saddle the latter countries with lower national incomes and higher unemployment rates than they would otherwise have. Thus, export-led expansion in some countries comes at the expense of import-imposed contraction in others, or – in Robinson's adaptation of Adam Smith's famous remark – export-led growth is a 'beggar-my-neighbour' policy. This analysis of conflictual trade relations stands in marked contrast to the conventional view of largely harmonious trade relationships – a view that ignores the existence of demand-side limits to global exports and allows for conflict only over the barter terms of trade.

The Post Keynesian approach includes critiques of conventional theories of automatic balance-of-payments adjustment. For example, in the 'specie-flow' mechanism of David Hume and David Ricardo, which applies to a fixed exchange rate system, a trade surplus (deficit) leads to an inflow (outflow) of monetary reserves (gold or hard currencies), which in turn raises (lowers) the money supply and causes a rise (fall) in the price level that makes a country's products less (more) competitive, and hence reverses the trade imbalance. Post Keynesians criticize this theory because (among other things) they deny that the supply of money determines the price level in a modern industrial economy, as well as because this theory ignores the role of capital flows in financing trade imbalances. As long as countries with trade surpluses run offsetting capital account deficits (that is, become net lenders) and countries with trade deficits run offsetting capital account surpluses (that is, become net borrowers), overall balance-of-payments equilibrium can be sustained without eliminating *trade* imbalances.

Another type of automatic stabilization mechanism involves flexible exchange rates. Traditional analyses presumed that countries with trade surpluses would have appreciating currencies and countries with deficits would have depreciating currencies, leading to the restoration of balanced trade. However, Post Keynesians argue that flexible exchange rates are driven primarily by financial capital flows and asset market speculation, and hence need not move in the 'right' direction for balancing trade – and, even when they do adjust, exchange rate changes may not generate the desired improvements in the trade balance due to low price elasticities or offsetting price changes. While these points are recognized by some mainstream economists, the implication that imbalanced trade will not follow comparative advantages is emphasized only by Post Keynesians (Blecker 2005a).

Post Keynesians in the Kaleckian tradition emphasize the feedback effects of international competition onto domestic profit mark-up rates, and hence on the distribution of income between profits and wages (Arestis and Milberg 1993–94). When a currency appreciates (or domestic costs rise relative to foreign), oligopolistic firms squeeze price–cost margins in order to 'price-to-market', which in turn leads to a fall in the profit share with possible negative repercussions for investment and growth (although this may be offset by a boost to domestic consumption arising from higher real wages and labour income). When a currency depreciates (or domestic costs fall relative to foreign), the opposite happens as domestic oligopolies are able to raise their price–cost margins without losing market share, income is redistributed from wages to profits, and the potential repercussions for investment and growth as well as for consumption are all reversed. Outcomes in which a redistribution of income towards wages is expansionary are known as 'wage-led' regimes, while outcomes in which a redistribution towards profits is expansionary are 'profit led'. Mainstream economists have recognized the flexibility of profit margins in response to exchange-rate fluctuations – what they call 'partial pass-through' – but they have not analysed the feedback effects onto income distribution, aggregate demand and economic growth. A number of empirical studies (surveyed by Blecker 2011) have tested whether various countries are wage or profit led in this sense, and a frequent conclusion is that the results may depend on the degree to which countries are open to international trade – with 'open economy' effects making countries more likely to be profit led (or less strongly wage led).

At the microeconomic level, Post Keynesians argue that trade generally follows absolute rather than comparative advantages (Milberg 1994). There are two different versions of this approach. For trade in standardized products, which can be manufactured in similar processes with comparable quality in a large number of countries, exports are based on *competitive advantages* in unit costs of production, principally unit labour costs (that is, wages adjusted for productivity, or 'wages in efficiency units'). Thus, the countries with the lowest unit costs in a certain product, taking into account current wages and other direct input costs (such as raw materials), relative to the productivity of labour and other inputs, and adjusted for prevailing exchange rates, will export that product, regardless of whether they have a 'true' comparative advantage in it. In labour-intensive industries in which technology is standardized, only low-wage countries will export the products, especially when capital is mobile and firms can locate production wherever production costs are lowest (Brewer 1985). Thus, Post Keynesians recognize some truth in the popular notion of low-wage competition, but only if it is understood in the proper context (that is, wages are adjusted for productivity, products are standardized and capital is internationally mobile).

However, there are many internationally traded goods for which neither production processes nor product qualities are standardized. For these goods, a few technological leaders either have absolutely superior (lower cost) technologies, or else produce absolutely higher qualities of the goods, than any other countries. In these industries, which include important sectors such as aerospace, machinery, software and medical equipment, trade is determined by *technological gaps* – that is, the countries with the superior technology or product are the exporters, and all other countries are importers (Dosi et al. 1990). Relative cost factors (such as wages or exchange rates) are not important in these sectors and product lines. Of course, individual products or components can shift over time from being innovative products traded according to technological gaps to standard-ized products traded according to competitive advantages. As a result, the small club of innovating countries (led by the United States in the postwar period, and joined more recently by Japan, Germany and others) needs to keep inventing newer innovative goods in order to stay ahead of the com-petitive curve (since such countries typically have high wages, and therefore cannot compete in standardized manufactures). The technology gap theory of trade in innovative products thus complements the absolute competitive advantages theory for standardized goods, allowing for a fairly complete characterization of most international trade especially in manufactures.

Other Post Keynesian views can be covered more briefly since they are discussed elsewhere in this volume. To deal with the volatility of flexible exchange rates as well as the deflationary biases in traditional adjustment mechanisms for deficit countries, some Post Keynesians have advocated a return to a Bretton Woods-like system of adjustable pegs, but accompa-nied by a mechanism to shift the burden of adjustment onto the surplus countries. Paul Davidson (1992–93) has called for the establishment of an international monetary clearing house, which would not only create an international reserve asset (international monetary clearing unit, or IMCU), but also require surplus countries to spend their surpluses and thus impart an expansionary bias to the global adjustment process. In addition, many Post Keynesians have advocated policies to discourage destabilizing flows of short-term capital and to prevent speculative attacks on currencies. However, Post Keynesian views on such policies vary, with some advocating Tobin taxes on foreign exchange transactions while others call for more direct forms of capital controls.

Finally, the theory of 'balance-of-payments-constrained growth' (McCombie and Thirlwall 2004) focuses on the long-term consequences if trade imbalances cannot be sustained indefinitely and countries are even-tually forced to balance their trade (or at least, to restrict trade imbalances to levels that can be financed through sustainable net capital flows). This view assumes that the long-run adjustment to balanced trade is effectu-ated mainly through changes in output quantities (income levels or growth rates), not by changes in relative prices (real exchange rates), as shown by

Alonso and Garcimartín (1998–99). The implication is that countries with slow export growth and high income elasticities of import demand are condemned to grow more slowly than their trading partners if they are forced to balance their trade in the long run. Note that, while the basic version of this model assumes balanced trade in the long run, it does not assume full employment or that the adjustment mechanisms that restore balanced trade are neutral or painless, and the model can be adapted to allow for capital flows.

Robert A. Blecker

See also:

Balance-of-payments-constrained Economic Growth; Bretton Woods; Exchange Rates; Export-led Growth; International Financial Reform; Kaleckian Economics; Tobin Tax; Wage- and Profit-led Regimes.

References

Alonso, J. and C. Garcimartín (1998–99), 'A new approach to the balance-of-payments constraint: some empirical evidence', *Journal of Post Keynesian Economics*, **21** (2), 259–82.

Arestis, P. and W. Milberg (1993–94), 'Degree of monopoly, pricing, and flexible exchange rates', *Journal of Post Keynesian Economics*, **16** (2), 167–88.

Blecker, R.A. (2005a), 'Financial globalization, exchange rates and international trade', in G. Epstein (ed.), *Financialization and the World Economy*, Cheltenham, UK and Northampton, MA, USA: Edward Elgar, pp. 183–209.

Blecker, R.A. (2005b), 'International economics after Robinson', in B. Gibson (ed.), *Joan Robinson's Economics: A Centennial Celebration*, Cheltenham, UK and Northampton, MA, USA: Edward Elgar, pp. 309–49.

Blecker, R.A. (2011), 'Open economy models of growth and distribution', in E. Hein and E. Stockhammer (eds), *A Modern Guide to Keynesian Macroeconomics and Economic Policies*, Cheltenham, UK and Northampton, MA, USA: Edward Elgar, pp. 215–39.

Brewer, A. (1985), 'Trade with fixed real wages and mobile capital', *Journal of International Economics*, **18** (1/2), 177–86.

Davidson, P. (1992–93), 'Reforming the world's money', *Journal of Post Keynesian Economics*, **15** (2), Winter, 153–79.

Deprez, J. and J.T. Harvey (eds) (1999), *Foundations of International Economics: Post Keynesian Perspectives*, London and New York: Routledge.

Dosi, G., K. Pavitt and L. Soete (1990), *The Economics of Technical Change and International Trade*, New York: New York University Press.

McCombie, J.S.L. and A.P. Thirlwall (eds) (2004), *Essays on Balance of Payments Constrained Economic Growth*, Abingdon and New York: Routledge.

Milberg, W. (1994), 'Is absolute advantage passé? Towards a Post Keynesian/Marxian theory of international trade', in M. Glick (ed.), *Competition, Technology and Money: Classical and Post-Keynesian Perspectives*, Aldershot, UK and Brookfield, VT, USA: Edward Elgar, pp. 220–36.

International Financial Reform

Post Keynesians support the active management of aggregate demand, trade and international finance, to maintain full employment, balance external accounts and provide a countercyclical weight to the positive feedbacks of the financial system. Endogenous credit, endogenous liquidity risk and endogenous expectations are all factors that create the boom–bust financial fragility best described by Hyman Minsky in the 1970s (Minsky 1975) in accordance with his reading of Keynes's *General Theory*. The Post Keynesian goal is to harness the creative power of financial markets while at the same time limiting their tendency to self-destruct.

Our advanced monetary system fosters a complex division of labour through an international network of sales and purchases. This production network is dependent on investment and the financing of balance-sheet positions. Money and credit is created endogenously simply by the credit and debit of interlinked balance sheets between financial institutions, firms, households, governments, central banks and similar international units. In this multidimensional interactive system, the solvency and financing of cash flows from unit portfolios – assets and liabilities – are uncertain. At a micro level the increase in liquidity of these portfolios, as investment markets become increasingly organized, makes the management of solvency and liquidity easier. But so too, as financial markets become more liquid, speculation becomes more pervasive and harmful. Keynes warned:

> Speculators may do no harm as bubbles on a steady stream of enterprise. But the position is serious when enterprise becomes the bubble on a whirlpool of speculation. When the capital development of a country becomes a by-product of the activities of a casino, the job is likely to be ill-done. (Keynes 1936, p. 159)

Post Keynesians view financial markets as power brokers that affect the character of production, income distribution and core–periphery dynamics. They are concerned over the growing 'financialization' of the economic system (Palley 2007) and the spillover costs of financial contagion to innocent bystanders. This is in dramatic contrast with the neoclassical or neoliberal paradigm, which has faith in the efficient operation of financial markets, while government management and regulation are seen as inefficient and/or ineffective. Under this view the functions of money, finance and financial markets are just a means to an end that: provide a medium of exchange, means of payment, and unit of account; allocate credit to its most productive use; lower costs by offering an efficient intermediary between savers and investors; smooth consumption over time; provide price and share risk, reducing the volatility of prices and incomes; aggregate information to create a fair value for assets that is arbitrage free; and innovate new instruments, which 'complete markets' and reduce uncertainty by better pricing future economic outcomes.

Neoclassical economists focus their attention on the exchange of goods and services, while money and private debt is regarded as neutral.

Speculation is seen as stabilizing, and rising market liquidity is synonymous with rising efficiency. After the 1970s, following the breakdown of Bretton Woods, this school successfully pushed the liberalization of finance around the world. For example, quantity constraints on bank loans were lifted; retail and wholesale banking was reintegrated; international capital flows were opened; micro-prudential controls and balance-sheet valuations came to rely on market prices; the highly innovative and sophisticated financial sector came to measure and manage its own risk; private credit rating agencies were promoted to centralize, decipher and disseminate information, lowering costs for other market participants; stock options were paid to managers to align their interests with those of shareholders; and central banking was limited to inflation targeting and market stability through interest rate adjustments rather than bank lending limits or modified reserve requirements. There were warnings that the creation of countercyclical policies or emergency lending facilities risked the creation of greater volatility, price distortions and moral hazard. The presence of asymmetric information (adverse selection and moral hazard) in financial markets called for transparency and competition through the privatization of services, both financial and real.

Post Keynesians challenge these conclusions and argue that the deregulation increased systemic risk and the frequency of financial crises at great cost to growth and development. While far from exhaustive, one can consolidate desired Post Keynesian international financial reform into five broad areas.

First, require countercyclical buffers on all financial entity balance sheets. At a micro level Minsky's concepts of interlocking balance sheets and cyclical finance explain higher valuations, excessive risk taking and financial expansion in good times, but lower valuations, insufficient risk taking and financial contraction in bad times. This procyclicality can be dampened by regulatory countercyclical margin requirements, leverage ratios, loan-to-asset-value ratios, liquidity ratios, capital provisioning against losses, asset-based reserve requirements (Palley 2004), and so on. These solvency measures also add tools to a central bank's monetary policy, which can be used to target asset prices rather than just focusing on inflation of consumer goods. Such countercyclical tools are especially needed when short-term interest rates have become procyclical with the increase in cross-border capital flows: higher interest rates attract foreign capital, easing domestic financing constraints, and the opposite occurs when interest rates are low (D'Arista and Griffith-Jones 2011).

Quantitative limits on financial firm balance sheets are necessary since financial markets follow 'beauty contest' dynamics where so-called 'fundamentals' are just conventions – they are what average opinion believes average opinion to be. Average opinion can be self-fulfilling and its reversal can be frighteningly sudden. Herding and volatility are accentuated by the increasing use of similar market-sensitive risk management techniques and trading strategies. As such, diversification strategies can fail as price correlations increase across heterogeneous securities and markets.

Second, reduce the volume of speculative capital flows. The volume of international capital flows has grown exponentially since the removal of capital controls in the post-Bretton Woods era. Search for yield by financial institutions means the movements of large swaths of capital and can produce local asset bubbles, which collapse when flows are reversed. Currency carry trades, where borrowings in a low-interest country are invested in a high-interest country, along with herd behaviour, have exacerbated global procyclicality. Various speed humps, tripwires and taxes have been suggested to dampen these whirlpools of speculative finance and instead promote long-term investment, especially in the emerging markets (Grabel 2004). Transaction taxes (a Tobin tax) would increase costs on short-term speculation, and even if it were too small to dampen volumes, it could raise substantial funds to finance emerging market development or financial regulation costs. Limits on commercial banks using federally guaranteed deposits for speculation are also popular among Post Keynesians.

Third, a new international reserve currency not linked to a key country to resolve global imbalances. The US dollar as international reserve currency began with Bretton Woods and the dollar's universal use as a medium for inter-central bank settlements. Since this time an increasing proportion of the world's monetary reserves came to be held in dollars rather than gold, and the capital market of US-denominated debt held off its shore grew rapidly. In 1951 the issuance of US net foreign assets became greater than that needed to finance US trade – at this point the US began a trend that would later mean the exporting of capital (foreign investment) and jobs overseas, rather than the exporting of manufactured goods (Kaldor 1971). With short-term foreign lending financing net long-term investment abroad, the US had become the world's central bank; its current account deficits provided the income to other countries to pay interest on debts to the US incurred due to US investment abroad. The recycling of these financial flows dwarfs those in terms of trade, raising concerns for the sustainability and growing fragility of the US. However, despite rising debt on US unit balance sheets there is much greater elasticity in their adjustment due to their reserve currency status. A US financial crisis can lead to 'flight to quality' or a rush into US$ liquid assets. Thus, the balance-sheet fragility of US entities may be exported to the periphery, often less-developed financial markets.

While the US$ reserve imparted enormous liquidity into the system, the cost of providing this 'international public good' was borne by the real side of the US economy through weakened export growth, a deindustrialization of the manufacturing base, transfer of resources to the financial sector, income inequality and wage stagnation, and a greater dependence on fiscal policy to maintain employment. Interestingly, some Post Keynesians have come to believe that deficit spending is not a solution to US unemployment when leakages to imports are so great.

The longstanding alternative to US$ international reserve is Keynes's international clearing union, a supranational central bank, which would resolve global imbalances and currency crises by generating a new currency called 'Bancor', held only by central banks. Davidson (2004) has proposed a modified version, though in keeping with Keynes he requires fixed exchange rates and a reserve that is not traded by private institutions. Other proposals, which argue that a new international reserve must be one traded in liquid private sector markets with flexible exchange rates, range from a revamp of the Special Drawing Rights (SDR) (which is pegged to a basket of key country currencies) (Stiglitz and Greenwald 2010) to a new currency backed by a pool of government infrastructure bonds from developing countries (D'Arista 2000). Kaldor's proposal for a commodity reserve currency also fits into this latter category but it has generally been ignored by Post Keynesians (Ussher 2009). This latter plan resolves the excess speculation in international commodity markets as well as addressing international resource security (Hart et al. 1964).

Fourth, institute an effective apolitical international lender of last resort. With increasing global trade and short-term capital flows, central banks have had to increase their reserve currency stock as self-insurance against a currency crisis. The stockpiling of reserves traps effective demand and effectively exports unemployment to deficit countries. Without this insurance, currency crises are resolved by IMF bailouts that usually impose deregulation and fiscal restrictions as conditionalities, stripping a country of its autonomy.

As private transnational financial units become bigger than individual countries, there is a need to broaden the lender of last resort facility beyond sovereign governments. The US Federal Reserve has played this role, offering swap lines and asset purchases to ever-wider groups of financial units in times of crisis – as too has the European Central Bank in its region. The creation of a global central bank that can expand international reserves and offer a lender of last resort facility could be formalized under the new international reserve plans of D'Arista (2000) or Stiglitz and Greenwald (2010).

Fifth, impose comprehensive regulation of all financial actors and activities. To avoid entrenching moral hazard by an international lender of last resort, a world financial authority would be needed (Eatwell and Taylor 2000) that can monitor and impose penalties and constraints, punishing excesses before financial units become too big to fail. The implementation of such regulation would be undertaken by regional institutions, but harmonized through one international authority. A comprehensive global supervisor will avoid regulatory arbitrage if all financial institutions are covered – national banks, foreign branches, hedge funds, private equity managers, money market funds, clearing houses, special purpose vehicles, insurance companies and so on. Universal coverage of all financial entities is far from being acceptable to most governments. But it is argued by a number of Post Keynesians that if such comprehensive agreements and monitoring arrangements could be implemented then countries would actually gain autonomy in their monetary and fiscal policy, allowing for a focus on employment and growth rather than monetary and financial stability (D'Arista and Griffith-Jones 2011).

Endogenous credit, endogenous liquidity risk and endogenous expectations are all factors that create cyclical financial fragility in financial markets. Without effective capital controls these markets are borderless. Some sort of international moderating countercyclical micro and macro architecture is required to stop the build-up of unsustainable imbalances. In order for regulation to be efficient, it is essential that the domain of the regulator be the same as the domain of the market that is being regulated. A new international reserve currency, an international clearing union, and a world financial authority are some of the visionary suggestions put forward by Post Keynesians that would make the financial sector handmaiden to the real side of the economy, rather than its master.

LEANNE USSHER

See also:

Efficient Markets Hypothesis; Exchange Rates; Financial Reform; Financialization; International Economics; Tobin Tax; Uncertainty.

References

D'Arista, J. (2000), 'Reforming the privatized international monetary and financial architecture', *Challenge*, **43** (3), 44–82.
D'Arista, J. and S. Griffith-Jones (2011), 'Reforming financial regulation: what needs to be done', in J.K. Sundaram (ed.), *Reforming the International Financial System for Development*, New York: Columbia University Press, pp. 143–68.
Davidson, P. (2004), 'The future of the international financial system', *Journal of Post Keynesian Economics*, **26** (4), 591–605.
Eatwell, J. and L. Taylor (2000), *Global Finance at Risk: The Case for International Regulation*, New York: New Press.
Grabel, I. (2004), 'Trip wires and speed bumps: managing financial risks and reducing the potential for financial crises in developing economies', prepared for the XVIIIth Technical

Group Meeting of the G-24 in Geneva, Switzerland, 8–9 March; published as G-24 Discussion Paper No. 33, November 2004, United Nations and Geneva.

Hart, A.G., N. Kaldor and J. Tinbergen (1964), 'The case for an international commodity reserve currency', Geneva, UNCTAD; reprinted in Kaldor (1980), *Essays on Economic Policy II*, Vol. IV of *Collected Economic Essays of Nicholas Kaldor*, New York: Holmes & Meier, pp. 131–77.

Kaldor, N. (1971), 'The dollar crisis', *The Times*, 6, 7, 8 September; reprinted in Kaldor (1978), *Further Essays on Applied Economics*, Vol. VI of *Collected Economic Essays* of *Nicholas Kaldor*, London: Duckworth, pp. 60–73.

Keynes, J.M. (1936), *The General Theory of Employment, Interest and Money*, London: Macmillan.

Minsky, H.P. (1975), *John Maynard Keynes*, New York: Columbia University Press.

Palley, T.I. (2004), 'Asset-based reserve requirements: reasserting domestic monetary control in an era of financial innovation and instability', *Review of Political Economy*, **16** (1), 43–58.

Palley, T.I. (2007), 'Financialization: what it is and why it matters', Working Paper No. 525, Levy Economics Institute of Bard College, Annandale-on-Hudson, available at: http://ssrn.com/abstract=1077923.

Stiglitz, J.E. and B. Greenwald (2010), 'Towards a new global reserve system', *Journal of Globalization and Development*, **1** (2), Article 10, available at: http://www.bepress.com/jgd/vol1/iss2/art10.

Ussher, L.J. (2009), 'Global imbalances and the key currency regime: the case for a commodity reserve currency', *Review of Political Economy*, **21** (3), 403–21.

Investment

The Post Keynesian theory of investment begins with the work of John Maynard Keynes and Michał Kalecki in the 1930s. Keynes's ideas about the determinants of investment in *A Treatise on Money* (1930 [1971]) and *The General Theory of Employment, Interest, and Money* (1936 [1964]) depart from the neoclassical theory mainly by emphasizing expectations of the profitability of investment spending and the expectations involved in the determination of financial market prices. The fundamental formulation of investment in neoclassical theory is that it is determined by the intersection of a downward-sloping schedule of the marginal productivity of increasing quantities of capital equipment relative to a given amount of the other factors of production with an upward-sloping schedule of the community's willingness to abstain from consumption to supply quantities of capital at different rates of return.

In the *Treatise* Keynes argued that the value of new investment goods would rise and fall relative to the cost of production of new investment, spurring changes in the level of investment, as the public and the banking system changed their opinions about the desirability of moving wealth between deposits and securities. A change in the willingness of the community to supply capital, that is, to save, would thus only change the level of physical investment if it also changed the level of financial investment in securities. The level of investment could change in turn, relative to the willingness to save, as the desirability of holding securities changed.

In the *General Theory* Keynes described the investment demand schedule as a schedule of the 'marginal efficiency' of capital. Although Keynes held that his marginal efficiency of capital schedule was equivalent to Irving Fisher's derivation of the 'rate of return over cost' from neoclassical optimizing behaviour, he was clear that his schedule stood for the expected profitability of additions to the capital stock and explicitly rejected the idea that the value of capital was determined by the productivity of capital. This schedule slopes downwards, Keynes wrote, since increased demand for capital goods raises the cost of producing them and an increased supply of any type of capital reduces its prospective yield. Later theorists were to say that as these factors influencing the profitability of additional capital were affected by the time period in which the capital is to be produced and installed, the schedule should be instead called the marginal efficiency of *investment*, or additions to the capital stock per unit of time.

Keynes saw the supply of finance for investment as coming from the willingness of the public and the banks to give up liquidity, which determined the relevant interest rate. The 'degree of excess bearishness', which determined the value of investment in the *Treatise*, became divided into the expectations of profitability of the marginal efficiency of capital schedule and the degree of liquidity preference for holding 'money' versus long-term debts, given the quantity of money supplied by the central bank.

Kalecki (1990, 1991) criticized Keynes's theory of investment on the grounds that it was insufficiently dynamic. That is, Kalecki questioned the idea of having investment determined by the intersection of a given marginal efficiency of capital schedule and the relevant mix of interest rates, because he held that changes in the level of investment so determined would feed back upon the marginal efficiency of capital schedule itself, first as, for example, increased investment increased aggregate demand and so the profitability of investment, and later as the new capital produced by the investment became available and so depressed the profitability of further investment.

Kalecki's depiction of how investment spending is determined thus requires a dynamic process in which investment interacts with output, profits and the level of the capital stock, as in the flexible accelerator or capital stock adjustment model, though his own models were specified in terms of investment, capital and profits, rather than output. Kalecki's theory of the financing of investment comes from his 'principle of increasing risk'. Addressing the question of what limits the size of the capital investment of any firm, Kalecki allowed that a firm which is large relative to the size of its market would be limited by this, but he held that there is another factor limiting firm expansion, which is the proportion of the owner's capital that is invested in the firm. For, Kalecki argued, the more of the wealth of any individual unit of capital that is sunk into one business, the more at risk is the individual's entire wealth position. This financial limit on investment means that there is a quantity constraint, as well as a price of funds constraint, on investment spending.

Keynes's ideas about 'borrowers' risk' and 'lenders' risk' in the *General Theory* make a similar point, but Keynes tended to place more emphasis on the psychological conventions governing the determination of financial market prices. That is, he argued that speculative activity directed towards the prices of long-term debt and corporate shares could significantly affect investment spending. In the face of the radical uncertainty of our knowledge of the future prospects of business, Keynes reasoned that stock market valuations of the marginal efficiency of capital would often represent the results of speculation about the psychology of the market rather than sensible forecasts of the long-term profitability of corporate capital. He discussed the ability of central bank policy to move long-term interest rates to achieve the desired level of investment, and he feared conditions under which monetary policy would not be able to overcome speculators' degree of liquidity preference sufficiently. He thus called for the state to take responsibility for ensuring an adequate level of investment through its direct actions.

James Duesenberry (1958 [1977]) combined the flexible accelerator, in which the level of investment is explained by the level of output relative to the level of existing productive capacity, with the financing effects on investment arising from current profit flows and a measure of the existing debt burden, based on Kalecki's ideas on the determination of investment finance, into a dynamic marginal efficiency of investment and marginal cost of funds determination of investment. Empirical work in the 1950s and early 1960s on this approach to investment demonstrated support for Kalecki's and Keynes's ideas.

Theoretical developments of the Post Keynesian theory of investment were made in the 1970s by Paul Davidson and Hyman Minsky. Davidson (1972 [1978]) specified the schedule of the demand price of capital goods as a function of entrepreneurial capitalists' subjective rate of discount, expectations of growth in product demand, their ability to raise the necessary financing, and their calculations of depreciation. His supply price schedule is given by the size of the existing capital stock and the increasing cost of production of new capital goods. Davidson's model is thus able to trace the effects of financial considerations and product market demand more clearly than Keynes's *General Theory* formulation, which appears to emphasize only the level of interest rates as the cost of finance, and stock market prices as the measure of the value of investment projects.

Minsky's (1975) formulation takes the cost of production of new capital to any one firm as given. It then takes the demand price to be the capitalized value of the expected cash flows from investment, which decreases as the level of investment rises into the range where use of external financing increases borrower's risk. In the region of external financing, Minsky depicted increasing lender's risk as a schedule raising supply price at an increasing rate above the cost of production of new capital. The intersection of the demand and supply price schedules gives the level of investment spending. Minsky's graphical exposition is somewhat similar to Duesenberry's, but he describes the details of financial concerns, in terms both of interest rate and debt burden effects, much more thoroughly and insightfully than anyone else. Minsky's dynamic treatment of the interactions among investment, profits and debt provides a financial counterpart to Kalecki's portrayal of investment, profits and capital interactions.

In the 1960s, interest in estimating a version of the neoclassical model of investment determination revived. Neoclassical economists claimed that profits or other flow measures of the availability of funds only appeared successful in investment regressions because they were highly correlated with, and thus were acting as a proxy for, the level of output, which all theories agreed to be a significant determinant of investment. In the 1980s, however, work by Steven Fazzari and several different co-authors offered empirical support to Post Keynesian ideas on investment. Fazzari and Tracy Mott (1986–87) was the earliest of these to demonstrate support for the role of output demand, internal finance and debt burden measures in explaining investment. In later studies, Fazzari and others showed further the importance of internal financing constraints, following the work of Kalecki, Minsky and some more recent work based on asymmetric information, in explaining investment.

Most of the theoretical and empirical work discussed above is concerned with the determinants of business fixed investment. Both Kalecki and Keynes also wrote about the factors governing inventory investment, arguing that inventory investment should be influenced by factors similar to those which determined fixed investment but be affected by shorter-term movements in the availability of finance and in expectations of sales relative to current stocks. Fazzari's empirical work on inventory investment has supported this.

Keynes and Kalecki also both tended to consider the question of the level of current investment apart from any questions of changes in technique, or capital intensity, which was arguably the main concern of marginal productivity theory. The 'Cambridge capital critique' has questioned the notion of 'capital intensity' as a measurable concept, and the claim that investment should be analysed as a process of changes in the ratio of 'capital' to labour in long-run equilibrium is something that no Post Keynesian would accept.

Of course, changes in the type of capital must be taken into account in any long-run analysis of investment. In the Post Keynesian literature these have been treated mainly under the heading of 'innovations'. Josef Steindl's (1952 [1976]) work on long-run growth within a Kaleckian perspective argues that in young industries investment is stimulated by the ability of 'progressive' firms to lower costs through expansion and innovation, and then to lower prices further in order to drive out higher-cost firms. This price-cutting maintains capacity utilization at high rates until only a small group of producers with similar cost structures remain. Price-cutting now offers no advantage to the remaining oligopolists, who thus abandon it. This in turn decreases the level of investment spending, unless new products or methods of production emerge. Steindl thus developed his ideas about 'absolute concentration' into a theory of a long-run tendency towards macroeconomic stagnation.

Post Keynesians have always acknowledged to some extent the importance of what Keynes called 'animal spirits' as a key influence on the level of investment spending. Some Post Keynesians have objected that this makes investment depend too heavily on the subjective reactions of managers to fundamental uncertainty, and therefore underestimates the objective determinants of investment. Kalecki's explanation of investment seems clearly to rest much more on objective factors, though he did allow that psychological matters might influence investment activity.

TRACY MOTT

See also:

Capital Theory; Expectations; Innovation; Kaleckian Economics; Keynes's *General Theory*; Keynes's *Treatise on Money*.

References

Davidson, P. (1972 [1978]), *Money and the Real World*, London: Macmillan.
Duesenberry, J. (1958 [1977]), *Business Cycles and Economic Growth*, Westport, CT: Greenwood Press.
Fazzari, S. and T. Mott (1986–87), 'The investment theories of Kalecki and Keynes: an empirical study of firm data, 1970–1982', *Journal of Post Keynesian Economics*, **9** (2), 171–87.
Kalecki, M. (1990, 1991), *Collected Works of Michał Kalecki*, Vols I and II, Oxford: Oxford University Press.
Keynes, J. M. (1930 [1971]), *A Treatise on Money*, London: Macmillan.
Keynes, J. M. (1936 [1964]), *The General Theory of Employment, Interest, and Money*, New York: Harcourt Brace.

Minsky, H. (1975), *John Maynard Keynes*, New York: Columbia University Press.
Steindl, J. (1952 [1976]), *Maturity and Stagnation in American Capitalism*, 2nd edn, New York: Monthly Review Press.

Italy

Post Keynesian economics in Italy represents a well-established research tradition in so far as scholars share various pre-analytical and methodological elements (see Laudan 1977), in particular the monetary nature of the economy, the antagonism between social groups, the role of uncertainty and historical time. The initial contributions were made by Luigi Pasinetti and Augusto Graziani, and these were developed in the works of their students and colleagues.

Pasinetti's main contribution to the Post Keynesian Italian research tradition regards the extension of the *General Theory* to the long run and the demonstration (Pasinetti 1962) that the profit rate is independent from the workers' propensity to save. His attention then shifted to classical themes (Pasinetti 1966, 1969; Scazzieri 2008), coming back to Keynesian studies in 1974 when he showed the compatibility of capital accumulation and cyclical fluctuations within a system featuring permanent structural changes. Pasinettian thought has been developed by different scholars, such as Mauro Baranzini, Enrico Bellino and Roberto Scazzieri. Baranzini (1992, p. 478) is particularly interested in the Pasinettian methodology, which he describes as a 'mixed classical/pure' Keynesian methodology, since it makes reference to three main interconnected thematic blocks: the theory of capital, the theory of income distribution and the theory of value. Baranzini (1991, p. iv) then tries to provide a microfoundation for the Pasinettian models of income distribution and economic growth, introducing some intertemporal and intergenerational analytical components, viewing the social classes as the 'outcome of long-term institutional behavior, and economic forces' and the antagonism among them as depending on the 'different inter-temporal and inter-generational allocations of consumption . . . life-cycle and bequest savings'.

Bellino, instead, tries to expand the Pasinettian contribution to the interpretation of Keynesian theory in terms of neo-Ricardianism. His approach consists of enriching Pasinetti's positive model, based on the classical framework, with normative prescriptions (see also Scazzieri 2007) in order to stimulate the convergence of the real economic system towards a so-called 'natural system'. In his latest work (Bellino 2011), for instance, by studying the natural configuration of the profit rate problem to find the critical element in current income distribution, he identifies it as the expansion of the economy's financial structure in relation to the particular accumulation conditions, historically and institutionally contextualized, and investigates them in terms of the mechanisms that can reduce the divergence of real profits from 'natural profit'.

One of the main contributions that Graziani (1990, 2003) made to the development of Post Keynesian theory in Italy concerns the renewal of the Keynesian monetary flow approach – known also as the monetary theory of production (hereafter MTP), or monetary circuit theory – developed in the *Treatise on Money* in order to sharpen the theory of capitalist instability. As Riccardo Realfonzo (2006, p. 105) remarks – followed by various authors such as Riccardo Bellofiore, Biagio Bossone, Lilia Costabile, Guglielmo Forges Davanzati, Giuseppe Fontana, Marcello Messori, Alberto Zazzaro and more recently, Emiliano Brancaccio, Stefano Lucarelli, Andrea Pacella, Guido Tortorella Esposito and others – the MTP approach in Italy 'is part of the broad and heterogeneous course of heterodox economic literature'. In general terms, MTP scholars agree that the economic process can be depicted in terms of a circular sequence of monetary flows, observing a continuity of thought in Keynes's works. In fact, by considering the *Treatise on Money* as the theory of capitalist reproduction in equilibrium, where money is used predominantly as a means of payment, and the *General Theory* as the theory of crises triggered by the lack of aggregate demand, in which money is used predominantly as a store of value (Realfonzo 1998; Fontana 2000; Fontana and Realfonzo 2005), they reject any hypothetical break points between the methodological approaches of these two works. Some of them, however, introduce heterogeneous elements into the basic circuit schema along Marxian lines (see, for example, Bellofiore 1989), Wicksellian/Keynesian lines (Pacella 2008), Schumpeterian lines (Messori 2004; Fumagalli and Lucarelli 2008) or, in the last few years, Veblenian lines (Forges Davanzati and Pacella 2010).

On the analytical plane there are two main issues that have inspired MTP research in Italy: income distribution and the theory of money. In general terms, Italian MTP scholars agree that income distribution depends on the bargaining power of firms reflected in the degree of mark-up (see, for example, Bellofiore et al. 2000; Forges Davanzati and Realfonzo 2005), investigating also the impact of workers' real wage expectations on the distributive dynamics (see Forges Davanzati and Realfonzo 2000). Within the circuitist debate on income distribution, MTP scholars explain the origin of monetary profits along two lines: the endogenous and the exogenous solutions. According to the first group, profits come from the productive sector as a result of the bankruptcy of inefficient firms (Messori and Zazzaro 2005), while others (for example, Zezza 2004) attribute the monetary profit to the banking system. The second group, instead, finds the solution in the external influxes of money guaranteed by private indebtedness (Forges Davanzati and Realfonzo 2009; Forges Davanzati and Pacella 2010). Within the recent debate on money, Fontana (2009) finds convergence points between the Post Keynesian theory of uncertainty and the related theory of unemployment with the monetary circuitist analysis in order to construct a general theory of money as both a stock and a flow of means of payments.

In the last few years there have been various attempts to expand the MTP from several points of view. Some MTP scholars, for instance, investigate the potentiality of the monetary circuit for the study of underdevelopment issues (see, for example, Bossone and Sarr 2002, 2005; Costabile 2005, 2007). Others instead (see Brancaccio 2008) try to link the classical approach with that of the MTP. Moreover, MTP scholars have recently joined the criticism of the New Consensus approach, arguing that output growth is demand-driven and that fiscal policies, as well as direct state intervention, are effective in stabilizing the macroeconomic system (see Forges Davanzati et al. 2009). Finally, different contributions have recently explored the current crisis. In particular, Italian MTP scholars identify it as an underconsumption crisis generated by labour market deregulation (see Forges Davanzati and Tortorella Esposito 2010; Forges Davanzati and Realfonzo 2011).

In conclusion, Post Keynesian economics in Italy initially developed along two lines of research: the Pasinettian one, consistent with the *General Theory* and the classical approach, and Graziani's approach, consistent instead with the *Treatise on Money*. Although many scholars remain close to the original models, an interesting debate between the two approaches is emerging in order to explain the current economic dynamics more effectively.

ANDREA PACELLA
GUIDO TORTORELLA ESPOSITO

See also:

Circuit Theory; Growth and Income Distribution; Keynes's *Treatise on Money*.

References

Baranzini, M. (1991), *A Theory of Wealth Distribution and Accumulation*, Oxford and New York: Oxford University Press.
Baranzini, M. (1992), 'Luigi Lodovico Pasinetti', in P. Arestis and M. Sawyer (eds), *A Biographical Dictionary of Dissenting Economists*, Aldershot, UK and Brookfield, VT, USA: Edward Elgar, pp. 477–86.
Bellino, E. (2011), 'Employment and income distribution from a Classical-Keynesian point of view: some tools to ground a normative analysis', in E. Brancaccio and G. Fontana (eds),

The Global Economic Crisis: New Perspectives on the Critique of Economic Theory and Policy, Abingdon and New York, Routledge, pp. 298–315.

Bellofiore, R. (1989), 'A monetary labor theory of value', *Review of Radical Political Economics*, **21** (1–2), 1–26.

Bellofiore R., G. Forges Davanzati and R. Realfonzo (2000), 'Marx inside the circuit: discipline device, wage bargaining and unemployment in a sequential monetary economy', *Review of Political Economy*, **12** (1), 403–17.

Bossone, B. and A. Sarr (2002), 'A new financial system for poverty reduction and growth', International Monetary Fund Working Paper 02/178, Washington, DC.

Bossone B. and A. Sarr (2005), 'Non-credit money to fight poverty', in Fontana and Realfonzo (eds.), pp. 187–201.

Brancaccio, E. (2008), 'Solvency and labour effort in a monetary theory of production', *European Journal of Economic and Social Systems*, **21** (2), 195–211.

Costabile, L. (2005), 'Towards a non-conventional circuit approach: credit, microcredit and property rights', in Fontana and Realfonzo (eds.), pp. 203–16.

Costabile, L. (2007), 'Labour commanded: micro-credit, the employment relation, and the property rights constraint', *Economia Politica*, **24** (2), 183–206.

Fontana, G. (2000), 'Post Keynesians and circuitists on money and uncertainty: an attempt at generality', *Journal of Post Keynesian Economics*, **23** (1), 27–48.

Fontana, G. (2009), *Money, Uncertainty and Time*, Abingdon and New York: Routledge.

Fontana, G. and R. Realfonzo (eds) (2005), *The Monetary Theory of Production*, Basingstoke: Palgrave Macmillan.

Forges Davanzati, G. and A. Pacella (2010), 'Emulation, indebtedness and income distribution: a monetary theory of production approach', *Intervention. European Journal of Economics and Economic Policies*, **7** (1), 145–65.

Forges Davanzati, G., A. Pacella and R. Realfonzo (2009), 'Fiscal policy in the monetary theory of production: an alternative to the "new consensus" approach', *Journal of Post Keynesian Economics*, **31** (4), 605–21.

Forges Davanzati G. and R. Realfonzo (2000), 'Wages, labour productivity and unemployment in a model of the monetary theory of production', *Économie Appliquée*, **53** (4), 117–38.

Forges Davanzati, G. and R. Realfonzo (2005), 'Bank mergers, monopoly power and unemployment: a monetary circuit approach', in Fontana and Realfonzo (eds), pp. 155–71.

Forges Davanzati, G. and R. Realfonzo (2009), 'Money, capital turnover and the leisure class. Thorstein Veblen's tips for MTP models', in J.F. Ponsot and S. Rossi (eds), *The Political Economy of Monetary Circuits*, Basingstoke: Palgrave Macmillan, pp. 116–37.

Forges Davanzati, G. and R. Realfonzo (2011), 'Low wages, consumer credit and the crisis: a monetary theory of production approach', in E. Brancaccio and G. Fontana (eds), *The Global Economic Crisis: New Perspectives on the Critique of Economic Theory and Policy*, Abingdon and New York: Routledge, pp. 144–63.

Forges Davanzati, G. and G. Tortorella Esposito (2010), 'Low wages, private indebtedness, and crisis. A monetary-theory-of-production approach', *European Journal of Economic and Social Systems*, **23** (1), 25–44.

Fumagalli, A. and S. Lucarelli (2008), 'Introduction', in 'Money and technological change: the role of financing in the process of evolution', *European Journal of Economic and Social Systems*, **21** (2), 151–63.

Graziani, A. (1990), 'The theory of monetary circuit', *Économies et Sociétés*, **24** (6), 7–36.

Graziani, A. (2003), *The Monetary Theory of Production*, Cambridge: Cambridge University Press.

Laudan, L. (1977), *Progress and Its Problems: Towards a Theory of Scientific Growth*, London: Routledge & Kegan Paul.

Messori, M. (2004), 'Credit and money in Schumpeter's theory', in R. Arena and N. Salvadori (eds), *Money, Credit and the Role of the State: Essays in Honour of Augusto Graziani*, Aldershot: Ashgate, pp. 175–202.

Messori, M. and A. Zazzaro (2005), 'Single-period analysis: financial markets, firms' failure and closure of the monetary circuit', in Fontana and Realfonzo (eds), pp. 111–23.

Pacella, A. (2008), 'The effects of labour market flexibility in the monetary theory of production', *Metroeconomica*, **59** (4), 608–32.

Pasinetti, L.L. (1962), 'Rate of profit and income distribution in relation to the rate of economic growth', *Review of Economic Studies*, **29** (4), 267–79.

Pasinetti, L.L. (1966), 'Changes in the rate of profit and switches of techniques', *Quarterly Journal of Economics*, **80** (4), 503–17.

Pasinetti, L.L. (1969), 'Switches of techniques and "the rate of return" in capital theory', *Economic Journal*, **79** (315), 508–31.

Pasinetti, L.L. (1974), *Growth and Income Distribution: Essays in Economic Theory*, Cambridge: Cambridge University Press.

Realfonzo R. (1998), *Money and Banking: Theory and Debate*, Cheltenham, UK and Northampton, MA, USA: Edward Elgar.

Realfonzo, R. (2006), 'The Italian circuitist approach', in P. Arestis and M. Sawyer (eds), *A Handbook of Alternative Monetary Economics*, Cheltenham, UK and Northampton, MA, USA: Edward Elgar, pp. 105–20.

Scazzieri, R. (2007), 'Back to the classics: labour productivity, technical progress and economic development', *Structural Change and Economic Dynamics*, **18** (2), 282–9.

Scazzieri, R. (2008), 'Reswitching of technique', in S. Durlauf and L. Blume (eds), *The New Palgrave Dictionary of Economics*, 2nd edn, Vol. 7, Basingstoke: Palgrave Macmillan, pp. 126–30.

Zezza, G. (2004), 'Some simple, consistent models of the monetary circuit', Working Paper No. 405, Levy Economics Institute of Bard College, Annandale-on-Hudson, NY.

Japan

John Maynard Keynes was a very famous economist in Japan even before the publication of the *General Theory*. His *Treatise on Money* (1930) had already been translated into Japanese in 1932–34 by Nisaburo Kito, and his *General Theory* (1936) was translated in 1941 by Tsukumo Shionoya. Korekiyo Takahashi is well known as the minister of finance who implemented a de facto Keynesian policy in 1932, before the publication of the *General Theory*, in order to resolve the 'Showa crisis' (that is, the Japanese result of the Great Depression).

In fact, Keynes's *General Theory* was translated into Japanese three times, first by Shionoya during the Second World War, then by his son Yuichi Shionoya in the 1980s, and more recently by Yosuke Mamiya in the 2000s. In the 1950s and 1960s, the main works of Joan Robinson, Michał Kalecki, Josef Steindl and Piero Sraffa were also translated into Japanese. At that time, Eiichi Asano, Mitsuharu Ito, Hiroshi Kawaguchi and Yoshikazu Miyazaki were well known as active Keynesian economists and Izumi Hishiyama was a prominent Sraffian economist. Toshiaki Hirai represents the younger generation of Keynesian scholars from the perspective of the history of economic thought in Japan. Thus Keynesian and Post Keynesian economics were quite popular in Japan from the beginning, but, up to the late 1970s, Japanese Keynesian and Post Keynesian economists were not well organized. The Japanese Society for Post Keynesian Economics (Post Keynes-ha Keizaigaku Kenkyu-kai: PK-ken) was established only relatively recently:

> The Japanese Society for Post Keynesian Economics was established in April 1980 in order to promote research into Post Keynesian economics in Japan and to stimulate communication among scholars who have an interest in Post Keynesian economics. The Society holds seminars (or meetings) about three times a year. The Society has a good partnership with Nihon Keizai Hyoronsha Ltd, a well-known publisher in Japan, which publishes a translation series on Post Keynesian economics. (Translated from the official home page)

The first book in this translation series was published in 1978 before the official establishment of the Society: Jan A. Kregel's *The Reconstruction of Political Economy* was translated by Toshio Ogata and Yoji Fukudagawa under the supervision of Hiroshi Kawaguchi. Up to 2010, 34 books had been translated into Japanese and published in this series, including books by Athanasios Asimakopulos, Victoria Chick, Paul Davidson, John Eatwell,

Duncan Foley, Richard M. Goodwin, Geoffrey C. Harcourt, Donald J. Harris, Richard Kahn, Nicholas Kaldor, Michał Kalecki, Peter Kriesler, Lynn Mainwaring, Hyman P. Minsky, Luigi L. Pasinetti, Joan Robinson, Malcolm C. Sawyer, Willi Semmler, Martin H. Wolfson and others.

Hiroshi Kawaguchi, who played an active role in establishing the Society, was Professor of Monetary Economics at Chuo University in Tokyo. At first the Society was based at Chuo University, but it was later relocated to Meiji University in Tokyo. Early active members included Tatsuhiko Aoki, Yuji Aruka, Eiichi Asano, Yoji Fukudagawa, Masahiko Hara, Yoshitaka Mori, Toshio Ogata, Shogo Sasahara and Katsumi Yamada. More recent members include Toichiro Asada, Yoriaki Fujimori, Yoshihiko Hakamata, Masao Ishikura, Denzo Kamiya, Manabu Kasamatsu, Ryuzo Kuroki, Kazuhiro Kurose, Yasutaka Niisato, Yasutoshi Noshita, Michiya Nozaki, Takashi Ohno, Yoshikazu Sato, Kazunori Watanabe, Yoshio Watanabe, Katsuyoshi Watarai, Takashi Yagi and Hiroyuki Yoshida.

Although the Society was founded by those who joined the translation series project, members regularly publish research papers and books. Most of these are written in Japanese, but some members publish papers in both English and Japanese, and the number of papers in English is increasing. During 2000–10, an average of 30 members attended every ordinary meeting. In September 2009, the Society held an international conference, 'The Ricardian–Post Keynesian Joint International Seminar' in Tokyo (organized by Takashi Yagi), attended by many internationally renowned Post Keynesian and neo-Ricardian economists, including Antonio d'Agata, Pierangelo Garegnani, Heinz Kurz and Neri Salvadori.

PK-ken is a free, open and loose organization with a varied membership, many of whom are also members of other economics organizations in Japan including JSHET (Japanese Society for the History of Economic Thought) and heterodox economics organizations such as JAFEE (Japan Association for Evolutionary Economics) and JSPE (Japan Society for Political Economy), as well as the mainstream JEA (Japanese Economic Association).

TOICHIRO ASADA

Joan Robinson's Economics

When Joan Robinson began to study economics in 1922, Marshallian theory, in the form of the version taught by A. C. Pigou, was economics in Cambridge (*CEP* I: vii; *CEP*, followed by the Roman number, stands for J.V. Robinson, *Collected Economic Papers*, Volumes I–V, Oxford:

Blackwell, 1951–79. Starred items indicate the second edition). In 1928–29 she attended the course on 'Advanced Theory of Value', given by Piero Sraffa – who was 'calmly committing the sacrilege of pointing out inconsistencies in Marshall' (*CEP* I: vii) – and met Richard Kahn, who was preparing his fellowship dissertation on the *Economics of the Short Period*; it was the beginning of a life-long collaboration.

Robinson's first publication, *Economics is a Serious Subject. The Apologia of an Economist to the Mathematician, the Scientist and the Plain Man*, was dedicated to Sraffa. By that time the book which was going to give her fame and academic respectability, *The Economics of Imperfect Competition*, was finished. Its starting-point was Sraffa's proposal 'to rewrite the theory of value, starting from the conception of the firm as a monopolist' (Robinson 1933 [1969], p. 6); its aim was to extend the marginal technique to all market forms. By this means she hoped to provide an answer to the challenge posed by Sraffa. However, twenty years later she repudiated the book as 'a blind alley' (Robinson 1978, p. x).

At the same time she was involved in the developments of Keynes's new ideas with the activity of the Cambridge 'Circus', which met between January and June 1931, writing two papers on issues being debated there. In 'A parable on saving and investment', she attacked Keynes's argument concerning the 'widow's cruse' contained in the *Treatise* because 'he was tacitly assuming that output was unchanged' (Robinson 1933 [1969], p. 82). In *The Theory of Money and the Analysis of Output* she urged Keynes to take the analysis of the *Treatise* to its logical conclusion, that is, that 'output may be in equilibrium at any number of different levels' (*CEP* I, p. 56). Finally, she was one of the recipients of the first proofs of the *General Theory*, which she commented on in June 1935.

Shortly afterwards she wrote some essays drawing 'a number of riders' from the *General Theory* (*CEP* V, pp. 185–6), which were published in 1937 with the title *Essays in the Theory of Employment*; in the same year she embarked on the project of writing a version of the *General Theory* suitable for teaching to first-year students, which became her *Introduction to the Theory of Employment*.

One of her articles collected in the *Essays* occasioned her encounter with Michał Kalecki (*CEP* V, p. 186). Robinson very soon realized that Kalecki's analysis was indeed as important as Keynes's, and took upon herself the task of 'blowing the trumpet for him' (ibid.); she later claimed that it was Kalecki, rather than herself, who 'brought imperfect competition in touch with the theory of employment' (Robinson 1933 [1969], p. viii).

Kalecki, who had drawn his inspiration from Marx's reproduction schemes, aroused her interest in them. She began to read Marx in 1940, with Maurice Dobb as 'tutor'. Her most substantial work on the subject,

An Essay on Marxian Economics, came out in 1942. The main conclusion of the book, while re-evaluating many points of Marxian analysis, was the rejection of Marx's value theory, and over the years she maintained a negative view of any attempt 'to solve the problem of transformation' (*CEP* I, p. 148).

The lesson drawn from the study of Marx in those years was later summed up by her with the sentence: 'For me, the main message of Marx was the need to think in terms of history, not of equilibrium' (Robinson 1973, p. x). The influence of Marx appears very clearly in her 1949 review of Harrod's *Towards a Dynamic Economics*, a book which threw in 'the challenge to develop a Keynesian analysis of accumulation in the long run' (*CEP* II*, p. iii).

The main programme of the 1950s in Cambridge was to develop a long-run analysis of accumulation, that is to develop an analysis 'which has freed itself from the need to assume conditions of static equilibrium' (*CEP* II*, p. iii). The stumbling-block to the dynamic analysis was given, according to her later recollection, by 'the lack of an adequate conception of the rate of profit' (*CEP* II*, p. vi). In fact, on the basis of Keynes's and Kalecki's theories of effective demand, the level of total profits can be determined, while to determine the rate of profit it is necessary to define the value of the stock of capital, but at the time 'no one seemed able to do' (Robinson 1978, p. xvi). She recorded having:

> innumerable discussions with Piero Sraffa but they always consisted in his heading off from errors; he would never say anything positive. Thus it was not till I found the 'corn economy' in his *Introduction* to Ricardo's *Principles* that I saw a gleam of light on the question of the rate of profit on capital. (Ibid., p. xvii)

The attempt to extend Keynes's short-period analysis to the theory of long-run development was thus conceived as a return to the 'classical' analysis of accumulation. Her famous books of the late 1950s and early 1960s, *Accumulation of Capital* (1956), *Exercises in Economic Analysis* (1960) and *Essays in the Theory of Economic Growth* (1962a) are directed against models of growth 'according as they exhibit some kind of inbuilt propensity to maintain full employment over the long run' (Robinson 1962a, p. 87). The 'golden-age method', that is, steady growth models with full employment, was provided to examine the relation between accumulation and the rate of profit (*CEP* V, p. 21). The difference between the equilibrium method and the 'historical' method was seen as a different treatment of time: 'To make a comparison between two situations, each with its own future and its own past, is not the same thing as to trace a movement from one to the other' (Robinson 1960, p. v).

The 'long struggle to escape' (*CEP* III*, p. 52) from a conception in which accumulation is seen as a substitution of labour for capital 'in a given state of technical knowledge' meant reinstating the possibility of the analysis of innovations and technical progress, as Adam Smith, David Ricardo and Karl Marx had done.

In her attempt to analyse the relationship between the rate of profit and the choice of techniques, Robinson was faced with the question of the meaning to be given to the expression 'quantity of capital'. In her 1953 article on 'The production function', and then in the *Accumulation of Capital*, she had invented a 'pseudo-production function', as Robert Solow later called it (*CEP* V, p. 82), in order to be able to list the techniques specified in a supposed 'book of blueprints', which represented the state of technical knowledge in a given point of time. The pseudo-production function was meant to show the possible equilibrium positions corresponding to different values of the rate of profit. So she encountered the phenomenon of reswitching, namely that:

> over certain ranges of a pseudo-production function the technique that becomes eligible at a higher rate of profit (with a correspondingly lower real wage-rate) may be less labour intensive (that is, may have a higher output per man employed) than that chosen at a higher wage rate, contrary to the rule of a 'well-behaved production function' in which a lower wage rate is always associated with a more intensive technique. (*CEP* IV, pp. 144–5)

With the publication in 1960 of Sraffa's *Production of Commodities by Means of Commodities* the basic tenets of his criticism of neoclassical theory could be seen more clearly. Sraffa's message has a twofold significance, according to Robinson: 'to knock out the marginal productivity theory' and to re-establish 'the classical doctrine that the rate of profit on capital depends upon the technical structure of production and the share of wages in net output' (*CEP* V, p. 95).

The conviction that it is possible to keep the scientific and ideological levels of analysis separate is at the core of Robinson's attitude to economics. In 1962 she presented her methodological ideas in *Economic Philosophy*, where she argued that in scientific discourse it is possible to distinguish empirical propositions from metaphysical propositions, as Karl Popper had maintained (Robinson 1962b, p. 3). Unfortunately, as she commented in her *Exercises in Economic Analysis*: 'Economics does not offer, like the well-developed natural sciences, a body of knowledge which the lay public can accept as established' (Robinson 1960, p. xv).

When she became Professor of Economics at Cambridge in 1965, she chose as the topic of her inaugural lecture, 'The new mercantilism', a denunciation of the mystique of free trade in historical practice and in the theoretical tradition since the time of Adam Smith (*CEP* IV, p. 4). She argued that contemporary neo-mercantilist philosophies and policies are always followed and theorized when the benefits of free trade are in danger (*CEP* IV, pp. 12–13).

In the early 1970s Robinson came insistently to the question of identifying the *pars construens* of her thought 'in the classical tradition, revived by Sraffa, which flows from Ricardo through Marx, diluted by Marshall and enriched by the analysis of effective demand of Keynes and Kalecki' (Robinson 1973, p. xii). However, in the work of reconstruction she found herself in disagreement with some of her allies in the battle against neoclassical economics. One point in particular became central in the discussion, that is, the maintenance of a concept of a long-run equilibrium in the context of historical analysis (Robinson 1980, p. 128).

It is the criticism of the concept of equilibrium, not only of neoclassical equilibrium, which she sees as the legacy of Keynes; therefore the main instrument with which to attack the neoclassical theory should be the distinction between historical time and logical time. In this respect she found Sraffa's language in *Production of Commodities* limited, because what it is offered is 'a purely logical structure – an elaborate thought experiment. There is no causation and no change' (Robinson 1980, p. 132). This is why she sees it as more promising to begin again with Keynes, who discusses events 'in terms of processes taking place in actual history' (Robinson 1979, p. xiv).

At the end of her life Robinson became increasingly dissatisfied with economics and more and more disillusioned with it as a body of knowledge which could be used to solve problems in the real world. She was increasingly concerned with those fundamental issues which are obscured rather than clarified by contemporary economic theory. Her last paper, published posthumously, originally had a telling title, 'Spring cleaning': 'We should throw out all self-contradictory propositions, unmeasurable quantities and indefinable concepts and reconstruct a logical basis for analysis with what, if anything, remains' (Robinson 1985, p. 160).

This is the legacy that Robinson has handed down to us (see Marcuzzo et al. 1996; Marcuzzo 2001, 2002; Gibson 2005; Harcourt and Kerr 2009).

MARIA CRISTINA MARCUZZO

See also:

Cambridge Economic Tradition; Capital Theory; Growth and Income Distribution; Growth Theory; Kaleckian Economics; Sraffian Economics; Time in Economic Theory.

References

Gibson, B. (ed.) (2005), *Joan Robinson's Economics: A Centennial Celebration*, Cheltenham, UK and Northampton, MA, USA: Edward Elgar.

Harcourt, G. and P. Kerr (2009), *Joan Robinson*, Basingstoke: Palgrave Macmillan.

Marcuzzo, M.C. (2001), 'Joan Robinson: une quête passionnée de la rationalité', in G.C. Harcourt (ed.), *L'Économie rebelle de Joan Robinson*, Paris: L'Harmattan, pp. 27–58.

Marcuzzo, M.C. (2002), 'The writings of Joan Robinson', in G.C. Harcourt and P. Kerr (eds), *Joan Robinson. Archive Edition*, Vol I, Basingstoke: Palgrave Macmillan, pp. xxii–lxxiii.

Marcuzzo, M.C., L.L. Pasinetti and A. Roncaglia (eds) (1996), *The Economics of Joan Robinson*, London and New York: Routledge.

Robinson, J. (1933), 'A parable on saving and investment', *Economica*, **13** (39), 75–84.

Robinson, J. (1933 [1969]), *The Economics of Imperfect Competition*, London: Macmillan.

Robinson, J. (1956), *The Accumulation of Capital*, London: Macmillan.

Robinson, J. (1960), *Exercises in Economic Analysis*, London: Macmillan.

Robinson, J. (1962a), *Essays in the Theory of Economic Growth*, London: Macmillan.

Robinson, J. (1962b), *Economic Philosophy*, London: Watts.

Robinson, J. (1973), 'Preface' to J.A. Kregel, *The Reconstruction of Political Economy: An Introduction to Post-Keynesian Economics*, London: Macmillan, pp. ix–xiii.

Robinson, J. (1978), *Contributions to Modern Economics*, Oxford: Blackwell.

Robinson, J. (1979), *The Generalization of the General Theory and other Essays*, London: Macmillan.

Robinson, J. (1980), *Further Contributions to Modern Economics*, Oxford: Blackwell.

Robinson, J. (1985), 'The theory of normal prices and reconstruction of economic theory', in G.R. Feiwel (ed), *The Theory of Normal Prices and Reconstruction of Economic Theory*, London: Macmillan, pp. 157–65.

Journal of Post Keynesian Economics

Political economy experienced a revival in the 1960s in many nations of the world, leading to the inception of many associations with journals to support a growing number of adherents and fellow-travellers. Post Keynesians never developed their own formal (multinational) association, and it was not until the late 1970s that specifically Post Keynesian journals emerged, starting in the UK with the *Cambridge Journal of Economics* in 1977. In the same year, the father of Post Keynesian economics in the United States, Sidney Weintraub (1914–83), along with a former student, Paul Davidson, sent out invitations to potential subscribers to another new journal. To their 'shock' and 'amazement' they received cheques from more than 400 subscribers within a month of the mail-out (Davidson 1998, p. 3). The first issue of the *Journal of Post Keynesian Economics* (*JPKE*) thus emerged in the autumn of 1978, published by M.E. Sharpe of New York, with an eminent international Honorary Board of Editors, and the editors Davidson and Weintraub overseeing the journal through the usual four issues a year.

The first issue of the journal included an editorial 'Statement of purposes' (Editors 1978, pp. 3–7), which made it clear that the journal was to be concerned with 'innovative theoretical work that can shed fresh light on contemporary economic problems' while 'contest[ing the] orthodoxy' that dominates journals in the US. The editors believed that '[i]nnovative ideas on inflation and unemployment have been routinely suppressed by prominent journals'. Such ideas have tried to 'explain the real world' as well as 'provide a reliable guide to public policy'. They cite some of the greats from the distant past, such as Adam Smith, David Ricardo, Karl Marx, J.S. Mill, W.S. Jevons, Alfred Marshall and J.M. Keynes, as well as others such as Joan Robinson, Nicholas Kaldor, Richard Kahn, Michał Kalecki, Abba Lerner, J.K. Galbraith and Hyman Minsky, as forging the central intellectual spirit of Post Keynesian economics.

Such a 'spirit' or 'vision' was to incorporate a monetary theory of production, where financial relationships influence economic processes in the short and long runs ('money matters'), due to hysteresis, path dependency and fundamental uncertainty. Money matters because the financial system generates credit for productive and financial activities, and the holding of money and credit influences velocity, money supply and thus GDP. Special reference would be given in the journal to the problems of uncertainty, credit and demand affecting inflation, unemployment, corporate power, capital–labour relations, demand management tools and 'strategies to enhance the general welfare – in the elemental, benign sense of that elliptical concept'. Significantly, the editors added: 'It is not a new sect that we seek to foster; it is instead a reasoned debate with a fair shake for innovative, unorthodox attitudes. The term "Post Keynesian" will thus be *broadly* interpreted, spotlighting new problems and revealing new theoretical perspectives' (emphasis added).

Apart from general articles, the journal has included many interesting symposia, comments, book reviews, an editorial corner and a series of lively and humanistic academic biographies (written often by board member Geoffrey Harcourt). Since the death of Weintraub in 1983, Paul Davidson has been the sole editor and main force behind the journal. His views have some bearing on the content and trend of the journal. For instance, he has never been too impressed by Sraffian themes, and has sought to differentiate Keynes's message from that of Kalecki (although *both* have affected the *JPKE*). Through its 35-year history the journal has concentrated on relating the core theory of Post Keynesian economics – concerning money, uncertainty and demand – to new developments, trends or problems in the world. For instance, in the 1970s and 1980s it paid special attention to the problem of stagflation; during the 1990s and early 2000s more attention was given to financial crises plus global imbalances and conflicts; while in the late 2000s and early 2010s it scrutinized the nature and impact of the subprime crisis and recession, including policies to reactivate fiscal policy, eschew the Washington Consensus, and institutionalize an independent global currency and central bank (see *JPKE*, Volume 33, 2010).

The principal themes of the core theory encouraged by Davidson seem to be, wittingly or unwittingly, a symbolic *reflection* of the composition of the Honorary Board of Editors. A core theme running through the journal, as Philip Arestis says (quoting Kalecki (1899–1970)), is that 'Post Keynesian analysis firmly embraces the view that "the institutional framework of a social system is a basic element of its economic dynamics"' (*JPKE*, Summer 1989, p. 611). This reflects the concerns of (especially) board members Arestis, Galbraith (Chair), Gunnar Myrdal (1898–1987), Daniel Fusfeld (1922–2007), Robert Heilbroner (1919–2005), Hyman Minsky (1919–96), Wallace Peterson and Warren Samuels (1933–2011). Of prime importance in this respect is an understanding of capitalism as a system, comprising a mixed economy – state and corporations; a heterogeneous series of social classes – workers, capitalists and salaried professionals; a corporate system of big and small firms; a complex system of finance – including banks, institutional investors and central authority; and a series of nation-states, global institutions and networks.

The main institutional themes of the journal link, directly or indirectly, to the theory of circular and cumulative causation (CCC), emanating especially from board members Myrdal, Nicholas Kaldor (1908–86), and Anthony Thirlwall. According to CCC, the main institutions and sectors of the economic system link together in a complex circuit of cybernetic feedback and interaction. Supply and demand are interdependent. For instance, households are not only consumers but also investors in durable structures, while governments spend not only on consumption items but also on investment. This requires a detailed analysis of habits, social conventions, procedural rationality and a hierarchy of needs from basics to luxuries (including Veblen goods and conspicuous consumption). Investment demand is associated with economies of scale/scope, new technology, complex dynamics, changes in capacity utilization and structural change. A proper system of government spending enhances infrastructure, knowledge and organization. And the 'balance-of-payments constraint' recognizes the impact of import elasticities, world income, and non-price competition on economic growth. Demand is the prime mover of the CCC circuit, since it links to the creation of new needs and changes to the systems of production and distribution; and hence links productivity and exports through economies of scale, learning by doing and structural modifications to needs and technologies. (See the debate on 'Effective demand', *JPKE*, Spring 2001, pp. 375–440; and the 'Symposium' on 'Thirlwall's Law and the BOPC', *JPKE*, Spring 1997, pp. 311–86.)

A primary source of change in a Post Keynesian world that is copiously developed in the journal is fundamental uncertainty, or non-ergodic dynamics; a theme expounded by Davidson as well as *JPKE* board members Donald Katzner, Minsky, G.L.S. Shackle (1903–92) and Douglas

Vickers. In their view, investment is largely affected by the prevailing business climate and demand, especially the degree of confidence in the future, and hence expected profits, as in chapter 12 of Keynes's *General Theory of Employment, Interest and Money* (1936). The future, however, is unknown and therefore uncertain (rather than strictly probabilistic): the greater the level of uncertainty the lower the expected rate of profit and rate of investment. Firms engage in routines, organizations and institutions, such as accounting notions of cash flow, net worth and mark-up pricing, to provide stability and structured activity in a world of uncertainty. This enables firms to invest in capital goods and consumer goods production – based substantially on credit – with some degree of confidence that profits will flow from such activities. But, despite all this, fundamental uncertainty and ignorance about the future still prevail, which periodically lead to booms and recessions of varying magnitudes. (See the 'Symposium' on 'Investment', *JPKE*, Summer 1992, pp. 423–96; the issue mainly on 'Uncertainty', Fall 1993, pp. 3–54; and the Spring 1996 issue.)

Editor Davidson has published a lot on demand and supply equations and conditions that are interdependent. The supply side links to work on non-price competition, 'degree of monopoly', mark-up pricing principles and the megacorp, especially by board members Alfred Eichner (1937–88), Fred Lee, J. Barkley Rosser Jr, Malcolm Sawyer and Nina Shapiro. National income, equating price level (p) times output (q), from the supply side (Y_s), equals:

$$Y_s = pq = (\kappa w/A)q.$$

Weintraub explained inflation through a wage–cost mark-up equation, $p = \kappa w/A$, where κ is the average mark-up of prices over unit wage (variable) costs, w/A, w the average money-wage rate and A the average product per worker. The mark-up by firms, κ, is said to be remarkably stable, dependent mainly on the relationship between wages and labour productivity (*JPKE*, Winter 1981–82, pp. 291–300). Inflation has thus been linked in the *JPKE* to wages upwardly deviating from productivity, leading firms to increase their prices accordingly.

National income in nominal terms, from the demand side (Y_d), includes workers' wages (W) and capitalists' profit (Π); which equals consumption (C) investment (I) government budget deficit (GD) and the trade surplus (TS):

$$Y_d = W + \Pi = C + I + GD + TS.$$

In simple Kaleckian models, workers spend all of their income, and capitalists receive what they spend. More complex models have been developed where workers and capitalists do not spend all their income. In the simple model, aggregate profit equals the consumption of capitalists plus investment plus the budget deficit and the trade surplus. Workers press for wage claims in the industrial relations arena, while firms seek claims through their target price mark-ups (*JPKE*, Fall 1991, pp. 93–110). The *JPKE* has published papers supporting the 'conflicting claims' theory, where inflation is due to aggregate nominal income claims – wages and profits – exceeding the total available income.

The *JPKE* specializes in developing endogenous explanations for economic phenomena, such as the creation of credit, business cycles, asset prices, financial crises and exchange rate instabilities. This material reveals that during business cycle upswings – such as 1984–87, 1996–2000 (1992–97 in parts of Asia) and 2004–07 – the generation of euphoria leads to a high rate of investment, as well as a stock market (and other assets) boom, financed largely by endogenous credit. According to Hyman Minsky's 'distance memory hypothesis', firms typically forget about previous financial crises and recessions and get caught up in the euphoric environment. Traders speculated in the late 1990s and 2000, for instance, about 'new rules to the game', and technology stocks not needing fundamentals in the 'new business environment', which supposedly 'justified' further credit expansion. The journal has explored endogenous money and credit responding to higher demand through instruments such as bank bills, certificates of deposit, capital inflow, financial innovations and reserve bank 'accommodation'. Forces endogenous to the upswing bring about a collapse of prospective yield, greater uncertainty, a speculative bubble crash, a declining rate of investment demand and financial crises: for instance, during 2000–02 and 2007–11 as euphoria turned to pessimism and recession (*JPKE*, Spring 1990; Winter 2000–01; Fall 2010; see Harvey 2010).

This leads the journal to concentrate on policies that moderate the instabilities of the business cycle, such as incomes policies, global institutions, basic income schemes, prudential financial policies and organizational arrangements (see *JPKE*, Winter 1997–98, Spring 2000, Summer 2000, Spring 2010). A recurring global policy proposal is monetary reform where the onus is on (current account) surplus nations increasing their effective demand, thereby restoring some degree of world balance. A cooperative global approach to balance-of-payments problems is seen to be better than one where deficit nations bear the brunt of adjustment through fiscal and monetary deflation (see *JPKE*, Summer 2004). The cooperative policy of enhancing productive aggregate demand is likely to moderate various conflicts, including distributional anomalies, war, terrorism and crime through the provision of global and regional stability, trust and accord.

While throughout most of the life of the journal Paul Davidson has taken a 'broad church' editorial approach to Post Keynesian economics, *personally* he prefers a more fundamentalist 'Keynes' approach to uncertainty, demand and policy making. Attempting to develop a school with greater coherence, he believes that a 'small tent' grouping is better. Davidson's (2003–04) narrower vision was explained in response to John King's (2002) history of the school, where King places Sraffian, Kaleckian and Minskian elements firmly within the Post Keynesian tradition, and advocates a united approach; as do Marc Lavoie, Fred Lee and many others. Davidson's reply is that none of these influences is Post Keynesian, since Sraffian approaches are not based on a real money economy, Kaleckians do not assume fundamental uncertainty and are based on rigidity of prices, while Minsky did not utilize Keynes's aggregate demand and supply framework. It seems strange for Davidson to conclude this when the editorial board and the journal has always had these broader influences embedded in the Post Keynesian mantle. Nevertheless it does raise important issues about coherence and the ability of a broad church of heterodox political economists to enhance the theoretical and empirical edifice of inquiry. (See *JPKE*, Winter 2003–04, Spring 2005, Spring 2010.)

Over the past 35 years the *Journal of Post Keynesian Economics* has been instrumental in promoting theoretical and policy insights that enhance the democratic and participatory workings of the economy in the pursuit of full employment and price stability. It has tracked and critically analysed the contemporary economic performance of US and world economies. The journal has done well to propagate a coherent alternative analysis of economic theory and policy in a difficult 'era of neoliberalism'. Advances in knowledge have been made in relation to a monetary theory of production, set in an environment of fundamental uncertainty, circular and cumulative causation and with interdependencies between supply and demand. The editor has encouraged the building of empirical evidence, the linking of theory and practice, and the development of policy prescriptions that are innovative yet relatively pragmatic; but always inspired by the need for fundamental reforms of capitalism. The ability of 'the journal' to withstand editorial, systemic and disciplinary instabilities, and progress further, will influence the future of Post Keynesian economics in the United States and elsewhere.

PHILLIP ANTHONY O'HARA

See also:

Galbraith's Economics.

References

Davidson, P. (1998), 'Twenty years old and growing stronger every day', *Journal of Post Keynesian Economics*, **21** (1), 3–5.

Davidson, P. (2003–04), 'Setting the record straight on *A History of Post Keynesian Economics*', *Journal of Post Keynesian Economics*, **26** (2), 245–72.

Editors (1978), 'A statement of purposes', *Journal of Post Keynesian Economics*, **1** (1), 3–7.

Harvey, J. (2010), 'Modeling financial crises: a schematic approach', *Journal of Post Keynesian Economics*, **33** (1), 61–81.

King, J.E. (2002), *A History of Post Keynesian Economics Since 1936*, Cheltenham, UK and Northampton, MA, USA: Edward Elgar.

Kaldorian Economics

Nicholas (Miklos) Kaldor (1908–86) was one of the most original and controversial economists of the twentieth century. The *Economist* newspaper once described him as 'the best known economist in the world not to have received the Nobel Prize'. In the 1930s and 1940s he made fundamental contributions to the theory of the firm, welfare economics, trade cycle theory, capital theory and Keynesian economics. In the 1950s, he turned his fertile mind to public finance and to growth and distribution theory, and was the joint architect with Joan Robinson and Richard Kahn of the Post Keynesian school of economics which extended Keynesian modes of thinking to the long run. Then in the 1960s he turned his attention to the applied economics of growth and initiated an enormous secondary literature related to the idea of manufacturing industry as the engine of growth based on static and dynamic increasing returns to scale. In the 1970s, he led worldwide the assault on the doctrine of monetarism which, as he described it, spread with the virulence of a plague from North America under the influence of Milton Friedman to infect academic thinking and policy making in several parts of the world, including most notably the United Kingdom during the government of Margaret Thatcher in the 1980s. He lost the battle but won the war because monetarism as a coherent intellectual doctrine is now dead.

It is clear from the above that Kaldor led several lives as an economist; his range of interests was wide, but he also had a vision of how capitalist economies function and a strong intuition concerning what is important and what is unimportant, what is cause and what is effect. There is a Kaldorian economics and an interesting story to tell.

Kaldor was Hungarian by birth. As a boy he attended the famous Minta school in Budapest, and then at the age of 17 attended the Humboldt University in Berlin to study economics for eighteen months before coming to the London School of Economics (LSE) in 1927, where he fell under the influence of Allyn Young (who tragically died in 1929 aged 53) and then of Lionel Robbins and (later) Friedrich von Hayek. In 1930 he graduated with first-class honours and stayed on at the LSE first as a research assistant and then as an assistant lecturer. The Keynesian revolution was still six years off, and his early research work was in the Austrian tradition – an analysis, for example, of the overcommitment of Austrian industry and the problem of the Danubian states. It was not long, however, before Kaldor crossed swords with Robbins and Hayek and became one of the first converts at the LSE to the thinking in Keynes's *General Theory*, along with Abba Lerner and Ursula Hicks. While Kaldor disagreed with some of the details of the *General Theory*, and made important contributions himself to its understanding, he never wavered from the thrust of its central message that monetary production economies are fundamentally different from barter economies, and that unemployment can exist for long periods of time even in the presence of wage and price flexibility, because of uncertainty associated with the peculiar properties of money.

Kaldor's first major theoretical contributions came in 1934–35 with four papers: 'A classificatory note on the determinateness of equilibrium', in which he was the first to coin the term 'cobweb theorem' to describe oscillations around an equilibrium; 'The equilibrium of the firm'; 'Mrs. Robinson's "Economics of imperfect competition"'; and 'Market imperfections and excess capacity'. In the next five years, including the first year of the war, there appeared a further spate of papers in diverse fields (Thirlwall 1987 and Targetti 1992 contain a full bibliography). There was his major survey of capital theory; his attack on A.C. Pigou's theory of how wage cuts affect unemployment – it must be through a reduction in the rate of interest; his critique of Edward Chamberlin and the distinction between monopolistic and imperfect competition; his debate with Hayek over capital intensity and the trade cycle; his introduction of compensation tests into welfare economies; his classic paper 'Speculation and economic stability', which John Hicks described in personal correspondence as 'the culmination of the Keynesian revolution in theory – you ought to have got more honour for it' (Thirlwall 1987, p. 75 n. 46); and his 1940 nonlinear model of the trade cycle.

During the Second World War, the LSE was evacuated to Cambridge, and Kaldor became more acquainted with the Cambridge economists, particularly Joan Robinson, Richard Kahn, Piero Sraffa, Pigou and Keynes himself. He spent most of the war years working on aspects of public policy, both national and international, related both to the war and preparations for the peace. In particular, he played a major role in the analysis and thinking behind the two Beveridge Reports, on Social Insurance (in 1942) and *Full Employment in a Free Society* (in 1944), and also the construction of national income accounts, then in their infancy. He emerged from the war with a high reputation as an incisive applied economist, which led to his appointment to several international commissions, and then in 1947 as Research Director of the Economic Commission for Europe in Geneva headed by Gunnar Myrdal. In 1949 he returned to Cambridge as a Fellow of King's College and a member of the Economics Faculty, where he remained for the rest of his life.

His interest in public finance, and particularly tax matters, deepened when he was appointed in 1951, along with John Hicks, to the Royal Commission on the Taxation of Profits and Income. Kaldor was the author of a trenchant Minority Report and also a classic book entitled *An Expenditure Tax*, arguing the case for taxing expenditure rather than income, both on grounds of equity and as a means of promoting growth. His tax expertise was later sought in several developing countries, and led to his appointment in the United Kingdom as a special tax adviser to the Chancellor of the Exchequer in two Labour governments (1964–69 and 1974–76).

Despite his multifarious contributions to economic theory and policy, Kaldor will be remembered in the history of economic thought largely for his work in growth economics and his challenge to equilibrium theory. In the mid-1950s and early 1960s there was his pioneering work on growth and distribution theory. In the mid-1960s there was his innovative thinking on the applied economics of growth, and then from the 1970s to his death there was his constant assault on the assumptions, predictions and usefulness of the Walrasian, general equilibrium framework of analysis for an understanding of the dynamics of capitalism in the real world. What are the mainsprings of growth in developed and developing countries? Does it make sense to separate capital accumulation and technical progress as in mainstream neoclassical growth theory? Why does the capital–output ratio remain roughly constant despite an ever-increasing ratio of capital to labour? Why does fast growth seem to be associated with industrialization? What determines the growth of industry in a closed economy (including the world) and in an open economy? Why is there a tendency for levels of development between regions and countries to become polarized, contrary to the predictions of neoclassical growth theory? These are the major questions that Kaldor attempted to answer in a series of profound and provocative papers over 40 years (Kaldor 1956, 1957, 1961, 1966, 1970, 1972, 1996).

In 1956, Kaldor revolutionized the theory of the functional distribution of income by showing that the share of profits in national income must be related to the share of investment in national income and the propensity to save out of wages and profits, and that the orthodox neoclassical theory of distribution based on relative factor prices and quantities is not only theoretically fraught with problems, but, in any case, unnecessary. The Kaldor theory of distribution is beautiful in its simplicity. Let full-employment income (Y) be divided between consumption (C) and investment (I), with consumption out of wages equal to $c_w W$ and consumption out of profits equal to $c_p P$ (where W is wages, P is profits and c_w and c_p are the propensities to consume out of wages and profits, respectively). Therefore, $Y = c_w W + c_p P + I$. But $P = Y - W$. Therefore $P = c_p P + I - s_w W$, where s_w is the propensity to save out of wages. The share of profits in income is therefore equal to $P/Y = (I/Y)/(s_p - s_w) - s_w/(s_p - s_w)$, where s_p is the propensity to save out of profits. Profits must be the dependent variable and investment the independent variable because capitalists can decide what to invest but they cannot decide what they earn.

Kaldor's 1957 and 1961 growth models introduce the innovation of the technical progress function (TPF) to replace the neoclassical production function, which makes what is an artificial distinction between movements along a function and shifts in the whole function. Kaldor was adamant that capital accumulation and technical progress go together; most technical progress requires capital accumulation for its embodiment and there is unlikely to be much new capital accumulation without technical progress. The TPF relates the rate of growth of output per worker (r) to the rate of growth of capital per worker (k). In linear form: $r = a + b(k)$. The position of the function (a) depends on 'autonomous' productivity growth (for example, learning by doing) and the slope of the function (b) depends on the technical dynamism of the economy. Equilibrium growth at a constant capital–output ratio is given by $r = a/(1 - b)$. Countries grow at different rates with the same capital–output ratio because of differences in the parameters of the technical progress function. The TPF is important not only because it provides a more realistic representation of the growth process, but also because it provides an explanation of why the capital–output ratio is no higher in rich countries than in poor countries, contrary to the prediction of orthodox neoclassical growth theory; countries are simply on different TPFs. Kaldor's TPF is thus the precursor, and true progenitor, of 'new' growth theory (or endogenous growth theory), which also seeks to explain why the marginal product of capital apparently does not fall as countries get richer and invest more. There are 'technological forces' that keep the capital–output ratio from rising, such as human capital formation, research and development and technological spillovers from trade.

Kaldor was not made a professor at Cambridge until 1966, aged 58, but in his famous Inaugural Lecture (Kaldor 1966) he turned his attention to the applied economics of growth and presented a series of growth laws which have subsequently been widely tested in different contexts. Kaldor's thesis was that manufacturing industry is the engine of growth for two major reasons. First, manufacturing industry is subject to increasing returns, which other sectors are not (at least to the same extent, and certainly not agriculture). This hypothesis is also known as Verdoorn's law (see McCombie et al. 2002), which Kaldor revived, it having lain effectively dormant for 17 years. Second, manufacturing industry generates fast growth because it draws resources in from sectors where the marginal product is less than the average, so that productivity growth is induced outside of the manufacturing sector. Today, the evidence for Kaldor's laws is most clearly seen in the newly industrializing countries of South East Asia, where GDP growth is rapid and the share of manufacturing industry in GDP is also rising fast.

But what determines the growth of industry? In the open economy it is the growth of exports in a circular and cumulative process (Kaldor 1970), although subject to a balance-of-payments constraint. In the closed economy, such as the world economy, it is land-saving innovations in agriculture that are crucial for industrial growth (and the performance of developed countries) as an offset to diminishing returns. In his 1986 Hicks Lecture on 'Limits to growth' (and elsewhere: for example, Kaldor 1996), he emphasizes the importance of an equilibrium terms of trade between the two sectors of agriculture and industry (developing and developed countries) for maximizing the growth rate of the economy as a whole.

In all these fields of theoretical and empirical enquiry mentioned above, Kaldor attracted many disciples, but also many adversaries. Academic hostility came from asking awkward questions about neoclassical economics in general and equilibrium theory in particular, and was understandably most prevalent in the USA. Kaldor's legacy to the profession is nearly 200 articles, pamphlets and books, many of the former being collected in his nine volumes of *Collected Essays*. Although he wrote no grand treatise, these volumes provide a lasting testimony and monument to the energy, creativity and endeavour of one of the greatest economists of the twentieth century. There are three main intellectual biographies of Kaldor: Thirlwall (1987), Targetti (1992) and King (2009).

A.P. THIRLWALL

See also:

Balance-of-payments-constrained Economic Growth; Cambridge Economic Tradition; Equilibrium and Non-equilibrium; Growth and Income Distribution; Growth Theory; Income Distribution.

References

Kaldor, N. (1956), 'Alternative theories of distribution', *Review of Economic Studies*, **23** (2), 83–100.
Kaldor, N. (1957), 'A model of economic growth', *Economic Journal*, **67** (268), 591–624.
Kaldor, N. (1961), 'Capital accumulation and economic growth', in F. Lutz (ed.), *The Theory of Capital*, London: Macmillan, pp. 177–222.
Kaldor, N. (1966), *Causes of the Slow Rate of Economic Growth of the United Kingdom*, Cambridge: Cambridge University Press.
Kaldor, N. (1970), 'The case for regional policies', *Scottish Journal of Political Economy*, **17** (3), 337–48.
Kaldor, N. (1972), 'The irrelevance of equilibrium economics', *Economic Journal*, **82** (328), 1237–55.

Kaldor, N. (1996), *Causes of Growth and Stagnation in the World Economy* (Mattioli Lectures), Cambridge: Cambridge University Press.
King, J.E. (2009), *Nicholas Kaldor*, Basingstoke: Palgrave Macmillan.
McCombie, J., M. Pugno and B. Soro (2002), *Productivity Growth and Economic Performance: Essays on Verdoorn's Law*, Basingstoke: Palgrave.
Targetti, F. (1992), *Nicholas Kaldor*, Oxford: Clarendon Press.
Thirlwall, A.P. (1987), *Nicholas Kaldor*, Brighton: Harvester Wheatsheaf.

Kaleckian Economics

Kaleckian economics may be broadly defined as the economic theories enunciated by Michał Kalecki (1899–1970), and the extensions of those theories by economists who were influenced by him. Kalecki was a Polish engineer and mathematician who taught himself economics in a left-wing political milieu during the 1920s, where the main intellectual influences were Austro-Marxism, Rosa Luxemburg, Mikhail Tugan-Baranovsky and Henryk Grossman. From 1929 to 1936 he was employed at the Institute for Research in Business Cycles and Prices in Warsaw, where the first national income statistics for Poland were constructed. In 1933 he published his first analysis of the business cycle under capitalism, arguing that it was due to the instability of investment, which in turn was caused by fluctuations in capitalists' profits. Investment was crucial. In a capitalist economy, in Kalecki's view, investment is the main determinant of aggregate demand. Investment also determines profits, where capitalists' costs are mainly accounted for by wages, which are by and large consumed. This was summarized in an aphoristic précis of Kalecki's theory (attributed by some to Joan Robinson, and by others to Nicholas Kaldor): 'Workers spend what they earn, capitalists earn what they spend'. This can easily be derived from the well-known Keynesian savings identity, in which saving (S) is by definition equal to gross investment (I), plus the fiscal deficit (government expenditure minus taxation, $G - T$), plus the trade surplus (exports minus imports, $X - M$). Assume that there are only two classes in society, capitalists and workers, earning profits and wages respectively, which can be saved or consumed. (Alternatively, it can be assumed that the other classes derive their incomes and expenditure from the expenditure and incomes of the two defining classes of capitalism.)

The saving identity therefore represents workers' and capitalists' saving (S_w and S_c):

$$S = I + (G - T) + (X - M) = S_w + S_c.$$

If workers' saving is deducted from both sides of the equation, then the saving identity shows only capitalists' saving:

$$S_c = I + (G - T) + (X - M) - S_w.$$

Since profits can only saved or consumed, adding capitalists' consumption (C_c) to the right-hand side of the equation gives an expression for profits (P):

$$P = C_c + S_c = I + (G - T) + (X - M) + C_c - S_w.$$

Profits are therefore equal to gross investment, plus the fiscal deficit, plus the trade surplus, plus capitalists' consumption, minus workers' saving. The greater is capitalists' expenditure on investment or their own consumption, or the fiscal deficit, or the expenditure of foreign residents on exports, the greater will be profits. Higher profits will tend to result in higher investment until excess capacity emerges and investment is reduced, causing profits to fall and a decline in economic activity to continue until excess capacity is eliminated and investment starts to rise. Higher profits then finance higher investment and stimulate a boom in economic activity.

In 1936 Kalecki left Poland for Stockholm and eventually for London, where Joan Robinson recruited him to Keynes's circle. Kalecki was critical of Keynes's reasoning, highlighting in particular the ephemeral character of the Keynesian short-period equilibrium, and the inadequacy of Keynes's theory of investment. These criticisms reveal the business-cycle approach that Kalecki took to economic analysis, by comparison with the Marshallian equilibrium methodology of Keynes. Kalecki participated in research on the business cycle at Cambridge, before transferring to Oxford in 1940. At Oxford, Kalecki made his mark with his contribution to discussions on rationing, war finance and, later, the possibilities of full employment under capitalism. At this time he developed his pricing analysis, in which the mark-up over prime costs is determined by imperfect competition, and an analysis of corporate finance in which external finance is a liability that enhances financial risks, as well as providing liquidity. After the Second World War, Kalecki worked for nearly 10 years for the United Nations, where he studied in detail the problems of developing countries. Out of this, in later years, came an analysis of economic development focusing on financial bottlenecks to capital accumulation in the developing countries, in a context of socio-economic 'structural' obstacles, poverty, rural backwardness and deficient food supply, to capitalist primary accumulation. In 1955 Kalecki returned to Poland. In the dislocation caused by Stalinist overinvestment, he emphasized the limited effectiveness of investment because of the need to maintain adequate levels of consumption and avoid excessive imports. He was a strong critic of market socialism, arguing that market mechanisms are less efficient than an effectively adjusted and centralized investment programme. Kalecki and his associates fell out of favour in the later 1960s, and succumbed to an anti-Semitic purge in 1968.

In the years after Keynes's death, Joan Robinson championed Kalecki's work for its radical criticism of capitalism, namely that capitalism is unstable (the business cycle), tends to regressive distributional values (cost-minimization holds down wages, while high profits are necessary to maintain investment), and is hostile to full employment (because it undermines labour discipline) (Robinson 1966). Kalecki's exposition of his analysis in the form of mathematical models based on national income identities made his work attractive to the first generation of Keynesian model-builders, in particular Lawrence Klein and David Worswick. They were attracted by models which gave a more systematic account of business cycles than Keynes's (Klein 1947).

During the 1950s Kalecki was influential in the monopoly capitalism school of Marxists, through the work of Paul Sweezy and Josef Steindl. Kalecki's analysis shows how the problem of realizing surplus value as profits, in twentieth-century capitalism, was alleviated by corporate investment and deficit spending by governments. At the same time, the absence of competition gives capitalists monopoly profits, which make excess capacity more tolerable. Such excess capacity in turn reduces the capitalists' inclination to invest, causing a tendency to economic stagnation (Steindl 1952; Baran and Sweezy 1966).

Kalecki's ideas were at the forefront of the emergence of Post Keynesian economics during the 1970s. Here Kaleckian economics provided a clear and consistent alternative to the neoclassical synthesis of Keynesian ideas with Walrasian general equilibrium. Kalecki could provide not only a theory of the business cycle (an essential element of any economic analysis after the return of economic instability to capitalism in the 1970s), but also microeconomic foundations, which are largely absent in Keynes's *General Theory*. Their absence had facilitated the neoclassical and monetarist interpretation of Keynesian unemployment as being due to wage inflexibility. Kalecki provided a more radical microeconomic explanation, in terms of monopoly and excess capacity reducing the propensity to invest out of profits (Sawyer 1985; King 1996; Lopez and Assous 2010). In this way Post Keynesian analysis spliced Kalecki's price and business-cycle theory onto more orthodox Keynesian monetary theory and concerns about aggregate demand and full employment.

However, Post Keynesians have, by and large, preferred to overlook two aspects in which the work of Kalecki and Keynes are less than compatible. The first of these arises out of their respective treatment of expectations and uncertainty. Expectations play a central role in Keynes's explanation of the instability of investment, to which both theorists attributed the business cycle. In Kalecki's view, business confidence is largely determined by current profits, so that further analysis of the subjective elements entering into businessmen's expectations is unnecessary. Uncertainty then plays a crucial role in Keynes's liquidity preference theory of money. Coming from outside the Marshallian tradition, Kalecki did not find it necessary to postulate any aggregate demand for and supply of money, outside the wholesale money markets, and he took it to be a central feature of capitalism that the banking system, or intra-business credit arrangements (trade bills and so on), accommodate business demand for credit. Money is therefore endogenous to the system, and uncertainty is less important in portfolio demand for money (Keynes's 'speculative' demand for money) than changes in short-term interest rates, relative to the long-term rate of interest.

Kalecki was also critical of Keynes's emphasis on the long-term rate of interest (the yield on long-term bonds) as a determinant of investment. That rate of interest was shown to be relatively stable, and therefore was of little use in explaining the instability of investment. Keynes resolved this problem by arguing that the expected return on investment that is in excess of the long-term rate of interest (his marginal efficiency of capital) is volatile, and therefore accounts for the instability of investment. Kalecki argued instead that investment is volatile because the internal liquidity of the corporate sector that is free of external financial liabilities (and is therefore available for investment without creditor's or debtor's risk) fluctuates with profits and the degree of external financing. This is Kalecki's 'principle of increasing risk'.

The principle derives from the work of an early collaborator, Marek Breit. It states that the financial risk of a business is determined by the ratio of that business's external borrowing in relation to the internal funds of the business (the money put into the business by the firm's managers and shareholders plus accumulated retained profits). The rate of interest that banks will charge on their lending to a business will therefore increase with the balance-sheet gearing (ratio of external indebtedness to internal funds) of the business. Kalecki drew two conclusions from this. First, the amount of investment that a firm may undertake is limited by the internal funds that a firm has and the limited borrowing that it allows. In aggregate, therefore, investment in the economy is determined by the liquidity of the non-financial business sector, rather than by the rate of interest on risk-free lending. Second, as Steindl was to detail, the principle explains the size distribution of firms at any one time (Steindl 1945, 1965). In the early 1960s W.H. Locke Anderson made a pioneering study in which he verified the validity of this principle (Anderson 1964). The chief exponent of Post Keynesianism as a theory of finance capital, Hyman Minsky, used

Kalecki's theory of the business cycle and, less explicitly, the principle of increasing risk. However, Minsky developed his own analysis of investment financing based on Keynesian expectations and Irving Fisher's debt deflation theory of economic depressions (Minsky 1986).

While Post Keynesians have tended to use Kalecki's analysis selectively to fill the lacunae in Keynes's economics, and the collapse of Communism has seriously limited the interest in Kalecki's economics of socialism, recurrent economic crises in developing and newly industrialized countries, and volatile financial conditions in the older capitalist countries offer scope for new developments in, and applications of, Kalecki's economics. This is most apparent in the work of Marc Lavoie (1992) and in the work of some of the German 'monetary Keynesians' (for example, Riese 2004).

JAN TOPOROWSKI

See also:

Business Cycles; Expectations; Financial Instability Hypothesis; Prices and Pricing; Profits; Socialism; Uncertainty; Underconsumption.

References

Anderson, W.H.L. (1964), *Corporate Finance and Fixed Investment: An Econometric Study*, Cambridge, MA: Harvard University Press.
Baran, P.A. and P.M. Sweezy (1966), *Monopoly Capital: An Essay on the American Economic and Social Order*, New York: Monthly Review Press.
Kalecki, M. (1990–97), *Collected Works of Michał Kalecki*, 7 vols, edited by Jerzy Osiatyński, Oxford: Clarendon Press.
King, J.E. (ed.) (1996), *An Alternative Macroeconomic Theory: The Kaleckian Model and Post-Keynesian Economics*, Boston, MA: Kluwer.
Klein, L.R. (1947), *The Keynesian Revolution*, New York: Macmillan.
Lavoie, M. (1992), *Foundations of Post-Keynesian Economic Analysis*, Aldershot, UK and Brookfield, VT, USA: Edward Elgar.
Lopez, J. and M. Assous (2010), *Michał Kalecki*, Basingstoke: Palgrave Macmillan.
Minsky, H.P. (1986), *Stabilizing an Unstable Economy*, New Haven, CT: Yale University Press.
Riese, H. (2004), *Money, Development and Economic Transformation*, Basingstoke: Palgrave.
Robinson, J. (1966), 'Kalecki and Keynes', in *Economic Dynamics and Planning: Essays in Honour of Michał Kalecki*, Oxford: Pergamon Press, pp. 335–41.
Sawyer, M.C. (1985), *The Economics of Michał Kalecki*, London: Macmillan.
Steindl, J. (1945), *Small and Big Business: Economic Problems of the Size Distribution of Firms*, Oxford: Blackwell.
Steindl, J. (1952), *Maturity and Stagnation in American Capitalism*, Oxford: Blackwell.
Steindl, J. (1965), *Random Processes and the Growth of Firms: A Study of the Pareto Law*, London: Charles Griffin.

Keynes's *General Theory*

Most economists recognize that Keynes's 1936 book, *The General Theory of Employment, Interest and Money*, was revolutionary. Unfortunately there is not a consensus as to what was revolutionary about this volume (Davidson 2009).

Some economists have argued that the aggregate accounting scheme used by Keynes was the revolutionary aspect. But Simon Kuznets had developed a system of aggregate income accounts by 1929, long before Keynes was even thinking about a general theory of employment, interest and money.

Many Old and New Keynesians believe that the Keynesian revolution is nested in supply-side market imperfections that result in the rigidity of money wages and prices, asymmetric information and lack of transparency. But throughout the nineteenth century classical economists had argued that monopoly elements in the market were the cause of unemployment and Keynes (1936, chapter 19) specifically denies that such supply-side elements are the fundamental cause of unemployment. Keynes claimed that it was on the demand side and not on the supply side that his revolution was embedded. Surely, then, price inflexibility was not a revolutionary idea in 1936.

Many scholars, for example Don Patinkin and Axel Leijonhufvud, have argued that Keynes's revolution was centred on the multiplier concept. Post Keynesians believe that there is a much more fundamental foundation for Keynes's revolution. After all, if the revolutionary essence was the multiplier, then the proper name would have been the Kahnian revolution, for Keynes merely transformed Kahn's employment multiplier measured in terms of employment units into an expenditure multiplier measured in either nominal or money-wage unit terms (ibid., p. 115). It would be hard to justify the canonization of Keynes in the economic literature if all he had done was to focus attention on a concept that a former student had developed and published years earlier.

Keynes (ibid., p. 192) was convinced that the assumption of less than perfect price flexibility made by the 'weaker [classical] spirits' was not necessary to explain persistent unemployment and that this assumption caused 'injury to . . . logical consistency'. Instead, Keynes developed an expanded demand classification system to demonstrate that Say's law 'is not the true law relating the aggregate demand and supply functions . . . [and hence] there is a vitally important chapter of economic theory which remains to be written and *without which all discussions concerning the volume of aggregate employment are futile*' (ibid., p. 26; italics added).

Say's law specifies that all expenditure (aggregate demand) on the products of industry is always exactly equal to the total costs of aggregate production (aggregate supply including gross profits). Letting D^w symbolize aggregate demand and Z^w aggregate supply (both measured in wage units, that is, nominal values deflated by the money-wage rate), then:

$$D^w = f_d(N) \tag{1}$$

and

$$Z^w = f_z(N). \tag{2}$$

Say's law asserts that:

$$f_d(N) = f_z(N) \tag{3}$$

'for all values of N, i.e., for all values of output and employment' (ibid., pp. 25–6; original stress). In other words, in an economy subject to Say's law, the total costs (including profits and rents) of the aggregate production of firms (whether in perfect competition or not) are recouped by the sale of output. There is never a lack of effective demand. The aggregate demand and aggregate supply curves coincide (see Figure 14). In a Say's law economy, there is never an obstacle to full employment, no matter what the degree of price flexibility in the system.

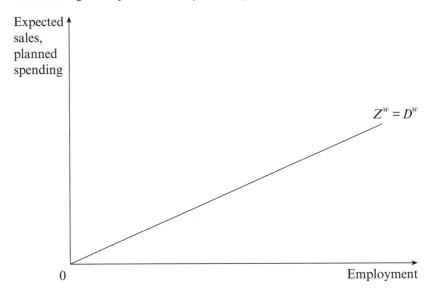

Figure 14   A Say's law economy

To develop the 'true law' relating D^w and Z^w for a monetary economy, Keynes produced a model where the aggregate demand and aggregate supply functions, $f_d(N)$ and $f_z(N)$, need not be coincident (see Figure 15); as the general case, there is no necessity for the determinants of the aggregate demand function to be identical with the determinants of aggregate supply.

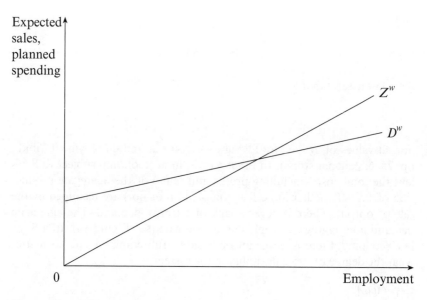

Figure 15   A Keynesian economy

Keynes differentiated his theory from classical economics by a taxonomic analysis of aggregate demand. As equation (1) suggests, classical theory fitted all expenditures into a single category, D^w, aggregate demand (which is created entirely by supply). Keynes, on the other hand, divided all types of expenditures into two demand classes, that is:

$$D^w = D_1^w + D_2^w = f_d(N),\qquad(4)$$

where D_1^w represented *all* expenditures which 'depend on the level of [current] aggregate income and, therefore, on the level of employment N' (ibid., p. 28). Thus:

$$D_1^w = f_1(N).\qquad(5)$$

Logically, therefore, D_2^w represents *all* expenditures *not* related to current income and employment:

$$D_2^w \neq f(N).\qquad(6)$$

Classical theory is a special case of Keynes's general analytical system that can occur only if additional axioms are imposed to force the aggregate demand function to consist solely of expenditures *equal* to current income at all levels of *N*. Demand will then have the same determinants as supply. The necessary additional classical postulates for Say's law are:

1. *the axiom of ergodicity*, which asserts that the future can be reliably calculated from past and present market data. In Old Classical theory ergodicity was usually subsumed when it was assumed that decision makers possessed foreknowledge of the future. In New Classical theory it is presumed that agents have rational expectations about a statistically reliably predictable future;
2. *the axiom of gross substitution*, so that flexible relative prices assure that all markets clear; and
3. *the neutral money axiom*, which assures that changes in the nominal money supply have no real effects.

Unfortunately, while Keynes was developing his principle of effective demand the modern axiomatic theory of value had not yet been developed, so that Keynes could not explicitly label the equivalents of the 'axiom of parallels' that had to be 'overthrown' (ibid. p. 16) to produce a general theory. Nevertheless, in 1933, Keynes (1933 [1973], pp. 408–9) specifically noted that in the new 'monetary theory of production' that he was developing, the neutral money axiom was not applicable in either the short run or the long run. Yet even today, Blanchard (1990, p. 828) proclaims that all macroeconomic New Classical and New Keynesian models 'impose the long-run neutrality of money as a maintained assumption. This is very much a matter of faith, based on theoretical considerations [that is, axiom-based], rather than on empirical science.'

Keynes's specification of the 'essential properties of money' in his general theory requires rejecting the classical postulate that money (and all other liquid assets) are *gross substitutes* for the products of industry. Money (and all other liquid) assets possess two essential properties (Keynes 1936, pp. 230–31). These are:

1. The elasticity of production of money is zero; in essence, money is non-producible by the use of labour in the private sector. *Money does not grow on trees.* Money (and all liquid assets) therefore cannot be harvested by hiring otherwise unemployed workers to harvest money trees whenever people demand to hold additional liquid assets as a store of value.
2. The elasticity of substitution between money (that is, liquid assets) and producible goods is zero. Accordingly, any increase in demand for liquidity (non-producibles to be held as a store of value), and resulting changes in relative prices between non-producible liquid assets and the products of industry, will not divert the demand for liquidity into

a demand for goods and services. Keynes (ibid., p. 241) insisted that 'the attribute of "liquidity" is by no means independent of these two [elasticity] characteristics' and therefore as long as savers store their wealth in assets whose 'elasticities of production and substitution may be very low', unemployment equilibrium can exist no matter what the supply-side conditions are.

Since classical theory assumes that only producibles provide utility, then, in the long run, only a 'lunatic' would want to hold a non-producible good as a liquid store of value. Keynes (ibid., chapter 12; 1937 [1973], pp. 112–15), on the other hand, used the concept of uncertainty to explain why, even in the long run, people would reveal a preference to hold non-producibles such as money as a store of value no matter how high its relative price rose *vis-à-vis* the products of industry. (The future is uncertain rather than merely risky in the probabilistic sense.) If non-producibility is an essential attribute of all assets that possess the characteristic of liquidity and the holding of liquid assets can provide a long-run security blanket against uncertainty, then liquid assets can provide utility in a way that producibles cannot.

Hahn demonstrated that unemployment occurs when 'there are in this economy resting places for savings other than reproducible assets' (1977, p. 31) and the existence of 'any non-reproducible asset allows for a choice between employment-inducing and non-employment inducing demand' (ibid., p. 39). In an uncertain world, he who hesitates to spend on producibles and holds liquid assets instead is free to make a decision another day. By jettisoning the classical axioms of ergodicity and gross substitution, Keynes could demonstrate that, as a general case, unemployment is possible and money is not neutral.

The axiomatic microfoundations of classical economic theory, on the other hand, ensure that all income is always spent on the products of industry. In the simplest case all current expenditures are equal to current income, as utility maximizers are constrained by their income (budget line constraint) in their choice between good A and all other producibles. To spend less than one's income is to reveal a preference below the budget line, and thereby to engage in non-utility-maximizing behaviour. The aggregate of all this microfoundational spending would be classified under D_1^w. The marginal propensity to spend out of current income is unity, and any additional supply (the micro equivalent is an upward shift in budget constraint lines) creates its own additional demand. (In an intertemporal setting with gross substitutability over time, agents plan to spend lifetime income on the products of industry over their life cycle. The long-run marginal propensity to spend is unity.) Consequently, in either the short run or the long run, $f_d(N) = f_z(N)$ for all values of N, and Figure 14 is relevant.

Keynes's taxonomy was a general analysis that could lead to non-classical results. Keynes's second expenditure category, D_2^w, was not equal to 'planned' savings (which can be defined as $f_z(N) - f_1(N)$). Only if D_2^w is assumed to be equal to planned savings are:

$$D_2^w = f_z(N) - f_1(N) \tag{7}$$

and

$$D^w = D_1^w + D_2^w = f_1(N) + f_z(N) - f_1(N) = f_z(N). \tag{8}$$

A comparison of equations (8) and (2) shows that if D_2^w is assumed equal to planned savings, then aggregate demand and supply are identical and Say's law holds.

To ensure that equations (7) and (8) did not represent a general case, Keynes asserted that the future is uncertain in the sense that it cannot be either foreknown or statistically predicted by analysing past and current market price signals. If the future is uncertain, then expected future profits, the basis for current D_2^w investment spending, can be neither reliably forecast from existing market information, nor endogenously determined from today's 'planned' savings function ($f_z(N) - f_1(N)$) (Keynes 1936, p. 210). Instead investment expenditures depend on the exogenous (and therefore by definition, sensible but not rational) expectations of entrepreneurs, or what Keynes called 'animal spirits'. Thus:

$$D_2^w \neq f(N) \tag{9}$$

in either the short or the long run.

Explicit recognition of the possibility of more classes of current demand for producible goods and services based on a smaller axiomatic foundation makes Keynes's analysis a more general theory than classical theory. The latter becomes 'a special case and not . . . the general case' (ibid., p. 3), where the category of 'all expenditures *not* related to current employment' is empty. In terms of equation (4), classical theory asserts:

$$D_2^w = 0 \tag{10}$$

and therefore

$$D^w = D_1^w = f_1(N) = f_z(N) = Z^w \tag{11}$$

for all values of N.

The next logical task for Keynes was to demonstrate that 'the characteristics of the special case assumed by classical theory happen not to be those of the economic society in which we actually live' (ibid., p. 3). In other words, Keynes had to demonstrate that even if $D_2^w = 0$, the D_2^w function would not be coincident with his macro-analogue of the age-old supply function for all values of N. To do this Keynes had 'to throw over' the classical axioms of neutral money (that is, the possession of money *per se* provides no utility) and gross substitution.

If these restrictive axioms are jettisoned, then some portion of a utility-maximizing agent's income might be withheld from the purchase of producible goods and diverted into purchasing non-producible money and/or other non-producible liquidity assets. The marginal propensity to spend out of current income on the products of industry would then be less than unity. In an uncertain world, the possession of money and other non-producible liquid assets provides utility by protecting the holder from fear of being unable to meet future liabilities. As long as producible goods are not gross substitutes for holding non-producible liquid assets (including money) for liquidity purposes, then no change in relative prices can induce income-earners to buy producibles with that portion of income they wish to use to purchase additional long-run security (against non-ergodic economic conditions) by holding liquid assets.

In sum, Keynes's general theory of employment must be applicable to an uncertain (non-ergodic) world. When money and all other liquid assets possess certain essential properties, then agents can obtain utility (by being free of fear of possible future insolvency or even bankruptcy) only by holding a portion of their income in the form of non-producible liquid assets. If the gross substitutability between non-producible liquid assets (including money) and producible goods is approximately zero (ibid., chapter 17; Davidson 1982–83, 2002), then when agents want to save (in the form of non-producible liquid assets) money is not neutral, even with perfectly flexible prices. Thus, the general case underlying the principle of effective demand is:

$$D_1^w = f_1(N) \neq f_2(N), \tag{12}$$

while planned savings $(f_z(N) - f_d(N))$ are equal to the amount out of current income that utility-maximizing agents use to increase their holdings of non-producible liquid assets. The decision to save today means 'a decision not to have dinner today. But it does not necessitate a decision to have dinner or to buy a pair of boots a week hence or a year hence or to consume any specified thing at any specified date' (Keynes 1936, p. 210).

By proclaiming a 'fundamental psychological law' associated with 'the detailed facts of experience', where the marginal propensity to consume is always less than unity, Keynes (ibid., p. 96) finessed the possibility that equation (9) is ever applicable. If the marginal propensity to consume is always less than unity, then $f_1(N)$ would never coincide with $f_z(N)$, even if $D_2^w = 0$, and the special classical case is not applicable to 'the economic society in which we actually live' (ibid., p. 3).

In sum, Keynes's principle of effective demand demonstrates that, in a non-ergodic world, it is the existence of non-producible assets that are held for liquidity purposes and for which the products of industry are not gross substitutes that is the fundamental cause of involuntary unemployment. The lack of perfect price flexibility is neither a necessary nor a sufficient condition for demonstrating the existence of unemployment equilibrium.

PAUL DAVIDSON

See also:

Bastard Keynesianism; Effective Demand; Liquidity Preference; Microfoundations; Money; Non-ergodicity; Say's Law; Uncertainty; Unemployment.

References

Blanchard, O.J. (1990), 'Why does money affect output?', in B.M. Friedman and F.H. Hahn (eds), *Handbook of Monetary Economics*, Vol. 2, New York: North-Holland, pp. 779–835.

Davidson, P. (1982–83), 'Rational expectations: a fallacious foundation for studying crucial decision making', *Journal of Post Keynesian Economics*, **5** (2), 182–96; reprinted in Davidson, *Inflation, Open Economies, and Resources*, edited by L. Davidson, London: Macmillan, 1991, pp. 123–38.

Davidson, P. (2002), *Financial Markets, Money and the Real World*, Cheltenham, UK and Northampton, MA, USA: Edward Elgar.

Davidson, P. (2009), *John Maynard Keynes*, rev. edn, Basingstoke: Palgrave Macmillan.

Hahn, F.H. (1977), 'Keynesian economics and general equilibrium theory', in G.C. Harcourt (ed.), *Microfoundations of Macroeconomics*, London: Macmillan, pp. 25–40.

Keynes, J.M. (1933), 'A monetary theory of production', in *The Collected Writings of John Maynard Keynes*, Vol. XIV, London: Macmillan for the Royal Economic Society, 1973, pp. 408–11.

Keynes, J.M. (1936), *The General Theory of Employment, Interest and Money*, New York: Harcourt Brace.

Keynes, J.M. (1937), 'The general theory of employment', *Quarterly Journal of Economics*, **51** (2), 209–23; reprinted in *The Collected Writings of John Maynard Keynes*, Vol. XIII, London: Macmillan for the Royal Economic Society, 1973, pp. 109–23.

Keynes's *Treatise on Money*

A Treatise on Money by John Maynard Keynes was published on 24 October 1930, after six years of deep thinking and practical work on, for example, the economic policies of the Liberal Party and the decline of the cotton industry. In the mind of Keynes, at that time already a well-known figure in world politics, the *Treatise* was designed to provide the most comprehensive and systematic analysis of monetary matters ever produced (Harrod 1951, chapter 10). It was to do for his academic reputation what political and cultural activities had already done in the public arena (Patinkin 1976). But the *Treatise* has had bad luck in a way that explains the fortunes and misfortunes of Keynesian economics more generally (Erturk 2006).

To modern students and most scholars Keynes means *The General Theory of Employment, Interest and Money* (1936). Keynes is the analyst of unemployment and the depression. He is the theorist of aggregate demand and equilibrium unemployment as well as the promoter of public expenditure. The *Treatise* is then at the best a prelude, in the words of Schumpeter, a collection of 'imperfect and embarrassed first statements of *General Theory* propositions' (Schumpeter 1946 [1952], p. 278). According to this orthodox interpretation of Keynes's work what is new and important in the *Treatise* is absorbed and developed in the *General Theory*, and the permanent value of the latter is the explanation of short-run unemployment. An alternative view starts with a more balanced reading of the *Treatise*. It defends the originality of that work but it also emphasizes the continuous evolution of what Keynes was later to call a monetary theory of production, that is, the search for a sound analytical framework based on the principle of non-neutrality of money (and non-neutrality of choice). This alternative view is also supported by early interpretations of the *Treatise*:

> The latter [the *General Theory*] was written somewhat in haste after Keynes had achieved in his own mind a wide theoretical synthesis . . . he was anxious to get this before the public quickly. The *Treatise*, by contrast, contains all his gathered wisdom about monetary matters . . . It is, I would submit, impossible to have an understanding of Keynes in depth, if one has not read the *Treatise*. (Harrod 1969, p. 163)

The *Treatise* consists of seven Books organized in two volumes, namely *The Pure Theory of Money* (Volume 1, Books I–IV) and *The Applied Theory of Money* (Volume 2, Books V–VII). Book I is concerned with the definition of the nature of money and the description of its historical origins. Book II deals with the laborious and complex description of various index numbers. An important outcome of those two books is the idea that aggregate concepts like the price level or the quantity of money are not adequate for explaining the behaviour of the main economic variables (Skidelsky 1992, chapter 10). Next follows the core of the *Treatise*, Books III–IV. There Keynes offers a formal and rigorous discussion of the static and dynamic problems of monetary theory, including the presentation of his Fundamental Equations. Book V considers the empirical magnitudes of his key variables, and Book VI deals with the institutional features of the banking system. Finally, Book VII lays out the implications of the analysis for both national and international stabilization policies.

The basic problem that Keynes sets out to analyse in the *Treatise* is the instability of market economies. The analysis is very clear: the initial and most influential cause of output fluctuations in modern economies is the change in the level of investment. Since profit is the 'mainspring' of those changes, a theory of profit is then essential for the explanation of economic fluctuations. Thus capital accumulation and income distribution are the main themes of the *Treatise* (Graziani 1981). At the same time Keynes argues that changes in the level of prices are the primary mechanism of reconciliation between the investment decisions of entrepreneurs and the distribution of income between wages and profit. These price movements are explained by means of the Fundamental Equations.

The analytical framework of the *Treatise* is grounded on the distinction between wage-earners and entrepreneurs, together with the related separation between expenditure on consumption goods and on capital goods:

> Saving is the act of the individual consumer and consists in the negative act of refraining from spending the whole of his current income on consumption. Investment, on the other hand, is the act of the entrepreneur whose function it is to make the decisions which determine the amount of the non-available output, and consists in the positive act of starting or maintaining some process of production or withholding liquid goods . . . The vital point to appreciate is this . . . the performance of the act of saving is in itself no guarantee that the stock of capital goods will be correspondingly increased. (Book III, pp. 155–8)

Saving and investment are made by two different groups of people, and for Keynes there is no spontaneous market mechanism that necessarily reconciles them. It is indeed in this divergence and the consequent disequilibrium process that Keynes envisages the source of profit creation. The story unfolds as follows. If investment runs ahead of (below) saving it means that entrepreneurs have decided to produce fewer (more) consumption goods than the amount wage-earners have decided to purchase. The price of those goods increases (decreases), as does the remuneration of entrepreneurs. Abnormal (or subnormal) profit – as Keynes called it – is then due to the divergence between investment and saving (equation (viii), Book III, p. 124).

The price of consumption goods plays a key role in Keynes's theory of income distribution. In equilibrium it is equal to average (long-period normal) cost but when, as in the case above, investment differs from saving, 'the price level, as determined by the first term [that is, cost], is upset by the fact that the division of the output between investment and goods for consumption is not necessarily the same as the division of the income between savings and expenditure on consumption' (Book III, p. 123). Changes in the price level of consumption goods have the role of reconciling, via the mechanism of forced saving ('involuntary abstention'), the production decisions of entrepreneurs with the expenditure plans of wage-earners. For instance, with investment running ahead of saving and under the assumption that abnormal profit is entirely saved, a redistribution of income from wage-earners to entrepreneurs takes place and equilibrium is again restored (Kahn 1984, pp. 67–8). Keynes formally derived these results from his definition of the price level of consumption goods as equal to the monetary cost of production per unit of output (what Keynes called 'the rate of efficiency earnings') plus any element of abnormal (or subnormal) profit per unit of output. This is the meaning of the first Fundamental Equation; the second Fundamental Equation extends this idea to the price level of output as a whole (Book III, pp. 122–4).

Thus booms and slumps derive from the difference between saving and investment. More importantly for what would later be argued in the *General Theory*, Keynes argues that 'voluntary abstinence' is no guarantee of prosperity. This idea is well illustrated in the famous banana parable describing a community in a state of equilibrium that is disturbed by a thrift campaign (Book III, chapter 12, sec. ii). With an increase in saving entrepreneurs are now forced to reduce the price of bananas (otherwise they will rot). The unexpected (abnormal) loss causes entrepreneurs to reduce their wage bills by laying off workers and/or cutting wages. But this does not help as long as the community continues to save more than it invests. Output declines until either 'the thrift campaign is called off or peters out as a result of the growing poverty; or . . . investment is stimulated by some means or another so that its cost no longer lags behind the rate of saving' (p. 160). A similar case, of course, could be argued for an increase of investment in, for example, new banana plantations. The crux of the whole parable is that saving can be made identical to investment as a result of a change in output though, as Robinson argued, Keynes may have failed fully to realize that he had actually elaborated a long-period analysis of output (Robinson [1933] 1960, p. 56).

In terms of the policy implications of the analysis, Keynes suggests that the banking system should try to eliminate economic fluctuations and in consequence to stabilize the purchasing power of money. By keeping the market rate of interest equal to the natural rate of interest, that is, to the notional rate 'at which saving and the value of investment are exactly balanced' (Book III, p. 139), the banking system would preserve the condition of zero (abnormal) profit. Keynes believed that in general the banking system could do the job. However, he also warned that the natural rate of interest relies on profit expectations of entrepreneurs, and hence it is independent of the objective technical conditions of production. A potential conflict may then arise between domestic and external equilibrium. In a severe slump, with profit expectations running very low, the banking system may not be able to afford effective reductions in the market rate without causing a large outflow of domestic currency. In this case Keynes suggested that 'the Government must itself promote a programme of domestic investment' (Book VII, p. 337).

Several authors have argued that the *Treatise* and the *General Theory* embody the same vision, the same appreciation of empirical observation and the same analytical structure (for example, Amadeo 1989, chapters 3–4). What really differentiates the *Treatise* from the *General Theory* is the formal method and the specific purpose of the analysis. Keynes had always in mind a close connection between theory and practice, but under the pressure of historical events his thought about the form of that connection went on changing. In 1930 Keynes was mainly concerned with the instability of market economies, the ups and downs that characterize the credit cycle. Output and employment were seen moving around some norm, and he aimed to explain the causal mechanism behind those movements. But by 1936 he felt that the problem was now not with fluctuations around a norm but with the norm itself. Persisting mass unemployment was the practical interest, and for the sake of getting his solution across, he was content to set aside some of his most brilliant though highly heterodox ideas. This is the ultimate link between his two major books and the main reason for reverting to the *Treatise*.

GIUSEPPE FONTANA

See also:

Business Cycles; Growth and Income Distribution; Keynes's *General Theory*; Monetary Policy; Money; Saving.

References

Amadeo, E.J. (1989), *Keynes's Principle of Effective Demand*, Aldershot, UK and Brookfield, VT, USA: Edward Elgar.
Erturk, K.A. (2006), 'Speculation, liquidity preference and monetary circulation', in P. Arestis and M. Sawyer (eds), *A Handbook of Alternative Monetary Economics*, Cheltenham, UK and Northampton, MA, USA: Edward Elgar, pp. 454–70.
Graziani, A. (1981), 'Keynes e il Trattato sulla Moneta' [Keynes and the Treatise on Money], in Graziani, C. Imbriani and B. Jossa (eds), *Studi di Economia Keynesiana* [*Studies in Keynesian Economics*], Napoli: Liguori, pp. 211–34.
Harrod, R.F. (1951), *The Life of John Maynard Keynes*, London: Macmillan.
Harrod, R.F. (1969), *Money*, London: Macmillan.
Kahn, R.F. (1984), *The Making of Keynes' General Theory*, Raffaele Mattioli Lectures, Cambridge: Cambridge University Press.

Patinkin, D. (1976), *Keynes's Monetary Thought. A Study of Its Development*, Durham, NC: Duke University Press.

Robinson, J. (1933 [1960]), 'The theory of money and the analysis of output', in Robinson, *Collected Economic Papers*, Vol. I, Oxford: Basil Blackwell, pp. 52–8.

Schumpeter, J.A. (1946 [1952]), 'J.M. Keynes', in Schumpeter, *Ten Great Economists*, London: Allen & Unwin, pp. 260–91.

Skidelsky, R. (1992), *John Maynard Keynes: The Economist as Saviour 1920–1937*, London: Macmillan.

Keynes's *Treatise on Probability*

The *Treatise on Probability* (Keynes 1921) is John Maynard Keynes's main philosophical work. The book had a long gestation period. The key idea was advanced in an undergraduate paper of 1904 before being expanded into a dissertation, awarded in 1909, for a fellowship at King's College, Cambridge. Publication was envisaged shortly thereafter, but extensive revisions and the First World War delayed its appearance until 1921. At the time, it established Keynes as a leading authority in the philosophy of probability, the ongoing interest in the work being indicated by at least eight reprints (1929, 1943, 1948, 1952, 1957, 1963, 1973 and 2004). Nowadays its influence continues, but in weaker vein.

It is important to note that this work is not a mathematical treatise on the probability calculus. Rather, it is a wide-ranging philosophical work which could easily have been entitled a *Treatise on Reason* or a *Treatise on Logic*. In general terms, its significance is threefold. First, it is a pioneering work advancing the earliest systematic exposition of the logical theory of probability and its differences from rival theories (on which, see Weatherford 1982). Second, this theory of probability forms part of a broader theory of rational belief and action under uncertainty. And third, Keynes's philosophizing across a range of topics throws light on various aspects of his thinking in economic theory, economic policy, politics and the arts.

Keynes began his analysis of probability and rational belief with a question. How are we to understand the large class of arguments encountered in many spheres of life that we regard as rational in some sense and yet we know are non-conclusive (or non-deductive)? His answer had two components – rationality implies a connection with logic, and non-conclusiveness implies a connection with probability. The synthesis of these two ideas led to his conception of probability as a general theory of logic, the subject matter of which is *rational but non-conclusive argument*. Traditional or deductive logic was embraced by the general theory as the special case of certainty.

Every argument, whether non-conclusive or conclusive, proceeds from a set of premises, h, to a conclusion, a. Probability, in Keynes's theory, is concerned with the relation between the two propositions, h and a. In the general (non-conclusive) case, h lends some support to a but not complete or conclusive support; that is, the premises partly entail the conclusion, but are insufficient for complete entailment. Keynes postulated that the relation between h and a is a logical relation, which he called the 'probability-relation'. It is a relation of partial support or entailment which is viewed as belonging to logic as much as the complete entailment of deductive logic. The distinctive symbol Keynes adopted for probability is a/h, read as the probability of a on premises h, this symbol emphasizing the essentially relational (or data-dependent) nature of probability.

The connection between probability and rational belief is then as follows. Assuming that h is true and that a deductively follows from h, then the probability of a on h would be unity ($a/h = 1$) and it would be rational to believe a with complete certainty. However, if h is true and only gives partial support to a, the probability of a on h would be less than unity ($a/h < 1$) and it would only be rational to believe a with a lower degree of certainty, this degree of certainty being given by the probability. If, for example, it has been raining for a week and no information indicates a cessation in the next few days, the probability of the proposition, 'it will rain tomorrow', will be high, and it will be rational to believe this proposition to a high degree, though not with complete certainty since it cannot be deduced from the given information. Note that rationality of belief in a is not tied to the truth of a. The fact that a might later turn out to be false does not mean it was irrational, on the evidence available at the time, to believe a to some degree.

Keynes's logical probability-relations thus express three aspects of arguments – degrees of partial inference (the extent to which a may be inferred from h), degrees of rational belief (the extent to which it is rational to believe a, given h), and degrees of certainty. The limits at either end of these ranges are the probabilities of unity and zero, both of which are given by deductive logic. Unit probability corresponds to full entailment and complete certainty. If a is fully entailed by h, then $a/h = 1$. Zero probability corresponds to contradiction or logical impossibility. If $-a$ is the contradictory of a, then $a/h = 0$ means that $-a/h = 1$, that is, h fully entails the contradictory of a, so that a is impossible and requires complete disbelief. Lying between these two extremes is the densely populated universe of Keynes's probability-relations ($0 \leq a/h \leq 1$).

Importantly, such probabilities are always objective and never subjective. Their objectivity derives from their status as relations of logic. Between any pair of propositions, a and h, the logical relation is unique and fixed independently of personal opinion or psychological belief. Probabilities are thus members of an immutable, non-natural realm of logical relations transcending human subjectivity. Keynes firmly insisted on the objectivity of his logical probabilities, and any accounts that portray his theory as dealing with subjective probabilities are not representing it in its own terms.

Knowledge of logical relations is arrived at by intellectual intuition – by careful reflection of the support *h* gives to *a* or, equivalently, by mental insight into the realm of logical relations. However, since mental ability varies across individuals and history, not all logical relations will be known to all individuals at all times. Depending on our powers of logical insight, some probabilities will be known and some unknown. Probabilities are more likely to be unknown when little relevant data are available, such situations being common in relation to the distant future. While unknown probabilities are not of much interest in a work devoted to probability, Keynes indicates that when probabilities are unavailable, rational agents will need to turn to non-probabilistic methods in decision making. Situations of unknown probability have been suggested as central to understanding the approach to rational decision making under fundamental uncertainty in the *General Theory* and associated writings.

The measurement of probabilities is an intriguing aspect of Keynes's theory. While other theories reduce probabilities to numerical (and hence universally comparable) form, Keynes's ordering of the probability space is far more complex. Three types of comparative relations are postulated:

1. cardinal comparison, which generates the relatively minor class of numerical probabilities. These only exist under the restrictive condition of equiprobability, which is established by careful use of the 'principle of indifference';
2. ordinal comparison, which generates the much bigger class of non-numerical probabilities. This class consists of many separate, incommensurable series whereby probabilities belonging to the same series are comparable in terms of greater or lesser, but probabilities belonging to different series are generally incapable of being compared in magnitude; and
3. non-comparability, which typically exists between numerical and non-numerical probabilities, and between non-numerical probabilities in different series.

Such heterogeneity in the ordering relations between probabilities greatly restricts the scope of the probability calculus in mathematical applications.

Keynes also contended that a second, independent variable, called 'the weight of argument', is also relevant to rational belief under uncertainty. Weight is positively associated with the data, *h*, and provides a measure of the 'well-foundedness' of non-conclusive argument and hence of the confidence that may be placed in the argument. Arguments of high weight are based on much information, are well founded and hence merit high degrees of confidence, regardless of whether their probability is high or low. Arguments of low weight rest on little information, are poorly founded and deserve low degrees of confidence even if their probability is high. All other things being equal, rational agents should choose the argument with the greatest weight.

After outlining the fundamental concepts in Part I of the book, Keynes applied these ideas to important issues in the remaining four parts. In Part II, he undertook the necessary task of deriving the probability calculus. Using definitions and axioms based on probability as the relation, *a/h*, he first arrived at the theorems of deductive logic, and then turned to probable inference to derive the theorems of the addition and multiplication of probabilities and of inverse probability.

In Part III, Keynes turned to induction, observing that logicians had not offered satisfactory accounts of this common form of argument. Claiming that every inductive argument was probabilistic in nature, he sought to explore both the analysis and logical justification of induction. His procedure was, first, to dissect inductive methods; second, to isolate the fundamental assumption(s) on which induction rested; and, third, to inspect these assumption(s) for their truth or self-evidence without resorting to appeals to experience which would involve circularity. The main assumption he saw underpinning induction was the principle of limited independent variety, which essentially says that the variety of the universe is limited because it derives from a finite number of independent generators. He then cautiously suggested that this principle was self-evidently true, thereby accepting the existence of synthetic a priori knowledge which, along with the role of intuition in his theories of probability and ethics, places the epistemology of his philosophical work in the rationalist tradition.

In keeping with much philosophy of the time, Keynes's treatment of chance and randomness in Part IV is based on determinism. On this view, chance, randomness and indeterminateness are not objective or inherent characteristics of the universe, but are purely subjective phenomena deriving from human ignorance. It is our lack of knowledge of the relevant causal mechanisms which leads us to say that certain events are due to chance or are random occurrences, when actually they are the product of causal influences of which we are (currently) ignorant.

Also in Part IV, Keynes addressed the vital question of 'what ought we to do?', but in only one chapter. His answer, which combined his logical theory of probability with the ethics of G.E. Moore, may be described as a probabilistic form of consequentialism. On this view, rational or right action is that which is judged to produce the greatest amount of probable goodness on the whole, appropriate attention being paid to weight and moral risk (see below). Broadly speaking, the assessment of an action involves a listing of its possible consequences and a means of combining the probabilities and values of these consequences into probable goodness on the whole. When numerical magnitudes can be ascribed to probabilities and values the procedure is straightforward, but, when probabilities and/or values are non-numerical in nature, Keynes appealed to direct judgement or intuition as the means by which we arrive at the probable goodness of the whole. If such judgement were not within our power, he accepted the matter as indeterminate. In such cases, suggestions were made that reason can turn to second-best options, including caprice.

In a criticism of mathematical expectations, Keynes introduced the concept of moral risk so as to draw particular attention to the probability of loss. It is most relevant to extreme cases where probable values derive from combinations of very low probabilities and very large gains, such as can occur in gambling or speculation. When the resulting probable values are the same as those associated with less risky ventures with higher probabilities and lower gains, mathematical expectations theory postulates indifference for rational agents. Keynes, however, argues that rationality requires the agent to examine both the probable value and the probability of loss. If the probability of losing whatever is wagered on the outcome is very high, and if this loss would be catastrophic for agents (and/or their associates), rational agents should be prudent and pursue actions with lower risks of loss. One should not bet all one's wealth on a horse race; winning might produce enormous wealth, but losing results in pauperism.

In the final part, Keynes investigated the logical basis of statistical inference. He analysed the law of large numbers, the theorems of Daniel Bernouilli, Siméon Poisson and Pafnuti Chebychev, Pierre Laplace's rule of succession, and the methods of Wilhelm Lexis, before concluding, all too briefly, with an outline of a constructive theory. His dual object was to uncover and discredit invalid inferences and to clarify and support valid inferences, his guiding principle throughout being that logic was the master and mathematics the servant. What drew his censure, here and in relation to mathematical methods generally, was loose thinking and inappropriate application, not valid and logically consistent use.

Questions naturally arise as to whether significant connections exist between Keynes's philosophical thought (as developed over the 1903–21 period) and his non-philosophical thought in areas such as economics, politics and the arts. Of central importance is the relationship between his major philosophical work and his major economic work, *The General Theory of Employment, Interest and Money*. Some of the key issues discussed have been whether substantial connections exist between: (i) the treatment of probability and uncertainty in the *Treatise on Probability* and the treatment of uncertainty and expectations in the *General Theory*; (ii) the non-neoclassical rationality of the *Treatise* and the non-neoclassical treatment of agent behaviour in the *General Theory*; (iii) the epistemology of the *Treatise* and his epistemological remarks in the *General Theory* and elsewhere; (iv) the approach taken to quantitative matters and formalism in the *Treatise* and his comments on mathematical methods in economics and econometrics in other writings; and (v) the ethics and theory of right action of the *Treatise*, and his thoughts on political philosophy and party politics in other works.

Such questions have generated considerable controversy. Some writers argue that various strong threads of continuity exist between the conceptual framework of the *Treatise* and major themes in Keynes's other thought. Others claim that his philosophical thinking changed significantly after 1921, thereby creating serious discontinuities between the *Treatise* and the *General Theory*. Debate has arisen over whether he remained an adherent of the logical theory of probability, or was converted shortly afterwards to Frank Ramsey's subjectivist theory. Discussion also surrounds rationality and irrationality, the influences of Sigmund Freud and Ludwig Wittgenstein, and whether or not Keynes's approach to fundamental uncertainty bears any relation to approaches based on non-ergodicity. For two views, out of the many available, on the relations between Keynes's philosophy and his other writings, see Carabelli (1988) and O'Donnell (1989).

Rod O'Donnell

See also:

Agency; Econometrics; Expectations; Keynes's *General Theory*; Non-ergodicity; Uncertainty.

Bibliography

Carabelli, A.M. (1988), *On Keynes's Method*, London: Macmillan.

Keynes, J.M. (1921), *Treatise on Probability*, London: Macmillan; republished (with different pagination) as Volume VIII of *The Collected Writings of John Maynard Keynes*, London: Macmillan, 1973.

McCann, C.R. (1994), *Probability Foundations of Economic Theory*, London and New York: Routledge.

O'Donnell, R.M. (1989), *Keynes: Philosophy, Economics and Politics. The Philosophical Foundations of Keynes's Thought and their Influence on his Economics and Politics*, London: Macmillan.

O'Donnell, R.M. (ed.) (1991), *Keynes as Philosopher–Economist*, London: Macmillan.
Runde, J. and S. Mizuhara (eds) (2003), *The Philosophy of Keynes's Economics*, London and New York: Routledge.
Weatherford, R. (1982), *Philosophical Foundations of Probability Theory*, London: Routledge & Kegan Paul.

Latin American Structuralism

Latin American structuralism constitutes a wide area of thought encompassing several fields: not only economics. Its origins lie in the ideas of Raúl Prebisch, which were deepened and fully developed by the United Nations Economic Commission for Latin America (ECLAC). Such ideas were greatly accepted throughout the region. Indeed, down to the 1980s, they had a significant impact on the design of economic policies throughout the subcontinent.

Structuralism can be divided into two great phases, which are linked to the challenges the Latin American region has faced in the last century. The first of such phases is associated with the 1930s Depression which, in the developed world, gave way to the Keynesian revolution and to a new approach in terms of economic policy making whereas, in Latin American countries, the crisis translated into a dramatic fall in both the price and the volume of exports. It was precisely in this context that the first wave of structural ideas emerged: their aim was to find a way for Latin American economies to come up with a sector capable of supplying the economic dynamism once provided by exports. The second phase of structuralism is associated with the economic crisis Latin America experienced during the 1980s, which led to a set of structural reforms known worldwide as the Washington Consensus. In this particular juncture, structuralism focused on an economic strategy based on achieving a transformation of production as well as on improving income distribution.

Since the 1950s, two main ideas have constituted the core of structural thinking: (i) peripheral economies tend to suffer balance-of-payments constraints which limit their economic growth, and (ii) such economies are structurally heterogeneous (Prebisch 1950). The first of these ideas has to do with the fact that economies see their growth limited by a lack of foreign currency, a subject which has been the focus of several studies including many countries, and from which Thirlwall's law emanates (Thirlwall 1979). The second idea, which stresses the structurally heterogeneous nature of developing economies, emphasizes that such a nature constitutes one of the key determinants of the income inequality endemically associated with Latin American nations. This is the case because structural heterogeneity implies the coexistence of economic sectors displaying very different productivity levels, a situation which tends to persist and which, in turn, results in the following: those who work in the low-productivity sectors receive very low incomes whereas those employed in the high-productivity sectors enjoy much higher incomes.

This entry will focus on these two main structuralist ideas and will concentrate on the period ranging from the 1950s up to the first decade of the twenty-first century. In order to overcome these two problems – external constraints on growth and structural heterogeneity – structuralism has insisted on the need for Latin American countries to industrialize. This demands government action in the form of industrial policies. However, through time, structuralism has experienced changes regarding how to tackle industrialization, how to define the interaction or relationship between the state and the market, how to promote economic development, and how to define or determine the profiles of industrial policies themselves.

According to early structuralist thought, the role played by Latin America since the 1850s in terms of the international division of labour – a provider of raw materials and agricultural products and a buyer of industrial goods – would result in the region lagging behind the developed countries, since Latin American growth would be permanently constrained by a shortage of foreign currency. This situation arises from the fact that the relative prices of the products exported by Latin America would tend to fall *vis-à-vis* those of industrial goods. This in turn is associated with two factors: (i) given the characteristics of labour markets in core countries, productivity increases registered there do not show up in the form of lower prices but in the form of higher real wages. At the same time, productivity increases achieved in peripheral countries do show up in lower prices, a phenomenon linked to the downward flexibility that wages display, which in turn is the result of the excess supply of labour which characterizes such countries, and (ii) the income elasticity of demand for primary products is lower than that for industrial products.

It is also important to highlight the fact that the basic reason why the Latin American region is in itself structurally heterogeneous is its role as provider of primary products for core countries. This is because, although the export sector permanently incorporates technological innovations and, therefore, does generate relatively high productivity levels, the slow growth of world demand for primary products implies that export industries are not capable of employing a significant part of the population. Hence the remaining labour force ends up employed in low-productivity activities.

Based on the external constraints to growth, as well as on structural unemployment, structuralism emphasized the urgency for Latin America to industrialize. Indeed, structuralism has always claimed that industry itself is a key sector in terms of economic development. Of course, this idea has been prevalent since the beginnings of development economics, when it was stressed that industrialization results in positive externalities, increasing returns to scale, intense forward and backward production linkages and spillover effects throughout the entire economy (Rosenstein-Rodan 1943; Hirschman 1958).

Taking into account the time in which it took place, the first phase of Latin American industrialization can be considered as one of late industrial development. Similarly, one of the main characteristics of this phase is the relevance of industrial policy, which led to a wide array of state actions and policies oriented towards achieving industrial development, such as particular trade, financing and exchange rate policies, as well as direct state investment in industrial sectors which were conceived as basic, that is, those dedicated to generating the inputs to be used by other industries.

Industrialization was supposed to contribute to solving the balance-of-payments constraint to growth by producing goods which, until then, had to be imported. Nevertheless, import substitution was not successful in this regard. This occurred because, in order for industrialization itself to be furthered, imports are required. Actually, Latin American industrialization started with the production of consumption goods and some basic inputs, such as steel. However, high-level industrial development demands certain inputs, raw materials and products which, by not being available in the home economy, in this case Latin American economies, had to be imported. The same happened regarding capital goods, which are a must for industrialization to be successful.

Another reason why import substitution was not the answer to the structural external constraint has to do with the fact that, although some countries of the region did achieve an important degree of industrialization, Latin America's exporting profile did not change significantly. Indeed, the primary sector, that is, exports of agricultural and mining products, remained as the main provider of the foreign currency the region required as industrialization proceeded. In other words, the industrial sectors of the region did not succeed in the international arena and, therefore, did not provide such currency at all, a phenomenon related to the highly protectionist nature acquired by industrial policy as time went by.

Industrialization was also expected to help in terms of overcoming the structural heterogeneity which characterizes the Latin American region and, in turn, improve income distribution. This process would take place following Lewis's model (Lewis 1954), according to which industrial growth and development allows labour employed in low-productivity activities to be incorporated into new, more-productive, industries. Consequently, productivity increases throughout the economy, gaps between economic sectors narrow and, in the long term, income distribution changes for the better.

By the 1960s, structuralism was already stressing that the foreign currency generated by exporting primary products resulted in constraints on economic growth that could only be overcome by exporting industrial goods instead. This demanded, in general, the rationalization of industrial policy and, in particular, high and indefinite trade barriers so that, gradually, the region was able to compete internationally. As a first approach to this process, structuralism called for the creation of free trade areas within Latin America itself (Prebisch 1963). However, the ample availability of international finance during the 1970s allowed Latin American countries to delay the opening of their industrial activities to international competition, an attractive and up to a point necessary measure given the political pressures naturally associated with such an opening. In this way, it was only in the 1980s when, in the context of the structural reforms associated with the Washington Consensus, integration into international markets took place; however, it occurred abruptly, not gradually.

Owing to extremely difficult foreign currency constraints, Latin American economies suffered greatly during the 1980s. In fact, with the aim of achieving trade surpluses and being able to meet their foreign debt, Latin American countries deflated economic activity on purpose. In order to overcome this situation, Latin American economies followed the Washington Consensus agenda. Structuralism proposed an alternative approach: the change of production patterns and achieving a better income distribution (CEPAL 1990). This approach did not abandon the main issues structuralism had always highlighted but did place them, and developed them, according to the new world economic context. In fact, the transformation of production emphasizes industrialization as the way to economic development. However, a key element is now added to the equation: the introduction of technological progress. This translates into supporting industrial development in general, as in the past, as well as particular economic sectors conceived as knowledge disseminators.

The rapid trade liberalization experienced by Latin America in the 1980s meant that South America remained mainly as an exporter of agricultural and mining products, whereas Mexico and some Central American countries turned into exporters of unskilled-labour-intensive industrial goods. This is what Fajnzylber (1990) labelled as 'trade integration based on spurious advantages', that is, on the ample availability of natural resources and cheap labour. This type of integration is completely different from one in which industry privileges activities based on technical progress, which, by their own nature, make such progress more dynamic while diffusing it throughout the whole economy. This scenario would allow Latin America to gradually replace its traditional competitiveness capabilities with what

Fajnzylber denominates as the basis for authentic competitiveness. In turn, all of this would contribute to sorting out the lack of foreign exchange which, as already explained, restricts economic expansion.

The transformation of production implies also a greater articulation of the economic system, that is, deeper and thicker linkages among sectors. This would allow for the growth of certain activities which, in turn, would encourage the development of others, both from the supply and the demand side of the economy, as well as through increased exports, which would incorporate more domestic value added into them, a situation which, in itself, would represent more economic growth.

In addition, the transformation of production should help in overcoming the structural heterogeneity of the economy and, in this way and at the same time, contribute to achieving equality. This would be the result of more articulation in the economic system, especially among firms of different sizes, capabilities and productivity levels, a key condition for narrowing productivity gaps and, of course, for increasing incomes throughout the economy, as well as improving income distribution.

Finally, the transformation of production strategy does attribute a key role to the state. The latter should be deployed through industrial policies in which both public and private agents are vigorously involved.

GERARDO FUJII

See also:

Balance-of-payments-constrained Economic Growth; Brazil; Development Finance; Economic Development; Economic Policy; Export-led Growth; Growth Theory.

References

CEPAL (1990), *Transformación Productiva con Equidad: la Tarea Prioritaria de América Latina y el Caribe en los Noventa* [*Productive Transformation with Equity: The Priority for Latin America and the Caribbean in the Nineties*], Santiago de Chile: United Nations.

Fajnzylber, F. (1990), 'Industrialización de América Latina: de la "Caja Negra" al "Casillero Vacíío". Comparación de Patrones Contemporáneos de Industrialización' ['The Industrialization of Latin America: from the 'Black Box' to the 'Empty Pigeonhole'. A Comparison of Current Patterns of Industrialization'], Santiago: CEPAL, Cuadernos de la CEPAL No. 60.

Hirschman, A. (1958), *The Strategy of Economic Development*, New Haven, CT: Yale University Press.

Lewis, W. A. (1954), 'Economic development with unlimited supplies of labour', *Manchester School*, **22** (2), 139–91.

Prebisch, R. (1950), *The Economic Development of Latin America and its Principal Problems*, Lake Success, NY: United Nations Department of Economic Affairs.

Prebisch, R. (1963), *Hacia una Dinámica del Desarrollo Latinoamericano* [*Towards a Dynamic of Development in Latin America*], México: Fondo de Cultura Económica.

Rosenstein-Rodan, P. (1943), 'Problems of industrialization of Eastern and South-Eastern Europe', *Economic Journal*, **53** (210/211), 202–11.

Thirlwall, A.P. (1979), 'The balance of payments constraint as an explanation of international growth rate differences', *Banca Nazionale del Lavoro Quarterly Review*, **128** (791), 45–53.

Liquidity Preference

The idea that 'the' rate of interest adjusts until the supply of savings is brought into equality with the demand for savings dates back at least as far as Henry Thornton. The proposition is exemplified by the loanable funds theory of the rate of interest, which Keynes attempted to over-throw in the *General Theory*. Ralph Hawtrey, Bertil Ohlin and Dennis Robertson were Keynes's primary adversaries, each subscribing to the idea that the rate of interest would settle at the point where the (flow) supply of savings and the (flow) demand for investible funds would be equal. According to the theory, an increase in savings (given the level of income) would bring 'the' rate of interest down just enough to stimu-late capital production to the point where the additional saving would be exactly exhausted by the additional demand for new investment. Accordingly, an increase in aggregate saving could alter the *composition* of aggregate demand (that is, less consumption and more investment), but it could not cause a reduction in the *level* of aggregate demand. Thus full employment could not be undermined by the preference of house-holds to save rather than spend money.

The experience of the Great Depression in the 1930s made it impos-sible to sustain the notion that capitalist economies were self-regulating. Moreover, it caused many economists to become dissatisfied with the quantity theory of money – the theory that holds that changes in the quan-tity of money are primarily responsible for causing changes in national income. By the logic of the quantity theory, it should have been possible for the central bank to stop the downward spiral by increasing the money supply. Keynes's liquidity preference theory offered a new perspective on these problems.

The difference between Keynes's analysis and the traditional theory of interest, which he considered 'a nonsense theory' (1936 [1964], p. 177), essentially amounts to a distinction between the economics of full employ-ment and the economics of unemployment. In Keynes's view, the tradi-tional analysis was flawed because it treated saving and investment as the determin*ants* of the system and the rate of interest as a determin*ate* when, in fact, savings and investment are the determin*ates* of the system, and the rate of interest is a determin*ant*. Moreover, he emphasized that because saving depends upon income and income depends upon investment, it was impossible to conceive of an independent shift in either schedule. According to Keynes, a shift in the savings schedule would, in general, cause a change in income 'with the result that the whole schematism based on the assumption of a given income breaks down' (ibid., p. 179).

An equally crucial blow to the traditional theory followed from Keynes's recognition that money, held in its barren form, yields no monetary reward. According to the loanable funds theory, interest was the reward for parting (today) with command over goods and services. But as Keynes pointed out, the act of saving, by itself, generates no necessary reward in the form of interest. Wealth can be stored in various forms (for example, idle balances, short- or long-term financial instruments, capital assets or other forms of income property), but interest will be forthcoming only if individuals agree to part with idle cash in favour of short- or long-term financial instruments. With this in mind, Keynes set out to discover why anyone, outside of a lunatic asylum, would ever choose to hold money in its barren form.

Initially, he offered three reasons: (i) the transactions motive, (ii) the precautionary motive and (iii) the speculative motive. The transactions motive refers to a desire to hold money for the purpose of meeting antici-pated expenditures (that is, bridging the time gap between known receipts and known expenditures). The precautionary motive, in contrast, has to do with the desire to hold cash for the purpose of meeting unanticipated expenditures. According to Keynes, increases (decreases) in the level of income would be associated with increases (decreases) in the size of the cash balances held to satisfy the transactions and precautionary motives. Like the precautionary motive, the speculative motive arises as a conse-quence of uncertainty. However, unlike the transactions and precaution-ary motives, an individual's desire to hold money to satisfy the speculative motive is a function of anticipated movements in a range of asset prices rather than changes in the level of income. Here, the idea is that individu-als hold money in order to hedge against a declining securities market. If, for example, bond prices are expected to rise, individuals will prefer to become less liquid today (that is, to transform idle money balances into bonds) in order to take advantage of anticipated capital gains. In contrast, if speculators expect bond prices to fall to a point where interest gains are outweighed by capital losses, they will prefer to become more liquid today (that is, to hold idle money balances instead of less liquid financial instru-ments). The money balances that are held to satisfy these three motives reflect the individual's degree of liquidity preference.

The desire to hold liquid assets (that is, coins, paper currency and bank deposits) can be analysed graphically by means of a liquidity preference function. Leaving aside the desire to hold money to satisfy the transactions and precautionary motives, Keynes proposed that the liquidity preference function could be envisaged as 'a continuous curve relating changes in the demand for money to satisfy the speculative motive and changes in the rate of interest as given by changes in the prices of bonds and debts of various maturities' (ibid., p. 197). Figure 16 depicts this relation.

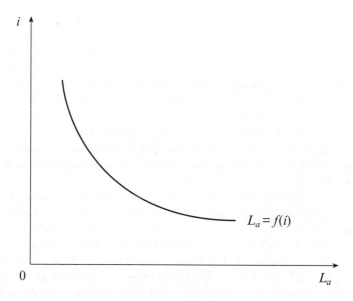

Figure 16   The liquidity preference function

The liquidity function L_a reflects the desire to hold money as an asset (that is, the desire to hold idle cash balances to satisfy the speculative motive). The curve shows the quantities of money that individuals, in the aggregate, will wish to hold at various rates of interest.

Keynes gave two reasons for the downward-sloping nature of the liquidity function. First, he explained that a fall (rise) in the rate of interest would be associated with an increase (decrease) in the demand for money as an asset, since the penalty for being liquid (that is, the forgone interest) has been reduced. Second, he suggested that a decline (rise) in the rate of interest would be associated with an increased (decreased) demand for cash balances to satisfy the speculative motive because some market participants will anticipate a future rise (fall) in the rate of interest.

As Keynes explained, both the position and the shape of the liquidity preference function depend upon the state of long-term expectations. What matters most are the expectations regarding the future path of asset prices. Thus, if speculators, who are constantly forming expectations about the future course of interest rates, believe that the market's estimate of future interest rates (as implied by current prices) is mistaken, they will attempt to profit from knowing better what the future will bring. If they believe that future rates will lie below those currently assumed by the market, they will have an incentive to reduce their liquidity by borrowing money today in order to purchase longer-term bonds. In contrast, if they expect future rates to lie above those assumed by the market, they will have an incentive to increase the liquidity of their portfolios by selling bonds today.

Only when the expected return on every financial asset in every portfolio is equal will market participants be satisfied with their existing holdings. Thus, in order for the money market to be in equilibrium, expectations must be such that investors are willing to hold the current mix of money and bonds, given the current structure of interest rates. In contrast to the loanable funds theory of the rate of interest, which treats 'the' rate of interest as the outcome of the forces equilibrating the flow supply of loanable funds with the flow demand for investible resources, this complex of rates will be determined by the stock demand for money relative to its stock supply.

Given the aggregate money supply, only the portion not desired to satisfy the transactions and precautionary motives is available to satisfy the speculative motive (that is, the stock demand for money). Figure 17 incorporates this constraint into the analysis. M_a is drawn as a vertical schedule, indicating the quantity of money available to satisfy the speculative motive. The interaction of these schedules determines not just the rate of interest on money but also the complex of rates on assets of various maturities. These rates can change either because the supply of money available to satisfy the speculative motive has been altered (that is, M_a shifts) or because the expectations that determine the position and shape of the liquidity preference function have changed (that is, L_a shifts).

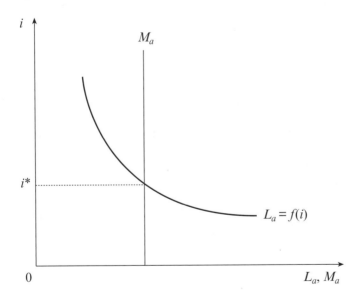

Figure 17   Determination of the rate of interest

At any interest rate above i^*, the stock of money available to be held as an asset exceeds the amount of money that individuals, in the aggregate, wish to hold to satisfy the speculative motive. In this situation, the rate of interest will have to fall until all of the money that is not desired for transactions or precautionary balances is willingly held to satisfy the speculative motive. Similarly, at any rate of interest below i^*, the quantity of money that market participants wish to hold as an asset exceeds the amount of money available to be held as an asset. Assuming that the banking system and the monetary authority do not respond by increasing the money supply, the rate of interest will have to rise to the point where the public is willing to hold the existing stock of money (or, more appropriately, the stock of existing securities). Thus the rate of interest is the premium required to induce market participants to hold less liquid assets.

Two important conclusions distinguish Keynes's analysis from the (neo) classical approach, which incorporated both loanable funds theory and the quantity theory of money. First, there is no reason to suppose that the rate of interest will settle at a price that is consistent with full employment. According to Keynes, saving and investment determine not the rate of interest but the aggregate level of employment. Moreover, an increase in the propensity to save (for example, a rise in liquidity preference) should be expected to increase interest rates, discourage investment and reduce employment – not reduce the interest rate and induce enough investment to maintain full employment. Second, changes in the money supply have a direct effect on interest rates (through portfolio adjustments) and only an indirect effect on national income. This does not imply that the monetary authority can simply manipulate the money supply until an interest rate consistent with full employment is achieved; changes in the state of long-term expectations can always disrupt any desired policy outcome. Keynes makes this clear in his attack on the quantity theory argument, cautioning that 'if . . . we are tempted to assert that money is the drink which stimulates the system to activity, we must remind ourselves that there may be several slips between the cup and the lip' (ibid., p. 173).

Generally speaking, Keynes's theory of liquidity preference remains an integral part of the Post Keynesian approach. But there are some notable exceptions. Basil Moore (1988), for example, argues that the liquidity preference theory actually undermines the rationale of *The General Theory*. According to Moore, liquidity preference theory is incompatible with endogenous monetary theory. Lavoie (1985) agrees, arguing that Post Keynesians must reject liquidity preference theory because it is relevant only in the context of an exogenously determined money supply.

The criticisms of Moore and Lavoie appear to follow from the manner in which Keynes treated the determination of the money supply in *The*

General Theory. According to Moore, Keynes should have retained the endogenous treatment of the money supply that he adopted in his *Treatise on Money* and designated the interest rate as an exogenously determined variable. If the interest rate is exogenously determined (by the monetary authority) and the supply of money is perfectly elastic at this rate, then an outward shift of the liquidity preference function cannot increase the rate of interest. Thus, for Moore and Lavoie, the problem appears to be this: if the supply of money always fully accommodates the demand for money (that is, the money supply is endogenous), then it cannot be true that an increase in the demand for money will increase the rate of interest.

Wray (1990) argues that liquidity preference and endogenous money are indeed compatible and that the criticisms of Moore and Lavoie are based on a failure to distinguish between the (stock) demand for money and the (flow) demand for credit. Davidson (1978), Kregel (1986), Dow and Dow (1989) and Wray (1990), emphasize the finance motive, which Keynes introduced in 1937 as a fourth motive for holding money. In this 1937 article, Keynes reasserts his commitment to the endogenous theory of money, explaining that as long as banks are willing to accommodate an increase in the demand for credit, there is no reason why the interest rate should rise with an increase in the level of planned activity. Thus, while changes in the (stock) demand for money can affect the rate of interest, changes in the (flow) demand for credit (that is, bank borrowing) need not.

When the concept of liquidity preference is extended to banks and other financial institutions, the rate of interest will be determined by the supply of money (determined endogenously within the banking system) and the liquidity preference of both commercial banks and the non-bank public. And, as we have observed in the wake of the Great Recession, when liquidity preference is high, both the demand for and the supply of loans tends to collapse. Until expectations improve and liquidity preference abates, banks will sit on mountains of excess reserves, and firms will refuse to invest in illiquid capital, leaving fiscal policy as the only viable tool for economic recovery.

STEPHANIE KELTON (*NÉE* BELL)

See also:

Banking; Expectations; Keynes's *General Theory*; Money; Rate of Interest; Uncertainty.

References

Davidson, P. (1978), *Money and the Real World*, London: Macmillan.
Dow, A.C. and S.C. Dow (1989), 'Endogenous money creation and idle balances', in J. Pheby (ed.), *New Directions in Post-Keynesian Economics*, Aldershot, UK and Brookfield, VT, USA: Edward Elgar, pp. 147–64.
Keynes, J.M. (1936 [1964]), *The General Theory of Employment, Interest and Money*, New York: Harcourt Brace.

Keynes, J.M. (1937), 'Alternative theories of the rate of interest', *Economic Journal*, **47** (186), 241–52.
Kregel, J. (1986), 'A note on finance, liquidity, saving, and investment', *Journal of Post Keynesian Economics*, **9** (1), 91.
Lavoie, M. (1985), 'Credit and money: the dynamic circuit, overdraft economics, and Post Keynesian economics', in M. Jarsulic (ed.), *Money and Macro Policy*, Boston, MA Dordrecht and Lancaster: Kluwer-Nijhoff, pp. 63–84.
Moore, B. (1988), *Horizontalists and Verticalists: The Macroeconomics of Credit Money*, Cambridge: Cambridge University Press.
Wray, L.R. (1990), *Money and Credit in Capitalist Economies: The Endogenous Money Approach*, Aldershot, UK and Brookfield, VT, USA: Edward Elgar.

Macroeconomic Methodology

Post Keynesian economics is mainly concerned with macroeconomic themes: theory and policy. Inspiration comes from the writings of John Maynard Keynes, especially *The General Theory*.

It was not until the early 1930s that Keynes started to emphasize that the main difference between his macroeconomic theory and the existing models was his applied methodology:

> On the one side are those who believe that the existing economic system is, in the long run, a self-adjusting system, though with creaks and groans and jerks and interrupted by time lags, outside interference and mistakes. (*CWK*, XIII, 1934, p. 486)

> On the other side of the gulf are those that reject the idea that the existing economic system is, in any significant sense, self-adjusting. (ibid., p. 487)

> The gulf between these two schools of thought is deeper, I believe, than most of those on either side of it are aware of. On which side does the essential truth lie? That is the vital question for us to solve. (p. 488)

In 1934 Keynes, at last, made explicit that there was a methodological 'gulf' between his new analytical macroeconomic model and the one employed by the dominant neoclassical economists represented by Pigou's *Theory of Unemployment* (1933). The relevance of Keynes's statements is still with us, because one crucial difference between modern mainstream (macro)economics (see, for instance Mankiw's 2000 textbook, *Macroeconomics*) and Post Keynesian economics is the choice of method, analytical model and the aim of macroeconomics.

The fundamental axioms lying behind most mainstream macroeconomic general equilibrium models are the following:

1. The perfect functioning market economic system has a general equilibrium solution determined by macroeconomic structures.
2. It is a predetermined and, at least in the longer-run, self-adjusting system.
3. Dynamic general equilibrium models build upon neoclassical microeconomic first principles of individual rationality by using representative agent theory and assuming rational expectations and market clearing.

Mainstream economics is divided into the hard-core equilibrium theory, often called real business-cycle theory, assuming continuous market clearing, and New Keynesian macroeconomics. In the hard-core models economic growth and business cycles are explained within a closed (that is, deterministic) system and caused by exogenous changes in the underlying economic structures and/or technology. New Keynesian macroeconomics employs the same underlying analytical framework of a general equilibrium closed model (see Rotheim 1998; Jespersen 2009). Short-run dynamics – deviations from general equilibrium such as involuntary unemployment – are caused by exogenous supply or demand shocks and propagated by market imperfections.

New Keynesian models have a rich menu of suggested market imperfections, for instance rigid nominal wages, prices, rates of interest or exchange rates, which make the adjustment process sluggish. Within mainstream macroeconomics the general equilibrium model is taken for granted; hence, research and policy recommendation are directed towards the causes and consequences of market imperfections and how to overcome them by increased wage and price flexibility.

In sum, one can say that the general equilibrium models are characterized by focusing on real sector activities, where:

1. Say's law prevails.
2. The financial sector's activities have no impact as long as the rate of interest is free to equalize saving and investment.
3. Money is 'a veil' and has no lasting effect on real business except the price level.

Within such an analytical, closed and predetermined market-clearing system, demand management policies can have no lasting real effect. If expansionary policies are pursued in the short run to overcome wage/price rigidities they have, according to the model, to be counterbalanced at a later stage to prevent an increase in the price level.

The general equilibrium model can be compared to a laboratory, where scientists have created an artificial and idealized picture of how a market system should work. The structures and dynamics of the model are not confronted with reality – it is based on axioms of individual rationality and market clearing, which are considered so obviously true that they do not have to be empirically verified.

Keynes's aim with macroeconomic analysis was fundamentally different. He wanted to understand the causal factors behind the real-world macroeconomic activities. In 1932 he changed the title of his university lectures from the 'pure theory of money' to a 'monetary theory of production'.

Thereby he signalled that the development of macroeconomics could not be divided into a real sector analysis, where money is just a veil, and a monetary theory, where financial variables only have a lasting impact on the price level.

Even more important was Keynes's emphasis on the theoretical importance of *uncertainty*. Lack of knowledge about the future, that is, uncertainty, is an unavoidable part of decision making in the real world at the individual as well as at the political level. The future is (partly) unknowable. But decisions have to be made and therefore have to be based on uncertain expectations.

The analytical challenge of Keynes's and Post Keynesian economics is to establish an analytical framework where economic behaviour based on expectations is incorporated. The analytical implications of individual uncertainty for macroeconomic theory are crucial, because the relevance of models relying on representative (individual) agent theory and rational expectations collapses. The unknowable future makes the hypothesis of rational expectations empirically false. Furthermore, there is no real-world evidence that continuous and simultaneous market clearing can happen, even if wages and prices are assumed to be fully flexible. As Keynes said in 1934, we do not know whether a perfect market economy entails a general market-clearing solution or not; but even if the model, by chance, did have a full-employment outcome, agents would not know about it and therefore cannot in advance behave in accordance with this abstract and unknowable information. Expectations will always be uncertain; that is the core of Post Keynesian economics and the real analytical challenge, which requires a specific methodology:

> The object of our analysis is, not to provide a machine, or method of blind manipulation, which will furnish an infallible answer, but to provide ourselves with an organized and orderly method of thinking out particular problems. (*CWK*, VII, p. 297)

Given the inherent state of uncertainty, the outcome of a realistic macroeconomic analysis could at best be a sketch of a few major tendencies of macroeconomic variables drawn through historical time. This means a set of context-related and path-dependent trends leading into a (partly) unknown future. Basically, macroeconomics is not a predictive science. The relevant framework is what critical realists would call an 'open-system' analysis. The outcome is from the very beginning (partly) indeterminate. A number of important variables have to be left out, because they cannot be quantified due to lack of information; see Dow (2002).

On the other hand a macroeconomic model which is open-ended, without a predetermined terminal point, does not preclude establishing subsections, so-called 'semi-closures', where parts of the system can be organized in a formalistic way (see Chick 2004). In these cases one could make a conditional qualitative or quantitative analysis of a specific hypothesis. One example is the multiplier analysis. In the case of reasonably stable structures and unchanged expectations it is possible to estimate a size of magnitude of the income multiplier, given the specific and changeable conditions. This calculation is, of course, context specific, and only valid if it is realistic to assume that the endogenous forces have entirely worked themselves out. Another example of a partial closure in the *General Theory* is the use of given long-term expectations to analyse investment and the later relaxation of this assumption to discuss 'shifting equilibrium' (Kregel 1976).

Although Keynes used the expression 'equilibrium' several times in the *General Theory*, it should not be confused with market clearing. Equilibrium is a state of the economy as a whole or of a relevant subsection of the economy, where the endogenous adjustment processes may exhaust themselves. For instance, the labour market can be in a state of equilibrium (standstill) with substantial involuntary unemployment, when effective demand is constant. This may be the case when expectations of decision makers are fulfilled and stay unchanged. In the real world, conditions will change continuously and any analytical equilibrium will at best be transitory. The concept of equilibrium is only an analytical tool, which might be useful to get a better understanding of causal factors behind specific macroeconomic phenomena such as, as mentioned, involuntary unemployment.

In sum, Post Keynesian economics is an attempt to understand reality. Hence, economic hypotheses need some empirical underpinning. Post Keynesian methodology emphasizes a constructive interplay between hypothetic deduction and empirical induction. Post Keynesian research usually starts with an ontological reflection of the macroeconomic phenomena under consideration. Hypotheses of possible and realistic explanations are established. These hypotheses have to be confronted with reality. Empirical support transforms hypothetical statements into conditional theory. Searching for empirical support is an established part of the Post Keynesian research procedure. Even negative empirical results may give inspiration for reformulation of the original hypotheses, which then can be re-tested and hopefully give a better understanding of reality. This reciprocal procedure is call 'retroduction' (a mix of deduction and induction) and takes inspiration from *critical realism*.

Post Keynesian economists have in varying forms adapted the open-system methodology; but there is no confirmed method shared by all Post Keynesian sub-schools. On the other hand it is hardly an exaggeration to summarize the actual state of the methodological debate in the following way: 'The coherence of Post Keynesian Economics lies principally at the methodological level' (Dunn 2004, p. 34). It is the rejection of the general equilibrium method as a relevant analytical tool to understand reality and the acceptance of open-system analyses which gives Post Keynesian macroeconomics a distinct profile. There is, to paraphrase Keynes, a deep gulf between mainstream and Post Keynesian methodologies.

This entry on Post Keynesian macroeconomic methodology could, therefore, for good reasons be finalized with a concluding quote from Keynes in 1937:

> Economics is a science of thinking in terms of models joined to the art of choosing models which are relevant to the contemporary world. It is compelled to be this, because, unlike the typical natural science, the material to which it is applied is, in too many respects, not homogeneous through time. (*CWK*, XIV, p. 296)

JESPER JESPERSEN

See also:

Critical Realism; Equilibrium and Non-equilibrium; Expectations; Keynes's *General Theory*; Non-ergodicity; Open Systems; Uncertainty.

References

Chick, V. (2004), 'On open systems', *Brazilian Journal of Political Economy*, **24** (1), 3–16.
Dow, S. (2002), *Economic Methodology: An Inquiry*, Oxford: Oxford University Press.
Dunn, S. (2004), 'Transforming Post Keynesian economics: critical realism and the Post Keynesian project', in P. Lewis (ed.), *Transforming Economics: Perspectives on the Critical Realist Project*, London and New York: Routledge, pp. 33–54.
Jespersen, J. (2009), *Macroeconomic Methodology: – A Post-Keynesian Perspective*, Cheltenham, UK and Northampton, MA, USA: Edward Elgar.
Keynes, J.M. (1972–89), *The Collected Writings of John Maynard Keynes*, 30 vols, London: Macmillan and Cambridge: Cambridge University Press for The Royal Economic Society. (Referred to as '*CWK*' and followed by the volume number in roman numerals; *CWK*, XIII, 1934, pp. 485–92 was originally submitted as a radio talk and later printed in *The Listener*, 21 November 1934, with the title 'Poverty in plenty: is the economic system self-adjusting?')
Kregel, J. (1976), 'Uncertainty: methods of Keynes and Post-Keynesians', *Economic Journal*, **86** (342), 209–25.
Mankiw, N.G. (2000), *Macroeconomics*, 4th edn, New York: Worth.
Pigou, A.C. (1933), *The Theory of Unemployment*, London: Macmillan.
Rotheim, R. (ed.) (1998), *New Keynesian Economics/Post Keynesian Alternatives*, London and New York: Routledge.

Marginalism

'Marginalism' is a term used to refer to the process of developing theoretical propositions from the imposition of conditions on the marginal values of variables. In modern neoclassical economics these conditions are derived from the assumption that economic agents engage in optimizing behaviour. In particular, the conditions are expressed as first-order conditions for optimization of the agents' objective function, along with the corresponding second-order conditions to ensure a maximum or minimum as appropriate to the problem. A standard example is derivation of the proposition that product supply curves are upward sloping in perfectly competitive markets. This proposition follows from finding that product price equal to marginal cost is the solution to the first-order condition for profit maximization by individual producers, while rising marginal cost with output is required to satisfy the corresponding second-order condition assuming a horizontal demand curve facing the producer.

The use of marginal conditions to develop theoretical propositions has a long tradition in economics. An early example is David Ricardo's analysis of the distribution of income between workers, capitalists and landowners in *The Principles of Political Economy and Taxation* (1817). Here, Ricardo determines the rent of land of varying quality by imposing the marginal condition that the rent of land at the extensive (or intensive) margin equal zero. He then imposes the conditions that capital accumulates until profits equal zero and that the wage of workers is driven to the subsistence level by the growth of population. In modern parlance, the growth of capital and population are each governed by a marginal condition.

Marginalism was established as an all-encompassing method of theoretical analysis in economics with the 'marginalist revolution' of the early neoclassical economists in the late nineteenth century. In the writings of Carl Menger, W.S. Jevons, Léon Walras and Vilfredo Pareto, Ricardo's analysis of production and supply based on conditions at the margin was extended by an analysis of demand conditions based on marginal utility. Alfred Marshall consolidated the revolution in his *Principles of Economics* (1890), providing a short-period marginal analysis of supply and demand to complement Ricardo's long-period supply analysis.

Modern neoclassical economics extends marginalism from its normative use in the theoretical analysis of an idealized economy in equilibrium to a positive use, namely using marginal conditions as the basis for policy making and empirical analysis. Machlup (1946) argues that the lack of realism in the assumptions of marginalism does not undermine its usefulness as a technique for predicting behaviour. To Machlup, decision makers can, and do, act 'as if' they are equating marginal conditions, even though they do not have the information necessary to calculate exact values. Errors in optimization are to be expected, but the 'way in which changes in the essential variables will affect the probable decisions and action of the business man is not much different if the curves which the theorist draws to depict their conjectures are a little higher or lower, steeper or flatter' (ibid., p. 536).

Today, marginal analysis dominates mainstream economics in both theory and practice. Students around the world are taught that marginal analysis constitutes the principles of economics. Applications of economics to business decisions and public policy are primarily based on evaluating changes in marginal conditions associated with hypothesized behaviour. Finally, estimation of economic relationships is generally based on assuming that economic agents optimize according to the solution of marginal conditions, but that they make errors that are normally distributed with zero mean.

Criticism of marginalism is fundamental to Post Keynesian economics. Indeed, the Keynesian revolution began with Keynes's critique of the application of marginal conditions for equilibrium in the labour market in *The General Theory of Employment, Interest and Money*. Keynes accepts the application of marginal analysis to the employment decisions of individual businesses and the labour supply decisions of workers, but argues persuasively that the marginal condition of wage equal to the value of the marginal product of labour is not sufficient to guarantee full employment in a capitalist economy. The problem noted by Keynes is that when wages and prices move together, a reduction in the money wage cannot be relied on to remove excess supply of labour. What is required is an increase in effective demand, which is most readily accomplished by government expenditure programmes.

Keynes's followers at Cambridge extended the critique of marginalism to other notions of equilibrium based on marginal conditions. Roy Harrod pointed to the fragility of full employment in a growing economy due to the knife-edge requirements for a balance between the growth in supply and growth in effective demand. Joan Robinson attacked the neoclassical parable of accumulation, noting that it ignores changes in relative prices required to maintain the marginal conditions for equilibrium in input markets with a change in the ratio of interest rate to wage rate. According to Robinson, these changes in relative prices destroy our ability to meaningfully measure a quantity of capital from the collection of heterogeneous productive equipment and structures used in the production process.

The attack on marginalism by Keynes and his followers emphasizes problems with its internal coherence, particularly problems encountered once marginal conditions for individual optimization decisions are aggregated to examine the behaviour of an economic system in either a static context or through time. Other Post Keynesians go further and reject the usefulness of marginalism in its entirety. A seminal contribution to this strand of critique is the pioneering study of business pricing behaviour by Hall and Hitch (1939). Hall and Hitch surveyed business executives responsible for price setting and concluded that prices are predominantly set by reference to average cost, suggesting the need for a pricing theory based on the full-cost principle rather than a theory based on the marginal conditions required for profit maximization. Machlup's (1946) argument about economic agents acting 'as if' they are engaged in optimizing behaviour was aimed directly at refuting the survey evidence provided by Hall and Hitch.

Both marginalists and followers of the full-cost principle now understand that there can be formal equivalence between a profit-maximizing price and a full-cost price. Indeed, there is recognition that many influences, such as increases in prices of variable inputs, have similar impact on prices in both approaches. However, as Lee (1990–91, p. 263) notes, 'it is clear that the Post Keynesian full cost pricing equation is radically different from its marginalist counterpart'. Particularly important to Lee as distinctive features of Post Keynesian pricing are (i) the absence of an influence of demand on prices, (ii) a role for social conventions in determining prices and (iii) the evolving nature of the firm such 'that prices and quantities have a historical/temporal dimension that effectively precludes a determinant relationship between price and quantity, and price–quantity and maximizing objectives' (ibid., p. 259).

In spite of the general hostility towards marginalism, some concepts with origins in marginal analysis have survived and prospered in Post Keynesian literature. A good example is the degree of monopoly. Lerner (1934) develops the degree of monopoly as the difference between price and marginal cost divided by price as a way of measuring the impact of monopoly on the efficiency of resource allocation, thereby providing a clear application of marginalism in economics. Lerner's definition is adopted in Kalecki's (1938) analysis of the distribution of income. Further, Kalecki (1940) subsequently provides his own derivation based on satisfying the marginal conditions for profit maximization under conditions of imperfect competition. However, Kriesler (1987) suggests that Kalecki's disenchantment with aspects of the marginalist derivation eventually led him to substitute a distinctly non-marginalist pricing equation as the basis for the degree of monopoly in his analysis of income distribution.

In summary, marginalism has not been banished completely from Post Keynesian economics, in spite of strong criticism by some Post Keynesians and outright rejection by others. This diversity of treatment is consistent with the open-systems ontology espoused by Post Keynesian methodologists. Rather than seek sole allegiance to a single method of analysis, as is the case with marginalism for our neoclassical colleagues, Post Keynesians recognize the virtue of using a variety of analytical methods in furthering our understanding of a complex and continually evolving economic system. In this context, Downward's (1999, chapter 6) assessment of the debate between marginalists and advocates of the full-cost pricing principle is particularly revealing.

HARRY BLOCH

See also:

Capital Theory; Effective Demand; Employment; Equilibrium and Non-equilibrium; Income Distribution; Macroeconomic Methodology; Open Systems; Prices and Pricing; Walrasian Economics.

References

Downward, P. (1999), *Pricing Theory in Post Keynesian Economics*, Cheltenham, UK and Northampton, MA, USA: Edward Elgar.

Hall, R.L. and C.J. Hitch (1939), 'Price theory and business behaviour', *Oxford Economic Papers*, **2** (1), 12–45.

Kalecki, M. (1938), 'The determinants of the distribution of national income', *Econometrica*, **6** (2), 97–112.

Kalecki, M. (1940), 'The supply curve of an industry under imperfect competition', *Review of Economic Studies*, **7** (2), 91–112.

Kriesler, P. (1987), *Kalecki's Microanalysis*, Cambridge: Cambridge University Press.

Lee, F.S (1990–91), 'Marginalist controversy and Post Keynesian price theory', *Journal of Post Keynesian Economics*, **13** (2), 249–63.

Lerner, A.P. (1934), 'The degree of monopoly', *Review of Economic Studies*, **1** (3), 157–75.

Machlup, F. (1946), 'Marginal analysis and empirical research', *American Economic Review*, **36** (4:1), 519–54.

Market Governance

In Post Keynesian economics, market governance refers to the processes of crafting and implementing laws and regulations to reduce instability and decrease uncertainty in the market, as part of the grand project of achieving a 'civilized society'. In contrast to neoclassical economics' portrayal of market governance as an apolitical and technical task to be managed by 'experts', Post Keynesians view it as a collective political process. Power plays a role in the process of governing. Conflict is unavoidable because social classes have different interests. Nevertheless, democracy is the way to solve disputes with the active participation of all social classes collectively, for market governance has significant implications for economic growth, income distribution, equity, environmental justice and the quality of life. First, we investigate the microeconomic foundations of market governance; second, we analyse the objectives of market governance in Post Keynesian economics; third, we examine the methods of governance; and finally we state the major findings.

Governance denotes the processes of governing the country by making rules that matter to the public collectively. As an act of governing, governance involves state, non-state and private actors. Economic governance encompasses all decision-making processes related to a country's economic activities and its relationships with other economies (UNDP 1997, p. 2). In the light of these two definitions, market governance can be defined as a system of regulating business enterprises' behaviour in the marketplace with the purpose of achieving the public interest.

For neoclassical economists, market governance denotes the deployment of the market mechanisms of supply and demand. In this view, private economic actors, institutions and mechanisms gain power and authority at the expense of public institutions in areas traditionally ruled by the states. In neoclassical economics, perfect competition allocates scarce resources efficiently. Markets are self-adjusting and business enterprises are price takers (Kitromilides 1985). The microeconomic foundation of market governance in Post Keynesian economics is based on the empirical observation that oligopolistic markets are the dominant market form, although it is also possible to observe competitive markets, especially in declining sectors of the economy or emerging industries. However, competitive markets are prone to consolidation eventually, which fuels instability and uncertainty. Overall, oligopolistic markets make up a significant portion of the economic structures in industrialized countries (Eichner 1976).

In oligopolistic markets, prices in product markets do not adjust automatically. Business enterprises have the power to determine prices (ibid., pp. ix–x). The megacorp, being the representative firm in the oligopolistic sector of the economy, is the price setter (Sawyer and Shapiro 2010, p. 86). Naturally, it earns more than the 'neoclassical proprietorship' and return on its investment is certain for two reasons. First, entry barriers prevent new entrants from gaining access to the market. Second, price coordination and the maintenance practices of the megacorp's industry protect it from price wars. Business enterprises sell their products under conditions of recognized interdependence and members of the industry engage in 'joint profit maximization' (Eichner 1976, p. 3). Price wars are not absent. They are rare, but can be destructive and destabilizing.

In neoclassical economics, the market is portrayed as being governed by the invisible hand, and impersonal imperatives such as supply and demand regulate it. Market governance is about creating a level playing field and leaving the market alone. In other words, the state is a referee to maintain the level playing field with minimal antitrust law enforcement. In Post Keynesian economics, both competitive and oligopolistic markets are prone to instability, which fuels uncertainty for different reasons. In competitive markets, business competition can be ruinous; labour may be left unemployed; there may be excess supply; prices may be too low to cover cost; there may be bankruptcies. In general, competitive markets are not self-adjusting (Sawyer and Shapiro 2010, p. 86). Instability and uncertainty are two immediate dangers that should be addressed by market governance mechanisms.

Oligopolistic markets have both positive and negative implications for the public interest as well. As the representative firm, the megacorp has market power and deploys it to extract higher prices from consumers (ibid., pp. 84–9). The megacorp's ability to mark up the prices of its products above their costs is a 'levy' for future investment and economic expansion. Competition between large business enterprises takes place on the basis of new products, new technology, product differentiation and product improvement (ibid.). Overall, the megacorp's power serves the public interest by promoting secular economic growth in the long run. Market power is also the source of stability in the market, compared to instability in competitive markets. Finally, the megacorp is the institutional form that achieves economies of scale and productive efficiency with its multi-plant structure and managerial talent (Eichner 1976, p. 1).

None the less, the megacorp is a private institution after all and market power can be the source of instability as well as uncertainty, for a number of reasons. First, higher pricing by the megacorp can fuel inflation. If strong trade unions in the oligopolistic sectors of the economy use their power, there is a high risk of price–wage inflation spiralling (ibid., pp. 1–2). Second, the megacorp may not use the levy for investment, if there are not profitable areas. Finally, the megacorp may abuse its power to drive its smaller and healthy competitors out of the market. There is a danger of long-term stagnation and exploitation of consumers in the oligopolistic sectors of the economy in the absence of carefully crafted market governance rules.

In Post Keynesian economics, market governance ultimately aims at creating a 'civilized society' which combines individualism with the public interest by preventing instability and uncertainty in the market. The idea of regulation reproducing the results of perfect competition is not acceptable. The fundamental assumption in the mainstream regulatory theory of allocative efficiency (price equals marginal cost) is strongly challenged. Productive efficiency, distributional equity, and the impact on market structure are the key concerns of good market governance (Wald 1979, pp. 126–8).

Instead of solely relying on Paretian pricing norms, there is a case for 'non-pricing efficiencies' to avoid uncoordinated production plans and the wasteful utilization of productive factors. There is support for preventing or minimizing anticompetitive restrictions that provide individual firms safe havens because of the inverse relationship between the market security of individual firms and the incentives to cost reduction, product improvement and innovation. There is a tendency for flexibility rather than a uniform application of antitrust/competition law without compromising the general validity of the antitrust rules. Eichner notes:

> Thus there is no model, or set of policies based on a model, that applies across the board to both the competitive and oligopolistic markets. Indeed, in the competitive sector, the government must make up for the lack of inter-firm coordination and planning, while in the oligopolistic sector, it must make sure that the private power to plan does not subvert any larger public interest. (Eichner 1979, p. 178)

Developing specific, flexible and well-defined antitrust/competition policy guidelines for separate markets, rather than applying the law uniformly in different markets, is the most important policy message in Post Keynesian economics.

In neoclassical economics, decisions are made by specialists and the decision-making process is technocratic, and thus isolated from political processes. Institutional autonomy and arm's-length relationships between government agencies and elected officials have been promoted by neoclassical economists over the past thirty years (Kitromilides 1985, p. 11). By contrast, Post Keynesians advocate the politicization of decision making by getting concerned social classes involved in the process. Law is a product of the democratic process and can be changed with the involvement of the social classes. Power becomes a determining factor in decision making.

Politics is the main place for individual citizens to get together, form political parties, and influence policy making. According to Pressman, 'Politics is the main arena in which people band together . . .. Politics is also the arena in which individuals assert power as a group in modern society' (Pressman 2006, p. 68). The state is not treated as an autonomous and independent actor alone. On the contrary, it is also perceived as an arena for contestation. Democratic governance is the foundation of the 'civilized society'. Minsky states:

> If amplified uncertainty, extremes of income distribution, and social inequality attenuate the economic underpinnings of democracy, then the market behavior that creates these conditions should be constrained. If it is necessary to give up a bit of market efficiency, or a bit of aggregate income, in order to contain democracy-threatening uncertainty, then so be it. (Minsky 1996, p. 364)

In sum, Post Keynesians value political debate and democratic decision making in market governance, instead of isolating important decisions from public influence. Market governance is seen as a collective and political decision.

Besides democratic decision making, good market governance requires a 'competent and committed state' as well (Arestis and Sawyer 1998, p. 192). The effectiveness of a bureaucracy and an uncorrupt civil service that implement laws and regulations are part of good market governance. Again, market governance is not equal to withdrawing the state from the market, but strengthening it to enforce laws properly. Overall, the effective, committed and competent bureaucracy is the tool for achieving good market governance.

This entry has demonstrated that market governance is a system that specifies the expected behaviour of market actors as well as state officials to regulate the market to achieve the ultimate aim of realizing the 'civilized society'. Good market governance is one that decreases market instability and uncertainty. The empirical observations that oligopolistic markets are the dominant market form in industrialized countries and that the megacorp is the representative firm serve as the basis of market governance in Post Keynesian economics. It does not mean that there are no competitive markets. They make up the smaller portion of the total economy and are prone to consolidation eventually. In either case, instability and uncertainty are the two issues to be addressed by market governance.

Market governance targets economic growth, stability, certainty, equity, environmental justice and quality of life. Rules and regulations should be flexible, specific and well-defined to achieve the goals. Active participation is necessary for achieving good market governance. Law is the product of political process where power becomes a crucial factor. A competent, efficient and effective bureaucracy is the main tool to achieve it. The state is both an autonomous actor as well as a site for political contention. Overall, market governance is a political process based on the principle of democratic decision making to reduce instability and uncertainty, not an expert business to create a level playing field only.

TUNA BASKOY

See also:

Competition; Galbraith's Economics; Prices and Pricing; Welfare Economics.

References

Arestis, P. and M. Sawyer (1998), 'Keynesian economic policies for the new millennium', *Economic Journal*, **108** (446), 181–95.

Eichner, A.S. (1976), *The Megacorp and Oligopoly: Micro Foundations of Macro Dynamics*, Cambridge: Cambridge University Press.

Eichner, A.S. (1979), 'A look ahead', in Eichner (ed.), *A Guide to Post-Keynesian Economics*, White Plains, NY: M.E. Sharpe, pp. 165–84.

Kitromilides, Y. (1985), 'The formation of economic policy: a question for economists?', in P. Arestis and T. Skouras (eds), *Post Keynesian Economic Theory: A Challenge to Neo Classical Economics*, Armonk, NY: M.E. Sharpe, pp. 7–23.

Minsky, H.P. (1996), 'Uncertainty and the institutional structure of capitalist economies', *Journal of Economic Issues*, **30** (2), 357–68.

Pressman, S. (2006), 'Economic power, the state, and Post-Keynesian economics', *International Journal of Political Economy*, **35** (4), 67–86.

Sawyer, M. and N. Shapiro (2010), 'The macroeconomics of competition: stability and growth questions', in M. Lavoie, L.-P. Rochon and M. Seccaraccia (eds), *Money and Macrodynamics: Alfred Eichner and Post-Keynesian Economics*, Armonk, NY: M.E. Sharpe, pp. 83–95.

United Nations Development Programme (UNDP) (1997), *Governance for Sustainable Human Development*, New York: United Nations Development Programme.

Wald, H.P. (1979), 'Comment: normative premises in regulatory theory', *Journal of Post Keynesian Economics*, **1** (3), 126–9.

Microfoundations

The term 'microfoundations' entered discussions of Post Keynesian theory from neoclassical analysis. In its broadest sense, the term refers to the specification for individual economic behaviour in macroeconomic models. In this broad sense, any behavioural theories of individual action as part of macroeconomic models constitute microfoundations.

The practical meaning of the term in mainstream discourse, however, is narrower, usually referring to the link between macroeconomic models and the maximization of utility and profit by individual agents. While this procedure dates back at least to the life-cycle model of consumption (Franco Modigliani) and the neoclassical model of investment (Dale Jorgenson), the New Classical macroeconomic revolution of the 1970s placed much greater emphasis on microfoundations in this sense. The reason for this methodological shift is the famous 'Lucas critique'. This idea arose initially from models that explore the neutrality of money with 'rational' expectations, but its implications have spread far beyond this context. The Lucas critique questions the usefulness of the predictions from any economic model that is not specified in terms of so-called 'deep, structural parameters' of taste and technology, for only these parameters are invariant to different policy regimes. This dictum has been used to dismiss a priori any analysis, theoretical or empirical, without microfoundations that explicitly link results to parameters of preference through utility maximization and parameters of technology through profit maximization.

Two issues from this debate are salient for Post Keynesian economics: the role of optimization as a foundation for behaviour and the specification of expectations. Post Keynesian writers have an eclectic approach to optimization. There are numerous examples of the use of optimization as the behavioural foundation in Keynesian and Post Keynesian research. Keynes's classical 'postulates' in chapter 2, section V of the *General Theory*, rely on a profit-maximization result to equate the marginal productivity of labour to the real wage. Davidson (1998) describes the point of effective demand in terms of the behaviour of 'profit maximizing entrepreneurs'. Fazzari et al. (1998) use maximization for a representative firm to explore the impact of imperfect competition on firms' employment and pricing decisions in a Keynesian macroeconomic model. Keynes's analysis of the marginal efficiency of capital in chapter 11 of the *General Theory* concludes that investment will equate the marginal efficiency of the capital stock to the market rate of interest, consistent with the results of a maximization model. Unlike the New Classical approach, however, there is no methodological restriction in Post Keynesian analysis that dictates the use of optimization as a behavioural axiom. Many relations are motivated by a broader and more eclectic perspective on individual behaviour that does not rely solely on optimization. For example, Keynes's 'fundamental psychological law' links consumption to income without reference to any explicit optimization conditions. More recently, Cynamon and Fazzari (2008) explain falling saving rates and rising indebtedness of US households prior to the 'Great Recession' that began in late 2007 as driven in large part by social norms rather than the atomistic optimization behaviour posited by the life-cycle model of consumer behaviour. However, as the examples above show, the use of optimization to explore microfoundations is a part of the Post Keynesian research programme.

A more significant difference between neoclassical and Post Keynesian microfoundations arises in the specification of expectation formation. The rational expectations approach specifies expectations from the actual statistical predictions of the model. In these models, expectations therefore have no independent existence; they are determined fully by the other structures in the model. To specify expectations, one solves the model for the expected values of variables that are consistent with model. If the model is specified in terms of parameters of preference and technology, then expectations are also a function of preference and technology. This approach contrasts sharply with the great emphasis put on an independent role for expectations by Post Keynesian research. In these models, the expectations of firms, households and participants in financial markets are central autonomous components of behaviour that cannot be reduced to technology or a narrow conception of preferences simply across goods. Changes in expectations can occur without any change in technology or preferences, and such independent changes in expectations significantly affect economic outcomes. This approach allows phenomena such as 'convention', 'confidence' and 'animal spirits' to affect macroeconomic outcomes. Although longstanding work on 'bounded rationality' and learning models has received some recent attention among neoclassical macroeconomists, a gulf remains between the microfoundations of expectations in the New Classical tradition and the Post Keynesian approach. (Crotty 1994 makes a similar point and links it insightfully to an assessment of the logic of grounding neoclassical models in the microfoundations of individual agent choices.)

This gulf in the conception of expectation formation reflects more than a difference in modelling strategy. It is linked inherently to the significant difference between orthodox and Post Keynesian conceptions of uncertainty. Uncertainty in neoclassical macroeconomic models is represented by probability distributions over ergodic stochastic processes. Most Post Keynesian writers reject this conception in favour of 'fundamental', 'true' or 'Keynesian' uncertainty, which implies that stable, objective probability distributions do not exist for key variables that affect microeconomic decisions. The microfoundations question for expectations, therefore, is not whether real-world agents do or do not behave in accordance with the rational expectations hypothesis. In the Post Keynesian perspective, there is no logical basis for rational expectations because the statistical information required for rational expectations simply does not exist.

Clearly, the concept of microfoundations plays a key role in understanding the difference between Post Keynesian and other forms of economic analysis. The remainder of this entry considers how these differences appear in three different contexts of central significance for macroeconomics: labour demand, the financing of investment and the role of nominal rigidity.

The first of Keynes's 'classical postulates' (*General Theory*, chapter 2) presents a theory of labour demand that appears consistent with the modern neoclassical microfoundations approach. That is, firms maximize profits constrained by their technology. Because Keynes maintains the first classical postulate, it appears on the surface that his theory is consistent with at least this aspect of neoclassical microfoundations. Such a conclusion, however, is misleading. While the Keynesian theory is consistent with the result that the real wage equals the marginal product of labour at an effective demand equilibrium, this result differs from the conclusion that the technologically determined marginal product of labour is the labour demand schedule. For as Davidson (1998, p. 825) and Fazzari et al. (1998, p. 534) argue, one cannot define the effective demand for labour in a Keynesian model without knowledge of the state of aggregate demand and its impact on firms' output markets. (The latter reference argues that this point becomes even more obvious in the realistic case of imperfect competition.) In a Keynesian model, the effective demand for labour is a single point on the marginal product of labour schedule, the point consistent with constraints on firm sales imposed by the state of aggregate demand.

These results demonstrate that the distinction between the Keynesian and neoclassical microfoundations for labour demand does not arise from behaviour at the level of individual agents: in both models, firms maximize profits. Rather, the distinction arises from a different conception of how microeconomic agents are embedded in the macroeconomic environment. In the Keynesian model, demand conditions constrain sales, a key factor that changes the microeconomic actions of business.

The link between finance and investment provides another example of an active research area in which the distinction between Post Keynesian and neoclassical microfoundations plays an important role. Keynes and many Post Keynesian authors, perhaps most prominently Hyman Minsky, have emphasized the connection between financial markets, the availability of financing, and investment spending. When Jorgenson and others developed neoclassical microfoundations for investment, however, consideration of financial constraints disappeared. Jorgenson explicitly linked this approach to the Modigliani–Miller theorem that establishes microfoundation conditions under which real firm investment decisions are independent of financial structure, largely eliminating finance from mainstream investment research for decades. In the 1980s, however, a deeper analysis of the microfoundations of investment decisions with asymmetric information between firms and lenders led to reconsideration of the independence of investment from finance. The result has been a large mainstream literature on financing constraints for investment, a change in microfoundations that appears to bring mainstream investment theory closer to the Post Keynesian approach.

The extent of this convergence has spawned controversy. A large body of mainstream empirical research supports the importance of financial conditions for investment, results that also broadly support Post Keynesian views. (Although controversy remains: see Brown et al. 2009, pp. 160–61 for recent references.) There is more debate on the theory of asymmetric information for the microfoundations of financing constraints. Fazzari and Variato (1994, pp. 359–61) point out that meaningful financing constraints require that potential lenders (or sources of external equity) refuse to fund investment projects that firms wish to undertake. They conclude that this outcome implies a systematic information asymmetry. Furthermore, they argue that asymmetric information is not a minor 'imperfection', it is a pervasive characteristic of decentralized market economies. Along similar lines, Dymski (1993) discusses the complementarity of asymmetric information and Post Keynesian microfoundations based on a Keynesian conception of uncertainty. In contrast, however, Van Ees and Garretsen (1993) argue that the kind of asymmetric information models that have been pursued in mainstream analysis cannot be reconciled with Post Keynesian theory because the mainstream models require an ergodic stochastic environment which is inconsistent with fundamental uncertainty. Crotty (1996) also explores the importance of expectations for investment with fundamental uncertainty. He argues that many important aspects of Keynesian investment theory and the linkages between investment and finance cannot be understood from microfoundations of asymmetric information models.

Finally, the mainstream literature known as 'New' Keynesian is largely motivated by microfoundations. This approach emphasizes nominal rigidity of either wages or prices (see Gali and Gertler 2007, for an accessible discussion). In the context of the Lucas critique, simply assuming nominal rigidity (perhaps motivated by empirical evidence on price rigidity) is considered *ad hoc*. New Keynesian macroeconomics therefore strives to explain nominal rigidity with optimizing models. This class of models has little relevance for Post Keynesian macroeconomics because the Post Keynesian approach does not require nominal rigidity to obtain effects of aggregate demand on output and employment (see Palley 2008 for further references).

Almost all economic models draw motivation from a specification of behaviour of economic agents. In this broad sense, microfoundations are part of virtually every economic theory, and the idea that microfoundations should be realistic and logically consistent seems uncontroversial. In much of mainstream macroeconomics, however, a particularly narrow perspective on what constitutes 'good' or even 'acceptable' microfoundations seems to have constrained theory in ways that block important insights about how the world really works. A broader conception of microfoundations that reflect an environment of uncertainty, norms of behaviour and demand constraints on economic activity is a distinctive feature of Post Keynesian theory.

STEVEN FAZZARI

See also:

Agency; Conventions; Credit Rationing; Effective Demand; Employment; Expectations; Financial Instability Hypothesis; Investment; Marginalism; New Classical Economics; New Keynesian Economics; Non-ergodicity; Uncertainty.

References

Brown, J.R., S.M. Fazzari and B.C. Petersen (2009), 'Financing innovation and growth: cash flow, external equity, and the 1990s R&D boom', *Journal of Finance*, **64** (1), 151–85.
Crotty, J.R. (1994), 'Are Keynesian uncertainty and macrotheory incompatible? Conventional decision making, institutional structures and conditional stability in Keynesian macromodels', in G. Dymski and R. Pollin (eds), *New Perspectives in Monetary Macroeconomics: Explorations in the Tradition of Hyman Minsky*, Ann Arbor, MI: University of Michigan Press, pp. 105–42.

Crotty, J.R. (1996), 'Is New Keynesian investment theory really "Keynesian"? Reflections on Fazzari and Variato', *Journal of Post Keynesian Economics*, **18** (3), 333–57.

Cynamon, B.Z. and S.M. Fazzari (2008), 'Household debt in the consumer age – source of growth and risk of collapse', *Capitalism and Society* (Berkeley Electronic Press), **3** (2), 1–30, available at: http://www.bepress.com/cas/vol3/iss2/art3.

Davidson, P. (1998), 'Post Keynesian employment analysis and the macroeconomics of OECD unemployment', *Economic Journal*, **108** (440), 817–31.

Dymski, G. (1993), 'Keynesian uncertainty and asymmetric information: complementary or contradictory?', *Journal of Post Keynesian Economics*, **16** (1), 49–54.

Fazzari, S.M., P. Ferri and E. Greenberg (1998), 'Aggregate demand and firm behavior: a new perspective on Keynesian microfoundations', *Journal of Post Keynesian Economics*, **20** (4), 527–58.

Fazzari, S.M. and A.M. Variato (1994), 'Asymmetric information and Keynesian theories of investment', *Journal of Post Keynesian Economics*, **16** (3), 351–69.

Gali, J. and M. Gertler (2007), 'Macroeconomic modeling for monetary policy evaluation,' *Journal of Economic Perspectives*, **21** (4), 25–45.

Palley, T.I. (2008), 'Keynesian models of deflation and depression revisited', *Journal of Economic Behavior and Organization*, **68** (1), 167–77.

Van Ees, H. and H. Garretsen (1993), 'Financial markets and the complementarity of asymmetric information and fundamental uncertainty', *Journal of Post Keynesian Economics*, **16** (1), 37–48.

Monetary Policy

Whatever its detailed variants, Post Keynesian monetary policy is unified by four characteristics, three of which stem directly from Keynes's *General Theory*. Of the three, the first is the dominant role given to aggregate demand in determining the level of economic activity; the second is the lack of any automatic tendency for that level of economic activity to coincide with the full-employment level of output; the third is the desire for a more equal distribution of income and wealth. The fourth characteristic, not present in the *General Theory* itself, is the acceptance of an endogenous money supply where the role of the central bank consists of setting the price at which it will make available the reserves required to validate the lending which banks wish to undertake, given the demand for loans. This 'price' is the central bank's official dealing rate and it provides the foundation for the level and structure of market rates. In the light of these interest rates and what is often called the 'state of trade', borrowers decide on the (flow) of new bank lending that they require and the resulting new loans create additional deposits, that is, 'money'. Thus monetary policy in Post Keynesian economics is interest rate policy (see, for example, Moore 1988).

In the Post Keynesian view, monetary policy affects *both* output *and* prices. Moreover, the effect upon prices runs *through* output. This is quite different from the more extreme versions of neoclassical economics where monetary policy is seen to affect only prices, and differs also from the more moderate versions where output may also be affected in the short run but as an unfortunate, simultaneous, byproduct of interest changes.

The immediate effect of a rise in interest rates falls upon demand, through five channels: a wealth effect as a result of falling asset prices; an increase in the price of consuming now as opposed to saving; a rise in the cost of credit; an increase in the external value of the currency; and a redistribution of spending power from the relatively poor to the better-off with higher propensities to save. Since firms are largely price-setting, quantity adjusters, the effect of the monetary tightening has its immediate effect upon output and eventually upon unemployment. Any downward pressure on prices occurs only subsequently as the result of prolonged underutilization of resources. And the slowing of monetary growth, so often misidentified in the orthodox literature as the *cause* of falling inflation, occurs only because firms' falling production requires less working capital in the form of bank loans.

This Post Keynesian analysis of how interest rate policy works is not far removed from that adopted by 'mainstream' economists with experience of the realities of central banking (Goodhart 1994) or from the statements of central banks themselves (Bank of England 1999). However, many Post Keynesians would query whether, if inflation is the demand-side phenomenon that orthodox economics claims, fiscal policy might be a superior alternative (Arestis and Sawyer 2002).

Given the belief that there are no automatic mechanisms for ensuring full employment and their tendency to support Keynes's proposition that it is more important to disappoint the rentier than the worker, there is a natural preference among Post Keynesians for a monetary (interest rate) policy that takes full employment as its primary objective. This is flatly at odds with the objectives of monetary policy as conducted by governments and central banks in developed countries for the last 25 years or so. In practice, the emphasis has been upon price stability (or at least low inflation) as the main or even only goal of monetary policy, achieved by sustained high real interest rates accompanied by chronically depressed output. Intellectually, this has drawn support from the 'rational expectations' and 'policy irrelevance' work of the 1970s, which argued that there is no sacrifice involved (in output or employment) since monetary policy *can* only affect prices. Minimizing inflation is a 'free lunch'. Such arguments amount to a restatement of the 'classical dichotomy' wherein money is a 'veil' whose quantity determines the overall level of prices but has no effect upon quantities, which are determined by 'real' forces. In its modern incarnation, this commitment to the classical dichotomy takes the form of inflation targeting, wherein interest rate policy is assigned the sole function of minimizing medium-term inflation and real magnitudes enter the picture only as indicators of likely future movements in inflation. This can be seen most clearly where central banks adopt a 'Taylor-type' rule for the setting of interest rates. Measurements of the output gap are important, but only because they provide *information* which can be used in the choice of interest rate whose sole purpose remains to minimize inflation. If central banks adhere rigidly to a Taylor rule and the object of monetary policy is solely the minimizing of inflation, then we are not far removed from the rule-governed monetary policy of the kind advocated by Milton Friedman and others in the 1960s. The interest rate replaces the stock of money as the instrument of policy and the instrument is set according to a rule which features output and real interest rates rather than the long-run growth of output.

To their credit, some mainstream economists (Laidler 1990; Blanchard et al. 1997) have consistently rejected this view, faced with clear evidence that the tightening of monetary policy in the early 1980s and 1990s clearly played a part in the accompanying recessions. The dramatic cuts in interest rates after the 2008 crisis and their subsequent maintenance at historically low levels suggests that central banks are also acutely aware that monetary policy affects real variables in a more than transient fashion. More importantly, the general public has always been sceptical of any argument that monetary policy does not affect their jobs and incomes. This has forced governments to recognize the danger that operating a tight monetary policy was likely to lead to electoral defeat if they were seen as authors of a policy in which the public perceived real costs. From this was born the belief that monetary policy was 'best' operated by an independent central bank which did not have to confront democratic preferences. The result has been a creeping privatization of monetary policy in which central banks have been reconstituted with charters giving them at least instrument independence (for example, the Bank of England in 1997) and in some cases the freedom to set the inflation target as well (the European Central Bank in 1999).

In the Post Keynesian view, therefore, monetary policy as operated has helped sustain an unwarrantedly high level of unemployment and loss of output. Furthermore, because monetary policy has become a 'one-club', interest rate, policy it also has distributional effects which work against broadly the same groups as are disadvantaged by chronic restrictions of output. The distributional effects of interest rates operate most obviously through agents' portfolios, in particular through their net holdings of floating rate assets. Where these holdings are positive, a rise in interest rates redistributes income in their favour (abstracting from any effects of the local tax regime). By the same mechanism, those with net floating rate liabilities lose. Thorbecke (1999) has shown that in periods of disinflationary policy the burden of adjustment is unequal between production sectors (construction and durables suffer most) and between social groups (low-income workers and minorities pay the highest price).

At the heart of Post Keynesian monetary policy, therefore, is not so much a body of technical analysis which cuts it off from the mainstream (or at least from its more realistic practitioners) but a desire to rid the *practice* of policy from its deflationary biases, to reassert the value of discretion in responding to monetary shocks and to restore accountability in the conduct of monetary policy. At the heart of Post Keynesian policy are lower interest rates. But it is widely recognized that such a policy will face severe constraints, especially in the form of reactions from global financial markets. Much discussion of what a Post Keynesian monetary policy might look like in practice is thus taken up with suggestions for intervention in and regulation of the financial system. For countries with independent central banks enjoying goal and instrument independence, legislation may be required to force a change in targets towards less deflationary policy. For central banks with only instrument independence, governments have retained the power to set less disinflationary targets. It remains to be seen whether the recent (2009–10) experience of monetary policy where central banks have been unable to reduce real interest rates further when the policy rate is at the zero lower bound, might encourage a rethink in favour of higher inflation targets. Any unilateral moves of this kind, however, especially if accompanied by a public commitment to a permanent shift in policy goals, would immediately bring an adverse reaction from foreign exchange markets. Post Keynesian monetary policy recognizes therefore the need for the redesign of the international monetary system aimed at reducing the scale and volatility of foreign exchange flows and creating a means whereby deficit countries can adjust without necessarily reducing demand. Some form of 'adjustable peg' system seems most appropriate and suggestions have been made by Davidson (1992). Lowering interest rates has the inevitable consequence of giving an immediate boost to the present value of all (including financial) assets, as well as increasing the demand for credit much of which may later find its way into asset price inflation rather than productive use. Such dangers could be overcome by a willingness to consider either lending ratios imposed upon financial institutions that could be encouraged by the appropriate use of such ratios to favour certain types of lending, or ratios (of loan to spending) imposed upon borrowers in the way that hire purchase agreements once used to specify minimum deposits (Arestis and Sawyer 1998).

PETER HOWELLS

See also:

Central Banks; Economic Policy; Financial Reform; Inflation; International Financial Reform; New Classical Economics; Rate of Interest.

References

Arestis, P. and M.C. Sawyer (1998), 'Keynesian economic policies for the new millennium', *Economic Journal*, **108** (446), 181–95.

Arestis, P. and M.C. Sawyer (2002), 'Can monetary policy affect the real economy?', Working Paper No. 355, Levy Economics Institute of Bard College, Annandale-on Hudson, NY.

Bank of England (1999), 'The transmission mechanism of monetary policy, *Bank of England Quarterly Bulletin*, May, 161–70.

Blanchard, O., A. Blinder, M. Eichenbaum, R. Solow and J.B. Taylor (1997), 'Is there a core of practical macroeconomics that we should all believe?', *American Economic Review*, **87** (2), 230–46.

Davidson, P. (1992), 'Reforming the world's money', *Journal of Post Keynesian Economics*, **15** (2), 153–79.

Goodhart, C.A.E. (1994), 'What should central banks do? What should be their macro-economic objectives and operations?', *Economic Journal*, **104** (427), 1424–36.

Laidler, D.E.W. (1990), *Taking Money Seriously*, Hemel Hempstead: Philip Allan.

Moore, B.J. (1988), *Horizontalists and Verticalists*, Cambridge: Cambridge University Press.

Thorbecke, W. (1999), 'Further evidence on the distributional effects of disinflationary monetary policy', Working Paper No. 264, Levy Institute of Bard College, Annandale-on Hudson, NY.

Money

This entry will first define money. This will allow us to discuss what we might call 'the nature of money' – what is money, what does money 'do', and why is money important. We then turn to two contrasting approaches to money – the 'exogenous' versus the 'endogenous' approaches. The first is adopted by most orthodox theory (most obviously, by monetarists) and the second by heterodoxy (most explicitly by Post Keynesians).

Defining money is a vexing problem for monetary theorists. Readers are familiar with the two usual approaches – defining money by its functions, or simply and arbitrarily choosing some empirical definition (as Keynes did in the *General Theory*: 'we can draw the line between "money" and "debts" at whatever point is most convenient' (Keynes 1936 [1964], p. 167). However, in the Post Keynesian approach, the critical distinction is between a unit of account and a thing that is denominated in a unit of account, following Keynes of the *Treatise*: 'the money-of-account is the description or title and the money is the thing which answers to the description' (Keynes 1930 [1976], p. 3). Many theorists make no such distinction, as they use the term sometimes to refer to the 'thing' (the medium of exchange) and at other times to refer to the 'title'. To avoid confusion, I shall carefully distinguish between money (the 'title', or dollar in the US), high-powered money (a particular money-thing – reserves and currency issued by the government), and bank money (another money-thing – demand deposits or private bank notes).

Post Keynesians are best known for their work on credit money and the endogenous money approach. First, however, we contrast the orthodox approach with the Post Keynesian approach to the nature of money; then we move to implications for theory and policy.

In the Post Keynesian view, money is not simply a handy *numéraire* in which prices, debts, and contracts happen to be denominated. This contrasts with a general equilibrium approach, in which we may choose any one good to serve as *numéraire*, converting relative values to nominal values in terms of the *numéraire*. Indeed, the typical story of the origin of money is really based on a *numéraire* approach, in which Robinson Crusoe decides to use 'tobacco, leather and furs, olive oil, beer or spirits, slaves or wives . . . huge rocks and landmarks, and cigarette butts' as 'money' (Samuelson 1973, pp. 275–6). When, say, seashells are chosen as money by Crusoe, he has simultaneously chosen a *numéraire* and designated which 'commodity money' will serve as the money-thing. Eventually, Crusoe discovers that gold – again, both a *numéraire* and a money-thing – has superior properties.

The conjectural history propagated by Samuelson (and many others) is dismissed by all serious historians and anthropologists. Interested readers are referred to numerous accounts that emphasize the social nature of the origins of money (see Wray 1998 for extensive references to the literature). In any case, our primary purpose in examining history and pseudo-history is to illuminate the nature of modern money. In my view, a system based on a commodity or *numéraire* money is not a 'money economy' as Keynes defined it. Rather, an economy in which money serves as nothing more than a *numéraire* is what Keynes called a 'barter' or 'real-wage' economy. Even if there really has been a historical stage in which there was a commodity money, I would argue that it sheds no light on the operation of our modern money system, in which both the unit of account and the money-things denominated in that account arise from social practices (Ingham 2000).

Thus Post Keynesians emphasize the difference between two approaches – what Goodhart (1998) has called 'C-form' (chartalist) and 'M-form' (metallist, or commodity money) – that is to say, between a theory in which money is a social unit of account and that in which money is nothing more than a *numéraire* commodity adopted for convenience. The C-form approach (or what has also been called the 'state money', or 'taxes-drive-money', theory) insists, as did Keynes, that the state 'writes the dictionary' (decides what will be the money of account – for example, the dollar in the USA) in all modern economies. This goes a long way towards explaining what would appear to be an otherwise extraordinary coincidence: the one-nation–one-currency rule. As Nobel laureate Robert Mundell's work makes clear, if money is simply a *numéraire* chosen to facilitate exchange, then one would expect use of a particular *numéraire* within an 'optimal currency area' (Goodhart 1998). There is no reason to expect such areas to be coincident with nation states. In fact, however, the one-nation–one-currency rule is violated so rarely that exceptions border on insignificance, and those few cases are easily explained away as special cases, as Goodhart demonstrates. The European Union thus represents a substantial and perhaps risky exception – with some member nations facing serious questions about government solvency in the early summer of 2011.

This leads us to an explanation of the use of money: why is money used? The orthodox story begins, as we have seen, with Crusoe and Friday, who grow tired of the inconveniences of barter. In any case, money comes out of the market. An alternative view that is consistent with a social approach to money argues that money derived from the pre-civilized practice of *Wergeld*; or to put it more simply, money originated not from a pre-money market system but rather from the penal system (Goodhart 1998; Wray 1998). *Wergeld*, an elaborate system of fines for transgressions, was developed and, over time, authorities transformed this system of fines paid to victims for crimes to a system that generated payments to the state. Until recently, fines made up a large part of the revenues of all states. Gradually, fees and taxes as well as rents and interest were added to the list of payments that had to be made to authority.

According to the C-form or taxes-drive-money approach, the 'state' (or any other authority able to impose an obligation – whether that authority is autocratic, democratic or divine) – imposes an obligation in the form of a generalized, social unit of account: a money. This does not require the pre-existence of markets, or of a *numéraire*, or of prices of any sort. Once the authorities can levy such an obligation, they can then name exactly what can be delivered to fulfil this obligation. They do this by denominating those things that can be delivered: in other words, by pricing them in the money unit.

Thus far we have only explained the money of account (the description). Once the state has named the unit of account, and imposed an obligation in that account, it is free to choose 'the thing' that 'answers to the description'. The state-money stage reaches full development when the state actually issues the money-thing answering to the description it has provided – that is, high-powered money. Economists often distinguish between a 'commodity money' (say, a full-bodied gold coin) and a 'fiat' paper money. However, regardless of the material from which the money-thing issued by the state is produced, the state must announce its value.

Indeed, in spite of the amount of ink spilled about the Gold Standard, it was actually in place for only a relatively brief period. Throughout most of history, the money-thing issued by the authorities was not gold-money, nor was there any promise to convert the money-thing to gold (or any other valuable commodity). It should be noted that, for most of Europe's history, the money-thing issued by the state was the hazelwood tally stick. Other government-issued money-things included clay tablets, leather and base metal coins, and paper notes. Why would the population accept otherwise 'worthless' sticks, clay, base metal, leather or paper? Because the state agreed to accept the same 'worthless' items in payment of obligations (fees, fines and taxes) to the state.

Georg Friedrich Knapp (1842–1926) distinguished between 'definitive' money accepted *by* the state in ('epicentric') payments of obligations *to* the state, and 'valuta' money used *by* the state in its own payments ('apocentric') (Wray 1998). In today's modern money systems, high-powered money fulfils both functions. Of course, it appears that the US government accepts bank money in payment of taxes, but in reality payment of taxes by bank cheque leads to a reserve drain from the banking system. Government spending, of course, takes the form of a Treasury cheque, which when deposited in a private bank leads to a reserve credit. Note that, so long as government does accept bank money in epicentric payments at par with high-powered money, from the point of view of the non-bank public there is no essential difference between bank money and high-powered money. This is not true for banks, which lose reserves when taxes are paid by bank cheque and gain reserves whenever Treasury cheques clear.

Finally, Knapp defined as 'paracentric' those payments made between non-government entities. In all modern economies, these mostly involve use of bank money and other money-things issued by the non-government sector (what can be called 'inside' or 'credit' money). There is a hierarchy or pyramid of money-things, with non-banks mostly using bank monies for net clearing and with banks using high-powered money for net clearing with other banks and with the government. Note that all these money-things are denominated in the unit of account, that is, the account in which obligations to the state are enumerated, and all credit money-things also represent a social relation – that between creditor and debtor.

Money-things are always IOUs, according to the C-form view. Even if government issues coins containing gold, they are a government debt with a value determined not by gold content but by their value in 'redemption' – that is, the value the government itself assigns to them when they are presented for payment. Government can, if it chooses, peg this value to gold or to a foreign currency, and can promise to convert its money-things to gold or foreign currency on demand at that rate. But its IOUs will be accepted without such a guarantee so long as those with obligations to the government need to use government's money-things in payment to government. A. Mitchell Innes (2004) argued that this is the fundamental law of credit: the issuer must accept its own debts in payment. For example, one can always repay a bank loan by presenting bank deposits (bank money-things that are bank IOUs) for payment. While money-things are always debts, we would not want to say that all debts are money-things. For a debt to become a money-thing it must become generalized and standardized. For example, demand deposits issued by the commercial banks in a given nation are a money-thing that has become standardized – widely accepted and cleared at par (deposits issued by one bank are accepted at any other bank at face value). On the other hand, the IOUs of individual households are not sufficiently standardized to gain general acceptability as money-things. One could see the rise of securitization (packaging individual loans and using them as collateral against a security) as a step in the direction of turning what were heterogeneous IOUs into something that is standardized and generally acceptable – in other words, a transformation of these into money-things. However, the global crisis that began with the collapse of securitized American subprime mortgages in 2007 halted that transformation – at least temporarily.

The evolving Post Keynesian endogenous approach to money offers a clear alternative to the orthodox neoclassical approach that is based on central bank control of an exogenous money supply through provision of reserves. That draws on the 'deposit multiplier' exposition in which each bank lends an amount equal to its excess reserves but the system as a whole expands lending and deposits by a multiple that is related to the required reserve ratio. So long as the multiplier is reasonably stable, if the central bank constrains the supply of reserves it can determine the growth of the money supply. Since reserves are a liability of the central bank, it would appear that by controlling its own creation of reserves the central bank can indeed control the amount of money created by private institutions. Monetarists link money growth to inflation; hence the central bank is said to determine not just the growth of money supply but also the rate of inflation. This led to experiments in the late 1970s and early 1980s to set money growth targets in an effort to control inflation. By almost all accounts this failed, as central banks did not hit money growth targets – although tight money policy pushed interest rates to very high levels, and deep recessions eventually brought down inflation. Although the exact cause–effect relations are still debated, central banks gave up money targets and instead use overnight interest rate targets to implement monetary policy. We shall briefly explore below the transition over the 1980s and 1990s to what is called the 'New Monetary Consensus' – an orthodox approach to policy making that was called into question by the disastrous global financial crisis and apparently impotent monetary policy after 2007.

Early Post Keynesian work emphasized uncertainty and was generally most concerned with hoards of money-things held to reduce 'disquietude', rather than with money-things 'on the wing' (the relation with spending). However, Post Keynesians always recognized the important role played by money in the 'monetary theory of production' that Keynes adopted from Marx. Circuit theory, mostly developed in France, focused on the role that money plays in financing spending. The next major development came in the 1970s, with Basil Moore's 'horizontalism' (somewhat anticipated by Nicholas Kaldor), which emphasized that central banks cannot control bank reserves in a discretionary manner. Reserves must be 'horizontal', supplied on demand at the overnight bank rate (fed funds rate) administered by the central bank. This also turns the textbook deposit multiplier on its head, as causation must run from loans to deposits and then to reserves.

This led directly to the development of the 'endogenous money' approach that was already apparent in the circuit and Marxist literature. When the demand for loans increases, banks normally make more loans and create more banking deposits (money-things), without worrying about the quantity of reserves on hand. Privately created credit can thus be thought of as a horizontal 'leveraging' of reserves, although there is no fixed leverage ratio. Central banks only control the overnight bank rate, which does not provide even indirect control over the money supply because it makes reserves completely horizontal.

This led to a debate between two camps of Post Keynesians, the 'horizontalists' and the 'structuralists'. Briefly, horizontalists insisted that not only is the supply of reserves horizontal (supplied on demand by the central bank that targets the overnight interest rate), but also that the supply of loans and deposits by banks is itself horizontal, completely accommodating the demand. Banks are presented as price setters (setting the loan and deposit rates) and quantity takers (creating loans and deposits on demand at those interest rates). (It is actually a bit more complicated than this: see Moore 1988.) Horizontalists accept that interest rates charged to borrowers do vary according to credit risk (riskier borrowers pay a higher rate), and will vary over time (rates charged holding individual credit risk constant will rise when the financial system as a whole appears more risky).

Structuralists argued that neither reserves nor the money supply should be treated as horizontal. They argued that the central bank can tighten policy and refuse to accommodate all demand for reserves. This causes banks to economize on reserve holdings (for example, by issuing types of deposits with lower reserve ratios); however, this typically increases bank costs, which they pass along in the form of higher interest rates on loans. Higher interest rates also induce innovations to get around reserve constraints. Hence, it is more proper to think of the money supply curve as upward sloping rather than horizontal.

In retrospect, this debate was to some extent arguing about two different time-frames. At a point in time, a central bank that is targeting the over-night interest rate must accommodate the demand for reserves or it will miss its interest rate target. Hence, the horizontalists are correct to envis-age a horizontal reserve supply. Yet, the structuralists are correct that over time banks are always economizing on reserves (since reserves pay little or no interest, banks want to minimize their holdings), and they are always innovating to get around required reserve ratios and any other constraints imposed by policy makers that interfere with profit making. But clearly the structuralists are talking about processes that take place over time, while the horizontalists are addressing a point in time. Still, I do not find the horizontalist view of a money supply curve to be appealing. It presumes that banks would make an 'infinite' amount of loans at a fixed loan rate of interest (adjusted as described above for credit risk). That is implausible – no honest banker would consider charging the same interest rate for loans of one thousand dollars and for loans of one billion dollars. An individual borrower's capacity to service debt depends on the size of debt relative to income flows. Similarly, an honest bank will not want to expose its entire equity to the possibility of loss on one loan – if a bank's capital is $5 million, it will not want to make a loan of $5 million to a single borrower, because default by just that one borrower would cause the bank to fail. Finally, a bank's total loan is also constrained by capital ratios. Hence for all these reasons it seems inappropriate to draw an infinitely elastic money supply curve.

To conclude, most economists now do accept a horizontal supply curve as an appropriate way to think about reserves. Even orthodox economists agree that in practice central banks accommodate the demand for reserves in order to hit overnight interest rate targets. That, in turn, means that we cannot treat the money supply as 'exogenous' in the sense that a central bank controls the private bank supply of deposits and loans. The money supply process is more contentious, but clearly banks respond to the demand for loans by creditworthy borrowers. To make loans, banks need to finance their position by issuing liabilities, mostly deposits of one kind or another. For this reason, we shall see loans and deposits growing more or less in step as banks finance economic activity. It is possible that central bank interest rate policy has some influence on willingness to borrow and to lend, in which case it will have an impact on money supply growth. However, as Keynes once remarked, there can be slips between lips and cups: raising rates might not squelch the growth of loans and deposits. Central banks could supplement interest rate policy with direct credit con-trols (for example, prohibiting mortgage loans to purchase real estate in an overheated market) that would probably be more effective in reducing loan and deposit growth. It is likely that there is an asymmetry involved: it might be easier to discourage lending in a boom than it is to encourage it in a slump. We conclude that it is far more sensible to think of the money supply as endogenous, mostly determined in the bargaining between lenders and borrowers.

Like Keynes, Post Keynesians have long emphasized that unemployment in capitalist economies has to do with the fact that these are *monetary* economies. Keynes had argued that the 'fetish' for liquidity (the desire to hoard) causes unemployment because it keeps the relevant interest rates too high to permit sufficient investment. While it would appear that monetary policy could eliminate unemployment, either by reducing overnight interest rates or by expanding the quantity of reserves, neither avenue will actually work. When liquidity preference is high, there may be no rate of interest that will induce investment in illiquid capital – and even if the overnight interest rate falls, this may not lower the long-term rate. Further, as the horizontalists make clear, the central bank cannot simply increase reserves in a discretionary manner, as this would only result in excess reserve holdings, pushing the overnight interest rate to zero without actually increasing the supply of private money-things. Indeed, when liquidity preference is high, the demand for, as well as the supply of, loans collapses. Hence there is no way for the central bank to simply 'increase the supply of money' in order to raise aggregate demand. This is why those who adopt the endogenous money approach reject IS–LM analysis, in which the authorities can eliminate recession simply by expanding the 'money supply' and shifting the LM curve out.

This was even accepted by the orthodox New Monetary Consensus that dominated central bank policy after the mid-1990s, which dropped the LM curve in favour of a Taylor-type rule. Essentially, it focused monetary policy on inflation targeting (even if no specific inflation rate target was chosen). Post Keynesians have been vocal critics of this policy. Some have argued that, since the central bank's only tool used to hit inflation targets is adjustment of the overnight interest rate, it does not have the power to actually influence inflation in any significant way. Others criticize the excessive focus on inflation, arguing that unemployment is usually a bigger problem. Still others argue that the large and frequent changes to interest rates cause unnecessary instability in financial markets (which are much more responsive to interest rate changes). And some want to return to Keynes's call for 'euthanasia of the rentier' by permanently lowering the overnight rate and keeping it close to zero. In any case, monetary policy failed to prevent a run-away speculative boom in the mid-2000s (especially in real estate in the US, the UK, Spain and some other nations), and proved even more impotent in its attempts to spur recovery after the global financial crash of 2007. While interest rates were pushed close to zero, economies failed to recover. This also leads us back to Keynes, who insisted that euthanasia of the rentier needs to be supplemented by fiscal policy to fill demand gaps, to allow the economy to operate closer to full employment.

L. RANDALL WRAY

See also:

Banking; Central Banks; Chartalism; Circuit Theory; Liquidity Preference; Monetary Policy.

References

Goodhart, C. (1998), 'The two concepts of money: implications for the analysis of optimal currency areas', *European Journal of Political Economy*, **14** (3), 407–32.

Ingham, G. (2000), '"Babylonian madness": on the historical and sociological origins of money', in J. Smithin (ed.), *What is Money?*, London and New York: Routledge, pp. 16–41.

Innes, A.M. (2004), *Credit and State Theories of Money: The Contributions of A. Mitchell Innes*, edited by L.R. Wray, Cheltenham, UK and Northampton, MA, USA: Edward Elgar.

Keynes, J.M. (1930 [1976]), *A Treatise on Money: Volume 1: The Pure Theory of Money*, New York: Harcourt Brace Jovanovich.

Keynes, J.M. (1936 [1964]), *The General Theory of Employment, Interest and Money*, New York: Harcourt Brace Jovanovich.

Moore, Basil J. (1988), *Horizontalists and Verticalists: The Macroeconomics of Credit Money*, Cambridge: Cambridge University Press.

Samuelson, Paul (1973), *Economics*, 9th edn New York: McGraw-Hill.

Wray, L.R. (1998), *Understanding Modern Money: The Key to Full Employment and Price Stability*, Cheltenham, UK and Northampton, MA, USA: Edward Elgar.

Money Manager Capitalism

In Hyman P. Minsky's 'stages' approach to the evolution of capitalism, money manager capitalism is the most recent stage that has developed in the US since the 1970s. In this period there has been a gradual shift in weight in the financial sector away from banks towards managed money. However, as many banks themselves are fund managers this distinction is somewhat elusive. It is probably easier to assert that it is traditional banking activities that have declined in importance while market-based financial activities have been booming. The latter quite often are housed in banking institutions. This new institutional structure is dominated by mutual, pension, hedge, money market mutual funds, university endowments, sovereign wealth funds and other leveraged institutional investors that have great influence upon economic outcomes. This entry will briefly discuss the rise of this latter form of capitalism and its consequences for the economy.

Minsky's 'stages' approach was a synthesis of John Maynard Keynes and Joseph Schumpeter. He built on Schumpeter's idea of the dynamic and destabilizing role of profit-seeking institutions as they responded to profit opportunities. To this he added his contribution of the important dynamics that the financing of investment created in the environment of fundamental uncertainty characteristic of capitalism. The latter, for Minsky, was an interpretation of Keynes's *General Theory*.

For Minsky, there is no unique capitalism. Rather, it comes in various forms that can even coexist at the same time. The institutional structure of the economy is constantly changing, affecting the manner in which social provisioning is conducted. He identified four stages in the evolution of US capitalism: commercial, finance, managerial and the most recent stage – money manager capitalism. The evolution of capitalism from commercial to manager money capitalism has been from a 'financial structure where external finance was mainly used for trade to an even greater use of market- or institution-based external funds to finance the long-term capital development of the economy' (Minsky 1996, p.3). As technology advanced, companies had to use expensive capital assets which often required outside financing. This gave rise to the *laissez-faire* finance capitalism of the pre-Great Depression era, characterized by small government and the dominance of bank-based finance. As this form of capitalism failed during the Great Depression, institutional constraints that greatly moderated uncertainty were placed upon the system. These were the 'Big Government', the 'Big Bank' and regulation. The outcome was a new form of capitalism, which Minsky called 'welfare state' or 'managerial' capitalism. Under this new system, high government deficits and lack of foreign competition ensured stable profits for firms and rising incomes for households. The stability was further cushioned by low levels of household and firm indebtedness and a large share of government bonds in private sector portfolios.

It was out of the relative stability of the managerial capitalism that money manager capitalism emerged as the Big Government and regulations were gradually dismantled and stagnating incomes created an ample opportunity for the financial sector to flourish. Under this form of capitalism, 'managers of money are replacing managers of industry as the leading players in the economy' (Minsky 1988, p. 5). Although managed money thrives when the economy is doing well, it is not merely a passive bystander. Rather, it changes the power structure in the society, affecting the behaviour of the economy.

The various funds that constitute managed money are arrangements which allow the beneficiaries of the fund to delegate the management of their wealth to a fiduciary – the money manager. Wealth owners have 'positions' in these funds. The money manager as the fiduciary is in charge of making portfolio allocation decisions on behalf of the fund owners. Money manager capitalism is characterized by the use of 'other people's money' (Minsky 1988). The managers of the enterprise are making decisions on behalf of the proximate owners of the corporation, while money managers act as the proximate owners of the corporation on behalf of the beneficiaries of the fund.

The goal of the money manager is to maximize total returns of the portfolio, which includes both the income flows (such as dividend or interest payments) and capital gains (asset price appreciation). It is the latter that money managers largely depend upon, which makes their time horizon very short (Wray 2009). Managed money is very volatile across different financial instruments, markets and even geographic boundaries: it will flow into the asset class or the country where it can get the highest total return.

Two main developments have followed the rise of money managers. First, by allocating a portion of their portfolios to corporate equity, they have become the proximate 'owners' of most US corporations, dictating the terms in which these firms are managed. Minsky argued that money managers, who themselves were under pressure to achieve high returns, would push corporate managers to take every possible step to increase their stock prices (Whalen 1997). When a company is owned by a single individual he/she has a genuine interest in its long-term success, in maintaining it as a 'going concern'. For money managers the company is as good as its ability to achieve high stock prices. Business managers are operating in an environment of increased uncertainty and have become very sensitive to the daily valuation of their firm (Minsky 1996). 'Managers of industry' are preoccupied with keeping up the price of their stocks rather than investing in productive activities, which often goes against the long-term survival of the firm.

It is not surprising that in the age of managed money 'shareholder value maximization' has become the dominant mantra of corporate governance. The application of this principle has changed the strategy of the management from the 'retain and reinvest' to the 'downsize and distribute' model (Lazonick and O'Sullivan 2000). In Minsky's terms this signifies the transition from managerial to managed money capitalism. Under the 'retain and reinvest' model, corporations had an incentive to retain a larger portion of their profits and reinvest it in plant and equipment, creating well-paying jobs. The 'downsize and distribute' model encouraged corporate managers to downsize their firms, which usually meant downsizing the labour force, so as to become more 'efficient'. The 'distribute' part meant that instead of retaining profits and reinvesting them, corporations were encouraged to use their earnings to increase shareholder value. This could be accomplished either by increasing the payout ratio (dividends) or by buying back the company stock to boost its price (ibid.).

The second major consequence of the rise of managed money is the growing financial fragility and the intensified tendency towards instability, which transformed into a financial crisis in 2007. The pools of managed money have an appetite for risk as they seek to earn maximum returns. They are also highly leveraged and are constantly looking to further diversify their portfolios (to achieve more stable returns). The movement of managed money into a certain class of assets causes the price of that asset to appreciate temporarily, increasing the return of the fund managers. This validates the employed strategy, motivating other money managers to do the same. In its quest for higher returns managed money bounces from one asset class to another, creating bubbles. When the bubble inevitably bursts, a portion of the managed money gets wiped out. But being as big as it is, it always makes a comeback and goes on to inflate another class of assets (Wray 2009).

Money managers are constantly looking for new financial products which will allow them to diversify their portfolios and to beat the average return, even if for a short period of time. Their trading activities create a demand for new financial products, facilitating financial engineering (often called 'financial innovation') by Wall Street, which is eagerly catering to managed money. Minsky recognized this a long time ago: 'In a mature managed money capitalism enterprises and governments will have to create instruments that are attractive to market participants' (Minsky 1988, p. 11). Block trading and the explosion of the type of exotic financial instruments such as collateralized debt obligations (CDOs), credit default swaps (CDSs), commodity futures and new processes such as securitization are just a few such examples. Money managers have been driving the process of securitizing any cash flow into standardized financial instruments that can be traded in secondary markets.

Managed money is largely unregulated, which means it can invest in almost any asset class, including mortgage-backed securities, synthetic securities, CDSs and other financial derivatives such as commodity future contracts, life-insurance settlements, carbon futures and so on. Nor do they usually have a guaranteed redemption value like the liabilities of banks. Except for a small portion of pension funds (defined benefit pension plans), the rest of managed money does not have governmental guarantees. This makes it subject to runs, as witnessed in the current crisis when the owners of money market mutual funds and hedge funds rushed to liquidate their positions in these funds. These, in turn, stopped rolling over the short-term debt of financial institutions and corporations, creating a refinancing crisis.

The rise of money managers was as much the result of the intensive pursuit of profits by the private sector as that of misguided economic policies that have their roots in mainstream economics. In particular, the growth of private and public (state and local governments) pension funds was largely facilitated by policies aimed at increasing 'national savings'. The rise of other institutions, such as mutual funds and money market mutual funds, was the result of Paul Volcker's monetarist experiment, more so than that of financial innovations driven by the profit motive.

Under managed money capitalism the financial system has evolved towards fragility, making another Great Depression possible. The financial sector has become so far separated from the productive sector that it essentially does not need the former to survive and grow. It simply lives off of asset price bubbles fuelled by debt which, although they don't create real wealth, allow the money managers to obtain high returns for short periods of time. It has also enhanced uncertainty and the economic insecurity of the population. Under this system everyone, from homeowners to pensioners, firms to governments, has become a hostage to the whims of the money managers.

According to Minsky, money manager capitalism has important consequences for economic stability, equity and democracy (Wray 2009). It enhances uncertainty and economic insecurity of large portions of the population, threatening democracy. If capitalism is to survive and become the successful system that it was in the golden age, then institutional constraints which limit uncertainty have to be strengthened once again.

YEVA NERSISYAN

See also:

Banking; Consumer Debt; Financial Instability Hypothesis; Financial Reform; Financialization; Galbraith's Economics; Institutionalism.

Bibliography

Lazonick, W. and M. O'Sullivan (2000), 'Maximizing shareholder value: a new ideology for corporate governance', *Economy and Society*, **29** (1), 13–35.

Minsky, H.P. (1987), 'Securitization', Levy Economics Institute of Bard College, Policy Note 2008/2, Annandale-on-Hudson, NY.

Minsky, H.P. (1988), 'Money manager capitalism, fiscal independence and international monetary reconstruction', paper prepared for a Round Table Conference: The Relationship Between International Economic Activity and International Monetary Reconstruction, Castle Szirak, Hungary, 25–26 August.

Minsky, H.P. (1993), 'Schumpeter and finance', in S. Biasco, A. Roncaglia and M. Salvati (eds), *Market and Institutions in Economic Development*, Basingstoke: Macmillan, pp. 103–15.

Minsky, H.P. (1996), 'Uncertainty and the institutional structure of capitalist economies', Working Paper No. 155, Levy Economics Institute of Bard College, Annandale-on-Hudson, NY, April.

Whalen, C. (1997), 'Money-manager capitalism and the end of shared prosperity', *Journal of Economic Issues*, **31** (2), 517–25.
Wray, L.R. (2009), 'The rise and fall of money manager capitalism: a Minskian approach', *Cambridge Journal of Economics*, **33** (4), 807–28.

Multiplier

A key aspect of John Maynard Keynes's impact upon political economy has been the role of the multiplier in justifying injections of government expenditure into an unemployment-prone capitalist economy. Fiscal injections were carried out across the world in response to the credit crisis of 2008, with the multiplier once again taking centre stage (see, for example, Almunia et al. 2010). For Keynes, writing in the depression of the 1930s, the possibility that each pound of Treasury expenditure could generate a multiplied effect on total income represented a valuable political argument. Borrowing from the work of his student, R.F. Kahn, Keynes was able to argue that each newly employed worker would carry out expenditure that resulted in a ripple effect of additional employment and income, the multiplier measuring the size of the total expansion. Moreover, this impact on total income would even generate sufficient savings to fund the initial injection of expenditure, with no cost to the Treasury.

To illustrate this argument, consider an initial injection of investment (ΔI) by firms. This injection generates new income in a series of rounds. In the first round there is an increase in income (ΔI), out of which expenditure increases according to the propensity to consume b. Hence in the second round income increases by $b\Delta I$. In the third round this newly generated income generates a further bout of expenditure resulting in an increment $b(b\Delta I)$. This process will continue until eventually the impacts peter out. The overall impact upon income is:

$$\Delta Y = (1 + b + b^2 + b^3 + \ldots)\Delta I. \tag{1}$$

Taking the sum of the polynomial contained in the brackets:

$$\Delta Y = \frac{1}{1 - b}\Delta I. \tag{2}$$

This is the multiplier relationship between increments in investment and income. So long as the propensity to consume b is less than 1, the multiplier takes a value more than 1. More income is generated than the initial injection in investment; the impact upon the economy is multiplied, hence the term multiplier.

Since the propensity to consume defines the proportion of income that is spent on goods and services, $1 - b$ is the propensity to save. It follows that $(1 - b)\Delta Y$ represents the total volume of savings (ΔS) generated by the injection of investment. Taking the denominator of the multiplier equation to the left-hand side we have the identity:

$$\Delta S = \Delta I. \tag{3}$$

This is the second politically attractive feature of the multiplier model: the injection of investment is financed out of savings generated by the income-generating process. Not only does investment generate more income than the initial outlay; it is also self-financing. There is a compelling argument, under circumstances of high unemployment, for the state to intervene to ensure that income is stimulated by new investment.

For Post Keynesians this analysis is fraught with difficulties because of the time that it takes for new savings to be generated by the multiplier process. New savings only match the initial injection of investment after a series of rounds in which consumer spending reacts to changes in income. Indeed, it has been argued that firms must borrow money in order to finance investment in the hope that savings will be forthcoming that can be used to pay off their debts, as the multiplier process works itself out. Since the multiplier process is not instantaneous, it is necessary to consider the way in which investment is financed.

The main source of finance is the banking system. Consider what happens when a bank agrees to make a loan for a new investment project. A remarkable institutional observation, which is now central to much of Post Keynesian thought, is that this loan is both an asset and a liability. After the loan is granted it is used by the firm to pay the supplier of new equipment and to hire new workers. The recipients now hold this outlay as deposits in the banking system. The initial loan therefore represents an asset (a promise by the firm to pay) and a liability (a promise by the banking system to pay).

For some Post Keynesians, this institutional observation has led to the conclusion that the multiplier process is not required as an explanation of how investment is financed. Since each loan is a deposit, the banking system is capable of financing investment without relying on a multiplier process to generate more income and savings. Indeed, for Moore (1994) an injection of investment is *instantaneously* equal to savings because of the deposits generated by each new loan (for recent discussion, see Gnos and Rochon 2008).

A similar position is adopted in the French circulation approach. Money is viewed as changing hands in a closed circuit, from banks to firms and households, and back to the banking system. The problem with the multiplier process is that changes in investment generate changes in income, but implicitly there is a dead weight of total income that remains unchanged. For Schmitt: 'If some incomes are "created" how can we explain that other incomes are simply maintained in "inertia" through time, where they are deemed to be neither created nor destroyed?' (Deleplace and Nell 1996, p. 125). In the circulation approach all income is generated by injections from the banking system that return back to the banking system as part of the money circuit. The multiplier is an obstacle to seeing clearly the conditions under which circuits are completed.

The importance of the multiplier can be defended, however, by arguing that even though the multiplier process is not a required condition for the finance of investment, its impacts should still be taken into account. A change in investment will still result in more workers being employed, and those workers will spend additional income on additional goods and services. Indeed by ignoring the multiplier it is possible to overestimate the amount of money that needs to be advanced by the banking sector in order to enable a complete circuit of money. Without multiplier effects that ripple between firms and households, banks are required to advance all of the money required for both consumption and investment purposes at the start of the circuit. In circuit theory the web of debt may appear larger and hence more prone to instability than is actually the case once the multiplier process is taken into account.

Although the multiplier has been considered thus far as a dynamic process, Chick (1983) demonstrates that in Keynes's *General Theory* this dynamic approach is defined alongside a comparative static interpretation. In the static variant there is a precise focus comparing different points of static equilibrium. Consider a closed economy in which income (Y) is made up of consumption (C) and investment (I):

$$Y = C + I. \tag{4}$$

Assuming that consumption is dependent upon income such that $C = bY$, with b representing the propensity to consume:

$$Y = bY + I, \tag{5}$$

which by manipulation can be written as:

$$Y = \frac{1}{1-b}I. \tag{6}$$

As before the term $1/1 - b$ is the multiplier, but here the relationship between aggregate income and investment is specified instead of the relationship between changes in these magnitudes. Paul Davidson argues that in comparative statics the multiplier should be used to compare two economic systems, each with identical propensities to consume, but different volumes of investment. Following an earlier insight provided by Joan Robinson, this can be viewed as a controlled experiment in which two systems are compared, holding everything else constant (Davidson 1994, pp. 40–41).

To some extent this interpretation limits the use that can be made of the multiplier. The multiplier is not used here as a method of explaining the actual course taken by a capitalist economy over time. The points of equilibrium can be compared but, in contrast to multiplier process analysis, there is no attempt to explain how an economy moves between two positions of equilibrium. As a consequence, Davidson contends that the multiplier is marginal to Keynes's system.

Moreover, Davidson argues that in the early 1930s Keynes had worked out the substance of the *General Theory* without the multiplier, only adding it in for political reasons. This contrasts directly with Patinkin's revealing quotation of Keynes: 'The essential role that the multiplier plays in the *General Theory* is attested to by Keynes' declaration to Beveridge, shortly after its publication, that "about half the book is really about it"' (Patinkin 1982, p. 199). Patinkin (p. 19) also relies on the multiplier to dismiss Michał Kalecki's claim to have discovered the substance of the *General Theory* prior to Keynes, arguing that this would be impossible as Kalecki did not discover the role of the multiplier in his system until 1943.

Aside from discussion about the origins of the *General Theory*, a case can be made for the analytical power provided by the multiplier in establishing the conditions that are required for full employment. Stated simply, the principle of effective demand shows that firms will not in general produce at full employment because of the leakage of savings from the economic system. As Chick (1983, p. 253) makes clear, the multiplier equation (6) 'says exactly what the Principle of Effective Demand says: that for a given level of income to be sustainable, the gap between income and consumption must be filled with investment'. Since consumers have positive savings, only a part of income is realized by consumer demand. The shortfall must be taken up by investment, and Keynes shows that in general private investment cannot be expected to do this job.

The importance of the multiplier in specifying the conditions required for full employment is testified by its relevance to long-run analysis. On the boundaries of Post Keynesian theory it has been argued that the principle of effective demand is only truly general in its applicability when extended to the long run. The key problem with Keynes's short-run period of analysis is that investment is viewed only as a component of aggregate demand. There is virtually no attention paid to the increase in productive capacity that will result in the next period. In the Harrod–Domar growth model the multiplier has a key role in identifying the necessary conditions for matching aggregate demand with productive capacity in the long run. Domar (1957) develops a dual approach to investment, one side of which is its capacity-generating role, the other its impact on demand via the multiplier. The requirements on aggregate demand to match this growth in capacity render the maintenance of full employment even more unlikely than is perceived in a short-run framework.

Long-run analysis also provides the basis for interaction with corresponding traditions in economic thought. Domar identified the close relationship between his growth model and Marx's reproduction schema, with the multiplier taking centre stage (Trigg 2006). Similarly, the multiplier is central to an emerging Sraffian literature on the relationship between effective demand and long-run capacity utilization (Serrano 1995). Common to both this and the Marxian approach is the observation that a monetary production economy must necessarily also be a surplus-producing economy. Investment goods that allow an expansion of productive capacity are by definition surplus goods. It should be noted, however, that in order to facilitate a simple macroeconomic exposition, this literature is limited to the narrow assumption that only one commodity is produced. Since monetary economies are necessarily multisectoral, with money providing the mechanism for exchanging heterogeneous commodities, the issue of aggregation requires close methodological attention – a challenge that applies with equal force to the models of circuit theory and multiplier process analysis.

ANDREW B. TRIGG

See also:

Circuit Theory; Consumption; Effective Demand; Fiscal Policy; Growth Theory; Keynes's *General Theory*.

References

Almunia, M., A. Bénétrix, B. Eichengreen, K.H. O'Rourke and G. Rua (2010), 'From Great Depression to Great Crisis: similarities, differences and lessons', *Economic Policy*, **25** (62), 219–95.
Chick, V. (1983), *Macroeconomics after Keynes*, Oxford: Philip Allan.
Davidson, P. (1994), *Post Keynesian Macroeconomic Theory*, Aldershot, UK and Brookfield, VT, USA: Edward Elgar.
Deleplace, G. and E.J. Nell (eds) (1996), *Money in Motion: The Post Keynesian and Circulation Approaches*, Basingstoke: Macmillan.
Domar, E.S. (1957), 'Expansion and employment', in Domar, *Essays in the Theory of Economic Growth*, New York: Oxford University Press, pp. 83–108.

Gnos, C. and L.-P. Rochon (eds) (2008), *The Keynesian Multiplier*, London: Routledge.
Moore, B.J. (1994), 'The demise of the Keynesian multiplier: a reply to Cottrell', *Journal of Post Keynesian Economics*, **17** (1), 121–34.
Patinkin, D. (1982), *Anticipations of the General Theory?*, Oxford: Basil Blackwell.
Serrano, F. (1995), 'Long period effective demand and the Sraffian supermultiplier', *Contributions to Political Economy*, **14**, 67–90.
Trigg, A.B. (2006), *Marxian Reproduction Schema: Money and Aggregate Demand in a Capitalist Economy*, London: Routledge.

New Classical Economics

New Classical economics is a school of thought that emerged in the early 1970s and aimed to complete the anti-Keynesian counter-revolution started by the monetarists by producing a radical U-turn in the methodology of macroeconomics. The name attributed to this school reflects the intention of Robert E. Lucas, its main founder and leader, to complete the euthanasia of macroeconomics in order to recover the fundamental unity of economic theory. Keynes had introduced the neologism 'macroeconomics' to emphasize its autonomy from the classical axioms of individual behaviour. On the contrary, according to Lucas and his followers, macroeconomics is nothing but the application of the classical axioms to the economy as a whole. The attempted euthanasia did not materialize as far as the terminology is concerned, since 'the split between micro and macroeconomists has probably grown sharper in recent decades, despite the methodological convergence' (Woodford 1999, p. 319); Lucas succeeded, however, in radically transforming the methodology of macroeconomics, exerting a deep influence also on schools that aimed to recover the Keynesian message in an updated form (New Keynesian economics) or tried to realize a new synthesis between the Keynesian and Classical approach (New Consensus). Therefore what follows focuses mainly on Lucas's method and its policy implications and is largely based on Vercelli (1991) as updated in recent works (in particular, Vercelli 2005 and 2010).

In Lucas there is no distinction between theory and model(s), as the theory 'is not a collection of assertions about the behaviour of the actual economy but rather an explicit set of instructions for building a parallel or analogue system' (Lucas 1981, p. 272). The object of macroeconomic theory is mainly the description and prediction of macroeconomic fluctuations.

The polar star of Lucas's method is the compelling requirement that sound macroeconomics be explicitly and rigorously founded on the stochastic general equilibrium model in the version of Kenneth Arrow and Gerard Debreu. In his opinion compliance with this requirement guarantees that a macroeconomic argument has thorough microfoundations on the classical principles (such as Say's law and the classical dichotomy). Also the mainstream Keynesianism of the Bretton Woods period, the so-called 'Neoclassical Synthesis', had sought rigorous foundations in the general equilibrium model (in particular with Paul Samuelson, Franco Modigliani and Don Patinkin), although from a completely different perspective; in this view the economy is not assumed to be necessarily in full-employment equilibrium and it is the persistent divergence from it, or the slow convergence towards it, that justify the adoption of Keynesian full-employment policies. On the contrary, in the new perspective suggested by Lucas, the conditions of market clearing and full-employment equilibrium are assumed to be always satisfied, while disequilibrium concepts (such as involuntary unemployment) and processes (such as endogenous fluctuations) are rejected as 'unintelligible'. This 'pure equilibrium' approach implies the systematic adoption of the rational expectations hypothesis, a move that from the very beginning was perceived as the hallmark of the new school of thought. The rational expectations hypothesis had been introduced by John Muth in 1961, but Lucas was the first to adopt it systematically in macroeconomics as he soon realized that this is the only expectations formation hypothesis consistent with the pure equilibrium method. As is well known, the rational expectations hypothesis assumes that the economic agents do not make systematic mistakes in their predictions; their mistakes as observed *ex post* are due exclusively to exogenous shocks and are thus unavoidable.

Lucas does not distinguish between theory and model, and macroeconomic theory is identified with business-cycle models; he provided in the 1970s the first prototype business-cycle model consistent with the principles of New Classical economics: the (monetary) equilibrium business cycle (see the anthology selected by the author in Lucas (1981) for its first version and a systematic justification). Macroeconomic fluctuations, previously interpreted as out-of-equilibrium dynamics, are seen instead as the consequence of oscillations of equilibrium itself induced by exogenous shocks. The main source of exogenous shocks is identified in the discretionary, and thus unpredictable, policies of monetary authorities. The stabilization of business cycles thus requires the adoption of well-defined, and properly announced, policy rules first and foremost by monetary policy authorities, as advocated for a long time by Milton Friedman. For that reason, the school of thought initiated by Lucas was first called 'Monetarism Mark 2', as similar policy conclusions were obtained through a different methodology. The emphasis on money, however, did not last more than a decade or so until Kydland and Prescott, who shared the basic tenets of Lucas's methodology but had a different view of the causal nexus between monetary and real variables, focused on real shocks as the main source of macroeconomic fluctuations (Kydland and Prescott 1982). The 'real business cycle' approach rapidly became the dominant stream of macroeconomic dynamics and was eventually accepted, after an initial resistance, also by Lucas. Whether we consider it as a different school (Woodford 1999) or as a stage of the evolution of New Classical economics, as we believe more sensible, its basic methodological stance is the same of Lucas.

The loss of welfare brought about by business cycles is seen as the consequence of the excessive interference by policy authorities on the market, weakening and distorting its self-regulation virtues. Therefore Lucas takes a position against countercyclical policies and macroeconomic 'fine-tuning', while he is in favour of structural policies and institutional reforms able to liberate the market (through privatization and deregulation) from state interference by adopting a minimal set of rigid and transparent policy rules. This viewpoint has been taken as providing scientific foundations for the policy strategies adopted since the early 1980s, called in Europe 'neo-liberal' and in the USA 'neo-conservative'. Lucas, however, took issue in different occasions with the practical implementation of these policies, considered to be inconsistent with the principles advocated by him and his followers (see, for example, Lucas in Klamer 1984, p. 51).

Lucas shows a keen awareness of the limits of his suggested paradigm but, at the same time, he does not conceal a strong belief in its superiority over the alternative paradigms. He recognizes that his approach can be applied only to a 'closed' world, stationary or ergodic, characterized by time-invariant regularities. He claims, however, that macroeconomic theory and policy are viable only under these restrictive hypotheses. In this case, he maintains, the requirements of sound scientific method do not offer credible alternatives to his paradigm. It is thus not surprising that mainstream macroeconomics, still deeply influenced by Lucas's method, was unable to predict and control the Great Recession triggered by the US subprime mortgage crisis, as the scope of New Classical economics is limited to 'white swans'.

The anti-Keynesian counter-revolution carried on by Lucas and the other exponents of New Classical economics has been successful also because it was in tune with growing mistrust in the state's interference in economic activity. However, this success did not remain unchallenged. We mention here only a few of the most important critiques. Although Lucas claimed to have (re-)introduced the standards of contemporary scientific method in macroeconomics, his concept of science is borrowed from Newtonian physics as it is based on the principle of 'uniformity of nature', believed to be a necessary requisite of rigorous science. This principle was made explicit by David Hume and was still upheld in natural science by John Stuart Mill, but the emergence of the evolutionary vision (the second law of thermodynamics) and of complex dynamics (structural instability of the solar system) have increasingly challenged the traditional view of science, even in physics. Whatever is believed to be right in natural sciences, it is difficult to deny that the economic system is 'open', that is, characterized by unpredictable evolution and structural change. Therefore the restriction of the scope of economics to invariant regularities is not justified, and would restrict its applicability to a very small subset of the empirical evidence, excluding some of the crucial phenomena: crises, industrial revolutions, institutional change and so on. The most interesting macroeconomic phenomena are black (or grey) swans, and we need a theory that does not exclude their frequent, sometimes quasi-periodic, appearance.

A second criticism is that the direct application of the perfectly competitive general equilibrium model to the empirical evidence is likely to give distorted results, taking into account the wide gap between its underlying assumptions and the features of real markets. Lucas's defence against this criticism resumes that of Friedman, who had maintained that what is important for sound theory is not the realism of hypotheses but the correctness of predictions. Lucas admits, however, that we are justified in being more confident in the prediction of a certain model if it 'mimics' the time series better than the other models. This limited concession to realism did not go deep enough into the reasons that explain why a model mimics the empirical evidence better than another one.

Further criticisms are often specifications of the first two. In particular the rational expectations hypothesis implies a series of counterfactual hypotheses such as the stationarity of stochastic processes, weak uncertainty, unbounded rationality, irrelevance of time and learning, and so on. As soon as we assume the possibility of disequilibrium, instability, strong uncertainty and structural change, we have to take account of the systematic mistakes made by the economic agents, which are excluded by the rational expectations hypothesis. This hypothesis thus plays the role of a Procrustean bed that strongly limits the empirical scope of macroeconomics. Analogously, the rejection by Lucas of the concept of involuntary unemployment has raised from the very beginning harsh criticisms, since it is difficult to deny that a situation of persistent slowdown of economic activity may severely restrict the range of job opportunities for unemployed people. The choice of giving the wallet to the robber is voluntary when the only alternative option is a gunshot. Analogously, the point underlined by Keynes is that the severe restriction of employment options that induces structural unemployment is independent of workers' will and severely limits their freedom and welfare.

As for the celebrated 'Lucas critique' (Lucas 1976), that plays a crucial role as support of the claim that New Classical economics is superior to Keynesian economics: it is a brilliant reformulation of a problem well known to the most astute macroeconomists before Lucas, including Keynes. Unfortunately the conviction that the New Classical economics fundamental parameters (tastes, technology) are invariant to policy rule changes is just wishful thinking. In any case, the influential prototype equilibrium business-cycle model can hope to mimic some of the basic features of the empirical evidence only by adding a propagation mechanism that converts the exogenous shocks in wavelike co-movements of the relevant variables (Lucas suggests learning and the accelerator). However, any specification of the propagation mechanisms introduces a disequilibrium process that slows down the process of adjustment, in blatant contradiction to the pure equilibrium method advocated by Lucas.

Notwithstanding the awareness shown by Lucas of the limits of his suggested approach, the latter has encouraged a dogmatic attitude. The old-fashioned view of science as formalization of time-invariant regularities and the conviction that all the rest is mere ideology imply that all the alternative approaches are seen as inconsistent with scientific standards. He rejects as such not only Keynesian economics but also, for example, Friedman's monetarism and Friedrich Hayek's and Ronald Coase's contributions (see De Vroey 2011, passim), while Post Keynesian economics is not even taken seriously (see Klamer 1984, p. 35). The deep impact of Lucas's methodology on contemporary macroeconomics contributes to explain why pluralism faded away in the last three decades. The assumptions on which this attitude rests are to be considered mere ideology according to Lucas's own definition, while weak pluralism is inconsistent with healthy science.

ALESSANDRO VERCELLI

See also:

Business Cycles; Economic Policy; Equilibrium and Non-equilibrium; Macroeconomic Methodology; Microfoundations; New Keynesian Economics; New Neoclassical Synthesis; Non-ergodicity; Open Systems; Pluralism in Economics; Underconsumption; Walrasian Economics.

References

De Vroey, M. (2011), 'Lucas on the relationship between theory and ideology', *Economics: The Open-Access, Open-Assessment E-Journal*, **5**, 2011–4, doi: 10.5018/economics-ejournal. ja.2011–4, http://dx.doi.org/10.5018/economics-ejournal.ja.2011–4.
Klamer, A. (1984), *The New Classical Macroeconomics. Conversations with New Classical Economists and Their Opponents*, Brighton: Wheatsheaf.
Kydland, F.E. and E.C. Prescott (1982), 'Time to build and aggregate fluctuations', *Econometrica*, **50** (6), 1345–70.
Lucas, R.E. Jr (1976), 'Econometric policy evaluation: a critique', *Carnegie-Rochester Conference Series on Public Policy*, **1**, 19–46.
Lucas, R.E. Jr (1981), *Studies in Business Cycle Theory*, Cambridge, MA: MIT Press.
Vercelli, A. (1991), *Methodological Foundations of Macroeconomics: Keynes and Lucas*, Cambridge: Cambridge University Press.
Vercelli, A. (2005), 'Rationality, learning and complexity', in B. Agarwal and A. Vercelli (eds), *Psychology, Rationality and Economic Behaviour: Challenging Standard Assumptions*, Basingstoke: Palgrave Macmillan, pp. 58–83.

Vercelli, A. (2010), 'Minsky moments, Russell chickens, and gray swans: the methodological puzzles of the financial instability analysis', in D. Tavasci and J. Toporowski (eds), *Minsky: Crisis and Development*, Basingstoke: Palgrave Macmillan, pp. 15–31.
Woodford, M. (1999), 'Revolution and evolution in twentieth-century macroeconomics', available at: http://www. Columbia.edu/~mw2230/.

New Keynesian Economics

Central to New Keynesian theory is the notion that wages and prices do not adjust rapidly enough to achieve the 'self-regulation' of classical and neoclassical economics. The latter theories assume frictionless markets, ensuring rapid correction whenever the economy deviates from its long-run equilibrium. New Keynesian theorists believe that market failures amplify and lengthen such deviations, accounting for business cycles. Although it is alleged to be a macroeconomic theory, its practitioners concentrate on establishing the microeconomic foundations of the price and wage stickiness generated by market failures. The absence of market clearing is supported by the argument that quantity rather than price adjustments are in the interest of both workers and firms, that is, that market participants behave rationally. In this way, New Keynesian economics purports to show that decisions at the microeconomic level are optimal while capable of generating adverse effects at the macroeconomic level. Mankiw and Romer (1991) provide a representative collection of New Keynesian works.

The claim that economic agents' rational behaviour not merely prevents the economy from absorbing shocks but amplifies and extends their effects is in stark contrast to the New Classical view that rational behaviour ensures a rapid return to equilibrium. Not surprisingly, the New Keynesian interventionist policy prescription creates a similar contrast. While agreeing that in some cases private actions will offset public policy, they argue that this is by no means always the case. They endorse built-in stabilizers and discretionary policy to reduce macroeconomic fluctuations, but are less optimistic about the power of policy than are Keynesians and Post Keynesians. New Keynesians warn against discretionary policy that initiates offsetting private action, and reject 'fine-tuning' as unrealistic. However, within these parameters, they view government action as a remedy, rather than as a cause of problems.

The beginning of New Keynesian theory is usually traced to work by Fischer (1977) and Phelps and Taylor (1977), but studies of wage and price inflexibilities as the result of rational behaviour substantially predate these works. For example, J.R. Hicks published work in the 1930s that stressed downward rigidity of nominal wages as a key contributor to 'fair' labour–employer relations that enhance efficiency. Okun (1975) considers 'fairness' in cementing firms' relations with customers to explain price rigidities. Buyers regard price increases in response to rising costs to be fair, but as 'gouging' if they are a response to rising demand. Other explanations of wage rigidity viewed labour as a long-term investment in human capital (Doeringer and Piore 1971). Lastly, Keynes himself stressed the importance of relative wages in explaining inflexibility. In all these examples, price and wage rigidities result from rational behaviour.

New Keynesians distinguish between nominal and real rigidities. A nominal rigidity prevents money prices from adjusting proportionately to changes in nominal output. Real rigidities, such as the stickiness of a real wage or of a relative wage or price, are traced to firms acting to increase efficiency. Early New Keynesian efforts concentrated on discovering why nominal wages are inflexible. Explanations included overlapping staggered wage contracts and efficiency wages. Overlapping contracts arise from the practice of labour and employers agreeing to wage contracts that commonly cover periods ranging from one to three years and that end at various times throughout the year. Consequently, although expectations may be revised as economic conditions change, nominal wages are fixed in contracts to be renegotiated at intervals during the ensuing three years, delaying the adjustment indicated by the revised expectations. Then, if demand falls, wage cuts are not possible, leaving layoffs as the only option.

The macroeconomic costs of these quantity adjustments can be very large, causing sometimes lengthy recessions while wage adjustments occur. Nevertheless, long-term wage contracts that impose quantity adjustments are preferred by both firms and workers. Their primary advantage is to reduce the high costs of negotiation borne by both firms and unions. These involve cash outlays as well as time, not only for the negotiations, but also to conduct the necessary research into existing wages and working conditions in comparable firms, and into assessing the economic conditions – inflation, employment, profits – likely to prevail over the life of the contract. A second advantage is the reduced opportunity for strikes, which are also costly to both labour and employers.

A second explanation of nominal wage rigidities attributes slow adjustment to the practice of paying efficiency wages. Efficiency wages pay a premium over the nominal wage predicted by traditional labour market analysis. The premium arises from the claimed dependence of productivity on the wage paid. The higher wage is expected to reduce slacking and absenteeism because workers believe that they are treated well by their employer, and enables firms to attract better-quality workers. It also increases workers' attachment to the firm, reducing costs associated with high turnover. The resulting productivity improvement is sufficient to justify the higher wage. Faced with an adverse demand shock, firms will not reduce the efficiency wage, since this would lower productivity and increase costs. Instead, the rational firm will cut employment.

Emphasis on the labour market was a natural first step for research in the Keynesian tradition. However, as long as profits are flexible, nominal wage stickiness is not sufficient to explain fluctuations in real output. For example, if profits are allowed to fall, nominal prices could fall, reducing or eliminating output fluctuations. The next phase of work emphasized price stickiness as a necessary condition for changes in real output, and dealt with the question of why nominal prices are not flexible enough to mirror changes in nominal output. In contrast to the competitive model used by New Classical theory, most New Keynesian analyses use a model of monopolistic competition, giving firms some control over price. The essential feature of this model is that price is always above marginal cost, so that firms are willing to sell more at the existing price when demand increases, while a perfect competitor would not sell more unless the price rose. However, following a change in demand, the model predicts adjustment of both price and quantity by the rational, profit-maximizing firm. Clearly, monopolistic competition alone cannot account for sticky prices. Some modification is needed to reconcile rationality and price stickiness.

One such modification has been the development of models of staggered price contracts, with strong parallels to the staggered wage models referred to above. These investigate the effects of staggered price setting for overlapping periods, starting from the premise that the length of the period during which the price remains fixed depends on the costs of adjustment. The staggering of price adjustments is attributed to firm-specific shocks occurring at different times. As with overlapping wage contracts, adjustment to changing demand conditions is achieved slowly and in a piecemeal fashion.

A core contribution to New Keynesian theory is the menu cost approach. Menu costs are associated with changing prices in response to changing demand, such as the cost of publishing new price lists and catalogues, and changing price tags. Broader definitions of menu costs also include managerial time taken as well as cash expenditures made to establish the need for change and to renegotiate contracts with suppliers. Faced with a drop in demand for its product, conventional analysis simply predicts that the profit-maximizing firm will reduce price. New Keynesian analysis suggests that reducing price will incur high menu costs, so that profit may well be maximized by keeping price constant (Akerlof and Yellen 1985). The rational firm will therefore cut output, not price. It is claimed that even small menu costs can cause severe recessions (Mankiw 1985).

Each explanation of the absence of market clearing has been subjected to criticism, usually by critics who implicitly accept the general framework of analysis. One such criticism of the menu cost approach is that while it stresses the costs of adjusting prices, it fails to address the costs attendant upon quantity adjustment. These would include costs of shutting down equipment, storing or scrapping semi-finished products, renegotiating contracts with input suppliers (or paying contractually agreed penalties) and, ultimately, reversing these to restore output levels later. In short, they bear great similarity to the menu costs of price adjustment. A second problem with this approach concerns the failure to consider menu costs in a dynamic context. The menu costs of a price reduction might wipe out profit for a period of time, after which profit would recover. This implicitly assumes that the time period equals or exceeds the period of depressed demand.

These are relatively minor criticisms compared with the general short-comings of New Keynesian economics. It is confusingly named, being neither Keynesian nor new. First, analyses of rigidity are typically framed in terms of a shock to a 'representative' firm, without regard for the variability of non-market-clearing responses and their causes. Empirical observation shows periods of price rigidity to be of extremely variable length, with prices changing frequently in some industries, and seldom in others (Carlton 1986). Carlton also found that small price changes (less than 1 per cent) are not uncommon, suggesting very low menu costs. His paper also considers industry structure, the type of product and the nature of relations between firms and customers; all have implications for pricing behaviour, and none is addressed by New Keynesian economics. Second, little effort is made to incorporate the propagation mechanisms central to macro-dynamic models. This neglect is consistent with the underlying assumption of New Keynesian literature that, imperfections notwithstanding, the economy is self-regulating, hovering around a macroeconomic equilibrium at the NAIRU (non-accelerating inflation rate of unemployment). Given this characteristic, New Keynesian models cannot be regarded as Keynesian; they are special cases of the neoclassical model. Finally, as suggested above, these ideas are not new, but reprise an older literature that treats wage and price rigidities. The earlier literature is richer in content, if less rigorously presented.

Rarely encountered in the literature for much of the 1990s, the term 'New Keynesian' is now frequently seen. Since the early 2000s, New Keynesian models have proliferated, ranging from the graphical three-equation models of Carlin and Soskice (2005), to dynamic stochastic general equilibrium models, which have become widely used by central banks and others to assess monetary policy options in the presence of imperfections (see, for example, Smets and Wouters 2003; Blanchard and Gali 2010). These recent models fail to address adequately the weaknesses listed above, and remain special cases of the neoclassical model. Beyond this, by ignoring or summarily dismissing fiscal policy, and treating monetary intervention as the only policy instrument worthy of the name, most recent studies have further distanced New Keynesian analysis from the central themes of Keynesian economics.

WENDY CORNWALL

See also:

Credit Rationing; Economic Policy; Microfoundations; New Classical Economics; New Neoclassical Synthesis; Price Rigidity; Prices and Pricing; Unemployment.

References

Akerlof, G. and J. Yellen (1985), 'A near-rational model of the business cycle with wage and price inertia', *Quarterly Journal of Economics*, **100** (5), Supplement, 823–38.

Blanchard, O.J. and J. Gali (2010), 'Labor markets and monetary policy: a New Keynesian model with unemployment', *American Economic Journal: Macroeconomics*, **2** (2), 1–30.

Carlin, W. and D. Soskice (2005), 'The 3-equation New Keynesian model – a graphical exposition', *Contributions to Macroeconomics*, **9** (3), 462–8.

Carlton, D.W. (1986), 'The rigidity of prices', *American Economic Review*, **76** (4), 637–58.

Doeringer, P. and M. Piore (1971), *Internal Labor Markets and Manpower Analysis*, Lexington, MA: D.C. Heath.

Fischer, S. (1977), 'Long-term contracts, rational expectations, and the optimal money supply rule', *Journal of Political Economy*, **85** (1), 191–205.

Mankiw, N.G. (1985), 'Small menu costs and large business cycles: a macroeconomic model of monopoly', *Quarterly Journal of Economics*, **100** (2), 529–38.

Mankiw, N.G. and D. Romer (eds) (1991), *New Keynesian Economics*, Cambridge, MA: MIT Press.

Okun, A. (1975), 'Inflation: its mechanics and welfare cost', *Brookings Papers on Economic Activity*, **2**, 351–401.

Phelps, E.S. and J.B. Taylor (1977), 'Stabilizing powers of monetary policy under rational expectations', *Journal of Political Economy*, **85** (1), 163–90.

Smets, F. and R. Wouters (2003), 'An estimated stochastic dynamic general equilibrium model of the euro area', *Journal of the European Economic Association*, **1** (5), 1123–75.

New Neoclassical Synthesis

Over the past couple of decades, a new framework for macroeconomic policy analysis has become immensely popular in the mainstream: the so-called 'New Consensus model' or the 'New Neoclassical Synthesis'. In advanced macroeconomic courses, often very little is done except building and solving 'Dynamic Stochastic General Equilibrium' (DSGE) models, as these models are referred to in more technical terms. Postgraduate textbooks such as Galí (2008) cover nothing but these models; advanced undergraduate textbooks such as Carlin and Soskice (2006) try to present at least a simplified three-equation version of the model.

The term 'New Neoclassical Synthesis' by itself implies a broad consensus, as it draws a parallel to the original neoclassical synthesis which has dominated textbooks over decades. In this original neoclassical synthesis, researchers of Keynesian origin such as Paul Samuelson or Franco Modigliani had attempted to find a compromise between the original IS–LM model, which only focused on aggregate demand, and the old neoclassical macroeconomic model which only focused on the supply side without allowing for situations in which aggregate demand falls short of aggregate supply. Just as the old consensus tried to include both neoclassical and Keynesian elements in its analysis, the New Neoclassical Synthesis tries to pull together the microfoundation and dynamic tools of (new classical) real business cycle (RBC) models and the work of New Keynesians on the consequences of labour and product market frictions and staggered price and wage setting for macroeconomic outcomes. A typical DSGE model is thus based on utility-maximizing representative agents with rational expectations (elements from the RBC tradition) and includes some staggered price setting and monopolistic competition (traditionally seen as New Keynesian elements).

Given the new classical RBC roots of the models, one might think that there is very little room for compromise with Post-Keynesian thought which in general rejects these models' priors. However, when solving the microeconomic maximization problems of a DSGE model, one comes up with three equations which bear some resemblance to traditional Keynesian models:

a so-called IS curve: $y_t = Ey_{t+1} - \dfrac{1}{\sigma}(i_t - E\pi_{t+1})$ (1)

a Phillips curve: $\pi_t = \beta E\pi_{t+1} + \kappa y_t$ (2)

a monetary policy reaction function: $i_t = r_t^* + \varphi_\pi \pi_t + \varphi_y y_t.$ (3)

Here E stands for expectations, y for the deviation of output from the steady-state value, i for the nominal interest rate, π for inflation, r^* for the natural real rate of interest, and κ, β, σ and φ are parameters.

The IS curve looks as if it has a spending multiplier much like the simple Keynesian aggregate demand model. Moreover, demand seems to be a function of the real interest rate, which could be rationalized by investment being a function of the interest rate just as in the standard IS–LM model. The Phillips curve seems to represent the fact that output above potential output leads to price increases.

Moreover, policy conclusions of the New Consensus also seem to be closer to Post Keynesian thinking than those from New Classical or monetarist models. In the New Classical Synthesis, the central bank sets its interest rate as a function of both inflation and the output gap. The money supply adjusts endogenously – a proposition which has long been held by Post Keynesian authors.

These ostensible parallels are illusory, however (Dullien 2011). It starts with the output gap. In a Keynesian understanding of the economy, the output gap would be the gap between potential output (leaving measurement issues aside) and current output. The existence of such a gap is explained by aggregate demand falling short of potential supply, thus preventing the economy from producing at potential output, that is, because of uncertainty and fluctuations (as Post Keynesians would claim) or because of sticky nominal wages due to labour market rigidities (as New Keynesians would emphasize). In the case of a negative output gap and hence employment below the (however defined) level of full employment, some individuals in the economy would like to work at the given wage rate, but are unable to find employment.

The mechanism in DSGE models is fundamentally different. Here, labour markets *always* clear. Maximization of the individuals' utility takes place through variations of the paths of their consumption demand, their labour supply and their money holdings over time. The central variation in output is thus caused by a variation of labour supply. If the real wage deviates from the steady-state value, individuals re-optimize their labour supply and change the number of hours worked, which in turn changes the output produced in the economy. Fluctuations in employment in the DSGE models are hence always an *optimal reaction* to changes in labour market conditions. A temporary increase of employment above the steady-state level is caused by an increase in the real wage, to which households react by cutting back their leisure and supplying more working hours. Similarly, a fall of employment below the steady-state level in the DSGE model is caused by a fall in the real wage. Households then react to the lower real wage by cutting back their labour supply. Hence, there is no involuntary unemployment in DSGE models, just voluntary unemployment as a reaction to changes in the wage or to changes in lifetime income. Or, to put it in a more graphic way: those who seem unemployed are just enjoying more leisure this year because they expect their real wages to be higher next year when they are in consequence going to work longer hours.

Changes in the interest rate also work through this mechanism: a cut in the interest rate makes consumption today relatively more attractive than consumption tomorrow. Hence, households will try to shift some of their lifetime consumption towards the current period. As both the goods market and the labour market had already cleared before the interest rate cut, this increase in consumption leads to excess demand. As firms try to hire new workers to satisfy this demand, nominal wages increase. As prices are (partly) sticky, this additional consumption demand leads to an increase in real wages and a compression of profits. Higher real wages in turn induce the households to offer more labour (substituting leisure for work), which in turn leads to a temporary new (higher employment) equilibrium in the labour market.

The reason for fluctuations in output and employment in DSGE models is hence not that wages are sticky, so that an adjustment of real wages to shocks cannot take place (as was the case in the fixed-wage version of the old neoclassical synthesis), but the assumption that nominal wages are flexible, but prices are sticky and hence demand shocks change nominal and real wages more quickly than prices, which leads to high-frequency changes in the labour supply.

Second, endogenous money in the DSGE world has little to do with Post Keynesian ideas of endogenous money. In the Post Keynesian debate, money is either endogenous because of the institutional set-up of central banks, which provide liquidity at a given interest rate freely, or because the central bank cannot just create it at will, but is subject to interaction with commercial banks, households and firms. If firms do not want to borrow, or commercial banks do not want to lend, there are limits to the expansion of the money supply by the central bank. Moreover, endogenous money in Post Keynesian thinking is a way to transfer purchasing power from surplus units (which save) to deficit units (which spend more than their cash flow) in the economy. As households are surplus units and firms are seen as deficit units, it is also possible to think of endogenous money as a means to transfer purchasing power from risk-averse, less entrepreneurial individuals to more risk seeking, more entrepreneurial individuals who use the purchasing power for the creation of fixed assets (Dullien 2004).

The logic of the money supply in DSGE models is fundamentally different. Money in DSGE models is not used to transfer purchasing power, neither between economic sectors nor between periods. As all individuals are identical (being a result of the representative agent assumption at least in the baseline DSGE models), there are no surplus and no deficit units. Everyone is just consuming what he/she is earning. By logic of aggregation, and also embedded in the market-clearing assumption for the goods market, consumption always equals output. Thus there are no savings in the simple DSGE model. While the baseline model includes a capital market, no agent is borrowing and no agent is lending in this market. The holding of bonds is exactly equal to zero in all periods. In consequence, the money supply is not determined (as in Post Keynesian thinking) by the private sector's willingness to incur debt and by the financial sector's willingness to extend loans, but by individuals' willingness to hold money for liquidity services.

The last major problem with the New Neoclassical Consensus from a Post Keynesian perspective is the working of fiscal policy: if a government sector is introduced in the DSGE model, one can show that increased government spending leads to higher output. However, the mechanism is again very different from what Post Keynesians would argue: a tax-financed increase in government spending in the DSGE world leads first to a negative income effect of the single household, as the tax money is taken away while the household does not have any utility from government spending. As a reaction, the households will cut back both on their consumption of goods and on their leisure time (as both consumption and leisure enter as imperfect substitutes into the utility function). The result is that the single household is supplying more labour. Firms demand this additional labour because they are faced with higher aggregate demand in the goods market (due to the additional government purchases). As the labour and the goods markets always clear, the households have no problems supplying more work. The labour market clears at a higher level of employment and the goods market clears at a higher level of production, but with lower private consumption than before.

This logic does not change fundamentally if government spending is deficit financed. As households now expect that they have to pay higher taxes in the future (to service the government debt), they again perceive the increase in government spending as a fall in their lifetime income and hence total wealth. Due to this negative wealth effect, they again cut back on current consumption as well as on current leisure, meaning that they supply more labour to at least partly make up for the taxes they will eventually have to pay. In contrast to the case described above without the government sector, these households now save. They hold government bonds exactly equal to the present value of their future tax liabilities caused by the government debt. As in the case for tax-financed government expenditure, output and employment increases, while private consumption falls.

Both of these reactions are very different from the traditional Keynesian narrative: in the DSGE model there is no income multiplier, no involuntarily unemployed workers being brought back to work, and no positive welfare effect of fiscal policy.

To cut a long story short: while the New Neoclassical Consensus has at first sight some resemblances to Post Keynesian ideas, analysing it in depth shows that this approach is little more than a New Classical real business cycle in disguise, rendering it all but useless to convey traditional Keynesian ideas.

SEBASTIAN DULLIEN

See also:

Bastard Keynesianism; Central Banks; Fiscal Policy; New Classical Economics; New Keynesian Economics; Unemployment.

Bibliography

Carlin, W. and D. Soskice (2006), *Macroeconomics: Imperfections, Institutions and Policies*, Oxford: Oxford University Press.

Dullien, S. (2004), *The Interaction of Monetary Policy and Wage Bargaining in the European Monetary Union: Lessons from the Endogenous Money Approach*, Basingstoke: Palgrave Macmillan.

Dullien, S. (2011), 'The New Consensus from a traditional Keynesian and Post-Keynesian perspective: a worthwhile foundation for research or just a waste of time?', *Économie Appliquée*, **44** (1), 173–200.

Galí, J. (2008), *Monetary Policy, Inflation, and the Business Cycle: Introduction to the New Keynesian Framework*, Princeton, NJ: Princeton University Press.

Goodfriend, M. (2007), 'How the world achieved consensus on monetary policy', *Journal of Economic Perspectives*, **21** (4), 47–68.

Woodford, M. (2009), 'Convergence in macroeconomics: elements of the new synthesis', *American Economic Journal: Macroeconomics*, **1** (1), 267–79.

Non-ergodicity

In response to the growing hegemony of the rational expectations revolution and the increasing complaint levelled against Post Keynesian economics that its concept of uncertainty had not been formalized or empirically evaluated, Paul Davidson introduced the notion that the Post Keynesian conception of uncertainty could be articulated with reference to a technical distinction between ergodic and non-ergodic processes. Building on Paul Samuelson's suggestion that economic knowledge about the future rested on the axiom of ergodicity, Davidson (1982–83) argued that the Post Keynesian conception of unknowledge was predicated on the rejection of the universality of the ergodic axiom. He suggested that the Post Keynesian view of time and discussion of the salience of uncertainty could be defined with respect to the absence of governing ergodic processes, which he labelled 'non-ergodicity'.

Ergodic theory has been explicitly developed in the theory of stochastic processes although the term itself arises from statistical mechanics (see Parry 1987 for a technical discussion). It refers to the property by which the time and space averages that originate and are computed from any data-generating process, either coincide for a series of infinite observations, or converge as the number of observations increases (with a probability of one) for a finite number. That is to say, averages from past realizations collapse on the objective probability distribution that governs current and future outcomes. Under such conditions the past reveals the future, and the rational expectations hypothesis that the process of competition forces agents to use all the amount of available information in forming expectations about the future which are efficient, unbiased and without persistent errors, appears reasonable – in the long run at least (see Table 1 below).

In Davidson's (1982–83) seminal paper he argued that the rational expectations hypothesis was a caricature of Keynes's recognition of the importance of uncertainty and expectations, because the ergodic assumption implies that the past reveals the future – that over time agents can predict the future with actuarial certainty equivalence. On the ergodic hypothesis, the passage of time does not affect the joint probability laws governing processes: history ultimately does not matter. In contrast, Davidson argued that agents would be truly uncertain under conditions of non-ergodicity, that is, in the absence of governing ergodic processes. This is not to deny a priori that some economic processes may be ergodic, at least for short periods of calendar time. But, under non-ergodic conditions, sampling from the past in the manner implied by the rational expectations theorists is not sensible since, *even if* agents have the ability to assemble and process all the relevant information pertaining to past and present outcomes, the future course of events will still not reveal itself. There are no governing social or economic laws to learn, and sensible agents will come to recognize their capacity to make their own history in the context of contemporaneous institutions.

The fact that most macroeconomic time series are non-stationary provides empirical evidence for this view. Indeed, Solow (1985, p. 328) recognized as much when he wrote that 'much of what we observe cannot be treated as a stationary stochastic process without straining credulity'. What is more, while the existence of co-integration or unit roots may be suggestive of an underlying ergodic relationship it may also be misleading, not least for the introduction of spurious stationarity. As Klein (1994, p. 37) argues:

> Stationarity means that in a time distribution of data, one could get the same moments of the distribution no matter what block of time. It is a mathematical property of a time series or other kind of collection of sample data. I do not think economic data are necessarily stationary or that economic processes are stationary. The technique of co-integration, to keep differencing data until stationarity is obtained and then relate the stationary series, I think can do damage [as it] may introduce new relationships, some of which we do not want to have in our analysis.

Nevertheless, the concepts of stationarity and non-stationarity should not be conflated with the ergodic–non-ergodic distinction. If the estimates of the time averages do not vary with the period under observation then a stochastic process can be said to be stationary. However, as some stationary stochastic processes are non-ergodic, for example, limit cycles, non-stationarity is not a necessary condition for the existence for non-ergodic processes. But all non-stationary processes are non-ergodic.

Non-stationarity is thus a sufficient condition for non-ergodicity and provides an empirical foundation for Post Keynesian claims about the relevance of history and uncertainty.

Nevertheless, Davidson's discussion seeks to go beneath purely stochastic considerations, identifying the underlying causal mechanisms and emergent properties and structures that generate non-ergodic time series. In a much-neglected aspect of his discussion of non-ergodicity, Davidson (1982–83, p. 192) emphasized the link to G.L.S. Shackle's concept of creative, crucial decision making, arguing that the existence of crucial decision making represents a sufficient condition for the existence of non-ergodic processes. Situations where purely processing information from the past provides insufficient information about the course of future events are suggestive of a creative role for human agency. Here 'crucial decisions' refers to non-routine decisions that take place in historical time. A crucial decision involves large transaction and sunk costs and cannot be unmade without loss; it calls attention to the fact that one is irrevocably tied (married) to one's decisions. Moreover, as this conceptualization relates both to consumption and production decisions that involve calendar time and large transaction costs, it moves beyond Keynes's apparently arbitrary distinction between 'autonomous' investment and 'non-autonomous' consumption decisions. It provides a more appropriate framework within which to elaborate Keynes's principle of effective demand and to outline the relevance of liquidity considerations and their nexus to the non-neutrality of money.

In linking non-ergodicity to Shackle's concept of crucial decision making, Davidson advocates a broader, creative view of agency than that contained within mainstream models of human behaviour. Accordingly he has expanded the concept to incorporate non-stochastic processes (Davidson 1991). Deterministic models of decision making which are elaborated in logical time require Leonard Savage's ordering axiom – the presumption, at least in principle, that agents can make a transitive ordering over all possible outcomes. This involves a pre-programmed future and invokes a substantive rationality that is inconsistent with the fecundity which Post Keynesians impute *a posteriori* to agents. Post Keynesians recognize that it is impossible to form a transitive ordering over a yet-to-be-created future in which circumstances inconceivable at the point of origination emerge.

Subsequently, and in response to the numerous meanings that could be imputed to non-ergodicity, as well as to encompass developments in complexity and chaos theory, Davidson (1996) has reformulated his discussion in terms of a distinction between immutable and transmutable economic processes. Immutability encompasses the ergodic and ordering axioms and embodies 'the presumption of a programmed stable, conservative system where the past, present and future reality are predetermined whether the system is stochastic or not' (ibid., pp. 480–81). In immutable models history is predetermined and choice is neither genuine nor matters. Under such a reformulation, immutability refers to attempts to elaborate (real or imagined) universal event regularities and to develop theoretical structures of the general form 'whenever event (type) X then event (type) Y'. Thus it closely parallels Lawson's discussion of closed systems (Dunn 2008). In contrast, the broader notion of transmutability encompasses the stochastic discussion of non-ergodicity within a creative and emergent conceptualization of history in which choice is genuine, matters, and can make a difference in the long run – not least in affecting liquidity considerations and influencing the employment path of an economy over time. On this view of economic processes, sensible agents recognize that the environment in which they make decisions is characterized by the absence of programmed and predetermined processes and is creative, open, emergent and uncertain.

This transmutable conception of economic processes provides for a delineation between the Post Keynesian approach to modelling and theorizing about economic processes and that of many Austrians, New Classicals, New Keynesian and New Institutionalist economists (see Table 1). It also underscores some of the methodological affinities between Post Keynesianism and the German historical school, the older institutionalists and critical realists, and provides for a renewed exchange of ideas with other potentially compatible approaches (ibid.).

This broader discussion of non-ergodicity underscores the Post Keynesian view of economic time and its nexus to the macroeconomics of modern credit money production economies. It provides for a strong critique of the rational expectations hypothesis, not rejecting it on the basis that it provides an unrealistic model of actual decision making, but rather in advancing a distinctive view of human agency that is broader than that contained within models of bounded rationality or complexity and provides a challenge to the conventional wisdom that markets work best without government intervention (Davidson 2007). Moreover, it can be used in theorizing in a positive fashion to clarify the informational foundations of monetary non-neutrality and transaction cost theory, as well as providing for a strategic conceptualization of the modern corporation (see Dunn 2008 and the references contained therein).

As Sir John Hicks conceded in personal correspondence with Davidson (12 February 1983): 'I have missed a chance, of labelling my own point of view as *non-ergodic*. One needs a name like that to ram a point home. I had

Table 1   Conceptualizations of economic processes

A.   IMMUTABLE REALITY (AN ERGODIC SYSTEM)

Type 1   In the short run, the future is known or at least knowable. Examples of theories using this postulate are:

(a)   classical perfect certainty models
(b)   actuarial certainty equivalents, such as rational expectations models
(c)   New Classical models
(d)   some New Keynesian theories

Type 2   In the short run, the future is not completely known due to some limitation in human information processing and computing power. Examples of theories using this postulate are:

(a)   bounded rationality theory
(b)   Knight's theory of uncertainty
(c)   Savage's expected utility theory
(d)   some Austrian theories
(e)   some New Keynesian models (e.g., coordination failure)
(f)   chaos, sunspot and bubble theories

B.   TRANSMUTABLE OR CREATIVE REALITY (A NON-ERGODIC SYSTEM)

Some aspects of the economic future will be created by human action today and/or in the future. Examples of theories using this postulate are:

(a)   Keynes's *General Theory* and Post Keynesian monetary theory
(b)   post-1974 writings of Sir John Hicks
(c)   G.L.S. Shackle's crucial experiment analysis
(d)   Old Institutionalist theory

Source: Reproduced from Davidson (1996, p. 485).

tried to read a book on stochastic processes, but I was not sharp enough to see the connections' (italics added).

STEPHEN P. DUNN

See also:

Agency; Austrian School of Economics; Conventions; Critical Realism; Expectations; Liquidity Preference; Money; Open Systems; Time in Economic Theory; Uncertainty.

References

Davidson, P. (1982–83), 'Rational expectations, a fallacious foundation for studying crucial decision-making processes', *Journal of Post Keynesian Economics*, **5** (2), 182–97.

Davidson, P. (1991), 'Is probability theory relevant for uncertainty? A Post Keynesian perspective', *Journal of Economic Perspectives*, **5** (1), 129–43.

Davidson, P. (1996), 'Reality and economic theory', *Journal of Post Keynesian Economics*, **18** (4), 479–508.

Davidson, P. (2007), *John Maynard Keynes*, Basingstoke: Palgrave Macmillan.

Dunn, S.P. (2008), *The Uncertain Foundations of Post Keynesian Economics*, Abingdon and New York: Routledge.

Klein, L. (1994), 'Problems with modern economics', *Atlantic Economic Journal*, **22** (1), 31–41.

Parry, W. (1987), 'Ergodic theory', in J. Eatwell, M. Milgate and P. Newman (eds), *The New Palgrave: A Dictionary of Economics*, Vol. 2, London, Macmillan, pp. 184–8.

Solow, R.M. (1985), 'Economic history and economics', *American Economic Review*, **75** (2), 328–31.

Open Systems

A feature of debates within Post Keynesian economics – and indeed within the emergent heterodox economics – in the 1970s onwards has been a strong methodological thread. By 'methodological' is meant philosophical work underpinning the theoretical and empirical analysis conducted in economics. Discussion of Keynes's early philosophical writing influenced debates about the appropriateness of existing methods and theories. Also, the philosophy of critical realism has influenced a number of heterodox economic schools in its critique of prevailing methods. Both of these contributions have sharpened existing Post Keynesian treatments of uncertainty.

'Open systems' is a concept that plays an important role in those methodological debates. The concept is amenable to existing strands of Post Keynesianism. Further, during the course of the debates, the meaning of 'open systems' has evolved. Arguably it has grown into a crucial concept which bridges the methodologies of mainstream and heterodox economics and encompasses many key debates in economic methodology, such as on the role of models, the realisticness of theory, the possibility of prediction, the choice of empirical method, and even the notion of a school of thought. For example, Lawson (2006) has argued that an ontology of open systems is the real essence of heterodox economics.

'Open systems' has multiple definitions, reflecting its different treatments in different fields. To complicate matters further, it has a dual status. It attempts to describe the world; and it is used to describe theories and models which are used to think about or describe the world. Set aside for now the fact that models, and so on, are themselves objects to be classified. Let us consider open (and closed) systems as real objects; and open (and closed) systems as theories, models and so on. It is useful to consider each separately; however, it is also crucial to consider the relation between the real object and the model used to describe it. Indeed, that consideration is one of the most important in economic methodology, and, the debate on open systems between Lawson, and Chick and Dow (2005), is on this particular point.

An open system can be defined in a number of ways. Critical realism defines open systems as systems in which event regularities do not occur. As a corollary, in closed systems, event regularities do occur. Lawson (2003, p. 15) distinguishes between event regularities which reflect causality and those which reflect concomitance (correlation). Clearly that is an important distinction. However, Chick and Dow (2005) and Mearman (2006) both criticize critical realist treatments of open systems as focusing on outcomes of systems rather than their nature and for being dualist, that is, defining open systems as opposite to closed systems. One of the many key contributions to the debate made by Chick and Dow is to point out that there are degrees of openness, according to which conditions of an open system an actual system displays and to what extent they display them.

Chick and Dow offer several main features of open systems. An important advantage of their treatment over critical realist treatments is that Chick and Dow make clear that open systems *are* systems. Such a notion is at best implicit in critical realist treatments through their notion of enduring structures. A system, drawing on treatments from the physical sciences, coheres; it contains elements and connections between them; and these are contained within a boundary. This boundary has two main properties in open systems: it is mutable, from actions by agents; and it is somewhat permeable. A permeable boundary allows the inflow of materials, energy and information. The UK economy is permeable to the flow of labour, capital (including finance) and physical goods; and in the wider sense it is permeable to solar energy and other aspects of climate and weather, and to geological factors.

Critical realism, in combination with other social theories, has contributed much to understanding the internal structures of these systems. In social systems, elements are agents. Connections are relationships between these agents. In open systems, agents are purposive and could do other than they actually do. Further, relations between agents may be internal (as in employer–employee) or external; but some common examples of external relations, such as those between buyers and sellers, are actually weak internal relations. Another feature of open systems is that these relations may change, either as a result of changes in the agents or changes in the structures in which the agents are embedded. Agents, for instance, may learn from past interactions and, as a result, change the relations between them. Further, agents may change the structures themselves, for example, by passing different laws. While structures such as cultural norms condition agents' actions, multifaceted agents also may (consciously or not) change cultural norms. Cultural norms may concern production (for example, working conditions) or consumption (for example, favouring organic food).

Thus open systems may be highly complex, changing objects; and one open system may be more open than another, by virtue of meeting more of the conditions for openness or by meeting those conditions more strongly. Consequently, understanding a system, for instance in order to predict outcomes in it, is rather difficult, and would entail some judgement on how open it is. The critical realist classification of systems in terms of event regularities may be seen as a short cut: if rough event regularities can be found, this may suggest that the system is somewhat closed. However, Chick and Dow's arguments would suggest that this conclusion could be problematic. A system which is strongly open on all criteria could still be roughly stable in terms of outcomes. One reason would be that humans may prefer stability and therefore create order, through conventions, laws and other limitations on behaviour.

How would an economist seek to understand these systems? This question is perennial. Alfred Marshall (1920, p. 288) wrote about the complexity and instability of systems, claiming that the movement of prices was subject to continual buffeting. His language suggests that he recognized the world as comprising open systems. Yet Marshall advocated partial equilibrium models and the *ceteris paribus* assumption. John Stuart Mill's method can be read similarly. From the perspective of open systems, both *ceteris paribus* and partial equilibrium are suspect. These methods presuppose that the market, or some causal mechanism, can be thought of in isolation from all the markets and mechanisms which surround it. Yet, in open systems, clearly markets and mechanisms are interconnected. *Ceteris* are not *paribus*. While the price changes, clearly many other things also change. An economic model has constant parameters attached to a fixed set of causal factors. A regression equation formalizes this arrangement with the device of an error term which apparently captures the effect of all other (unimportant) factors. It has been argued that the error term is simply analogous to closing the laboratory door; but of course in the laboratory the data are created, whereas in the regression, the door is closed after the data are created. For these reasons, Lawson (*passim*) has argued against the use of traditional modelling methods unless there is evidence that the system from which the data are drawn is closed (or closed enough). Similarly, Keynes demanded that users of econometrics justify its use by providing evidence that its context was appropriate.

Practising economists and methodologists have explored the possibilities for economic research in the light of Lawson's arguments. The conclusions from that discussion are considered shortly. First, though, it should be noted that Lawson takes a strict position: closed models or methods are only applicable to closed systems. This implies that it is always invalid to impose partitions on reality or exclusions from it. Further, the requirement to match the openness of methods with the openness of systems before engaging in analysis imposes a large practical burden on economists. Collectively these requirements would render any enquiry impossible. All forms of analysis, it seems, involve the partitioning of reality, at least temporarily. Even historical analysis invokes themes, experiments with trends, or imposes a theoretical framework on historical events.

Chick and Dow argue for a more permissive, practical approach. As they put it: 'Our difference with critical realists is that we see no need for such a strong reluctance to acknowledge the need for boundaries . . . as a means of building theories, or even for using models as one tool of theorising' (2005, p. 376). They argue for tools such as closure (in the mind), the use of *ceteris paribus* clauses, partial equilibrium, and the like, as temporary devices in theorizing. *Theories* remain open systems, and as such are open to external influences; they change over time and evolve through, for example, resolution of internal contradictions. Similarly, schools of thought can be conceptualized as open systems: thus Post Keynesianism has an internal coherence and is different from other schools of thought, but it is open to influence from them, and in some cases it may overlap or share fuzzy boundaries with them. Indeed, it can be argued that a difference between heterodox and mainstream economics is that both acknowledge the problem of open systems (see Marshall), but mainstream economists are more prepared than are heterodox economists to use methods which impose strict closure on reality.

The consequences of the above discussion are varied. Methodologically, open systems demand that economists take seriously the nature of the objects they were studying. In practice, an economist would look carefully at the history and structure of the system, and the system within which it resides. Although it would remain legitimate to study the firm as a (temporarily) distinct object, the firm's history and structure would need to be studied in the context of its market and its economy. Clearly, in open systems, the path of the system is important. An open system would be path dependent, in the sense that structures endure to some extent and therefore would constrain and enable all present and future outcomes. Thus, incorporating the historical development of the system can enhance considerably the explanatory power of any theory.

Further, the tools that the economist uses to study the system may vary, from the more formal and quantitative to 'qualitative' techniques. Chick and Dow's (2005) view is consistent with regarding all analysis as provisional. Downward and Mearman (2007) have argued that the nature of open systems is such that no technique is likely to provide exhaustive insight and that a triangulation or mixing of methods is necessary. That in turn has implications for the meaning of Post Keynesianism, because subsystems within the school, such as neo-Ricardianism, need not be excluded on the basis of the choice of analytical tool.

Perhaps more fundamentally, in open systems the concept of equilibrium is suspect. Equilibrium has a range of meanings that include: no tendency to change (either for the system or agents within it), satisfied expectations, and a balance of forces. However, in open systems all of these are questionable as states of reality. Agents with curiosity generate change in highly complex systems, in which the conditions for completely satisfied expectations are unlikely to hold. Similarly, in open systems the changing and sometimes on/off nature of mechanisms mean that systems are unlikely to settle into a state of balance or position of 'rest'. However, as with *ceteris paribus*, it is not automatic that equilibrium in theorizing should be ditched. Indeed, that principle is well-established in Post Keynesianism, through the work of Keynes, as discussed by Jan Kregel and Chick, among others. Consistent with later arguments on provisional closure of systems in thought, Chick has discussed the notion of provisional equilibrium (Chick and Caserta 1997).

The concept of open systems has had a significant impact on Post Keynesianism. One reason is that, in the light of debates over the coherence of Post Keynesianism, the school was defined by some in terms of ontology; Lawson (2006) has done the same with heterodox economics. As discussed above, though, 'open systems' was kicking at an open door in the school which had for so long emphasized uncertainty. Although uncertainty is inherently a property of people, Post Keynesians tend to argue that the nature of reality, rather than lack of computational capacity or irrationality, creates uncertainty. Open systems also help explain how a prediction is unlikely to be realized. In turn, predictive success ought not be the criterion for assessment of theory. Further, Post Keynesians have argued that realistic theories are more useful than those based on fictions, and the focus on ontology entailed by open systems supported that position.

ANDREW MEARMAN

See also:

Agency; Critical Realism; Econometrics; Equilibrium and Non-equilibrium; Keynes's *Treatise on Probability*; Macroeconomic Methodology; Uncertainty.

References

Chick, V. and M. Caserta (1997), 'Provisional equilibrium and macroeconomic theory', in P. Arestis, G. Palma and M. Sawyer (eds), *Markets, Unemployment and Economic Policy: Essays in Honour of Geoff Harcourt*, Vol. 2, London and New York: Routledge, pp. 223–37.
Chick, V. and S. Dow (2005), 'The meaning of open systems', *Journal of Economic Methodology*, **12** (3), 363–81.
Downward, P. and A. Mearman (2007), 'Retroduction as mixed-methods triangulation in economic research: reorienting economics back into social science', *Cambridge Journal of Economics*, **31** (1), 77–99.
Lawson, T. (2003), *Reorienting Economics*, London and New York: Routledge.

Lawson, T. (2006), 'The nature of heterodox economics', *Cambridge Journal of Economics*, **30** (4), 438–505.

Marshall, A. (1920), *Principles of Economics*, London: Macmillan.

Mearman, A. (2006), 'Critical realism in economics and open system ontology: a critique', *Review of Social Economy*, **64** (1), 47–75.

Pluralism in Economics

Pluralism has been a rallying cry for openness and broad-mindedness in economics since the early 1980s, when heterodox economists' longstanding challenges to the methodological and epistemological monism of post-Second World War economics were joined and extended by 'old Chicago' (McCloskey 1983). Fortified by this extended base of support, the pluralist campaign reached new heights in 1992, when the *American Economic Review* (*AER*) published a petition signed by 44 leading economists, including four Nobel laureates, calling for 'a new spirit of pluralism in economics, involving critical conversation and tolerant communication between different approaches' and demanding that this new pluralist spirit be 'reflected in the character of scientific debate, in the range of contributions in its journals, and in the training and hiring of economists' (Hodgson et al. 1992, p. xxv).

Although issues of pluralism (that is, the analysis and advocacy of 'many-ness') arise in many domains, including theories of human behaviour and social structure, they have been most commonly associated with the aims and methods of economic science and education. My focus in this short entry will be the meaning and importance of pluralism in these two fundamental areas. Although debates between monist and pluralist perspectives on economics education and economics *qua* science are still in their infancy, they have already generated enough range, clarity and substance to warrant our attention here.

Pluralists see economics as a polycentric discipline consisting of 'not one, but many sciences of economics' (Denis 2009, p. 7). Monists, in contrast, presuppose a scientific consensus about 'good economics' – a core of foundational concepts, methods and propositions that is 'accepted by all but a few extreme left-wing and right-wing writers' (Samuelson 1967, pp. 197–8). The notion of a singular economic way of thinking is a hallmark of Samuelsonian monism.

Economic science took a monist turn after the Second World War (Weintraub 2002), a significant departure from the pluralist environment of the 1920s and 1930s in which 'it was possible to hold a number of different economic beliefs and to do economics in many different ways without being out of place or necessarily forfeiting the respect of one's peers' (Morgan and Rutherford 1998, p. 4). This shift reflected professional economists' wartime successes in the development and application of new analytic tools – formal modelling, econometric testing, and hypothetico-deductive reasoning – which had become widely revered as the *sine qua non* of a rigorous social science (ibid., p. 9).

Additional impetus for economists' postwar monism came from the international unity-of-science movement (Richardson 2006). Upon arrival in the US, many émigré economists from interwar Europe championed methodological uniformity as 'a wall against irrational and authoritarian threats to inquiry' (McCloskey 1998, p. 169). By the 1960s and 1970s, however, the noble aims of the interwar period had hardened into a more authoritarian ethos. Mainstream economists were increasingly predisposed to dismiss alternative economic theories or methods *tout court* as unscientific, making the lines of demarcation between mainstream and non-mainstream approaches more rigid and polarizing.

One pluralist response to the monism of mainstream economics was a 'fight science with science' strategy, as leading Austrian, Marxian, Sraffian, Post Keynesian and institutionalist theorists advanced systematic alternatives to the prevailing dominant paradigm. These critics were monist in their pursuit of stand-alone alternatives to mainstream theory. Yet they were pluralist in one important sense: against the grain of a heavy-handed orthodoxy, these purveyors of 'revolutionary science' (Kuhn 1962) sought to make truth and method contestable in economic inquiry.

By the early 1990s, however, many non-mainstream economists had begun to embrace a new genre of pluralism, not just polite tolerance among parallel schools, each with its own truth, but active dialogue and mutual learning among self-consciously partial perspectives. This post-Kuhnian shift in pluralist thinking became visible in the 1992 *AER* petition, and in the creation of an international consortium (ICARE, the International Confederation of Associations for the Reform of Economics) in 1993, but achieved a new level of prominence in 2000 and 2001, when a series of petitions from young economists in France, the UK, the US and Italy ignited the international Post-Autistic Economics (PAE) movement (Fullbrook 2003). This student-led movement called for a more open and scientific economics, guided by a philosophically principled pluralism:

> [a pluralism] that regards the various 'schools' of economics, including neoclassicalism, as offering different windows on economic reality, each bringing into view different subsets of economic phenomena [and] rejects the idea that any school could possess final or total solutions, but accepts all as possible means for understanding real-life economic problems. (Ibid., pp. 8–9)

This temporal juxtaposition of first- and second-wave pluralism is of course stylized. Most pluralist economists embrace key elements of both perspectives. Yet the epistemological assumptions and goals of the two genres are notably divergent. First-wave pluralists place a high value on paradigmatic self-sufficiency. Their ideal is a self-contained school of thought whose practitioners require no intellectual resources beyond their own tradition. In contrast, second-wave pluralists aspire to a Millian pluralism: a 'positive valuing of a diversity of views in the minimal sense that one who is so committed would not want to reduce the number of available narratives or views' (Hargreaves-Heap 2001, p. 356). On this view, inter-paradigmatic conversation is perennially fruitful and necessary since it promotes exchange, trust, *Verstehen* and learning among rival schools of thought, none of whom is epistemically self-sufficient.

Tensions between monist and pluralist ideals – singularlity vs. multiplicity, self-sufficiency vs. interdependence, closure vs. openness – are generating important lines of debate and discovery. Is it still accurate or useful to classify mainstream economics (or heterodox economics) as a single body of thought? Should non-mainstream economists aspire to produce a unified alternative to neoclassical economics? Are mainstream economists becoming more pluralistic? Are heterodox economists as pluralistic as they claim to be? Does the mainstream/heterodox distinction empower non-mainstream traditions or deepen their marginality and thus hasten their demise? Does every citizen in the 'republic of science' have a duty to exercise the virtues of pluralist scholarship? If so, would broad adherence to such an ethic among economists enhance or retard the pace of intellectual progress?

Economics education emerged as a leading frontier of pluralist work over the past decade, as the PAE movement ignited fresh efforts to rethink the goals and methods of graduate and undergraduate economics programmes. The main line of demarcation between monist and pluralist approaches is once again the perceived singularity or diversity of economics itself. From a monist perspective, the main task of economics education is to teach the prevailing orthodoxy, since all relevant ideas from previous thinkers are assumed to be embodied in the prevailing mainstream consensus. For pluralists, the depiction of economics as a 'single coherent view' is factually misleading and pedagogically counterproductive. As Ferber argues, 'It is difficult, if not impossible, to teach economics effectively while pretending that there is consensus in the discipline about either theory or policy . . . Ignoring these issues deprives students of learning about the most thought-provoking discussions of the profession' (1999, pp. 137–8). Pluralists believe that every graduate and undergraduate economics programme should introduce students to the intellectual diversity of economic science.

Against this common backdrop, the literature on pluralism in economics education currently exhibits two overlapping yet distinct approaches. One is a 'contending perspectives' approach in which the presence or absence of pluralism is tied to the presence or absence of competing paradigms in economics courses and curricula. This approach has been substantially shaped by the pluralist course and curriculum proposal outlined by Barone (1991), including a required, intermediate-level survey of radical/Marxian, old institutionalist, Austrian, Post Keynesian and steady-state paradigms.

Barone's contending perspectives model was based on the widespread (though not unanimous) heterodox view that mainstream economics is monist and heterodox economics is pluralist. On this dualist view, mainstream and heterodox economics are strictly separate, and the main *pluralist* goal of the contending perspectives course is to provide a 'basic introduction to heterodox economics' (ibid., p. 16). A secondary premise of this approach is that the main faultlines – points of contention – in economics lie between mainstream and heterodox perspectives or perhaps among heterodox perspectives, but not within mainstream economics.

Of equal importance to the present discussion are the ways in which Barone's pluralism resists this dualist logic. The dialogical inflection of the term 'contending' (rather than 'opposing' or 'alternative') signifies a deliberate emphasis on 'healthy contention rather than competition that forces clear-cut choices of one perspective over another' (ibid., p. 20). Barone is also keen to avoid the problem of reverse monism. He argues that 'all perspectives have something to contribute' and that an integrated, multi-paradigmatic curriculum can enhance students' knowledge of economic theory (mainstream and heterodox) and their capacity for critical, self-directed thought (pp. 18–22). The inclusion of Austrian economics is particularly significant in this regard, since Austrian perspectives are often excluded from heterodoxy due to their non-conformity with the left-leaning ideologies that heterodox economists are generally (if erroneously) presumed to share.

A second approach to pluralist education in economics is closely associated with the notion of critical thinking (Freeman 2007). On this approach, the presence or absence of pluralism is determined *not* by the paradigmatic diversity of a particular course or curriculum but by the learners' intellectual capabilities.

Inspired by a larger shift from teacher- to student-centred (or learning-centred) visions of education, the critical thinking approach has added a new dimension to the monist/pluralist debate in economics education, namely the critical differences between monocentric and polycentric views of the educational process. Teacher-centred approaches are monocentric inasmuch as they presuppose a view of education as a one-way transfer of knowledge from authorities (teachers, textbooks) to novices, whereas student- or learning-centred approaches are polycentric since they conceive student learning as a byproduct of decentralized interactions among many minds, including the 'mind' of the subject matter itself. The monist/

pluralist contrast here is not simply 'top-down' versus 'bottom-up' modes of learning. Pluralists recognize that all educational processes include 'top-down' elements due to the hierarchical relationship between instructors and students. The difference lies in the pluralist commitment to liberal education as an epistemically *inclusive* enterprise wherein students and instructors interact as partners (though never as equals) in the process of inquiry.

An important corollary of the shift towards student- and learning-centred perspectives is that pluralist education itself is more and more being defined in terms of learning outcomes and processes rather than course content. In a teacher-centred view of pluralist education, the definition of a pluralist course is primarily content based: the more paradigmatically diverse the course materials, the more 'pluralist' the course. This is the contending perspectives model. In the 'critical thinking' view, however, education is a process of intellectual capacity building, not the delivery and retention of information. Measures of learning focus less on 'what' students learn and more on 'how' they learn (pedagogy) and what they are able to do (capabilities) as a result of their learning. Teaching competing paradigms may be one way to foster pluralist capabilities, but for many educators it is no longer the defining feature of pluralist education.

In economics education, as in the realm of economic science, the ultimate ground for pluralist positions is not heterodox theory but philosophical liberalism. Long before the PAE movement hoisted the pluralist flag, the Socratic–liberal goal of teaching students to think for themselves was shared by a diverse array of mainstream and heterodox economics educators. As expressed by the British economist George Shackle:

> The first task of the University teacher of any liberal art is surely to persuade his students that the most important things he will put before them are questions and not answers. He is going to put up for them a scaffolding, and leave them to build within it. He has to persuade them that they have not come to the University to learn as it were by heart things which are already hard-and-fast and cut-and-dried, but to watch and perhaps help in a process, the driving of a causeway which will be made gradually firmer by the traffic of many minds. (Shackle 1953, p. 18)

Shackle's felicitous image of liberal learning is still cherished by many economics educators. But the pedagogical ideals of this 'silent majority' have never gained much professional standing, in part because its leading advocates – mainstream and heterodox – have been unable to sustain collaborative ties across the methodological, ideological and sociological divisions of our profession.

Economics education promises to remain an active site of pluralist (re)-thinking in our discipline. Pluralist educators of all stripes increasingly agree, for instance, that student learning is inhibited by the doctrinaire monism of conventional economics textbooks, curricula and pedagogies. Yet disagreement persists over the goals and contents of pluralist alternatives. At a superficial level, this debate looks like a familiar heterodox/ orthodox standoff, pitting those who favour a larger role for heterodox theories in economics education against those who contend that 'economics students are entitled to a solid disciplinary training in prevailing economic theory' (Vromen 2007, p. 64). But as serious thinkers on all sides wrestle with how to revamp the standard aim of teaching students to 'think like economists' (Siegfried et al. 1991) in our nascent post-Samuelsonian era, the central questions are shifting. Rather than simply 'whose paradigm(s) should be taught?', leading educators across the heterodox/mainstream spectrum are looking to expand the notion of 'thinking like an economist' to include the liberal arts of creative, critical inquiry and reflective judgement. Herein we see a fundamental sense in which the future vitality of economic science depends upon the cultivation of pluralism in economics education, and vice versa.

ROB GARNETT

References

Barone, C.A. (1991), 'Contending perspectives: curricular reform in economics', *Journal of Economic Education*, **22** (1), 15–26.

Denis, A. (2009), 'Editorial: pluralism in economics education', *International Review of Economics Education*, **8** (2), 6–21.

Ferber, M.A. (1999), 'Guidelines for pre-college economics education: a critique', *Feminist Economics*, **5** (3), 135–42.

Freeman, A. (2007), 'Catechism versus pluralism: the heterodox response to the national undergraduate curriculum proposed by the UK Quality Assurance Agency', unpublished paper, available at: http://econpapers.repec.org/paper/pramprapa/6832.htm (accessed 14 December 2010).

Fullbrook, E. (ed.) (2003), *The Crisis in Economics: The Post-Autistic Economics Movement: The First 600 Days*, London: Routledge.

Hargreaves-Heap, S. (2001), 'Postmodernism, rationality, and justice', in S. Cullenberg, J. Amariglio and D. Ruccio (eds), *Postmodernism, Economics, and Knowledge*, London and New York: Routledge, pp. 354–73.

Hodgson, G.M., U. Mäki and D.N. McCloskey (1992), 'Plea for a pluralistic and rigorous economics', *American Economic Review*, **82** (2), xxv.

Kuhn, T.S. (1962), *The Structure of Scientific Revolutions*, Chicago, IL: University of Chicago Press.

McCloskey, D.N. (1983), 'The rhetoric of economics', *Journal of Economic Literature*, **31** (2), 434–61.

McCloskey, D.N. (1998), *The Rhetoric of Economics*, 2nd edn, Madison, WI: University of Wisconsin Press.

Morgan, M.S. and M. Rutherford (eds) (1998), *From Interwar Pluralism to Postwar Neoclassicism*, Durham, NC: Duke University Press.

Richardson, A.W. (2006), 'The many unities of science: politics, semantics, and ontology', in S. Kellert, H. Longino and K. Waters (eds), *Scientific Pluralism*, Minneapolis, MN: University of Minnesota Press, pp. 1–25.

Samuelson, P.A. (1967), *Economics*, 7th edn, New York: McGraw-Hill.

Shackle, G.L.S. (1953), *What Makes an Economist?*, Liverpool: Liverpool University Press.
Siegfried, J.J., R.L. Bartlett, W.L. Hansen, A.C. Kelley, D.N. McCloskey and T.H. Tietenberg (1991), 'The status and prospects of the economics major', *Journal of Economic Education*, **22** (3), 197–224.
Vromen, J. (2007), 'In praise of moderate plurality', in J. Groenewegen (ed.), *Teaching Pluralism in Economics*, Cheltenham, UK and Northampton, MA, USA: Edward Elgar, pp. 64–94.
Weintraub, E.R. (2002), *How Economics Became a Mathematical Science*, Durham, NC: Duke University Press.

Price Rigidity

When one thinks of price rigidity and the term 'Keynesian', one generally does not think first of Post Keynesian economists but rather of New Keynesian economists. These economists have indeed contributed a lot of theoretical and empirical work on the observed phenomenon of price rigidity (prices that respond slowly and/or incompletely to changes in demand). However, Post Keynesians are not absent from the story, and have an interpretation to provide that relies above all on the way prices are determined *and* on the rigidity of profit margins. This Post Keynesian conception of sticky prices is fundamentally different from the New Keynesian interpretation. To understand the Post Keynesian view, one has to answer two distinct questions: why are prices sticky, and do sticky prices really have an impact on macroeconomic fluctuations?

After the Second World War, the Neoclassical Synthesis used a fixed wage and price assumption to derive effective demand effects. This hypothesis was soon criticized by New Classical economists on the basis that it was not founded on rational individual behaviour. Assuming that prices do not adjust to supply and demand disequilibrium is the same as saying that agents do not achieve gains from trade or, as Robert Lucas often stated, that they leave $500 bills on the sidewalk. Thus this question has no place in the New Classical framework, where price rigidity is not really an issue. Some authors, however, refused to abandon the Keynesian theory because of its weak microeconomic foundations and decided to try to derive strong theoretical support for the rigidity of prices: this was the birth of New Keynesian economics. The problem is that in order to explain why prices are sticky, one must explain two things: first, that firms have power over prices, and, second, that these firms do not change their prices when demand changes. To meet the first problem, New Keynesians usually refer to 'imperfect competition'. If competition were perfect, firms would be forced to accept the market price. But competition is imperfect, and this gives firms some power: firms are price setters. Then, to explain why firms do not change prices in the face of a change in demand, New Keynesians developed several specific theories.

The main New Keynesian theories of price rigidity are as follows:

Menu costs: The principle is that firms face costs of changing prices, because they have to write prices on tags, menus and catalogues. When demand changes, firms do not change their prices because the cost of changing would be greater than the potential gain.

Implicit contracts: In this theory, firms are supposed to make implicit arrangements with customers to stabilize prices, and with workers to stabilize money wages. The idea is that firms seek to build long-term relationships with their customers and employees, and do not want to antagonize them.

Nominal contracts: Firms are committed to written fixed-term contracts and cannot change prices before the end of the contract.

Coordination failure: The principle here is that firms do not change their prices because they do not want to be the first to do it, and wait for another competitor to go first.

Cost-based pricing: In this view firms base their prices on costs and do not change them until costs change, leading to an insensitivity of prices to demand variations.

Constant marginal cost: If marginal costs are constant throughout the business cycle, movements in demand do not affect the price (it is, however, also necessary that demand curves be isoelastic).

Non-price competition: Firms prefer to change other characteristics instead of price when demand changes (for example, delivery delays and product quality).

Pricing threshold: Some prices are set at a psychological level ($9.99, for example), rendering it difficult to change them.

Link between quality and price: Some firms fear that a change in price could be interpreted as a change in the quality of their product (this is especially relevant to a fall in price).

Beyond their academic success, the New Keynesian theories of prices also achieved real empirical success. This success came from Alan Blinder, who was the first to test these theories empirically by asking businesspeople directly what they thought of them. Following his amazing results, many central banks across the world decided to conduct similar studies for their own countries. The results of these studies are twofold: they confirm the existence of price stickiness, and they show that some theories are more popular among businesspeople than others. Without being able to derive a precise hierarchy of all these theories, one can nevertheless say that among the winners would probably figure the implicit contract, the nominal contract, coordination failure and cost-based pricing theories. Among the losers is the theory of menu costs, despite it being the first theory to be developed and one of the most popular of its time (see Fabiani et al. 2007 for European results, and Melmiès 2010 for a global overview).

Thus it would be difficult at first sight to say something from a Post Keynesian point of view that would differ from the New Keynesian analysis of the reasons for price rigidity. This New Keynesian analysis could seem all the more convincing in that it relies on imperfect competition, which was precisely developed by Post Keynesian authors (especially Joan Robinson), who also discussed the question of price rigidity.

However this conclusion would be an illusion. To understand why, it is necessary to specify precisely in what sense the New Keynesian and Post Keynesian theories of price differ. New Keynesians still refer to a framework where firms set prices that maximize their profits. In that case, in the face of a change in demand, firms would like to change their price but prefer not to do so because costs, contracts or coordination failures dissuade them from doing it. It is thus a theory of *constrained price stickiness*. On the contrary, Post Keynesians do not invoke the maximizing framework. Empirical data just suggest that firms are goal driven and do not try to maximize profits (Lee 1998; Downward 1999). But then the problem is this: if firms do not set prices in order to maximize profits, what is the function of prices? Post Keynesians argue that firms seek to survive, maintain and reproduce themselves and grow in the market. They have to engage in sequential transactions in decentralized markets, and they thus have to set a price.

Relying on Gardiner Means's theory of administered prices, the Post Keynesian analysis underlines the fact that firms deliberately administer and maintain the price of their product for several transactions. Using pricing procedures such as mark-up, full cost or target return pricing, firms often set prices according to a standard or normal level of output and do not change them for a given period, even if demand is not at the standard level and varies during the 'pricing period' (for example three months, six months or one year). The notion of standard output is central to understanding why prices do not change with the level of sales: short-term changes in demand are not what firms are looking at. Seeking to maintain themselves in the market, and seeking to grow, they look at the long-term level of demand. Short-term changes in the level of sales will not affect the price. Firms will maintain this price for a period of time whatever the level of demand during the period, thus underlining a *deliberated price stickiness*. In fact, even if New Keynesians have abandoned the existence of the auctioneer, they have argued *as if* firms were their own auctioneer and behave with 'auctioneer type rationality', adjusting their price to meet demand/supply disequilibria. This is not the case in Post Keynesian economics, where the absence of the auctioneer leads to fundamentally different behaviour.

However, this does not mean that prices never change. The most frequent causes of price changes are cost changes, especially changes in labour and material costs, suggesting that profit margins are at least as rigid as prices themselves (see Blinder et al. 1998 and Downward 1999). Indeed, Post Keynesians have a theory of profit margins which can explain their rigidity. If some authors still refer to an explanation of profit margins based on the price elasticity of demand (an explanation which can also be found in New Keynesian economics), another branch of Post Keynesians explains profit margins by the need for internal finance for investment. Based on Eichner's analysis of the megacorp and price leadership (Eichner 1976), this analysis can explain why firms will try to restore their profit margins by raising prices when costs increase: they need these margins to generate internal funds. Whereas in mainstream and New Keynesian economics margins are a residual profit that firms 'extort' from the market due to their market power, in the Post Keynesian explanation firms add a mark-up for the purposes of reproduction and self-financing, thus allowing them to invest in the future. Thus what emerges is that, in a Post Keynesian perspective, the observed price stickiness is not a phenomenon in its own right but is due to three other phenomena: relative inertia in costs (especially labour costs), pricing procedures which do not rely on the actual level of activity but rather on a normal level which is anchored in the long run, and rigidity of profit margins, which are a strategic financial variable for firms.

Concerning the second question, the importance of sticky prices in economic fluctuations, the central point that must be made from a Post Keynesian perspective is that New Keynesian authors have a very specific (and contentious) use of the term 'Keynesian'. For them, price rigidity is a necessary condition to get effective demand effects and to derive policy recommendations based on demand stimulation. If prices were perfectly flexible, money and aggregate demand would not affect output and there could be no underemployment equilibrium. This conception could seem seductive, if it were not precisely what Keynes denied in 1936! As Davidson (1992) has shown, Keynes's goal was precisely to demonstrate that supply does *not* create its own demand, and that demand can affect the economy *even if* prices are perfectly flexible and *even if* competition is perfect. Considering this, labelling New Keynesian economists 'Keynesians' seems very misleading.

To conclude: New Keynesians and Post Keynesians have a totally different view of prices and especially of price stickiness. From a Post Keynesian perspective, one can analyse prices which seem 'sticky' and analyse the way in which prices are determined, because this is an important strategic variable for the firm's reproduction, and an important variable in the distribution of income. But in Post Keynesian economics price rigidity cannot be held responsible for demand affecting output.

JORDAN MELMIÈS

See also:

Competition; Galbraith's Economics; Investment; Marginalism; New Keynesian Economics; Prices and Pricing; Profits.

References

Blinder, A., E.R.D. Canetti, D.E. Lebow and J.B. Rudd (1998), *Asking About Prices: A New Approach to Understanding Price Stickiness*, NewYork: Russell Sage Foundation.
Davidson, P. (1992), 'Would Keynes be a "New" Keynesian?', *Eastern Economic Journal*, **18** (4), 449–63.
Downward, P. (1999), *Pricing Theory in Post Keynesian Economics: A Realist Approach*, Cheltenham, UK and Northampton, MA, USA: Edward Elgar.
Eichner, A.S. (1976), *The Megacorp and Oligopoly: Micro Foundations of Macro Dynamics*, Cambridge: Cambridge University Press.
Fabiani, S., C.S. Loupias, F.M.M. Martins and R. Sabbatini (2007), *Pricing Decisions in the Euro Area: How Firms Set Prices and Why*, New York: Oxford University Press.
Lee, F.S. (1998), *Post Keynesian Price Theory*, Cambridge: Cambridge University Press.
Melmiès, J. (2010), 'New-Keynesians versus Post Keynesians on the theory of prices', *Journal of Post Keynesian Economics*, **32** (3), 445–65.

Prices and Pricing

Post Keynesians see the discipline of economics as being concerned with explaining the process that provides the flow of goods and services required by society to meet the needs of those who participate in its activities. Consequently, Post Keynesian economic theory is the theoretical explanation of this social provisioning process in a capitalist economy. Hence Post Keynesian theory is concerned with explaining those factors that are part of the process, including the setting of prices by business enterprises.

The business enterprise is a specific social organization for coordinating and carrying out activities associated with the provisioning process. It consists of an organizational component, a production and cost component, a series of routines that transmit information (such as costs, sales and prices) which enable workers and management to coordinate and carry out their activities, and a management that makes strategic decisions about prices (as well as investment). When making decisions, management is motivated by different goals, such as growth of sales, developing new products, entering new geographical regions or markets, generating dividends for shareholders and/or attaining political power. Hence management views price setting, or pricing, as strategic decisions designed to meet these goals (Eichner 1976; Lee 1998; Downward 1999).

To set a price of a product, the pricing administrators of the business enterprise first determine its cost base. Utilizing costing procedures derived from the management accounting procedures used by the enterprise, the pricing administrators determine the product's average direct costs (ADC), average overhead costs (AOC), and average total costs (ATC) at normal output. The relevance of normal output is that it enables the pricing administrators to determine the product's normal costs. That is, since ADC, AOC and ATC vary as output changes, it is necessary to select a particular level of output if costs for pricing are to be determined before production takes place and the actual costs of production are known. With the normal costs administratively determined, the pricing administrators select a profit mark-up to be applied to the normal costs to set the price. This pricing procedure means that the price of the good is set before the good is produced and exchange takes place. The pricing administrators then take the administratively determined price (which is determined outside the market) and administer it to (or impose it on) the market.

There have been several Post Keynesian taxonomies or classifications of pricing procedures – for instance, Lavoie (1992) and Lee (1998). Since prices are determined through both costing procedures and profit mark-up processes, they incorporate these two idiosyncratic dimensions in their pricing classifications. In other words, one group of the pricing procedures which they identify is predicated on different costing procedures, taking the rate of profit mark-up simply as given whatever the mark-up process is, whereas the other group is defined according to the profit mark-up processes, taking their relevant cost base as given whatever the costing procedure is. Thus, it is necessary to differentiate between the two perspectives on pricing procedures and identify them as two different taxonomies: the *costing-oriented pricing taxonomy* and the *mark-up-oriented pricing taxonomy*, respectively. However, it should be noted that this does not mean that the previous pricing classifications are simply falsified; rather they reflect the reality of their own time period in terms of pricing procedures which are supposed to be historically contingent. The two taxonomies suggested here are developed and extended from the previous perspectives, with the intention of taking into consideration recent developments in accounting systems and pricing practices in the business world since the early 1990s; indeed, the fundamental structures and properties of prices and pricing remain unchanged in a capitalist economy (Wolman 2007).

The costing-oriented pricing taxonomy is a pricing classification predicated primarily on various costing procedures, including both traditional and newly invented costing techniques. The traditional costing system uses a volume-based driver such as direct labour hours for overhead cost allocation. The main problem with the traditional allocation system is that a product's consumption of overhead resources may not be strictly related to units produced. Given that the portion of overhead costs has increased significantly, whereas that of direct labour cost has decreased gradually, the traditional cost management system has become less and less efficient in providing accurate cost information to the business entrepreneurs. Activity-based costing (ABC) has attracted high levels of interest from both academics and practitioners since its emergence in the mid-1980s. ABC is a method of assigning indirect or overhead costs according to the factors that cause the costs. The traditional costing procedure is easy and inexpensive to implement, but the information obtained could be too raw to be accurate, whereas the ABC procedure solves the problem but is expensive and time-consuming to implement. Given the strengths and weaknesses of the two costing systems, business enterprises rely on both of them with varying degrees of scope and sophistication of their ABC applications, rather than choosing and operating only one of the discrete alternatives (Stratton et al. 2009).

At the centre of the pricing procedures in the costing-oriented taxonomy are direct cost pricing, total cost pricing and ABC cost pricing. It should be remembered that their cost base always begins with average cost – either average direct cost or average total cost – at normal output. Thus the terms 'direct cost', 'total cost' and 'ABC cost' pricing should be preceeded by 'normal average', but this is omitted below for simplicity.

Direct cost pricing consists of marking up average direct cost based on the normal volume of output to set the price, with the mark-up being sufficient to cover overhead costs and produce profits:

$$\text{direct cost pricing: price} = (\text{NADC})(1+k),$$

where NADC is normal average direct cost, and k is the mark-up for overhead costs and profits.

Total cost pricing has two forms: one is to mark up NADC to cover overhead costs, which gives NATC, and then apply a profit mark-up to NATC to set a price; the other applies the profit mark-up directly to NATC to set the price:

$$\text{total cost pricing: price} = (\text{NADC})(1+g)(1+r) \text{ or price} = (\text{NATC})(1+r),$$

where g is the mark-up for overhead costs based on normal output, and r is the mark-up for profits.

As the most advanced pricing procedure, ABC cost pricing can be formulated in the following manner:

$$\text{ABC cost pricing: price} = (\text{NADC})(1 + \sum_{i=1}^{n} x_i)(1+r),$$

where x_i is the mark-up to cover an allocated part of ith overhead cost according to the product's consumption of the activity that causes the overhead cost.

It should be noted that the difference between total cost pricing and ABC cost pricing consists in the specific method by which to determine the mark-up for the overhead costs. With more than one product that a business enterprise produces, total cost pricing allocates the total amount of the overhead costs to each product based on each product's normal volume, which may be irrelevant to the causes of the overhead costs, whereas ABC cost pricing utilizes each product's relative consumption of each overhead cost to allocate the total amount of the overhead costs among its products.

The mark-up-oriented pricing taxonomy is the other pricing classification, in which pricing procedures are differentiated according to a variety of profit mark-up processes after presupposing a cost base such as normal average direct or total cost, regardless of what its costing procedure is. The best-known pricing procedures identified by this taxonomy are fair rate of return pricing and target rate of return pricing. In addition, there is also a refined pricing procedure, which can be divided into three subgroups: product-based mark-up pricing, competitor-motivated mark-up pricing and class-induced mark-up pricing.

First, *fair rate of return pricing* is a cost-plus pricing procedure in which the mark-up is predetermined by convention or a fair rate of profit, based on the industry norms, which are customs and practices established within an industry and with which firms must comply. These customs and practices are known by the industry, and the industry will expect that all business and trading conform to these customs and practices. In the context of pricing, these customs and practices will be manifest as 'acceptable' and 'expected' mark-ups and margins; such margins will be known, particularly where products have little differentiation.

Second, *target rate of return pricing* is a cost-plus pricing procedure in which the mark-up is determined exclusively by organizational conditions. Suppose that a new business enterprise installs plant and equipment to produce a product, and aims to generate a desired flow of funds from that investment for whatever it wants to achieve. A possible target rate of return pricing consists of marking up NATC by a certain percentage to generate a volume of profits at normal output that will produce a specific rate of return with respect to the value of the enterprise's capital assets connected with the production of the product. That is, given the value of the capital assets (VCA) associated with the production of the product, the pricing administrators want to obtain a specific target rate of return (TRR) on those assets. Therefore, the profit required to meet the target rate of return is TRR × VCA = target profits, P_t. To incorporate the target profit figure into the price, P_t is first divided by normal output (*no*) to get the targeted costing margin, cm_t, and then divided by NATC to get the targeted profit mark-up (t):

$$\text{target rate of return pricing: price} = (NATC)(1 + t)$$
$$= (NATC)[1 + TRR \times VCA/(no)NATC].$$

Given the targeted profit mark-up, if the business enterprise produces at normal output, enough profits will be generated to attain the desired target rate of return on the capital assets (Eichner 1976; Lavoie 1992; Lee 1998; Downward 1999). Because actual output can differ from the normal output, the business enterprise will not always achieve its target rate of return or desired profits, sometimes being above it and other times being below it over the business cycle.

Third, *product-based mark-up pricing* is a cost-plus pricing procedure in which the mark-up is predominantly adjusted to reflect characteristics or life cycles of products. Product characteristics have much to do with complementarity and supplementarity between the enterprise's products; business enterprises sometimes use a joint mark-up rate for a group of complementary products. Product life cycles are mostly determined by technological changes and market growth; the mark-up rates of unfashionable products are occasionally curtailed. This procedure is closely related to specific pricing practices or tactics such as price bundling and skimming pricing.

Fourth, *competitor-motivated mark-up pricing* is a cost-plus pricing procedure in which the mark-up is set mainly to be responsive to the strategies of competitors in the same industry. Depending on the price leader–follower relations, business enterprises position themselves in setting mark-up rates and thus prices. Practically there are four possible tactics: leader pricing, parity pricing, low-price supplier and opportunistic pricing. In the majority of industries, large business enterprises set the rules of the game, leaving smaller ones with limited price discretion and no other option than to follow the leader's (or leaders') pricing initiatives, since the price leader tends to maintain its superiority in technology.

Lastly, *class-induced mark-up pricing* is a cost-plus pricing procedure in which the mark-up differs primarily according to its primary target class. More often than not, business enterprises aim to create markets for their products and set desirable mark-up rates by manipulating the purchasing habits of their consumers – for example, developing conspicuous consumption by the upper class – by means of pricing practices such as perceived-value pricing, price signalling and image pricing. They sometimes try to increase their total profits by providing discounts for the lower class – that is, expanding their customer group – in the case of reference pricing and second-market discounting.

The prices set by pricing administrators using normal cost-based pricing procedures have five properties. The first is that the price is not based on or related to actual costs, and immediate or current market forces do not affect the profit mark-up. That is, irrespective of the pricing procedures used by pricing administrators, the shape of the enterprise's average direct cost curve or its average total cost curve is immaterial for pricing purposes. The costs used for pricing are determined prior to production and are based on normal output. Consequently, the shape of the ADC cost curve or ATC curve is not important for price-setting purposes. Instead the price is based on normal costs, while actual costs vary around it as actual output varies around normal output. As for the profit mark-up, the evidence strongly suggests that it remains stable for significant periods of time, so that in some cases it is considered customary by pricing administrators; that it is based on long-term competitive forces and will change when those forces change; and that it is unaffected by momentary fluctuations in sales. To explain theoretically the magnitude and the relative stability of the profit mark-up, Post Keynesians have utilized either market structure arguments or investment-determining mark-up arguments. However, neither argument has much empirical support. Thus the profit mark-up remains theoretically underexplained in Post Keynesian theory (Wood 1975; Eichner 1976; Capoğlu 1991; Lavoie 1992; Sawyer 1995; Downward 1999). The establishment of pricing procedures in the mark-up-oriented taxonomy can be viewed as an attempt to theorize the complexities of profit mark-up processes.

Given normal costs and the stability of the profit mark-up, it follows that the second property of administered prices is that they are stable: they remain unchanged for extended periods of time and for many sequential transactions. Consequently, administered prices are neither exchange-specific prices nor prices that reflect the impact of immediate variations in sales. This implies that markets that have stable, normal cost-based prices are not organized like auction markets or oriental bazaars, where the retailer engages in individual price negotiation for each transaction. Rather, an enterprise that desires to enter these unorganized markets must first announce a price for its product and then enter into direct buyer–seller interaction to obtain sales. Since buyer–seller interactions take place both simultaneously and through time, business enterprises find that stable prices are cost efficient in terms of selling costs, reduce the threat of price

wars and facilitate the establishment of goodwill relationships with customers (Lee 1998; Downward 1999).

The third property of administered prices is that they are set largely
without reference to an inverse price–sales relationship and are not set to
achieve a specific volume of sales. In studies of price determination, business enterprises have stated that variations of their prices within practical
limits, given the prices of their competitors, produced virtually no change
in their sales and that variations in the market price, especially downward,
produced little if any changes in market sales in the short term. Moreover,
when the price change is significant enough to result in a significant change
in sales, the impact on profits has been negative enough to persuade enterprises not to try the experiment again. Consequently, administered prices
are maintained for a variety of different outputs over time.

The fourth property of administered prices is that they change over
time. The pricing administrators of business enterprises maintain pricing
periods of three months to a year in which their administered prices
remained unchanged; and then, at the end of the period, they decide on
whether to alter them. The factors which are most important to the enterprises in this regard are changes in labour and material costs, changes in
the mark-up for profit and changes in normal output. Factors prompting
the enterprises to alter their profit mark-ups include short- and long-term
competitive pressures, the stage that the product has reached in its life cycle
and the need for profit. Moreover, since normal output is administratively
determined, it is possible for pricing administrators to alter it cyclically
over the business cycle, resulting in the NATC increasing in the downturn
and decreasing in the upturn. If the mark-ups for profit remain constant,
then the pricing administrators would be setting countercyclical prices.
Consequently, administered prices can change from one pricing period
to the next in any direction, irrespective of the state of the business cycle.
However, evidence does suggest that within short periods of time (such as
two-year intervals), change in costs will dominate price changes, whereas
over longer periods changes in the mark-up will play a more important role
(Lee 1998; Downward 1999).

The fifth and final feature of administered prices is their role in the
reproduction of the business enterprise. That is, pricing administrators use
cost-based pricing procedures to set prices that would enable the enterprise
to engage in sequential acts of production over time and thereby reproduce itself and grow. More specifically, because market conditions facing
the enterprise's many products are not uniform and change over time,
its pricing administrators utilize a variety of multitemporal, open-ended
pricing strategies designed to achieve time-specific and temporally unde-
fined goals. The compendium of pricing strategies is known as the enter-

prise's pricing policy, and the prices that the pricing administrator applies to the various markets are based on one or more of these strategies. Thus, the administered prices of a business enterprise are strategic prices whose common and overriding goals are reproduction and growth (Eichner, 1976; Lavioe, 1992; Lee, 1998; Downward, 1999).

GYUN CHEOL GU
FREDERIC S. LEE

See also:

Competition; Galbraith's Economics; Income Distribution; Kaleckian Economics; Price Rigidity; Production.

References

Capoğlu, G. (1991), *Prices, Profits and Financial Structures*, Aldershot, UK and Brookfield, VT, USA: Edward Elgar.
Downward, P. (1999), *Pricing Theory in Post Keynesian Economics*, Cheltenham, UK and Northampton, MA, USA: Edward Elgar.
Eichner, A.S. (1976), *The Megacorp and Oligopoly*, Cambridge: Cambridge University Press.
Lavoie, M. (1992), *Foundations of Post-Keynesian Economic Analysis*, Aldershot, UK and Brookfield, VT, USA: Edward Elgar.
Lee, F.S. (1998), *Post Keynesian Price Theory*, Cambridge: Cambridge University Press.
Sawyer, M.C. (1995), *Unemployment, Imperfect Competition and Macroeconomics*, Aldershot, UK and Brookfield, VT, USA: Edward Elgar.
Stratton, W., R. Lawson and T. Hatch (2009), 'Activity-based costing: is it still relevant?', *Management Accounting Quarterly*, **10** (3), 31–40.
Wolman, A. (2007), 'The frequency and costs of individual price adjustment', *Managerial and Decision Economics*, **28** (6), 531–52.
Wood, A. (1975), *A Theory of Prices*, Cambridge: Cambridge University Press.

Production

It can be argued that, in the mainstream neoclassical theoretical apparatus, the role of production is subsidiary to that of exchange. The core of that approach, which explores how scarce commodities are allocated among alternative uses through the price mechanism, can be represented using a model of exchange with given endowments of non-produced commodities. Production can be introduced into this model at a later stage to show how resources are transformed into goods through the production function, without fundamentally altering the basic insights to be drawn from the approach. In contrast, in Post Keynesian economics, as in classical–Marxian political economy, production takes a more central role.

The centrality of production in Post Keynesian economics can be related to some of its main concepts, such as effective demand, historical time and uncertainty (see Dutt and Amadeo 1990). Perhaps the key concept common to all varieties of Post Keynesianism is effective demand, and its role in determining employment in the short run and the rate of accumulation and growth in the long run. Since effective demand determines these by determining the level and rate of change of production, production naturally takes a central place in the Post Keynesian approach. Another important idea stressed in Post Keynesian economics is historical time, as opposed to logical time in which historical processes and irreversibilities are not adequately captured. Chick (1983, pp. 16–21) discusses how major economic decisions such as consumption, saving, investment and especially production can be portrayed as being made over historical time. In this sequence, production decisions have to be made prior to sales, but with the expectation of sales affecting how much firms produce. These expectations are referred to as short-period expectations, which are different from the long-period expectations which govern investment decisions. A related concept, stressed more in some varieties of Post Keynesianism than in others, is that of uncertainty, which is distinguished from risk because objective probabilities cannot be assigned to the consequences of many economic decisions as is assumed in the analysis of risk. While the concept of uncertainty is stressed in discussions of investment and asset-holding decisions, it has also been invoked in discussion of production. In uncertain situations firms and other economic agents are often seen as following conventions and rules of thumb, behaviour which may be much more sensible than doing detailed cost–benefit calculations of their actions.

An examination of the theory of production at the level of individual producers illustrates the importance of some of these ideas. Since Post Keynesian economics follows several different approaches, it is useful to consider two different approaches to such a theory, one derived from the Marshallian tradition of Keynes's *General Theory* presentation, and the other the Kaleckian approach which stresses imperfect competition.

In the Keynesian approach the firm is assumed to operate in a purely competitive environment, in the sense that it expects to sell any amount at the going price. Since the firm has to make its production decision without knowing the price which will prevail when its produce will be brought to the market it is assumed to form short-period expectations, which take the form of an expected price. With the money wage assumed to be given, the firm is then taken to maximize profit by equating its marginal product of labour (assuming diminishing returns and a given stock of capital) to the ratio of the wage to the expected price. This determines the firm's market-period equilibrium level of employment and output. Once each firm makes its production and employment plans and carries them out, income flows are generated in the form of wages and profits, and these determine the level of consumption, while firms make investment plans depending on their exogenously given long-period expectations. Assuming that aggregate effective demand depends on the price level (perhaps because of its effect on the real wage, and hence on consumption demand with differential propensities to consume out of wage and profit income), the price is assumed to vary to equate demand to total market-period equilibrium. There is no guarantee that the expected price of firms (for simplicity assumed to be the same for all firms) will be equal to the market-period equilibrium price. If they are different, firms will adapt by adjusting their expectations, and thereby (under certain conditions) arrive at the short-period equilibrium level of production, at which not only does the market clear but the firms' short-period expectations are also fulfilled, although long-period expectations are still taken as given. The short-period equilibrium level of output depends on the level of investment spending, among other things, and may well be below the full-employment level of output. This approach can be seen as providing a simple formalization of the role of effective demand in determining output, of historical time in which different periods are carefully distinguished, and of uncertainty, through its invocation of short- and long-period expectations. Moreover, the approach can be used as a basis for examining changes in long-period expectations and its relation to short-period expectations, which can be shown to lead to various kinds of path dependencies in the determination of the aggregate level of production (see Dutt 1997). However, some Post Keynesians exhibit some hostility to it and to the aggregate demand–aggregate supply analysis related to it, given its closeness to marginalist traditions following from its assumptions of pure competition and production functions that exhibit diminishing returns.

These Post Keynesians prefer the Kaleckian approach, in which firms in oligopolistic situations enjoy some degree of monopoly power. In this approach, given the uncertainty concerning the level of aggregate demand and the behaviour of other firms, firms use the rule of thumb of setting their price as a mark-up on their unit prime or variable costs. On the assumption of a fixed unit labour requirement, a fixed money wage, that labour is the only variable factor, and a fixed mark-up (which depends on factors such as the level of industrial concentration), the price becomes constant, and the firms adjust their level of output to the level of demand for their product, while maintaining excess capacity given their stock of capital. In this approach the level of production for each firm is determined by the demand for the firm's product. The aggregate level of production in the economy is therefore determined by aggregate effective demand, and will in general be consistent with excess capacity and unemployed labour. This approach represents a more radical departure from neoclassical economics, because of its assumption of fixed unit labour requirements, which can be allowed to vary due to changes in technology and in the social relations of production as in Marxian and radical presentations, rather than due to factor substitution. The approach can also be used to illustrate different sources of path dependence in the determination of output and its growth rate (see Dutt 2009).

The feature common to both approaches is the role of aggregate effective demand. There cannot be a self-contained microeconomic theory of production: the level of output depends on the demand for each firm, which depends on macroeconomic factors such as aggregate consumption and other sources of demand (and some rule according to which total demand is apportioned between firms).

However, the discussion presented so far leaves open the possibility that, although unemployment equilibrium can occur in the short run, there may be forces in the economy which change the level of production of firms in a direction which will drive aggregate production to fully employ all the economy's resources in the longer run. Unemployment can lead to a fall in the wage or the price level, which increases the real supply of money, which through wealth effects on demand or through a reduction of the interest rate can induce firms to invest more, and thereby increase the demand for goods. These forces can take the economy to positions of full employment, as suggested by the 'Neoclassical Synthesis' Keynesian approach and imply that aggregate demand does not determine output in the long run.

To negate this, Post Keynesians argue that the money wage is determined by institutional factors rather than by the automatic forces of supply and demand. Thus, the importance given to relative wages by workers in the wage-bargaining process may prevent wage reductions, as argued by Keynes (1936) himself, or issues such as efficiency wages or insider–outsider considerations may explain wage rigidity. While this wage rigidity interpretation of Keynesian macroeoconomics is common in mainstream circles, it would make Keynesian economics little different from that of the pre-Keynesians, who were quite aware that wage rigidity could result in unemployment.

More distinctively, Post Keynesians emphasize that wage reductions need not take the economy to full employment, following Keynes's own lead in chapter 19 of the *General Theory*. Thus, they argue that money supply in a credit-money economy is demand determined, so that a fall in the wage and price level, rather than automatically reducing the interest rate because of an excess supply of money, will simply reduce the supply of money endogenously. Moreover, even if the interest rate does fall, when the wage and price falls, firms – caught in an uncertain situation – may not increase investment, and asset holders may simply wish to hold more money. Thus, standard mechanisms of expansion relying on asset market considerations are short-circuited. A fall in wages and prices may actually reduce the cash receipts of firms from the sale of goods and, given pre-committed costs, might lead them to cut back investment, and even worse, declare bankruptcy in extreme cases. More generally, deflation will redistribute wealth from debtors to creditors, thereby possibly reducing aggregate demand. A fall in the money wage, if it results in a fall in the real wage, can also redistribute income from wage-earners to profit recipients with a lower marginal propensity to consume, which also reduces aggregate demand. Moreover, neo-Ricardian Keynesians argue that a fall in the interest rate may not increase aggregate investment if one takes into account the fact that capital goods are produced inputs, and that changes in the interest rate or profit rate can cause changes in the relative prices of capital goods and lead to 'perverse' changes in aggregate investment demand. In the absence of automatic tendencies which take output to full employment, it may be supposed that this will be achieved by governments, especially through fiscal and monetary policies. However, such policies can be ineffective or slow to take effect, and there may be political constraints on full-employment policies, as discussed by Kalecki (1971). Post Keynesians also argue that even if the economy does adjust to the so-called full employment or non-accelerating inflation rate of unemployment and natural rate of growth, these levels and rate of growth are themselves dependent on aggregate demand (Dutt and Ros 2007). For all these reasons, even in the longer run, production is determined by aggregate demand considerations rather than supply-side factors.

AMITAVA KRISHNA DUTT

See also:

Effective Demand; Expectations; Kaleckian Economics; Keynes's *General Theory*; Marginalism; Prices and Pricing; Sraffian Economics; Time in Economic Theory; Uncertainty.

References

Chick, V. (1983), *Macroeconomics After Keynes. A Reconsideration of the 'General Theory'*, Cambridge, MA: MIT Press.

Dutt, A. (1997), 'Equilibrium, path dependence and hysteresis in post-Keynesian models', in P. Arestis and M. Sawyer (eds), *Markets, Unemployment and Economic Policy: Essays in Honour of G.C. Harcourt*, Vol. 2, London and New York: Routledge, pp. 238–53.

Dutt, A.K. (2009), 'Path dependence, equilibrium and economic growth', in P. Arestis and M. Sawyer (eds), *Path Dependency in Macroeconomics*, Basingstoke: Palgrave Macmillan, pp. 119–61.

Dutt, A. and E. Amadeo (1990), *Keynes's Third Alternative? The Neo-Ricardian Keynesians and the Post Keynesians*, Aldershot, UK and Brookfield, VT, USA: Edward Elgar.

Dutt, A. and J. Ros (2007), 'Aggregate demand shocks and economic growth', *Structural Change and Economic Dynamics*, **18** (1), 75–99.

Kalecki, M. (1971), *Selected Essays on the Dynamics of the Capitalist Economy*, Cambridge: Cambridge University Press.
Keynes, J.M. (1936), *The General Theory of Employment, Interest and Money*, London: Macmillan.

Profits

While profits are literally the difference between the revenue from sales and the costs of production, the scope of the term 'profit' varies according to what is admitted as a cost. If one believes that all value is produced by labour (aside from natural non-reproducible resources), then only labour incomes are costs and all non-labour incomes accrue as profits. If, on the other hand, tangible capital is thought to contribute to the production process, then dividends and other returns to the owners of plant and machinery are netted out of profits.

Profit, under any economic definition, represents a return from financing acts which produce a good or service. It does not, in economics, include winnings from zero-sum activities such as gambling or arbitrage. Nor would most economists accept that it includes net capital gains, although the difference between current profits and capital gains is temporal (higher profit expectations raise the current value of an asset) and may be irrelevant to the firm if the asset is realized. Profits are a flow arising from current production. Lack of clarity among authors about what they include in the term 'profits', as well as lack of recognition of the non-uniqueness of the definition, can be a source of confusion for readers and remains a barrier to interschool-of-thought discussions.

Profits are received for advances of money or resources made in the expectation of future benefits, whether these moneys are used to buy the services of current or intermediate inputs into the production process, as exemplified by David Ricardo's corn model, or so-called 'investment goods' whose use may last beyond a single production cycle. However, a convention used in economic analysis (but not accounting), is to regard profits earned on working capital as secondary details, in order to focus on the more complex relationship between investment goods and profits. Most likely, this convention was established because expenditures made with respect to longer time horizons exhibit greater volatility and uncertainty. Accordingly, investments which are expected to furnish returns beyond a year will, in general, be more important determinants of other economic phenomena than investments that repay within a week.

From a single firm's perspective, funds advanced in each time period equal the amount of working capital advanced to cover the costs of producing the good or service: payments to labour, leasing costs (direct or implicit owner costs) of using reproducible plant, equipment or intangible assets, and rents on non-reproducible inputs. From the point of view of the whole economy, however, rents are not true costs but transfer payments (as there are no opportunity costs), and the costs of producing the reproducible assets can be decomposed in a similar way according to the costs of the respective investment-goods businesses. Taken to its limit, each production process can be reduced to labour and non-reproducible inputs, with the only true cost of production being a dated series of labour inputs, as revealed by Sraffa's (1960) scheme of prices. However, in each stage of production, a surplus exists after the firm has paid for the costs of labour and non-labour inputs. And this, summed over all firms, is gross aggregate profit.

If the costs of using capital goods (Alfred Marshall's 'quasi-rents'), that is, capital consumption or depreciation, are essentially released flows of stored labour, then what accounts for the existence and size of profits? Why isn't all income paid to labour? In order to understand the determinants of profits it is important to recognize the importance of the ownership of financial capital and the power of finance over economic resources. Rentiers and firms will not invest in production, or any given project, unless they expect it to return a minimum or normal rate of profit (the ratio of profits accrued to funds advanced). Rentiers and firms are not compelled to invest and they can, when they desire, keep their finances as secure financial assets. Furthermore, economic resources cannot be mobilized without financial backing. Borrowing cannot replace this backing but can only supplement collateral (see Kalecki 1939). Hence, profits form the incentive for rentiers to invest.

The two components of *ex ante* normal profits include default-free interest payments and returns to compensate for the 'normal' uncertainty associated with doing business. The default-free interest rate is set by central banks and represents a totally secure alternative way for capital owners to place their funds. Owners of financial assets, or their banking intermediaries, will not lend to businesses for investment unless they are assured of a greater return than what they would receive from these default-free bill rates. To the extent that these central banks offer an elastic supply of these bills, then the rate of interest becomes the minimum supply price for rentiers of financial capital. However, non-zero default-free banking rates constitute a net injection of funds into the economy, and the cost to the public of this convention or policy action may be a redirection of funds from the central government's normal budgetary policies. That is, the higher are the interest payments governments need to make to meet their interest obligations, the more funds are diverted, in the first instance, from their portfolios for appropriations.

Even if the default-free rate were set at zero, businesses would still require a positive return in order to commit themselves to production. There are substantial uncertainties associated with investments, and unless some compensation is forthcoming a rational rentier would place funds in a sequence of government bills instead. While the premium for uncertain risk is undoubtedly positive (to the extent that business people are risk averse), there are few theories to explain how much is required to compensate the rentier for his/her risk of investing in a business, as the evaluation of *uncertainty* is subjective. Knight (1921) recognized that, at the limit, profits are not required to compensate for *risk* (actuarial-based risk). If people have complete information about the probabilities of all possible contingencies, then they can objectively estimate an expected value and at the limit, repeated instances of the risky situation will produce a certain expected outcome. Accordingly, at the limit, no premium is required to compensate for actuarial risk, only for non-actuarial risk (or uncertainty).

Clearly if the business expects a project to return greater-than-normal profits, we expect that it will proceed with the project and consider the windfall (pure) above-normal profits as a reward for recognizing an overlooked and unexploited opportunity. In this way, theory predicts that expected profits attract the attention of entrepreneurs who will shift resources into or out of markets with a speed determined by the magnitude of the difference between demand and supply. However, this seemingly commonsensical prediction is not supported by the evidence. According to Geroski, empirical studies show that market entry is slow to respond to expected profits and '[d]ifferences in profitability between industries are extremely stable and persistent (much of the same applies to differences in profitability between firms)' (1995, p. 428).

Part of the reason for this paradox is because the distinction between monopoly profit and 'normal' returns is not as clear as it sounds. Where does the 'normal' premium for uncertainty end and above-normal profits begin? Pursuit of profits is also the pursuit of monopoly profits. According to Brozen (1971) and Demsetz (1973), endogenous barriers to entry are natural outcomes of firms striving for profits via efficiency under conditions of uncertainty, resource heterogeneity and factor immobility. (Also see Lippman and Rumelt (1982) for a discussion of these issues. This theory is close to the body of hypotheses that management theorists included under the 'resource-based view' of the firm.)

Barriers are created since rivals of successful firms have difficulty replicating the entire successful accumulation path. In this context, some industries are more inherently risky than others, and firms which aggressively pursue monopoly profits by investing in uncertain and unpredictable intangible capital would expect to be compensated by a higher premium for uncertainty. Until this issue has been resolved, no explanation can exist for the level of normal profits and it would be difficult in practice to identify whether firms or industries are receiving monopoly profits.

While positive *ex ante* profits are required for *ex ante* investment, these profits do not always materialize. *Ex post* profits can vary for reasons related more to macroeconomic factors than the behaviour or expectations of the specific firm. For example, as recognized by Kalecki, while firms can set their profit mark-up on unit costs, they cannot determine how much they will sell and consequently how much total profit they will make.

There are relatively few theories which seek to explain the size of *ex post* aggregate profits and thus the extent to which *ex ante* expectations can be simultaneously realized. Neoclasssical aggregate production function theories, such as Robert Solow's 1956 model, have been used in conjunction with J.B. Clark's marginal productivity theory to show that the rate of profits is simply the value of the marginal product of (aggregate) capital. As such, the level of profits reflects the innate productivity of aggregate tangible plant and equipment. However, all measures of aggregate capital (needed to calculate a VMP_K) use the prices of capital goods and thus an embedded rate of profit. This endogenous value measure of aggregate capital does not therefore constitute an *independent* explanation of the rate of profit (Harcourt 1992).

The nineteenth-century theory of Ricardo defined the level of profits per unit of output to be the difference between the subsistence wage for labourers per unit of output and the average product of labour on the most marginal land in the economy. The level of production was consistent with full employment. However, this theory is less relevant where the average wage rate can and does vary over time and where subsistence is culturally defined.

Kalecki (1939) has one of the most comprehensive theories of the determination of profits. Using a simple two-sector macroeconomic model (with no government or foreign sectors) he uses the two identities:

$$Y \equiv C_w + C_K + I$$

$$Y \equiv W + P,$$

where Y is output, C_w is workers' consumption, C_K is capitalists' consumption, I is investment demand, W is the wage bill and P is total profits. If it is assumed that workers do not save, such that $C_W = W$, but capitalists consume a small portion of their incomes, such that $C_k = A + \lambda P$ (where

A is a given constant and λ is the marginal propensity to consume out of profits), then $P = (A + I)/(1 - λ)$. Since *I* can be determined by the deliberate decisions of businesses (and *A* and λ by rentiers) but *P* cannot, the direction of causation must run from *I*, *A* and λ to *P*. Introducing workers' saving complicates, but does not destroy, this basic conclusion. Kalecki also had a microeconomic theory of the minimum *ex ante* rate of profit (which he took as exogenous to the economy) and average profit per unit of output (which depended on the rate of competition). However, the *ex post* rate and level of profits for each firm depend on the aggregation of all microeconomic investment decisions, and accordingly are out of the hands of any individual business.

Finally, a word about how entrepreneurs or business managers actively seek to make profits. Classical and neoclassical theories commonly portray the flow of profit-seeking funds as action like water passively seeking an even level. In contrast to this, contemporary Post Keynesian, Austrian and evolutionary theories, which have a genesis in Joseph Schumpeter and G.L.S. Shackle, endow the entrepreneur with a more aggressive and less mechanical role. These theories begin with the postulate that any activity which aims to maximize profits, implicitly aims to maximize monopoly profits. Monopoly or above-normal profits are received through exploiting some special demand or cost advantage that creates economic distance between the firm and its nearest market rivals. Thus, firms aim to develop endogenous barriers to entry.

This assertive profit-seeking behaviour by firms involves intangible investments in the development of marketing and distribution channels, R&D, workforce training and management strategies. Investing in tangible plant and equipment *per se* will not create above-normal profits, as there is nothing unique or difficult to copy about such goods and they do not therefore result in the creation of endogenous barriers to entry. Tangible capital can be bought off the shelf and reproduced *ad infinitum* at a constant cost. Intangible assets, by contrast, are heterogeneous and difficult to copy primarily because they are heavily embodied in diverse human beings. It is investment in intangible capital that creates monopoly profits and endogenous barriers to entry.

Essentially, this brings the discussion of the source of profits back to the original point that profits are incomes accruing to non-labour inputs. If, on the one hand, profits are received by owners of financial wealth but, on the other, their size depends on the behaviour of other human beings, then an incongruity may exist within the incentive structure between the creators of monopoly profits and its beneficiaries.

ELIZABETH WEBSTER

See also:

Capital Theory; Competition; Income Distribution; Innovation; Investment; Kaleckian Economics; Sraffian Economics; Uncertainty.

References

Brozen, Y. (1971), 'The persistence of "high rates of return" in high-stable concentration industries', *Journal of Law and Economics*, **14** (2), 501–12.

Demsetz, H. (1973), 'Industry structure, market rivalry and public policy', *Journal of Law and Economics*, **16** (1), 1–9.

Geroski, P. (1995), 'What do we know about entry?', *International Journal of Industrial Organization*, **13** (4), 421–40.

Harcourt, G. (1992), 'The Cambridge controversies: old ways and new horizons – or dead-end?', in C. Sardoni (ed.), *On Political Economists and Modern Political Economy, Selected Essays of G.C. Harcourt*, Routledge, London and New York, pp. 101–29.

Kalecki, M. (1939), *Essays in the Theory of Economic Fluctuations*, Oxford: Clarendon Press.

Knight, F.H. (1921), *Risk, Uncertainty and Profit*, Boston, MA: Houghton Mifflin.

Lippman, S. and R. Rumelt (1982), 'Uncertain imitability: an analysis of interfirm differences in efficiency under competition', *Bell Journal of Economics*, **13** (2), 418–38.

Sraffa, P. (1960), *Production of Commodities by Means of Commodities*, Cambridge: Cambridge University Press.

Rate of Interest

Interest is the price for the use of capital in production – the 'pure' remuneration of capital whatever the form of its employment, whether financial or real. If production is carried out with the firm's own capital, interest constitutes its opportunity cost and as such will enter into that normal cost which in the long run tends to be equated with the unit price. Firms would not continue to replace plant which is wearing out unless the prices for their commodities were such that they could not do better for themselves by investing their depreciation funds in gilt-edged securities; conversely, commodity prices could not permanently involve rates of return on the firms' funds exceeding the relevant rates of interest – those to be earned in the market on long-term fixed-interest securities in which there is no element of risk – by more than a normal remuneration for the 'risk and trouble' of productively employing capital. The case of share capital does not alter the fundamentals of this picture. It may be presumed that the nearest competing alternative to shares is long-term bonds, and that ordinary shares will be held only if the expected yield on them exceeds the yield on long-term bonds. As there is a significant section of the investing public ready to switch from one kind of investment to the other, this tends to maintain their respective yields at a steady level. That is to say, at any given time there will be a certain relationship between the prices of the various classes of securities: a shift in the price of one large class must be followed by a general shift in the whole range of prices. Thus a rise in prices for long-term government bonds – a fall in the long-term rate of interest resulting from the pursuing of a cheap-money policy – will be followed by a rise in prices of securities generally. But a higher quotation for existing equities implies that companies can raise capital by issuing shares on more-favourable terms; in the words of Keynes, a high quotation for existing equities has 'the same effect as if (companies) could borrow at a low rate of interest' (1936 [1964], p. 151, n.1). So the issue of common stocks, as a method of financing investment available to joint-stock companies, will also become cheaper (or dearer) in the face of a persistent fall (or rise) in interest rates. We may conclude, therefore, that quite irrespective of the kind of capital employed in production, a lasting lowering (or raising) of interest rates tends to make normal costs stand lower (or higher) than they would otherwise have done, and thus, by the competition among firms within each industry, to affect prices correspondingly. Given the level of money wages, any such change in the price level brought about by a lasting change in interest rates would then be accompanied by a change in the same direction in the level of prices in relation to the level of money wages, thereby causing changes in income distribution. A prolonged fall in interest rates should cause a fall in prices relative to the wage level and thereby bring about a lower rate of profit and a higher real wage, while a prolonged rise in interest rates should raise the rate of profits, and thus reduce the real wage.

Although economic theory has always looked at interest as the price for the use of capital in production, it has however also generally regarded it as a subordinate phenomenon. In the words of Joan Robinson: '[o]ver the long run, the interest rate rentiers can exact is dominated by the profits that entrepreneurs can earn, not the other way round' (1979, p. xxii). In fact, according to both classical and neoclassical economists there is, between the normal rate of profit and the money rate of interest, a long-run causal relationship going from the former to the latter, so that the rate of interest is ultimately determined by those real forces which explain the course of the normal rate of profit: the real wage rate and production techniques, in the classical theory of distribution up to David Ricardo; the 'fundamental phenomena' of productivity and thrift, as far as the neoclassical theory is concerned. An important implication of this way of conceiving the relation between interest and profit is the denial of any substantial power on the part of the monetary authorities. Given the state of the real forces governing normal profit – the 'natural real rate' – the impact on the price level or on real output and accumulation of any lasting discrepancy between the courses of the two rates would force the monetary authorities to act so as to make the rate of interest move in sympathy with the normal rate of profit. An autonomous lowering of the lending rate by the monetary authorities would drive the price level *up*, contrary to what has been outlined in the previous paragraph; this is because overall monetary expenditure would expand as a consequence of the difference which would be created between the lending rate and the 'natural real rate'. In actual experience, however, rising prices very rarely coincide with low or falling interest rates and the opposite is the general rule (the so-called 'Gibson paradox' or 'price puzzle'). Instead of assuming a lowering of interest rates by the monetary authorities, other things being equal, one would then simply have to make the alternative assumption that a difference between the natural real rate and the actual money rate generally arises because it is *the former* which rises or falls, while the latter remains unchanged and only belatedly follows (see Wicksell 1906 [1962], pp. 204–5). The 'natural rate' notion also permeates the so-called 'New Consensus monetary policy model'. Indeed, inflation targeting postulates the existence of a long-run equilibrium real rate of interest, to which the interest rate policy instrument must be adjusted in order to check fluctuations in inflation and keep output at potential (see Pivetti 2010 for a critical discussion of the inflation targeting framework).

As to Keynes's views on interest, an unprejudiced observation of concrete reality clearly played a significant part in his interpretation of the rate of interest as a 'monetary phenomenon'. Unfortunately, the persistence in Keynes's analysis of some traditional neoclassical premises seriously weakens his concept of the rate of interest as a magnitude determined by monetary factors. In particular, the idea of an investment demand schedule constitutes an obstacle which a monetary theory of interest cannot easily overcome. Notwithstanding the statement in the *General Theory* that he 'no longer' regards Wicksell's notion of a 'natural real rate' as 'a most promising idea' (Keynes 1936 [1964], p. 234), the natural rate is still there, as the rate that would ensure equality between full-employment saving and investment decisions. Keynes's underemployment equilibrium is ultimately the result of the presence in the economic system of factors that hinder the possibility of bringing the actual rate of interest down to its 'natural' or full-employment level. It is, in other words, the result of a limited flexibility of the money rate of interest. This limited flexibility is actually all that Keynes has to offer as a basis for his non-orthodox concept of interest as a monetary phenomenon. But if one takes into account the fact that even in Wicksell there is no automatic gravitation of the money rate towards the level of the natural real rate (banking policy having to perform the task), then the difference between the two authors will not appear that marked. They both share the idea of an inverse relation between the rate of interest and investment decisions, while the conflict of opinion is essentially centred upon the degree of the (non-automatic) flexibility of the rate of interest, in the face of discrepancies between full-employment savings and investment decisions. One can say that it was largely in the light of this comparison that the Neoclassical Synthesis could successfully argue that Keynes's views on interest, while adequate for showing that the flexibility of the rate of interest is not of an automatic nature, are, however, insufficient to sustain the thesis of a *limited* flexibility of the rate of interest. And if the current money interest rate can normally be brought to, and kept at, its 'natural' level – provided the monetary authority applies to its action 'a modest measure of persistence and consistency of purpose' (ibid., p. 204) – then the neoclassical real forces of productivity and thrift may still be regarded as the ultimate determinants of the equilibrium rate of interest.

Things are quite different if there is no such thing as a 'natural' rate of interest – a normal rate of profit, that is to say, determined independently by real forces and which can be taken as the *primum movens*. We would be back in this case to the picture outlined at the beginning of this entry, that is, it would be difficult not to acknowledge that, given money wages and production techniques, a lowering (raising) of interest rates by the monetary authorities would actually drive the price level *down* (up), owing to the adaptation of prices to normal costs caused by competition. There would thus be nothing 'paradoxical' in the positive correlation between interest and prices that one generally finds in actual experience. And at a given level of real output, the rate of interest would also regulate the quantity of money in active circulation – a quantity that adapts itself to the needs of trade – via its influence on the price level: interest, prices and the quantity of money would all move in the same direction, with the policy-determined interest rate acting as the *primum movens* of the process.

The 'monetary' explanation of distribution that I started to develop 20 years ago (see Pivetti 1991) is precisely an attempt to emancipate us from any real explanation of the rate of interest – an attempt prompted by Sraffa's suggestion that in the necessary long-run connection between normal profit and money interest it is the latter which is susceptible to setting the pace (see Sraffa 1960, p. 33). By focusing on the actual mechanism whereby the rate of interest is likely to set the pace in its connection with normal profit, eventually I got hold of the notion of money interest as an autonomous determinant of normal money production costs which governs the ratio of prices to money wages. As pointed out earlier, this interpretation of interest does not require any particular assumption as to the kind of capital employed in production: borrowed, in the form of shares, or a firm's own capital. For any given situation of technique, there is a price level that depends on the money wage and on the money rate of interest, with the latter acting as the regulator of the ratio of the price level to the money wage. This ratio is thus seen as the connecting link between the rate of interest and the rate of profit: by the competition among firms within each industry, a persistent change in the rate of interest causes a change in the same direction in the level of prices in relation to the level of money wages, thereby generating a corresponding change in the rate of profits and an inverse change in the real wage. Wage bargaining and monetary policy come out of this analysis as the main channels through which class relations act in determining distribution. Class relations are seen as tending to act primarily upon the profit rate, via the money rate of interest, rather than upon the real wage as maintained by both the English classical economists and Marx. Indeed, the level of the real wage prevailing in any given situation is viewed as the *final result* of the whole process by which distribution of income between workers and capitalists is actually derived. Interest rate determination is thus not seen as constrained by some natural, technical or accidental circumstances – be they the relative scarcity of capital and labour, a 'subsistence' real wage, or the rate of growth of the economic system. Rather, the rate of interest is regarded as a policy-determined variable, a conventional monetary phenomenon 'determined from outside the system of production' (Sraffa 1960, p. 33) and not subject to any general law. One can describe interest rate determination in terms of sets of objectives and constraints, on the action of the monetary authorities, which have different weights both among the various countries and for a particular country at different times (see Pivetti 1991, pp. 11–17, 33–6), and with which, to a very large extent, the parties' relative strength is ultimately intertwined.

MASSIMO PIVETTI

See also:

Bastard Keynesianism; Income Distribution; Liquidity Preference; Monetary Policy; New Neoclassical Synthesis; Sraffian Economics.

References

Keynes, J.M. (1936 [1964]), *The General Theory of Employment, Interest and Money*, London: Macmillan.
Pivetti, M. (1991), *An Essay on Money and Distribution*, London: Macmillan.
Pivetti, M. (2010), 'Interest and the general price level: some critical notes on "the new consensus monetary policy model"', in A. Birolo, D.K. Foley, H.D. Kurz, B. Schefold and I. Steedman (eds), *Production, Distribution and Trade: Alternative Perspectives. Essays in Honour of Sergio Parrinello*, London and New York: Routledge, pp. 216–32.
Robinson, J. (1979), *The Generalisation of the General Theory and other Essays*, London: Macmillan.
Sraffa, P. (1960), *Production of Commodities by Means of Commodities*, Cambridge: Cambridge University Press.
Wicksell, K. (1906 [1962]), *Lectures on Political Economy. Volume II: Money and Credit*, London: Routledge & Kegan Paul.

Regional Monetary Policy

Over the last few decades, there has been a growing interest in the economic literature on the role that money, monetary policy and banks play in the process of regional economic development (for a survey of the literature, see Dow and Rodríguez-Fuentes 1997; Rodríguez-Fuentes and Dow 2003; and Rodríguez-Fuentes 2006, pp. 73–113).

This growing interest has been partially motivated by the establishment of the third and final stage of the European Monetary Union in January 1999, whereby some European countries became regions within the euro area, raising concerns over the regional implications of the European Central Bank (ECB) monetary policy.

The interest in regional financial matters has come to question, to some extent, the orthodox assumption that neither money nor banks have ever played a significant role in the regional development process.

Orthodox economic theory has usually assumed that monetary policy has no role to play in economic development, since money is considered as a separate variable whose only role is to ease the exchange of goods already produced. Consequently, all that monetary policy can do is to affect the general level of prices (when money is supplied in excess for exchange purposes) but not real output (at least in the long run). Additionally, according to the orthodox framework financial factors play no role in regional development since, once the central bank sets the money supply in accordance with real needs (the transactions motive in the demand for money) and the money multiplier determines the total available supply of bank credit, the banking system simply (and passively) distributes the total (and limited) amount of available credit among regions according to demand pressures.

For that reason, from the orthodox perspective the regional effects of monetary policy are reduced either to the existence of structural differences which cause some regions to have 'different' (higher/lower) responses to national monetary policy shocks (regional business cycles), or to market imperfections (asymmetric or imperfect information) that reduce interregional capital flows and produce a spatial misallocation of financial resources (regional credit rationing). Consequently, and leaving aside market 'imperfections', according to this view, national monetary policies may have a regional differential effect only if regional differences in terms of economic structure exist. Otherwise all regions would be equally affected by national monetary shocks, either positively or negatively. But it is important to note that the 'real cause' of the regional impact of monetary policy in this analysis is not money itself, but instead regional structural differences that have nothing to do with monetary policy.

The traditional orthodox view described above has been challenged by the contributions that, built on the basic principles of Post Keynesian monetary theory, have broadened the scope of the analysis by stressing the role that the banking system and the liquidity preference of economic agents (including banks) play in the transmission of central banks' monetary policy decisions to regions within a country, or countries within a currency union (Dow 1987a, 1987b, 1992; Chick and Dow 1988; Dow and Rodríguez-Fuentes 1997; Rodríguez-Fuentes 1998, 2006). The introduction of these two variables, the stage of banking development and liquidity preference, means that the analysis of the regional impact of monetary policy cannot be restricted to the so-called 'structural effect', but should also pay close attention to the influence of monetary policy on financial behaviour (the 'behavioural effect'). The set of variables shown in Table 2 provides a framework for studying both factors. The structural effect suggests that monetary policy would affect regions differently because these

Table 2   *Relevant variables for analysing the regional impact of monetary policy: structural and behavioural effects*

Structural effect	
Sectoral mix	• Sectors' sensitivity to business cycles: interest rate elasticity
Aggregate demand mix	• Consumption (durable and non-durable) and investment (fixed capital, construction, etc.) responses to changes in: interest rates, national income and credit restrictions
	• Export and import responses to exchange rates, interest rates, credit restrictions. Regional differences in degree of openness to trade, marginal and average propensity to export and import, export specialization and import composition
Business structure	• Firms' size, differences in terms of sources of finance, costs and availability of bank credit, collateral, and so on.
Degree of competition	• Internal competition: degree of segmentation in regional financial markets (information costs gathering, administrative and risk evaluation costs, regional financial assets and inter-mediaries, isolation and distance from 'financial centres', etc.)
Behavioural effect	
Regional supply of funds	• Banks' ability to expand credit (banking development) and liquidity preference
	• Central banks' financial regulation and monetary policy influences
	• Savers' portfolio preferences
Regional demand for funds	• Borrowers' willingness to borrow (invest), liquidity preference, firms' size (dependence on bank lending, bargaining power, etc.)

Source: Rodríguez-Fuentes and Dow (2003, p. 976).

are structurally different from the economy for which the monetary policy is actually being designed. However, this argument only applies to a world of exogenous money, where the central bank unilaterally (and exogenously) determines the quantity of money that fits the real needs of exchange and banks passively determine the volume of credit money. Nevertheless this view ignores the influence that central banks' monetary policy decisions may have on banks' and borrowers' liquidity preference which, particularly in the more financially developed economies, may influence banks' and borrowers' willingness to lend and borrow (the behavioural effect). Consequently, from a regional perspective it is relevant to study the spatial differences in terms of banking development and liquidity preference, as well as the influence that monetary policy may have on such variables. One of the consequences of the Post Keynesian framework is that the proper analysis of the regional impact of monetary policy should explicitly take into account the spatial differences in terms of banking development and liquidity preference, as well as the influence that monetary policy may have on such variables (the *behavioural effect*), and not only the structural differences that might produce regional asymmetric responses to exogenous monetary policy shocks (the *structural effect*).

The Post Keynesian analysis specifically suggests that monetary policy affects regional credit availability through its influence on banks' and borrowers' liquidity preference and that regional differences in terms of banking development and liquidity preference may produce higher instability in credit availability in less developed regions. This argument clearly contrasts with the orthodox one, which assumes that regional credit shares mirror regional GDP shares, since money is considered to be a means of payment and, consequently, its demand is determined only by the transaction motive.

Consequently, for the Post Keynesian regional credit theory the availability of credit is determined not only by the 'efficient allocation process' carried out by banks, but also (and more importantly) by the changes in liquidity preference in different phases of the business cycle and the regional differences in terms of banking development. One important implication that arises from this view is that credit availability may systematically fluctuate in different phases of the business cycle, as liquidity preference does, this pattern being more pronounced for the less developed regions (see Rodríguez-Fuentes 1998 and Rodríguez-Fuentes and Dow 2003). Consequently, rather than focusing on why a perfect flow of financial resources among regions does not exist, the Post Keynesian literature on regional money and credit takes market imperfection as the norm, and focuses on the study of regional patterns of credit creation and how these may vary from one region to another. In so doing Post Keynesian theory makes use of both Chick's stages of banking development (Chick and Dow 1988; Chick 1993) and the Keynesian principle of liquidity preference. For a fuller account of this approach, see Rodríguez-Fuentes (2006, pp. 100–103).

A particular feature of the Post Keynesian theory is that its analysis addresses both the supply and the demand side of the regional credit market (see Figure 18). For that reason Post Keynesian analysis does not see regional credit rationing as a uni-causal situation explained by regional-discriminatory behaviour on the part of the financial system (mainly banks) which, in turn, leads to an uneven regional distribution of credit, but instead as a multi-causal situation in which all sectors in the region are involved.

One implication that follows from the Post Keynesian theoretical

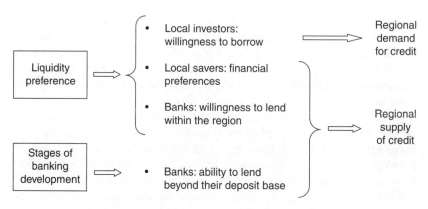

Source: Rodríguez-Fuentes (2006, p. 100).

Figure 18   Post Keynesian theory of regional credit

framework is that having sound and developed regional financial institutions is important for securing the supply of the necessary credit to finance regional investment and growth. However, as Dow (1992) has noted, this is only a necessary condition, since banks can always choose to ration the local demand for credit when they have strong preferences for liquid assets. Thus when uncertainty rises, banks might try to satisfy their preferences by replacing the risky assets in their portfolios (bank credit) by others, which may not be available locally (if they are only supplied in central regions) or, if they are, they might not be serving the needs for working capital or productive investment. When this happens, the 'defensive financial behaviour' of banks (Dow 1992), which leads them to focus on short-term and riskless operations, might interfere with the availability of credit for working capital as well as for new long-term profitable investment projects in the region. Consequently, the 'defensive financial behaviour' of banks may become an important obstacle to securing funds for many small and medium-sized enterprises simply because they have no other option of funding sources besides banks.

In the case of peripheral regions, it is important to highlight two important aspects in relation to credit dynamics. The first one is concerned with microeconomic implications, specifically with the formal credit risk assessment processes, which are more difficult and costly to carry out in remote regions, and the liquidity preference of economic agents, which tends to be higher than in central regions. Thus, in peripheral regions more rigid and rationed credit markets are likely to be found, with correspondingly higher interest rates and collateral requirements.

The second point, being more macroeconomic in nature, is related to the procyclical changes in the liquidity preferences of all agents, which reinforce (reduce) the agents' willingness to borrow (public) and lend (banks) in expansions (recessions). These are more pronounced in peripheral regions, and therefore the financial system reinforces the volatile character of such regional economies rather than promoting economic growth in the long run: there is a more unstable pattern of credit availability, and thus the credit creation process fuels expansions and enhances recessions (Rodríguez-Fuentes 2006, pp. 100–103).

CARLOS J. RODRÍGUEZ-FUENTES

See also:

Banking; Central Banks; Credit Rationing; Economic Policy; Financial Reform; International Financial Reform; Liquidity Preference; Monetary Policy.

References

Chick, V. (1993), 'The evolution of the banking system and the theory of monetary policy', in S.F. Frowen (ed.), *Monetary Theory and Monetary Policy: New Tracks for the 1990s*, London: Macmillan, pp. 79–92.

Chick, V. and S.C. Dow (1988), 'A Post-Keynesian perspective on the relation between banking and regional development', in P. Arestis (ed.), *Post-Keynesian Monetary Economics: New Approaches to Financial Modelling*, Aldershot, UK and Brookfield, VT, USA: Edward Elgar, pp. 219–50.

Dow, S.C. (1987a), 'Money and regional development', *Studies in Political Economy*, **23** (2), 73–94; reprinted in Dow, *Money and the Economic Process*, Aldershot, UK and Brookfield, VT, USA: Edward Elgar, 1993, pp. 141–58.

Dow, S.C. (1987b), 'The treatment of money in regional economics', *Journal of Regional Science*, **27** (1), 13–24; reprinted in Dow, *Money and the Economic Process*, Aldershot, UK and Brookfield, VT, USA: Edward Elgar, 1993, pp. 98–110.

Dow, S.C. (1992), 'The regional financial sector: a Scottish case study', *Regional Studies*, **26** (7), 619–31.

Dow, S.C. and C.J. Rodríguez-Fuentes (1997), 'Regional finance: a survey', *Regional Studies*, **31** (9), 903–20.

Rodríguez-Fuentes, C.J. (1998), 'Credit availability and regional development', *Papers in Regional Science*, **77** (1), 63–75.

Rodríguez-Fuentes, C.J. (2006), *Regional Monetary Policy*, Abingdon and New York: Routledge.

Rodríguez-Fuentes, C.J. and S.C. Dow (2003), 'EMU and the regional impact of monetary policy', *Regional Studies*, **37** (9), 973–84.

Saving

What is the relationship between saving behaviour in capitalist economies and their macroeconomic performance? This question is a hardy perennial in the history of economics, and one that has carried great theoretical and practical significance through its many revivals. It is easy to see why this is so, since any economy that aspires to long-term increases in productivity and average living standards must devise effective means of raising the quantity and quality of its capital stock. The role of saving is central to this process, though how exactly it exerts influence has long been a matter of contention.

Debates on how saving behaviour affects long-term growth and business cycles stretch back to those between David Ricardo and Robert Malthus on whether Say's law of markets that 'supply creates its own demand' can be violated, thereby creating the possibility for 'general gluts' or depressions. The Keynesian revolution, of course, was also focused on this issue, as Keynes rebelled against the 1934 'Treasury View' that higher saving rates were a necessary precondition for stimulating investment and lifting the British economy out of depression. Arguing against the intuitively appealing notion that an adequate pool of saving must exist before the funds for investment can be drawn, Keynes and Richard Kahn developed the concept of the multiplier to demonstrate the counter-intuitive point that higher levels of saving will generate higher saving as well. Many of the most pressing policy concerns of today – including the intense debates on fiscal deficits and crowding out in the aftermath of the 2008–09 Great Recession – remain centred on the relationship between investment and macroeconomic performance (Pollin 2010).

What is saving? The answer is not obvious. Moreover, answering the most basic questions about the impact of saving on macroeconomic activity – including whether saving rates are rising or falling – depends on how one defines and measures the term (this discussion follows Pollin 1997). Two standard approaches to measuring saving are as an increase in net worth and as the residual of income after consumption. As accounting categories, these two saving measures should be equal in value. But making this distinction raises a major question: when one considers the category of asset-specific saving, should the value of assets be measured at historical costs or market values? Only the historical cost measure is equivalent conceptually to residual saving. Measured at market values, asset-specific saving will of course fluctuate along with fluctuations in asset prices themselves.

Another major issue is distinguishing *gross* saving, including depreciation allowances, and *net* saving, which excludes depreciation. In principle, net saving measures the funds available to finance economic growth, while gross saving would also include funds set aside for replacing worn-out capital stock. In practice, however, depreciation allowances do not simply finance replacement. Rather, they are primarily used to finance investment in capital stock that represents some advance over previous vintages. As such, depreciation funds are also utilized to promote economic growth.

What is the most appropriate definition of saving? In fact, for the purposes of economic analysis, there are legitimate reasons to examine each concept. There are three basic reasons for considering saving patterns by any measure. The first is to observe households' portfolio choices, in which case asset-specific saving is obviously the only option. The second purpose would be to understand consumer behaviour. Here we would want to measure consumption directly relative to income, making saving a residual. However, asset-specific saving at market values would also be important here in so far as it contributes to understanding consumer behaviour. The third reason for measuring saving is with respect to examining its role in determining credit supply, that is, the source of funds available to finance investment and other uses of funds. This role for saving is clearly the primary consideration among analysts seeking to understand the relationship between saving and macroeconomic performance. In fact, however, the connections between any given measures of saving, the provision of credit, and overall rates of economic activity are quite loose. We can see some indication of such loose connections through Table 3, on the US economy.

The first three rows of the table show annual figures on net, gross and net worth saving in the US relative to nominal GDP between 1960 and 2007 . The data are grouped on a peak-to-peak basis according to National Bureau of Economic Analysis business cycles. The last two rows of the table show, respectively, measures of credit supply and overall activity: first the ratio of total lending in the US economy relative to gross private saving, then the average annual growth rate of real GDP.

To begin with, the table shows significant differences in the cycle-to-cycle behaviour of the three saving ratios. For example, between the 1980–90 and 2001–07 cycles, the net saving ratio fell dramatically from 8.6 to 4.8 per cent, while the declines for the gross saving ratio (from 18.6 to 15.1 per cent) and the net worth ratio (from 27.1 to 25.0 per cent) were much more modest. Meanwhile, between these same two cycles, the lending/saving

Table 3   *Saving rates, credit supply and GDP growth for the US economy*
(in percentages)

	1960–69	1970–79	1980–90	1991–2000	2001–07
Net private saving/ GDP	9.7	9.8	8.6	6.6	4.8
Gross private saving/ GDP	17.2	18.5	18.6	16.1	15.1
Net worth private saving/GDP	20.4	28.7	27.1	27.9	25.0
Total lending/gross private saving	60.3	86.7	109.0	103.6	174.1
Real GDP growth	4.4	3.3	2.9	3.4	2.4

Note: For brevity, two sets of cycles – 1970–73/1974–79 and 1980–81/1982–90 – have been merged.

Sources: US National Income and Product Accounts; US Flow of Funds Accounts.

ratio rose sharply from 109.0 to 174.1 per cent, while the rate of GDP growth fell from 2.9 to 2.4 per cent.

At the very least, one can conclude from these patterns that we cannot take for granted any analytic foundation through which we assume a simple one-way pre-Keynesian causal connection whereby, as James Meade (1975, p. 82) put it, 'a dog called saving wagged its tail labelled investment' instead of the Keynesian connection in which 'a dog called investment wagged its tail labelled saving'.

The pre-Keynesian orthodox view held that the saving rate is the fundamental determinant of the rate of capital accumulation, because the saving rate determines the interest rate at which funds will be advanced to finance investment. Keynes's challenge to this position constituted the core of the ensuing Keynesian revolution in economic theory. Nevertheless, what we may call the 'causal saving' view was nevertheless restored fairly quickly to its central role in the mainstream macroeconomic literature and continues to play a central role in the contemporary literature (Feldstein 2006).

Despite neglect among mainstream economists, the 'causal investment' perspective has advanced substantially since the publication of Keynes's *General Theory* (1936). One major development has been precisely to establish a fuller understanding of the interrelationship among saving, financial structures and real activity. This has brought recognition that the logic of the causal investment position rests on the analysis of the financial system as well as the real-sector multiplier–accelerator model.

Of course, the multiplier–accelerator analysis is the basis for the 'paradox of thrift', that is, low saving *rates* (saving as a proportion of income) can yield high *levels* of saving and vice versa when real resources are not fully employed. However, considered by itself, the multiplier–accelerator analysis neglects a crucial prior consideration: that the initial increment of autonomous investment must be financed, and the rate at which financing is available will influence the size of this investment increment and the subsequent expansion of output, income and saving.

Kaldor (1939) was an early critic of the multiplier–accelerator causal investment position, and his argument was revived by Asimakopulos (1983). Their critique focuses on the interregnum between an autonomous investment increase and the attainment, through the multiplier–accelerator process, of a new level of saving–investment equilibrium. The Kaldor–Asimakopulos position is that, as a general case during such interregnum periods, intermediaries could not be expected to accept a reduction in liquidity without receiving an interest rate inducement to do so. Rather, for intermediaries to supply an increased demand for credit would require either a rise in interest rates or a prior increase in saving. As such, low rates of saving again yield high interest rates and a dampening of investment – an argument, in other words, that returns us to the causal saving position.

In fact, Keynes himself addressed this issue, working from his theory of liquidity preference and interest rate determination. But this dimension of his argument is far less well known than the consumption function and multiplier analysis, at least in part because it is less fully developed in the *General Theory* itself.

Holding the level of saving constant, Keynes argued that the banking system – private institutions as well as the central bank – was capable of financing investment growth during the interregnum without necessarily inducing a rise in interest rates. That is, as he put it, 'In general, the banks hold the key position in the transition from a lower to a higher scale of activity' (1938[1973], p. 222). Keynes based his position on a central institutional fact, that private banks and other intermediaries, not ultimate savers, are responsible for channelling the supply of credit to non-financial investors. The central bank can also substantially encourage credit growth by increasing the supply of reserves to the private banking system, thereby raising the banks' liquidity. But, even without central bank initiative, the private intermediaries could still increase their lending if they were willing to accept a temporary decline in their own liquidity. The reason why the fall in the intermediaries' liquidity would be only temporary is that liquidity would rise again, even before the completion of the multiplier, when the recipients of the autonomous investment funds deposited those funds with an intermediary. Moreover, the completion of the multiplier process would mean that an increase in saving equal to the investment increment had been generated. Overall, then, it is through this chain of reasoning that Keynes reached what he called 'the most fundamental of my conclusions within this field', that 'the investment market can become congested through a shortage of cash. It can never become congested through a shortage of saving' (ibid., p. 222).

This more fully developed Keynesian position emphasizes clearly the central role of financial institutions in establishing the relationship between saving and macroeconomic activity. More recent literature has developed this idea in several directions. One area of recent research has been debates around the distinction between 'liquidity preference' and 'loanable funds' and the implications of those distinctions for the analysis of macro finance (see, for example, Leijonhufvud 2006 and Hayes 2010). When Keynes argued that the 'investment market can become congested through a shortage of cash' but never through a 'shortage of saving', he was emphasizing the importance of how financial markets produce liquid assets – 'cash' – among the full array of available assets; and why agents demand to hold these liquid assets rather than less liquid alternatives. This consideration is entirely distinct from assuming that the saving rate – however measured – itself determines the quantity of liquid assets in the market or the interest rate at which these can be attained. The data in Table 3 showing the lending/saving ratio as rising from 60.3 to 174.1 per cent between 1960–69 and 2001–07 make clear that 'saving' does not translate into 'loanable funds' without first getting channelled through the system of intermediation that creates liquid assets, based on the preferences of agents.

Other researchers have broadened further this investigation as to the relationship between saving, institutional structures and macro activity. Indeed, in the 1990s a substantial literature developed arguing that financial systems that channelled savings within a tighter regulatory structure tended to outperform economies in which capital markets operated more freely (Pollin 1995 reviews this literature). Countries categorized as having more tightly regulated 'bank-based' financial systems were Germany, France, Japan and, among the less developed Asian countries, South Korea. The US and the UK represented the less regulated 'capital marked-based' system. But, by the mid-1990s, the debate over the relative merits of these systems was short-circuited by two factors: first the stock market bubble in the United States, which lent temporary credence to the idea that capital market-based systems could operate more effectively; and, second, the global ascendance of neoliberal economic policies – centred around deregulation of financial markets, including in economies such as Japan, France and Korea (Arestis and Sawyer 2005). The neoliberal policy framework contributed, in turn, to rising financial instability throughout the global economy.

In the aftermath of the collapses of both the stock market bubble in 2001, producing the 2001 recession, and, even more emphatically, the real estate bubble in 2008, which brought the global Great Recession, it is now clear that the unregulated neoliberal policy framework for managing the flows of saving, finance and investment is not viable (Jarsulic 2010). As such, a restoration of this line of research on alternative financial institutional environments and regulatory systems will be critical for developing new policy regimes that can promote more stable as well as more egalitarian growth prospects (Pollin 2009; Epstein and Pollin 2011).

More broadly within the realm of policy, there always have been clear important normative issues at play in the debates over saving behaviour. The agenda following from a causal saving perspective consists of seeking to raise national saving rates through measures such as providing preferential tax treatment to capital income, eliminating government deficit spending, or even paying off completely outstanding government debts. These will normally also generate a less equal distribution of income. Building from a causal investment analytic framework points to policy approaches that directly encourage higher investment while also promoting egalitarian distributional outcomes. Such measures would include increasing aggregate demand and employment through fiscal and monetary interventions or more equal income redistribution, or, through various institutional reforms, giving preferential access to credit for productive private investment relative to unproductive speculative expenditures. The policy ideas that flow from a causal investment perspective are committed to utilizing most effectively the interconnections observed in research between growth, stability and distributional equity.

ROBERT POLLIN

See also:

Consumption; Keynes's *General Theory*; Multiplier; Say's Law.

References

Arestis, P. and M. Sawyer (2005), 'Financial liberalization and the finance-growth nexus: what have we learned?', in Arestis and Sawyer (eds), *Financial Liberalization: Beyond Orthodox Concerns*, London: Palgrave Macmillan, pp. 1–43.

Asimakopulos, A. (1983), 'Kal_ki and Keynes on finance, investment and saving', *Cambridge Journal of Economics*, 7 (3–4), 221–33.

Epstein, G. and R. Pollin (2011), 'Regulating Wall Street: exploring the political economy of the possible', in P. Arestis (ed.), *Microeconomics, Macroeconomics, and Economic Policy: Essays in Honour of Malcolm Sawyer*, New York: Palgrave Macmillan, pp. 268–87.

Feldstein, M. (2006), 'The return of saving', *Foreign Affairs*, 85 (3), 87–93.

Hayes, M.G. (2010), 'The loanable funds fallacy: saving, finance and equilibrium', *Cambridge Journal of Economics*, 34 (4), 807–20.

Jarsulic, M. (2010), *Anatomy of a Financial Crisis: A Real Estate Bubble, Runaway Credit Markets, and Regulatory Failure*, Basingstoke: Palgrave Macmillan.

Kaldor, N. (1939), 'Speculation and economic activity'; reprinted in Kaldor, *Essays on Economic Stability and Growth*, London: Duckworth, 1960, pp. 17–58.

Keynes, J.M. (1936), *The General Theory of Employment, Interest and Money*, New York: Harcourt Brace.

Keynes, J.M. (1938), 'The "ex ante" theory of the interest rate', in *The Collected Writings of John Maynard Keynes, Volume XIV. The General Theory and After: Defence and Development*, London: Macmillan for the Royal Economic Society, 1973, pp. 215–23.

Leijonhufvud, A. (2006), 'Keynes as a Marshallian', in R.E. Backhouse and B.W. Bateman (eds), *The Cambridge Companion to Keynes*, Cambridge: Cambridge University Press, pp. 58–77.

Meade, J. (1975), 'The Keynesian revolution', in M. Keynes (ed.), *Essays on John Maynard Keynes*, Cambridge: Cambridge University Press, pp. 82–8.

Pollin, R. (1995), 'Financial structure and egalitarian economic policy', *New Left Review*, **214**, 26–61.

Pollin, R. (1997), 'Financial intermediation and the variability of the saving constraint', in Pollin (ed.), *The Macroeconomics of Saving, Finance and Investment*, Ann Arbor, MI: University of Michigan Press, pp. 309–66.

Pollin, R. (2009), 'Tools for a new economy: proposals for a new financial regulatory system', *Boston Review*, **34** (1), 9–13.

Pollin, R. (2010), 'Austerity is not a solution: why the deficit hawks are wrong', *Challenge*, **53** (6), 6–36.

Say's Law

Say's law, also known as the law of markets, is a set of ideas and propositions that were originally formulated during the classical period in the history of economics. Despite the name, Jean-Baptiste Say was neither the inventor of the law nor was he its clearest and most coherent advocate. Important contributions to the development of the law were made by Adam Smith, James Mill, David Ricardo and John Stuart Mill. After the demise of classical political economy and the rise to dominance of neoclassical economics, Say's law remained essentially unchallenged, even though economists paid much less attention to it. Say's law has always generated opponents. During the classical period, Thomas Robert Malthus, J.C.L. Simonde de Sismondi and Karl Marx were some of the most important critics; in modern times, John Maynard Keynes undoubtedly provided the most radical and clearly articulated critique of Say's law. Only Keynes, however, succeeded in convincing a significant part of the profession that the law was incorrect and had to be rejected (for a thorough historical reconstruction of the debate on Say's law, see Sowell 1972, but also Baumol 1977).

The basic idea underlying the 'law of markets' is that there cannot be any obstacle to economic growth deriving from an insufficient level of aggregate demand. Whatever the level of aggregate supply, it will give rise to an equal level of aggregate demand. If there are obstacles to growth, they depend on other factors, such as, for Ricardo, decreasing returns in agriculture. In the analyses of markets carried out by classical adherents to Say's law, the production and sale of goods generates an income which is either spent on consumption or saved. What is saved, however, is also spent, as it is devoted to investment. Thus production gives rise to purchasing power of equal value that is entirely spent to buy the current production itself. Situations in which aggregate supply exceeds aggregate demand are therefore impossible.

The analysis was based on the assumption that the exchange of goods through money is conceptually the same as barter, in which it is impossible that any divergence between demand and supply arises because sellers are necessarily at the same time buyers. Money was regarded merely as a device to facilitate exchanges, which was therefore demanded only for this function. It was assumed that people do not draw any utility from holding money in a larger amount than that required to exchange commodities. The law in its classical formulation also implied that the existing productive capacity of the economy is always fully utilized, even though this does not mean that labour is fully employed: the existing productive capacity might be insufficient to employ the entire labour force. In other words, if there is unemployment, it does not result from an insufficient level of demand but from an insufficient growth of capital.

It is hard to find Say's law expressed in these terms by any post-classical economist. None the less, neoclassical economics left the law of markets essentially unchallenged. Its basic aspects were accepted: money was still regarded essentially as a mere device to make exchanges more efficient, and it was held that saving is necessarily transformed into investment. However, there were some significant differences between the classical and neoclassical versions of the law. First, classical economists simply assumed that saving is investment, so that any discrepancy between the two variables is impossible; neoclassical economists, instead, admitted the possibility that saving and investment diverge. Such a divergence, however, would be eliminated by some equilibrating mechanism. Second, for the classics, the law only implied the full employment of capital, whereas, for neoclassical economics, the validity of the law also implied the full employment of labour. Also in this case, unemployment of labour would be eliminated by an equilibrating mechanism.

For Smith, Ricardo, and so on, the transformation of saving into investment was essentially a direct process, in the sense that savers themselves were those who invested. For the neoclassicals, the process was essentially indirect: saving and investment decisions are not necessarily made simultaneously and by the same people. For this reason saving and investment may diverge; but market mechanisms take care of this by ensuring that the equality is restored. The variable that plays this equilibrating role is the rate of interest. Abstaining from present consumption (saving, that is, the supply of capital) is a direct function of the interest rate, and investment (the demand for capital) is an inverse function, so that any divergence between the two variables is eliminated by variations in the interest rate. For the classics, the possible existence of unemployment did not give rise to any adjusting mechanism that would bring the economy to the full employment of labour; for neoclassical economists, variations of the (real) wage rate bring the economy to full employment. If there is an excess supply of labour, a decrease in the real wage rate would induce firms to increase their demand for labour and eliminate unemployment.

These analytical differences between classical and neoclassical economists can also be pointed out by expressing Say's law in two different ways: as an identity and as equality. Classical economists, by assuming that saving is investment, accepted the law as an identity (the equality between aggregate supply and demand is always true); neoclassical economists, by concentrating on equilibrating mechanisms, accepted the law as an equality, which is true only in equilibrium (see, for example, Sowell 1972, pp. 34–8).

Keynes held that, before him, Malthus went closest to a satisfactory criticism of Say's law, but he was probably far too generous to Malthus's critique of Say and Ricardo. Malthus did not provide a coherent alternative analytical framework, as he maintained the assumption that saving is investment. It was Marx (1968) who developed a more satisfactory critique of the law of markets, which resembles Keynes's own criticism in several respects (Sardoni 1991). In Marx, as well as in Keynes, the rejection of Say's law is based on the idea that the analysis of the working of the economy must be carried out by taking account of money, which plays a more crucial role than merely being a device to facilitate exchange. For Marx, the existence of money breaks the unity between selling and buying; the exchange of commodities through money is not conceptually the same as barter. Those who own money can always decide not to convert it into commodities and, hence, break the unity of exchange. In particular, capitalists can decide to keep money 'idle' instead of investing, whenever they expect that producing commodities will not be profitable.

Turning now to consider Keynes, it is useful to distinguish between two different analytical levels at which he developed his critique of Say's law. On the one hand, he carried out a critique of the law that is addressed to the essential theoretical foundations on which it rests; on the other hand, especially in the *General Theory*, he also developed a criticism that is more complex and articulated, as it takes into account analytical aspects that are typical of the neoclassical version of the law.

Keynes's essential critique hinges on the idea that what makes the law untenable is that the economy of the world in which we live is a *mon-*

etary economy, that is, an economy in which money plays a much more fundamental role than the advocates of the law implied. The income of the factors of production, which is generated by production, is not necessarily spent entirely on current output; income not spent on consumption goods can be kept in the form of money rather than being transformed into goods. The explanation of why individuals may wish to hold money as a store of value is one of the key elements of Keynes's theory. He was deeply convinced that the economic and social environment is dominated by uncertainty, which cannot be reduced to risk and treated with the traditional tools of probability theory. But, notwithstanding uncertainty, individuals have to make decisions and to act. They do so by pretending that the calculation of the probabilities of a series of prospective advantages and disadvantages is possible. In order to behave in such a way, some techniques are devised, which essentially are conventions, like assuming that the present is a reliable guide to the future despite the past evidence to the contrary, or trying to conform to the behaviour of the majority.

These are, for Keynes, 'flimsy foundations for decision making', and they are subject to sudden and violent changes. It is in this context that money plays a crucial role, different from its function as a medium of exchange. Money demanded as a store of value is, for Keynes, an indicator of people's distrust of their conventions concerning the future. When conventions break down and expectations become more uncertain, demanding money is a sort of insurance against uncertainty. The demand for money, however, is in no way similar to the demand for any other good or service: an increase in the demand for it, which means a decrease in the demand for some other goods or services, does not give rise to a corresponding increase in its production. Money has a zero elasticity of production (Keynes 1936, p. 230). Thus, as in Marx's analysis, money can be demanded and kept idle rather than being spent on goods or services. This is the basic reason why Say's law does not hold.

Keynes, however, criticized the law in its neoclassical version; therefore, he also had to consider those specific aspects on which neoclassical economists concentrated. In particular, he had to reject the idea that there is an equilibrating mechanism that brings aggregate supply and demand to equality by ensuring the equality between saving and investment. For Keynes, saving is not necessarily transformed into investment. The act of saving does not imply the supply of a corresponding amount of funds to those who wish to invest. Once the amount of saving has been decided, the individual has to decide whether to keep it in the form of money or to part with it for a certain time, that is, to lend it. Such a decision depends on the individual's liquidity preference. This vision of saving decisions implies that the interest rate is not a return to saving, to waiting as such.

In fact, 'if a man hoards his saving in cash, he earns no interest though he saves as much as before. The interest rate, instead, is the reward for parting with liquidity' (ibid., p. 167). Therefore, the rate of interest cannot play the equilibrating role that is given to it in neoclassical analysis. There can be situations in which liquidity preference is so high that the interest rate is at too high a level to allow investment to reach its full-employment level, that is, that level that ensures the level of aggregate demand associated with the full employment of labour and capacity. In other words, it is not true that any level of supply whatsoever generates an equal level of demand.

Keynesian economists of the neoclassical synthesis accepted Keynes's rejection of Say's law but in their analyses, based on the IS–LM model, they concentrated on the more technical aspects of the reasons why the interest rate cannot guarantee the full-employment level of investment (for example, the so-called 'liquidity trap'), while Keynes's deeper critique of market economies and his notion of uncertainty were essentially neglected. Post Keynesian economists, by emphasizing the importance of decision making under uncertainty, more clearly link the rejection of Say's law to an alternative notion of the essential features of market economies. Contemporary mainstream economics has essentially returned to the full acceptance of Say's law, even though macroeconomists hardly ever mention it in their analyses. The acceptance of the law is particularly evident in long-period models of growth. In these models, all inspired more or less directly by Solow's famous growth model (1956), it is always assumed that all savings are invested; there is no problem of effective demand and attention is focused on other aspects, like the role of technological progress, investment in human capital, and so on. In short–medium period models, since it is usually assumed that imperfect or monopolistic competition prevails in all markets, it is recognized that firms' production is demand-constrained: firms do not produce all the output they could with their productive capacity because such output could not be sold at its normal price.

CLAUDIO SARDONI

See also:

Bastard Keynesianism; Conventions; Effective Demand; Keynes's *General Theory*; Liquidity Preference; New Neoclassical Synthesis; Rate of Interest; Uncertainty; Unemployment; Walrasian Economics.

References

Baumol, W.J. (1977), 'Say's (at least) eight laws, or what Say and James Mill may really have meant', *Economica*, **44** (174), 145–62.
Keynes, J.M. (1936), *The General Theory of Employment Interest and Money*, London: Macmillan.

Marx, K. (1968), *Theories of Surplus Value*, Vol. II, Moscow: Progress Publishers.

Sardoni, C. (1991), 'Marx and Keynes: the critique of Say's law', in G.A. Caravale (ed.), *Marx and Modern Economics: Volume 2: The Future of Capitalism and the History of Thought*, Aldershot, UK and Brookfield, VT, USA: Edward Elgar, pp. 219–39.

Solow, R.M. (1956), 'A contribution to the theory of economic growth', *Quarterly Journal of Economics*, **70** (1), 65–94.

Sowell, T. (1972), *Say's Law: An Historical Analysis*, Princeton, NJ: Princeton University Press.

Socialism

Most Post Keynesians are not socialists. But almost all are reformers, who advocate major reforms of capitalism, designed not only to help stability, but also to increase equality. There is nothing incompatible between advocating major reforms in the short run and advocating a complete change to socialism in the long run. So a minority of Post Keynesians are also socialists.

What is meant by socialism? Fortunately, the Soviet Union is dead and buried. So we can ask what a Post Keynesian approach to socialism may be. If one wants to consider something called socialism, there are three questions to be asked: the role of democracy in socialism, the plan versus the market in socialism, and the degree of equality in socialism.

All Post Keynesian socialists are agreed that any socialist society must be democratic. To understand the issue fully, however, the long and convoluted history of this issue must be briefly mentioned. Marx and Engels fought in the 1848 revolution for democracy in Germany and they supported every movement for democracy in their lifetimes. European socialist parties, from the German Social Democrats to the British Labour Party grew up in a struggle for the extension of democracy, including suffrage rights for male workers and for women.

After the Bolshevik revolution of 1917 in Russia, however, the embattled Bolsheviks became less and less democratic, with 60 years of one-party dictatorship. Their defence was a parody of Marxism: they argued that the Soviet Union had only one class, the working class, so it needed only one party to be democratic. In truth, it was a dictatorship over workers and everyone else – and the horrors of that dictatorship set back the cause of anything called socialism by many decades.

Socialism means that the people rule over the economy, not a small group of capitalists or a small group of bureaucrats appointed by a dictator. A precise definition would be that socialism means the extension of democracy from the political sphere into the economic sphere. Some of the procedural necessities and safeguards in the political sphere under socialism are spelled out in detail by Ralph Miliband (1994). In the economic sphere, two types of democratic procedures have been advocated. One is to have local, state and national ownership by a democratically elected government. The other procedure is to have corporate boards democratically elected by the employees of each enterprise. Of course, there may be any mix of these two forms – even a role for a democratic government representative on the board of an employee-run enterprise. This poses the question of the manner of control of the economy.

Post Keynesian socialists are divided on what would be the best way to coordinate a socialist economy. Some – probably a minority at present – favour some form of democratic central planning. Others – perhaps a majority – favour a market type of socialism (for a good introduction to the debate among socialists, see Ollman 1998).

The Soviet Union had extreme central planning with dictatorship. In that model, almost all industry and about half of agriculture was directly owned and run by the government. A group of planners, appointed by the ruling party, drew up a plan for the whole economy. To do this, they had to know (i) the available resources, including all known raw materials, every type and quality of labour, and every type and quality of capital. They also had to know (ii) the preferences of the government and all consumers. Finally, they had to know (iii) all the technological coefficients telling them what could be produced with a given amount of resources. Of course, even with the best presently available information network, collecting all such information down to the enterprise level would be impossible in any limited amount of time, such as six months to a year. So they dealt instead with broad aggregates of each industry, divided at most into about 500 categories. With that general information, they calculated several variants of a national plan. It was then up to the government dictatorship to decide on which variant would be used, depending on its time preferences between present production and investment for future expansion. The plan which was adopted was then handed down as law to the managers appointed by the dictatorship. Although some discussion was allowed in the early stages, criticism of the final plan was not allowed, nor was it healthy for employees to criticize the managers.

Such excessive planning in a dictatorial setting nevertheless managed to transform the economy from an underdeveloped, mainly rural and agricultural one, to the second-largest industrialized economy in the world. From 1928 to 1989 – excluding the Second World War – the Soviet economy never suffered a decline in aggregate output. Moreover, it had full employment that entire time. So it has been argued that, whatever its other problems, central planning can provide for full employment, development out of underdevelopment, and rapid growth rates for at least a time. On the other side, it was clear that the Soviet economy suffered from a high level of inefficiency. That inefficiency grew worse as the economy became more complex and the problems of central planning grew. So it has been argued that central planning always leads to enormous inefficiency – though whether it is worse than the crises of capitalism is another question.

The truth, however, is that the Soviet experience gave us very limited lessons. It was not democratic planning, but planning under a one-party dictatorship. Dictatorships must lead to vast inefficiency in government-owned enterprises. There can be no criticism of Cabinet decisions on the plan, there can be no criticisms of the details of planning at the lower levels, and there can be no criticism of management (until after they are fired). There can be no freedom for scientists to choose the direction of scientific research because the ultimate decisions on the direction and funding of research will be under political control. Thus one cannot say whether Soviet inefficiency resulted from excessive planning, from dictatorship, or from their combination. If it was the combination, how should the blame and the praise be allocated?

Those who argue that central planning always leads to unacceptable inefficiency argue that socialism would be better with a market form. Managers could be told to maximize profit, rather than follow a plan. But most advocates of market socialism would argue for employee-controlled enterprises, since this would provide a high level of direct democracy. Of course, government could control some functions, such as environmental regulations, while employees controlled the rest. The only extensive experience known of a form of market socialism with employee control of enterprises. was in Yugoslavia – but that again was conditioned by a one-party dictatorship that affected the results. Yugoslavia did seem to have considerable enterprise efficiency, such as better quality control than the Soviet Union. But as Yugoslavia moved from central planning to independent enterprises, it also witnessed all the problems of capitalism, including monopoly profits, inflation, and cycles of boom and bust with cyclical unemployment. It also moved toward a society with great emphasis on consumerism, and with feelings of helplessness by unemployed or employees in firms doing poorly or going bankrupt. There was plenty of food and other goods in the stores, but an unequal income distribution which meant that many people could not buy an adequate bundle of goods. Many people began to work in more than one job. So market socialism has been attacked as leading to instability and alienation.

Many Post Keynesian socialists conclude that, under present technological and social circumstances, a feasible socialism must combine market and plan. The smallest businesses could remain private. Medium-sized business could all be employee controlled so as to provide incentives and efficiency with internal democracy. To stabilize the economy, the giant conglomerates require direct public control and planning. Even the largest, government-owned firms would leave many functions, such as safety, hours and forms of the production process, to internal democratic decisions. This is not a vision of utopia, but it would mean the end of extraction of profits from employees by a small elite and it would mean a large degree of economic democracy through planning by democratic governments at local, state, national and world levels, as well as a large measure of internal democracy for firms with the most employees.

There is vast inequality under capitalism. John Maynard Keynes advocated greater equality of income distribution, both to increase the stability of capitalism and for ethical reasons. All Post Keynesians advocate more equality under capitalism and would surely endorse more equality under socialism.

Socialism by itself does not necessarily mean equality. If all capitalist ownership and profits are eliminated, then the single largest source of inequality will be eliminated. In addition, democratic control of the economy may bring a decision for greater equality, but it could mean a decision to continue wide disparities of income. Under centrally planned socialism, where all income is determined by planners and politicians, it is possible for a democratically elected government to reduce drastically the inequality of wages and salaries, but it is also possible to increase wage and salary inequality. In a market socialist economy, the market decides; so one person might earn $5,000 a year, while another earns $1,000,000 a month.

In the old Soviet Union, Stalin decided that the conservative argument, that great income inequalities are necessary to provide great incentives, was correct. Therefore, for much of Soviet history, the degree of inequality of wage and salary income was about the same as in the United States. It is true that private profit income was outlawed, but the elite did receive secret income and very important non-monetary privileges, including villas, chauffeured cars, and medical specialists.

At the other extreme, in the utopia described by Edward Bellamy (1887[1987]) there was central planning with equal wages for everyone – with only a few medals or lesser hours for the most dirty, dangerous and difficult jobs. But given the present psychology of employees under capitalism, it is true that equal wages would enormously reduce incentives to work. Perhaps decades of new experience and propaganda would change that psychology, but that is speculation.

Still more utopian is the world described by Ursula Le Guin (1974), in which there is central planning, but there is no money or prices, so everyone can take what they need – with only peer pressure as a goad to work or a limit on demand. With present psychology, that would mean almost no work and unlimited demand – an impossible situation. And, aside from incentive and demand problems, central planning with no explicit prices or money would be very difficult in any complex economy.

Most Post Keynesians would urge fiscal means to reduce inequality. They advocate highly progressive taxes together with government spending to provide certain free goods and services to everyone with negligible effect on incentives. If the items are necessities, such as health care, then there will be only a limited increase in demand.

Health care is provided to some extent by every industrialized country other than the United States. In the United States, over 40 million people have no guaranteed health care. If a socialist society provided free health care to all, that would reduce inequality, provide for a basic need, and increase productivity. Another area of struggle in many capitalist countries is the provision of free higher education. If a socialist society wished to go further, it could ensure that everyone has a minimum necessary amount of food to eat, a certain minimum level of housing, and free public transport – with no economic disruption if this is done gradually.

HOWARD J. SHERMAN

See also:

Kaleckian Economics; Transition Economics.

References

Bellamy, E. (1887[1987]), *Looking Backward*, New York: Modern Library.
Le Guin, U. (1974), *The Dispossessed*, New York: Harper Prism.
Miliband, R. (1994), *Socialism*, New York: Verso.
Ollman, B. (1998), *Market Socialism: The Debate among Socialists*, London and New York: Routledge.

Sraffian Economics

Among the many unsettled issues within Post Keynesian economics, one of the most divisive concerns the relationship between Keynes's theoretical framework and the analytical tradition associated with Piero Sraffa (1898–1983). In the 1970s, Sraffian economics was generally regarded not only as compatible with Post Keynesianism, but as an important branch of it. (The essays in Nell (1980), for example, were the culmination of a project to integrate Keynesian, Kaleckian, Sraffian and Marxian insights into a unified Post Keynesian account of postwar capitalism.) By the end of the 1980s, however, this view had largely given way to the presumption that the two frameworks are distinct and, in at least some key respects, incompatible.

Sraffa is best known as the author of *Production of Commodities by Means of Commodities* (1960), which provided the basis for a capital-theoretic critique of the neoclassical theory of distribution. Orthodox theory explains income distribution in terms of the interaction of the demand for and supply of scarce factors of production. The theory requires (i) that the endowment of each factor of production be known *prior* to the determination of prices and distribution; and (ii) that the demand for any factor declines as the price of its productive services increases. Sraffa's analysis suggested that in a long-period setting neither of these conditions can be presumed to hold for the factor called 'capital'. Since capital is composed of many different kinds of produced means of production, whose prices themselves depend upon the real wage and the profit rate, the endowment of capital, specified as a value magnitude, cannot be known prior to distribution. Moreover, changes in distribution can cause the prices of capital goods to vary in highly complex ways, so that no systematic relation can be established between the profit rate and the capital intensity of production. The upshot of all this is that the substitution mechanisms that underpin the price-elastic factor demand functions of neoclassical theory lack solid foundations. But these substitution mechanisms are precisely what justify the orthodox claim that, in the absence of impediments to the adjustment of prices, market forces will push the economy toward full employment.

The capital critique was part of a larger constructive agenda that motivated Sraffa's scientific work from the late 1920s. His objective was to lay a foundation for the reconstruction of the classical political economy approach pioneered by Adam Smith, David Ricardo and Karl Marx that had been, as Sraffa (1960, p. v) put it, 'submerged and forgotten' with the rise of neoclassical economics. A distinctive feature of the classical theory is its treatment of income distribution not in terms of the equilibrating interaction of price-elastic supply and demand functions, but as the outcome of the interplay of class interests in a historically conditioned institutional setting. Profits are conceived as a residual, or surplus, appropriated by the owners of capital after the replacement of the material inputs – including the wage goods consumed by workers – used up in the production of aggregate output; for this reason the classical theory is sometimes called the 'surplus approach'.

In their analysis of value and distribution the classicals treated the following variables as parametric: (i) the size and composition of the social product; (ii) the technical conditions of production; and (iii) the real wages of workers. The equation systems of Parts I and II of *Production of Commodities* establish that these data are sufficient to determine relative prices and the profit rate. (Sraffa's formulation fixes the profit rate and determines the real wage as a residual; but it makes no difference to the logic of the theory which distribution variable is taken as parametric.) From the same equations Sraffa derived a trade-off, between the real wage and the profit rate, that corresponds to the classical–Marxian conception of distribution as grounded in the opposition of class interests.

Sraffa's analysis and Keynes's theory of effective demand intersect at several junctures. First, by knocking out the foundations of neoclassical distribution theory the capital critique buttresses Keynes's contention that there is no mechanism within capitalism capable of ensuring that the labour market will tend to clear. Second, the classical theory of value and distribution – including Sraffa's modern formulation of it – is open-ended with regard to the determination of the level and composition of the social product. Some variation on the Keynes–Kalecki effective demand mechanism could therefore provide an explanation of outputs that is compatible with the classical surplus framework.

Third, Sraffa's analysis calls into question some aspects of Keynes's articulation of the theory of effective demand, and helps to account for the theory's assimilation, in weakened form, into mainstream economics. Keynes incorporated into *The General Theory* two elements of Marshallian orthodoxy: the proposition that in equilibrium the real wage must equal the marginal product of labour; and the notion that investment demand is a decreasing function of the interest rate. The capital critique undermines both of these claims. The Sraffian literature on Keynes maintains, furthermore, that by adopting them he opened the way for the interpretation of *The General Theory* in terms of the neoclassical synthesis, according to which, under conditions of wage and price flexibility, the Keynes effect and the real balance effect ensure that the labour market tends to clear in the long run. On this interpretation Keynes's argument applies to the short period or to circumstances in which persistent market imperfections prevent the price adjustments that would otherwise bring about full employment. In failing to detach himself fully from his Marshallian roots, Keynes produced 'an inherently unstable compromise' that in the end fell short of its revolutionary promise (Garegnani 1978–79; see also Milgate 1982).

Sraffa appears to have harboured reservations about *The General Theory* (Kurz 2010). His manuscripts at Trinity College, Cambridge, indicate that he disliked the liquidity preference theory of interest, but this by itself seems inadequate to account for his scepticism. It is possible that Sraffa recognized earlier and more clearly than other members of Keynes's circle that the book's argument was susceptible to assimilation into the orthodox framework that Keynes wanted to scuttle. The way past this difficulty, most Sraffian writers would contend, lies in jettisoning the Trojan horses Keynes incorporated into *The General Theory* – the Marshallian elements that are anyway vulnerable to the capital critique.

Throughout most of the formative period of Post Keynesian economics, from 1960 until the mid-1980s, the affinities between the Keynes–Kalecki effective demand mechanism and Sraffa's work were not a matter of dispute. Since then, however, the Post Keynesian project of integrating Keynes, Kalecki and Sraffa has lost momentum, and something of a rift appears to have developed between the Sraffian camp and many of those who identify themselves as Post Keynesians. The history of this rift remains to be sorted out, though it appears to be connected, no doubt as both cause and effect, to the failure of the Trieste summer school to achieve one of its principal goals – the forging of a unified methodological and analytical foundation for the Post Keynesian project. The tensions are largely unnecessary, and at least some Post Keynesian resistance to the Sraffian view is based on a misunderstanding of it. There are of course genuine differences of perspective, but these do not render the two traditions incompatible with each other.

Much of the Post Keynesian literature exhibits a strong antipathy towards attempts to explain economic phenomena in terms of equilibrating forces, and the classical surplus approach has come in for some criticism because of its utilization of models of long-period gravitation to explain aspects of income distribution and price determination. There is no disputing the practical importance of the themes emphasized by Post Keynesians – uncertainty, expectations, disequilibrium; what is at issue is how to incorporate these phenomena into a coherent account of social processes. Uncertainty, technical change and coordination failure account for much of the complexity of economic life. A Sraffian would argue that it is the very complexity of these issues that justifies the indispensability of a long-period theory of value and distribution: disequilibrium processes can best be understood by reference to the gravitational forces they disrupt. There is no necessary incompatibility on methodological grounds between the Post Keynesian and Sraffian frameworks; the two complement each other, each providing a different set of tools for different sorts of analytical problems.

Similarly, the Sraffian approach to money is not incompatible with a broad Post Keynesian perspective. The Sraffian framework allows for the non-neutrality of money via the effect of the money rate of interest on distribution. Panico (1985) and Pivetti (1985), developing a hint from Sraffa (1960, p. 33), have argued that the rate of interest fixed by the monetary authorities regulates the rate of return on non-financial capital. The argument starts from the familiar stylized fact that central banks can regulate interest rates but cannot generally control the money supply; the reasoning is therefore consistent with the endogeneity of money, a defining Post Keynesian premise. In the models developed along this line, money is not neutral at all: the monetary authorities, by setting the interest rate, influence distribution, and this has consequences for the composition, level and growth of aggregate output, and for employment. Related work (for example, Stirati 2001) has drawn upon the Kaleckian view of inflation as a manifestation of the conflicting claims of labour and capital over the distribution of net income. Here we see that Sraffa prices are not at all incompatible with another key element of Post Keynesian economics – mark-up pricing. The analysis provides an alternative to the NAIRU (non-accelerating inflation rate of unemployment) as a framework for understanding how unemployment and inflation interact with each other in a modern market economy. All of these models illuminate important aspects of the distributional role of finance. The question is not *whether* money is non-neutral – on this, the Sraffian and Post Keynesian positions are not in conflict – but *how* it is non-neutral.

Underlying the Sraffian argument is a presumption that what we can say about money depends on how we conceive value and distribution. One of the reasons the Post Keynesian literature relies so heavily on the pervasiveness of uncertainty is that it is not solidly grounded in a theory of value and distribution; this deficiency is partly a byproduct of the rift with the Sraffians. Post Keynesian arguments about uncertainty are not so much wrong as extremely limited in what they can explain. Long before the publication of *The General Theory*, Keynes's neoclassical predecessors understood that uncertainty and fluctuations in business confidence could disrupt the market's coordinating mechanisms. If, as many Post Keynesians contend, the monetary nature of capitalist production is what accounts for unemployment, it would appear to follow that in a non-monetary economy the postulates of neoclassical theory hold, and that such an economy would tend towards full employment. But the capital critique undermines the neoclassical theory of distribution, and hence its theory of employment, *whether the economy utilizes money or not*. The Sraffian analysis of money and interest suggests furthermore that the non-neutrality of money does not reside – or at any rate does not reside exclusively – in the uncertainty inherent in monetary exchange regimes. Non-neutrality is indeed incompatible with the neoclassical theory of distribution; but there is no evident incompatibility between the non-neutrality of money and the classical surplus approach of Sraffa.

Over the past quarter of a century a robust Sraffian literature has emerged which explicitly integrates Post Keynesian elements into the framework of the classical surplus approach. Much of this work has focused on a theoretical device known as the 'Sraffian supermultiplier', which combines the standard Keynesian spending multiplier with an accelerator mechanism in such a way as to enable aggregate demand to determine long-period levels of employment, aggregate income and aggregate productive capacity (see Serrano 1995). Because they start from a non-neoclassical approach to the theory of distribution, models that incorporate the Sraffian supermultiplier can accommodate the possibility that aggregate demand drives macroeconomic processes even in a long-period context. In this respect, the device buttresses Keynes's theory against the claim that effective demand is relevant only in the short period, while in the long run the economy is resource constrained and the conventional neoclassical conclusions hold. Other work in a similar vein has argued that consumption spending reacts asymmetrically to increases and decreases in aggregate income. Since consumption patterns and living standards tend to become entrenched over time, the reductions in consumption spending that follow a decline in aggregate income in a cyclical downturn are proportionally smaller relative to income than the increases in consumption spending that occur during a boom. As a result, consumption spending tends to ratchet upwards, creating a stimulus to permanent capacity expansion, that is, investment (see Garegnani and Trezzini 2010). Like the supermultiplier model, to which it is complementary, this argument provides a grounding for demand-driven endogenous growth.

Fuller discussions of the issues discussed here can be found in the essays contained in Eatwell and Milgate (1983). For a general overview of Sraffa's scientific legacy, see Mongiovi (2002).

GARY MONGIOVI

See also:

Cambridge Economic Tradition; Capital Theory; Equilibrium and Non-equilibrium; Income Distribution; Rate of Interest; Uncertainty.

References

Eatwell, J. and M. Milgate (eds) (1983), *Keynes's Economics and the Theory of Value and Distribution*, Oxford: Duckworth.
Garegnani, P. (1978–79), 'Notes on consumption, investment and effective demand, parts I & II', *Cambridge Journal of Economics*, 2 (4) and 3 (1), 335–53 and 63–82.
Garegnani, P. and A. Trezzini (2010), 'Cycles and growth: a source of demand-driven endogenous growth', *Review of Political Economy*, 22 (1), 119–25.
Kurz, H.D. (2010), 'Keynes, Sraffa, and the latter's "secret scepticism"', in B.W. Bateman, T. Hirai and M.C. Marcuzzo (eds), *The Return to Keynes*, Cambridge, MA: Harvard University Press, pp. 184–204.
Milgate, M. (1982), *Capital and Employment*, London: Academic Press.
Mongiovi, G. (2002), 'Classics and moderns: Sraffa's legacy in economics', *Metroeconomica*, 53 (3), 223–41.
Nell, E.J. (ed.) (1980), *Growth, Profits and Property*, Cambridge: Cambridge University Press.

Panico, C. (1985), 'Market forces and the relation between the rates of interest and profit', *Contributions to Political Economy*, **4**, 37–60.

Pivetti, M. (1985), 'On the monetary explanation of distribution', *Political Economy: Studies in the Surplus Approach*, **1**, 73–103.

Serrano, F. (1995), 'Long period effective demand and the Sraffian supermultiplier', *Contributions to Political Economy*, **14**, 67–90.

Sraffa, P. (1960), *Production of Commodities by Means of Commodities*, Cambridge: Cambridge University Press.

Stirati, A. (2001), 'Inflation, unemployment and hysteresis: an alternative view', *Review of Political Economy*, **13** (4), 427–51.

Stagflation

The term 'stagflation' describes the simultaneous occurrence of inflation and stagnation, the latter consisting of prolonged slow growth and high (or even rising) unemployment. The term gained popularity in the early 1970s with the simultaneous increase in rates of inflation and unemployment throughout the developed capitalist economies. Hitherto during the post-Second World War period, the behaviour of inflation and unemployment rates conformed to an inverse relationship formalized in the Phillips curve, which became an integral part of Keynesian macroeconomics.

The stagflation episode of the 1970s posed a serious challenge to the dominance of Keynesian macroeconomics and fuelled the emergence of a radically different set of beliefs. The simultaneous occurrence of rising unemployment and inflation rates allegedly constituted definite proof of fundamental flaws in Keynesian theory and its application as a tool for forecasting (Lucas and Sargent 1978). To Post Keynesians – indeed, to all macroeconomists mindful of the complexity of real-world economies – this response was but another example of the dangers of relying on gross correlations to substantiate or refute economic theory. In fact, by simply taking account of additional influences on inflation rates that were prominent during the stagflation period, the negative relationship assumed in the original Phillips curve remains unchallenged. In isolating the critical historical events responsible for stagflation in this fashion, it is necessary to give a more precise definition of the term. Hereafter, stagflation will refer to the simultaneous occurrence of unemployment and inflation rates that are high relative to those of the postwar 'golden age' (1948–73).

Figure 19 shows average annual rates of inflation and unemployment in the seven largest OECD (Organisation for Economic Co-operation and Development) economies from the closing years of the golden age to the onset of the Great Recession. Three distinct eras are evident in this figure. The first, running from the late 1960s to the early 1980s, is characterized

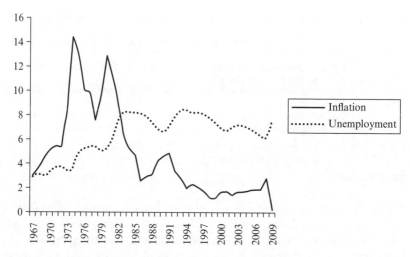

Note: Data include West Germany prior to 1993; thereafter, data for the unified Germany are used.

Source: OECD Historical Statistics.

Figure 19   *Average annual rates of inflation and standardized*
unemployment for the G7 countries, 1967–2009

by a pronounced upward trend in unemployment rates accompanied by high average rates of inflation. These trends combined resulted in a decade of stagflation. The second era – from the early 1980s to the early 1990s – witnessed continued high average rates of unemployment, even as inflation rates fell. Moreover, Figure 19 illustrates that when unemployment did fall during this second era – from the mid-1980s until the recession of the early 1990s – the small decline in unemployment rates from historic highs was sufficient to trigger a sharp rise in inflation rates by 1990. Only in the early 1990s, with the return of unemployment rates to approximately 2½ times their golden-age rates, was inflation once again checked. Finally, Figure 19 reveals a third era, from the early 1990s up to the beginning of the Great Recession. During this third era, there is evidence of a modest trend decline in unemployment, even as inflation rates fell through the late 1990s and then remained roughly constant thereafter. These developments were more pronounced in some economies than in others. In the US, for example, the annual average rates of unemployment and inflation fell from 7.1 and 6.7 per cent (respectively) during the 1974–89 period, to 5.6 and 3.0 per cent (respectively) during 1990–2000 and then to 5.2 and 2.7 per cent (respectively) during 2001–2007. The performance of the US economy during these last two periods compares favourably to its performance during the second half of the golden age.

The stagflation episode (and the subsequent events described above) raised several questions, the answers to which are still a matter of dispute. First, why did unemployment rates rise and remain high for so long after the early 1970s? Second, if, as Post Keynesians maintain, stimulative aggregate demand policies are effective in reducing unemployment when unemployment is involuntary, why were such policies not implemented? Third, what were the causes of the decade-long period of stagflation? And, fourth, why did it require a prolonged period of high unemployment to rid the system of high inflation, and why was it subsequently possible (at least in some of the G7 economies) for unemployment to decline without reigniting inflation?

To those of a neoclassical persuasion, capitalism is a self-regulating system. From this perspective, the long-run upward trend in unemployment rates after the golden age was caused by a rising 'equilibrium' rate of unemployment, alternatively referred to as the NAIRU (non-accelerating inflation rate of unemployment) or natural rate of unemployment. This is a rate of unemployment determined solely by supply-side forces. It implies that aggregate demand policies can alter unemployment permanently only at the cost of ever-increasing (or-decreasing) rates of inflation. To Post Keynesians, much if not most of the prolonged high unemployment after the early 1970s could be explained by deficient aggregate demand. A sustained, policy-induced increase in aggregate demand would have produced a permanent reduction in unemployment, with increased (but *not* ever-increasing) inflation rates, because the unemployment was largely involuntary. In other words, the long-run Phillips curve was downward sloping. Why, then, did policy makers allow the unemployment rate to remain so high?

The opinion of governments and central bankers was that if stimulative policies strong enough to maintain the economy at golden age unemployment rates had been introduced any time before the mid-late 1990s, inflation would have risen to politically unacceptable (although not necessarily ever-increasing) rates. Unlike the golden age period, when the goals of full employment and acceptable rates of inflation could be realized simultaneously, the early 1970s saw the emergence of an inflationary bias throughout the OECD – that is, an inability of economies to reach full employment without experiencing unacceptable rates of inflation. A shift in the Phillips curve outward to the right had taken place. Recovery in unemployment required more than a stimulation of aggregate demand; it required measures to contain inflation at full employment. When these proved unavailable, the full-employment goal was sacrificed in the interests of restraining inflation. This leads to the third question: what initiated the episode of stagflation?

Figure 19 reveals a sharp rise in inflation in the late 1960s to rates well above their previous golden-age rates and then, in 1973–74, the first of two explosions in inflation rates. Underlying these price movements was a series of 'shocks', beginning with the 'wage explosion' of the second half of the 1960s, continuing with the breakdown of the Bretton Woods agreement, the rapid run-up of commodity prices and the prices of foodstuffs in the early 1970s and finally the explosion in oil prices in 1973–74. In each case the impacts of the shocks were then magnified by the activation of wage–wage and wage–price inflationary mechanisms, and propagated throughout the OECD. By themselves the disturbances provided a plausible explanation of the Great Inflation up to the mid-1970s and, when account is taken of a second oil shock in 1979–80, of the strong inflationary trend until 1980. Thus, even without taking further account of the wage explosion, the episode of stagflation could be explained as large price disturbances dominating the effects of policy-induced unemployment increases on inflation outcomes. (See, for example, Blinder and Rudd 2008 for a contemporary restatement of this view.)

Without denying the influence of shocks on inflation, such an interpretation ignores the lasting impact of developments leading up to the explosion in money wages that had preceded the other shocks just cited. While the increase in unemployment rates worked to restrain wage and thereby price increases, influences other than shocks and rising unemployment rates had a major impact on wage settlements and therefore on price movements throughout the period covered in Figure 19. These influences were labour market institutions, including the income and employment expectations and aspirations of the average worker. During the golden age, wage and hence price dynamics were constrained by 'social bargains' – *quid pro quo* arrangements in which unionized workers exercised wage restraint (forgoing the bargaining power inherent in low unemployment rates) in return for commitments, on the part of firms and the state, to steadily rising living standards and full employment (Cornwall and Cornwall 2001). But by the end of the golden age, a growing proportion of the labour force had become accustomed to steadily rising standards of living and 'guaranteed' full employment. The subsequent inflation of their aspirations generated growing demands upon the system and caused the social bargains to break down. The so-called 'wage explosion' of the late 1960s was thus a symptom of profound institutional change that had a lasting effect on inflation and unemployment.

Evidence supporting the lasting effects of the breakdown of social bargains can be seen in the behaviour of wage and price inflation in the mid-1970s. In 1975–76, inflation fell in response to restrictive policies (which raised unemployment and so reduced the bargaining power and hence the wage demands of workers) and a decline in commodity prices, including oil. However, only a slight reduction in unemployment rates in 1977–78 led to an increase in inflation rates once again, as workers sought to act on their increased bargaining power to maximize their wage increases (see Figure 19). Events of the 1980s provide further evidence of the short-lived effects of restrictive policies on wage and price inflation during the 1970s and 1980s. Restrictive policies successfully reduced inflation in the first half of the 1980s to levels little different from those of the golden age, but at a large unemployment cost (again, see Figure 19). However, beginning in 1987 with a rather moderate fall in unemployment rates from existing historically high rates, inflation again rose sharply until it was checked once again by the recession of 1990.

This leads to the fourth question. Since the overriding concern of the authorities after 1973 was to reduce inflation through restrictive aggregate demand policies, eventually permitting a reduction in unemployment ('short-term pain for long-term gain'), why did the reduction of inflation rates to their golden-age levels take so long and why, since the early 1990s, has it been possible for some OECD economies to reduce unemployment without increasing inflation? The mainstream explanation stresses the persistent effects of the 'inflationary psychology' that built up during the 1970s. Reversing the deeply ingrained expectations of continued high inflation required an equally long period of time – and hence persistent restrictive policies and accompanying high unemployment – before unemployment rates could be successfully reduced.

An alternative explanation, offered by Post Keynesians (Cornwall and Cornwall 2001) and others (Phelps Brown 1971, 1975; Salvati 1983), focuses on institutional developments in the labour market. As previously discussed, the transitory effect of restrictive policies on inflation reflected the breakdown of the golden age social bargains, and the consequent willingness of workers to exercise any market power vested in them by low unemployment in the pursuit of wage gains. In addition, the restrictive policies initiated to fight the Great Inflation confirmed labour's suspicion that they were to be made the victims of the fight against inflation. This antagonized the conflictual labour relations that ultimately made full employment incompatible with acceptable rates of inflation for fully two decades after 1973.

However, the impact of prolonged high unemployment and the attendant stagnation of real earnings on income and job expectations and aspirations eventually worked to reduce wage demands. Equally if not more important were other, extensive changes to labour market institutions that took place after 1980 – especially in economies such as the US – which included deunionization, changes in labour law, the introduction of periodic 'downsizing' exercises, and increases in part-time and temporary employment. These institutional changes created an 'incomes policy based on fear', as a result of which the very structure of the labour market and the employment relationship restricts the bargaining power of workers (and hence their ability to bid up wages) even when unemployment is low (Setterfield 2006, 2007). It is these developments that explain why the trend reduction in unemployment after the early 1990s evident in Figure 19 did not reignite inflation, and why economies such as the US – where construction of the incomes policy based on fear proceeded furthest and fastest – succeeded in finally conquering both components of stagflation (high inflation *and* high unemployment).

According to Post Keynesians, quite apart from its fundamental inequity, an important weakness of the incomes-policy-based-on-fear regime is its propensity to depress workers' *real* income growth, so that the capacity of the economy to generate sufficient aggregate demand to maintain full employment becomes overly dependent on the willingness and ability of households to accumulate ever more debt – a potentially unsustainable process (Palley 2002; Cynamon and Fazzari 2008). The Great Recession can be interpreted as a manifestation of this weakness. Whether or not the Great Recession and its aftermath will have lasting institutional effects, and how these events shape the subsequent behaviour of inflation and unemployment rates, remains to be seen.

JOHN CORNWALL†
REVISED AND UPDATED BY MARK SETTERFIELD

See also:

Bretton Woods; Economic Policy; Inflation; Unemployment.

References

Blinder, A.S. and J.B. Rudd (2008), 'The supply-shock explanation of the great stagflation revisited', NBER Working Paper No. 14563, New York.
Cornwall, J. and W. Cornwall (2001), *Capitalist Development in the Twentieth Century: An Evolutionary–Keynesian Analysis*, Cambridge: Cambridge University Press.
Cynamon, B.Z. and S. Fazzari (2008), 'Household debt in the consumer age: source of growth – risk of collapse', *Capitalism and Society*, **3**, Article 3, available at: http://www.bepress.com/cas/vol3/iss2/art3/.
Lucas, R. and T. Sargent (1978), 'After the Phillips curve: persistence of high inflation and high unemployment', in *After Keynesian Economics*, Federal Reserve Bank of Boston, pp. 49–72.
Palley, T.I. (2002), 'Economic contradictions coming home to roost? Does the US economy face a long-term aggregate demand generation problem?', *Journal of Post Keynesian Economics*, **25** (1), 9–32.

Phelps Brown, E.H. (1971), 'The analysis of wage movements under full employment', *Scottish Journal of Political Economy*, **18** (3), 233–43.

Phelps Brown, E.H. (1975), 'A non-monetarist view of the pay explosion', *Three Banks Review*, **105**, 3–24.

Salvati, M. (1983), 'Political business cycles and long waves in industrial relations: notes on Kalecki and Phelps Brown', in C. Freeman (ed.), *Long Waves in the World Economy*, London: Butterworths, pp. 202–24.

Setterfield, M. (2006), 'Balancing the macroeconomic books on the backs of workers: a simple analytical political economy model of contemporary US capitalism', *International Journal of Political Economy*, **35** (3), 46–63. (See also 'Erratum', *International Journal of Political Economy*, **37** (4), 2008–09, 104.)

Setterfield, M. (2007), 'The rise, decline and rise of incomes policies in the US during the post-war era: an institutional–analytical explanation of inflation and the functional distribution of income', *Journal of Institutional Economics*, **3** (2), 127–46.

Stock–Flow Consistent Modelling

Stock–flow consistent (SFC) models have been developed over the past decade following the seminal model of Godley (1999). The reference models of the subsequent SFC literature are those of Lavoie and Godley (2001–02), Zezza and Dos Santos (2004) and Godley and Lavoie (2007). SFC models belong to the family of accounting-based macroeconomic models inspired by the modelling methodology developed by Richard Stone for the Cambridge Growth Project, a research project set up at the Department of Applied Economics (DAE) of the University of Cambridge (UK) in 1960 and ending in 1987. One of Stone's main innovations was to propose applied macroeconomic models whose core structure was based on a *social accounting matrix*.

A social accounting matrix (SAM) represents the national accounting framework in a matrix form. In a SAM every transaction by one sector implies an equivalent transaction by another sector (every purchase implies a sale) and every entry on the balance sheet of one sector has a counterpart in another entry on the same balance sheet. With such a framework 'everything comes from somewhere and everything goes somewhere' so that 'there is no black hole (Godley and Lavoie 2007, p. 13). Stone's methodology is based on the principle that, for the dynamics of a macroeconomic model to be consistent, the behavioural equations defining the flows between sectors have to be compatible with the budget constraints facing the decision makers in the economy, as summarized in the SAM. Therefore, for the accounting of a model to be right, the latter should integrate in its equations all the accounting identities issued from its associated SAM *but one*. Indeed, a model which takes into account the budget constraints of $(n–1)$ sectors is necessarily consistent with the flow budget constraint of the nth sector. The use of a SAM in accordance with the latter principle, which can be referred to as 'Walras's law of flows', is the cornerstone of Stone's modelling methodology.

The SAM and its associated accounting identities provide only the skeleton of a macroeconomic model. For this accounting framework to come to life as an economic model, one has to introduce behavioural equations explaining all the entries of the matrix not defined through accounting identities. It is at this stage of modelling that the various SAM-based models differ from one another and reflect the theoretical choices of their builder. The most important theoretical choice comes down to the 'closure' of the model, that is to deciding which variables should be exogenous or endogenous in order to make sure that the equation system issued from the SAM and the behavioural equations has a solution. This choice sets the direction of causality in the model.

In the late 1970s and early 1980s various SAM-based research programmes were developed independently in the United Kingdom and the United States with different aims and scope, using a wide range of theoretical assumptions and closures. The SFC literature developed over the past decade traces its intellectual roots to two of them: the SAM-based portfolio models developed at Yale by James Tobin and his associates (Backus et al. 1980) and the New Cambridge models developed at the DAE by Wynne Godley, Ken Coutts and Francis Cripps.

Yale portfolio models were developed along five features put in evidence by Tobin (1982) in his Nobel lecture. These five features all apply to SFC models as well. The first feature, *Walras's law and adding-up constraints*, states that, for a macroeconomic model to be consistent, its core structure should be based on a SAM. With regard to this point, Yale and SFC models are not different from other Stone-inspired types of models. Their only specificity lies in the fact that their accounting skeleton is issued from a peculiar type of SAM, labelled the 'transactions–flow matrix'. The main advantage of the latter, compared to a traditional SAM, is to facilitate the representation of firms' inventories, which play a great role in most of SFC models. In a transactions–flow matrix, every row represents a monetary transaction, and every column corresponds to a sector account. The latter is divided into a current and a capital account. Sources of funds appear with plus signs and uses of funds are indicated by negative signs. The sum of every row must equate to zero as each transaction always simultaneously corresponds to a source and a use of funds. Equally, the sum of each column must be zero as each account (or sub-account) is balanced.

The second feature, *the tracking of stocks*, asserts that a consistent macro model must respect not only the *flow* constraints synthesized in the transactions–flow matrix, but also the *stock* constraints. The stock constraint of a given economic sector arises from the concept of 'net wealth' which consists of the sum of the sector's assets minus the sum of its liabilities. This constraint states that, when a sector is managing its balance sheet by reallocating its financial assets (liabilities), the sum of all the net claims (commitments) it wishes to hold (undertake) must equal its net wealth (debt). In SFC models, as in Yale models, both stock and flow constraints are respected for all sectors, hence their name.

The third feature, *several assets and rates of return*, refers to the use of Tobinian portolio choices in order to model the behaviour of financial markets. In SFC models, agents decide to allocate their wealth between various assets so that: (a) the demand for each asset varies positively with its own real rate of return and negatively with the rates of other assets (that is, assets are imperfect substitutes); (b) stock constraint requirements are fulfilled (any increase in wealth is allocated to some asset and any increase in the demand for a particular asset is met by a compensating reduction in demand for some other asset). This Tobinian representation of financial markets became over the years a key component of all Stone-inspired macroeconomic models that deal with financial markets. However it is usually rejected by other model builders because problems of collinearity among asset rates of return make the econometric estimation of asset demand functions problematic.

The fourth feature, *precision regarding time*, corresponds to the idea that the short-run determination of macroeconomic variables is one among several steps of a dynamic sequence, not a repetitive equilibrium in which the economy settles. Therefore macroeconomic models have to be conceived as dynamic systems. In SFC models, business cycles stem from the interaction between *stocks* of assets and monetary *flows*. One can describe the SFC representation of economic cycles through a 'predator–prey' metaphor based on a closed natural system with foxes (predators) and rabbits (prey). Fluctuations in both species' populations (though of course subject to exogenous shocks) are generated endogenously by the combination of reproduction and predation mechanisms. Moreover, an increase in the number of foxes will reduce the number of rabbits, which in turn will have a negative impact on the future number of predators. This means that to represent properly the dynamic behaviour of a given economic system the SFC methodology takes account of the fundamental principle that current economic flows modify the levels of existing stocks of real and financial assets, which in turn have an impact on agents' economic behaviour and future economic flows.

The last feature, *modelling of financial and monetary policy operations*, states that a macroeconomic model should describe in detail how the stocks of the various financial assets are supplied to the economy by monetary authorities and the government. With regard to this point SFC models are Tobinian in spirit but not in form. Yale portfolio models did indeed use a conventional LM closure that assumes an exogenous money supply and represents the interest rate as the price emerging from the money market equilibrium. On the contrary SFC models use a Post Keynesian closure where money is supplied endogenously by the central bank and the latter sets the level of the key interest rate. Such a closure is more consistent with contemporary macroeconomics, since most economists now agree on the fact that central banks use the interest rate as their policy variable and pay little attention to monetary aggregates.

Although SFC models are built in accordance with Tobin's principles, they 'trek along paths that were not suggested by [Yale models], paths that generally have a post-Keynesian flavour' (Godley and Lavoie 2007, pp. 12–13). For this reason, the common view is that the theoretical framework of SFC models is closer to the New Cambridge models developed by Godley and Cripps (1983) in order to analyse, among other issues, the consequences of the balance-of-payments problems of the United Kingdom. As their name indicates, these models were deeply rooted in the Cambridge tradition of economics. However these applied models were based on a very basic accounting framework. The latter was reduced to the identity which says that, measured in current prices, the government's budget deficit less the current account deficit is equal, by definition, to private saving minus investment (an accounting identity put in evidence by Michał Kalecki). As such, these models have in fact little in common with Godley's (1999) model, a purely theoretical construct that aims to illustrate the behaviour of a *monetary production economy* with a complex institutional structure comprising households, (non-financial) firms, banks and the government (including the central bank). A few years later Lavoie and Godley (2001–02) incorporated further Kaleckian and Kaldorian elements into the core structure of this model and produced a Post Keynesian growth model that is now considered as the archetypal SFC model; a theoretical model built in accordance with the five features of the Yale approach and whose behavioural equations and closure are chosen in reference to Post Keynesian economics. Among the Post Keynesian concepts that are integrated into the equations of SFC models, one can mention for instance the principle of effective demand, endogenous money, imperfect information, cost-plus pricing, Kaleckian capacity utilization and profits, liquidity preference and procedural rationality.

Although they were not inspired directly by Godley's New Cambridge models nor by Lavoie's Post Keynesian insights, at least two modern research programmes based on the Stone–Tobin methodology fit with the definition of an SFC model given above: Lance Taylor's (2004) theoretical structuralist models on one side, and the Keynes–Metzler–Goodwin

(KMG) family of models developed by Carl Chiarella and Peter Flaschel (2000) on the other. Both types of models trace their intellectual roots to Kalecki, Nicholas Kaldor and Keynes, so that the real difference with Godley and Lavoie's models is not to be found at the level of the theoretical assumptions but rather at the level of the period length used for writing the models and studying their properties. Most of the SFC models are indeed written in discrete time and thus are not solved analytically but simply studied through computing simulations. On the contrary, Taylor and Flaschel's models favour the use of models written in continuous time and solved analytically in order to study macroeconomic issues.

TARIK MOUAKIL

See also:

Econometrics; Effective Demand; Kaldorian Economics; Kaleckian Economics; Liquidity Preference; Prices and Pricing.

References

Backus, D., W. Brainard, G. Smith and J. Tobin (1980), 'A model of U.S. financial and non-financial economic behavior', *Journal of Money, Credit and Banking*, **12** (2), 259–93.

Chiarella, C. and P. Flaschel (2000), *The Dynamics of Keynesian Monetary Growth: Macro Foundations*, Cambridge: Cambridge University Press.

Godley, W. (1999), 'Money and credit in a Keynesian model of income determination', *Cambridge Journal of Economics*, **23** (4), 393–411.

Godley, W. and F. Cripps (1983), *Macroeconomics*, London: Fontana.

Godley, W. and M. Lavoie (2007), *Monetary Economics: An Integrated Approach to Credit, Money, Income, Production and Wealth*, Basingstoke: Palgrave Macmillan.

Lavoie, M. and W. Godley (2001–02), 'Kaleckian models of growth in a coherent stock–flow monetary framework: a Kaldorian view', *Journal of Post Keynesian Economics*, **24** (2), 277–311.

Taylor, L. (2004), *Reconstructing Macroeconomics: Structuralist Proposals and Critiques of the Mainstream*, Cambridge, MA: Harvard University Press.

Tobin, J. (1982), 'Money and the macroeconomic process', *Journal of Money, Credit and Banking*, **14** (2), 171–204.

Zezza, G. and C. Dos Santos (2004), 'The role of monetary policy in Post-Keynesian stock–flow consistent macroeconomic growth models', in M. Lavoie and M. Seccareccia (eds), *Central Banking in the Modern World: Alternative Perspectives*, Cheltenham, UK and Northampton, MA, USA: Edward Elgar, pp. 183–208.

Sustainable Development

Sustainable development as a concept came into common usage with the contemporaneous publication of the 'Bruntland Report' (WCED 1987) and the environment pamphlet from the World Bank (1987). In a general popular sense, sustainable development refers to economic development which 'meets the needs of the present without compromising the ability of future generations to meet their own needs' (WCED 1987, p. 8). Many

actions can be implemented in aiming towards this sustainable development concept by people, organizations (especially businesses) and governments, including energy efficiency, recycling, reduced planned obsolescence
and improved mass public transport. All such actions have been dubbed
'green' and can significantly address the climate change challenge that was
conclusively acknowledged in the 2007 report of the Intergovernmental
Panel on Climate Change (IPCC). Thus this concept deals with policy
action for future path(s) of economic systems.

This entry addresses broadly how economic development can be 'sustainable' (leaving the microeconomic issues of natural resource policy
and environmental economics to another entry in this book). From a
Post Keynesian perspective, Vercelli (1998, p. 268) specifies a viable policy
definition which states that economic development can be 'considered
sustainable only when future generations are guaranteed a set of options
at least as wide as that possessed by the current generation'. The power
of this definition is that as a policy guide it underscores the need to keep
viable options open; otherwise there is a danger of path dependence (or
'lock-in') on strategies that may turn out to be unsustainable in the future.
For example, adopting any renewable energy car (for example, electric,
hydrogen cell) as the major transport option prevents consideration of
alternative, possibly more viable configurations than the 'personal car/road
network' system. As Winnett (2005, p. 92) argues cogently, '[w]hat society
acquires by keeping options open is not just the negative avoidance of bad
outcomes but also the positive good of maintaining options for future
learning as more information accrues'.

Despite the excellent Vercelli starting-point, and given that it is supposedly a 'broad church', there is precious little Post Keynesian theoretical discussion of this concept or policy guidance related to it (Berr
2009). Ric Holt, in a series of papers – the latest is Holt (2009) – details
the relevance of Post Keynesian analysis for sustainable development.
Mearman (2009) has tried to explain, using survey and interviews, why
Post Keynesians have 'inadequately dealt' with environmental issues.
Acknowledging their lack of expertise and interest in the myriad of
micro-environment issues, this does not absolve them from their non-
contribution to the macroeconomic systems-based sustainable development issue. However, as the Post Keynesian approach emerged out
of concern with unemployment, there seems to be a view that any
consideration of this issue will be through trade-off with employment.
Geoffrey Harcourt responded to Mearman's inquiry with the view that
historically the 'Great Depression', and huge concomitant unemployment, was the major issue that shaped the pioneers' approach. To
consider themselves relevant to the major issues of the day, the massive

climate change challenge needs to engage Post Keynesians in the debate on the way to expunge the 'so-called' employment–environment trade-off. This entry aims to connect this challenge with the historical roots of the pioneers, identify constructive elements of such an effort, and use the standard Keynesian aggregate demand function to pull together the limited research effort that has been conducted mostly in the past decade. Hopefully, out of this will come an effort to construct a coherent and unified Post Keynesian theory of sustainable development which intersects with the theory of growth (in advanced economies) and the theory of development (in less developed economies). Michał Kalecki was a significant contributor to both theories; thus this entry ends with some reflective suggestions along Kaleckian lines.

Berr (2009) presents a persuasive history of thought account that Keynes's philosophy has elements in common with operationalizing sustainable development by the 'strong sustainability' rule in which natural (capital) resources are not substitutable with man-made (capital) resources. This non-substitutability is counter to neoclassical economists' monetary valuation of the environment, which enables all production factors, including natural capital, to be substitutable at high enough prices. Keynes recognizes that economic value is disconnected from ecological values, and irreversibility of historical time leads to fundamental uncertainty with a need for precaution in decision making. His view, expressed to Roy Harrod, that the practice of discounting future values is 'a polite expression for rapacity and the conquest of reason by passion' (Vercelli 1998, p. 266) fuses both his ethical and probabilistic concerns with entrepreneurial actions being justified by economists' modelling. This provides a basis for Post Keynesians to initiate a unique effective demand and cyclical instability framework towards the sustainable development debate that is acutely absent at present. As Berr (2009) notes, Keynes's underestimation of natural resources and the power of vested interests to use economics to justify their actions points to Kalecki as the other pioneer who can inspire this framework for a deeper and stronger Post Keynesian sustainability analysis.

Kalecki, during the Second World War at the Oxford Institute of Statistics, worked with E.F. (Fritz) Schumacher (of *Small is Beautiful* fame) on postwar reconstruction, with emphasis on the capitalist periphery of Europe. This was a pragmatic effort in combining the theories of growth and development for a broad sustainability objective. However, they recognized the limits of capitalism when recovering from the ravages of war. Together they wrote a paper on continued draining of liquid reserves by surplus countries under proposed US and UK international clearing regimes. Kalecki also identified limits in developed countries to full employment, and limits in less developed countries due to insufficient productive capacities. The response to these limits is demand-side perspective planning with what Sachs (1996) calls 'variant thinking'. This is 'a set of procedures to promote the societal debate on the "project", to stimulate the social imagination' (ibid., 1996, p. 318). Sachs co-authored a paper with Kalecki on foreign aid, and has since developed this Kaleckian approach to planning and development with 'environmental prudence' in many papers and books. What emerges is a 'designing rationality' over historical time, in which the consequences of decisions taken in the recent past crucially influence future rational decisions. In this way structural transformation to an ecologically sustainable society comes from the planning and development process.

A few specific analyses and policies developed by that rare breed of Post Keynesian 'strong sustainability' pioneers exist, but often with no reference or linkage to the other works, and not within some broad sustainability transformation as established above. These pioneers are all working 'in the dark'. Brief outlines of these works are described using, as the organizing agenda, the Keynesian aggregate demand function of consumption, investment, government and trade (and development).

Consumption has been a significant problem for sustainability ever since J.K. Galbraith's *The Affluent Society* (1958) and Vance Packard's *The Waste Makers* (1960), with Marc Lavoie tying the bits together to form the Post Keynesian lexicographic ordering of consumer choice. Lavoie (2009) explores the implications of income boundaries to consuming specific class of goods and services depending on the level of need/desire. Such demand constraint limits price- and incentive-based substitution effects, opening up possibilities through income effects to adopt public policies that can reduce certain classes of consumption goods and/or services that through designing rationality are considered unsustainable. Jespersen (2004) applies tradable work permits equally to all employed persons as a first step to sustainable development, reducing average working hours with unchanged real income. This introduces an equality-based environmental constraint, limiting higher-order foreign goods and replacing them with lower-order domestic goods. This re-orders priorities, and over time these permits can be lowered if required. Work permits has links to a standard Post Keynesian policy tool of incomes policy, when in the early 1990s Gowdy (1991) and Mathieu (1993) proposed a negative income tax linked to sustainability to limit conspicuous consumption and provide 'ecobonuses' for low carbon emissions. Reviewing this incomes policy suggestion, Ozay Mehmet (1995) shows how it can create employment, thus revoking the employment–environment trade-off. The problem is that all these articles were published in *Ecological Economics*, and so no doubt were missed by most Post Keynesians. A 'ghetto' problem remains in the heterodox economics communities.

Investment continues to remain, as Kalecki called it, the *pièce de résistance* of economics, and even more so when one appreciates that investment drives business cycles and the resulting capital stock delivers long-term structural change. Since the Industrial Revolution, investment has powered the economically unstable and ecologically unsustainable trajectory of accumulation and growth. Galbraith in *The Affluent Society* recognized environmental degradation and identified investment in infrastructure and technology as elements in this degradation. Using a Kaleckian accumulation framework, Courvisanos (2009a) explains how investment has been the demand-based 'adaptation mechanism' that directed supply-based innovation into historically unstable path-dependent economic development, and has been preserved by monopoly capitalism's structure of production (*à la* Baran and Sweezy). This is the fount of the Post Keynesian investment analysis of sustainable development. In effect, just as earlier technological revolutions (steam, electricity, energy) delivered the 'wealth of nations' through the accumulation process, so investment in 'eco-innovation' – defined as environment-informed and -driven knowledge-based activities that reduce net environmental impacts – needs to deliver the entrepreneurial opportunity for a path to sustainable development. Based on the growth path analysis conducted by Adolph Lowe, Courvisanos (2009b) argues that market-based economic regions or nations lack relevant ecologically supportive physical and social infrastructure. Thus there is insufficient order and coherence to impel the creation of, and the market demand for, eco-innovation by the private sector on its own.

In the two-sided Kaleckian investment framework, profits are expected as a result of investment commitments, and the retained profits from prior investment enable future investment. Inadequate profits from eco-innovation severely limit this Kaleckian cycle. Coherence in sustainability needs large undertakings of both private and public investment in eco-innovation, both physical and knowledge-based activities. Physical investment needs to be in areas that support strong sustainability, but currently lack technological embeddedness and a market niche to secure adequate funding. Knowledge (or intangible) investment needs to cover the wide gamut of activities that require patient and long-term funding, notably R&D, education, training, learning and development systems and property rights regulation. In a series of papers – the latest is Courvisanos (2009b) – an eco-sustainable framework is set out as a policy guide for a public–private sector cooperative process of innovation and investment that underpins appropriate satisficing paths to sustainable development. The satisficing approach adopts what Vercelli (1998) calls adaptive

procedural (or bounded) rationality, which involves cumulative and itera-
tive social learning with the investment commitments in the short run
developing over time strong market share and effective demand for eco-
innovations. Acceptable adaptive non-optimal conventions and rules are
required to be incorporated in the investment decisions by both public and
private organizations in a 'mixed economy' (for example, Kalecki's lower
real depreciation and better utilization resources coefficients). Finally,
Kalecki's (1992) perspective planning allows short-term adjustments along
the Lowe path of instrumental analysis.

Governments can use fiscal policy to stimulate sustainable development.
Despite this instrument being an obviously quite powerful Post Keynesian
form of intervention, there has been very little formal theoretical research
conducted linking fiscal policy to sustainable development. At the policy
and practice level, left-Keynesian green political economy has emerged in
the early part of the twenty-first century with strong active fiscal policy
prescriptions of infrastructure investment, tax credits, loan guarantees and
carbon pricing (tax or cap-and-trade) aimed at shifting economies away
from the dominant oil-based heavy pollution, high-carbon industrial structure. The 2008–10 global financial crisis provided a strong focus around
the concept of a 'green new deal' as the basis of government stimulus out
of deep recession. The UK New Economics Foundation was the first off
the mark (July 2008) in coining this term, followed quickly by the United
Nations Environment Programme (UNEP) and the European Green
parties. In the same way, the Political Economy Research Institute (PERI)
at the University of Massachusetts–Amherst, led by Robert Pollin, has
concentrated on providing a set of programmes for building a clean-energy
US economy while creating employment and reducing poverty.

None of the above left-Keynesian green political economy initiatives,
or the recently established *International Journal of Green Economics*, have
been incorporated into a Post Keynesian theoretical structure. The one
specific exception is the work of researchers linked to the University of
Missouri–Kansas City, led by Mathew Forstater who, in a series of papers
– the latest is Forstater (2006) – has explained how green jobs can be created
using the countercyclical policy of the state as employer of last resort (discussed in other entries). Public sector jobs can be designed to support the
Lowe–Kalecki eco-sustainable framework. The jobs would be designed
based on functional financing to avoid structural bottlenecks in a market
economy, using 'appropriate technology' (for example, recycling, recondi-
tioning, energy-saving refitting, rooftop gardening, electric van pooling)
and provide skilling-up to work, and consume and live in an ecologically
sustainable society. This fiscal approach again discredits the mainstream
employment–environment trade-off argument, and chapters by Mitchell

and Watts (2009) and Tcherneva (2009) develop this functional finance for sustainability in more detail. Also, from the alternative Kaleckian balanced budget fiscal approach, Courvisanos et al. (2009) outline a tax on greenhouse gases, allied with fiscal incentives for entrepreneurs to accelerate obsolescence of existing high greenhouse gas emissions capital stock and undertake eco-innovation in new low emissions technological investment. This can have a similar countercyclical effect, while adopting an environmental tax would assist in structural change to sustainable development.

International trade through the balance-of-payments constraint on growth has been a significant area of Post Keynesian research, yet the implications of this for sustainable development have not been investigated. There is potential for research in this aspect, along with Kaleckian income distribution effects, to examine international trade which is currently 'rigged against the poor' (Sachs 2004, p. 1809). Two Kalecki-influenced scholars have begun to develop a trade and development link to sustainable development. Lance Taylor with A.K. Dutt and J.M. Rao, in a 10-year World Institute for Development Economics Research project (Taylor 1996), indicate that income distributional improvements can lower import intensity in less developed economies and ease constraints on balance of payments. Ignacy Sachs (2004, p. 1803) goes further by stating that: 'import-sensitivity stems from the structure of the national economy. It does not depend on the degree of economic openness and on the relative share of foreign trade in GDP.' Sachs points to conspicuous consumption of urban elites in less developed countries supporting a public administration and state that are parasitical. Sachs develops a Kaleckian perspective planning approach for import of crucial inputs in a 'mixed economy' form to create a socially inclusive, environmentally sustainable and economically sustained development process. This aims to create social and eco-efficient domestic industries, especially exploring competitive strengths in their country's biodiversity, such that employment elasticity of growth becomes a variable – not a parameter – in development planning towards full employment.

At the beginning of this entry, the problem of a unified Post Keynesian sustainability approach was identified. The suggestion is that a framework around the Kaleckian elements discussed above provides a unique contribution, but only in concert with other heterodox work on sustainability. The evolutionary school's approach to sustainability via innovation policies is well developed, and is discussed in Courvisanos (2009b). Significant pragmatic policies for fostering technological and knowledge-based innovation have been developed at the micro- and meso-economic levels, but they need to be incorporated into an effective demand–income distribution macroeconomic model that will counter the austerity-bound neoliberal global regime. 'Global Keynesianism' and sustainability is a world-systems perspective that, Köhler (1999) deduces, lends itself to integration with Post Keynesian analysis, so that globalization processes can be tackled, beginning with exchange rate reform (which has been one area of Post Keynesian interest stemming from monetary theory). Finally, all this needs to be modelled with complex sustainability dynamics, as suggested by Rosser and Rosser (2006).

JERRY COURVISANOS

See also:

Balance-of-payments-constrained Economic Growth; Consumer Theory; Employer of Last Resort; Environmental Economics; Full Employment; Galbraith's Economics; Innovation; International Economics; Investment; Kaleckian Economics, Technology and Innovation; Unemployment.

References

Berr, E. (2009), 'Keynes and sustainable development', *International Journal of Political Economy*, **38** (3), 22–38.
Courvisanos, J. (2009a), 'Political aspects of innovation', *Research Policy*, **38** (7), 1117–24.
Courvisanos, J. (2009b), 'Optimise versus satisfice: two approaches to an investment policy for sustainable development', in R.F. Holt, S. Pressman and C.L. Spash (eds), *Post Keynesian and Ecological Economics: Confronting Environmental Issues*, Cheltenham, UK and Northampton, MA, USA: Edward Elgar, pp. 279–300.
Courvisanos, J., A.J. Laramie and D. Mair (2009), 'Tax policy and innovation: a search for common ground', *Intervention: European Journal of Economics and Economic Policies*, **6** (2), 271–87.
Forstater, M. (2006), 'Green jobs: public service employment and environmental sustainability', *Challenge*, **49** (4), 58–72.
Gowdy, J. (1991), 'Bioeconomics and Post Keynesian economics: a search for common ground', *Ecological Economics*, **3** (1), 77–87.
Holt, R.F. (2009), 'The relevance of post-Keynesian economics to sustainable development', in P. Lawn (ed.), *Environment and Employment: A Reconciliation*, Abingdon and New York: Routledge, pp. 146–59.
Jespersen, J. (2004), 'Macroeconomic stability: sustainable development and full employment', in L. Reisch and I. Røpke (eds), *The Ecological Economics of Consumption*, Cheltenham, UK and Northampton, MA, USA: Edward Elgar, pp. 233–49.
Kalecki, M. (1992), 'Outline of a method of constructing a perspective plan (based on Polish experience)', in J. Osiatyński (ed.), *Collected Works of Michał Kalecki, Volume III: Socialism – Functioning and Long-run Planning*, Oxford: Clarendon Press, pp. 221–31 [originally published in Polish in 1962].
Köhler, G. (1999), 'Global Keynesianism and beyond', *Journal of World-Systems Research*, **V** (2), 253–74.
Lavoie, M. (2009), 'Post Keynesian consumer choice theory and ecological economics', in R.F. Holt, S. Pressman and C.L. Spash (eds), *Post Keynesian and Ecological Economics: Confronting Environmental Issues*, Cheltenham, UK and Northampton, MA, USA: Edward Elgar, pp. 141–57.
Mathieu, K.-H. (1993), 'Bioeconomics and Post Keynesian economics: a search for common ground', *Ecological Economics*, **8** (1), 11–16.
Mearman, A. (2009), 'Why have Post-Keynesians (perhaps) inadequately dealt with issues related to the environment?', in P. Lawn (ed.), *Environment and Employment: A Reconciliation*, Abingdon and New York: Routledge, pp. 97–125.

Mehmet, O. (1995), 'Employment creation and green development strategy', *Ecological Economics*, **15** (1), 11–19.

Mitchell, W. and M. Watts (2009), 'A comparison of the macroeconomic consequences of basic income and job guarantee schemes', in P. Lawn (ed.), *Environment and Employment: A Reconciliation*, Abingdon and New York: Routledge, pp. 206–23.

Rosser, J.B. Jr and M.V. Rosser (2006), 'Institutional evolution of environmental management under global economic growth', *Journal of Economic Issues*, **40** (2), 421–9.

Sachs, I. (1996), 'What state, what markets, for what development? The social, ecological and economical dimensions of planning', *Social Indicators Research*, **39** (3), 311–20.

Sachs, I. (2004), 'From poverty trap to inclusive development in LDCs', *Economic and Political Weekly*, **39** (18), 1802–11.

Taylor, L. (1996), 'Sustainable development: an introduction', *World Development*, **24** (2), 215–25.

Tcherneva, P. (2009), 'Evaluating the economic and environmental viability of basic income and job guarantees', in P. Lawn (ed.), *Environment and Employment: A Reconciliation*, Abingdon and New York: Routledge, pp. 184–205.

Vercelli, A. (1998), 'Sustainable development, rationality and time', in S. Faucheux, M. O'Connor and J. van der Straaten (eds), *Sustainable Development: Concepts, Rationalities and Strategies*, Dordrecht: Kluwer Academic Publishers, pp. 259–76.

Winnett, A. (2005), 'Natural capital: hard economics, soft metaphor?', *Environmental Education Research*, **11** (1), 83–94.

World Bank (1987), *Environment, Growth and Development*, World Bank Development Committee Pamphlet 14, Washington, DC.

World Commission on Environment and Development (WCED) (1987), *Our Common Future*, Oxford: Oxford University Press.

Technology and Innovation

Technical change and innovation are at present considered determining factors of competitiveness and economic growth. However, economic literature has not always considered technology and economic dynamics to be an analytical priority. It has been in the last few decades when theoretical and empirical research has started to pay special attention to the study of this connection.

There exists a consensus in all schools of thought as to the positive effect that technical change has on economic growth. The difference between the various schools lies mainly in the way of understanding how and via which mechanisms technical change affects economic growth. Thus, in the case of Robert Solow's neoclassical model, technical change is considered to be an exogenous variable. This exogenous nature means that his model will only be valid for the purpose of describing the effects of innovation on companies and growth, but will not be able to explain the process by which innovation takes place. In the New Neoclassical theory of economic growth, the idea of exogeneity in terms of innovation develops into an endogenous variable.

To understand how the Post Keynesian school ties in with the study of innovation and technical change, one needs to previously establish some of the core ideas that characterize this paradigm of thought.

Post Keynesian theory assumes that economic agents operate within an environment characterized by the existence of uncertainty, thus rejecting the perfect information hypothesis contained in neoclassical theory. The presence of uncertainty compels one to work with the concept of historical time, as opposed to the concept of logical time – which is predominant in neoclassical equilibrium models. This means that the economic process is conceived as an evolutionary process that is subject to ruptures of a structural nature. The idea of *normal times* which appears in works by Keynes can be identified with the idea of stability associated with an institutional configuration that may temporarily help to control tensions generated by interactions among agents (Ferreiro and Serrano 2009). In other words, stability in terms of relationships between variables concealed by the concept of logical time is always a result rather than a starting-point for economic analysis.

It is clear that among the many variables that can have a bearing on economic dynamics, technical change is one of the most relevant. Its effects on the productivity of the workforce and, as a corollary, on profits and therefore on investment and economic growth, make it one of the determining aspects in understanding the dynamics of market economics.

Indeed, the macroeconomic theory of Post Keynesian inspiration has had a special bearing on our understanding of how innovation interacts with economic growth while none the less avoiding the microeconomic dimension, that is, the study of those factors that have a bearing on the development of innovative activity. The evolutionary school, however, which shares some of the methodological keys to Post Keynesian thought, may help to cover this microeconomic dimension.

Joan Robinson lays down the foundations for a conceptualization of technical change in the Post Keynesian theory of economic growth. Technical change is considered to be an exogenous variable. However, by relating it to investment, it takes on an 'endogenous' dimension in the sense that technical change is the result of the search on the part of companies for cheaper and more efficient means of production. Robinson also considers technical change to act as a stimulus for investment. One of the restrictions of the Robinson model is that it works with the hypothesis that the economy finds itself in a situation in which its production capacity is being fully exploited.

Nicholas Kaldor, for his part, admits that technical progress is both the cause and the result of economic growth, although he does not concern himself with explaining the process via which technical change comes about. His analysis is based on the notion of *circular causation*, according to which a higher growth rate gives rise to a higher rate of technical progress and, in turn, the latter has an influence on the growth rate. The Kaldor model also evidences a major restriction, which is that it assumes that the economy is in a situation of full employment.

Michał Kalecki also considered the fact that basic innovations were essentially exogenous, at least for the part of the economy he attempted to explain, that is, for the study of the impact of basic (exogenous) innovations in investment cycles in the economy. Kalecki's model, like those of Robinson and Kaldor, also has no bearing on the microeconomic dimension of innovation. More specifically, he studies the relationship between investment, the economic cycle and economic growth. He considers that when an innovation takes place, this has a positive effect on investment, which in turn influences the economic cycle and therefore economic growth. According to Kalecki, technical change permits an increase in profits of a temporary nature, albeit sufficient for the purpose of generating increases in effective demand that will promote economic growth. He also recognizes Kaldor's causal relationship, according to which the investment rate determines the innovation rate. However, for Kalecki, the endogenous nature acquired by innovation in this sequence has an important side-effect, and is explained by small improvements or adaptations made to existing capital resources. For him, it is the economic cycle itself that induces innovation processes. A central feature of the study of long-term growth in Kalecki is that it relaxes some of the restrictions that appear in the Kaldor and Robinson models, as part of the assumption that the economy operates in general terms with underutilization of the capital stock, and that the possibility exists of full employment not being attained.

Recently, some authors (Courvisanos and Verspagen 2002; Courvisanos 2009) have attempted to make advances in developing a new framework for analysing innovation within the Post Keynesian paradigm, by supporting the approaches taken by Kalecki and the neo-Schumpeterian school. These works open up new lines of research in which innovation may be of an endogenous nature and, via this hypothesis, help to explain economic dynamics. At the same time and given the essentially microeconomic nature of the neo-Schumpeterian economy, this might be able to contribute basic micro-economic principles to Post Keynesian macroeconomic models.

Evolutionary economics (Nelson and Winter 1982) has developed some theoretical elements related to innovative activity that are consistent with Post Keynesian approaches. This theory has given rise to a large amount of literature, above all of an empirical nature, making its interest manifestly clear in understanding real processes. Evolutionary approaches are inspired by works by Joseph Schumpeter, although they keep their distance from his approaches, considering themselves to be attached to the neo-Schumpeterian school.

Evolutionary theory, like Post Keynesian theory, rejects the concept of neoclassical equilibrium; rather it emphasizes the idea of the *dynamic process*. The economy, from the evolutionary standpoint, is perceived as a system that is continually being disturbed by technological change. Structural changes and, in the last analysis, economic growth, would be the result of an explosion of substantially new technologies in the economic system.

Evolutionary thought considers innovation and technological progress to be *endogenous processes* and the main drivers of economic growth. The innovation process is considered to be the result of strategic decisions taken by the company, by means of which it decides – in an uncertain world – as to which resources it wishes to set aside for the development of new processes and products. This endogenous concept of innovation is reinforced by the idea that innovation is an *accumulative* learning process in the sense that the innovators of today are more likely to become the innovators of the future.

Another feature associated with the innovation process in the evolutionary paradigm is its *uncertain* nature. The transfer of knowledge to new products and processes does not follow a linear and sequential path from the basic research stage to applied research and the market, as neoclassical theory proclaims. The path to innovation is *unpredictable* and is characterized by complex feedback mechanisms among diverse agents. Among these players, the market is included as one more agent that helps define the type of innovation that is going to take place. Demand recovers a space within this framework which was denied it by the neoclassical context, ensuring that all responsibility for innovation falls on centres that produce science and technology.

This way of understanding innovation processes and technical change places the importance of institutions at the heart of the analysis in order to explain economic dynamics. Institutions intervene in the economic system as guarantors of a set of rules that act as a framework for the courses of action taken by agents and reduce the uncertainty associated with innovation. The institutional framework defined as such manages to contain company dynamics over a period of time. However, there comes a time when the technical change experiences advances which are so fast and so radical that they may help to break this framework. The establishment of a new institutional framework adapted to new conditions that emerge might help to re-establish an equilibrium.

The concept of logical time would be compatible with the institutional framework that facilitates the containment of innovative dynamics and enables a certain equilibrium to exist in the economic system. The structural crisis would enable profit rates to recover. The *normal times* idea is consistent with the existence of a stable technical change dynamic within a specific institutional framework. When there is a rupture in the institutional structures, the pressure generated by technical change in order to repair profit rates finds itself in contradiction with the current institutional framework. At the present time, we might be witnessing a similar situation to the one described, in which it was noted that the framework of labour relations – which helped over previous decades to contain the predominant innovative dynamic during that stage – started to break down. This breakdown is giving rise to a situation involving a structural rupture that demands reflection on change that needs to take place within the framework of labour relations, in order for it to be compatible with the innovative activity of modern times.

Post Keynesian macroeconomic models recognize the importance of innovation and technology for economic growth. However, Post Keynesian thought has not placed innovation at the heart of its analysis. The main interest in Post Keynesian works has been the study of the connection between investment and economic growth and, in some cases, the study of this relationship has been enriched by incorporating innovation as an essentially exogenous variable.

There also exists a substantial rupture in Post Keynesian economics, between its macroeconomic models that recognize innovation and the rare microeconomic models existing that are still unable to explain it. Given the interest on the part of Post Keynesian economics in reflecting on reality and studying real problems, it would appear sensible to consider that the Post Keynesian theory should delve more into an analysis of innovation – on both a macro- and a microeconomic level. Evolutionary economics might be able to constitute a major reference point for making advances in knowledge of endogenous innovation processes, as this school accepts much of the original elements of the Post Keynesian vision. Schumpeterian models might also help to equip the macroeconomic Post Keynesian approach with basic microeconomic fundamentals.

AMAIA ALTUZARRA

See also:

Business Cycles; Growth Theory; Innovation; Institutionalism; Investment; Joan Robinson's Economics; Kaldorian Economics; Uncertainty.

References

Courvisanos, J. (2009), 'Political aspects of innovation', *Research Policy*, **38** (7), 1117–24.
Courvisanos, J. and B. Verspagen (2002), 'Innovation and investment in capitalist economies 1870–2000: Kaleckian dynamics and evolutionary life cycles', paper presented to the Seventh International Post Keynesian Workshop, University of Missouri, Kansas City, USA, 29 June–3 July.
Ferreiro, J. and F. Serrano (2009), 'Institutions, expectations and aggregate demand', in G. Fontana and M. Setterfield (eds), *Macroeconomic Theory and Macroeconomic Pedagogy*, Basingstoke: Palgrave Macmillan, pp. 309–22.
Nelson, R.R. and S.G. Winter (1982), *An Evolutionary Theory of Economic Change*, Cambridge, MA: Belknap Press of Harvard University Press.

Time in Economic Theory

Conventional (neoclassical) economics allows no place for time in the sense of a historical, unidirectional process. While Alfred Marshall observed that time was 'the source of many of the greatest difficulties in economics' (*Principles of Economics*, 8th edn, p. 92), neither he nor his descendants were able to incorporate meaningful time into their theory. Equilibrium analysis, whether of a partial or a Walrasian form, must be of an atemporal nature. Contrary to textbook authorities, the short and long runs of neoclassical theory do not refer to the passage of historic (calendar) time, but are mere analytic concepts that allow 'time enough' for whatever logically needs to happen to permit the equilibrium outcomes intrinsic to the argument to unfold. In the general equilibrium world, time is essentially excluded from the theory because everything happens simultaneously – there is no process or sequence of events taking place over real time. Further, reading time out of the argument opens the door to 'plastic capital' or 'putty', thus sidestepping the problems associated with real investment decisions in a real economy where accumulation is the main objective of those decisions. A machine is not a machine produced in real time with specific technological characteristics, but simply a lump of putty that can be manipulated to conform to the equilibrium requirements of the moment. 'Putty investment . . . can be undone and squeezed into another form while still representing the same "quantity of capital"' (Robinson 1980, p. 51).

Various attempts have been made to deal with time in a more realistic fashion, but still retain the notion of equilibrium states to which the economy is always tending. Such efforts, since they are contained within an equilibrium framework, must reduce time to some non-historic meaning: economic actions must be reversible and the future must be knowable if equilibrium outcomes are to obtain. As the neoclassical equilibrium argument is of a mechanical nature, similar to the inner workings of a clock-like machine, one can trace the sequence of events through a system of interconnected variables (gears) in any direction: a deterministic outcome will always obtain and no 'arrow of time' is permitted by the argument. Hicks's 'weeks' are not to be confused with the passage of real time (Hicks 1939). Week 2 does not historically follow week 1, because the equilibrium adjustment process undergone in week 1 could just as logically follow that of week 2: 'weeks' are interchangeable. And, if actions are reversible and the future knowable, any expectations admitted in this theory (if the assumption of full information is dropped) must also be reversible. There can be no fundamental uncertainty in the sense that we simply do not know what the future state(s) will be. At best, uncertainty is seen as probabilistic risk, the calculation of which requires knowledge of that future.

While recent developments within the neoclassical framework may seem to incorporate time, this is illusory. The 'New Neoclassical Synthesis' (Goodfriend and King 1997), for example, does feature intertemporal modelling, and does include what appear to be expectations and uncertainty in the Keynesian sense. However, such theoretical work remains bound by equilibrium considerations and thus, cannot embrace real, historical time, and uncertainty in a Keynesian sense disappears: 'I assume *complete financial markets*, that is, that available financial assets completely span the relevant uncertainty faced by households about future income, prices, taste shocks, and so on' (Woodford 2003, p. 64; emphasis in original). In other words, the future is known and markets in the present can and (under specified conditions) *will* adjust accordingly. In a recent work dedicated to demonstrating why modern neoclassicism is more realistic and more theoretically sound than that of past decades in which a 'sterile, mechanistic, view of human nature and a reductionist vision of society' dominated (Coyle 2007, p. 5), there is no index entry for time, uncertainty, expectations or money.

For mainstream theorists then, time is simply an intellectual construct developed to conform to the equilibrium requirements of the theory itself. Assumptions of perfect knowledge of past, present and future states – where there are no disappointed expectations in the past and where the future is known – 'emasculate the very concepts of time and uncertainty in economics' (Davidson 1978, p. 14). But, '(a)s soon as the uncertainty of the expectations that guide economic behaviour is admitted, equilibrium drops out of the argument and history takes its place' (Robinson 1980, p. 48).

For Keynes, and those economists who follow his lead, time is of crucial importance in understanding the workings of a monetary (capitalist) economy, and is inextricably linked to *fundamental* uncertainty and to money itself. Economic processes occur in real time, where actions taken today that cannot be undone have unknowable consequences for the future. In particular, in this form of economic organization, contractual relations are of utmost economic significance, and contracts are written in calendar time. This position contains the essential Post Keynesian criticism of neoclassical equilibrium analysis: since adjustment processes necessitate change, and change can take place only in real time, by the time the logical process leading to equilibrium could work itself out, the conditions on which the equilibrium outcome was specified have all been altered. No deterministic outcome is possible: 'economic decisions are made by human beings facing an uncertain and unpredictable future while they are moving away from a fixed and *irreversible past*' (Davidson 1991, p. 32; original italics). For Keynes, neoclassical equilibrium analysis was just a 'pretty, polite technique which tries to deal with the present by abstracting from the fact that we know very little about the future' (Keynes 1936 [1987], p. 115). (For some purposes Keynes did employ a concept of logical time, but such usage was confined to countering standard theory's arguments on its own terms or in establishing preliminary statements identifying various causal relations; this is of little interest in analysing his general theory, which is conducted in historical time; see Robinson 1980.)

This difference in perspective raises an issue that transcends mere economic theorizing. As noted by the elder Hicks, in his struggle to separate himself from the younger Hicks, '[i]t is because I want to make economics more human that I want to make it more time-conscious' (1976, p. 149).

Equilibrium theory essentially denies meaningful human decision making. 'Conventional economics is not about choice, but about acting according to necessity. Economic man obeys the *dictates* of reason, follows the *logic of choice*. . . . The theory which describes conduct under these assumptions is a theory of structure, not creation of history' (Shackle 1961, p. 272; emphasis in original). Humans become, in Thorstein Veblen's felicitous phrase, mere 'self-contained globule[s] of desire'. In a world of real time, humans must exercise imagination in making decisions in the face of an uncertain future that, while disorderly to be sure, is not utterly chaotic. 'In time' theorizing brings humans to centre stage. '*[O]ur imaginative perception of the possibilities inherent in it* determines what we do in our choice-decision moments, and because of the way in which the passing of time qualifies our stance at the decision points we experience' (Vickers 1994, p. 105; emphasis in original).

Keynes's position on money and uncertainty requires a theoretical stance on time, where economic *processes* (as counterpoised to equilibrium *states*) occur in real time and within a distinct form of economic organization that cannot be analysed on the basis of universal laws deduced from a reductionist (individual agent) foundation. Production processes obviously occur through time, but this fact, while important for Keynes, was not the defining aspect of a monetary economy. Production occurs in all forms of economic organization, but a monetary economy differs in its fundamental nature from non-monetary economies. In a monetary (capitalist) economy, the objective of production is to produce not goods, but money. In his early drafts of *The General Theory*, Keynes, following Marx, was very specific in his formulation of such an economy as M-C-M', where money is required to purchase inputs to produce commodities that are then sold for money. The objective, of course, is that the money at the end of the circuit (M') is greater than that at the beginning – a profit is made.

For Keynes and the Post Keynesians, such an economy is driven by aggregate spending. If current spending is limited to income received in the previous period, spending cannot increase beyond the level of that period – M' could not exceed M. As capitalist production is undertaken primarily on the expectation that M' will grow, such an economy requires a source of spending in excess of current income – debt (and its dialectical opposite, credit). Indeed, the production process in a monetary economy must begin with debt, because workers must be paid and capital goods purchased *before* income-yielding output is produced. Hence the owners of productive property must not only incur debt to allow production, but must also *hope* that sufficient spending will occur in the future so that M' exceeds M and debt can be cleared (or at least serviced). The capitalist market, then, is not a *device* to clear goods through changes in prices, but a *process* to clear debt. And, as a lender makes loans today on the promise of payment in the future, this process requires the creation of *dated* contracts; these in turn require the establishment of a unit of account that allows the recording of debt:

> Money of account comes into existence along with debts, which are contracts for deferred payment, and price lists, which are offers of contracts for sale or purchase. Such debts and price lists . . . can only be expressed in terms of a money of account.
>
> Money itself . . . derives its character from its relationship to the money of account, since the debts and prices must first have been expressed in terms of the latter. . . . Money proper . . . can only exist in relation to a money of account. (Keynes 1930 [1971], p. 3)

But, since the future cannot be known, it is impossible to make accurate predictions as to the outcome of any production-exchange process. Hence, in a monetary economy, production cannot be undertaken on the basis of a known, quantifiable (or even probabilistic) calculation, as is supposed in neoclassical models. 'Animal spirits' (or 'spontaneous optimism') drive investment and production in a world where historical time is of real importance and thus *fundamental* uncertainty is a fact of life.

In a monetary economy, the owners of productive property have obviously separated that property from the control of the larger community. Since capitalists produce goods only in the expectation of future gain, the community cannot depend on such individuals for its economic well-being. Nor can the capitalist depend on the community should he or she encounter economic (financial) difficulties: the capitalist faces an uncertain future.

To protect themselves against the vagaries of this uncertain future, capitalists must accumulate stocks of wealth. These stocks will not be in the form of real goods (use values), for such forms of wealth are not readily convertible into other goods (they are not very liquid), and they entail large carrying costs. Thus, the capitalist will hold wealth in the form of money. Since this appears objectively irrational (one cannot 'eat' money), such actions can only be comprehended within an economic organization where time is important and the future is unknowable. '*[T]he importance of money essentially flows from its being a link between the present and the (uncertain) future*' (Keynes 1936 [1987], p. 293; emphasis in original).

For Keynes, then, historical time is one of the core features of his general theory. It is only through the inclusion of time that one can understand the uncertainty that is central to the decision-making process under capitalism, and it is only through an analysis of uncertainty that one can understand the nature of money. And money, of course, is the central characteristic of a monetary economy. In Hyman Minsky's succinct words,

'Once a financial perspective is adopted, time cannot be interpreted away as just adding additional commodities (Walrasian money) to the economy' (Minsky 1982, p. 62).

JOHN F. HENRY

See also:

Agency; Equilibrium and Non-equilibrium; Expectations; Keynes's *General Theory*; New Neoclassical Synthesis; Non-ergodicity; Uncertainty; Walrasian Economics.

References:

Coyle, D. (2007), *The Soulful Science: What Economists Do and Why It Matters*, Princeton, NJ: Princeton University Press.

Davidson, P. (1978), *Money and the Real World*, 2nd edn, New York: John Wiley & Sons.

Davidson, P. (1991), *Controversies in Post Keynesian Economics*, Aldershot, UK and Brookfield, VT, USA: Edward Elgar.

Goodfriend, M. and R. King (1997), 'The new neoclassical synthesis and the role of monetary policy', *NBER Macroeconomics Annual*, **12**, 231–83.

Hicks, J.R. (1939), *Value and Capital*, Oxford: Clarendon Press.

Hicks, J.R. (1976), 'Some questions of time in economics', in A. Tang, F. Westfield and J. Worley (eds), *Evolution, Welfare, and Time in Economics*, Lexington, MA: Lexington Books, pp. 135–52.

Keynes, J.M. (1930), *Treatise on Money*, in *The Collected Writings of John Maynard Keynes*, Vol. 5, D. Moggridge (ed.), London: Macmillan, 1971.

Keynes, J.M. (1936), *The General Theory of Employment, Interest, and Money* in *The Collected Writings of John Maynard Keynes*, Vol. 7, D. Moggridge (ed.), London: Macmillan, 1987.

Minsky, H. (1982), *Can 'It' Happen Again?*, Armonk, NY: M.E. Sharpe.

Robinson, J. (1980), 'History vs. equilibrium', in J. Robinson, *Collected Economic Papers*, Vol. 5, Cambridge, MA: MIT Press, pp. 45–58.

Shackle, G. (1961), *Decision, Order, and Time in Human Affairs*, Cambridge: Cambridge University Press.

Vickers, D. (1994), *Economics and the Antagonism of Time*, Ann Arbor, MI: University of Michigan Press.

Woodford, M. (2003), *Interest and Prices: Foundations of a Theory of Monetary Policy*, Princeton, NJ: Princeton University Press.

Time-series Econometrics

Post Keynesian economists approach the use of time-series econometric methods with the same caution as they approach the use of econometric techniques in general. This caution derives from the very different way in which Post Keynesian and neoclassical economists view the world. In the neoclassical conceptualization of the world, economic events take place in 'logical' rather than 'historical' time. Their emphasis is on the inherent equilibrating tendencies of a world consisting of 'atomistic' individuals in which fundamental uncertainty does not exist. In such an environment, it is safe to assume that past and future economic variables follow the same probability distribution, or at least that 'probabilities regarding future prospects at the moment of choice govern future outcomes' (Davidson 1991, p. 131). In contrast, central to the Post Keynesian approach is the view that we live in a world characterized by fundamental uncertainty, where the economic system evolves in an irreversible and unidirectional time sequence.

The same criticisms that Post Keynesian economists direct towards the use of econometric techniques remain valid for time-series econometrics. However, there is an additional difficulty in time-series models. As a starting-point, time-series models are largely constructed independently of the formulation of a conceptual framework provided by economic theory to explain the relationship among economic variables. Traditional econometric methods draw on economic theory to specify the model. However, time-series econometric models are largely 'atheoretical' and 'agnostic'.

A time series is a sequence of observations of the same variable at equal intervals of time. For example, GDP is measured or estimated quarterly. Most economic variables are observed through time and, hence, formal empirical research in the areas of macroeconomics, microeconomics, finance, industrial organization and trade are largely based on time series. Univariate time-series models are constructed in such a way that the endogenous variable is explained only in terms of its own lagged values and current and lagged values of random disturbances. These models ignore the impact of past and current values of other relevant variables in the system. Multivariate econometric models are more complex and allow for the variable(s) in question to be affected (simultaneously or not) by the current and/or lagged values of other time series.

Depending on whether or not the time-series process satisfies a set of conditions imposed on the mean, variance and error terms, the series may be classified as stationary or non-stationary. In stationary series, the effect of the shocks from previous periods dissipates through time and eventually becomes zero. In non-stationary series, shocks from previous periods tend to become larger through time, eventually reaching infinity. Non-stationarity means that a variable has no tendency to return to its mean or linear trend.

Central to mainstream empirical research in economics is the testing of hypotheses and the estimation of relationships among aggregate economic variables that, more often than not, follow non-stationary stochastic processes. Applying conventional statistical and econometric methods to dynamic and interrelated series that have a unit root (are non-stationary) resulted in 'spurious regressions'. The development of time-series econometric techniques, such as Granger's (1981) *degree of integration* or error-correction models, to deal with such 'ill-behaved' economic variables, allowed for the modelling of non-stationary processes and the construction of 'statistically sound' models.

The development of time-series econometrics, however, could not overcome the more fundamental methodological difficulties derived from the uncertain, non-ergodic and dynamic nature of historically embedded capitalist economies. Davidson (1993) argued that the belief 'that there is a scientific basis for calculating the economic future through differencing past observations is incompatible with a world of Keynesian uncertainty' (p. 311). The search for stationary higher-order differences is ultimately based on the premise that there must exist a long-run economic equilibrium relationship 'determined solely by some real thing(s) that is (are), in the long run, time and path independent' (p. 312). Uncertainty and non-ergodicity implies, however, that 'a long-run statistical average about which the system will fluctuate as it moves from the present to an uncertain future need not exist' (p. 313). In fact, Kregel (1976) argued that Keynes had a model of shifting equilibrium and there is no predetermined path to which the economy will converge since the model is only consistent with 'an actual path of the economy over time chasing an ever changing equilibrium – it need never catch it' (p. 217).

Furthermore, the common feature among the long list of different time-series models, as argued before, is that economic theory plays a limited role. In particular, Box–Jenkins and VAR models are largely driven by data. Economic theory is only relevant in selecting individual or a group of time-series processes to be included in the model. Sims (1980) sees this feature as an advantage in that time-series models can then overcome 'identification problems'. In VAR models, a system of equations is estimated and each variable is explained by its own lagged values and the current and lagged values of all the other variables in the system. There is no structural modelling involved in this process, and, therefore, no input from economic theory. The data largely speak for themselves.

Alternatively, the Hendry/LSE approach combines structural modelling and time-series analysis. The LSE approach follows a 'general to simple' methodology and allows for the continual interaction between data and theory. This approach generally involves two steps. The data-generating process (DGP) draws on economic theory in structuring the model. The statistical-generating process (SGP) remains fictitious in the sense that it involves assumptions made about the probability distribution of the stochastic process in question and provides the basis for estimation and inference (Gilbert 2002). In this sense, economic theory is seen as providing a well-specified model to be estimated. This led Gilbert to argue that while the 'textbook approach' to time-series econometrics is not methodologically consistent with Post Keynesianism, the LSE approach 'offers a radical methodology in the sense of allowing for an interactive approach between economic theory and empirical evidence' (p. 129).

Central to the mainstream position is the proposition that 'there must be a generating mechanism that produces the group of stochastic processes known as "the economy"' (Granger 1996, p. 360). And therefore time-series econometric techniques are useful in constructing time-series models that 'in some way approximate the central generating mechanism' (p. 559). It is clear from the passage above that mainstream economists theorize about a closed and deterministic system. In such a system, empirical regularities can, in principle, be isolated and the group of diverse stochastic processes 'known as the economy' may be logically reduced to a 'central generating mechanism'. Mainstream economists, ultimately, base the performance of time-series econometric models on their forecasting or predictive power and little importance is given to inference. Once a time-series model is formulated and tested, it can be used to make predictions about the future value of economic outcomes and to formulate economic policies accordingly.

Most Post Keynesian economists emphasize a critical realist approach to methodology. In an open system approach, it is not possible to reduce economic processes to a 'central generating mechanism'. Event regularities, if observable, are the outcome of the continual interaction of human agency and structure in an uncertain and non-ergodic world, and, hence, comprise a plurality of 'partial regularities' and processes (Downward 2002). Post Keynesian ontology is incompatible with mainstream rhetoric. The economy is not merely a collection of stochastic processes, and no universal event regularities exist. Post Keynesian economists are, therefore, not surprised by the lack of predictive power of time-series models.

As argued by Lawson (1997), the sorts of concerns put forward by Keynes in the beginning of the previous century are still relevant today and explain why Post Keynesian economists remain largely hostile to the use of time-series econometric models. Keynes questioned the general applicability of statistical probability distributions to complex 'organic' social systems in which most economic events are unique. He argued that 'the method of multiple correlation to complex economic problems lies in the apparent lack of any adequate degree of uniformity in the environment' (Keynes 1939, p. 567). In this context, the use of statistical probability becomes inappropriate in terms of representing the uncertainty attached to a particular statistical event, since in such a world, the past is not a reliable guide to the future, and 'there is no scientific basis on which to form any calculable probability whatever. We simply do not know' (Keynes 1937, p. 214).

While Davidson (1991, p. 132) concludes that 'the application of the mathematical theory of stochastic processes to macroeconomic phenomena [is] highly questionable, if not invalid in principle', not all Post

Keynesians have completely banned the use of time-series econometric methods from empirical investigation. Some Post Keynesians take the position that the use of such techniques is justifiable, and even necessary, to critically engage with mainstream economists at the same level of mathematical/statistical sophistication. Others argue that the careful use of these techniques can make important contributions to the development of Post Keynesian theory itself.

Downward (1995), for example, applies the techniques associated with VAR models and the LSE approach to investigate the dynamics of manufacturing pricing in the UK to provide additional evidence that supports the Post Keynesian price theory. Downward's position is that 'econometric evidence may have a constructive role to play for Post Keynesians' (2002, p. 144). He invokes Lawson's intrinsic closure condition to defend the use of econometrics when the interactions between theory and data are considered, given a particular context. In his words, 'a combination of prior theoretical insight and statistical analysis, firmly grounded in a particular context, provides a use of econometrics that would also be in keeping with a realist methodological position' (ibid., p. 157). According to him, empirical evidence increases the 'weight of the argument' as it provides new evidence that may increase the belief that a particular proposition is more or less reliable.

In summary, the consensus among Post Keynesian economists is that the 'abusive' use of time-series econometrics reflects the simplistic neoclassical view of real-world phenomena and the unrealistic prior assumptions made as to the nature of economic processes and relationships. There is no place for a 'torturing-the-numbers-until-they-confess' kind of method in Post Keynesian methodology. Quite the contrary: 'theories should be relevant in that they should represent reality as accurately as possible and should strive to explain the real world as observed empirically' (Arestis 1996, p. 116). In this sense, there are no absolute truths and, hence, theories should be *diverse* and *context specific* while subject to constant revision as history unfolds, in the light of new facts, evidence and knowledge. Time-series econometrics may still remain an instrument at the disposal of Post Keynesians as long as it is used conscientiously and cautiously.

FLAVIA DANTAS

See also:

Critical Realism; Econometrics; Non-ergodicity; Open Systems; Uncertainty.

References

Arestis, P. (1996), 'Post-Keynesian economics: towards coherence', *Cambridge Journal of Economics*, **20** (1), 111–35.

Davidson, P. (1991), 'Is probability theory relevant for uncertainty? A Post Keynesian perspective', *Journal of Economic Perspectives*, **5** (1), 129–43.
Davidson, P. (1993), 'The elephant and the butterfly: or hysteresis and Post Keynesian economics', *Journal of Post Keynesian Economics*, **15** (3), 309–22.
Downward, P.M. (1995), 'A Post Keynesian perspective of UK manufacturing pricing', *Journal of Post Keynesian Economics*, **17** (3), 403–26.
Downward, P.M. (2002), 'Realism, econometrics and Post Keynesian economics', in S.C. Dow and J. Hillard (eds), *Post Keynesian Econometrics, Microeconomics and the Theory of the Firm*, Cheltenham, UK and Northampton, MA, USA: Edward Elgar, pp. 144–61.
Gilbert, B. (2002), 'The role of econometrics in a radical methodology', in S.C. Dow and J. Hilliard (eds), *Post Keynesian Econometrics, Microeconomics and the Theory of the Firm*, Cheltenham, UK and Northampton, MA, USA: Edward Elgar, pp. 110–32.
Granger, C. (1981), 'Some properties of time series data and their use in econometric model specification', *Journal of Econometrics*, **16** (1), 121–30.
Granger, C. (1996), 'Time series econometrics', in D. Greenway, M. Bleaney and I. Stewart (eds), *A Guide to Modern Economics*, London and New York: Routledge, pp. 360–72.
Keynes, J.M. (1937), 'The general theory of employment', *Quarterly Journal of Economics*, **51** (2), 209–23.
Keynes, J.M. (1939), 'Professor Tinbergen's method', *Economic Journal*, **44** (195), 558–68.
Kregel, J.A. (1976), 'Economic methodology in the face of uncertainty: the modelling methods of Keynes and the Post Keynesians', *Economic Journal*, **86** (342), 209–25.
Lawson, T. (1997), *Economics and Reality*, London and New York: Routledge.
Sims, C.A. (1980), 'Macroeconomics and reality', *Econometrica*, **48** (1), 1–47.

Tobin Tax

In his 1972 Janeway lecture at Princeton, James Tobin (1974) proposed a tax on foreign exchange transactions as a way of limiting speculation, enhancing the efficacy of macroeconomic policy, and raising tax revenues; Davidson (1997) opposes this view. Keynes, in the *Treatise on Money* and in the *General Theory*, had already suggested that a tax on foreign lending to contain speculative capital movements might be necessary (see also Haq et al. 1996). Official interest in the Tobin tax has been expressed repeatedly. The United Nations Development Programme (1994) emphasized its potential for raising large amounts of money that could be used to finance development. The Tobin tax has been gaining reasonable popularity since then. More recent contributors in favour of the idea of a Tobin tax are, for example, Ehrenstein et al. (2005) and Westerhof (2003). Contributions against the Tobin tax idea have also made their views public, such as Aliber et al. (2003) and Grahl and Lysandrou (2003). It must be readily admitted, though, that although governments and international fora have shown approval or willingness to discuss it, not much more has been in evidence. More recently, a cautiously expressed renewed interest has emerged in view of the Great Recession; but no more than that. A good example is the International Monetary Fund (IMF) approach to the G20 contributions. The idea in this context is that although a financial transactions tax could be considered by the IMF, and should not be excluded, the conclusion reached, however, is that a financial stability contribution tax and a financial activity tax are thought to be more efficient ways of raising tax than a financial transactions tax.

In Arestis and Sawyer (1997) four sets of rationales are advanced in support of the Tobin tax. In a world of floating exchange rates, the large volume of transactions is viewed as generating volatility in the exchange rate, with consequent detrimental effects on the real economies. The second rationale is simply its revenue potential. Tobin (1978) suggested it as a byproduct of a financial transaction tax, not as the main aim – a financial transaction tax of 0.05 per cent could have raised $150 billion a year over the 1995–2000 period. The third rationale concerns the possibility of enhancing the autonomy of national economic policy, and reducing the constraints on such policy imposed by financial markets. In this context a financial transaction tax increases the independence of policy makers by reducing foreign exchange rate volatility through hitting the most frequent transactors the hardest. The fourth is that this tax can potentially tackle the problems just alluded to more flexibly than the introduction of financial controls, especially quantitative exchange controls, which are usually viewed as rigid.

Three reasons for the increased interest in the Tobin tax are mentioned in Arestis and Sawyer (1997). The first is the growing volume of foreign exchange trading. The second reason is that a transactions tax is now seen as important, not merely by policy makers and others concerned with foreign exchange market volatility, but also by those who attach significance to public financing of world development. The third reason is an increasing realization that foreign exchange markets do not operate in the efficient manner portrayed in the rational expectations literature. Foreign exchange markets suffer from asymmetric information, herd behaviour and moral hazard, and from the possibility of multiple equilibria; the implication of all these is persistent misalignments and unstable exchange rate regimes. Most, if not all, of these problems have been highlighted recently in view of the emergence of the Great Recession.

One common argument raised against the Tobin tax relates to its possible distortionary effects. The argument is that such a tax leads in a competitive market to an equilibrium that involves a lower quantity of transactions, and fewer resources being allocated to that particular market. There are three points to be made in connection with this argument. First, the financial sector may at present be relatively lightly taxed, and the 'products' of the financial sector are generally not subject to general sales or value-added taxes or to specific excise taxes and the like. This would mean that the imposition of a financial transaction tax might in effect be removing some distortions rather than imposing them. To the extent that this view is accepted, the introduction of a financial transaction tax would help to reduce the distortionary effect of the tax system.

Second, the distortionary nature of a tax arises from some potentially beneficial trades not taking place that would otherwise have happened. This leads to the question of whether there are gains from the current volume of exchange transactions, which would not arise with a substantially smaller volume. Some further doubt is cast on the distortionary argument by the observation that, while the two parties to a foreign exchange trade may believe that they will gain from the trade (through a favourable price movement), both cannot do so; that is, it is a zero-sum game.

Third, the analysis of distortions is an equilibrium one, and it is equilibrium trades that are discouraged. But there is a sense in which much of the trading in currency markets is disequilibrium trading in terms of seeking to take advantage of price changes. Thus the conventional analysis of distortions does not apply to this situation, and if it is the case that the amount of 'noise trading' is excessive, then a tax is beneficial rather than distortionary.

Assuming that the tax was fully passed on to consumers, it is clear that there could be a substantial impact on the volume of international trade (Davidson 1997). However, a rather low rate of taxation, and the fact that the tax may be absorbed by producers rather than passed on to consumers, are distinct possibilities. In evaluating the overall balance of effects of a financial transaction tax on international trade, due consideration would need to be given to the effects of reduced volume of exchange transactions, of reduced volatility, enhanced independence of national economic policies and the probable stimulus to worldwide aggregate demand. These latter factors would stimulate international trade, and the overall net effect of such a tax on international trade cannot be readily predicted.

It is expected that the introduction of a Tobin tax would be a major economic and political development. At the same time it would have to be introduced on a 'big bang' basis, for otherwise foreign exchange dealings would quickly move to those countries that were not applying the tax.

It is also expected that a financial transactions tax would have a significant impact on worldwide aggregate demand. Besides the obvious point that the aggregate demand effects will depend on the use to which the tax revenue is put, it is quite reasonable to assume that a financial transaction tax would be levied on those with a low propensity to spend, and the redistribution would be towards those with a much higher propensity to spend. Hence aggregate demand may well increase. This would be an additional effect to the enhanced capability of national governments to pursue economic policies that stimulate a higher level of demand. Furthermore, to the extent to which the tax revenue does not lead (at the national and/ or international level) to increased government expenditure, there would obviously be some reduction in budget deficits. Some would argue that the reduction in budget deficits would lead to a reduction in interest rates, with some stimulus to investment.

The appropriate definition of the transaction should be as follows: any transaction that involves the exchange of a financial asset denominated in one currency for a financial asset denominated in another currency. This was Tobin's initial suggestion when he wrote:

> [T]he tax would apply to all purchases of financial instruments denominated in another currency – from currency and coin to equity securities. It would have to apply . . . to all payments in one currency for goods, services, and real assets sold by a resident of another currency area. I don't intend to add even a small barrier to trade. But I see off-hand no other way to prevent financial transactions disguised as trade. (Tobin 1978, p. 159)

A number of proposals have been put forward on the way to distribute the tax proceeds (see UNDP 1994). To the extent that it is the IMF or World Bank who are the intermediate recipients, a further proposal may be to enhance the lending capabilities of these institutions especially to the Third World countries, which could embrace development and anti-pollution projects. The workings of the tax could be reinforced by making the administration of a Tobin tax a condition of membership of the IMF. It should be conceded, though, that this may not be sufficient to prevent the growth of offshore dealings. This is so since a small country would have very little to gain from membership of the IMF as compared with the potential revenue as the location of offshore financial markets.

There is widespread agreement that the tax would have to be implemented on a coordinated international basis. It may not be necessary for there to be full agreement over the tax rate, though there would be strong pressures towards a degree of uniformity (and probably a requirement for a minimum rate to avoid competitive undercutting of the tax rate between countries). It is clear that there would be very considerable differences in the amount of tax collected in each country. Part of the international agreement could clearly be that a proportion of the tax collected be paid over to an international body and/or used for agreed development and environmental purposes. The obvious difficulty which arises here is obtaining international agreement over the introduction and the rate of the tax when the revenue from the tax would be so unequally distributed across countries (and to the extent to which countries fear that their financial centres would be reduced in size, the costs also unequally distributed). Furthermore, a substantial retention of revenue at the national level obviously reduces the funds available for international development and global environmental purposes. It should also be expected that the economic and political influence of the financial markets would be much reduced; indeed the imposition of such a tax would be a clear signal that the influence of the financial sector was in decline. The point should be made, though, that the high-yield UK securities transaction tax, known as stamp duty, was maintained in one of the most sophisticated financial markets. It has not obviously met with any serious opposition from these sophisticated financial markets, nor have there been cries of tax evasion in a market where players are most likely to find mechanisms to evade such a tax.

Most advocates of a financial transaction tax recognize that it would have to be 'universal and uniform'. This requirement may well be the most important practical obstacle to the implementation of such a tax. It would clearly require the cooperation of all countries with significant foreign exchange dealings within their borders, although there would be incentives for countries to apply a lower tax rate within their jurisdiction. Given the IMF's considerable expertise in international financial markets, it would be in a good position to undertake such a task. Furthermore, recognition of the IMF's central objectives of the promotion of international monetary cooperation to maintain exchange rate stability and orderly exchange arrangements among its members, substantially strengthens the argument that the IMF should play a central role in its implementation.

A Tobin tax is expected to diminish the volatility of exchange markets and raise in revenue substantial sums of taxation. Its introduction could face political problems; and yet it has been gaining popularity, including the Commission of the European Union. It might be more appropriate to use the Tobin tax as one of several policy instruments to combat speculation on the world's foreign exchanges, and to finance development.

PHILIP ARESTIS

See also:

Development Finance; Economic Policy; Exchange Rates; International Economics; International Financial Reform.

References

Aliber, R.Z., B. Chowdhry and S. Yan (2003), 'Some evidence that a Tobin tax on foreign exchange transactions may increase volatility', *European Finance Review*, **7** (3), 481–510.
Arestis, P. and M. Sawyer (1997), 'How many cheers for the Tobin financial transaction tax?', *Cambridge Journal of Economics*, **21** (6), 753–68.
Davidson, P. (1997), 'Are grains of sand in the wheels of international finance sufficient to do the job when boulders are often required?', *Economic Journal*, **107** (442), 671–86.
Ehrenstein, G., F. Westerholf and D. Stauffer (2005), 'Tobin tax and market depth', *Quantitative Finance*, **5** (2), 213–18.

Grahl, J. and P. Lysandrou (2003), 'Sand in the wheels or spanner in the works? The Tobin tax and global finance', *Cambridge Journal of Economics*, **27** (4), 597–621.

Haq, M., I. Kaul and I. Grunberg (eds) (1996), *The Tobin Tax: Coping with Financial Volatility*, Oxford: Oxford University Press.

Tobin, J. (1974), *The New Economics One Decade Older: The Eliot Janeway Lectures on Historical Economics in Honour of Joseph Schumpeter, 1972*, Princeton, NJ: Princeton University Press.

Tobin, J. (1978), 'A proposal for international monetary reform', *Eastern Economic Journal*, **4** (3–4), 153–9; reprinted in Tobin, *Essays in Economics: Theory and Policy*, Cambridge, MA: MIT Press, 1982 pp. 488–94.

United Nations Development Programme (UNDP) (1994), *Human Development Report 1994*, New York and Oxford: Oxford University Press.

Westerhof, F. (2003), 'Heterogeneous traders and the Tobin tax', *Journal of Evolutionary Economics*, **13** (1), 53–70.

Transition Economies

The term 'transition economy' can be applied to any economy moving from one dominating mechanism for coordinating its economy to another; since 1989, the term has been applied specifically to the post-communist, formerly centrally planned economies of Eastern and Central Europe. Before 1989, these economies were predominantly characterized by a high degree of administrative planning, absence of the market mechanism in the allocation of resources and a relative scarcity of consumer goods as compared to the advanced Western industrialized economies. Since 1989, however, as they moved to adopt more 'Western' capitalist features, certain structural or behavioural 'maladaptions' appeared preventing the successful completion of this transition. This can be seen most clearly in their response to the global financial crisis of 2008–09: all of them suffered more severe recessionary pressures than the Western economies.

In the decades before 1989, the appearance of various inefficiencies and distortions put pressure for some sort of change, especially after the 1970s, when it became clear that the area's previously high growth rates could no longer be maintained. After the collapse of the Soviet Union, many policy makers and economists in the area believed that adopting the market mechanism, privatizing industry and using the profit motive as an incentive would be necessary to improve their economic performance. The record of achievement was mixed to begin with. As the World Bank noted in 2000: 'Ten years after the breakup of the Soviet System, what is perhaps most striking about the European and Central Asia (ECA) region is its diversity. A decade ago, all countries in the region seemed to face similar challenges of transition from a planned centralized system to a market economy' ('Europe and Central Asia: Introduction', World Bank 2000, p. 63).

At that time, the explanation for this diversity was partly made in terms of the presence or absence of those supportive, usually non-economic, institutions that make market mechanisms work and market-oriented behaviour feasible. Those Eastern European economies such as Hungary, Poland, the Czech Republic and Slovenia, which were already more diversified, fared better than others, most notably the Russian Federation and Ukraine, which experienced negative growth and were struggling to regain levels of GDP reached before the Soviet collapse. After 2000, and before the global recession, the ECA countries benefited from their opening up to the global economy, and saw improved growth as well as rising living standards. But all this ended in 2008, and recovery, in 2011, seems to be dependent on yet more difficult adjustments.

Many of the current problems stem from their earlier reaction to poor economic performance, even though, starting in the 1980s, some of them were already beginning to reduce the role of bureaucratic decision making. This had originally been instituted as a way to jump-start an industrialization process after the Second World War, and those countries falling within the Soviet sphere of influence shared certain characteristics.

Because they had wanted to catch up to the Western industrialized economies as quickly as possible, planners gave preference to the production of investment and intermediate goods. Enterprises were operating entities, not decision makers, responsible only for fulfilling the plan's targets with the resources allocated to them. Planning was taut: targets were set high, assuming full employment with little slack. Also, the Soviet Union encouraged specialization in different countries; when it collapsed, each separate economy was not very diversified. A price system existed as an accounting device, not as an incentive or allocative mechanism; firms did not need to respond to financial incentives. At the outset, prices were more or less in accordance with resource (opportunity) costs, but they diverged considerably over time: planners were either slow to respond to changing supply conditions or they manipulated the data for various political purposes. As a result, prices ceased to be aligned with either opportunity costs or world prices for similar items.

Hence various distortions and imbalances appeared, but the structure and functioning of these economies prevented their elimination. For example, enterprises faced a soft budget constraint, meaning that they could manipulate external financing and/or negotiate taxes, grants and credits in order to avoid bankruptcy: there were no penalties for failure (Kornai 1980). Even though shortages and bottlenecks resulted, thus justifying investment plans to eliminate them, resource limitations prevented plan fulfilment. One example of this problem was the ubiquitous existence of queues, evidence of consumer goods' shortages. To sum up, these economies were high-investment, resource-constrained economies, not (effective) demand-constrained economies like Western capitalist market economies. In addition, innovative responses were absent because enterprises were not decision makers, and their managers responded to political, not economic, stimuli; even now, such entrenched interest groups persist. Managers also had little incentive to respond innovatively for fear that plan targets would be revised upwards.

Although some changes were beginning to take place, whether they would have resulted in more effective performance became irrelevant following the events of 1989–90. At that time, the collapse of communist-dominated governments in the region initiated both political and economic pressures towards the adoption of more democratic political processes and the market mechanism.

Economic advisers to many of the new governments favoured a three-prong approach to economic restructuring: replace planning with a market mechanism; privatize government-owned productive assets; and adopt a price system to coordinate economic activity, with financial incentives replacing quantitative targets. Advisers also recommended speed, the so-called 'shock therapy' approach, in spite of its short-term costs. These costs of adjustment could include a rise in unemployment as enterprises shed excess workers, or balance-of-payments deficits as economies opened up to western imports.

The assumption that markets are the best mechanisms for coordinating economic activity underlay these recommendations, an assumption shared with the standard economics model that focuses on self-interested individuals making rational choices in order to maximize utility/income/welfare/profits. In the transition economies, enterprises are central because they both generate and respond to price signals once they become financially self-sufficient. That is, they are subject to a hard budget constraint with real penalties for failure because they no longer simply carry out the central bureaucracy's orders.

However, marketization is not a universally applicable solution, which partly explains the problems the transition economies then encountered. Because the standard model was devised with the already-mature capitalist market economies in mind, it assumed that all the necessary institutions and behaviour patterns (including, for example, appropriate legal and educational systems, well-functioning capital markets, and a competent civil service), were in place. Such assumptions could not be made in the transition economies. Instead, an approach that takes account of their history, culture, institutional development, and values is needed, plus recognizing that it may take a long time for those institutions supportive of an effective modern mixed economy to take root.

For example, private ownership of productive resources will only produce socially favourable results if a legal system specifying property rights, and the corresponding rights *and obligations* associated with them, is in place. Initially, the very concept of private property had to be legitimized, and it takes time for the necessary legal changes to be put in place and accepted. Enterprises can only respond to financial incentives if there is a well-developed financial system made up of banks and other financial institutions to replace government's role as finance provider. Procedures to enforce accountability, which could include proper accounting systems, bankruptcy laws, and an independent financial press, for example, are also needed.

Using prices assumes that not only is there some way of estimating the relation between opportunity costs and market prices, but also that there are monetary institutions capable of ensuring adequate liquidity and stability in the system. Replacing planning with the market mechanism requires new behaviour patterns too. For example, enterprise owners and managers must be able to respond to price signals, and the incentive system should harmonize the actions of consumers, employees and managers in an acceptable way. However, desired behaviour patterns are not inherent, but learned, so the mechanisms necessary for teaching and learning them have to be put into place.

An essential requirement for the transition economies is reworking the role of the state. Market economies rely on a strong effective state to provide the necessary framework within which private action can take place. The state has a role to play in providing infrastructure, enforcing the 'rules of the game', and in education, for example. There is also an important role for government to use appropriate policies for when things go wrong – to ameliorate market failures and maintain the level of effective demand, because there is no automatic self-correcting mechanism in a capitalist market economy. This is vital once the dynamic role of (privately generated) investment in a global economy subject to uncertainty, and where historical time is uni-directional, is recognized. Long-term problems also cannot be solved by market forces alone. Of particular concern here is the environmental degradation caused by the transition economies' earlier focus on industrialization at all costs, which ignored the negative externalities associated with rapid resource exploitation and use.

These considerations perhaps help explain why the transition economies suffered more than the Western market economies during the global financial crisis and recession that began in 2008. Anxious to take advantage of the opening up of their economies, many welcomed large amounts of foreign capital, but later were unable to service huge debt levels once the global crisis hit and their domestic economies shrank. One extreme example was Ukraine, whose economy contracted by 14 per cent in 2009. Both Ukraine and Russia are instructive for other reasons. Both began privatization schemes, price liberalization and other structural reforms, but neither diversified sufficiently to moderate any external shock. Russia is heavily dependent on commodity exports (predominantly oil, natural gas and primary aluminium), and on steel, so is extremely vulnerable to boom/bust cycles and volatile swings in global commodity prices. Because Ukraine remains dependent on Russia for its energy supplies (as in the old pre-transition days), it too is subject to the same cyclical swings (CIA 2010). Some of the transition economies suffer from political instability. Many have continued state interference in industry, which does nothing to help improve their global competitiveness. In Russia, privatization resulted in highly concentrated equity ownership dominated by politically connected oligarchs, and growing income inequality. Few are free of ongoing problems with political corruption and incompetent government bureaucracies.

Even those which seemed best placed to gain from the end of state planning faced problems they are poorly equipped to handle. For example, Estonia, which had one of the region's highest per capita income levels, saw its GDP fall by 15 per cent in 2009, and is becoming known for the growth of the illegal drug trade and related money laundering (ibid.). The pattern of adopting both the best and the worst of Western economies, along with inherited problems, characterizes many of the transition economies.

While few countries in the world remained immune from the global financial crisis and recession, these problems help demonstrate that the transition economies need to do more than simply replace bureaucratic decision making and material balances planning with the profit motive, private property and the market mechanism. They do need all the institutions and processes that make a private enterprise economy function well, plus those that are needed when it falters.

Policy options compatible with a Post Keynesian approach start from the (often difficult) realization that improved economic functioning depends on effective operations in many different areas. Simply removing bureaucratic intervention and leaving markets alone so that the price system can work its magic is insufficient.

Certain key elements of policy can be identified. First, the necessary legal, social, political and economic institutional arrangements that coordinate and promote effective economic behaviour should be put into place, and continually re-evaluated to meet changing circumstances. These include finance-granting institutions, with controls to ensure that an adequate amount of liquidity exists: money and monetary institutions are not neutral, and do influence economic activity.

Second, those elements contributing to effective behaviour patterns – which are not inherent but learned – should be developed. Included here would be different levels of formal and informal educational and training institutions, information collection, analysis and dispersion (as with a free press), and control and accountability mechanisms (such as accounting rules and procedures).

Third, because a market system is not automatically self-correcting, it is necessary to develop various policy options to deal with market failures, such as excessive market power. Also, macroeconomic policies to maintain aggregate demand and employment at appropriate levels, and to stabilize prices are needed. Here, the dynamic aspects of economic growth and development are too important to be left to chance. Hence, investment, its level and distribution, in order to promote growth given an uncertain and unknowable future, needs to be attended to. It would also be appropriate to put a social safety-net in place, not only to provide income security for its traditional clientele (including the retired, sick and disabled) but also to encourage risk taking and innovation by cushioning the hardships of failure.

While it is possible to identify and describe many other specific aspects of policy, it is important to encourage flexibility. The goal of a pluralist, democratic and open market system cannot be reached through a rigid commitment to a single official blueprint.

CHRISTINE RIDER

See also:

Economic Policy; Institutionalism; Socialism.

Bibliography:

Central Intelligence Agency (CIA) (2010), *The World Factbook*, available at: www.cia.gov (accessed 24 January 2010).
International Monetary Fund (2009), *World Economic Outlook: Crisis and Recovery*, Washington, DC: IMF, April.
Kornai, J. (1980), *The Economics of Shortage*, Amsterdam: North-Holland.
Rider, C. (1993), 'The pricing problems of Eastern Europe', in I. Rima (ed.), *The Political Economy of Global Restructuring*, Vol. I, Aldershot, UK and Brookfield, VT, USA: Edward Elgar, pp. 86–99.
Rider, C. (1996), 'Ethical policy making in the transition economies', in E.J. O'Boyle (ed.), *Social Economics: Premises, Findings and Policies*, London and New York: Routledge, pp. 178–90.
Rosser, J.B. Jr and M.V. Rosser (1996), *Comparative Economics in a Transforming World Economy*, Chicago, IL: Irwin.
World Bank (2000), *Annual Report 2000*, International Bank for Reconstruction and Development, Oxford: Oxford University Press.
World Bank (2009), *The World Bank in Russia*, No. 20, available at: www.worldbank.org.ru, (accessed 24 January 2010).

Traverse

The traverse defines the movement of the economy outside equilibrium. It plays a particularly important role in Post Keynesian theory, as most Post Keynesian economists have serious doubts about the relevance and usefulness of equilibrium analysis.

Economics and political economy have almost always relied on some concept of equilibrium as a central organizing concept. A major methodological difference between different schools of thought has been the operational significance that each ascribed to that concept. For some economists, the concept of equilibrium is important for organizing ideas, and as an idealized point of reference. Others see it as being descriptive, with actual economies showing strong tendencies towards equilibrium, which would be achievable except for constant shocks. However, despite the importance of the concept of equilibrium, little was usually said about the process whereby the economy achieved it. For equilibrium to serve the function which economists have for so long assigned to it, there must be forces pushing the economy towards equilibrium, and the path the economy takes towards that equilibrium, that is, its adjustment path, must not influence the equilibrium to which it is tending. In the absence of these conditions, analyses of equilibria, independent of the 'traverse' become pointless. Hicks, who first introduced the term 'traverse' into economics, characterized it as 'the path which will be followed when the steady state is subjected to some kind of disturbance' (Hicks 1973, p. 81). In other words, the traverse describes the economy's dynamic out-of-equilibrium adjustment path in historical time. The importance of historical time is its unidirection, time can only move forward, with the link between time periods given by the stock of capital inherited from the past, and the expectations embodied in it (Robinson 1974; Setterfield 1995; Kriesler 1999). Although initially the traverse was used to describe the path between equilibria, later the traverse itself was seen to be the end of the story. Post Keynesian economists, among other heterodox economists (especially evolutionary and institutional economists), have been vocal about the fruitlessness of studying the equilibrium properties of an economic system without considering the question of whether the economy will actually get there. In other words, they have voiced their doubts about the comparative static method which dominates modern economics. More pointedly, Joan Robinson often criticized the separation of equilibrium analysis from the analysis of the traverse, as she believed that the actual equilibrium which an economy achieves (if it is capable of achieving one) will be vitally dependent on the path it takes, so that equilibrium would always be path dependent (Robinson 1974).

The traverse is of relevance both to economists who deny that the economy is attracted to any equilibrium, as well as to those who accept that the economy will tend towards equilibrium, but argue that the final equilibrium position is path determined, in the sense associated with hysteresis where current outcomes are determined by past values. Hicks and Lowe undertook detailed analysis of the adjustment paths economies take outside equilibrium. They considered the question of whether the market would send the correct signals to allow the structure of production to adjust as a response to a shock. 'The necessary *adjustment path* requires both *time* and *costs*, and faces difficulties which arise from disproportions between sectors and misleading market signals' (Hagemann 1992, p. 235; italics in original).

Hicks's initial analysis of the traverse utilizes a two-sector, fixed-coefficients model making use of the methods of the classical economists, with similarities to Piero Sraffa's model. In a two-sector model the one capital good can freely be moved between the capital- and consumption-goods sectors. Without the complications implied by structural disproportionalities, Hicks concludes that a full-employment path to equilibrium is only possible if the consumption-goods sector is more mechanized than the capital-goods sector. Even if this condition is fulfilled, a full-employment traverse is not guaranteed but must satisfy a series of technologically determined conditions with respect to the man/machine ratios in the two sectors. Hicks reaches the important conclusion that 'smooth adjustment may not be possible', with prices providing inappropriate guides to decision makers (Hicks 1965). In his later work, Hicks moved away from the 'classical' traverse, and attempted to analyse the traverse within a hybrid neoclassical/Austrian framework. In order to get a unique and unambiguous period of production, he resorted to the uninteresting case of the 'simple profile', for reasons related to the capital controversies. Unfortunately, this becomes essentially a one-commodity model, and is not, therefore, particularly enlightening. In any case, the neo-Austrian model cannot incorporate a specific machine-goods sector, or adequately treat fixed capital (Hagemann 1992), and so abstracts from the main problems. This attempt by Hicks to analyse the traverse within a neoclassical framework may be contrasted with the efforts of Kalecki and Lowe, and illustrates the difficulty of using the neoclassical approach to meaningfully discuss disequilibrium phenomena (Lavoie and Ramirez-Gaston 1977; Kriesler 1999).

Lowe (1976), in a return to the concerns of the classical economists, sees the main problem of economics as the description of the 'path of economic growth', which is not normally of the steady-state equilibrium type. He specifically analyses the traverse, and concentrates on the implications of structural change. For this reason, he focuses on the nature of changes in the structure of production and on intersectoral relations, in a manner reminiscent of the classical economists. To examine this problem, Lowe developed a three-sector model which incorporated not only the concept of historical time but also two important aspects of production: the specificity of capital goods and the importance of reproduction, which is necessary for the incorporation of intersectoral relations. Specificity is dealt with by differentiating two subsectors of the capital-goods sector. In the first subsector, capital goods are produced which can either reproduce themselves or produce capital goods for the consumption-goods sector. Although, at this stage, there is no distinction between the capital goods, specificity becomes important when the capital goods produced in this sector are installed, as on installation they lose their generality and, in an irreversible process, become specific to the production of capital goods for the consumption-goods sector. These capital goods may be considered a separate branch of production. The capital-goods output of this sector is installed in the consumption-goods sector to produce consumption goods.

Lowe uses this model to examine the nature of the traverse. From an initial stationary state, the implications for the traverse of changes and restrictions on variables are analysed. The model is used to consider the structural changes within the capital-goods sector which are necessary to facilitate, for example, changes in technology and in the rate of growth of the labour force, and their implications for intersectoral relations.

An important conclusion to emerge is Lowe's demonstration that, although there may very well be a traverse which leads to a new full-employment steady state, it is unlikely to be achieved within a decentralized market system. This, in part, results from the market transmitting the 'wrong' signals in terms of the optimal structure of production and intersectoral flows.

While the Hicks/Lowe traverse analysis concentrates on the supply-side questions of the responses of the structure of production, Kalecki's emphasis was on the demand side. For Kalecki, the structure of demand was the key to the adjustment process, with the essence of the problem being what happens to the composition of demand as a result of the changes in the distribution of income during the cycle. As a result, although Kalecki, like Lowe, disaggregated the economy into three sectors, the disaggregation served different purposes. For Kalecki the division of the economy into a capital-goods sector and two consumption-goods sectors, differentiating workers' consumption from that of capitalists, was the result of his emphasis on the problems associated with realization in the form of effective demand.

He did, however, share Lowe's concern with reproduction and with intersectoral relations, but concentrated on flows of commodities and of incomes between sectors. Kalecki saw the main determinant of income and growth in mature capitalist economies as being the level of effective demand. Crucial to this was the dual role of investment, which, on the one hand, was part of effective demand (so that the higher the level of investment, the greater the level of employment in that period), while, on the other, it contributed to the creation of extra capacity (so that the higher the level of investment, the larger would be the problem with achieving full employment in subsequent periods). This 'paradox', according to Kalecki struck at the heart of the capitalist system: 'The tragedy of investment is that it causes crisis because it is useful. Doubtless many people will consider this theory paradoxical. But it is not the theory which is paradoxical, but its subject – the capitalist economy' (Kalecki 1990–97, Volume I, p. 318).

Although Kalecki concentrated on the role of effective demand in his analysis of capitalist economies, in his work on socialist economies the structure of production, rather than effective demand, was seen as the important constraint on economic activity. Here he came much closer to the traverse analysis of Hicks and Lowe, and in many ways their efforts are complementary. In a capitalist economy, a reduction in investment causes a reduction in profits, which feeds through to a multiplied reduction in income and aggregate demand. Kalecki contrasts this with the effects of a reduction in investment in a socialist economy, where he argues that there need be no problem with effective demand:

> The workers released from the production of investment goods would be employed in the consumption goods industries. The increased supply of these goods would be absorbed by means of a reduction in their prices. Since profits of the socialist industries would be equal to investment, prices would have to be reduced to the point where the decline in profits would be equal to the value of the fall in investment. (Ibid., Volume II, pp. 254–5)

In his analysis of 'the structure of investment in socialist economies', he acknowledged the possibility of short-run problems in adjustment caused by capacity bottlenecks, in the sense of too much (or too little) capacity in the capital-goods sector. It is here that his work touches on issues raised by Hicks and Lowe. Using a two-sector model, and differentiating investment in the capital-goods sector from aggregate investment, he showed that changes in the growth rate of the economy will necessitate deviations between the growth rate of investment and that of the economy, during the transition period. However, 'there exists a ceiling to the deviation of the rate of growth of investment from that of national income which is determined by the productive capacity of the investment sector' (Ibid., Volume IV, p. 102).

Kalecki's two-sector model suffers from its inability to sufficiently disaggregate the structure of the investment-goods sector. This is of particular importance when the problem is that of differential growth rates between the consumption- and investment-goods sectors, with investment goods being provided to both sectors. It is here that Lowe's model can supplement Kalecki's discussion of structural problems, as well as showing the difficulty of getting rid of excess capacity.

The denial of equilibrium and the emphasis on path dependency is also a major theme of evolutionary economists. They see the major components of the economy, particularly firms and industries, as evolving due to changes in their environment. Both the environmental changes and the adaptations are strongly path determined. Recently, Post Keynesian economists have been incorporating evolution into their models, and this work represents an extremely important direction for future research (Rosser 2002; Setterfield 2002; Hart 2009).

There are many other examples of traverse analysis in economic theory. The literature on path dependency, hysteresis, cumulative causation (Setterfield 2002) and lock-in are some examples. The general conclusion of this literature is that, without serious analysis of the traverse, all economic theory utilizing some concept of equilibrium (including the long-run equilibrium analysis of the Sraffians) is vacuous. Without some demonstration that there are forces in the economy which push it to equilibrium, without influencing the position to which the economy is gravitating, it is difficult to foresee any useful role for such equilibrium theory. However, such a demonstration is unlikely, as 'without a visible hand, the invisible hand is likely to guide us on to the wrong path; this is perhaps the most important conclusion from the analysis of the traverse' (Halevi and Kriesler 1992, p. 233).

PETER KRIESLER

See also:

Equilibrium and Non-equilibrium; Expectations; Growth Theory; Kaleckian Economics; Sraffian Economics; Time in Economic Theory.

References

Hagemann, H. (1992), 'Traverse analysis in a post-classical model', in J. Halevi, D. Laibman and E. Nell (eds), *Beyond the Steady State: A Revival of Growth Theory*, Basingstoke: Macmillan, pp. 235–63.
Halevi, J. and P. Kriesler (1992), 'An introduction to the traverse in economic theory', in J. Halevi, D. Laibman and E. Nell (eds), *Beyond the Steady State: A Revival of Growth Theory*, Basingstoke: Macmillan, pp. 225–34.
Hart, N. (2009), 'Marshall's equilibrium and evolution: then and now', PhD dissertation, School of Economics, University of New South Wales, Sydney.
Hicks, J.R. (1965), *Capital and Growth*, Oxford: Oxford University Press.

Hicks, J.R. (1973), *Capital and Time*, Oxford: Clarendon Press.

Kalecki, M. (1990–97), *Collected Works of Michał Kalecki*, 7 Vols, Oxford: Clarendon Press.

Kriesler, P. (1999), 'Harcourt, Hicks and Lowe: incompatible bedfellows?', in C. Sardoni and P. Kriesler (eds), *Themes in Political Economy: Essays in Honour of Geoff Harcourt*, London and New York: Routledge, pp. 400–417.

Lavoie M and P. Ramirez-Gaston (1977), 'Traverse in a two-sector Kaleckian model of growth with target-return pricing', *Manchester School*, **65** (2), 145–69.

Lowe, A. (1976), *The Path of Economic Growth*, Cambridge: Cambridge University Press.

Robinson, J. (1974), 'History versus equilibrium', in Robinson, *Collected Economic Papers*, Vol. V, Oxford: Blackwell, 1979, pp. 48–58.

Rosser, J.B. Jr (2002), 'Complex dynamics and Post Keynesian economics', in M. Setterfield (ed.), *The Economics of Demand-led Growth*, Cheltenham, UK and Northampton, MA, USA: Edward Elgar, pp. 74–98

Setterfield, M. (1995), 'Historical time and economic theory', *Review of Political Economy*, **7** (1), 1–27.

Setterfield, M. (2002), 'A model of Kaldorian traverse: cumulative causation, structural change and evolutionary hysteresis', in Setterfield (ed.), *The Economics of Demand-led Growth*, Cheltenham, UK and Northampton, MA, USA: Edward Elgar, pp. 215–33.

Uncertainty

Economics texts commonly define a situation of *risk* as one in which an individual with a decision to make is able to assign numerical probabilities to all outcomes that could possibly follow from that decision. If probabilities cannot be assigned, a situation of *uncertainty* is then said to obtain. These texts characteristically focus their attention on the 'risk' situation thus specified: having defined uncertainty, they simply ignore it. Some mainstream theorists take a different tack and assume that economic agents can *always* identify, and assign probabilities to, the whole range of possible future 'states of the world'. This group has no need to make a distinction between risk and uncertainty: for them, uncertainty itself is inherently quantifiable.

The passion for numerical probability shown by mainstream economists is no accident. For their central concept of 'rational' optimizing choice, developed under assumptions of perfect knowledge, can seem somewhat irrelevant to the real world, where certainty is never obtainable. However, if knowledge of probabilities attaching to alternative possible future scenarios is assumed to be available, then (statistically) expected values can be calculated. These can, in turn, provide a basis for a theory of optimal decisions in a world in which perfect knowledge is lacking. In this way, many orthodox economists believe they have remedied a major perceived deficiency in their theoretical apparatus.

For Post Keynesian economists, in contrast, the future is characterized by *fundamental uncertainty*. They take their cue from Keynes, who rejected the possibility of a theory of optimal choice under uncertainty, observing that 'human decisions affecting the future . . . cannot depend on strict mathematical expectation, since the basis for making such calculations does not exist' (Keynes 1936, pp. 162–3). Drawing primarily on the work of Paul Davidson, the discussion which follows tries to explain the concept of fundamental uncertainty in broad terms and to show why it occupies such an important place in Post Keynesian economic theory. As a first step, it is appropriate to review some important concepts developed by George Shackle, since his theories have been a major influence on the way Post Keynesian economists in general think about uncertainty and on Davidson's ideas on the subject in particular.

Any 'question about the future' represents what Shackle (1955 [1968], p. 63) calls an 'experiment'. He defines a 'divisible' experiment as one consisting of 'a series of trials all in some sense alike and each important only as it contributes to the total result of the series' (p. 64). For instance, a firm might regard any sale to a prospective customer as a trial. Its sales 'experiment' would then be a divisible one, if (as is likely) its management were primarily interested in the total revenue generated by its sales effort and not in the outcome of its dealings with any specific customer.

Shackle accepts that it might in principle be possible to calculate numerical probabilities in divisible experiments, provided that frequency distributions could be derived from '"suitably uniform" circumstances and a "large" number of [past] repetitions' (p. 4). His point, however, is to challenge what that would achieve. For, suppose our firm *could* draw up reliable frequency data from individual customer records and so meet these preconditions for calculating numerical probabilities. Its total monthly sales revenue could then be forecast with considerable accuracy and could not be described as being a matter over which its management was in any real sense uncertain. Thus, Shackle argues, a situation in which numerical probabilities *could* be calculated 'has nothing whatever to do with ignorance or uncertainty: it is knowledge' (p. 4). His argument implies that the orthodox economists whose approach was outlined above delude themselves in imagining they have developed theories that have anything to do with real uncertainty.

An even more potent concept developed by Shackle is that of the 'crucial experiment'. This he explains as follows:

> An experiment can be such that . . . the making of it will radically alter the situation . . . so that it will subsequently be impossible . . .to perform another experiment of a relevantly similar kind. Napoleon could not repeat the battle of Waterloo a hundred times in the hope that, in a certain proportion of cases, the Prussians would arrive too late. His decision to fight on the field of Waterloo was what I call a crucial experiment . . . Had he won, repetition would . . . have been unnecessary; when he lost, repetition was impossible. (p. 25)

Shackle's main point is not that the 'average' outcome of a large number of 'similar' experiments is hypothetical when the experiment is crucial. Rather, it is that any such average is *of no interest* to the crucial experimenter, because the latter is never going to be in a position to offset a poor outcome now with better ones later. Shackle's position can perhaps be summarized as follows: when numerical probability calculations are relevant, the situation is not uncertain; when the situation *is* uncertain, they are not relevant.

Shackle insisted that '[t]he difficulty of obtaining reliable frequency ratios is the lesser strand of my argument' (p. 4). Although drawing on Shackle's concepts, Davidson's efforts have, however, been directed at showing just how serious that 'difficulty' is. Now Keynes (1921 [1973], p. 468) castigated the 'Professors of probability [who are] often and justly derided for arguing as if nature were an urn containing black and white balls in fixed proportions'. Nevertheless, Davidson insists that the conceptions of these professors' modern-day counterparts must be used if the case against them is to be demonstrated. To follow Davidson's analysis it is therefore helpful to begin by considering what the world would be like if nature *were* akin to Keynes's urn.

The outcome of any drawing from the urn will be a *stochastic* (random) event, so that we can possibly think of a series of outcomes in a succession of drawings as resulting from a stochastic *process*. Furthermore, if these drawings take place at consecutive points in time, they will yield a *time series*, from which an average outcome, a *time average*, can be calculated. This series could be infinite. It is not so easy to conceive of all possible outcomes of a drawing at a *single* point in time as existing simultaneously in a universe or *ensemble* (Davidson 1982–83, p. 189) of alternative 'logical' worlds. However, having made this conceptual leap, we can grasp the idea of a 'space average', the mean value taken by a (finite or infinite) set of such drawings (ibid.).

On this basis, we can begin to understand the following definition of an 'ergodic process', Davidson's formal equivalent to nature's urn:

> If, and only if, the stochastic process is ergodic, then for an infinitely large realization [that is, set of drawings from the urn] the time statistics and the space statistics will coincide. For finite realizations of ergodic processes, time and space statistics coincide except for random errors. In other words, calculated time and space statistics tend to converge (with the probability of unity) as the number of observations increase. (Davidson 2007, p. 32; see also Davidson 1982–83, p. 185)

The importance of this concept in Davidson's work is measured by the frequency with which more or less this same terse definition is restated in his writings. It is the basis on which he asserts the existence of what he calls the 'ergodic axiom', the assumption that economic events are broadly governed by ergodic processes. This axiom, he suggests, is the ultimate logical foundation of orthodox theorizing (Davidson 1996, p. 494; 2007, pp. 31–5). For the convergence of averages in an ergodic system implies that, over a long enough period of time, events will tend to follow repetitive patterns, and it is central to Davidson's argument that just this kind of conception lies behind the orthodox belief in an inherent tendency in market economies towards a long-run (full-employment) equilibrium (Davidson 1996, p. 496).

Of course, Davidson's purpose in highlighting the importance to orthodox theory of an ergodic axiom is only to demonstrate that belief in it is untenable. This he seeks to do on both empirical and logical grounds. Now, simply stated, a time series is stationary if all observations that go to make it up are drawn from distributions with the same mean and variance, and his empirical objection is that real-world time-series data often fail to exhibit evidence of stationarity. As he points out, non-stationarity is, formally, a sufficient condition for non-ergodicity (ibid., pp. 494–5).

Davidson's logical objection is perhaps the more fundamental. He observes, referring to Shackle's concept, that '[w]hen agents make *crucial decisions*, they necessarily destroy any ergodic processes that may have hitherto existed' (Davidson 1982–83, p. 192). Furthermore, if crucial decisions are 'all pervasive' (Shackle 1955 [1968], p. 63) or even just 'very common' (Davidson 1982–83, p. 192), then the economy as a whole will be in a state of constant change as economic agents continually alter the pre-existing state of things by taking them. That will in turn represent 'a sufficient condition for a non-ergodic world' (ibid.; see also Davidson 1996, pp. 497, 500). In that world, decision makers will typically operate in an environment of fundamental uncertainty, since it will be impossible to base a whole range of significant economic decisions on forecasts derived from past data.

The significance of this analysis for Post Keynesian theory is immense. For, as Davidson (1996, pp. 501, 506; 2007, pp. 90–96) insists:

1. individuals will exhibit long-term liquidity preference only under conditions of fundamental uncertainty;
2. the Post Keynesian contention that money is not neutral even in the long run assumes the possibility of long-term liquidity preference;
3. the Post Keynesian critique of the notion that market economies have an automatic tendency towards full-employment equilibrium is based on a denial of the neutrality of money; and
4. Post Keynesian policy analysis, with its emphasis on government intervention and the need for protective institutions, arises out of that critique.

As has been shown, the essential premise of the first of this argument's four steps is the proposition that the crucial experiment is, at the very least, a 'common' phenomenon in the economic sphere. But if 'crucial-ness' is important in the real world, why do orthodox theorists fail even to acknowledge it as a possibility? The answer would seem to be that, conceiving nature as an urn like Keynes's professors of probability, they cannot do so. For that would be tantamount to accepting that the proportions of black and white balls in the urn could be changed by human decisions and would make it impossible to view cause and effect simply in terms of the operation of stochastic processes.

The idea of a stochastic process, it is reasonable to argue, implies a metaphysical view of the world that is at odds with human experience. This is because:

> the existence of a process implies that the outcome today stands at the end, in real time, of a chain of causation and may be different from what it was yesterday because of prior changes somewhere along the length of that causal chain. Processes are in reality the polar opposite of repeated drawings from some eternally subsisting distribution. In other words, in place of a genuine process there is, within the stochastic scheme of things, only the isolated, accidental outcome, dissociated from any determining cause/effect relationship with anything that has gone before. (Glickman 1997–98, p. 262)

Davidson has noted: 'If observed economic events are not the result of stochastic processes then objective probability structures do not even fleetingly exist' (1994, p. 90). The historical/causal conception of a process just outlined offers a realistic alternative account of how economic events are determined that can help us understand *why* uncertainty is fundamental in economics.

MURRAY GLICKMAN

See also:

Agency; Conventions; Expectations; Keynes's *General Theory*; Keynes's *Treatise on Probability*; Liquidity Preference; Non-ergodicity.

References

Davidson, P. (1982–83), 'Rational expectations: a fallacious foundation for studying crucial decision-making processes', *Journal of Post Keynesian Economics*, **5** (2), 182–97.
Davidson, P. (1994), *Post Keynesian Macroeconomic Theory*, Aldershot, UK and Brookfield, VT, USA: Edward Elgar.
Davidson, P. (1996), 'Reality and economic theory', *Journal of Post Keynesian Economics*, **18** (4), 479–508.
Davidson, P. (2007), *John Maynard Keynes*, Basingstoke: Palgrave Macmillan.
Glickman, M. (1997–98), 'A Post Keynesian refutation of Modigliani–Miller on capital structure', *Journal of Post Keynesian Economics*, **20** (2), 251–74.
Keynes, J.M. (1921), *The Treatise on Probability*; reprinted as *The Collected Writings of John Maynard Keynes*, Vol. VIII, edited by D.E. Moggridge, London: Macmillan for the Royal Economic Society, 1973.
Keynes, J.M. (1936), *The General Theory of Employment, Interest and Money*, London: Macmillan.
Shackle, G.L.S. (1955 [1968]), *Uncertainty in Economics*, Cambridge: Cambridge University Press.

Underconsumption

Although Keynes wrote about underconsumption at some length, the term is seldom used these days by Post Keynesians. Some of the central issues continue to resonate, however, in discussions of economic growth and the relationship between wages and employment.

Keynes devoted chapter 23 of the *General Theory* to 'Notes on Mercantilism, the usury laws, stamped money and theories of under-consumption', revealing considerable sympathy for seventeenth- and eighteenth-century work on the dangers of excessive saving. He also quoted Malthus and provided a critical commentary on such later under-consumptionists as J.A. Hobson and Major C.H. Douglas. The 'primary evil' identified by these writers, Keynes concluded, was ' a propensity to save in conditions of full employment more than the equivalent of the capital which is required, thus preventing full employment except when there is a mistake of foresight' (Keynes 1936, pp. 367–8). By 'the capital that is required' he seems to have meant the addition to the capital stock needed to cater for the increase in output as a whole (not just consumption goods), while 'the mistake in foresight' referred to the belief of Hobson and other underconsumptionists that unemployment would normally result unless entrepreneurs wrongly invested more than was justified by this requirement.

In chapter 22, 'Notes on the trade cycle', Keynes declared his support for 'all sorts of policies for increasing the propensity to consume' (ibid., p. 325), and offered a numerical example to illustrate what might be required:

> [If] the average level of output of to-day is 15 per cent below what it would be with continuous full employment, and if 10 per cent of this output represents net investment and 90 per cent of it consumption – if, furthermore, net invest-ment would have to rise 50 per cent in order to secure full employment, with the existing propensity to consume, so that with full employment output would rise from 100 to 115, consumption from 90 to 100 and net investment from 10 to 15:– then we might aim, perhaps, at so modifying the propensity to consume that with full employment consumption would rise from 90 to 103 and net investment from 10 to 12. (pp. 325–6)

Quite how this was to be achieved, Keynes did not say. The earliest under-consumptionists had called for a larger share of national income to go to the idle rich, who could be relied upon not to save very much of it. Subsequently, liberal and socialist writers urged redistribution in favour of the poor, on the grounds that the propensity to consume out of wages and salaries was considerably higher than that out of profits (and rents).

This is where Keynes –or at least his left-wing supporters – met Marx. The brief references to Marxism in the *General Theory* are disparaging, though in a 1933 draft Keynes had been much less critical. There was in fact a long tradition of underconsumptionism in the Marxian literature on economic crises and – not surprisingly – it featured prominently in analyses of the Great Depression by socialist theorists such as Otto Bauer, Natalie Moszkowska and Eugen Varga. The inexorable tendency of capitalist production, they argued, was towards an increase in the rate of exploitation, and hence in the share of profits in net output. This had become even more pronounced in the latest, monopoly stage of capitalism, which was dominated by what Paul Baran and Paul Sweezy subsequently termed 'the law of the rising surplus'. The decline in the wage share had rendered the system liable to crises of overaccumulation, with the capital stock growing more rapidly than was warranted by the increase in consumption. Thus, even if higher saving were to stimulate higher investment, the situation was inherently unsustainable. Any boom would end in a severe cyclical downturn, or perhaps (in the most dramatic versions of the argument) in the complete breakdown of the system. The maturity of capitalism was therefore synonymous with stagnation, according to the Austrian 'left Keynesian' Josef Steindl (King 2002, chapter 2).

Of all Keynes's close allies, it was Joan Robinson who was most receptive to these ideas. While she criticized Marx for trying to work out a theory of crisis in which Say's law continued to hold, she also saw considerable merit in his reproduction models. They could be used, Robinson suggested, as the basis for a theory in which

> consumption by the workers is limited by their poverty, while consumption by the capitalists is limited by the greed for capital which causes them to accumulate wealth rather than to enjoy luxury. The demand for consumption goods (the product of group II) is thus restricted. But if the output of the consumption-goods industries is limited by the market, the demand for capital goods (group I) is in turn restricted, for the constant capital of the consumption-good industries will not expand fast enough to absorb the potential output of the capital-good industries. Thus the distribution of income, between wages and surplus, is such as to set up a chronic tendency for a lack of balance between the two groups of industries. (Robinson 1942, p. 49)

In this interpretation Robinson was heavily influenced by Michał Kalecki who, though not himself an underconsumptionist, had absorbed the closely related work of Mikhail Tugan-Baranovsky and Rosa Luxemburg while still a young man in Poland. In a celebrated passage Kalecki wrote of 'the tragedy of investment', which adds both to effective demand and to the capital stock, simultaneously stimulating growth and undermining it (Kalecki 1939 [1991], p. 284).

In formal terms, there are certain similarities between models of underconsumption and the accelerator principle that is central to Harrod–Domar growth theory, itself a major influence on Post Keynesian thinking about economic growth. It is significant that both Roy Harrod and Evsey Domar acknowledged their debt to Hobson. As Domar wrote:

Keynes analysed what happened when savings (of the preceding period) are not invested. Hobson, on the other hand, went a step further and stated the problem in this form: suppose savings are invested. Will the new plants be able to dispose of their products? Such a statement of the problem was not, as Keynes thought, a mistake. It was a statement of a different, and possibly also a deeper problem. (Domar 1957, p. 52)

Some intricate analytical issues are involved here, in particular the precise specification of the accelerator principle (does investment depend on the rate of increase in consumption or the rate of increase in total output?), and the relationship between underconsumption and what has been termed the 'underinvestment' theory that is implicit in the Harrod–Domar model (Schneider 1996, pp. 77–83).

If growth theory is one area in which underconsumptionist thinking continues to influence Post Keynesian macroeconomics, another is wage and employment theory. Sidney Weintraub (1956) approached this question from the perspective of Keynes's aggregate supply–aggregate demand analysis. An increase in the general level of money wages would shift the aggregate supply curve upwards, by increasing firms' costs of production, and would therefore tend to reduce employment. But it might also shift the aggregate demand curve up, through increasing consumption by wage-earners; alternatively, it could reduce aggregate demand by depressing the marginal efficiency of capital and discouraging investment. Weintraub distinguished three possibilities: the classical case, where employment falls as money wages rise; what he termed the Keynesian case, where shifts in aggregate supply and aggregate demand cancel each other out; and the underconsumptionist case, where employment increases as money wages rise.

While Weintraub focused on money wages, Amit Bhaduri and Stephen Marglin (1990) provided a formal analysis of the effects on aggregate demand of an exogenous change in the *real* wage. They distinguished 'stagnationist' and 'exhilarationist' regimes, the former (which corresponds to the classic underconsumptionist position) prevailing when investment responds weakly to a reduction in profitability while consumption increases substantially if real wages rise. The case for the stagnationists, they argued, is stronger in the context of a closed economy than in an open economy, where effective demand can be increased by a currency devaluation that lowers the real wage.

The policy issues that are involved here are evidently very important, and potentially very divisive. Kalecki angrily criticized those self-proclaimed 'workers' friends' who urged trade unions to accept money-wage reductions in the interests of increased employment (Kalecki 1939 [1991], p. 318), although this did not make him an advocate of wage inflation as the route to full employment. Instead he suggested that higher money wages were likely to generate price inflation, leaving *real* wages – and real consumption – unchanged. Only a reduction in the product market and labour market power of the capitalists, Kalecki concluded, would permanently raise real wages and reduce the share of profits in national income.

Is it possible that both workers and capitalists might gain from an increase in real wages that increases effective demand, thereby raising capacity utilization and increasing total profits? Bhaduri and Marglin contrast the social democratic ideology of economic cooperation between the classes with the conservative (and Marxian!) view that conflict over income distribution is inescapable in any capitalist economy. In their model, the values of the parameters determine precisely when cooperation will give way to conflict, and it proves impossible to establish an unambiguous association between the stagnationist regime and class cooperation on the one hand, and the exhilarationist regime and class conflict on the other (Bhaduri and Marglin 1990, Figure 3, p. 389).

The evidence on the relationship between real wages and aggregate employment is also rather mixed. In the late 1930s Keynes was convinced by 'friendly critics', among them Kalecki, John Dunlop and Lorie Tarshis, that increased employment was associated with higher, not lower, real wages. More recent research suggests that he (and they) may well have been mistaken. Empirically no less than theoretically, underconsumption remains one of the more contentious questions in Post Keynesian economics, even if the term itself is rarely used nowadays. In one sense, the issues raised by theorists of underconsumption have become more pertinent since the late 1970s, when the labour share in total output began to fall in most advanced capitalist economies. The analysis does need to be revised, however, to allow for the emergence of working-class saving and, especially, working-class debt. The aphorism attributed to Kalecki, 'capitalists get what they spend, workers spend what they get', was true a century ago, when the assets of most working families were restricted to a few sticks of furniture and their only debts were 'on the slate' at the corner shop. By the early twenty-first century this was palpably no longer the case, with the great majority of wage- and salary-earners deeply embroiled in financial markets, as both creditors (with houses and superannuation accounts) and debtors (mortgages, credit cards and overdrafts). Thus the subprime mortgage crisis of the mid-2000s in the United States had its roots in declining real wages and a falling labour share, as the underconsumptionists might have expected (Barba and Pivetti 2009; Palley 2009). But it manifested itself in financial instability, and was transmitted to the 'real' economy through the money markets – precisely the areas that the original theorists of underconsumption often tended to ignore.

J.E. KING

See also:

Consumer Debt; Growth and Income Distribution; Growth Theory; Income Distribution; Kaleckian Economics; Saving; Wage- and Profit-led Regimes.

References

Barba, A. and M. Pivetti (2009), 'Rising household debt: its causes and macroeconomic implications – a long-period analysis', *Cambridge Journal of Economics*, **33** (1), 113–37.
Bhaduri, A. and S. Marglin (1990), 'Unemployment and the real wage: the economic basis for contesting political ideologies', *Cambridge Journal of Economics*, **14** (4), 375–93.
Domar, E.S. (1957), 'Expansion and employment', *American Economic Review*, **47** (1), 34–55.
Kalecki, M. (1939), *Essays in the Theory of Economic Fluctuations*, London: Allen & Unwin; reprinted in *Collected Works of Michał Kalecki*, Vol. I, Oxford: Clarendon Press, 1991.
Keynes, J.M. (1936), *The General Theory of Employment, Interest and Money*, London: Macmillan.
King, J.E. (2002), *A History of Post Keynesian Economics Since 1936*, Cheltenham, UK and Northampton, MA, USA: Edward Elgar.
Palley, T. (2009), 'After the bust: the outlook for macroeconomics and macroeconomic policy', in E. Hein, T. Niechoj and E. Stockhammer (eds), *Macroeconomic Policies on Shaky Foundations? Whither Mainstream Economics*, Marburg: Metropolis, pp. 371–91.
Robinson, J. (1942), *An Essay on Marxian Economics*, London: Macmillan.
Schneider, M.P. (1996), *J.A. Hobson*, London: Macmillan.
Weintraub, S. (1956), 'A macroeconomic approach to the theory of wages', *American Economic Review*, **46** (5), 835–56.

Unemployment

In capitalist economies, individuals and families are largely responsible for providing for their own well-being. In all industrialized and many developing economies, most workers do not have the means of production to provide for their own subsistence, but rather must obtain the means of purchase and means of payment (money) necessary for buying the means of subsistence by selling their labour power in the market. In addition, the requirement that taxes be paid in government currency means that even those possessing the means of production to provide for their own subsistence nevertheless must usually enter the labour market to obtain that which is necessary to settle their tax obligations.

Unemployment, the failure to obtain employment that earns wages or salaries paid in money, thus has a dire impact on the jobless, and is also associated with tremendous social and economic costs for society as a whole. Whereas, in neoclassical economics, market systems possess an inherent tendency to full employment, in Post Keynesian economics unemployment is seen as a normal feature of capitalist economies. The *effective demand problem* means that capitalist economies have trouble *attaining* full employment, while the *structural change problem* means that capitalist economies have trouble *maintaining* full employment, even if it could be attained. In addition, some Post Keynesians – echoing Marx – have identified the *functionality* of unemployment, which presents obstacles to Post Keynesian economic policies to eliminate unemployment. Nevertheless, Post Keynesian economics does suggest policies that might assist capitalist economies in attaining and maintaining full employment, without resulting in other macroeconomic problems, such as inflation. Moving from macroeconomic theory to policy implementation may be assisted by combining legislative efforts with grassroots activism at the local level, perhaps led by the unemployed and underemployed themselves.

Unemployment has tremendous social and economic costs (see, for example, Piachaud 1997). Unemployment causes permanent losses of output of goods and services. The unemployed are faced with financial insecurity, resulting in poverty and indebtedness. Certain kinds of criminal activity are directly related to unemployment. Many studies have linked unemployment to family disruption, suicide, ill health (physical and mental), drug addiction, homelessness, malnutrition, poor prenatal care, school dropouts, racial and ethnic antagonism, and other social problems (see, for example, Jahoda 1982). Unemployment also differentially affects certain sectors of the population, so that disadvantaged minorities, those with little education, and youth, for example, can suffer from rates of unemployment two to ten times the overall rate.

Unemployment also can destabilize business expectations, as fears of low demand cool private investment. Related to this, unemployment can also lead to technological stagnation. If, as Marx and others suggest, high levels of employment stimulate technical innovation, unemployment would be associated with less innovation. Firms with high and stable levels of demand have the resources and the incentive to support going high-tech; with high unemployment and thus cheap labour, firms lack the resources and the incentive to retool. It has also been shown that unemployment leads to deterioration in labour skills. All of this suggests that unemployment may lead to lower productivity growth.

Unemployment is the direct and indirect cause of many social and economic problems. It can also lead to political instability. Since Keynes, Post Keynesians have dedicated significant attention to the problems of unemployment. Since unemployment is the cause of so much social and human misery, it is of great interest whether capitalist economies tend to full employment or whether unemployment is a normal feature of capitalism, and thus a target for government intervention.

In neoclassical economics, market systems tend to utilize all resources fully, including labour. Perfectly flexible wages, prices and interest rates constitute the self-adjusting mechanism that will tend to eliminate unemployed resources in the long run. In the neoclassical version of Say's law, if there is unemployment wages will adjust to increase labour demand, and interest rates will adjust to ensure that the excess of aggregate income over aggregate consumption at the full-employment level of output will be invested. There is no *involuntary* unemployment in the long run, unless there are market imperfections such as 'sticky' wages, government interference, or other institutional rigidities (for example, unions). For neoclassical economics, if there is unemployment, government should stay out and let the market correct itself; if there are market imperfections, government may promote conditions under which the self-adjusting mechanism works most smoothly, for example, deregulation, antitrust, and so on.

In *The General Theory of Employment, Interest, and Money*, Keynes overthrew Say's law and demonstrated the possibility and the likelihood that market systems do not tend to fully utilize resources, even under competitive conditions, due to insufficient effective demand. Keynes criticized the neoclassical theory of saving and investment, arguing that traditional loanable funds theory holds income constant when looking at savings and abstracts from expectations when analysing investment. If aggregate saving is primarily a function of income, not interest rates, and investment is determined by the expected profitability of investors and lending institutions, then saving does not determine investment through variations in the rate of interest, and the economy does not automatically tend to full employment. Instead private investment determines savings through changes in income, but there is no reason to expect that the full-employment level of investment will always be undertaken. Keynes's analysis takes place in historical rather than notional (or logical) time. The past is unchangeable and the future is unknown and unknowable. Money must be understood as an institution for dealing with radical uncertainty. The result is that capitalist economies tend to operate with excess capacity and unemployment. It is therefore unlikely for a capitalist economy, on its own, to attain full employment.

But capitalist economies have problems maintaining full employment, even if it could be attained, due to ongoing structural and technological change, such as changes in labour supply and the supply of natural resources, labour- and capital-displacing technical change, and changes in the composition of final demand. An economy running at full capacity and full employment would be unable to respond to such changes, and sectoral imbalance is here added to aggregate imbalance as a further cause of unemployment. Bottlenecks and rigidities mean that full employment is likely to be inflationary. Structural change will soon result in unemployment, as technology displaces workers in one sector and fails to absorb them in another, the formation of real capital fails to keep up with the pace of a growing labour supply, or declining demand in one sector fails to be offset by demand for new products. Work such as Lowe (1976) and Pasinetti (1981) offers structural models that demonstrate the great unlikelihood of capitalist economies maintaining full employment, even if it could be attained.

The effective demand and structural change problems are economic causes of unemployment. But Post Keynesians such as Michał Kalecki have noted that there may also be political obstacles to full employment. Since unemployment in Keynes is a negative byproduct of capitalism, it is viewed as serving no purpose in the capitalist system and so is clearly undesirable for all. Kalecki, Josef Steindl and others, however, have highlighted that unemployment may be functional in capitalism, an insight that is drawn from Marx's analysis of the reserve army of labour.

In Marx, unemployment serves several functions. First, it provides the system with a pool of available labour from which to draw when the pace of accumulation increases. Second, unemployment serves to discipline workers, who may not fear being laid off in an environment of full employment. Third, unemployment holds down wages, since one of the ways in which unemployment disciplines workers is to decrease their bargaining power and thus keep wages from rising. Thus, in this view, unemployment is not only a natural byproduct of capitalism, it is essential to its smooth operation.

Marx postulated a number of different components of the reserve army of labour. The 'latent reserve' includes those currently outside of the market system, either performing unpaid household labour or eking out a meagre subsistence in the periphery of Third World economies. The 'stagnant reserve' includes those who are almost never employed, boom or bust. Members of the 'floating reserve' alternate between employment and unemployment, with the ups and downs of the business cycle. 'Paupers' is the term Marx used to identify those who are now often referred to as the 'underclass'. Recently, it has been suggested that changes in global capitalism have rendered some of these components no longer functional. And this has resulted in an environment conducive to policies that may promote the elimination of the emerging 'surplus population', with scary genocidal and racist connotations (Darity 1999).

Policies to address unemployment must recognize both the effective demand and structural change problems, as well as the functionality of unemployment and the emergence of a hard-core, 'unemployable' sector no longer functioning as a reserve army. Traditional Keynesian policies initially attempted to stimulate aggregate demand through fiscal and monetary policies. Stimulating the private sector to full employment may address the aggregate demand problem but not the structural change one. In fact, since the structural change problem emerges most forcefully at higher levels of capacity utilization and employment, stimulating private sector demand may increase this problem. Some Post Keynesians would utilize incomes policies to deal with some of the symptoms. Other routes would include promoting public works and the 'socialization of invest-ment'. These latter approaches, if designed correctly, may be more effec-tive than conventional fiscal stimulus in dealing with the structural change problem. In the framework of a capitalist economy, full employment requires a policy – or a set of policies – that can increase effective demand without bringing on structural rigidity and that can eliminate unemploy-ment while finding some institutional mechanism for dealing with the functionality question.

More recently, Post Keynesians have suggested that such a policy is avail-able in the form of a kind of permanent Works Progress Administration (Wray 1998). Hyman Minsky (1986) referred to this as government as 'employer of last resort'. Under such a policy, the government would provide a public service employment (PSE) job to anyone ready and willing to work. As the economy expands (contracts), the private sector demand for labour would increase (decrease), and the PSE sector would shrink (grow). PSE workers would be employed in all kinds of social and public services that would benefit the community. Elimination of long periods of unemployment would preserve and potentially enhance labour productiv-ity. The social and economic costs of unemployment due to income insecu-rity and poverty would decline, and society would experience a significant benefit in the form of less crime and other social problems associated with unemployment. The effective demand problem would be solved by main-taining aggregate income at high levels, but the PSE approach, unlike tra-ditional demand stimulus, would address the structural change problem as well (Forstater 1998). Instead of workers alternating between employment and unemployment, sectoral and aggregate change would alter only the proportion of private and public sector employment. PSE can also address environmental problems. Stimulating the private sector to full employment would surely result in greater pollution and exhaustible resource utiliza-tion, while PSE activities may be designed to pollute less, use less fossil fuel and perform a variety of environmental services (that is, green jobs).

A PSE approach to full employment and price stability can also serve as the basis for humanistic social policies. Under such a programme, a wide variety of social policies may be introduced that otherwise would not stand a chance. To understand how this might work, consider that workers will always have the option to take a public service job. Now imagine what might happen if the public service wage–benefits package included health insurance. Employers in the private sector would have to match the public service wage–benefits, either line by line, or in some other compensating way. Private businesses would be encouraged by 'market' pressures to either offer health insurance or compensate in some alternative way (higher salary, more chance for advancement, other benefits or some other attractive part of the offer). Likewise, since the public sector wage would be the de facto minimum wage (remember that the real minimum wage in an economic society with a semi-permanent pool of unemployed is zero), increases in the public sector wage could also be used to pressure businesses to raise wages (or some other compensating feature of their offer). Consider what might happen if the public sector job came with child care. Likewise, worker health and safety issues and general job environment. The list of ways in which public sector employment might be used as a 'benchmark' to increase the quality of private sector jobs is limited only by the imagination.

Next, consider the possibilities offered by millions of new workers available to do public service. Suddenly, there is no longer any financial or labour constraint to the provision of public and community services (other than the 'real' constraints of population size, skills and education, and so on): Habitat for Humanity and Meals on Wheels are never wanting for labour; public libraries and community centres are open every night; additional helping hands in playgrounds, at subway stations, in nursing homes, and at recycling centres. The environment benefits are numerous, from clean-up to parks and recreation to tree-planting to new hiking trails. We know from the history of the Works Progress Administration (WPA) and other successful public service programmes just how productive the contributions can be (we can also learn from the mistakes of such programmes – for example, race and gender discrimination must not be tolerated).

A public service jobs programme could also be used to redefine just what constitutes valuable work in our society. Presently, the market is used as the measuring rod, so if you cannot make your way in the private sector, your life-calling must not be valuable. Under the PSE programme, society is free to decide what qualifies as a public service job. Musicians and artists might be free to follow their calling. Oral histories can be documented and preserved through interviews with the elderly. Community gardens can thrive, with public service chefs preparing meals. Addressing the historical legacy of patriarchy and gender exploitation, care for one's own children and one's own home can be considered valid public service work.

A number of observers have noted that the Post Keynesian theory of the state is not well developed, or that Post Keynesians view the state as benevolent and rational, overlooking the political pressures weighing against sensible policies (see, for example, Danby 2004). Those involved in the early stages of the drafting of the 1946 Employment Act and the 1978 Humphrey–Hawkins bill in the United States witnessed employment guarantees eliminated from the final legislation. More recently, advocates of the NREGA in India saw the programme limited to one hundred days a year, and the Argentine *Jefes* programme included only 'heads of households' despite supporters at the highest levels of government. History teaches that successful efforts at utilizing governmental institutions are enhanced by pressures stemming from grassroots activism and popular organization (Rose 1995). Organizing the unemployed, the underemployed, and even the homeless, with employed and unemployed working together, may prove effective (Groff 1997). Neighbourhood and community unemployment councils may play important roles in the future, as they have in the past (Ervin 1994).

Unemployment is at the root of many of the economic and social problems of capitalism. Some would argue that, instead of tinkering with capitalism, a new economic system should be sought in which the right to a job as put forward in the United Nations Universal Declaration of Human Rights is realized. Perhaps in a post-capitalist society the employment–money link will be severed and a new mode of social and economic organization will make unemployment extinct and irrelevant. Until such a time, however, there is no good economic reason not to go immediately to full employment with a guaranteed public service job for anyone ready and willing to work. Political obstacles may be more effectively negotiated by complementing policy advocacy with grassroots campaigns at the community level.

MATHEW FORSTATER

See also:

Economic Policy; Effective Demand; Employer of Last Resort; Employment; Full Employment; Kaleckian Economics; Keynes's *General Theory*; Say's Law.

References

Danby, C. (2004), 'Contested states, transnational subjects: toward a Post Keynesianism without modernity', in E.O. Zein-Elabdin and S. Charusheela (eds), *Postcolonialism Meets Economics*, Abingdon and New York: Routledge, pp. 253–70.
Darity, W.A. Jr (1999), 'Who loses from unemployment?', *Journal of Economic Issues*, 33 (2), 491–6.
Ervin, L.K. (1994), *Anarchism and the Black Revolution*, Philadelphia, PA: Monkeywrench Press.
Forstater, M. (1998), 'Flexible full employment: structural implications of discretionary public sector employment', *Journal of Economic Issues*, 32 (2), 557–63.
Groff, R. (1997), 'Class politics by any other name: organizing the unemployed', *Studies in Political Economy*, 54, 91–117.
Jahoda, M. (1982), *Employment and Unemployment: A Social–Psychological Analysis*, Cambridge: Cambridge University Press.
Lowe, A. (1976), *The Path of Economic Growth*, Cambridge: Cambridge University Press.
Minsky, H.P. (1986), *Stabilizing an Unstable Economy*, New Haven, CT: Yale University Press.

Pasinetti, L. (1981), *Structural Change and Economic Growth*, Cambridge: Cambridge University Press.

Piachaud, D. (1997), 'A price worth paying? The costs of unemployment', in J. Philpott (ed.), *Working for Full Employment*, London and New York: Routledge, pp. 49–62.

Rose, N. (1995), *Workfare or Fair Work: Women, Welfare, and Government Work Programs*, New Brunswick, NJ: Rutgers University Press.

Wray, L.R. (1998), *Understanding Modern Money: The Key to Full Employment and Price Stability*, Cheltenham, UK and Northampton, MA, USA: Edward Elgar.

University of Missouri–Kansas City

The University of Missouri–Kansas City (UMKC) was chartered in 1929 as the University of Kansas City, and its first entering class was in 1933. In 1963 it became UMKC when it joined the University of Missouri (UM) system. Economics courses were initially taught in the Department of Business Administration. It was not until 1939 that the Department of Economics was established. One of its early members was Abba Lerner, who was appointed in 1941 and stayed two years. However, the department's heterodox intellectual heritage did not begin until the hiring of John Hodges as the department chair in 1946. As a student of Clarence Ayres and the Institutionalist school of the University of Texas, Hodges was one of a number of young institutional economists who populated mid-west and southwest colleges and universities from the 1930s through to the 1960s. In 1947 Horace B. Davis joined the department. This was a daring appointment since Davis was a Marxist economist (and also a member of the Communist Party). He got caught up in McCarthyism and was dismissed from his tenured position by the university in 1954. The latter part of the 1950s was one of decline for the university and the department in terms of faculty, students and courses, so that in 1961 Hodges was the only economist left. In the midst of this financial crisis facing UMKC, an offer was made by a community leader to donate over US $10 million to the university if 'the executive could name the president of the University, if the faculty be purged of liberal incumbents, and that the Economics Department in particular be completely re-oriented in its political and social philosophy' (Wagner 1999, p. 4). The university trustees turned down the offer. The subsequent admission to the UM system combined with postwar baby-boomers going to college; both the university and the department grew from this low point and never looked back.

The next phase of the department, running from 1962 to 1992, started with the hiring of Gene Wagner in 1962, who later became engaged in activities of the Union for Radical Political Economics (URPE) circa 1970. Next to be hired in 1963 was Robert (Bob) Brazelton. He obtained his doctorate from the University of Oklahoma where he was introduced to institutional economics (Brazelton 2004) which he put alongside his deep interest in Keynes's *General Theory*. Later in 1979, he was the first heterodox economist to clearly bring together Post Keynesian and institutional economics. A third hire was Joe Brown, also a student of Ayres, who came to UMKC in 1966 and remained until he died in 1978. The final 'institutional–heterodox' hire was James Sturgeon, who arrived in 1977. He was a student of Hodges and Brown and also obtained his doctorate from the University of Oklahoma. Mainstream economists were also hired during this thirty-year period, so the department was pluralistic. However, Hodges and the heterodox hires maintained a strong institutional and Keynesian presence in both the undergraduate economics major and in the MA economics degree. In particular, a course in institutional economics was required in both, a requirement that reaches back to 1946 for the economics major and 1950 for the MA degree and continues to this day (2011). Thus the department has the longest uninterrupted BA and MA programmes in which institutional economics is required and taught in the United States and indeed the world.

The third phase of the department started in 1992 when UMKC established an Interdisciplinary PhD (IPhD) programme, which the department joined. Prior to this, the department, along with many others, was prevented from offering a doctoral degree because it would 'duplicate' the doctoral degree offered by the flagship of the UM system, UM–Columbia. To circumvent this, Sturgeon and others worked very hard to establish the IPhD programme, pointing to its interdisciplinary nature as its differentiating characteristic from the doctoral programmes at Colombia. During its first 10 years, eight doctorates in economics were awarded.

In the mid-1990s, Sturgeon and Brazelton began expanding the programme. Anticipating the retirement of four members of the department, they developed a plan to more deeply ground the IPhD programme (and indeed the department as a whole) in institutional and Post Keynesian economics and thereby elevate its regional institutional reputation to a national and even international institutional–Post Keynesian reputation. That plan was executed in 1999 when Randall Wray (a student of Hyman Minsky and Washington University) and Mathew Forstater (a student of Robert Heilbroner and New School University) were hired and followed soon thereafter with the hiring of Frederic Lee (2000, a student of Alfred Eichner and Rutgers University), Stephanie Kelton (*née* Bell) (2002, a student of Ed Nell and New School University), Erik Olsen (2005, a student of Richard Wolff and Stephen Resnick and University of Massachusetts–Amherst), and Linwood Tauheed (2006, a student of Sturgeon and UMKC) all of whom are heterodox economists: institutionalists, Post Keynesians, and/or Marxists with some social and feminist economics thrown into the mix. Other faculty who have joined the department in various capacities include John Henry, who joined the department in 2002 after retiring from the California State University–Sacramento and counts Wray and Kelton as his students before they went on to graduate school; Jan Kregel, who joined the department as a visiting research professor and was a student of Paul Davidson and also taught Lee when he was a graduate student at Rutgers University; lecturers Ben Young and Mike Kelsay, who both received their MAs at UMKC before completing their PhDs at Oklahoma and Tennessee, respectively; and William Black, who joined the department with a joint appointment in the Law School in 2006.

Overall, the department's undergraduate and graduate economics programmes introduce students to Post Keynesian, institutionalist and other heterodox perspectives. In the undergraduate programme, the required microeconomics and macroeconomics courses include a discussion of both mainstream and heterodox theory. In addition, majors are required to take a course in institutional economic theory and another in the history of economic thought. A number of elective courses are offered, such as radical political economy, monetary theory, environment, urban, economic history and race and gender, in which heterodox approaches play a dominant role. Moreover, most of the undergraduate courses include aspects of the history of thought. For the MA programme, the required courses include advanced microeconomics, macroeconomics, econometrics and institutional theory. While the micro course covers mainstream micro, it does so from a very critical historical perspective, starting with the students reading Alfred Marshall's *Principles of Economics*. In contrast, in the macro course, students are presented with both mainstream and Post Keynesian views. The elective courses include those listed above as well as advanced political economy, economic policy and monetary theory.

The IPhD programme in economics is perhaps unique in the world. It consists of two components: a major concentration in economics consisting of 10–12 courses and a minor concentration in some area outside of economics, such as mathematics, history or geosciences, consisting of 4–5 courses. Part of the IPhD programme is based on the required courses in the MA programme as well as required doctoral courses in microeconomics, macroeconomics, political economy, history of thought and econometrics. The programme embraces heterodox economics to an even greater extent than at the undergraduate or the MA level. The microeconomics course concentrates solely on heterodox micro, while the macro course places a much greater emphasis on Post Keynesian macroeconomics and the political economy course covers the provisioning process, feminist economics, black political economy and the origins of capitalism. In addition, there are doctoral elective courses on advanced heterodox theory, financial macroeconomics, the history of economic thought, and monetary theory and policy. Finally, the comprehensive theory examination, which covers micro, macro, political economy and their interrelationship, emphasizes institutional, Post Keynesian, Marxian and other heterodox theories.

The strengths of the UMKC doctoral programme in terms of its contribution to heterodox economics lie in four areas: Post Keynesian macroeconomics and chartalism, institutional–social economics, heterodox microeconomics, and, in a very particular way, the history of economic thought. Each of these areas created a range of activities that promoted and developed doctoral education and transformed the department's regional reputation into a national and international reputation. When Forstater and Wray arrived at UMKC in 1999, they brought with them the Center for Full Employment and Price Stability (C-FEPS). Started circa 1996 with the support of Warren Mosler, C-FEPS was initially an informal policy institute whose mission was to promote research in the areas of functional finance and chartalism and public discussion of issues relating to monetary, budgetary and employment theory, history and policy. However, once at UMKC, it became a formal research institute, with Forstater as its director, Pavlina Tcherneva as its associate director, Wray as its research director, and Kelton as a senior research associate. Since its inauguration, C-FEPS has brought in Kregel on an annual basis to teach a course in financial macroeconomics, as well as many guest speakers, including James K. Galbraith, Harald Hagemann, Alain Parguez, Gary Dymski, Ed Nell, Nancy Ros and Sumner Rosen. But perhaps the most enduring contribution of C-FEPS to heterodox economics at UMKC was its sponsorship of the Post Keynesian International Workshop and summer school from 2002 to 2008. At this biannual extravaganza in Post Keynesian–institutional–heterodox economics, students and professors from UMKC and around the world talked, argued, discussed and learned from each other. Many former students to this day remember with fondness the intellectual excitement of the summer schools. Given the faculty's interest in Post Keynesian macroeconomics and chartalism, combined with the support of C-FEPS, a number of outstanding dissertations have been written on the US budget (Joëlle Leclaire 2006), central banking (Éric Tymoigne 2006), foreign direct investment and China's economic development (Yan Liang 2007), full employment and price stability in developing countries (Fadhel Kaboub 2006), fiscal policy (Pavlina Tcherneva 2008) and an instrumental approach to full employment (Michael Murray 2010).

As noted above, institutional economics has been a defining feature of the department since 1946. In addition to the taught courses, there is a monthly seminar on pragmatism and institutional economics. Moreover, doctoral students are encouraged to join the Association for Evolutionary Economics (AFEE) and the Association for Institutional Thought (AFIT) and present papers at their annual meetings. And they have done so with enthusiasm, with 10–15 former and current students presenting papers at these annual meetings and 10 students getting the AFIT Student Research Award between 2006 and 2010. Along with institutional economics, the department also introduces students to social economics and supports their interest in Catholic social thought and teaching. Consequently, many dissertations are quite infused with institutionalist ideas and arguments; another was written on the institutional approach to economic development (Jairo Parada 2005), and others have been written on Catholic social thought (Douglas Meador 2007; David Harris 2008; Jeremy O'Connor 2010).

UMKC is one of a very few places where undergraduate students are introduced to heterodox microeconomics as a component of their introductory and intermediate micro courses. The doctoral students, on the other hand, are required to take a course in it. The course covers the 'conventional' topics found in any microeconomics course: circular production, business enterprise, production and cost theory, pricing, demand, market governance and the microfoundations of macroeconomics. It is supplemented by courses on heterodox linear production models, American economic history and industrial economics and by the various heterodox summer schools and international conferences held at UMKC. Two excellent dissertations that engage with heterodox micro topics have been written: one on the microfoundations of effective demand (Tae-Hee Jo 2007) and the second on the household in heterodox economic theory (Zdravka Todorova 2007), with the latter winning the Veblen 150 Prize Competition sponsored by the European Association for Evolutionary Political Economy (EAEPE) and AFEE.

The history of economic thought has a rather particular place in the department. As noted above, doctoral students are required to take a course in the history of thought and the department offers two additional seminars in thought and history of economics. Its main purpose in the programme is to provide historic context for the theoretical issues that are raised in the process of the department's training of heterodox economists. Unlike most (orthodox) graduate programmes, which provide no such context, it is this department's philosophy that to properly appreciate theory and theoretical controversies, one must have some understanding of the issues, debates and surrounding social environment within which such theoretical structures first appeared, how they were modified over time, and the extent to which they were challenged (successfully or not) in the past. The department is also concerned with introducing students to theoretical perspectives that have little or no currency in the present, but which represent possible avenues through which current problems or issues can be more successfully addressed than through conventional theory. Essentially, the history of thought component of the doctoral programme is not to see it as a 'stand-alone' segment, but to complement and support the main theoretical directions of the department and to provide students with a better sense of the contexts within which theories were developed.

In the mid-1990s Sturgeon and Brazelton concocted a plan to put UMKC on the national and international heterodox map – and their plan is a resounding success. Since 2000, its faculty and their former students held positions in eight heterodox associations, were members of the editorial boards of five heterodox journals, and are among the most active heterodox economists; in addition Lee is the editor of the *American Journal of Economics and Sociology* while former student Jo is the co-editor of the *Heterodox Economics Newsletter*. Additional evidence of success is a recent ranking of mainstream and heterodox departments, where UMKC is ranked among the top thirty of all US economic departments and in the top two of heterodox departments (Lee 2010). Finally, and perhaps the most tangible proof of success in producing doctoral students, nine former and current UMKC students are contributors to this volume: Flavia Dantas, Gyun Cheol Gu, Yeva Nersisyan and Robert Scott, in addition to the previously mentioned Jo, Leclaire, Tcherneva, Todorova and Tymoigne.

FREDERIC S. LEE

See also:

Budget Deficits; Employer of Last Resort; Expectations; Households; Institutionalism; Liquidity Preference; Money; Money Manager Capitalism; Prices and Pricing; Time in Economic Theory; Time-series Econometrics; Unemployment; Welfare Economics.

Bibliography

Brazelton, W.R. (2004), 'The Oklahoma "institutionalist" school', in W.J. Samuels (ed.), *Research in the History of Economic Thought and Methodology*, Vol. 22-C, *Wisconsin, 'Government and Business' and the History of Heterodox Economic Thought*, Amsterdam: Elsevier, pp. 245–60.

Lee, F.S. (2005), 'Teaching heterodox microeconomics', *Post-Autistic Economics Review*, **31** (16 May), article 3, available at: http://www.btinternet.com/~pae_news/review/issue31.htm.

Lee, F.S. (2009), *A History of Heterodox Economics: Challenging the Mainstream in the Twentieth Century*, Abingdon and New York: Routledge.

Lee, F.S. (2010), 'A heterodox teaching of neoclassical microeconomic theory', *International Journal of Pluralism and Economics Education*, **1** (3), 203–35.

Lee, F.S., T.C. Grijalva and C. Nowell (2010), 'Ranking economics departments in a contested discipline: a bibliometric approach to quality equality between theoretically distinct sub-disciplines', *American Journal of Economics and Sociology*, **69** (5), 1345–75.

Phillips, R. (1995), *Economic Mavericks: The Texas Institutionalists*, Greenwich, CT: JAI Press.

Wagner, E. (1999), 'Part I of the history of the Economics Department at UMKC', UMKC Department of Economics, Kansas City, MO, Newsletter **3** (Spring), pp. 1, 3–4, available at: http://cas.umkc.edu/economics/history.asp.

Wagner, E. (2001), 'A generation of political economists: part II of the history of the Department of Economics', UMKC Department of Economics, Kansas City, MO, Newsletter, **4** (Spring), pp. 3–4; available at: http://cas.umkc.edu/economics/history2.asp.

Wage Deflation

The Post Keynesian approaches hold that deflation is rooted in wage deflation. There is no fully-fledged Keynesian deflation theory yet, and only a small amount of Post Keynesian literature exists on the subject. Mainstream theories cannot offer a common theory of deflation, but most see sticky nominal wages – and hence, too high real wages – as the most important problem of deflation. Thus nominal wage flexibility is idealized as a means to achieve full employment, even under deflation. If sticky nominal wages are taken as an unalterable fact of the modern 'real-world' economies (for whatever reason), deflation is considered highly problematic by most practitioners in central banks for a number of reasons.

Prior to the mid-1990s, the problems of deflation and wage deflation had largely been dismissed as problems of the past. Then the Japanese deflation surprised many economists and reignited their interest in the subject. Economics textbooks ignored deflation, stipulating wage flexibility and a vertical long-run aggregate supply curve as guarantors of full employment. The main reason for the predominant belief in the irrelevance of deflation was the assumption that it could be easily prevented by an increase in money supply, given prudent monetary policy informed by the lesson of 1929. 'It' cannot happen again.

There are various currents of thought in the mainstream of economics regarding the causes of deflation. For Knut Wicksell, deflation emanates from too high monetary interest rates caused by tight monetary policy as compared to the 'natural' interest rate, conversely for inflation. Milton Friedman advocated moderate stable deflation for reasons of allocational efficiency and for keeping money neutral, with a nominal interest rate of zero. This would imply continuous wage deflation, since holding money would be remunerated according to the deflation rate and not be punished, as would be the case under inflation. Bordo and Filardo (2005) rediscovered the prevalence of deflation in many cases in the nineteenth century, as well as during the 'golden 1920s' in the US with moderate growth. Hence, they argued that deflation must not be seen only through the lens of the Great Depression. In a similar vein, still others distinguish between good and bad deflation. They regard 'good deflation' as being supply side, caused by improvements to technology (pushing the aggregate supply curve downward to intersect the aggregate demand curve at a higher output level). 'Bad deflation' is characterized by negative demand shocks. Under both good and bad deflations, nominal wage deflation would be necessary to prevent them from turning into bad or disastrous deflations. However, a few mainstreamers such as De Long and Summers (1986) have raised doubts about whether price flexibility (including wage flexibility) is capable of stabilizing an economy. The orthodoxy is far from being uniform.

Surprisingly, Keynes confined himself both in the *Treatise on Money* (1930 [1971]) and in the *General Theory of Employment, Interest and Money* (1936 [1973]) to the analysis of price and wage flexibility, rather than deflation. Irving Fisher's (1933) debt deflation theory of depressions was not perceived by Keynes, but rather by Minsky, who forged it into a Keynesian framework. Palley (2008), following Tobin (1975), and Herr (2008) elaborated the most advanced approaches to a full Post Keynesian theory of deflation, with wage deflation as its cornerstone.

In the *General Theory*, Keynes rejected the notion that wage cuts could remedy unemployment and return an economy to a state of full employment (chapter 19). He discussed seven important repercussions of money wage reduction, and concluded that probably none of them is capable of strengthening aggregate demand, and thereby employment. In his last repercussion effect, he hinted at the increased real debt effect of lower prices with adverse effects on investment and business confidence, without mentioning deflation or the 'Fisher effect' (as this was coined later). In principle, a lower wage and price level might increase the real money supply and reduce interest rates (later dubbed the 'Keynes effect'). However, monetary policy is better suited to lowering interest rates without negative side-effects. In sum, a stable unemployment equilibrium would emerge due to the failure of wage and price flexibility to restore full employment. Instead, Keynes advocated stable money wages as a nominal anchor for the price level, assuming that overall productivity is given. Needless to say, this implies dismissing the quantity theory of money and also departing from the Gold Standard. The latter requires inflation or deflation as the international adjustment mechanism for surplus and deficit countries, with regard to the trade balance.

A.C. Pigou rejected Keynes's proposition of unemployment equilibrium by implying a real wealth effect (or real balance effect), which Keynes ignored in chapter 19. With a given nominal money supply, a drop in the price level would increase the value of the money supply, which is considered a part of national wealth. The latter would trigger additional consumption, which would pull output and employment up towards equilibrium. This 'Pigou effect', later called the 'Patinkin resolution', was disputed on several grounds (see Minsky 1986 [2008], pp. 196 ff.). The effect applies only to outside money that is not coupled with debt, and is therefore small. Further, it is likely to be offset by the various negative effects of a reduced price level, in particular the increased real debt of the debtors (see Kalecki 1944).

In the *Treatise*, Keynes (1930 [1971], pp. 111 ff.) established that the main determinants of the price level in a goods market equilibrium are aggregate nominal wages and aggregate profits. For Keynes (in both the *Treatise* and the *General Theory*), profits depend basically on the profit rate on fixed capital. Given the profit per unit of output, the price level in a closed economy depends primarily on the average wage per unit of output (that is, on unit labour costs). The profit rate is not dependent on nominal wages, but rather on the nominal interest rate, risk, the degree of monopoly and a number of other factors. It is not money supply, but the nominal 'wage unit' that anchors the price level, as long as wage per worker increases alongside productivity advances. Demand inflation increases prices relative to costs; hence it is also profit inflation. Cost inflation is mainly the result of wage inflation, but is also influenced by fluctuations in the price of other inputs and exchange rate depreciation. Continuous demand inflation will trigger wage increases. Hence, in a dynamic inflationary process, it is always wage–price or price–wage inflation, which leads to the same result. More money in circulation, or an increase in the velocity of money, accommodates this process, unless monetary policy tightens, which affects both output and prices. This conception was endorsed by many Post Keynesian authors, notably by Weintraub (1959), who proposed a productivity-led incomes policy to maintain price stability, in contrast to a stop-and-go monetary policy. Rowthorn (1977) described this cost–push theory of wage–price inflation as 'conflict inflation'. By analogy, wage deflation then is essential for causing deflation. There is, too, an element of 'conflict deflation' in this. However, wage deflation is not simply symmetrical to wage inflation; the issue is more complex.

How can deflation and wage deflation emerge? Most theorists focus on a strong drop in aggregate demand, which is suspected to cause a fall in the price level since the aggregate supply curve is either vertical or, under sticky wages, upward sloping in the short run. In contrast, if demand falls but the price level is guaranteed by the nominal wage anchor, only a one-time profit deflation might occur. However, this will not result in a continuous deflationary process. Output and employment would fall, without deflation. Only if, due to the impact of unemployment, the nominal anchor bursts, will money wages fall, dragging prices down – and wage deflation is on the way.

Fisher argued that all severe depressions that trigger deflation are 'debt deflations', such as the Great Depression. Debt deflations are caused by overindebtedness resulting from such factors as loose monetary policy, speculation and excessive optimism. After debtors begin to default, a sequence of steps leads to deflation, starting with distress selling, the slowing of the velocity of circulation and a fall in the price level; then the sequence continues with a fall in the net worth of businesses that precipitates bankruptcies, a fall in profits, a loss of business confidence, hoarding of money and finally a rise in the real interest rate. Wage deflation is not mentioned, nor is a liquidity trap. Fisher concentrates on falling demand, Keynes and most Post Keynesians on supply, particularly on wages. Key steps in the deflationary process are the increase in real debt, later called the 'Fisher effect', and the increase of real interest rates due to either the zero bound for the nominal interest rate, or at a level above zero due to an interest rate floor. By reflation this process could easily be terminated. Otherwise, the process would lead to a near 'universal bankruptcy', which Fisher terms the 'natural way' out of deflation (p. 346). Although Fisher embedded this process in classical theory, its essence is compatible with Keynes's key ideas. It was Minsky (1986 [2008], pp. 192 ff.) who incorporated debt deflation into his financial instability hypothesis that focuses on the formation of credit bubbles, which Fisher had described only briefly.

Palley (2008) builds on a theory of deflation from Tobin (1975) in a model with exogenous money (endogenous money would not alter the results). Tobin distinguished a one-time change in the price level from deflation, which includes deflationary expectations. Following the Mundell–Tobin effect, a rise in inflation will be accompanied by a smaller rise in the nominal interest rate, since agents hold less in money balances and more in other assets. Thus real interest rates fall with inflation; the demand for money and real interest rates rise, the velocity of money falls – and conversely under deflation. With deflationary expectations, purchases of goods tend to be delayed, which impedes aggregate demand. Including the Pigou and the Keynes effects, the Fisher effect and expectation effects, it is shown that continuous deflation reduces aggregate demand, especially under *expected* deflation. Price and wage flexibility aggravate the deflation problem, as Keynes had stated (1936[1973], p. 269); the notion that wage rigidity is a special case leading to disequilibrium is rejected. Instead, downward rigidity in prices is a stabilizing factor. Wage deflation is not explicitly addressed by Palley as the focus is on aggregate demand, but is tacitly included.

Herr (2008) proposes a typology of demand and cost inflation and/or deflation. Demand inflation is Keynes's profit inflation, cost inflation is mainly wage inflation, and conversely deflation. Deflation is both wage and demand deflation, exacerbated by the Fisher effect, whereas the Keynes and Pigou effects are no longer paid attention. Wage deflation combined with demand inflation occurs seldom, mainly only under strong external demand. Applying the wage deflation concept to the Japan's moderate but enduring deflation since the mid-1990s, the key proposition is that the nominal wage anchor broke down, thus giving rise to a downward wage–price spiral. Unit labour costs and the inflation rate have moved downward in tandem since 1997, after a collapse of the traditional wage formation pattern. Deflation led to bad debt, cautious bank lending (and even a credit crunch), a liquidity trap and capital outflows; these were only alleviated by highly expansionary fiscal policy. Monetary policy is paralysed in the face of zero-bound interest rates, apart from 'quantitative easing'. Accomplishing anything beyond low growth under such a regime is not possible. Cleaning balance sheets of firms and banks will not suffice to return to growth. Wage deflation is not simply a result of deflation, but a necessary precondition. Herr's analysis shows that deflation can have diverse features, as witnessed during the Great Depression and other deflation episodes.

JAN PRIEWE

See also:

Economic Policy; Financial Instability Hypothesis; Inflation; Monetary Policy; Price Rigidity; Uncertainty.

References

Bordo, M. and A. Filardo (2005), 'Deflation and monetary policy in a historical perspective: remembering the past or being condemned to repeat it?', *Economic Policy*, **20** (44), 799–844.
De Long, B. and L. Summers (1986), 'Is increased price flexibility stabilizing?', *American Economic Review*, **76** (5), 1031–44.
Fisher, I. (1933), 'The debt-deflation theory of great depressions', *Econometrica* **1** (4), 337–57.
Herr, H. (2008), 'The labour market in a Keynesian economic regime: theoretical debate and empirical findings', *Cambridge Journal of Economics*, **33** (5), 949–65.
Kalecki, M. (1944), 'Professor Pigou on "The classical stationary state": a comment', *Economic Journal*, **54**, (213), 131–2.
Keynes, J.M. (1930 [1971]), *A Treatise on Money*, London: Macmillan and Cambridge: Cambridge University Press.
Keynes, J.M. (1936 [1973]), *The General Theory of Employment, Interest and Money*, London: Macmillan and Cambridge: Cambridge University Press.
Minsky, H.P. (1986 [2008]), *Stabilizing an Unstable Economy*, New York: McGraw-Hill.
Palley, T.I. (2008), 'Keynesian models of deflation and depression revisited', *Journal of Economic Behavior and Organization*, **68** (1), 167–77.
Rowthorn, R.E. (1977), 'Conflict, inflation and money', *Cambridge Journal of Economics*, **1** (3), 215–39.
Tobin, J. (1975), 'Keynesian models of recession and depression', *American Economic Review*, **65** (2), 195–202.
Weintraub, S. (1959), *A General Theory of the Price Level, Output, Income Distribution, and Economic Growth*, Philadelphia, PA: Chilton.

Wage- and Profit-led Regimes

Post Keynesian investment-driven distribution and growth models apply Keynes's principle of effective demand also to the long run (Kurz and Salvadori 2010). Broadly speaking, two basic approaches can be distinguished. First, there is the Kaldor–Pasinetti–Robinson (Cambridge) approach, in which saving adjusts to investment in the long run by means of changes in functional income distribution, with the propensity to save out of wages falling short of the propensity to save out of profits. In these models it is assumed that productive capacities given by the capital stock are fully utilized in the long run – or that an exogenously given 'normal' rate of capacity utilization is attained. Nicholas Kaldor's and Luigi Pasinetti's models are also set in a full-employment natural rate of growth framework, whereas Joan Robinson's are not. Changes in investment, determined by 'animal spirits' and the expected profit rate, trigger changes in the price level and, with rigid nominal wages, in real wages and hence the wage share. Capital accumulation and the real wage rate, and thus the wage share, are therefore inversely related; a higher rate of accumulation will be associated with a lower wage share.

Second, there are the Kaleckian distribution and growth models, which contain a variable rate of capacity utilization in the long run (Blecker 2002). In these models income distribution is determined by mark-up pricing of firms over variable unit costs, and is hence mainly affected by the degree of price competition in the goods market, by overhead costs (that is, management salaries, interest costs), by the relative power of firms and workers in the labour market, and by the relationship of variable material costs to variable labour costs. Investment decisions of firms, determined by expected sales and internal profits, determine capacity utilization, capital accumulation and growth. Saving adjusts to investment in the long run by means of changes in the degree of utilization of productive capacity given by the capital stock, that is, by changes in income and in capital stock.

In the 'stagnationist' variant of the Kaleckian model, pioneered by Rowthorn (1981) and Dutt (1984), changes in distribution have unique effects on the long-run growth equilibrium: rising wage shares cause higher rates of capacity utilization, capital accumulation and growth, and also a higher profit rate, because a strong accelerator effect in the investment function is assumed.

In contrast to this approach, the seminal paper by Bhaduri and Marglin (1990) has shown that in a Kaleckian framework different regimes of demand, accumulation and growth are possible. Taking into account the effects of redistribution between wages and profits on consumption demand, on the one hand, and on investment of the firm sector via costs of production and hence unit profits, on the other, demand may be wage led ('stagnationist') or profit led ('exhilarationist'), that is, a higher profit share may lead to lower or higher equilibrium rates of capacity utilization. Also, capital accumulation and growth may be wage or profit led, depending on the parameter values in the saving and the investment functions. A higher profit share may thus cause higher or lower rates of capital accumulation and growth.

In order to analyse the effects of changes in distribution on economic activity, capital accumulation and growth, following the Bhaduri and Marglin approach, we start with the goods market equilibrium condition for an open economy without economic activity of the state and with constant technical conditions of production: planned saving (S) has to be equal to net investment (I) and net exports (NX), the difference between exports (X) and imports (M) of goods and services:

$$S = I + X - M = I + NX. \tag{1}$$

For convenience, equation (1) is normalized by the capital stock (K), and therefore we get the following goods market equilibrium relationship between the saving rate ($\sigma = S/K$), the accumulation rate ($g = I/K$) and the net export rate ($b = NX/K$):

$$\sigma = g + b. \tag{2}$$

Saving consists of saving out of profits (S_Π) and saving out of wages (S_W). The propensity to save out of wages (s_W) is assumed to fall short of the propensity to save out of profits (s_Π), because the latter includes retained earnings of firms, in particular. Since the rate of capacity utilization is the relation of output to potential output ($u = Y/Y^p$) and the capital–potential output ratio relates the capital stock to potential output ($v = K/Y^p$), we obtain for the saving rate:

$$\sigma = \frac{S_\Pi + S_W}{K} = \frac{s_\Pi \Pi + s_W(Y - \Pi)}{K}$$

$$= [s_W + (s_\Pi - s_W)h]\frac{u}{v}, \quad 0 \le s_W < s_\Pi \le 1. \tag{3}$$

Investment and hence capital accumulation is a positive function of the profit rate, which can be decomposed into the profit share, the rate of capacity utilization and the capital–potential output ratio ($r = hu/v$). With a constant coefficient technology, investment is therefore positively affected by the profit share and by capacity utilization. Increasing unit profits and hence a rising profit share have a positive effect on investment because internal funds for investment finance improve, *ceteris paribus*. Increasing capacity utilization has a positive effect on investment because the relation between (expected) sales and productive capacity improves. For capital accumulation to be positive, the expected rate of profit has to exceed a minimum rate (r_{min}), given by the foreign rate of profit or by the rate of interest in financial markets, which are both considered to be exogenous here:

$$g = \alpha + \beta u + \tau h, \quad \alpha, \beta, \tau > 0, \quad g > 0 \text{ only if } r > r_{min}. \tag{4}$$

The net export rate is positively affected by international competitiveness, provided that the Marshall–Lerner condition can be assumed to hold and the sum of the price elasticities of exports and imports exceeds unity. Under this condition, the real exchange rate will have a positive effect on net exports. We assume that the real exchange rate is positively related to the profit share because redistribution at the expense of wage incomes is usually obtained by lower nominal unit labour cost growth and hence lower inflation. Net exports also depend on the relative rates of growth of foreign and domestic demand. If domestic demand grows at a faster rate than foreign demand, net exports will decline, *ceteris paribus*. With foreign demand given, the domestic rate of capacity utilization as an indicator for domestic demand will thus have a negative impact on net exports:

$$b = \psi e_r(h) - \phi u, \quad \psi, \phi, \frac{\partial e_r}{\partial h} > 0. \tag{5}$$

Stability of the goods market equilibrium requires that saving responds more elastically to a change in the endogenous variable, the rate of capacity utilization, than investment and net exports do together:

$$\frac{\partial \sigma}{\partial u} - \frac{\partial g}{\partial u} - \frac{\partial b}{\partial u} > 0 \Rightarrow [s_W + (s_\Pi - s_W)h]\frac{1}{v} - \beta + \phi > 0. \tag{6}$$

The equilibrium rates (*) of capacity utilization and capital accumulation are given by:

$$u^* = \frac{\alpha + \tau h + \psi e_r(h)}{[s_W + (s_\Pi - s_W)h]\frac{1}{v} - \beta + \phi}, \tag{7}$$

$$g^* = \alpha + \frac{\beta[\alpha + \tau h + \psi e_r(h)]}{[s_W + (s_\Pi - s_W)h]\frac{1}{v} - \beta + \phi} + \tau h. \qquad (8)$$

Whereas equilibrium capacity utilization indicates equilibrium activity with given productive capacities, equilibrium capital accumulation determines the growth of productive capacities and hence of potential output. The effects of a change in the profit share on the equilibrium rates of capacity utilization and capital accumulation can be calculated from equations (7) and (8):

$$\frac{\partial u}{\partial h} = \frac{\tau - (s_\Pi - s_W)\frac{u}{v} + \psi\frac{\partial e_r}{\partial h}}{[s_W + (s_\Pi - s_W)h]\frac{1}{v} - \beta + \phi}, \qquad (7a)$$

$$\frac{\partial g}{\partial h} = \frac{\tau\left[\frac{s_w}{v} + \phi + \frac{h}{v}(s_\Pi - s_W)\right] + \beta\left[\psi\frac{\partial e_r}{\partial h} - \frac{u}{v}(s_\Pi - s_W)\right]}{[s_W + (s_\Pi - s_W)h]\frac{1}{v} - \beta + \phi}. \qquad (8a)$$

Equation (7a) shows that an increasing profit share will have no unique effect on equilibrium capacity utilization. From the numerator it can be seen that the total effect of redistribution in favour of profits is composed of three effects: first, there is a positive effect via investment demand, τ; second, a negative effect via consumption demand, $-(s_\Pi - s_W)(u/v)$; and third, a positive effect via net exports, $\psi(\partial e_r/\partial h)$. If $(\partial u/\partial h) > 0$, the demand regime will be profit led; and if $(\partial u/\partial h) < 0$, the demand regime will be wage led. For equilibrium capital accumulation a similar result holds, as can be seen in equation (8a). There is a positive effect of the profit share on equilibrium capital accumulation via the positive impact of the profit share on investment decisions,

$$\tau\left[\frac{s_w}{v} + \phi + \frac{h}{v}(s_\Pi - s_W)\right].$$

But there is also the indirect effect via the accelerator term in the investment function,

$$\beta\left[\psi\frac{\partial e_r}{\partial h} - \frac{u}{v}(s_\Pi - s_W)\right],$$

which may be positive or negative. If $(\partial g/\partial h) > 0$, the accumulation and growth regime will be profit led; and if $(\partial g/\partial h) < 0$, the accumulation and growth regime will be wage led.

Following this approach, the identification of the demand, accumulation and growth regime in a certain country in a certain period of time becomes a question of concrete historical and empirical analysis, and the Bhaduri and Marglin (1990) model has increasingly inspired empirical work. The focus of this research so far has been on the demand regime and it has concentrated on the determinants of changes in GDP, because potential output and thus capacity utilization are difficult to measure empirically. Starting with the work by Bowles and Boyer (1995), most of the empirical studies have applied single-equation estimation procedures. Since the change in GDP can be decomposed into changes in its expenditure components, consumption (C), investment (I) and net exports (NX), the overall effect of a change in the profit share on aggregate demand is the sum of the effects on the expenditure components:

$$\frac{\frac{\partial Y}{Y}}{\partial h} = \frac{\frac{\partial C}{Y}}{\partial h} + \frac{\frac{\partial I}{Y}}{\partial h} + \frac{\frac{\partial NX}{Y}}{\partial h}. \tag{9}$$

As outlined above, the following signs of the partial derivatives can be expected from theory:

$$\frac{\frac{\partial C}{Y}}{\partial h} < 0, \frac{\frac{\partial I}{Y}}{\partial h} > 0, \frac{\frac{\partial NX}{Y}}{\partial h} > 0 \Rightarrow \frac{\frac{\partial Y}{Y}}{\partial h} = ?. \tag{9a}$$

The single-equation estimation studies therefore start with estimating the consumption, investment, export and import functions (or net export functions), calculate the partial effects of changes in the profit share on each of these demand components, and finally sum up the partial effects in order to obtain the overall effect. As surveyed in Hein and Vogel (2008), most of the studies find domestic demand, that is, the sum of investment and consumption demand, in developed capitalist economies to be wage led. Usually a strong effect of redistribution on consumption demand is obtained, due to considerably higher estimates for the propensity to consume out of wage income than out of profit income, and only weak or statistically insignificant estimated effects of the profit share on investment of the firm sector. The latter is found to be mostly driven by aggregate demand or capacity utilization, that is, by the accelerator term in the investment functions. Including the external sector, that is, foreign trade and globalization effects, aggregate demand remains wage led in most of the countries, although redistribution at the expense of labour in many studies has a significantly positive effect on net exports (see, for example, Stockhammer et al. 2011 on Germany). In small open economies this effect may turn a domestically wage-led aggregate demand regime into an overall profit-led demand regime (see, for example, Stockhammer and Ederer 2008 on Austria).

The economic policy implications drawn from this kind of analysis are quite straightforward: pursuing strategies of profit-led growth via the net export channel, that is, depressing domestic wages and domestic demand, and therefore relying on a kind of 'beggar thy neighbour' policy, may be a successful way for small open economies. But it cannot be recommended for larger and less open economies. Such a strategy will not only be harmful for the trading partners of the respective countries and, if generally pursued, in the long run hence for the world economy as a whole. It will also lower aggregate demand in the large, less open economies following such a strategy in the short run. Wage-led strategies are therefore more promising, but may be more difficult to obtain, in particular if economies become increasingly open to foreign competition.

ECKHARD HEIN

See also:

Economic Policy; Kaleckian Economics; Underconsumption.

References

Bhaduri, A. and S. Marglin (1990), 'Unemployment and the real wage: the economic basis for contesting political ideologies', *Cambridge Journal of Economics*, **14** (4), 375–93.
Blecker, R.A. (2002), 'Distribution, demand and growth in neo-Kaleckian macro-models', in M. Setterfield (ed.), *The Economics of Demand-Led Growth*, Cheltenham, UK and Northampton, MA, USA: Edward Elgar, pp. 129–52.
Bowles, S. and R. Boyer (1995), 'Wages, aggregate demand, and employment in an open economy: an empirical investigation', in G.A. Epstein and H.M. Gintis (eds), *Macroeconomic Policy after the Conservative Era*, Cambridge: Cambridge University Press, pp. 143–71.
Dutt, A.K. (1984), 'Stagnation, income distribution and monopoly power', *Cambridge Journal of Economics*, **8** (1), 25–40.
Hein, E. and L. Vogel (2008), 'Distribution and growth reconsidered – empirical results for six OECD countries', *Cambridge Journal of Economics*, **32** (3), 479–511.
Kurz, H.D. and N. Salvadori (2010), 'The post-Keynesian theories of growth and distribution: a survey', in M. Setterfield (ed.), *Handbook of Alternative Theories of Economic Growth*, Cheltenham, UK and Northampton, MA, USA: Edward Elgar, pp. 95–107.
Rowthorn, R. (1981), 'Demand, real wages and economic growth', Thames Papers in Political Economy, Thames Polytechnic, London, Autumn.
Stockhammer, E. and S. Ederer (2008), 'Demand effects of the falling wage share in Austria', *Empirica*, **35** (5), 481–502.
Stockhammer, E., E. Hein and L. Grafl (2011), 'Globalization and the effects of changes in functional income distribution on aggregate demand in Germany', *International Review of Applied Economics*, **25** (1), 1–23.

Walrasian Economics

Walrasian economics originated in the work of Léon Walras (1874) and was one of several neoclassical approaches emerging from the marginal revolution in the late nineteenth century. Its hallmark was the focus on the interrelations of markets and their simultaneous, or general, equilibrium. Walrasianism was, therefore, distinct from Marshallian neoclassicism, which sought analytic devices to neutralize interdependencies so as to allow partial equilibrium analysis of particular sectors of the economy. And it was different, too, from the neoclassicism of J.B. Clark, who resorted to extensive aggregation to avoid the complexities resulting from interdependence. Since Walras's early formulation, his general equilibrium theory has been increasingly refined, and it became the dominant form of microeconomic orthodoxy during the twentieth century, only recently being displaced by game theory.

The neoclassical quality of Walrasian economics is evident in the derivation of agents' choices, or supplies and demands, from particular types of maximization. It is assumed that each consumer's domain of choice (commodity space), preferences (typically represented as a utility function) and assets (labour capacities, physical possessions and financial securities and debts), and each producer's technology (input–output combinations) are exogenously specified, and economic interaction takes place only through competitive markets. Every consumer is depicted as maximizing utility subject to a budget constraint, and every producer maximizes profit constrained only by technology. A set of prices that allows these optimizations to be realized simultaneously, so making demands and supplies compatible, and markets clear, is a Walrasian equilibrium.

Two varieties of Walrasian economics can be distinguished: Arrow–Debreu intertemporal equilibrium theory and temporary equilibrium analysis. They differ in their treatment of time: that is, in how agents relate to the future. The Arrow–Debreu version classifies commodities not only by their physical properties and locational attributes, but also by their date of availability and the 'state of the world' at each date, which specifies the values of variables that were previously uncertain. The rationale for this is straightforward. All of these characteristics can affect utilities and profits, and therefore demands and supplies. For example, consumers' preferences are generally sensitive to a commodity's physical properties and the location where consumption occurs, as well as embodying time preferences and attitudes towards risk. But the implications of conceptualizing commodities in this fourfold way are dramatic. When coupled to the usual assumption that agents can completely rank consumption bundles and input–output combinations, it means that there will be a single decision date for all agents and a comprehensive set of futures markets and contingent commodity, or insurance, markets. Agents will form supplies and demands for every date and for every contingency, and will determine all of their choices in the very first period.

Walrasian temporary equilibrium theory implicitly recognizes the unreasonableness of assuming that agents have complete rankings of commodity bundles. Instead, they are likely to be uncertain as to what commodities and technologies will be available in the future and what their preferences will be, as well as the exact composition and value of their assets. And typically they will encounter transaction costs that are especially high for trading in futures markets and contingent commodities. Thus markets will be incomplete, and at least some trading will take place sequentially. An Arrow–Debreu equilibrium will be impossible, and any equilibrium will be 'temporary'. J.R. Hicks (1939) formalizes the matter as follows. There are a number of periods and, at the beginning of each, spot markets exist together with *some* futures markets and contingent commodity markets. Agents can trade on the markets that exist, and will do so on the basis of expectations about future prices for commodities that are not presently tradable. Equilibrium is defined only in terms of clearance on those markets that exist, and these are not comprehensive. At the beginning of the next period, markets reopen, and new trading can occur on spot markets and newly available markets for forward contracts. Expectations formed at the beginning of the first period may turn out to be incorrect, and will be revised, so that market prices in the second period will reflect new expectations. At the start of the third period markets reopen again. And so on. The economy thus moves in a sequence of temporary equilibria.

The causation structure of both types of Walrasian theory is clear-cut. The equilibrium values of the endogenous variables (prices and quantities traded) are determined by the exogenously specified preferences, asset endowments, technologies, optimizing behaviours and agents' expectation formation rules. The endogenous variables are, of course, the microeconomic components of the macroeconomic variables and the time path of these aggregates can be very complex in both forms of Walrasian model. However, no matter how complicated, equilibria will always involve market clearance, so there will be no involuntarily unemployed labour or underutilized productive capacity in the Keynesian sense of these terms. (There can be excess supplies in Walrasian equilibria, providing that there is free disposal, but they will correspond to zero prices.)

Five problems have been examined in both types of Walrasian theory. First, under what conditions do equilibria exist? Second, when will the economy be stable, in the sense of disequilibrium proving transitory? Third, what are the efficiency properties of equilibria? Fourth, what circumstances will guarantee a unique equilibrium, and, fifth, generate definite comparative static results? Overall, coordination through prices as depicted by Walrasianism is shown to be a delicate matter. Very restrictive assumptions are required to ensure existence, stability, efficiency, uniqueness and definite comparative statics. For example, take the existence question, that is, the problem of determining what types of consumers' preferences, producers' technologies, asset distributions and expectation formation mechanisms will ensure that there is a vector of prices that will clear all markets simultaneously. Since Walrasianism is essentially a set of propositions about the properties of equilibria, the significance of the problem is difficult to exaggerate. But the assumptions required to guarantee existence are stringent. In particular, they must ensure that demands and supplies vary *continuously* with prices. This requires, *inter alia*, that bankruptcies do not occur at any set of prices! Further restrictive assumptions are required to guarantee that, if equilibrium exists, it is unique, efficient and stable, and that parameter shifts engender definite changes in endogenous variables. This has led some eminent orthodox theorists to suggest that Walrasianism is *not* a sensible route to proceed along in analysing real economies, or, alternatively, that it should quickly lead into a more secure non-Walrasian path (Arrow and Hahn 1971; Hahn and Solow 1995).

Such caution is notably absent from orthodox macroeconomics, whether monetarist, New Classical, or real business cycle theory. Here actual economies are modelled as oscillating between two types of Walrasian temporary equilibrium, those with rational expectations and those deviating from rational expectations. The deviations may be the result of monetary or real shocks, and are regarded as quickly self-correcting. Walrasian equilibria thus prevail continuously and are each treated as unique, stable and exhibiting definite comparative statics. Since it is difficult to justify any of this in terms of the theorems proved by Walrasian theorists, orthodox macroeconomists usually take refuge within the confines of Milton Friedman's instrumentalist methodology to justify their extreme modelling simplifications, most notably their resort to heroic aggregation, where markets are reduced to a very small number and where there is a single, infinitely long-lived economic agent with well-behaved preferences and constraints. Random shocks in the form of unanticipated price changes, shifts in productivity and alterations in regulations generate fluctuations in macro variables through the optimizing recalculations of the representative agent. In such a context, the problems of ensuring the existence, stability, uniqueness and efficiency of equilibrium are eliminated and definite comparative static results are easy to generate. New Classical and real business cycle theorists ignore this deficiency of their work, yet claim that their conclusions are robust because they are immune from the 'Lucas critique' of traditional forecasting methods as a result of being derived from the microfoundations of neoclassical choice theory.

This truncated type of general equilibrium analysis is now referred to as dynamic stochastic general equilibrium modelling (usually abbreviated as DSGE), and has been adopted by New Keynesians, although in more complex forms involving several types of agent and recognizing sticky prices and wages. This stickiness means that markets may not continuously clear in the face of shocks, and unemployment may not be solely the result of voluntarily substituting leisure for labour intertemporally, as it is in New Classical and real business cycle theory. (It is of course these results that account for the DSGE models that generate them being designated as Keynesian.) Such models have been commonly used by central banks, and help explain why the recent financial crisis and the deep recession that followed went wholly unanticipated by those responsible for macroeconomic management.

Beginning in the 1960s, more theoretically inclined Keynesians insightfully exposed the key assumption guaranteeing market clearance as a property of equilibria in Walrasian theory, and showed that this assumption has nothing to do with the presence of price flexibility as New Keynesians claim. Clower (1965) and Leijonhuvud (1968) argued that market clearance resulted from treating agents as formulating their demands and supplies in the belief that they can always trade whatever quantities they desire, providing only that they deliver equivalents in exchange. This seems innocuous, but is in fact crucial, as can be appreciated by considering a Walrasian disequilibrium. By definition, in such a situation not all agents' choices can be realized simultaneously, and some will be rationed if trades actually occur. Then it is not unreasonable to imagine that this rationing will affect choices. For example, a consumer who is quantity constrained in the sale of labour and expects this to continue at future dates will not necessarily alter the supply of labour from that resulting from a Walrasian maximization of utility, but will probably reduce consumption demands, thereby contributing to an effective demand deficiency. A producer who is quantity rationed in the sale of output, and expects this to continue at future dates, will not necessarily reduce the supply of output below the Walrasian level, but is likely to reduce demand for labour inputs, again contributing to a shortfall in demand. Agents' supplies and demands will not, therefore, be correctly specified by neoclassical maximizations, and their equilibration may involve significant deviations from market clearance. If a new equilibrium occurs it can be Keynesian, in the sense of there being excess supplies of commodities, including the involuntary unemployment of labour, without the corresponding prices being zero.

Post Keynesians have been even more critical of Walrasian theory, including all notions of optimization and equilibrium. Key assumptions of neoclassical theory regarding the neutrality of money and the probabilistic nature of future events are subjected to scrutiny and found to be seriously deficient (Davidson 2009). Radical uncertainty, it is claimed, is not only something irreducible to a probabilistic calculus; it cannot be sensibly treated as affecting only the way expectations are formed. Instead, it will result in behaviour that cannot be modelled as maximization subject to constraints. Post Keynesians have also explained exactly why the financial sector has unique properties that systematically engender instability in the whole economy (Minsky 1986 [2008]). The historical processes that result from all this are unlikely to be representable as equilibria because – speaking in Walrasian terms – the determinants of equilibria will undergo change in the process itself. Thus 'the notion of general equilibrium is irrelevant to a world of ignorance and uncertainty, where irreversible decisions must be taken in calendar time and equilibrium states are (if indeed they are attained) invariably path dependent' (King 1995, p. 245).

M.C. HOWARD

See also:

Bastard Keynesianism; Equilibrium and Non-equilibrium; Macroeconomic Methodology; Marginalism; New Classical Economics; New Keynesian Economics; New Neoclassical Synthesis; Say's Law.

References

Arrow, K.J. and F.H. Hahn (1971), *General Competitive Analysis*, Edinburgh: Oliver & Boyd.
Clower, R.W. (1965), 'The Keynesian counter-revolution: a theoretical appraisal', in F.H. Hahn and F. Brechling (eds), *The Theory of Interest Rates*, London: Macmillan, pp. 103–25.
Davidson, P. (2009), *John Maynard Keynes*, London: Palgrave Macmillan.
Hahn, F.H. and R. Solow (1995), *A Critical Essay on Modern Macroeconomic Theory*, Cambridge, MA: MIT Press.
Hicks, J.R. (1939 [1946]), *Value and Capital*, 2nd edn, Oxford: Oxford University Press.
King, J.E. (1995), *Conversations with Post Keynesians*, London: Macmillan.
Leijonhuvud, A. (1968), *On Keynesian Economics and the Economics of Keynes*, Oxford: Oxford University Press.
Minsky, H.P. (1986), *Stabilizing an Unstable Economy*, New Haven CT: Yale University Press; republished New York: McGraw-Hill, 2008.
Walras, L. (1874), *Elements of Pure Economics*, Edition Définitive, 1926, London: Allen & Unwin, 1954.

Welfare Economics

Post Keynesians, in radical contrast to neoclassical economists, argue that the provisioning process through the capitalist market system does not guarantee general welfare improvement as well as full employment. Nor does the system of welfare policy or the welfare state necessarily achieve the desirable standard of well-being for all people, since a policy is politically selected and the effect of a policy is uncertain. In a world of fundamental uncertainty, therefore, the capitalist economic system is inherently unstable and thereby a person's life is vulnerable.

While welfare figures prominently in their inquiry into real-world problems, the Post Keynesian theory of welfare is still at an infant stage (Hargreaves Heap 1989; King 1995, pp. 61, 130–31, 149–50). The objective of this entry is to argue that the theoretical core of Post Keynesian economics lends itself to a theory of welfare that is an alternative to the market- and efficiency-based theory of welfare. Let us first deal with why Post Keynesian welfare economics is underdeveloped, then move on to the possibility of constructing a Post Keynesian welfare theory.

In the modern capitalist economy, the welfare of the population is closely associated with capital accumulation, business cycles, income distribution, inflation, economic growth, employment, market structure, socio-economic institutions, culture and globalization. In so far as Post Keynesian economics is concerned, changes in aggregate economic activity are mainly driven by unstable business investment that is circumscribed by fragile business expectations of cash flows. Macroeconomic instability grows as the economy becomes more financialized and more globalized. The vicious circle extends to individuals whose livelihood is dependent upon the market system. This implies that welfare involves both macro and micro instability. To cope with macro instability *vis-à-vis* the welfare of the public, Post Keynesians support active government intervention in markets including, but not limited to, the socialization of demand. A 'good' macro policy is thus assumed to improve the quality of individual life, the capability of individuals, and social justice (Keynes 1936; Minsky 1986). The making of the welfare state in major industrialized societies after the Second World War was supported theoretically by just such a (Post) Keynesian idea. In this macroeconomic context, welfare is reduced to a matter of policy effectiveness. More importantly, it is the state that is able and ought to make people better off by stabilizing the market system.

Legitimate doubts arise regarding the efficacy of macroeconomic policy. Is there any policy that serves the interests of all class segments in the society? Is the capitalist state able to achieve full employment? And can macroeconomic stabilization policy reduce the vulnerability in people's lives caused by the market activities? Indeed, Post Keynesian macroeconomic policy is, on the one hand, effective and relevant in the monetary production economy where less than full employment and uncertainty are prevalent. It has come to Post Keynesians' notice, on the other hand, that macroeconomic policy alone is insufficient to achieve such goals as full employment and improving general welfare since it relies on the power relation between classes, a current dominant ideology, and the political preferences of the state (Kalecki 1943; Eichner 1987, p. 702; Henry 1986; Samuels 1994, p. 668).

The limitation of aggregate demand policy is perhaps attributed to the limited vision of the capitalist state. Many Post Keynesians tend to believe that the capitalist state is benevolent and class neutral, and that its primary role is reducing uncertainty or, using Minsky's succinct words, 'stabilizing an unstable economy'. This 'liberal' political philosophy is unquestionably linked to Keynes's ideas underlying his *General Theory*, which is criticized by radical political economists (see Sawyer 1985, chapter 9; Howard and King 1992, chapter 5). Consequently, as the latter's point of view indicates, liberal policy not only leaves vested interests and the capitalist socio-economic order unchallenged, but also lends justification to the values and forces that create the underprovisioning of welfare for the working and dependent classes. That said, there is a theoretical lacuna between macroeconomic policy and the state. To make any welfare-oriented policy more realistic and effective (as opposed to an optimal and efficient policy in neoclassical economics), Post Keynesians should reassess the role of the state in the monetary production economy beyond the benevolent administrator.

Another theoretical issue that is conducive to the underdevelopment of Post Keynesian welfare economics is the scant attention paid to social agency. When welfare is viewed only from the macroeconomic or structuralist perspective, an increase in aggregate production and employment is linearly translated into an increase in social welfare. This is rendered possible either by assuming that individual agents have an 'equal capacity for satisfaction' (Kaldor 1939, p. 551) or by making a theory agency free. Although Post Keynesians in general reject the interpersonal comparability of individual utility and, hence, a neoclassical-type social welfare function that relies on a static, partial analysis, they do not pay much attention to the roles played by social agency whose deliberate actions can alter existing social structures. In its place are structural and persistent forces that determine the well-being of the public. The important implication of social agency, however, is that welfare is neither determined by the efficient market allocation process nor predetermined by existing socio-economic structures; rather, welfare is dependent upon the decisions made by dominant agents in the society such as the business enterprise and the state who make actual decisions on production, investment, price and employment. Structures (like neoclassical markets) do not act by themselves. It is fallible and deliberate human actions, grounded in a particular set of values, which direct their own welfare.

Bearing the aforementioned theoretical shortcomings in mind, we can move on to illustrating a Post Keynesian approach to welfare that is consistent with the theoretical core of Post Keynesian economics. In so doing, the analytical focus is given to the surplus approach and the principle of effective demand in the context of the capitalist social provisioning process.

Let us first describe what the social provisioning process means and how it is relevant to the account of welfare in the monetary production economy. Human beings engage in economic, social, political and cultural activities to sustain their socially constructed lifestyle. The provisioning of surplus goods and services is of the utmost importance for the survival and reproduction of individuals as well as the society as a whole. Thus economic activities are organized in such a way as to access and/or control the social provisioning process. Had it not been for the engagement in the provisioning process or, at least, social assistance, one cannot continue a meaningful lifestyle. The existence of the welfare state implies, on the one hand, that the capitalist economic system is unable to secure 'the greatest happiness for the greatest number of people'. On the other hand, the role played by the state has been changing, along with the changes in power relations in a particular society. Therefore, suffice it to say that the fundamental basis of welfare is not the exchange, but the production of surplus goods and services.

The emphasis on production rather than exchange is found in the Post Keynesian tradition as well as in classical political economy. With the social provisioning perspective delineated above, the total social product and, hence, the social surplus are determined by agent-based expenditure decisions (that is, by effective demand). Employment decisions follow. Actual profits are in turn realized in the market. What this suggests is that, unlike the Sraffian surplus approach, the social product is not given and the surplus is not a residual. More importantly, the principle of effective demand, coupled with the surplus approach, demonstrates that wage incomes are given to workers so as to enable them to purchase surplus goods and services. The welfare of working-class households has nothing to do with the efficiency of market exchange or individual workers' capability; that is, workers' welfare is a sort of residual that is subservient to business enterprises' or, in general, ruling elites' expenditure decisions.

The structural deficiency of the market system requires the state. The state is in principle able to maintain or raise the level of effective demand by means of social expenditure (including welfare transfers). This does not necessarily cause crowding out of resources available to the private business enterprises. Nor does it harm private profits; rather, increasing welfare spending and thereby consumption expenditure by households would generate additional profits, as long as economy is not at full employment.

Alternatively, the state directly produces surplus goods and services at lower prices than private enterprises charge. As a result, the redistribution of income between wages and profits would take place, since dependent individuals' real income increases and private enterprises are not making any profits from those public goods. The provision of public goods would also create new demand for those goods. Some individuals are even able to gain access to such services as health care and education without limit (Cesaratto 2008). However, it should be noted that the state is a political entity. The state transfers incomes and provides public goods for its own political sake. It may thus be argued that the primary goal of social expenditure is not to improve the welfare of the public (or those who do not gain access to the provisioning process), but to supplement effective demand that is necessary for the accumulation of capital and/or the stabilization of the market system. The business enterprise together with the capitalist state requires surplus labour and surplus goods to maintain the status quo in the capitalist economy.

In short, the Post Keynesian approach to welfare draws on the principle of effective demand and the surplus approach in the context of the social provisioning process. The implications are noteworthy. First, the material welfare of the general public depends upon the decisions made by dominant agents in the society. Since the foremost concern of the private business enterprise is the survival and expansion of the business over time, welfare improvement is not guaranteed by market activities. Even during a period of rapid capital accumulation, the welfare of the subservient class is not necessarily increasing. Second, at any given point in history, there is a standard of welfare that is socially acceptable, and that is governed by historically contingent social institutions (for example, the welfare state) and the power relations between classes. A Post Keynesian approach to welfare suggested here reveals that the central difficulty in provisioning social welfare lies not merely in the uncertainty of welfare policy, but also in the structure of capitalist system that governs actual decisions made by those agents controlling the social provisioning process.

TAE-HEE JO

See also:

Agency; Economic Policy; Effective Demand; Galbraith's Economics; Income Distribution; Institutionalism; Production; Sraffian Economics.

References

Cesaratto, S. (2008), 'The classical "surplus" approach and the theory of the welfare state and public pensions', in G. Chiodi and L. Ditta (eds), *Sraffa: Or an Alternative Economics*, Basingstoke: Palgrave Macmillan, pp. 93–113.

Eichner, A.S. (1987), *The Macrodynamics of Advanced Market Economies*, Armonk, NY: M.E. Sharpe.

Hargreaves Heap, S.P. (1989), 'Towards a Post-Keynesian welfare economics', *Review of Political Economy*, **1** (2), 144–62.

Henry, J.F. (1986), 'On economic theory and the question of solvability', *Journal of Post Keynesian Economics*, **8** (3), 371–86.

Howard, M.C. and J.E. King (1992), *A History of Marxian Economics: Volume II, 1929–1990*, Princeton, NJ: Princeton University Press.

Kaldor, N. (1939), 'Welfare propositions of economics and interpersonal comparisons of utility', *Economic Journal*, **49** (195), 549–52.

Kalecki, M. (1943), 'Political aspects of full employment', *Political Quarterly*, **14** (4), 322–31.

Keynes, J.M. (1936), *The General Theory of Employment, Interest and Money*, London: Macmillan.

King, J.E. (1995), *Conversations with Post Keynesians*, New York: St. Martin's Press.

Minsky, H.P. (1986), *Stabilizing an Unstable Economy*, New Haven, CT: Yale University Press.

Samuels, W.J. (1994), 'On macroeconomic politics', *Journal of Post Keynesian Economics*, **16** (4), 661–71.

Sawyer, M.C. (1985), *The Economics of Michał Kalecki*, Armonk, NY: M.E. Sharpe.

Name index

Page references to authors of entries in this volume are in bold type.

Subject index

Numbers in bold type refer to entries in this volume.